THE COMPLETE PLAYS OF

D. H. LAWRENCE

The Complete Plays of D.H.Lawrence

THE VIKING PRESS · NEW YORK

Published in 1966 by The Viking Press, Inc.
625 Madison Avenue, New York, N.Y. 10022

Published simultaneously in Canada by
The Macmillan Company of Canada Limited

Library of Congress catalog card number: 66-11829
Printed in U.S.A.

Second printing March 1967

All inquiries regarding performance rights of these plays should be di-
rected to Margery Vosper Ltd., 54A Shaftesbury Avenue, London W.1.

David was originally published by Alfred A.
Knopf, Inc., and is used by their permission.

Contents

The Widowing of Mrs Holroyd   9

David   63

The Married Man   155

The Daughter-in-Law   203

The Fight for Barbara   269

Touch and Go   321

The Merry-Go-Round   387

A Collier's Friday Night   469

Altitude   531

Noah's Flood   549

In several cases alternative drafts of the plays in this volume exist in manuscript form, but the versions here printed are regarded as being the most complete.

The date in brackets under the title of each play indicates the year of completion of the text.

The Widowing of Mrs Holroyd

A PLAY IN THREE ACTS

(1914)

CHARACTERS

MRS HOLROYD

HOLROYD

BLACKMORE

JACK HOLROYD

MINNIE HOLROYD

GRANDMOTHER

RIGLEY

CLARA

LAURA

MANAGER

TWO MINERS

The action of the play takes place in the Holroyds' cottage

ACT I

SCENE I

The kitchen of a miner's small cottage. On the left is the fireplace, with a deep, full red fire. At the back is a white-curtained window, and beside it the outer door of the room. On the right, two white wooden stairs intrude into the kitchen below the closed stair-foot door. On the left, another door.

The room is furnished with a chintz-backed sofa under the window, a glass-knobbed painted dresser on the right, and in the centre, toward the fire, a table with a red and blue check tablecloth. On one side of the hearth is a wooden rocking-chair, on the other an arm-chair of round staves. An unlighted copper-shaded lamp hangs from the raftered ceiling. It is dark twilight, with the room full of warm fireglow. A woman enters from the outer door. As she leaves the door open behind her, the colliery rail can be seen not far from the threshold, and, away back, the headstocks of a pit.

The woman is tall and voluptuously built. She carries a basket heaped full of washing, which she has just taken from the clotheslines outside. Setting down the basket heavily, she feels among the clothes. She lifts out a white heap of sheets and other linen, setting it on the table; then she takes a woollen shirt in her hand.

MRS HOLROYD (*aloud, to herself*): You know they're not dry even now, though it's been as fine as it has. (*She spreads the shirt on the back of her rocking-chair, which she turns to the fire.*)
VOICE (*calling from outside*): Well, have you got them dry?
    MRS HOLROYD *starts up, turns and flings her hand in the direction of the open door, where appears a man in blue overalls, swarfed and greased. He carries a dinner-basket.*
MRS HOLROYD: You—you—I don't know what to call you! The idea of shouting at me like that—like the Evil One out of the darkness!

BLACKMORE: I ought to have remembered your tender nerves. Shall I come in?

MRS HOLROYD: No—not for your impudence. But you're late, aren't you?

BLACKMORE: It's only just gone six. We electricians, you know, we're the gentlemen on a mine: ours is gentlemen's work. But I'll bet Charles Holroyd was home before four.

MRS HOLROYD *(bitterly)*: Ay, and gone again before five.

BLACKMORE: But mine's a lad's job, and I do nothing!—Where's he gone?

MRS HOLROYD *(contemptuously)*: Dunno! He'd got a game on some-where—toffed himself up to the nines, and skedaddled off as brisk as a turkey-cock. *(She smirks in front of the mirror hanging on the chimney-piece, in imitation of a man brushing his hair and moustache and admiring himself.)*

BLACKMORE: Though turkey-cocks aren't brisk as a rule. Children playing?

MRS HOLROYD *(recovering herself, coldly)*: Yes. And they ought to be in.

> She continues placing the flannel garments before the fire, on the fender and on chair-backs, till the stove is hedged in with a steaming fence; then she takes a sheet in a bundle from the table, and goes up to BLACKMORE, who stands watching her.

Here, take hold, and help me fold it.

BLACKMORE: I shall swarf it up.

MRS HOLROYD *(snatching back the sheet)*: Oh, you're as tiresome as everybody else.

BLACKMORE *(putting down his basket and moving to door on right)*: Well, I can soon wash my hands.

MRS HOLROYD *(ceasing to flap and fold pillow-cases)*: That roller-towel's ever so dirty. I'll get you another. *(She goes to a drawer in the dresser, and then back toward the scullery, from which comes the sound of water.)*

BLACKMORE: Why, bless my life, I'm a lot dirtier than the towel. I don't want another.

MRS HOLROYD *(going into the scullery)*: Here you are.

BLACKMORE *(softly, now she is near him)*: Why did you trouble now? Pride, you know, pride, nothing else.

MRS HOLROYD *(also playful)*: It's nothing but decency.

BLACKMORE *(softly)*: Pride, pride, pride!

A child of eight suddenly appears in the doorway.

JACK: Oo, how dark!

MRS HOLROYD *(hurrying agitated into the kitchen)*: Why, where have you been—what have you been doing now?

JACK *(surprised)*: Why—I've only been out to play.

MRS HOLROYD *(still sharply)*: And where's Minnie?

A little girl of six appears by the door.

MINNIE: I'm here, mam, and what do you think——?

MRS HOLROYD *(softening, as she recovers equanimity)*: Well, and what should I think?

JACK: Oh, yes, mam—you know my father——?

MRS HOLROYD *(ironically)*: I should hope so.

MINNIE: We saw him dancing, mam, with a paper bonnet.

MRS HOLROYD: What——?

JACK: There's some women at New Inn, what's come from Nottingham——

MINNIE: An' he's dancin' with the pink one.

JACK: Shut up, our Minnie. An' they've got paper bonnets on——

MINNIE: All colours, mam!

JACK *(getting angry)*: Shut up, our Minnie! An' my dad's dancing with her.

MINNIE: With the pink-bonnet one, mam.

JACK: Up in the club-room over the bar.

MINNIE: An' she's a lot littler than him, mam.

JACK *(piteously)*: Shut up, our Minnie— An' you can see 'em go past the window, 'cause there isn't no curtains up, an' my father's got the pink bonnet one——

MINNIE: An' there's a piano, mam——

JACK: An' lots of folks outside watchin', lookin' at my dad! He can dance, can't he, mam?

MRS HOLROYD *(she has been lighting the lamp, and holds the lamp-glass)*: And who else is there?

MINNIE: Some more men—an' *all* the women with paper bonnets on.

JACK: There's about ten, I should think, an' they say they came in a brake from Nottingham.

    MRS HOLROYD, *trying to replace the lamp-glass over the flame, lets it drop on the floor with a smash.*

JACK: There, now—now we'll have to have a candle.

BLACKMORE *(appearing in the scullery doorway with the towel)*:
What's that—the lamp-glass?

JACK: I never knowed Mr Blackmore was here.

BLACKMORE *(to* MRS HOLROYD*)*: Have you got another?

MRS HOLROYD: No. *(There is silence for a moment.)* We can
manage with a candle for to-night.

BLACKMORE *(stepping forward and blowing out the smoky flame)*:
I'll see if I can't get you one from the pit. I shan't be a minute.

MRS HOLROYD: Don't—don't bother—I don't want you to.

He, however, unscrews the burner and goes.

MINNIE: Did Mr Blackmore come for tea, mam?

MRS HOLROYD: No; he's had no tea.

JACK: I bet he's hungry. Can I have some bread?

MRS HOLROYD *(she stands a lighted candle on the table)*: Yes, and you
can get your boots off to go to bed.

JACK: It's not seven o'clock yet.

MRS HOLROYD: It doesn't matter.

MINNIE: What do they wear paper bonnets for, mam?

MRS HOLROYD: Because they're brazen hussies.

JACK: I saw them having a glass of beer.

MRS HOLROYD: A nice crew!

JACK: They say they are old pals of Mrs Meakins. You could hear her
screaming o' laughin', an' my dad says: "He-ah, missis—here—a
dog's-nose for the Dachess—hopin' it'll smell samthing"— What's
a dog's-nose?

MRS HOLROYD *(giving him a piece of bread and butter)*: Don't ask me,
child. How should I know?

MINNIE: Would she eat it, mam?

MRS HOLROYD: Eat what?

MINNIE: Her *in* the pink bonnet—eat the dog's-nose?

MRS HOLROYD: No, of course not. How should I know what a dog's-
nose is?

JACK: I bet he'll never go to work to-morrow, mother—will he?

MRS HOLROYD: Goodness knows. I'm sick of it—disgracing me.
There'll be the whole place cackling *this* now. They've no sooner
finished about him getting taken up for fighting than they begin on
this. But I'll put a stop to it some road or other. It's not going on,
if I know it: it isn't.

She stops, hearing footsteps, and BLACKMORE *enters.*

BLACKMORE: Here we are then—got one all right.

MINNIE: Did they give it you, Mr Blackmore?

BLACKMORE: No, I took it.

He screws on the burner and proceeds to light the lamp. He is a tall, slender, mobile man of twenty-seven, brown-haired, dressed in blue overalls. JACK HOLROYD *is a big, dark, ruddy, lusty lad.* MINNIE *is also big, but fair.*

MINNIE: What do you wear blue trousers for, Mr Blackmore?

BLACKMORE: They're to keep my other trousers from getting greasy.

MINNIE: Why don't you wear pit-breeches, like dad's?

JACK: 'Cause he's a 'lectrician. Could you make me a little injun what would make electric light?

BLACKMORE: I will, some day.

JACK: When?

MINNIE: Why don't you come an' live here?

BLACKMORE *(looking swiftly at* MRS HOLROYD*)*: Nay, you've got your own dad to live here.

MINNIE *(plaintively)*: Well, you could come as well. Dad shouts when we've gone to bed, an' thumps the table. He wouldn't if you was here.

JACK: He dursn't——

MRS HOLROYD: Be quiet now, be quiet. Here, Mr Blackmore. *(She again gives him the sheet to fold.)*

BLACKMORE: Your hands *are* cold.

MRS HOLROYD: Are they?—I didn't know.

BLACKMORE *puts his hand on hers.*

MRS HOLROYD *(confusedly, looking aside)*: You must want your tea.

BLACKMORE: I'm in no hurry.

MRS HOLROYD: Selvidge to selvidge. You'll be quite a domestic man, if you go on.

BLACKMORE: Ay.

They fold the two sheets.

BLACKMORE: They are white, your sheets!

MRS HOLROYD: But look at the smuts on them—look! This vile hole! I'd never have come to live here, in all the thick of the pit-grime, and lonely, if it hadn't been for him, so that he shouldn't call in a public-house on his road home from work. And now he slinks past on the other side of the railway, and goes down to the New Inn instead of coming in for his dinner. I might as well have stopped in Bestwood.

BLACKMORE: Though I rather like this little place, standing by itself.

MRS HOLROYD: Jack, can you go and take the stockings in for me? They're on the line just below the pigsty. The prop's near the apple-tree—mind it. Minnie, you take the peg-basket.

MINNIE: Will there be any rats, mam?

MRS HOLROYD: Rats—no. They'll be frightened when they hear you, if there are.

The children go out.

BLACKMORE: Poor little beggars!

MRS HOLROYD: Do you know, this place is fairly alive with rats. They run up that dirty vine in front of the house—I'm always at him to cut it down—and you can hear them at night overhead like a regiment of soldiers tramping. Really, you know, I *hate* them.

BLACKMORE: Well—a rat is a nasty thing!

MRS HOLROYD: But I s'll get used to them. I'd give anything to be out of this place.

BLACKMORE: It *is* rotten, when you're tied to a life you don't like. But I should miss it if you weren't here. When I'm coming down the line to the pit in the morning—it's nearly dark at seven now— I watch the firelight in here. Sometimes I put my hand on the wall outside where the chimney runs up to feel it warm. There isn't much in Bestwood, is there?

MRS HOLROYD: There's less than nothing if you can't be like the rest of them—as common as they're made.

BLACKMORE: It's a fact—particularly for a woman—But this place is cosy— God love me, I'm sick of lodgings.

MRS HOLROYD: You'll have to get married— I'm sure there are plenty of nice girls about.

BLACKMORE: Are there? I never see 'em. *(He laughs.)*

MRS HOLROYD: Oh, come, you can't say that.

BLACKMORE: I've not seen a single girl—an unmarried girl—that I should want for more than a fortnight—not one.

MRS HOLROYD: Perhaps you're very particular.

She puts her two palms on the table and leans back. He draws near to her, dropping his head.

BLACKMORE: Look here!

He has put his hand on the table near hers.

MRS HOLROYD: Yes, I know you've got nice hands—but you needn't be vain of them.

BLACKMORE: No—it's not that— But don't they seem—*(he glances swiftly at her; she turns her head aside; he laughs nervously)*— they sort of go well with one another. *(He laughs again.)*

MRS HOLROYD: They *do*, rather—

> *They stand still, near one another, with bent heads, for a moment. Suddenly she starts up and draws her hand away.*

BLACKMORE: Why—what is it?

> *She does not answer. The children come in—*JACK *with an armful of stockings,* MINNIE *with the basket of pegs.*

JACK: I believe it's freezing, mother.

MINNIE: Mr Blackmore, could you shoot a rat an' hit it?

BLACKMORE *(laughing)*: Shoot the lot of 'em, like a wink.

MRS HOLROYD: But you've had no tea. What an awful shame to keep you here!

BLACKMORE: Nay, I don't care. It never bothers me.

MRS HOLROYD: Then you're different from most men.

BLACKMORE: All men aren't alike, you know.

MRS HOLROYD: But do go and get some tea.

MINNIE *(plaintively)*: Can't you stop, Mr Blackmore?

BLACKMORE: Why, Minnie?

MINNIE: So's we're not frightened. Yes, do. Will you?

BLACKMORE: Frightened of what?

MINNIE: 'Cause there's noises, an' rats—an' perhaps dad'll come home and shout.

BLACKMORE: But he'd shout more if I was here.

JACK: He doesn't when my uncle John's here. So you stop, an' perhaps he won't.

BLACKMORE: Don't you like him to shout when you're in bed?

> *They do not answer, but look seriously at him.*

CURTAIN

The same scene, two hours later. The clothes are folded in little piles on the table and the sofa. MRS HOLROYD *is folding a thick flannel undervest or singlet which her husband wears in the pit and which has just dried on the fender.*

MRS HOLROYD *(to herself)* : Now, thank goodness, they're all dried. It's only nine o'clock, so he won't be in for another two hours, the nuisance. *(She sits on the sofa, letting her arms hang down in dejection. After a minute or two she jumps up, to begin rudely dropping the piles of washed clothes in the basket.)* I don't care, I'm not going to let him have it all *his* way—no! *(She weeps a little, fiercely, drying her eyes on the edge of her white apron.)* Why should *I* put up with it all?—He can do what he likes. But I don't care, no, I don't—

She flings down the full clothes-basket, sits suddenly in the rocking-chair, and weeps. There is the sound of coarse, bursting laughter, in vain subdued, and a man's deep guffaws. Footsteps draw near. Suddenly the door opens, and a little, plump, pretty woman of thirty, in a close-fitting dress and a giddy, frilled bonnet of pink paper, stands perkily in the doorway. MRS HOLROYD *springs up; her small, sensitive nose is inflamed with weeping, her eyes are wet and flashing. She fronts the other woman.*

CLARA *(with a pert smile and a jerk of the head)*: Good evenin'!

MRS HOLROYD : What do you want?

CLARA *(she has a Yorkshire accent)*: Oh, we've not come beggin'— this is a visit.

She stuffs her handkerchief in front of her mouth in a little snorting burst of laughter. There is the sound of another woman behind going off into uncontrollable laughter, while a man guffaws.

MRS HOLROYD *(after a moment of impotence—tragically)*: What——!

CLARA *(faltering slightly, affecting a polite tone)*: We thought we'd just call——

She stuffs her handkerchief in front of her explosive laughter

—the other woman shrieks again, beginning high, and running down the scale.

MRS HOLROYD: What do you mean?—What do you want here?

CLARA *(she bites her lip)* : We don't want anything, thanks. We've just called. *(She begins to laugh again—so does the other.)* Well, I don't think much of the manners in this part of the country. *(She takes a few hesitating steps into the kitchen.)*

MRS HOLROYD *(trying to shut the door upon her)*: No, you are not coming in.

CLARA *(preventing her closing the door)*: Dear me, what a to-do! *(She struggles with the door. The other woman comes up to help; a man is seen in the background.)*

LAURA: My word, aren't we good enough to come in?

MRS HOLROYD, *finding herself confronted by what seems to her excitement a crowd, releases the door and draws back a little—almost in tears of anger.*

MRS HOLROYD: You have no business here. What do you want?

CLARA *(putting her bonnet straight and entering in brisk defiance)*: I tell you we've only come to see you. *(She looks round the kitchen, then makes a gesture toward the arm-chair.)* Can I sit here? *(She plumps herself down.)* Rest for the weary.

A woman and a man have followed her into the room. LAURA *is highly coloured, stout, some forty years old, wears a blue paper bonnet, and looks like the landlady of a public-house. Both she and* CLARA *wear much jewellery.* LAURA *is well dressed in a blue cloth dress.* HOLROYD *is a big blond man. His cap is pushed back, and he looks rather tipsy and lawless. He has a heavy blond moustache. His jacket and trousers are black, his vest grey, and he wears a turn-down collar with dark bow.*

LAURA *(sitting down in a chair on right, her hand on her bosom, panting)*: I've laughed till I feel fair bad.

CLARA: 'Aven't you got a drop of nothink to offer us, mester? Come, you are slow. I should 'ave thought a gentleman like you would have been out with the glasses afore we could have got breaths to ask you.

HOLROYD *(clumsily)*: I dunna believe there's owt in th' 'ouse but a bottle of stout.

CLARA *(putting her hand on her stomach)*: It feels as if th' kettle's going to boil over.

She stuffs her handkerchief in front of her mouth, throws back her head, and snorts with laughter, having now regained her confidence. LAURA *laughs in the last state of exhaustion, her hand on her breast.*

HOLROYD : Shall ta ha'e it then?

CLARA: What do you say, Laura—are you having a drop?

LAURA *(submissively, and naturally tongue-tied)*: Well—I don't mind —I will if *you* do.

CLARA *(recklessly)*: I think we'll 'ave a drop, Charlie, an' risk it. It'll 'appen hold the rest down.

There is a moment of silence, while HOLROYD *goes into the scullery.* CLARA *surveys the room and the dramatic pose of* MRS HOLROYD *curiously.*

HOLROYD *(suddenly)*: Heh! What, come 'ere——!

There is a smash of pots, and a rat careers out of the scullery. LAURA, *the first to see it, utters a scream, but is fastened to her chair, unable to move.*

CLARA *(jumps up to the table, crying)*: It's a rat— Oh, save us! *(She scrambles up, banging her head on the lamp, which swings violently.)*

MRS HOLROYD *(who, with a little shriek, jerks her legs up on to the sofa, where she was stiffly reclining, now cries in despairing falsetto, stretching forth her arms)*: The lamp—mind, the lamp!

CLARA *steadies the lamp, and holds her hand to her head.*

HOLROYD *(coming from the scullery, a bottle of stout in his hand)*: Where is he?

CLARA: I believe he's gone under the sofa. My, an' he's a thumper, if you like, as big as a rabbit.

HOLROYD *advances cautiously toward the sofa.*

LAURA *(springing suddenly into life)*: Hi, hi, let me go—let me go— Don't touch him— Where is he? *(She flees and scrambles on to* CLARA'S *arm-chair, catching hold of the latter's skirts.)*

CLARA: Hang off—do you want to have a body down— Mind, I tell you.

MRS HOLROYD *(bunched up on the sofa, with crossed hands holding her arms, fascinated, watches her husband as he approaches to stoop and attack the rat; she suddenly screams)*: Don't, he'll fly at you.

HOLROYD: He'll not get a chance.

MRS HOLROYD: He will, he will—and they're poisonous! *(She ends on a very high note. Leaning forward on the sofa as far as she dares, she stretches out her arms to keep back her husband, who is about to kneel and search under the sofa for the rat.)*

HOLROYD: Come off, I canna see him.

MRS HOLROYD: I won't let you; he'll fly at you.

HOLROYD: I'll settle him——

MRS HOLROYD: Open the door and let him go.

HOLROYD: I shonna. I'll settle him. Shut thy claver. He'll non come anigh thee.

> *He kneels down and begins to creep to the sofa. With a great bound,* MRS HOLROYD *flies to the door and flings it open. Then she rushes back to the couch.*

CLARA: There he goes!

HOLROYD *(simultaneously)*: Hi!—Ussza! *(He flings the bottle of stout out of the door.)*

LAURA *(piteously)*: Shut the door, do.

> HOLROYD *rises, dusting his trousers knees, and closes the door.* LAURA *heavily descends and drops in the chair.*

CLARA: Here, come an' help us down, Charlie. Look at her; she's going off.

> *Though* LAURA *is still purple-red, she sinks back in the chair.* HOLROYD *goes to the table.* CLARA *places her hands on his shoulders and jumps lightly down. Then she pushes* HOLROYD *with her elbow.*

Look sharp, get a glass of water.

> *She unfastens* LAURA's *collar and pulls off the paper bonnet.* MRS HOLROYD *sits up, straightens her clothing, and tries to look cold and contemptuous.* HOLROYD *brings a cup of water.* CLARA *sprinkles her friend's face.* LAURA *sighs and sighs again very deeply, then draws herself up painfully.*

CLARA *(tenderly)*: Do you feel any better—shall you have a drink of water?

*(*LAURA *mournfully shakes her head;* CLARA *turns sharply to* HOLROYD.)*

She'll 'ave a drop o' something.

> HOLROYD *goes out.* CLARA *meanwhile fans her friend with a handkerchief.* HOLROYD *brings stout. She pours out the stout, smells the glass, smells the bottle—then finally the cork.*

Eh, mester, it's all of a work—it's had a foisty cork.

At that instant the stairfoot door opens slowly, revealing the children—the girl peering over the boy's shoulder—both in white nightgowns. Everybody starts. LAURA *gives a little cry, presses her hand on her bosom, and sinks back, gasping.*

CLARA *(appealing and anxious, to* MRS HOLROYD*)* : You don't 'appen to 'ave a drop of brandy for her, do you, missis?

MRS HOLROYD *rises coldly without replying, and goes to the stairfoot door where the children stand.*

MRS HOLROYD *(sternly, to the children)* : Go to bed!

JACK : What's a matter, mother?

MRS HOLROYD : Never you mind, go to bed!

CLARA *(appealingly)* : Be quick, missis.

MRS HOLROYD, *glancing round, sees* LAURA *going purple, and runs past the children upstairs. The boy and girl sit on the lowest stair. Their father goes out of the house, shamefaced.* MRS HOLROYD *runs downstairs with a little brandy in a large bottle.*

CLARA : Thanks, awfully. *(To* LAURA*)* Come on, try an' drink a drop, there's a dear.

They administer brandy to LAURA. *The children sit watching, open-eyed. The girl stands up to look.*

MINNIE *(whispering)* : I believe it's blue bonnet.

JACK *(whispering)* : It isn't—she's in a fit.

MINNIE *(whispering)* : Well, look under th' table—JACK *peers under* —there's 'er bonnet. *(*JACK *creeps forward.)* Come back, our Jack.

JACK *(returns with the bonnet)* : It's all made of paper.

MINNIE : Let's have a look—it's stuck together, not sewed.

She tries it on. HOLROYD *enters—he looks at the child.*

MRS HOLROYD *(sharply, glancing round)* : Take that off!

MINNIE *hurriedly takes the bonnet from her head. Her father snatches it from her and puts it on the fire.*

CLARA : There, you're coming round now, love.

MRS HOLROYD *turns away. She sees* HOLROYD'S *eyes on the brandy-bottle, and immediately removes it, corking it up.*

MRS HOLROYD *(to* CLARA*)* : You will not need this any more?

CLARA : No, thanks. I'm very much obliged.

MRS HOLROYD *(does not unbend, but speaks coldly to the children)*: Come, this is no place for you—come back to bed.

MINNIE : No, mam, I don't want to.

MRS HOLROYD *(contralto)* : Come along!

MINNIE : I'm frightened, mam.

MRS HOLROYD : Frightened, what of?

MINNIE : Oo, there *was* a row.

MRS HOLROYD *(taking* MINNIE *in her arms)* : Did they frighten you, my pet? *(She kisses her.)*

JACK *(in a high whisper)* : Mother, it's pink bonnet and blue bonnet, what was dancing.

MINNIE *(whimpering)*: I don't want to go to bed, mam, I'm frightened.

CLARA *(who has pulled off her pink bonnet and revealed a jug-handle coiffure)*: We're going now, duckie—you're not frightened of us, are you?

> MRS HOLROYD *takes the girl away before she can answer.* JACK *lingers behind.*

HOLROYD : Now then, get off after your mother.

JACK *(taking no notice of his father)* : I say, what's a dog's-nose?

> CLARA *ups with her handkerchief and* LAURA *responds with a faint giggle.*

HOLROYD : Go thy ways upstairs.

CLARA : It's only a small whiskey with a spoonful of beer in it, my duck.

JACK : Oh!

CLARA : Come here, my duck, come on.

> JACK *curious, advances.*

CLARA : You'll tell your mother we didn't mean no harm, won't you?

JACK *(touching her earrings)* : What are they made of?

CLARA : They're only earrings. Don't you like them?

JACK : Um! *(He stands surveying her curiously. Then he touches a bracelet made of many little mosaic brooches.)* This is pretty, isn't it?

CLARA *(pleased)* : Do you like it?

> She takes it off. Suddenly MRS HOLROYD *is heard calling, 'Jack, Jack!'* CLARA *starts.*

HOLROYD : Now then, get off!

CLARA *(as* JACK *is reluctantly going)* : Kiss me good night, duckie, an' give this to your sister, shall you?

> She hands JACK *the mosaic bracelet. He takes it doubtfully. She kisses him.* HOLROYD *watches in silence.*

LAURA *(suddenly, pathetically)*: Aren't you going to give me a kiss, an' all?

JACK *yields her his cheek, then goes.*

CLARA *(to* HOLROYD): Aren't they nice children?

HOLROYD: Ay.

CLARA *(briskly)*: Oh, dear, you're very short, all of a sudden. Don't answer if it hurts you.

LAURA: My, isn't he different?

HOLROYD *(laughing forcedly)*: I'm no different.

CLARA: Yes, you are. You shouldn't 'ave brought us if you was going to turn funny over it.

HOLROYD: I'm not funny.

CLARA: No, you're not. *(She begins to laugh.* LAURA *joins in in spite of herself.)* You're about as solemn as a roast potato. *(She flings up her hands, claps them down on her knees, and sways up and down as she laughs,* LAURA *joining in, hand on breast.)* Are you ready to be mashed? *(She goes off again—then suddenly wipes the laughter off her mouth and is solemn.)* But look 'ere, this'll never do. Now I'm going to be quiet. *(She prims herself.)*

HOLROYD: Tha'd 'appen better.

CLARA: Oh. indeed! You think I've got to pull a mug to look decent? You'd have to pull a big un, at that rate.

She bubbles off, uncontrollably—shaking herself in exasperation meanwhile. LAURA *joins in.* HOLROYD *leans over close to her.*

HOLROYD: Tha's got plenty o' fizz in thee, seemly.

CLARA *(putting her hand on his face and pushing it aside, but leaving her hand over his cheek and mouth like a caress)*: Don't, you've been drinking. *(She begins to laugh.)*

HOLROYD: Should we be goin' then?

CLARA: Where do you want to take us?

HOLROYD: Oh—you please yourself o' that! Come on wi' me.

CLARA *(sitting up prim)*: Oh, indeed!

HOLROYD *(catching hold of her)*: Come on, let's be movin'—*(he glances apprehensively at the stairs).*

CLARA: What's your hurry?

HOLROYD *(persuasively)*: Yi, come on wi' thee.

CLARA: I don't think. *(She goes off, uncontrollably.)*

HOLROYD (*sitting on the table, just above her*): What's use o' sittin' 'ere?

CLARA: I'm very comfy: I thank thee.

HOLROYD: Tha'rt a baffling little 'ussy.

CLARA (*running her hand along his thigh*): Aren't you havin' nothing, my dear? (*Offers him her glass.*)

HOLROYD (*getting down from the table and putting his hand forcibly on her shoulder*): No. Come on, let's shift.

CLARA (*struggling*): Hands off!

> She fetches him a sharp slap across the face. MRS HOLROYD is heard coming downstairs. CLARA, *released, sits down, smoothing herself.* HOLROYD *looks evil. He goes out to the door.*

CLARA (*to* MRS HOLROYD, *penitently*): I don't know what you think of us, I'm sure.

MRS HOLROYD: I think nothing at all.

CLARA (*bubbling*): So you fix your thoughts elsewhere, do you? (*Suddenly changing to seriousness.*) No, but I *have* been awful to-night.

MRS HOLROYD (*contralto, emphatic*): I don't want to know anything about you. I shall be glad when you'll go.

CLARA: Turning-out time, Laura.

LAURA (*turtling*): I'm sorry, I'm sure.

CLARA: Never mind. But as true as I'm here, missis, I should never ha' come if I'd thought. But I had a drop—it all started with your husband sayin' he wasn't a married man.

LAURA (*laughing and wiping her eyes*): I've never knowed her to go off like it—it's after the time she's had.

CLARA: You know, my husband was a brute to me—an' I was in bed three month after he died. He was a brute, he was. This is the first time I've been out; it's a'most the first laugh I've had for a year.

LAURA: It's true, what she says. We thought she'd go out of 'er mind. She never spoke a word for a fortnight.

CLARA: Though he's only been dead for two months, he was a brute to me. I was as nice a young girl as you could wish when I married him and went to the Fleece Inn—I was.

LAURA: Killed hisself drinking. An' she's that excitable, she is. We s'll 'ave an awful time with 'er to-morrow, I know.

MRS HOLROYD (*coldly*): I don't know why I should hear all this.

CLARA: I know I must 'ave seemed awful. An' them children—aren't they nice little things, Laura?

LAURA: They are that.

HOLROYD (*entering from the door*): Hanna you about done theer?

CLARA: My word, if this is the way you treat a lady when she comes to see you. (*She rises.*)

HOLROYD: I'll see you down th' line.

CLARA: You're not coming a stride with us.

LAURA: We've got no hat, neither of us.

CLARA: We've got our own hair on our heads, at any rate. (*Drawing herself up suddenly in front of* MRS HOLROYD.) An' I've been educated at a boarding school as good as anybody. I can behave myself either in the drawing-room or in the kitchen as is fitting and proper. But if you'd buried a husband like mine, you wouldn't feel you'd much left to be proud of—an' you might go off occasionally.

MRS HOLROYD: I don't want to hear you.

CLARA (*bobbing a curtsy*): Sorry I spoke.

> She goes out stiffly, followed by LAURA.

HOLROYD (*going forward*): You mun mind th' points down th' line.

CLARA'S VOICE: I thank thee, Charlie—mind thy own points.

> He hesitates at the door—returns and sits down. There is silence in the room. HOLROYD sits with his chin in his hand. MRS HOLROYD listens. The footsteps and voices of the two women die out. Then she closes the door. HOLROYD begins to unlace his boots.

HOLROYD (*ashamed yet defiant, withal anxious to apologize*): Wheer's my slippers?

> MRS HOLROYD sits on the sofa with face averted and does not answer.

HOLROYD: Dost hear? (*He pulls off his boots, noisily, and begins to hunt under the sofa.*) I canna find the things. (*No answer.*) Humph!—then I'll do be 'out 'em. (*He stumps about in his stockinged feet; going into the scullery, he brings out the loaf of bread; he returns into the scullery.*) Wheer's th' cheese? (*No answer—suddenly*) God blast it! (*He hobbles into the kitchen.*) I've trod on that broken basin, an' cut my foot open. (MRS HOLROYD *refuses to take any notice. He sits down and looks at his sole—pulls off his stocking and looks again.*) It's lamed me for life. (MRS

HOLROYD *glances at the wound.)* Are 'na ter goin' ter get me öwt for it?

MRS HOLROYD: Psh!

HOLROYD: Oh, a' right then. *(He hops to the dresser, opens a drawer, and pulls out a white rag; he is about to tear it.)*

MRS HOLROYD *(snatching it from him)*: Don't tear that!

HOLROYD *(shouting)*: Then what the deuce am I to do? (MRS HOLROYD *sits stonily.)* Oh, a' right then! *(He hops back to his chair, sits down, and begins to pull on his stocking.)* A' right then—a' right then. *(In a fever of rage he begins pulling on his boots.)* I'll go where I *can* find a bit o' rag.

MRS HOLROYD: Yes, that's what you want! All you want is an excuse to be off again—"a bit of rag"!

HOLROYD *(shouting)*: An' what man'd want to stop in wi' a woman sittin' as fow as a jackass, an' canna get a word from 'er edgeways.

MRS HOLROYD: Don't expect me to speak to you after to-night's show. How dare you bring them to my house, how dare you?

HOLROYD: They've non hurt your house, have they?

MRS HOLROYD: I wonder you dare to cross the doorstep.

HOLROYD: I s'll do what the deuce I like. They're as good as you are.

MRS HOLROYD *(stands speechless, staring at him; then low)*: Don't you come near me again——

HOLROYD *(suddenly shouting, to get his courage up)*: She's as good as you are, every bit of it.

MRS HOLROYD *(blazing)*: Whatever I was and whatever I may be, don't you ever come near me again.

HOLROYD: What! I'll show thee. What's the hurt to you if a woman comes to the house? They're women as good as yourself, every whit of it.

MRS HOLROYD: Say no more. Go with them then, and don't come back.

HOLROYD: What! Yi, I will go, an' you s'll see. What! You think you're something, since your uncle left you that money, an' Blackymore puttin' you up to it. I can see your little game. I'm not as daft as you imagine. I'm no fool, I tell you.

MRS HOLROYD: No, you're not. You're a drunken beast, that's all you are.

HOLROYD: What, what—I'm what? I'll show you who's gaffer, though. *(He threatens her.)*

MRS HOLROYD *(between her teeth)*: No, it's not going on. If *you* won't go, I will.

HOLROYD: Go then, for you've always been too big for your shoes, in my house——

MRS HOLROYD: Yes—I ought never to have looked at you. Only you showed a fair face then.

HOLROYD: What! What! We'll see who's master i' this house. I tell you, I'm goin' to put a stop to it. *(He brings his fist down on the table with a bang.)* It's going to stop. *(He bangs the table again.)* I've put up with it long enough. Do you think I'm a dog in the house, an' not a man, do you——

MRS HOLROYD: A dog would be better.

HOLROYD: Oh! Oh! Then we'll see. We'll see who's the dog and who isna. We're goin' to see. *(He bangs the table.)*

MRS HOLROYD: Stop thumping that table! You've wakened those children once, you and your trollops.

HOLROYD: I shall do what the deuce I like!

MRS HOLROYD: No more, you won't, no more. I've stood this long enough. Now I'm going. As for you—you've got a red face where she slapped you. Now go to her.

HOLROYD: What? What?

MRS HOLROYD: For I'm sick of the sights and sounds of you.

HOLROYD *(bitterly)*: By God, an' I've known it a long time.

MRS HOLROYD: You have, and it's true.

HOLROYD: An' I know who it is th'rt hankerin' after.

MRS HOLROYD: I only want to be rid of you.

HOLROYD: I know it mighty well. But *I* know him!

    MRS HOLROYD *sinking down on the sofa, suddenly begins to sob half-hysterically.* HOLROYD *watches her. As suddenly, she dries her eyes.*

MRS HOLROYD: Do you think I care about what you say? *(Suddenly.)* Oh, I've had enough. I've tried, I've tried for years, for the children's sakes. Now I've had enough of your shame and disgrace.

HOLROYD: Oh, indeed!

MRS HOLROYD *(her voice is dull and inflexible)*: I've had enough. Go out again after those trollops—leave me alone. I've had enough. (HOLROYD *stands looking at her.*) Go, I mean it, go out again. And if you never come back again, I'm glad. I've had enough. *(She keeps her face averted, will not look at him, her attitude expressing thorough weariness.)*

HOLROYD : All right then!

He hobbles, in unlaced boots, to the door. Then he turns to look at her. She turns herself still farther away, so that her back is towards him. He goes.

CURTAIN

ACT II

The scene is the same, two hours later. The cottage is in darkness, save for the firelight. On the table is spread a newspaper. A cup and saucer, a plate, a piece of bacon in the frying tin are on the newspaper ready for the miner's breakfast. MRS HOLROYD *has gone to bed. There is a noise of heavy stumbling down the three steps outside.*

BLACKMORE'S VOICE: Steady, now, steady. It's all in darkness. Missis!—Has she gone to bed?
  He tries the latch—shakes the door.
HOLROYD'S VOICE *(He is drunk.)*: Her's locked me out. Let me smash that bloody door in. Come out—come out—ussza! *(He strikes a heavy blow on the door. There is a scuffle.)*
BLACKMORE'S VOICE: Hold on a bit—what're you doing?
HOLROYD'S VOICE: I'm smashing that blasted door in.
MRS HOLROYD *(appearing and suddenly drawing the bolts, flinging the door open)*: What do you think you're doing?
HOLROYD *(lurching into the room, snarling)*: What? What? Tha thought tha'd play thy monkey tricks on me, did ter? *(Shouting.)* But I'm going to show thee. *(He lurches at her threateningly; she recoils.)*
BLACKMORE *(seizing him by the arm)*: Here, here—! Come and sit down and be quiet.
HOLROYD *(snarling at him)*: What?—What? An' what's thäigh got ter do wi' it *(Shouting.)* What's thäigh got ter do wi' it?
BLACKMORE: Nothing—nothing; but it's getting late, and you want your supper.
HOLROYD *(shouting)*: I want nöwt. I'm allowed nöwt in this 'ouse. *(Shouting louder.)* 'Er begrudges me ivry morsel I ha'e.
MRS HOLROYD: Oh, what a story!
HOLROYD *(shouting)*: It's the truth, an' you know it.
BLACKMORE *(conciliatory)*: You'll rouse the children. You'll rouse the children, at this hour.

HOLROYD *(suddenly quiet)*: Not me—not if I know it. *I* shan't disturb 'em—bless 'em.

He staggers to his arm-chair and sits heavily.

BLACKMORE: Shall I light the lamp?

MRS HOLROYD: No, don't trouble. Don't stay any longer, there's no need.

BLACKMORE *(quietly):* I'll just see it's alright.

He proceeds in silence to light the lamp. HOLROYD *is seen dropping forward in his chair. He has a cut on his cheek.* MRS HOLROYD *is in an old-fashioned dressing-gown.* BLACKMORE *has an overcoat buttoned up to his chin. There is a very large lump of coal on the red fire.*

MRS HOLROYD: Don't stay any longer.

BLACKMORE: I'll see it's alright.

MRS HOLROYD: I shall be all right. He'll go to sleep now.

BLACKMORE: But he can't go like that.

MRS HOLROYD: What has he done to his face?

BLACKMORE: He had a row with Jim Goodwin.

MRS HOLROYD: What about?

BLACKMORE: I don't know.

MRS HOLROYD: The beast!

BLACKMORE: By Jove, and isn't he a weight! He's getting fat, must be——

MRS HOLROYD: He's big made—he has a big frame.

BLACKMORE: Whatever he is, it took me all my time to get him home. I thought I'd better keep an eye on him. I knew you'd be worrying. So I sat in the smoke-room and waited for him. Though it's a dirty hole—and dull as hell.

MRS HOLROYD: Why did you bother?

BLACKMORE: Well, I thought you'd be upset about him. I had to drink three whiskies—had to, in all conscience—*(smiling)*.

MRS HOLROYD: I don't want to be the ruin of you.

BLACKMORE *(smiling)*: Don't you? I thought he'd pitch forward on to the lines and crack his skull.

HOLROYD *has been sinking farther and farther forward in drunken sleep. He suddenly jerks too far and is awakened. He sits upright, glaring fiercely and dazedly at the two, who instantly cease talking.*

HOLROYD *(to* BLACKMORE*)*: What are thäigh doin' 'ere?

BLACKMORE: Why, I came along with you.

HOLROYD: Thou'rt a liar, I'm only just come in.

MRS HOLROYD *(coldly)*: He is no liar at all. He brought you home because you were too drunk to come yourself.

HOLROYD *(starting up)*: Thou'rt a liar! I niver set eyes on him this night, afore now.

MRS HOLROYD *(with a "Pf" of contempt)*: You don't know what you *have* done to-night.

HOLROYD *(shouting)*: I s'll not ha'e it, I tell thee.

MRS HOLROYD: Psh!

HOLROYD: I s'll not ha'e it. I s'll ha'e no carryin's on i' my 'ouse——

MRS HOLROYD *(shrugging her shoulders)*: Talk when you've got some sense.

HOLROYD *(fiercely)*: I've as much sense as thäigh. Am I a fool? Canna I see? What's *he* doin' here then, answer me that. What——?

MRS HOLROYD: Mr Blackmore came to bring *you* home because you were *too drunk* to find your own way. And this is the thanks he gets.

HOLROYD *(contemptuously)*: Blackymore, Blackymore. It's him tha cuts thy cloth by, is it?

MRS HOLROYD *(hotly)*: You don't know what you're talking about, so keep your tongue still.

HOLROYD *(bitingly)*: I don't know what I'm talking about—I don't know what I'm talking about—don't I? An' what about him standing there then, if I don't know what I'm talking about?—What?

BLACKMORE: You've been to sleep, Charlie, an' forgotten I came in with you, not long since.

HOLROYD: I'm not daft, I'm not a fool. I've got eyes in my head and sense. You needn't try to get over me. I know what you're up to.

BLACKMORE *(flushing)*: It's a bit off to talk to me like that, Charlie, I must say.

HOLROYD: I'm not good enough for 'er. She wants Mr Blackymore. He's a gentleman, he is. Now we have it all; now we understand.

MRS HOLROYD: I wish you understood enough to keep your tongue still.

HOLROYD: What? What? I'm to keep my tongue still, am I? An' what about *Mr Blackymore*?

MRS HOLROYD *(fiercely)*: Stop your mouth, you—you vulgar, low-minded brute.

HOLROYD: Am I? Am I? An' what are you? What tricks are you up to, an' all? But that's alright—that's alright. *(Shouting.)* That's alright, if it's *you*.

BLACKMORE: I think I'd better go. You seem to enjoy—er—er—calumniating your wife.

HOLROYD *(mockingly)*: Calamniating—calamniating—I'll give you calamniating, you mealy-mouthed jockey: I'll give you calamniating.

BLACKMORE: I think you've said about enough.

HOLROYD: 'Ave I, 'ave I? Yer flimsy jack—'ave I? *(In a sudden burst.)* But I've not done wi' thee yet?

BLACKMORE *(ironically)*: No, and you haven't.

HOLROYD *(shouting—pulling himself up from the arm-chair)*: I'll show thee—I'll show thee.

   BLACKMORE *laughs.*

HOLROYD: Yes!—yes, my young monkey. It's thäigh, is it?

BLACKMORE: Yes, it's *me*.

HOLROYD *(shouting)*: An' I'll ma'e thee wish it worn't, I will. What—? What? Tha'd come slivin' round here, would ta? *(He lurches forward at BLACKMORE with clenched fist.)*

MRS HOLROYD: Drunken, drunken fool—oh, don't.

HOLROYD *(turning to her)*: What?

   She puts up her hands before her face. BLACKMORE *seizes the upraised arm and swings* HOLROYD *round.*

BLACKMORE *(in a towering passion)*: Mind what tha'rt doing!

HOLROYD *(turning fiercely on him—incoherent)*: Wha'—wha'——!

   He aims a heavy blow. BLACKMORE *evades it, so that he is struck on the side of the chest. Suddenly he shows his teeth. He raises his fists ready to strike* HOLROYD *when the latter stands to advantage.*

MRS HOLROYD *(rushing upon BLACKMORE)*: No, no! Oh, no!

   She flies and opens the door, and goes out. BLACKMORE *glances after her, then at* HOLROYD, *who is preparing, like a bull, for another charge. The young man's face lights up.*

HOLROYD: Wha'—wha'——!

As he advances, BLACKMORE *quickly retreats out-of-doors.*
HOLROYD *plunges upon him.* BLACKMORE *slips behind the door-
jamb, puts out his foot, and trips* HOLROYD *with a crash upon
the brick yard.*

MRS HOLROYD: Oh, what has he done to himself?

BLACKMORE *(thickly)*: Tumbled over himself.

    HOLROYD *is seen struggling to rise, and is heard incoherently
cursing.*

MRS HOLROYD: Aren't you going to get him up?

BLACKMORE: What for?

MRS HOLROYD: But what shall we do?

BLACKMORE: Let him go to hell.

    HOLROYD, *who has subsided, begins to snarl and struggle
again.*

MRS HOLROYD *(in terror)*: He's getting up.

BLACKMORE: Alright, let him.

    MRS HOLROYD *looks at* BLACKMORE, *suddenly afraid of him
also.*

HOLROYD *(in a last frenzy)*: I'll show thee—I'll——

    He raises himself up, and is just picking his balance when
BLACKMORE, *with a sudden light kick, sends him sprawling
again. He is seen on the edge of the light to collapse into stupor.*

MRS HOLROYD: He'll kill you, he'll kill you!

    BLACKMORE *laughs short.*

MRS HOLROYD: Would you believe it! Oh, isn't it awful! *(She
begins to weep in a little hysteria;* BLACKMORE *stands with his
back leaning on the doorway, grinning in a strained fashion.)* Is
he hurt, do you think?

BLACKMORE: I don't know—I should think not.

MRS HOLROYD: I wish he was dead; I do, with all my heart.

BLACKMORE: Do you? *(He looks at her quickly; she wavers and
shrinks; he begins to smile strainedly as before.)* You don't know
what you wish, or what you want.

MRS HOLROYD *(troubled)*: Do you think I could get past him to
come inside?

BLACKMORE: I should think so.

    MRS HOLROYD, *silent and troubled, manœuvres in the door-
way, stepping over her husband's feet, which lie on the threshold.*

BLACKMORE: Why, you've got no shoes and stockings on!

MRS HOLROYD: No. (*She enters the house and stands trembling before the fire.*)

BLACKMORE (*following her*): Are you cold?

MRS HOLROYD: A little—with standing on the yard.

BLACKMORE: What a shame!

> *She, uncertain of herself, sits down. He drops on one knee, awkwardly, and takes her feet in his hands.*

MRS HOLROYD: Don't—no, don't!

BLACKMORE: They are frightfully cold. (*He remains, with head sunk, for some moments, then slowly rises.*) Damn him!

> *They look at each other; then, at the same time, turn away.*

MRS HOLROYD: We can't leave him lying there.

BLACKMORE: No—no! I'll bring him in.

MRS HOLROYD: But——!

BLACKMORE: He won't wake again. The drink will have got hold of him by now. (*He hesitates.*) Could you take hold of his feet— he's so heavy.

MRS HOLROYD: Yes.

> *They go out and are seen stooping over HOLROYD.*

BLACKMORE: Wait, wait, till I've got him—half a minute.

> MRS HOLROYD *backs in first. They carry* HOLROYD *in and lay him on the sofa.*

MRS HOLROYD: Doesn't he look awful?

BLACKMORE: It's more mark than mar. It isn't much, really.

> *He is busy taking off* HOLROYD'S *collar and tie, unfastening the waistcoat, the braces and the waist buttons of the trousers; he then proceeds to unlace the drunken man's boots.*

MRS HOLROYD (*who has been watching closely*): I shall never get him upstairs.

BLACKMORE: He can sleep here, with a rug or something to cover him. *You* don't want him—upstairs?

MRS HOLROYD: Never again.

BLACKMORE (*after a moment or two of silence*): He'll be alright down here. Have you got a rug?

MRS HOLROYD: Yes.

> *She goes upstairs.* BLACKMORE *goes into the scullery, returning with a ladling can and towel. He gets hot water from the boiler. Then, kneeling down, he begins to wipe the drunken*

man's face lightly with the flannel, to remove the blood and dirt.

MRS HOLROYD *(returning)*: What are you doing?

BLACKMORE: Only wiping his face to get the dirt out.

MRS HOLROYD: I wonder if he'd do as much for you.

BLACKMORE: I hope not.

MRS HOLROYD: Isn't he horrible, horrible——

BLACKMORE *(looks up at her)*: Don't look at him then.

MRS HOLROYD: I can't take it in, it's too much.

BLACKMORE: He won't wake. I will stay with you.

MRS HOLROYD *(earnestly)*: No—oh, no.

BLACKMORE: There will be the drawn sword between us. *(He indicates the figure of* HOLROYD, *which lies, in effect, as a barrier between them.)*

MRS HOLROYD *(blushing)*: Don't!

BLACKMORE: I'm sorry.

MRS HOLROYD *(after watching him for a few moments lightly wiping the sleeping man's face with a towel)*: I wonder you can be so careful over him.

BLACKMORE *(quietly)*: It's only because he's helpless.

MRS HOLROYD: But why should you love him ever so little?

BLACKMORE: I don't—only he's helpless. Five minutes since I could have killed him.

MRS HOLROYD: Well, I don't understand you men.

BLACKMORE: Why?

MRS HOLROYD: I don't know.

BLACKMORE: I thought as I stood in that doorway, and he was trying to get up—I wished as hard as I've ever wished anything in my life——

MRS HOLROYD: What?

BLACKMORE: That I'd killed him. I've never wished anything so much in my life—if wishes were anything.

MRS HOLROYD: Don't, it *does* sound awful.

BLACKMORE: I *could* have done it, too. He ought to be dead.

MRS HOLROYD *(pleading)*: No, don't! You know you don't mean it, and you make me feel so awful.

BLACKMORE: I do mean it. It is simply true, what I say.

MRS HOLROYD: But don't say it.

BLACKMORE: No?

MRS HOLROYD: No, we've had enough.

BLACKMORE: Give me the rug.

She hands it him, and he tucks HOLROYD *up.*

MRS HOLROYD: You only do it to play on my feelings.

BLACKMORE *(laughing shortly)*: And now give me a pillow—thanks.

There is a pause—both look at the sleeping man.

BLACKMORE: I suppose you're fond of him, really.

MRS HOLROYD: No more.

BLACKMORE: You *were* fond of him?

MRS HOLROYD: I was—yes.

BLACKMORE: What did you like in him?

MRS HOLROYD *(uneasily)*: I don't know.

BLACKMORE: I suppose you really care about him, even now?

MRS HOLROYD: Why are you so sure of it?

BLACKMORE: Because I think it is so.

MRS HOLROYD: I did care for him—now he has destroyed it——

BLACKMORE: I don't believe he can destroy it.

MRS HOLROYD *(with a short laugh)*: Don't you? When you are married you try. You'll find it isn't so hard.

BLACKMORE: But what did you like in him—because he was good-looking, and strong, and that?

MRS HOLROYD: I liked that as well. But if a man makes a nuisance of himself, his good looks are ugly to you, and his strength loathsome. Do you think I *care* about a man because he's got big fists, when he is a coward in his real self?

BLACKMORE: Is he a coward?

MRS HOLROYD: He *is*—a pettifogging, paltry one.

BLACKMORE: And so you've really done with him?

MRS HOLROYD: I have.

BLACKMORE: And what are you going to do?

MRS HOLROYD: I don't know.

BLACKMORE: I suppose nothing. You'll just go on—even if you've done with him—you'll go on with him.

There is a long pause.

BLACKMORE: But was there nothing else in him but his muscles and his good looks to attract you to him?

MRS HOLROYD: Why? What does it matter?

BLACKMORE: What did you *think* he was?

MRS HOLROYD: Why must we talk about him?

BLACKMORE : Because I can never quite believe you.

MRS HOLROYD : I can't help whether you believe it or not.

BLACKMORE : Are you just in a rage with him, because of to-night?

MRS HOLROYD : I know, to-night finished it. But it was never right between us.

BLACKMORE : Never?

MRS HOLROYD : Not once. And then to-night—no, it's too much; I can't stand any more of it.

BLACKMORE : I suppose he got tipsy. Then he said he wasn't a married man—vowed he wasn't, to those paper bonnets. They found out he was, and said he was frightened of his wife getting to know. Then he said they should all go to supper at his house— I suppose they came out of mischief.

MRS HOLROYD : He did it to insult me.

BLACKMORE : Oh, he was a bit tight—you can't say it was deliberate.

MRS HOLROYD : No, but it shows how he feels toward me. The feeling comes out in drink.

BLACKMORE : How does he feel toward you?

MRS HOLROYD : He wants to insult me, and humiliate me, in every moment of his life. Now I simply despise him.

BLACKMORE : You really don't care any more about him?

MRS HOLROYD : No.

BLACKMORE *(hesitates)* : And you would leave him?

MRS HOLROYD : I would leave him, and not care *that* about him any more. *(She snaps her fingers.)*

BLACKMORE : Will you come with me?

MRS HOLROYD *(after a reluctant pause)* : Where?

BLACKMORE : To Spain : I can any time have a job there, in a decent part. You could take the children.

 The figure of the sleeper stirs uneasily—they watch him.

BLACKMORE : Will you?

MRS HOLROYD : When would you go?

BLACKMORE : To-morrow, if you like.

MRS HOLROYD : But why do you want to saddle yourself with me and the children?

BLACKMORE : Because I want to.

MRS HOLROYD : But you don't love me?

BLACKMORE : Why don't I?

MRS HOLROYD : You don't.

BLACKMORE : I don't know about that. I don't know anything about love. Only I've gone on for a year, now, and it's got stronger and stronger——

MRS HOLROYD : What has?

BLACKMORE : This—this wanting you, to live with me. I took no notice of it for a long time. Now I can't get away from it, at no hour and nohow. *(He still avoids direct contact with her.)*

MRS HOLROYD : But you'd *like* to get away from it.

BLACKMORE : I hate a mess of any sort. But if you'll come away with me—you and the children——

MRS HOLROYD : But I couldn't—you don't love me——

BLACKMORE : I don't know what you mean by I don't love you.

MRS HOLROYD : I can feel it.

BLACKMORE : And do you love *me*? *(A pause.)*

MRS HOLROYD : I don't know. Everything is so—so——
      There is a long pause.

BLACKMORE : How old are you?

MRS HOLROYD : Thirty-two.

BLACKMORE : I'm twenty-seven.

MRS HOLROYD : And have you never been in love?

BLACKMORE : I don't think so. I don't know.

MRS HOLROYD : But you must know. I must go and shut that door that keeps clicking.
      She rises to go upstairs, making a clatter at the stairfoot door. The noise rouses her husband. As she goes upstairs, he moves, makes coughing sounds, turns over, and then suddenly sits upright, gazing at BLACKMORE. *The latter sits perfectly still on the sofa, his head dropped, hiding his face. His hands are clasped. They remain thus for a minute.*

HOLROYD : Hello! *(He stares fixedly.)* Hello! *(His tone is undecided, as if he mistrusts himself.)* What are—who are ter? (BLACKMORE *does not move;* HOLROYD *stares blankly; he then turns and looks at the room.)* Well, I dunna know.
      He staggers to his feet, clinging to the table, and goes groping to the stairs. They creak loudly under his weight. A door-latch is heard to click. In a moment MRS HOLROYD *comes quickly downstairs.*

BLACKMORE : Has he gone to bed?

MRS HOLROYD *(nodding)* : Lying on the bed.

BLACKMORE: Will he settle now?

MRS HOLROYD: I don't know. He is like that sometimes. He will have delirium tremens if he goes on.

BLACKMORE *(softly)*: You can't stay with him, you know.

MRS HOLROYD: And the children?

BLACKMORE: We'll take them.

MRS HOLROYD: Oh!

> *Her face puckers to cry. Suddenly he starts up and puts his arms round her, holding her protectively and gently, very caressingly. She clings to him. They are silent for some moments.*

BLACKMORE *(struggling, in an altered voice)*: Look at me and kiss me.

> *Her sobs are heard distinctly.* BLACKMORE *lays his hand on her cheek, caressing her always with his hand.*

BLACKMORE: My God, but I hate him! I wish either he was dead or me. (MRS HOLROYD *hides against him; her sobs cease; after a while he continues in the same murmuring fashion.*) It can't go on like it any more. I feel as if I should come in two. I can't keep away from you. I simply can't. Come with me. Come with me and leave him. If you knew what a hell it is for me to have you here—and to see him. I can't go without you, I can't. It's been hell every moment for six months now. You say I don't love you. Perhaps I don't, for all I know about it. But oh, my God, don't keep me like it any longer. Why should *he* have you—and I've never had anything.

MRS HOLROYD: Have you never loved anybody?

BLACKMORE: No—I've tried. Kiss me of your own wish—will you?

MRS HOLROYD: I don't know.

BLACKMORE *(after a pause)*: Let's break clear. Let's go right away. Do you care for me?

MRS HOLROYD: I don't know. *(She loosens herself, rises dumbly.)*

BLACKMORE: When do you think you *will* know?

> *She sits down helplessly.*

MRS HOLROYD: I don't know.

BLACKMORE: Yes, you do know, really. If he was dead, should you marry me?

MRS HOLROYD: Don't say it——

BLACKMORE: Why not? If wishing of mine would kill him, he'd soon be out of the way.

MRS HOLROYD: But the children!

BLACKMORE: I'm fond of them. I shall have good money.

MRS HOLROYD: But he's their father.

BLACKMORE: What does that mean——?

MRS HOLROYD: Yes, I know—*(a pause)* but——

BLACKMORE: Is it *him* that keeps you?

MRS HOLROYD: No.

BLACKMORE: Then come with me. Will you? *(He stands waiting for her; then he turns and takes his overcoat; pulls it on, leaving the collar turned up, ceasing to twist his cap.)* Well—will you tell me to-morrow?

> *She goes forward and flings her arms round his neck. He suddenly kisses her passionately.*

MRS HOLROYD: But I ought not. *(She draws away a little; he will not let her go.)*

BLACKMORE: Yes, it's alright. *(He holds her close.)*

MRS HOLROYD: Is it?

BLACKMORE: Yes, it is. It's alright.

> *He kisses her again. She releases herself but holds his hand. They keep listening.*

MRS HOLROYD: Do you love me?

BLACKMORE: What do you ask for?

MRS HOLROYD: Have I hurt you these months?

BLACKMORE: *You* haven't. And I don't care what it's been if you'll come with me. *(There is a noise upstairs and they wait.)* You will soon, won't you?

> *She kisses him.*

MRS HOLROYD: He's not safe. *(She disengages herself and sits on the sofa.)*

BLACKMORE *(takes a place beside her, holding her hand in both his)*: You should have waited for me.

MRS HOLROYD: How wait?

BLACKMORE: And not have married him.

MRS HOLROYD: I might never have known you—I married him to get out of my place.

BLACKMORE: Why?

MRS HOLROYD: I was left an orphan when I was six. My Uncle

John brought me up, in the Coach and Horses at Rainsworth. He'd got no children. He was good to me, but he drank. I went to Mansfield Grammar School. Then he fell out with me because I wouldn't wait in the bar, and I went as nursery governess to Berryman's. And I felt I'd nowhere to go, I belonged to nowhere, and nobody cared about me, and men came after me, and I hated it. So to get out of it, I married the first man that turned up.

BLACKMORE: And you never cared about him?

MRS HOLROYD: Yes, I did. I did care about him. I wanted to be a wife to him. But there's nothing at the bottom of him, if you know what I mean. You can't *get* anywhere with him. There's just his body and nothing else. Nothing that keeps him, no anchor, no roots, nothing satisfying. It's a horrible feeling there is about him, that nothing is safe or permanent—nothing is anything——

BLACKMORE: And do you think you can trust *me*?

MRS HOLROYD: I think you're different from him.

BLACKMORE: Perhaps I'm not.

MRS HOLROYD *(warmly)*: You are.

BLACKMORE: At any rate, we'll see. You'll come on Saturday to London?

MRS HOLROYD: Well, you see, there's my money. I haven't got it yet. My uncle has left me about a hundred and twenty pounds.

BLACKMORE: Well, see the lawyer about it as soon as you can. I can let you have some money if you want any. But don't let us wait after Saturday.

MRS HOLROYD: But isn't it wrong?

BLACKMORE: Why, if you don't care for him, and the children are miserable between the two of you—which they are——

MRS HOLROYD: Yes.

BLACKMORE: Well, then I see no wrong. As for him—he would go one way, and only one way, whatever you do. Damn him, he doesn't matter.

MRS HOLROYD: No.

BLACKMORE: Well, then—have done with it. Can't you cut clean of him? Can't you now?

MRS HOLROYD: And then—the children——

BLACKMORE: They'll be alright with me and you—won't they?

MRS HOLROYD: Yes——

BLACKMORE: Well, then. Now, come and have done with it. We

can't keep on being ripped in two like this. We need never hear of him any more.

MRS HOLROYD: Yes—I love you. I do love you——

BLACKMORE: Oh, my God! *(He speaks with difficulty—embracing her.)*

MRS HOLROYD: When I look at him, and then at you—ha—*(She gives a short laugh.)*

BLACKMORE: He's had all the chance—it's only fair—Lizzie——

MRS HOLROYD: My love.

> *There is silence. He keeps his arm round her. After hesitating, he picks up his cap.*

BLACKMORE: I'll go then—at any rate. Shall you come with me?
> *She follows him to the door.*

MRS HOLROYD: I'll come on Saturday.

BLACKMORE: Not now?

CURTAIN

ACT III

Scene, the same. Time, the following evening, about seven o'clock.
The table is half-laid, with a large cup and saucer, plate, etc.,
ready for HOLROYD'S *dinner, which, like all miners, he has*
when he comes home between four and five o'clock. On the
other half of the table MRS HOLROYD *is ironing. On the hearth*
stand newly baked loaves of bread. The irons hang at the fire.
JACK, *with a bowler hat hanging at the back of his head,*
parades up to the sofa, on which stands MINNIE *engaged in*
dusting a picture. She has a soiled white apron tied behind her,
to make a long skirt.

JACK: Good mornin', missis. Any scissors or knives to grind?

MINNIE *(peering down from the sofa)*: Oh, I can't be bothered to
come downstairs. Call another day.

JACK: I shan't.

MINNIE *(keeping up her part)*: Well, I can't come down now. (JACK
stands irresolute.) Go on, you have to go and steal the baby.

JACK: I'm not.

MINNIE: Well, you can steal the eggs out of the fowl-house.

JACK: I'm not.

MINNIE: Then I shan't play with you.

> JACK *takes off his bowler hat and flings it on the sofa; tears*
> *come in* MINNIE'S *eyes.*

> Now I'm *not* friends. *(She surveys him ruefully; after a few*
> *moments of silence she clambers down and goes to her*
> *mother.)* Mam, he won't play with me.

MRS HOLROYD *(crossly)*: Why don't you play with her? If you
begin bothering, you must go to bed.

JACK: Well, I don't want to play.

MRS HOLROYD: Then you must go to bed.

JACK: I don't want to.

MRS HOLROYD: Then what do you want, I should like to know?

MINNIE: I wish my father'd come.

JACK: I do.

MRS HOLROYD : I suppose he thinks he's paying me out. This is the third time this week he's slunk past the door and gone down to Old Brinsley instead of coming in to his dinner. He'll be as drunk as a lord when he does come.

The children look at her plaintively.

MINNIE : Isn't he a nuisance?

JACK : I hate him. I wish he'd drop down th' pit-shaft.

MRS HOLROYD : Jack!—I never heard such a thing in my life! You mustn't say such things—it's wicked.

JACK : Well, I do.

MRS HOLROYD *(loudly)*: I won't have it. He's your father, re-member.

JACK *(in a high voice)*: Well, he's always comin' home an' shoutin' an' bangin' on the table. *(He is getting tearful and defiant.)*

MRS HOLROYD : Well, you mustn't take any notice of him.

MINNIE *(wistfully)*: 'Appen if you said something nice to him, mother, he'd happen go to bed, and not shout.

JACK : I'd hit him in the mouth.

MRS HOLROYD : Perhaps we'll go to another country, away from him—should we?

JACK : In a ship, mother?

MINNIE : In a ship, mam?

MRS HOLROYD : Yes, in a big ship, where it's blue sky, and water and palm-trees, and——

MINNIE : An' dates——?

JACK : When should we go?

MRS HOLROYD : Some day.

MINNIE : But who'd work for us? Who should we have for father?

JACK : You don't want a father. I can go to work for us.

MRS HOLROYD : I've got a lot of money now, that your uncle left me.

MINNIE *(after a general thoughtful silence)*: An' would my father stop here?

MRS HOLROYD : Oh, he'd be alright.

MINNIE : But who would he live with?

MRS HOLROYD : I don't know—one of his paper bonnets, if he likes.

MINNIE : Then she could have her old bracelet back, couldn't she?

MRS HOLROYD : Yes—there it is on the candlestick, waiting for her.

There is a sound of footsteps—then a knock at the door. The children start.

MINNIE *(in relief)*: Here he is.

MRS HOLROYD *goes to the door.* BLACKMORE *enters.*

BLACKMORE: It is foggy to-night— Hello, aren't you youngsters gone to bed?

MINNIE: No, my father's not come home yet.

BLACKMORE *(turning to* MRS HOLROYD*)*: Did he go to work then, after last night?

MRS HOLROYD: I suppose so. His pit things were gone when I got up. I never thought he'd go.

BLACKMORE: And he took his snap as usual?

MRS HOLROYD: Yes, just as usual. I suppose he's gone to the New Inn. He'd say to himself he'd pay me out. That's what he always does say, "I'll pay thee out for that bit—I'll ma'e thee regret it."

JACK: We're going to leave him.

BLACKMORE: So you think he's at the New Inn?

MRS HOLROYD: I'm sure he is—and he'll come when he's full. He'll have a bout now, you'll see.

MINNIE: Go and fetch him, Mr Blackmore.

JACK: My mother says we shall go in a ship and leave him.

BLACKMORE *(after looking keenly at* JACK: *to* MRS HOLROYD*)*: Shall I go and see if he's at the New Inn?

MRS HOLROYD: No—perhaps you'd better not——

BLACKMORE: Oh, he shan't see me. I can easily manage that.

JACK: Fetch him, Mr Blackmore.

BLACKMORE: Alright, Jack. *(To* MRS HOLROYD.*)* Shall I?

MRS HOLROYD: We're always pulling on you—— But yes, do!

BLACKMORE *goes out.*

JACK: I wonder how long he'll be.

MRS HOLROYD: You come and go to bed now: you'd better be out of the way when he comes in.

MINNIE: And you won't say anything to him, mother, will you?

MRS HOLROYD: What do you mean?

MINNIE: You won't begin of him—row him.

MRS HOLROYD: Is he to have all his own way? What *would* he be like, if I didn't row him?

JACK: But it doesn't matter, mother, if we're going to leave him——

MINNIE: But Mr Blackmore'll come back, won't he, mam, and dad won't shout before him?

MRS HOLROYD *(beginning to undress the children)*: Yes, he'll come back.

MINNIE: Mam—could I have that bracelet to go to bed with?

MRS HOLROYD: Come and say your prayers.

They kneel, muttering in their mother's apron.

MINNIE *(suddenly lifting her head)*: Can I, mam?

MRS HOLROYD *(trying to be stern)*: Have you finished your prayers?

MINNIE: Yes.

MRS HOLROYD: If you want it—beastly thing! *(She reaches the bracelet down from the mantelpiece.)* Your father must have put it up there—I don't know where I left it. I suppose he'd think I was proud of it and wanted it for an ornament.

> MINNIE *gloats over it.* MRS HOLROYD *lights a candle and they go upstairs. After a few moments the outer door opens, and there enters an old woman. She is of middling stature and wears a large grey shawl over her head. After glancing sharply round the room, she advances to the fire, warms herself, then, taking off her shawl, sits in the rocking-chair. As she hears* MRS HOLROYD'S *footsteps, she folds her hands and puts on a lachrymose expression, turning down the corners of her mouth and arching her eyebrows.*

MRS HOLROYD: Hello, mother, is it you?

GRANDMOTHER: Yes, it's me. Haven't you finished ironing?

MRS HOLROYD: Not yet.

GRANDMOTHER: You'll have your irons red-hot.

MRS HOLROYD: Yes, I s'll have to stand them to cool. *(She does so, and moves about at her ironing.)*

GRANDMOTHER: And you don't know what's become of Charles?

MRS HOLROYD: Well, he's not come home from work yet. I supposed he was at the New Inn— Why?

GRANDMOTHER: That young electrician come knocking asking if I knew where he was. "Eh," I said, "I've not set eyes on him for over a week—nor his wife neither, though they pass th' garden gate every time they go out. I know nowt on 'im." I axed him what was the matter, so he said Mrs Holroyd was anxious because he'd not come home, so I thought I'd better come and see. Is there anything up?

MRS HOLROYD: No more than I've told you.

GRANDMOTHER: It's a rum 'un, if he's neither in the New Inn nor the Prince o' Wales. I suppose something you've done's set him off.

MRS HOLROYD: It's nothing I've done.

GRANDMOTHER: Eh, if he's gone off and left you, whativer shall we do! Whativer 'ave you been doing?

MRS HOLROYD: He brought a couple of bright daisies here last night—two of those trollops from Nottingham—and I said I'd not have it.

GRANDMOTHER *(sighing deeply)*: Ay, you've never been able to agree.

MRS HOLROYD: We agreed well enough except when he drank like a fish and came home rolling.

GRANDMOTHER *(whining)*: Well, what can you expect of a man as 'as been shut up i' th' pit all day? He must have a bit of relaxation.

MRS HOLROYD: He can have it different from that, then. At any rate, I'm sick of it.

GRANDMOTHER: Ay, you've a stiff neck, but it'll be bowed by you're my age.

MRS HOLROYD: Will it? I'd rather it were broke.

GRANDMOTHER: Well—there's no telling what a jealous man will do. *(She shakes her head.)*

MRS HOLROYD: Nay, I think it's my place to be jealous, when he brings a brazen hussy here and sits carryin' on with her.

GRANDMOTHER: He'd no business to do that. But you know, Lizzie, he's got something on *his* side.

MRS HOLROYD: What, pray?

GRANDMOTHER: Well, I don't want to make any mischief, but you're my son's wife, an' it's nothing but my duty to tell you. They've been saying a long time now as that young electrician is here a bit too often.

MRS HOLROYD: He doesn't come for my asking.

GRANDMOTHER: No, I don't suppose he wants for asking. But Charlie's not the man to put up with that sort o' work.

MRS HOLROYD: Charlie put up with it! If he's anything to say, why doesn't he say it, without going to other folks . . . ?

GRANDMOTHER: Charlie's never been near me with a word—nor 'as he said a word elsewhere to my knowledge. For all that, this is going to end with trouble.

MRS HOLROYD : In this hole, every gossiping creature thinks she's got the right to cackle about you—sickening! And a parcel of lies.

GRANDMOTHER : Well, Lizzie, I've never said anything against you. Charlie's been a handful of trouble. He made my heart ache once or twice afore you had him, and he's made it ache many, many's the time since. But it's not all on his side, you know.

MRS HOLROYD *(hotly)* : No, I don't know.

GRANDMOTHER : You thought yourself above him, Lizzie, an' you know he's not the man to stand it.

MRS HOLROYD : No, he's run away from it.

GRANDMOTHER *(venomously)* : And what man wouldn't leave a woman that allowed him to live on sufferance in the house with her, when he was bringing the money home?

MRS HOLROYD : "Sufferance!"—Yes, there's been a lot of letting him live on "sufferance" in the house with me. It is *I* who have lived on sufferance, for his service and pleasure. No, what he wanted was the drink and the public house company, and because he couldn't get them here, he went out for them. That's all.

GRANDMOTHER : You have always been very clever at hitting things off, Lizzie. I was always sorry my youngest son married a clever woman. He only wanted a bit of coaxing and managing, and you clever women won't do it.

MRS HOLROYD : He wanted a slave, not a wife.

GRANDMOTHER : It's a pity your stomach wasn't too high for him, before you had him. But no, you could have eaten him ravishing at one time.

MRS HOLROYD : It's a pity you didn't tell me what he was before I had him. But no, he was all angel. You left me to find out what he really was.

GRANDMOTHER : Some women could have lived with him happy enough. An' a fat lot you'd have thanked me for my telling.

There is a knock at the door. MRS HOLROYD *opens.*

RIGLEY : They tell me, missus, as your mester's not hoom yet.

MRS HOLROYD : No—who is it?

GRANDMOTHER : Ask him to step inside. Don't stan' there lettin' the fog in.

RIGLEY *steps in. He is a tall, bony, very roughly hewn collier.*

RIGLEY: Good evenin'.

GRANDMOTHER: Oh, is it you, Mr Rigley? *(In a querulous, spiteful tone to* MRS HOLROYD.) He butties along with Charlie.

MRS HOLROYD: Oh!

RIGLEY: Au' han yer seen nowt on 'im?

MRS HOLROYD: No—was he all right at work?

RIGLEY: Well, e' wor nowt to mention. A bit short, like: 'adna much to say. I canna ma'e out what 'e's done wi' 'issen. *(He is manifestly uneasy, does not look at the two women.)*

GRANDMOTHER: An' did 'e come up i' th' same bantle wi' you?

RIGLEY: No—'e didna. As Ah was comin' out o' th' stall, Ah shouted, "Art comin', Charlie? We're a' off." An' 'e said, "Ah'm comin' in a minute." 'E wor just finishin' a stint, like, an' 'e wanted ter get it set. An' 'e 'd been a bit roughish in 'is temper, like, so I thöwt 'e didna want ter walk to th' bottom wi' us. . . .

GRANDMOTHER *(wailing)*: An' what's 'e gone an' done to himself?

RIGLEY: Nay, missis, yo munna ax me that. 'E's non done owt as Ah know on. On'y I wor thinkin', 'appen summat 'ad 'appened to 'im, like, seein' as nob'dy had any knowings of 'im comin' up.

MRS HOLROYD: What is the matter, Mr Rigley? Tell us it out.

RIGLEY: I canna do that, missis. It seems as if 'e niver come up th' pit—as far as we can make out. 'Appen a bit o' stuff's fell an' pinned 'im.

GRANDMOTHER *(wailing)*: An' 'ave you left 'im lying down there in the pit, poor thing?

RIGLEY *(uneasily)*: I couldna say for certain where 'e is.

MRS HOLROYD *(agitated)*: Oh, it's very likely not very bad, mother! Don't let us run to meet trouble.

RIGLEY: We 'ave to 'ope for th' best, missis, all on us.

GRANDMOTHER *(wailing)*: Eh, they'll bring 'im 'ome, I know they will, smashed up an' broke! An' one of my sons they've burned down pit till the flesh dropped off 'im, an' one was shot till 'is shoulder was all of a mosh, an' they brought 'em 'ome to me. An' now there's this. . . .

MRS HOLROYD *(shuddering)*: Oh, don't, mother. *(Appealing to* RIGLEY.) You don't know that he's hurt?

RIGLEY *(shaking his head)*: I canna tell you.

MRS HOLROYD *(in a high hysterical voice)*: Then what is it?

RIGLEY *(very uneasy)*: I canna tell you. But yon young electrician —Mr Blackmore—'e rung down to the night deputy, an' it seems as though there's been a fall or summat. . . .

GRANDMOTHER: Eh, Lizzie, you parted from him in anger. You little knowed how you'd meet him again.

RIGLEY *(making an effort)*: Well, I'd 'appen best be goin' to see what's betide.

  He goes out.

GRANDMOTHER: I'm sure I've had my share of bad luck, I have. I'm sure I've brought up five lads in the pit, through accidents and troubles, and now there's this. The Lord has treated me very hard, very hard. It's a blessing, Lizzie, as you've got a bit of money, else what would 'ave become of the children?

MRS HOLROYD: Well, if he's badly hurt, there'll be the Union-pay, and sick-pay—we shall manage. And perhaps it's *not* very much.

GRANDMOTHER: There's no knowin' but what they'll be carryin' him to die 'i th' hospital.

MRS HOLROYD: Oh, don't say so, mother—it won't be so bad, you'll see.

GRANDMOTHER: How much money have you, Lizzie, comin'?

MRS HOLROYD: I don't know—not much over a hundred pounds.

GRANDMOTHER *(shaking her head)*: An' what's that, what's that?

MRS HOLROYD *(sharply)*: Hush!

GRANDMOTHER *(crying)*: Why, what?

  MRS HOLROYD *opens the door. In the silence can be heard the pulsing of the fan engine, then the driving engine chuffs rapidly: there is a skirr of brakes on the rope as it descends.*

MRS HOLROYD: That's twice they've sent the chair down—I wish we could see. . . . Hark!

GRANDMOTHER: What is it?

MRS HOLROYD: Yes—it's stopped at the gate. It's the doctor's.

GRANDMOTHER *(coming to the door)*: What, Lizzie?

MRS HOLROYD: The doctor's motor. *(She listens acutely.)* Dare you stop here, mother, while I run up to the top an' see?

GRANDMOTHER: You'd better not go, Lizzie, you'd better not. A woman's best away.

MRS HOLROYD: It is unbearable to wait.

GRANDMOTHER: Come in an' shut the door—it's a cold that gets in your bones.

MRS HOLROYD *goes in.*

MRS HOLROYD: Perhaps while he's in bed we shall have time to change him. It's an ill wind brings no good. He'll happen be a better man.

GRANDMOTHER: Well, you can but try. Many a woman's thought the same.

MRS HOLROYD: Oh, dear, I wish somebody would come. He's never been hurt since we were married.

GRANDMOTHER: No, he's never had a bad accident, all the years he's been in the pit. He's been luckier than most. But everybody has it, sooner or later.

MRS HOLROYD *(shivering)*: It *is* a horrid night.

GRANDMOTHER *(querulous)*: Yes, come your ways in.

MRS HOLROYD: Hark!

There is a quick sound of footsteps. BLACKMORE *comes into the light of the doorway.*

BLACKMORE: They're bringing him.

MRS HOLROYD *(quickly putting her hand over her breast)*: What is it?

BLACKMORE: You can't tell anything's the matter with him—it's not marked him at all.

MRS HOLROYD: Oh, what a blessing! And is it much?

BLACKMORE: Well——

MRS HOLROYD: What is it?

BLACKMORE: It's the worst.

GRANDMOTHER: Who is it?—What does he say?

MRS HOLROYD *sinks on the nearest chair with a horrified expression.* BLACKMORE *pulls himself together and enters the room. He is very pale.*

BLACKMORE: I came to tell you they're bringing him home.

GRANDMOTHER: And you said it wasn't very bad, did you?

BLACKMORE: No—I said it was—as bad as it could be.

MRS HOLROYD *(rising and crossing to her* MOTHER-IN-LAW, *flings her arms round her; in a high voice)*: Oh, mother, what shall we do? What shall we do?

GRANDMOTHER: You don't mean to say he's dead?

BLACKMORE: Yes.

GRANDMOTHER *(staring)*: God help us, and how was it?

BLACKMORE: Some stuff fell.

GRANDMOTHER (*rocking herself and her daughter-in-law—both weep-ing*): Oh, God have mercy on us! Oh, God have mercy on us! Some stuff fell on him. An' he'd not even time to cry for mercy; oh, God spare him! Oh, what shall we do for comfort? To be taken straight out of his sins. Oh, Lizzie, to think he should be cut off in his wickedness! He's been a bad lad of late, he has, poor lamb. He's gone very wrong of late years, poor dear lamb, very wrong. Oh, Lizzie, think what's to become of him now! If only you'd have tried to be different with him.

MRS HOLROYD (*moaning*): Don't, mother, don't. I can't bear it.

BLACKMORE (*cold and clear*): Where will you have him laid? The men will be here in a moment.

MRS HOLROYD (*starting up*): They can carry him up to bed——

BLACKMORE: It's no good taking him upstairs. You'll have to wash him and lay him out.

MRS HOLROYD (*startled*): Well——

BLACKMORE: He's in his pit-dirt.

GRANDMOTHER: He is, bless him. We'd better have him down here, Lizzie, where we can handle him.

MRS HOLROYD: Yes.

> She begins to put the tea things away, but drops the sugar out of the basin and the lumps fly broadcast.

BLACKMORE: Never mind, I'll pick those up. You put the children's clothes away.

> MRS HOLROYD *stares witless around. The* GRANDMOTHER *sits rocking herself and weeping.* BLACKMORE *clears the table, putting the pots in the scullery. He folds the white tablecloth and pulls back the table. The door opens.* MRS HOLROYD *utters a cry.* RIGLEY *enters.*

RIGLEY: They're bringing him now, missis.

MRS HOLROYD: Oh!

RIGLEY (*simply*): There must ha' been a fall directly after we left him.

MRS HOLROYD (*frowning, horrified*): No—no!

RIGLEY (*to* BLACKMORE): It fell a' back of him, an' shut 'im in as you might shut a loaf 'i th' oven. It never touched him.

MRS HOLROYD (*staring distractedly*): Well, then——

RIGLEY: You see, it come on 'im as close as a trap on a mouse, an' gen him no air, an' what wi' th' gas, it smothered him. An' it wouldna be so very long about it neither.

MRS HOLROYD *(quiet with horror)*: Oh!

GRANDMOTHER: Eh, dear—dear. Eh, dear—dear.

RIGLEY *(looking hard at her)*: I wasna to know what 'ud happen.

GRANDMOTHER *(not heeding him, but weeping all the time)*: But the Lord gave him time to repent. He'd have a few minutes to repent. Ay, I hope he did, I hope he did, else what was to become of him. The Lord cut him off in his sins, but He gave him time to repent.

RIGLEY *looks away at the wall.* BLACKMORE *has made a space in the middle of the floor.*

BLACKMORE: If you'll take the rocking-chair off the end of the rug, Mrs Holroyd, I can pull it back a bit from the fire, and we can lay him on that.

GRANDMOTHER *(petulantly)*: What's the good of messing about—— *(She moves.)*

MRS HOLROYD: It suffocated him?

RIGLEY *(shaking his head, briefly)*: Yes. 'Appened th' after-damp——

BLACKMORE: He'd be dead in a few minutes.

MRS HOLROYD: No—oh, think!

BLACKMORE: You mustn't think.

RIGLEY *(suddenly)*: They commin'!

MRS HOLROYD *stands at bay. The* GRANDMOTHER *half rises.* RIGLEY *and* BLACKMORE *efface themselves as much as possible A man backs into the room, bearing the feet of the dead man, which are shod in great pit boots. As the head bearer comes awkwardly past the table, the coat with which the body is covered slips off, revealing* HOLROYD *in his pit-dirt, naked to the waist.*

MANAGER *(a little stout, white-bearded man)*: Mind now, mind. Ay, missis, what a job, indeed, it is! *(Sharply.)* Where mun they put him?

MRS HOLROYD *(turning her face aside from the corpse)*: Lay him on the rug.

MANAGER: Steady now, do it steady.

SECOND BEARER *(rising and pressing back his shoulders)*: By Guy, but 'e 'ings heavy.

MANAGER: Yi, Joe, I'll back my life o' that.

GRANDMOTHER : Eh, Mr Chambers, what's this affliction on my old age. You kept your sons out o' the pit, but all mine's in. And to think of the trouble I've had—to think o' the trouble that's come out of Brinsley pit to me.

MANAGER : It has that, it 'as that, missis. You seem to have had more'n your share; I'll admit it, you have.

MRS HOLROYD *(who has been staring at the men)* : It is too much!
	BLACKMORE *frowns*; RIGLEY *glowers at her.*

MANAGER : You never knowed such a thing in your life. Here's a man, holin' a stint, just finishin', *(He puts himself as if in the holer's position, gesticulating freely.)* an' a lot o' stuff falls behind him, clean as a whistle, shuts him up safe as a worm in a nut and niver touches him—niver knowed such a thing in your life.

MRS HOLROYD : Ugh!

MANAGER : It niver hurt him—niver touched him.

MRS HOLROYD : Yes, but—but how long would he *be (She makes a sweeping gesture; the MANAGER looks at her and will not help her out.)*—how long would it take—ah—to—to kill him?

MANAGER : Nay, I canna tell ye. 'E didna seem to ha' strived much to get out—did he, Joe?

SECOND BEARER : No, not as far as Ah'n seen.

FIRST BEARER : You look at 'is 'ands, you'll see then. 'E'd non ha'e room to swing the pick.
	The MANAGER goes on his knees.

MRS HOLROYD *(shuddering)* : Oh, don't!

MANAGER : Ay, th' nails is broken a bit——

MRS HOLROYD *(clenching her fists)* : Don't!

MANAGER : 'E'd be sure ter ma'e a bit of a fight. But th' gas 'ud soon get hold on 'im. Ay, it's an awful thing to think of, it is indeed.

MRS HOLROYD *(her voice breaking)* : I can't bear it!

MANAGER : Eh, dear, we none on us know what's comin' next.

MRS HOLROYD *(getting hysterical)* : Oh, it's too awful, it's too awful!

BLACKMORE : You'll disturb the children.

GRANDMOTHER : And you don't want *them* down here.

MANAGER : 'E'd no business to ha' been left, you know.

RIGLEY : An' what man, dost think, wor goin' to sit him down on his hams an' wait for a chap as wouldna say "thank yer" for his cump'ny? 'E'd bin ready to fall out wi' a flicker o' the candle, so

who dost think wor goin' ter stop when we knowed 'e on'y kep
on so's to get shut on us.

MANAGER : Tha'rt quite right, Bill, quite right. But theer you are.

RIGLEY : Ah' if we'd stopped, what good would it ha' done——

MANAGER : No, 'appen not, 'appen not.

RIGLEY : For, not known——

MANAGER : I'm sayin' nowt agen thee, neither one road nor t'other.
(There is general silence—then, to MRS HOLROYD.*)* I should think
th' inquest'll be at th' New Inn to-morrow, missis. I'll let you
know.

MRS HOLROYD : Will there have to be an inquest?

MANAGER : Yes—there'll have to be an inquest. Shall you want anybody in, to stop with you to-night?

MRS HOLROYD : No.

MANAGER : Well, then, we'd best be goin'. I'll send my missis down
first thing in the morning. It's a bad job, a bad job, it is. You'll
be a' right then?

MRS HOLROYD : Yes.

MANAGER : Well, good night then—good night all.

ALL : Good night. Good night.

> The MANAGER, *followed by the two bearers, goes out, closing
> the door.*

RIGLEY : It's like this, missis. I never should ha' gone, if he hadn't
wanted us to.

MRS HOLROYD : Yes, I know.

RIGLEY : 'E wanted to come up by 's sen.

MRS HOLROYD *(wearily)* : I know how it was, Mr Rigley.

RIGLEY : Yes——

BLACKMORE : Nobody could foresee.

RIGLEY *(shaking his head)* : No. If there's owt, missis, as you
want——

MRS HOLROYD : Yes—I think there isn't anything.

RIGLEY *(after a moment)* : Well—good night—we've worked i' the
same stall ower four years now——

MRS HOLROYD : Yes.

RIGLEY : Well, good night, missis.

MRS HOLROYD AND BLACKMORE : Good night.

> The GRANDMOTHER *all this time has been rocking herself to
> and fro, moaning and murmuring beside the dead man. When*

RIGLEY *has gone* MRS HOLROYD *stands staring distractedly be-fore her. She has not yet looked at her husband.*

GRANDMOTHER : Have you got the things ready, Lizzie?

MRS HOLROYD : What things?

GRANDMOTHER : To lay the child out.

MRS HOLROYD *(she shudders)* : No—what?

GRANDMOTHER : Haven't you put him by a pair o' white stockings, nor a white shirt?

MRS HOLROYD : He's got a white cricketing shirt—but not white stockings.

GRANDMOTHER : Then he'll have to have his father's. Let me look at the shirt, Lizzie. (MRS HOLROYD *takes one from the dresser drawer.)* This'll never do—a cold, canvas thing wi' a turndown collar. I s'll 'ave to fetch his father's. *(Suddenly.)* You don't want no other woman to touch him, to wash him and lay him out, do you?

MRS HOLROYD *(weeping)* : No.

GRANDMOTHER : Then I'll fetch him his father's gear. We mustn't let him set, he'll be that heavy, bless him. *(She takes her shawl.)* I shan't be more than a few minutes, an' the young fellow can stop here till I come back.

BLACKMORE : Can't I go for you, Mrs Holroyd?

GRANDMOTHER : No. *You* couldn't find the things. We'll wash him as soon as I get back, Lizzie.

MRS HOLROYD : Alright.

She watches her mother-in-law go out. Then she starts, goes in the scullery for a bowl, in which she pours warm water. She takes a flannel and soap and towel. She stands, afraid to go any further.

BLACKMORE : Well!

MRS HOLROYD : This is a judgment on us.

BLACKMORE : Why?

MRS HOLROYD : On me, it is——

BLACKMORE : How?

MRS HOLROYD : It is.

BLACKMORE *shakes his head.*

MRS HOLROYD : Yesterday you talked of murdering him.

BLACKMORE : Well!

MRS HOLROYD : Now we've done it.

BLACKMORE: How?

MRS HOLROYD: He'd have come up with the others, if he hadn't felt—felt me murdering him.

BLACKMORE: But we can't help it.

MRS HOLROYD: It's my fault.

BLACKMORE: Don't be like that!

MRS HOLROYD (*looking at him—then indicating her husband*): I daren't see him.

BLACKMORE: No?

MRS HOLROYD: I've killed him, that is all.

BLACKMORE: No, you haven't.

MRS HOLROYD: Yes, I have.

BLACKMORE: *We* couldn't help it.

MRS HOLROYD: If he hadn't felt, if he hadn't *known*, he wouldn't have stayed, he'd have come up with the rest.

BLACKMORE: Well, and even if it was so, we can't help it now.

MRS HOLROYD: But we've killed him.

BLACKMORE: Ah, I'm tired——

MRS HOLROYD: Yes.

BLACKMORE (*after a pause*): Shall I stay?

MRS HOLROYD: I—I daren't be alone with him.

BLACKMORE (*sitting down*): No.

MRS HOLROYD: I don't love him. Now he's dead. I don't love him. He lies like he did yesterday.

BLACKMORE: I suppose, being dead—I don't know——

MRS HOLROYD: I think you'd better go.

BLACKMORE (*rising*): Tell me.

MRS HOLROYD: Yes.

BLACKMORE: You want me to go.

MRS HOLROYD: No—but *do* go. (*They look at each other.*)

BLACKMORE: I shall come to-morrow.

> BLACKMORE *goes out.*
>
> MRS HOLROYD *stands very stiff, as if afraid of the dead man. Then she stoops down and begins to sponge his face, talking to him.*

MRS HOLROYD: My dear, my dear—oh, my dear! I can't bear it, my dear—you shouldn't have done it. You shouldn't have done it. Oh—I can't bear it, for you. Why couldn't I do anything for you? The children's father—my dear—I wasn't good to you. But

you shouldn't have done this to me. Oh, dear, oh, dear! Did it
hurt you?—oh, my dear, it hurt you—oh, I can't bear it. No,
things aren't fair—we went wrong, my dear. I never loved you
enough—I never did. What a shame for you! It was a shame.
But you didn't—you didn't try. I *would* have loved you—I tried
hard. What a shame for you! It was so cruel for you. You
couldn't help it—my dear, my dear. You couldn't help it. And I
can't do anything for you, and it hurt you so! *(She weeps
bitterly, so her tears fall on the dead man's face; suddenly she
kisses him.)* My dear, my dear, what can I do for you, what can
I? *(She weeps as she wipes his face gently.)*
      Enter GRANDMOTHER.

GRANDMOTHER *(putting a bundle on the table, and taking off her
  shawl)*: You're not all by yourself?

MRS HOLROYD: Yes.

GRANDMOTHER: It's a wonder you're not frightened. You've not
  washed his face.

MRS HOLROYD: Why should I be afraid of him—now, mother?

GRANDMOTHER *(weeping)*: Ay, poor lamb, I can't think as ever
  you could have had reason to be frightened of him, Lizzie.

MRS HOLROYD: Yes—once——

GRANDMOTHER: Oh, but he went wrong. An' he was a taking lad,
  as iver was. *(She cries pitifully.)* And when I waked his father
  up and told him, he sat up in bed staring over his whiskers, and
  said should he come up? But when I'd managed to find the shirt
  and things, he was still in bed. You don't know what it is to live
  with a man that has no feeling. But you've washed him, Lizzie?

MRS HOLROYD: I was finishing his head.

GRANDMOTHER: Let me do it, child.

MRS HOLROYD: I'll finish that.

GRANDMOTHER: Poor lamb—poor dear lamb! Yet I wouldn't wish
  him back, Lizzie. He must ha' died peaceful, Lizzie. He seems to
  be smiling. He always had such a rare smile on him—not that
  he's smiled much of late——

MRS HOLROYD: I loved him for that.

GRANDMOTHER: Ay, my poor child—my poor child.

MRS HOLROYD: He looks nice, mother.

GRANDMOTHER: I hope he made his peace with the Lord.

MRS HOLROYD: Yes.

GRANDMOTHER : If he hadn't time to make his peace with the Lord, I've no hopes of him. Dear o' me, dear o' me. Is there another bit of flannel anywhere?

MRS HOLROYD *rises and brings a piece. The* GRANDMOTHER *begins to wash the breast of the dead man.*

GRANDMOTHER : Well, I hope you'll be true to his children at least, Lizzie. (MRS HOLROYD *weeps—the old woman continues her washing.*) Eh—and he's fair as a lily. Did you ever see a man with a whiter skin—and flesh as fine as the driven snow. He's beautiful, he is, the lamb. Many's the time I've looked at him, and I've felt proud of him, I have. And now he lies here. And such arms on 'im! Look at the vaccination marks, Lizzie. When I took him to be vaccinated, he had a little pink bonnet with a feather. *(Weeps.)* Don't cry, my girl, don't. Sit up an' wash him a' that side, or we s'll never have him done. Oh, Lizzie!

MRS HOLROYD *(sitting up, startled)* : What—what?

GRANDMOTHER : Look at his poor hand!

She holds up the right hand. The nails are bloody.

MRS HOLROYD : Oh, no! Oh, no! No!

Both women weep.

GRANDMOTHER *(after a while)* : We maun get on, Lizzie.

MRS HOLROYD *(sitting up)* : I can't touch his hands.

GRANDMOTHER : But I'm his mother—there's nothing I couldn't do for him.

MRS HOLROYD : I don't care—I don't care.

GRANDMOTHER : Prithee, prithee, Lizzie, I don't want thee goin' off, Lizzie.

MRS HOLROYD *(moaning)* : Oh, what shall I do!

GRANDMOTHER : Why, go thee an' get his feet washed. He's setting stiff, and how shall we get him laid out?

MRS HOLROYD, *sobbing, goes, kneels at the miner's feet, and begins pulling off the great boots.*

GRANDMOTHER : There's hardly a mark on him. Eh, what a man he is! I've had some fine sons, Lizzie, I've had some big men of sons.

MRS HOLROYD : He was always a lot whiter than me. And he used to chaff me.

GRANDMOTHER : But his poor hands! I used to thank God for my children, but they're rods o' trouble, Lizzie, they are. Unfasten his belt, child. We mun get his things off soon, or else we s'll have such a job.

    MRS HOLROYD, *having dragged off the boots, rises. She is weeping.*

CURTAIN

David

A PLAY IN SIXTEEN SCENES

(1926)

CHARACTERS

DAVID, son of Jesse
SAUL, King of Israel
SAMUEL, Prophet of God
JONATHAN, son of Saul
ABNER, leader of Saul's host
AGAG, King of Amalek
MERAB, daughter of Saul
MICHAL, daughter of Saul
WOMAN-SERVANT
MAIDENS
JESSE, father of David
ELIAB, ABINADAB, SHAMMAH, brothers of David
Fourth, Fifth, Sixth, and Seventh Brothers of David
ADRIEL the Meholathite
Captains, Fighting-Men, Herald, Armour-Bearer, Elders,
Neighbours, Prophets, Herdsmen, and Lad

SCENE I
Courtyard of Saul's house in Gilgal

SCENE II
A room in Ramah

SCENE III
An open place in the village of Bethlehem

SCENE IV
A courtyard in Jesse's house

SCENE V
Saul's house in Gilgal

SCENE VI
Yard of Saul's house in Gilgal

SCENE VII
Camp of the Israelites at Elah

SCENE VIII
The King's tent at Elah

SCENE IX
Outside the courtyard of Saul's house in Gilgal

SCENE X
Courtyard of Saul's house in Gilgal

SCENE XI
Room in King's house at Gilgal

SCENE XII
The well at Gilgal

SCENE XIII
A room in David's house in Gilgal

SCENE XIV
The same as for Scene XIII

SCENE XV
Naioth in Ramah

SCENE XVI
A rocky place outside Gilgal

SCENE I

Courtyard of SAUL'S *house in Gilgal: sort of compound with an adobe house beyond.* AGAG, *bound, seated on the ground, and fastened by a rope to a post of the shed. Men with spears. Enter* MERAB *and* MICHAL, *daughters of* SAUL, *with tambourines.* MAIDENS.

MERAB *(running and dancing)*: Saul came home with the spoil of the Amalekite.

MAIDENS: Hie! Amalekite! Hie! Amalekite!

MICHAL: Saul threw his spear into the desert of Shur, through the heart of the Amalekite.

MAIDENS: Struck the Amalekite, pierced him to the ground.

MICHAL: Wind of the desert blows between the ribs of Amalek, only the jackal is fat on that land. Who smote the Amalekite, as a sand-storm smites the desert?

MAIDENS: Saul! Saul! Saul is the slayer and the death of Amalek.

MERAB *(before* AGAG*)*: What is this dog with a string round his neck?

MAIDENS: What dog is this?

MICHAL: I know this dog, men used to call it King!

MAIDENS: Look at this King!

MERAB: Agag, Agag, King of the Amalekites! Dog on a string at the heel of mighty Saul!

MICHAL *(speaking to* AGAG*)*: Are you the King of the Amalekites?

AGAG: I am he, maiden!

MICHAL: I thought it was a dog my father had brought home, and tied to a post.

MERAB: Why are you alone, Agag? Where are all your armed men, that ran like lions, round the road to Egypt? Where are your women, with gold on their foreheads? Let us hear the tinkle of the bracelets of your women, O King, King Agag, King of mighty Amalek!

MAIDENS *(laughing—shaking tambourines in* AGAG'S *face—spitting on him)*: Dog! Dog! Dog of an Amalekite!

MICHAL: Who hung on the heels of Israel when they journeyed out of the wilderness of Shur, coming from Egypt, in the days of our fathers, in the day of Moses, our great deliverer?

MAIDENS: Ay! Ay! Who threw their spears in the backs of the wandering Israelites?

MICHAL: Who killed our women, and the weary ones, and the heavy-footed, in the bitter days of wandering, when we came up out of Egypt?

MERAB: Who among our enemies was accursed like the Amalekite? When Moses held the rod of God uplifted in his hand, Joshua smote the Amalekite till the sun went down. But even when the sun was gone, came the voice of the Almighty: *War, and war with Amalek, till Amalek is put out from under heaven.*

MICHAL: Dog! Son of dogs that lay in wait for us as we passed by! Dog! Why has Saul left you eyes to see, and ears to hear!

SAUL *(coming from house)*: Agag is among the maidens!

MICHAL: See, Father, is *this* a king?

SAUL: Even so.

MICHAL: It is a dog that cannot scratch his own fleas.

SAUL: Even so, it is a king: King of rich Amalek. Have you seen the presents he has brought for the household of Saul?

MICHAL: For the daughters of Saul, Father?

SAUL: Surely for Merab and Michal, daughters of Saul. *(To a man.)* Ho! Bring the basket of spoils for the daughters of the King.

MICHAL: Listen! Listen! King Agag seeks a wife in Gilgal! Oh, Father, I do not like him! He looks like a crow the dogs have played with. Merab, here is a King for your hand!

MERAB: Death is his portion, the Amalekite.

MICHAL: Will you put him to death, Father? Let us laugh a little longer at his Amalek nose.

> *Enter man with basket—also* JONATHAN *and* ABNER.

SAUL: See the gifts of Agag, King of Amalek, to the daughters of Saul! Tissue from Egypt, head-veils from Pharaoh's house! And see, red robes from Tyre, and yellow from Sidon.

MICHAL *(screams)*: That for *me*, Father, that for me! Give the other to Merab.—Ah! Ah! Ah!—Thank you, King Agag; thank you, King of Amalek.

SAUL: Goldsmith's work for arms and ankles, gold and dropping silver, for the ears.

MICHAL : Give me those! Give me those! Give the others to Merab! Ay! Ay! Maidens! How am I?—See, Agag, noble Agag, how am I now? Listen! *(She dances, the ornaments clink.)* They say: *Noble Agag!—King of Givers!* Poor draggled crow that had gold in its nest! Caw! King Agag! Caw! It's a daughter of Saul, of long-limbed Saul, smiter of Amalek, who tinkles with joys of the Amalekite.

JONATHAN : Peace, maiden! Go in and spin wool with the women. You are too much among the men.

MICHAL : Art thou speaking, O Jonathan, full of thy own manhood?

JONATHAN : Take in these spoils from the eye of men, and the light of day. Father, there came one saying that Samuel sought you in Carmel.

SAUL : Let him find me in Gilgal.

ABNER : They are calling even now at the gate. *(Moves to gate.)*

SAUL *(to girls)* : Go to the house and hide your spoil, for if this prophet of prophets finds the treasure of the Amalekite upon you, he will tear it away, and curse your youth.

MICHAL : That he shall not! Oh, Merab, you got the blue shawl from me! Run! Maidens! Run! Farewell, King Agag, your servant thanks your lordship!—Caw!—Nay, he cannot even say caw!

        *Exit—running—*MICHAL, *and other* MAIDENS *follow.*

ABNER : It is so, my lord. Samuel even now has passed the stone of directions, seeking Saul in Gilgal.

SAUL : It is well. He has come to bless our triumph.

JONATHAN : Father, will you leave that man in the sight of Samuel?

SAUL : No! Go you quickly into the house, O Agag! Take him quickly, men, and let no mouth speak his name.

        Exeunt AGAG *and men.*

JONATHAN : I have a misgiving, Father, that Samuel comes not in peace, after Saul in Gilgal.

SAUL : Has Saul laid low the Amalekite, to fear the coming of an old prophet?

ABNER : Samuel is a jealous man, full of the tyranny of prophecy. Shall we wait him here, or go into the house and be seated on the mats? Or shall we go forth from the gate towards him?

SAUL : I will stay here, and brighten my sword-edge in the waiting.

ABNER *(at the gate—calling)*: He is coming across the field; an old man in a mantle, alone, followed by two of his prophets.

JONATHAN *(joining* ABNER*)*: It is he. And coming in anger.

ABNER: In anger against whom?

JONATHAN: Against my father. Because we have not destroyed the Amalekite utterly, but have saved the best spoil.

ABNER: Nay, but it is a foolish thing, to throw fine linen into the fire, and fat young oxen down a dry well.

JONATHAN: It was the commandment.

ABNER: Why should the maidens not rejoice in their ornaments, and the God of the Unknown Name enjoy the scent of blood-sacrifice?

> *They retreat from the gate;* SAUL *sharpens his sword. After a pause, enter* SAMUEL, *followed by the prophets.*

SAUL *(laying down his sword)*: Blessed be thou of the Lord! I have performed the commandment of the Lord.

SAMUEL: What meaneth the bleating of the sheep in my ears, and the lowing of the oxen which I hear?

SAUL: They have brought them from the Amalekites. The people spared the best of the sheep, and of the oxen, to sacrifice unto thy God, but the rest we have utterly destroyed.

SAMUEL: Stay, and I will tell thee what I have heard out of the inner darkness, this night.

SAUL: Say on.

SAMUEL: When thou wast little in thine own sight, wast thou not made the chieftain of the tribes of Israel, and the Deep poured His power over thee, to anoint thee King? And the Voice out of the deeps sent thee on a journey, saying: Go, and utterly destroy the sinners the Amalekites, and fight against them until they be consumed.—Why then did you not obey the Voice, instead of flying upon the spoil, and doing evil in the sight of the Unclosing Eyes?

SAUL: Yea, I have obeyed the Voice from the beyond. I have gone the way which the Great One sent me, and have brought Agag the King of Amalek prisoner, and have utterly destroyed the Amalekites. But the people took the spoil, sheep and oxen, the chief of the things which should have been utterly destroyed, to sacrifice in Gilgal unto the Lord thy God.

SAMUEL: Does the Breather of the skies take as great delight in

sacrifice and burnt offerings as in obedience to the Voice that
spoke on the breath of the night? Behold, to obey is better than
sacrifice, and to hearken than the fat of rams.

SAUL: Is not God the sender of life, and the bread of life? And
shall we deny the meat and destroy the bread that is sent?

SAMUEL: Behold, is the Lord my God a sutler, to stock the larders
of Saul? Lo, He heeds not the fat beef nor the fine raiment, but
threshes out His anger in the firmament. Amalek has defied the
living Breath, and cried mockery on the Voice of the Beyond.
Therefore the living Wrath will wipe out the Amalekite, by the
hand of His servant, Israel. And if the Nameless is without compunction, whence the compunction of Saul?

SAUL: I feared the people, and obeyed their voice.

SAMUEL: Yea, that was bravely done! Thou didst not fear the Great
Lord thou fearedst the people, smaller than thyself. Thou didst
not obey the Cry from the midst of the dark, but the voice of the
people!—I tell thee, rebellion is as the sin of witchcraft, and
stubbornness is as iniquity and idolatry. Because thou hast rejected the word of the Lord the Lord hath also rejected thee from
being King.

SAUL: Shall a King not hearken to the voice of his people?

SAMUEL: The people cried for a King, in the frowardness of their
hearts. But can they make a King out of one of themselves? Can
they whistle a lion forth from a litter of dogs? The people cried
for a King, and the Lord gave to them. Even thee, Saul. But why
art thou King? Because of the voice of the people?

SAUL: Thou didst choose me out.

SAMUEL: The finger of the Thunder pointed me to thee, and the
Wind of Strength blew me in thy way. And thou art King because from out of the middle world the great Wish settled upon
thee. And thou art King because the Lord poured the oil of His
might over thee. But thou art disobedient, and shuttest thine ears
to the Voice. Thou hearest the barkings of dogs and the crying of
the people, and the Voice of the Midmost is nothing to thee.
Therefore thou hast become as nothing unto the Lord, and He
that chose thee rejecteth thee again. The power of the Lord shall
fall away from thee, and thou shalt become again a common
man, and a little thing, as when the Lord first found thee.

SAUL: I have sinned. For I have transgressed the commandments of the Lord, which thou didst hear out of the deeps of the night. Because I feared the people, and obeyed their voice. But now, I pray thee, pardon my sin, and turn again with me, that I may find the Lord, to worship Him.

SAMUEL: I will not return with thee: for thou hast rejected the word of the Lord, and the Lord hath rejected thee from being King over Israel. (SAMUEL *turns away.* SAUL *catches hold of the hem of* SAMUEL'S *garment and it tears in his hand.*) The Lord hath rent the Kingdom of Israel away from thee this day, and hath given it to a neighbour of thine, that is better than thou *(pause);*—and the Mighty One that moveth Israel will not lie, nor repent towards thee again: for He is not a man that He should repent.

SAUL: I have sinned, I have sinned, I have turned my face the wrong way. Yet honour me now, I pray thee! Honour me before the elders of my people, and before Israel, and turn again with me, that I may find the Lord thy God, and worship Him.

SAMUEL *(turning)*: Thou hast turned away from the Hidden Sun, and the gleam is dying from out of thy face. Thou hast disowned the Power that made thee, and the glow is leaving thy limbs, the glisten of oil is waning on thy brow, and the vision is dying in thy breast. Yet because thou art the Lord's anointed I will bless thee again in the sight of the elders. Yet if the Lord hath decided against thee, what avails an old man's blessing?

SAUL: Yet bless me, my Father.

SAMUEL *(lifting his hand)*: The Lord be with thee! The Lord's strength strengthen thee! The power and the might of the Lord brighten thine eyes and light thy face: the Lord's life lift thy limbs and gladden the walls of thy breast, and put power in thy belly and thy hips! The Lord's haste strengthen thy knees and quicken thy feet!

SAUL *(lifting both hands to heaven)*: Lo, I have sinned, and lost myself, I have been mine own undoing. But I turn again to Innermost, where the flame is, and the wings are throbbing. Hear me, take me back! Brush me again with the wings of life, breathe on me with the breath of Thy desire, come in unto me, and be with me, and dwell in me. For without the presence of the awful Lord, I am an empty shell. Turn to me, and fill my heart, and forgive my transgression. For I will wash myself clean of Amalek, to the last speck, and remove the source of my sinning. *(Drops his hands—turns to* SAMUEL.*)* Is it well, O Samuel?

SAMUEL: May it be well! Bring me hither Agag, King of the Amalekites.

SAUL: Ho, Jonathan, send here Agag the Amalekite. And send thou the chief of the herdsmen, O Abner, for we must wipe away the stain of Amalek swiftly, out of Gilgal.

Exeunt JONATHAN *and* ABNER.

SAUL *(to* SAMUEL*)*: The Lord shall be with me again this day, that the Kingdom be not rent from me.

SAMUEL: Who knoweth the ways of the Deep? I will entreat, ah! for thee in the night-time, and in the day. But if He hath turned His face away, what am I but an old man crying like an infant in the night!

Enter AGAG—*coming forward delicately.*

AGAG: Surely the bitterness of death is past.

SAMUEL *(seizing* SAUL'S *sword):* As thy sword hath made women childless, so shall thy mother be childless among women. *(Rushes on* AGAG *with sword—*AGAG *steps behind a wall,* SAMUEL *upon him.)*

Enter HERDSMAN.

JONATHAN: Better it had been in battle, on the field of the fight.

ABNER: It is a sacrifice.

SAUL *(to* HERDSMAN*)*: Gather together the cattle of the Amalekite which came as spoil, and fasten them in a pen. Leave out no sheep and no calf, nor any goat, but put them all in.

HERDSMAN: It shall be as Saul says.

Exit HERDSMAN.

SAMUEL *(entering with red sword)*: I have hewed him in pieces before the Lord, and his blood has gone up to the Most High; it is in the nostrils of the God of Wrath.

SAUL: Come now, I pray thee, within the house, and let them bring water for thy feet and food to gladden thine heart.

SAMUEL: It may not be. But I must go to Ramah to entreat for thee before the Lord, and even now must I go. And may the Might be with thee.

CURTAIN

SCENE II

A room in Ramah. Night. SAMUEL *in prayer.*

SAMUEL : Speak to me out of the whirlwind, come to me from behind the sun, listen to me where the winds are hastening. When the power of the whirlwind moves away from me, I am a worthless old man. Out of the deep of deeps comes a breath upon me, and my old flesh freshens like a flower. I know no age. Oh, upon the wings of distance turn to me, send the fanning strength into my hips. I am sore for Saul, and my old bones are weary for the King. My heart is like a fledgling in a nest, abandoned by its mother. My heart opens its mouth with vain cries, weak and meaningless, and the Mover of the deeps will not stoop to me. My bowels are twisted in a knot of grief, in a knot of anguish for my son, for him whom I anointed beneath the firmament of might. On earth move men and beasts, they nourish themselves and know not how they are alive. But in all the places moves Unseen Almighty, like a breath among the stars, or the moon, like the sea turning herself over. I eat bread, but my soul faints, and wine will not heal my bones. Nothing is good for me but God. Like waters He moves through the world, like a fish I swim in the flood of God Himself. Answer me, Mover of the waters, speak to me as waves speak without mouths. Saul has fallen off, as a ripe fig falls and bursts. He, anointed, he moved in the flood of power, he was God's, he was not his own. Now he is cast up like a fish among the dry stones, he beats himself against the sun-licked pebbles. He jumped out from the deeps of the Lord, the sea of God has seen him depart. He will die within the smell of his own violence. Lord, Lord, Ocean and Mover of oceans, lick him into the flood of Thyself. Wilt Thou not reach for him with the arm of a long wave, and catch him back into the deeps of living God? Is he lost from the sway of the tide for ever and for ever? When the rain wets him, will it wet him Godless, and will the wind blow on him without God in it? Lord, wilt Thou not reach for him, he is Thine anointed? Bitter are the waters of old age, and tears fall inward on the heart. Saul is the son whom I anointed, and Saul has crawled away from God, he creeps up the rocks in vanity, the stink of him will rise up like a dead crab. Lord, is it verily so with Saul, is he gone out from Thee for ever, like a creeping thing crawled in vanity from the element of elements? I am old, and my tears run inward, they deaden my heart because of Saul. For Saul has crawled away from the Fountain of Days, and the Ancient of Days will know him no more. I hear the voice of the Lord like waters washing through the night, saying: *Saul has fallen away and is no more in the way of the power of God.* Yea, what is love, that I should love him! He is fallen away, and stinketh like a dead crab, and my love stinks with him. I must wash myself because of Saul, and strip myself of him again, and go down into the deeps of God. Speak, Lord, and I will obey. Tell me, and I will do it. I sink like a stone in the sea, and nothing of my own is left me. I am gone away from myself, I disappear in the deeps of God. And the oracle of the Lord stirs me, as the fountains of the deep. Lo! I am not mine own. The flood has covered me and the waters of the beginning sound in the shell of my heart. And I will find another King for Israel, I shall know him by the whispers of my heart. Lo, I will fill the horn with oil again, with the oil from the body of Him, and I will go into the hills of Judah. I will find out one, in whom the power sleeps. And I will pour potency over his head and anoint him with God's fecundity, and place him beyond forgetting. I will go into the hills of Judah, where the sheep feed among the rocks, and find a man fresh in the morning of God. And he shall be King. On the morrow I will gather myself and go, silently, carrying the kingship away from Saul, because the virtue is gone out of him. And Saul will kill me with a spear, in one stroke, for rage he will kill me, if I tell him. But I shall not tell him. I shall say: I must away to the land of Judah, it is the time to sacrifice in the place of Bethlehem, the appointed time is at hand.—So I shall go away from Saul for ever, and never shall I see his face again. I shall hide myself away from his face, lest he hurt himself, slaying me. I shall go in the morning with sure feet, but the shell of my heart will be weary. For I am the Lord's and servant of the Lord, and I go in obedience, even with the alacrity of willingness. But alas, that I should have loved Saul, and had pride in him! I am old.

CURTAIN

David

S C E N E   I I I

Bethlehem: an open place in the village. An old man on a roof
calling aloud and kindling a signal fire.

1ST ELDER *(calling, on the roof)*: Come in! Come in! Come in!
Come all men in! Come all in to the place of counsel! Gather
into the place of counsel, all men gather now. Come in! Come
in!

2ND ELDER *(on the plaza)*: What now?

3RD ELDER: The watchman on the fourth hill saw a host of
prophets coming, even Samuel among them.

2ND ELDER: Yea! What does this bode?

JESSE: What have we done wrong, that Samuel comes down upon
us? If he curses us we are dead men.

4TH ELDER: Dread is on me. The sun looks darkened.

3RD ELDER: Nay, let us wait. It may be he comes in peace.

ELIAB *(brother of* DAVID*)*: Why do we, who are men that fear not
the lion nor the bear, nor even the Philistine, tremble before the
raging of these prophets?

2ND ELDER: Hush then! For the Bolt is above us, and can strike
out of a clear sky. Canst thou hear His meaning, or know His
vision, Who is secret save to the prophets? Peace then, hush thy
mouth.

JESSE: Verily, there is no open vision, and the word of One is
precious. Without Samuel, we should stare with the stare of deaf
men, and the fixed eyes of the blind. We should run our faces
against the wall, and fall with our feet into a hole. We should
not hear the lion roaring upon us.

ELIAB: Not so, my Father. Without a prophet I seek the lion when
he roars about the herd, I slay him without advice from the Lord.
We live our lives as men, by the strength of our right hand. Why
heed the howlings of priests in linen ephods, one or many!

JESSE: My son, shut thy teeth on such words. Seal thy heart to
silence. The strength of a man lasts for a little time, and wastes
like the oil in a lamp. You are young, and your lamp is unbroken.
But those that live long needs must renew their strength again,

and have their vessel replenished. And only from the middle-
middle of all the worlds, where God stirs amid His waters, can
strength come to us.

ELIAB : Will it not come without Samuel?

JESSE : There is a path that the gazelle cannot follow, and the lion
knows not, nor can the eagle fly it. Rare is the soul of the
prophet, that can find the hidden path of the Lord. There is no
open vision, and we, who can see the lion in the thicket, cannot
see the Lord in the darkness, nor hear Him out of the cloud. But
the word of One is precious, and we perish without it.

ELIAB : *I* cannot bow my heart to Samuel. Is he a King to lead us
into battle, and share the spoil with us? Why should we fare
worse without him?

JESSE : My son, day follows day, and night travels between the
days. But the heart of man cannot wander among the years like
a wild ass in the wilderness, running hither and thither. The
heart at last stands still, crying: *Whither? Whither?* Like a lost
foal whinnying for his dam, the heart cries and nickers for God,
and will not be comforted. Then comes the prophet with the
other vision in his eyes, and the inner hearing in his ears, and
he uncovers the secret path of the Lord, Who is at the middle-
most place of all. And when the heart is in the way of God, it
runs softly and joyously, without weariness.

ELIAB : I would sooner follow the King, with spear and shield.

JESSE : Samuel is more precious than the King, and more to be
obeyed. As God is to Samuel, Samuel to the King is God. The
King is as a boy awaiting his father's bidding, uneasy till he is
told what he shall do. Even so Samuel speaks to Saul, with the
mouth of authority, to be obeyed. For he is the lips of God.

ELIAB : For me, give me the right arm of Saul.

> SAMUEL *enters—followed by wild prophets. The* ELDERS *go
> to meet him.*

1ST ELDER : The Lord be with thee!

SAMUEL : The Lord keep this people!

1ST ELDER : Comest thou in peace?

SAMUEL : In peace. I come to sacrifice unto the Lord. Sanctify yourselves and come to sacrifice, according to your families. Renew
your clothes and purify yourselves.

1ST ELDER : Into which house will you go?

SAMUEL: Into the house of Jesse.

JESSE: I am here, my lord.

SAMUEL: Call your household together, and sanctify yourselves, for we will sacrifice a heifer to the Lord this day, in your house. And it shall be a feast unto you.

CURTAIN

SCENE IV

JESSE'S *house. A small inner courtyard: a rude altar smoking, and blood sprinkled round:* SAMUEL *before the altar, hands bloody. In another part a large red fire with a great pot seething, and pieces of meat roasting on spits.* JESSE *turning the spits. It is evening, sun going down.*

SAMUEL: Call your sons. Call them one by one to pass before me. For I will look on them, before we sit around to the feast of the sacrifice.

JESSE: They are in the house, waiting. I will call the first-born first. *(Calling.)* Eliab, come forth! Samuel asks for thee!

ELIAB *(entering)*: The Lord be with you.

SAMUEL *(aside)*: Surely the Lord's anointed is before Him! *(Gazes at* ELIAB *who is big and handsome.)*

SAMUEL *(aside)*: I shall not look on his countenance, nor on the height of his stature. For the voice of my soul tells me he is rejected. The Lord sees not as men see. For man looketh on the outward appearance, but the Lord looketh on the heart.

SAMUEL *(to* JESSE*)*: Him hath the Lord not chosen. Call thy other son.

JESSE: Ha! Abinadab! And, Eliab, gather all thy brothers together, for the feast shall be set forth.

        Exit ELIAB.

ABINADAB *(entering)*: The Lord be with you.

SAMUEL *(gazing on* ABINADAB*)*: Neither hath the Lord chosen this.

JESSE: Go thou, Abinadab! Be all thy brethren ready in the house?

ABINADAB: They be all there, waiting for the sacrifice meat.

JESSE *(calling)*: Come, Shammah! And when I call, come you others in your order, one by one.

SHAMMAH *(entering)*: The Lord be with you.

SAMUEL *(slowly)*: Neither hath the Lord chosen this.

JESSE: Go thou! Nay! Rather go to the fire and turn the spitted meat.

SHAMMAH: Yea! For it should not singe.

JESSE *(calling)*: Ho! Son! Come forward!

FOURTH SON: The Lord be with you!

SAMUEL: Neither hath the Lord chosen this.

JESSE: Go thou hence, and wait yet a while.

FOURTH SON: What wouldst thou then with me?

JESSE *(calling)*: Ho! Son! *(To him who waits.)* Nay, go or stay, as thou wilt. But stand aside. *(He stands aside.)*

FIFTH SON: The Lord be with you.

JESSE: Turn thy face to the sun, that it may be seen.

SAMUEL: Neither hath the Lord chosen this.

JESSE: Thou art not he whom Samuel seeks. Stand thou aside. *(Calling.)* Ho! Son! *(To him who waits.)* Bring in thy brother.
  Enter SIXTH SON: *all the other brothers edge in after him.*

SIXTH SON: The Lord be with you!

SAMUEL: Neither hath the Lord chosen this.

SIXTH SON: Wherefore hast thou called me, my Father?

JESSE: Samuel would look on the faces of all my sons. Go now! Who then was not called? Who among you has not come forward?

SEVENTH SON: I! Wilt thou me?

JESSE: Nay, but come into the light before the prophet of God.

SAMUEL: Neither hath the Lord chosen this.

JESSE: Nay, then it is finished, for there be no more.

SAMUEL: Are here all thy children?

JESSE: Yea, verily, there remaineth yet the youngest. And behold he keepeth the sheep.

SAMUEL: Send and fetch him. For we will not sit down till he come hither.

JESSE: Go thou, Shammah, for he will be coming in now. I will see——!
  Exit JESSE, *also* SHAMMAH.

ELIAB: My lord, will the Lord of Hosts anoint a King, while Saul
yet liveth?

SAMUEL: My son, out of the deep cloud the lightning cometh, and
toucheth its own. Even so, from the whirlwind of the whole
world's middle, leaneth out the Wonderful and toucheth His
own, but whether the anointing be for prophecy or priesthood,
or for a leader or a King over Israel, the Mover of all hath it in
His own deeps.

ELIAB: Yea! But if the Lord anoint a man to be King, can the Lord
again take back the anointing, and wipe out the oil, and remove
the gift, and undo the man He has made?

SAMUEL: The power is beyond us, both before and after. Am I not
anointed before the people? But if I should say: *The power is
my own; I will even do my own bidding*, then this is the sin of
witchcraft, which stealeth the power of the whirlwind for its
own. And the power will be taken from me, and I shall fall into
a pit.

ELIAB: It is a hard thing, to be the Lord's anointed.

SAMUEL: For the froward and irreverent spirit, it is a thing wellnigh impossible.

     Enter JESSE *with* DAVID.

JESSE: This is David, the last of the sons of Jesse.

     Enter SHAMMAH.

SAMUEL *(aside)*: I shall arise and anoint him. For this is he.
(Aloud.) The Lord hath chosen this one. *(Takes the horn of oil
and holds it over* DAVID'S *head.)* The skies will anoint thee with
their glory, the oil of the Sun is poured over thee, and the strength
of His power. Thou shalt be a master of the happenings among
men. Answer then. Does thy soul go forth to the Deep, does the
Wonderer move in thy soul?

DAVID: Yea, my lord. Surely my soul leaps with God!

SAMUEL *(anointing* DAVID*)*: The Glory pours Himself out on thee.
The Chooser chooseth thee. Thou shalt be no more thine own, for
the chosen belongs to the Chooser. When thou goest in, it shall
be at the whisper of the Mover, and when thou comest out, it
shall be the Lord. Thy strength is at the heart of the world, and
thy desires are from thence. The walls of thy breast are the front
of the Lord, thy loins are the Deep's, and the fire within them is
His. The Lord looketh out of thy eyes and sits on thy lips. Thou

closest thy fist on the Deep, and thy knees smile with His strength. He holdeth the bow of thy body erect, and thy thighs are the pillars of His presence. Henceforward thou art not thine own. The Lord is upon thee, and thou art His.

DAVID *(making an obeisance)* : I am thy servant, my lord.

SAMUEL : Ye shall sit around, and divide the meat, and eat of the feast, and bid the neighbours to your feast of sacrifice this night.

> *They move around, fetching trenchers of wood, and a huge dish, and a heap of flat bread. They begin to take the meat from the fire, and with a cry lift down the pot.*

JESSE : David is a child, and the Lord hath chosen him. What shall become of him? Make it plain to us, O Samuel, this night!

SAMUEL : Ask not, for none knoweth. Let him live till such time as the Unseen stretcheth out His hands upon him. When the time is fulfilled, then we shall know. Beforehand no man knoweth. And now the meat is ready from the fire, and the feast of sacrifice is prepared, and I have done. Eat you of the feast, and live before the Lord, and be blessed. Speak nothing of this hour, lest mischance befall you. I go my way. Do not seek to stay me. Call whom ye will to meat, eat then what is before you, for this is your hour.

JESSE : The sun has gone down, and it is night. Wilt thou verily go forth?

> *Exit* SAMUEL.

ELIAB : He has anointed the youngest, and the oldest he has passed over.

JESSE : It is the Lord. Go, Abinadab, and bid in the neighbours to the feast.

ELIAB : Nay, it is Samuel, who envies a strong man his strength, and settles on the weak.

JESSE : These things, at this hour, thou shalt not say. Is my son David chosen beneath the heavens, and shall Eliab his brother cast it up a reproach to him? Yea! pile up the dish from the pot, that it may cool, and not burn the hand of him that tasteth.

ELIAB *(to* DAVID*)* : Wilt thou be a priest in a blue ephod?

DAVID : I know not. To-day and to-morrow I shall keep my father's sheep. More I know not.

ELIAB : Canst thou see the Bolt within the cloud? Canst thou hear His voice out of the ground?

DAVID : I know not. I wish the Lord be with me.

ELIAB : Is He nearer thee, than thine own father?

DAVID : My father sits before me and I see his face. But the Lord is in my limbs as a wind in a tree, and the tree is shaken.

ELIAB : Is not the Lord also in me, thou stripling? Is thine the only body that is visited?

DAVID : I know not. My own heart I know. Thou knowest thine own. I wish the Lord be with me.

ELIAB : Yea, I know my own heart indeed. Neither is it the heart of a whelp that minds the sheep, but the heart of a man that holds a spear. Canst thou draw my bow, or wield my sword?

DAVID : My day is not yet come

JESSE : It is enough. The guests we have bidden are here! O David, my son, even carry out their portion to the womenfolk, for they may not come here. And think thou no more of this day. The Lord will move in His own time, thou canst not hasten Him. *Exit* DAVID. *(To the* NEIGHBOURS.) Nay, come! And sit ye to meat! For we will eat this night of the sacrifice that Samuel hath slain before the Lord.

NEIGHBOURS : Peace be to this house! And is Samuel at once gone forth? Yea! Good seemeth thy feast, O Jesse!

JESSE : An heifer, of the first year, fat and goodly! Reach forth thy hand.

> *They all sit around the huge, smoking platter.* JESSE *dips in his hand, and carries the mess to his mouth.*

NEIGHBOUR : Yea! Good is the feast! And blessed be Samuel, who came to Bethlehem this day!

> *Re-enter* DAVID : *sits down and eats. They all dip their hands in the great platter, and eat in silence.*

Verily, this is a great feast! Surely the Lord hath visited thy house this day, O Jesse!

CURTAIN

SCENE V

SAUL'S *house in Gilgal.* MERAB *and* MICHAL *in the courtyard, spinning wool, with their maidens. They are laughing and giggling.*

1ST MAIDEN : Now I'll ask one! I'll ask one.

MERAB : Ask then!

3RD MAIDEN : Why does a cow look over a wall?

MICHAL : Yah! Yah! We know that old one. We all know it.

MERAB : Who knows the answer? Hold your hand up.
        Only MICHAL *holds up her hand.*

3RD MAIDEN : There! There! They don't know it! Why does a cow look over a wall?

1ST MAIDEN : To see what's on the other side.

MICHAL : Wrong! Wrong! How silly! *(Laughter.)*

2ND MAIDEN : Because it wants to get out.

MICHAL : Wrong! And it's such an easy one.

3RD MAIDEN : Why does a cow look over a wall?

4TH MAIDEN : To scratch its neck. *(Much laughter.)*

3RD MAIDEN : Wrong! Wrong! All wrong! Give it up!

MICHAL : No! No! Let them guess again. Why does a cow look over a wall?

1ST MAIDEN : To see if David's coming to drive her to pasture *(Wild laughter.)*

MICHAL : That's wrong! That's not the answer!

MERAB : Give it up?

3RD MAIDEN *(laughing wildly)* : To see if David's coming to drive her to pasture!

MICHAL : That's not the answer, *Stupid!*

1ST MAIDEN : Why not, say I? It's as good as the real answer.— The cows of Jesse will have to look a long time over a wall. *(Much laughter.)* No doubt they're looking at this moment. *(Shrieks of laughter.)* Mooo-oo! Moo-oo! David, come home. *(Hysterical laughter.)*

MICHAL : Fool! Fool! That's not the answer.

1ST MAIDEN : Yes. That's the answer in Bethlehem. Why does a

Bethlehem cow look over a wall?—Because David's come to Gilgal. *(Much laughter.)*

MICHAL: That's wrong! That's wrong!

2ND MAIDEN: It's not wrong for a Bethlehem cow.

MICHAL: But it's not a Bethlehem cow. *(Much laughter.)*

1ST MAIDEN: Is it the heifers of Gilgal? *(Wild laughter.)*

4TH MAIDEN: Why do the heifers of King Saul look over the wall in Gilgal?

1ST MAIDEN: Listening to the music. *(Wild laughter.)*

MERAB *(amid her laughter)*: If my father hears us!

MICHAL: You are all fools! You don't know the right answer. You can't guess it! You can't guess it.

2ND MAIDEN: Well, what is it then? Only Michal knows what the cow is looking for! *(Laughter.)*

MAIDENS: Go on! Go on! Tell us, Michal!

MICHAL: Because she can't see through it. *(Laughter.)*

1ST MAIDEN: See through what? *(Wild laughter.)*

MAIDENS: See through what? *(All laughing.)*

2ND MAIDEN: Because who can't see through what? *(Shrieks of laughter.)*

1ST MAIDEN: What a senseless answer! *Because she can't see through it! (Shrieks of laughter.)*

MICHAL: You are all fools! fools! fools! You know *nothing*. You don't know *anything*.

Enter SAUL—*angry.*

SAUL: Enough! Enough! What is all this? Is there a madness among the women? Silence, I say!

MICHAL: We are but telling riddles.

SAUL: It shall not be! What! am I to hear the shrieks of my daughters' folly spoiling the morning? I will riddle you a riddle you shall not care for. (MAIDENS *steal away.*)

MERAB: We had thought my father was abroad among the men.

SAUL: You had thought, had you! And your father's being abroad was timely to let loose your ribaldry!

MICHAL: Nay, Father, there was no ribaldry. The maid did only ask, why does a cow look over a wall?

SAUL *(shouting)*: Be still! Or I will run this spear through your body. Am I to wrestle with the Lord and fail because of the

wantoning of my daughters among their maidens! Oh! cursed
in my offspring as in all things!

    MERAB *steals away.*

Cursed above all in my womenfolk!

MICHAL: Could we not help you, Father, to strive with the Lord?
They say the wise women can command the spirits of the
deep.

SAUL: Art thou then a seeress? art thou amongst the witches?

MICHAL: Not so. But Saul my father is among the wondrous. Should
not his daughter be as wise as the wise women who can see into
the mysteries?

SAUL *(groaning)*: This is the sin of witchcraft! The hand of my
children is against me!

MICHAL: Nay, Father, we would indeed be for you, and not against
you.

SAUL: I have sworn to wipe out the sin of witchcraft from the land,
I have sworn the death of all who lure the people with spirits
and with wizardry. I have killed the soothsayers in the towns
and the villages.

MICHAL: But, Father, might I not see the Bolt in a cloud, or call
the Spirits out of the earth! I am your daughter, is that to be a
witch?

SAUL: Thou art a spawn of evil, and I will run thee through.

MICHAL: But why! Oh, why!

SAUL: Thy soul is a soul of a witch that workest against thy father.
I call on the Lord, and my heart foams, because He will not hear
me. I know it now. It is thee, thou witch! *(Wanting to strike her
with the spear.)*

MICHAL *(weeping)*: It is not so! It is not so! The people say of thee,
the Lord has departed from thee, and I would only help thee with
the Lord, as Jonathan helps thee against the Philistines.

SAUL *(horrified)*: Is the Deep a Philistine! Nay, now I know thou
art the brood of witches, who catch the powers of the earth by
cunning. Now I will surely pierce thee through, that my house
may be pure, and the Fire may look on me again.

MICHAL *(screams)*: My lord! My lord!

SAUL: I will pierce thee through. For I have sworn the death of all
witches, and such as steal the powers of earth and sky by their
cunning. It will be as good a deed in the sight of the Lord, as

when the prophet of God slew Agag, and Samuel will turn to me again. For I am empty when the Lord abandons me. And evil spirits break into my empty place, and torture me.—I will surely slay this witch, though she were seven times my youngest. For she lifts the latch to the evil spirit that gets into my soul unawares.

MICHAL : My lord! My lord! I am no witch! I am not!

SAUL : Thou art a witch, and thy hand worketh against me, even when thou knowest not. Nay, thou art a witch and thy soul worketh witchcraft even when thou sleepest. Therefore I will pierce thee through. And I will say unto the people : Saul hath slain the witch that gnawed nearest into his heart.

MICHAL : I will not be slain! *(Shrieks.)*

> *Enter* JONATHAN *and* DAVID, *running.*

JONATHAN : My Father!

DAVID : O King!

SAUL : This is the witch that hinders me with the Lord!

JONATHAN : This, Father! Why, Michal is a child, what can she know of witchcraft?

SAUL : It is in her will. My soul tells me that women with their evil intentions are playing against me, with the Lord. And this is she. She shall die as the others, seeresses, died, to cleanse the land before the Lord God.

DAVID : But yet, O King, thy servant has heard it is a hard thing to be a witch, a work of silent labour and of years. And this maiden your daughter is not silent, I think, nor does she seem to waste her young brows in secret labours.

JONATHAN : This is true enough. She is a feather-brain.

SAUL : Yet is her spirit against her father's.

MICHAL *(still weeping)* : No! No! I would help him.

DAVID : If some spirit of evil hinder King Saul with the Lord of Hosts, it will be more than the whims of a girl. The spirits that hamper the soul of the King cannot be children and girls.

SAUL : It may be so. Yet though I wrestle, the spirit of the Deep will not come to me. And the wound is greater than a wound in battle, bleeding inwardly. I am a strange man unto myself.

DAVID : Yet Saul is King, comely in his pride, and a great leader in battle. His *deeds* cry unto the whirlwind and are heard. Why should Saul wrestle with the Lord? Saul speaks in actions, and in

the time of action the spirit of God comes upon him, and he is
King in the sight of all men.

SAUL: It is even so. Yet my soul does not cease to ache, like the
soul of a scorned woman, because the Lord will not descend upon
me and give me peace in strength.

DAVID: Who is strong like Saul, in Israel?

SAUL: Yet his strength is as a drunken man's—great with despair.

DAVID: Nay, O King! These are fancies. How can my lord speak of
despair, when victory is with him, and the light is on his brow
in the sight of all Israel!

SAUL: Can I so deceive myself?

DAVID: Surely the King deceives himself.

JONATHAN: Surely, Father, it is a strange self-deception you put on
yourself.

SAUL: Can it be so? Yet if so, why does Samuel visit me no more,
and withhold his blessing? And why do I feel the ache in me,
and the void, where the Full should be? I cannot get at the
Lord.

MICHAL: May I speak, my Father?

SAUL: Yea!

MICHAL: Why not laugh as you used to laugh, Father, and throw
the spear in sport, at a mark, not grip it in anger? Saul is beautiful among men, to make women weep for joy if he smile at them.
Yet his face is heavy with a frown.

SAUL: Why should I smile at thee, witch?

MICHAL: To gladden me, Father. For I am no witch.

SAUL: And when dost thou need gladdening, say?

MICHAL: Now, Father, even here!

SAUL: Thy sorrows are deep, I warrant me.
    Touches her cheek with his fingers.

MICHAL: Yea! Did not this strange young man—indeed he is but a
boy—find me chidden and disgraced and in tears before the King?

SAUL: And what then?

MICHAL: Who is this boy from the sheepfolds of Bethlehem, that he
should think lightly of the King's daughter in Gilgal?

DAVID: Nay! What man could think lightly of Michal the daughter
of Saul? Her eyes are like the stars shining through a tree at
midnight.

MICHAL: Why through a tree?

SAUL *(laughing suddenly)*: Thou bird of the pert whistle! Run! Run, quail! Get thee among the maidens! Thou hast piped long enough before the men.

MICHAL: Even if I run my thoughts run with me.

SAUL: What thoughts, bird of mischief?

MICHAL: That this boy, ruddy with the shepherd's sun, has seen my tears and my disgrace.

DAVID: Surely the tears of Michal are like falling stars in the lonely midnight.

MICHAL: Why, again, in the night?

SAUL *(laughing aloud)*: Be gone! Be gone! No more!

    Exit MICHAL.

SAUL: She is a chick of the King's nest! Think not of her, David!

DAVID: But she is pleasant to think of.

SAUL: Even when she mocks thee?

DAVID: Very pleasant.

SAUL: The young men flee from a mocking woman.

DAVID: Not when the voice is sweet.

SAUL: Is Michal's voice sweet? To me at times it is snarling and bad in my ears.

DAVID: That is only when the harp-strings of the King's ears are unstrung.

SAUL: It may be. Yet I think I am cursed in my womenfolk. Was not the mother of Jonathan a thorn in my heart? What dost thou prescribe for a thorn in the heart, young wiseling?

DAVID: Pluck it out, O King, and throw it aside, and it is forgotten.

SAUL: But is it easy to pluck out a rancorous woman from the heart?

DAVID: I have no certain knowledge. Yet it should not be hard, I think.

SAUL: How?

DAVID: A man asks in his heart: *Lord, Who fannest the fire of my soul into strength, does the woman cast fuel on the Lord's fire within me, or does she cast wet sand?* Then if the Lord says: *She casts wet sand,* she departs for ever from a man's presence, and a man will go nigh unto her no more, because she seeks to quench the proper fire which is within him.

SAUL: Thou art wiser than if thou hadst been many times wived. Thou art a cocksure stripling.

DAVID : My brothers say of me, I am a cocksure malapert. Yet I do not wish to be! Why am I so, my lord?

SAUL *(laughing)* : It must be the Lord made thee so.

DAVID : My brother has struck me in the face, before now, for words in which I saw no harm.

SAUL *(laughing)* : Didst see the harm afterwards?

DAVID : Not I. I had a bruised mouth, and that was harm enough. But I thought still the words were wise.

SAUL *(laughing)* : Dost think so even yet?

DAVID : Yea, they were wise words. But unwisely spoken.

SAUL *(laughing heartily)* : The Lord sends the wisdom, and leaves thee to spend it! You offer a tit-bit to a wolf, and he takes your fingers as well.

DAVID : I shall learn in the King's household.

SAUL : Among the wolves?

DAVID : Nay, the lion is nobler than the wolf.

SAUL : He will not grudge thee thy callow wisdom.—I go to speak with Abner.

DAVID : Can I serve the King in anything?

SAUL : Not now.

    Exit SAUL.

DAVID : He has gone in good humour.

JONATHAN : We found him in an evil one.

DAVID : Evil spirits out of the earth possess him, and laughter from a maiden sounds to him as the voice of a hyena sounds to a wounded man stricken in the feet.

JONATHAN : It is so. He rails at his daughter, and at the mother who bore me, till my heart swells with anger. Yet he was not always so. Why is it?

DAVID : He has lost the Lord, he says.

JONATHAN : But how? Have I lost the Lord, too?

DAVID : Nay! You are good.

JONATHAN : I wish I knew how my father had lost the Lord.—You, David, the Dawn is with you. It is in your face.—Do you wrestle before the Lord?

DAVID : Who am I, that I should wrestle before the Lord? But when I feel the Glory is with me, my heart leaps like a young kid, and bounds in my bosom, and my limbs swell like boughs that put forth buds.—Yet I would not be vainglorious.

JONATHAN : Do you dwell willingly here in Gilgal?

DAVID : I am strange here, and I miss my father, and the hills where the sheep are, in Bethlehem. Yet I comfort myself, turning my soul to the Nameless; and the flame flares up in my heart, and dries my tears, and I am glad.

JONATHAN : And when my father has been bitter and violent, and you go alone in tears, in a strange place—I have seen the tears, and my heart has been sad—then do you yearn for Bethlehem, and your own?

DAVID : I am weak still.—But when I see the stars, and the Lord in darkness alive between them, I am at home, and Bethlehem or Gilgal is the same to me.

JONATHAN : When I lie alone in camp, and see the stars, I think of my mother, and my father, and Michal, and the home place.—You, the Lord becomes a home to you, wherever you are.

DAVID : It is so. I had not thought of it.

JONATHAN : I fear you would never love man nor woman, nor wife nor child, dearly.

DAVID : Nay! I love my father dearly, and my brothers and my mother.

JONATHAN : But when the Lord enters your soul, father or mother or friend is as nothing to you.

DAVID : Why do you say so?—They are the same. But when the Lord is there, all the branches are hidden in blossom.

JONATHAN : Yea!—I, alas, love man or woman with the heart's tenderness, and even the Lord cannot make me forget.

DAVID : But nor do I forget.—It is as if all caught fire at once, in the flame of the Hope.

JONATHAN : Sometimes I think the Lord takes from me the flame I have. I love my father. And my father lifts the short spear at me, in wild anger, because, he says, the Fire has left him, and I am undutiful.

DAVID : The King is the Lord's anointed. The King has known, as none know, the strong gladness of the Lord's presence in his limbs. And then the pain of wanting the Lord, when He cometh not, passes the pain of a woman moaning for the man she loves, who has abandoned her.

JONATHAN : Yet we love the King. The people look up to him. Abner, the chief captain, is faithful to him unto death. Is this nothing to a man?

DAVID: To a man, it is much. To the Lord's anointed, it is much riches. But to the King whom the Lord hath rejected, even love is a hurt.

JONATHAN: Is my father truly rejected from being King, as Samuel said? And merely that he spared Agag and a few Amalekite cattle? I would not willingly have drawn the sword on naked Agag.

DAVID: Who knows? I know not.—When a people choose a King, then the will of the people is as God to the King. But when the Lord of All chooses a King, then the King must answer to the Lord of All.

JONATHAN: And the Lord of All required the death of defenceless Agag?

DAVID: Amalek has set his will against the Whirlwind. There are two motions in the world. The will of man for himself, and the · desire that moves the Whirlwind. When the two are one, all is well, but when the will of man is against the Whirlwind, all is ill, at last. So all is decreed ill, that is Amalek. And Amalek must die, for he obstructs the desire of the breathing God.

JONATHAN: And my father?

DAVID: He is King, and the Lord's anointed.

JONATHAN: But his will is the will of a man, and he cannot bend it with the Lord's desire?

DAVID: It seems he cannot. Yet I know nothing.

JONATHAN: It grieves me for my father. Why is it you can soothe him? Why cannot I?

DAVID: I know not. It is the Lord.

JONATHAN: And why do I love thee?

DAVID: It is the Lord.

JONATHAN: But do you love me again, David?

DAVID: If a man from the sheep dare love the King's son, then I love Jonathan. But hold it not against me for presumption.

JONATHAN: Of a surety, lovest thou me, David?

DAVID: As the Lord liveth.

JONATHAN: And it shall be well between us, for ever?

DAVID: Thou art the King's son. But as the Lord liveth and keepeth us, it shall be well between me and thee. And I will serve thee.

JONATHAN: Nay, but love my soul.

DAVID: Thy soul is dear to my soul, dear as life.

They embrace silently.

JONATHAN: And if my father sends thee away, never forget me.

DAVID: Not while my heart lives, can I forget thee.—But David will easily pass from the mind of the son of the King.

JONATHAN: Ah never! For my heart is sorrowful, with my father, and thou art my comfort. I would thou wert King's son, and I shepherd in Bethlehem.

DAVID: Say not so, lest thine anger rise on me at last, to destroy me.

JONATHAN: Nay, it will not.

CURTAIN

SCENE VI

Yard of SAUL'S *house in Gilgal.* MICHAL, *with tambourine, singing or talking to herself.*

MICHAL: As for me, I am sad, I am sad, I am sad, and why should I not be sad? All things together want to make me sad. I hate the house when the men are gone to war. All the men are gone out against the Philistine. Gone these many days. And never a victory. No one coming home with spoil, and no occasion to dance. I am sad, I am sad, my life is useless to me. Even when they come, they will not bring David. My father looked pleasantly on him for a while, then sent him away. So are men! Such is a king! Sent him away again! And I know, some day when the Lord has left Saul, he will marry me to some old sheik. —Unless he dies in the war. Anyhow, everybody is gone, and I am dull, dull. They say it is the Lord. But why should the Lord make the house of Saul dreary? As for me, I don't know whether the Lord is with me, or whether He is not with me. How should I know? Why should I care? A woman looks with different eyes into her heart, and, Lord or no Lord, I want what I want. I wish I had a sure charm to call back David, son of Jesse. The spells I have tried were no good. I shall try again with the sand and the bones. *(She puts a little sand, and three small white bones, in her tambourine—mutters and bends—tosses her tambourine softly and drops it on the ground. Kneels and gazes intently.)* Bones, bones, show me the ways in the sand. Sand, lie still; sand, lie still and speak. Now then, I see the hills of Judah, where Bethlehem is. But David is not there, he is gone. At least I don't see him. In the sand is a road to Gilgal, by the white crown-bone. But he is not coming this way, that I can see. Where else? Where else? This must be Elah in the sand, where my father is. And there is Shochoh, opposite, where the Philistines are. Ah yes, two hills, and a valley between, with a brook in the bottom. And my father with our men on one slope, the Philistines on the other. Ah yes, that will be my father among our men; at least that is his black tent. But Jonathan is not there. O woe, if Jonathan were killed! My heart is afraid for Jonathan. Though how should I know Jonathan as a speck of sand, anyhow? There is nothing in the sand. I am no wise woman, nor a seeress, even though I would like to be. How dull it is! How dull it is here! How dull it is to be a woman! *(Throws away her tambourine.)* Why do they sit in front of the Philistines without defeating them!

WATCHMAN *(entering from the gate)*: Men are coming, from the host of Saul. They come with a litter.

SOLDIER *(entering)*: The Lord strengthen you.

MICHAL: Who comes? Is it news of victory?

SOLDIER: No, lady! Jonathan is wounded in the knee, and comes home to rest.

MICHAL: Wounded in the knee? And what else?

SOLDIER: How, else?

MICHAL: Oh, slow-witted! What other news? Are the Philistines defeated and slaughtered?

SOLDIER: Nay, they are not.

MICHAL: Then what has happened?

SOLDIER: Naught has happened.

MICHAL: Where is the King? Is all well with him?

SOLDIER: The King is with the host at Elah, and all is well with him.

MICHAL: Then where are the Philistines?

SOLDIER: The Philistines are arranged over against us, on the opposite hill at Shochoh.

MICHAL: And what has happened? Do Israel and the Philistines sing songs to one another?

SOLDIER: Nay! A portion of the men go forth to fight, wellnigh each day. And the champions of the Philistines come each day to challenge us.

MICHAL: And who answers out of Israel?

SOLDIER: None answers.

MICHAL: None answers! Yea, that is news to hear! Has Israel never a champion? Is my father, the King, sick?

SOLDIER: Many champions have we, forsooth. But we are men. And this Philistine is huge: he is out of the old days, before the Flood. He is a huge giant, whose great voice alone shakes the tents.

MICHAL: And not one man answers his challenge?

SOLDIER: Nay, where shall we find a huge giant among us, to answer him?

MICHAL: If he were a mountain, I would prick him with my needle.

SOLDIER: Yes, and would you might prick the eyeballs of him!
Enter litter-bearers with JONATHAN.

MICHAL: This is most strange!—Ah, Jonathan, and art thou wounded in the knee?

JONATHAN: Yea!

MICHAL: The Lord be praised it is not in the calf!

JONATHAN: Hush, shrew!

MICHAL: Did the Philistine giant wound thee in the knee, O Jonathan?

JONATHAN: A Philistine wounded me.

MICHAL: But I hear they boast a giant, a champion.

JONATHAN: Yea, verily.

MICHAL: A huge unheard-of giant.

JONATHAN: Huge enough: and heard daily.

MICHAL: What does he say, daily?

JONATHAN: Oh—he asks that we send down a man to fight with him. And if he, the Philistine of Gath, slay our man, then shall all Israel be servant to the Philistines. But if our man slay this Goliath, then the Philistines shall be our servants. And seeing that this giant be so large, no ordinary man can get past his sword to attack him, therefore the King is not willing that the fight be settled between champions, lest we lose our freedom in a moment.

MICHAL: And dare no man go up against this huge one?

JONATHAN: Nay, many dare. And many a man seeks to go. I myself would willingly go. Though I know I should die. But what would I care about dying, if the Philistine died first? Yet I doubt *I* should die first, and Israel be delivered into bondage. Hence the King will accept no champion from our midst. But we shall sally forth in daily companies, and defeat the Philistines at length.

MICHAL: At a great length.

JONATHAN: Hast thou wounds or pain, to find it so?

MICHAL: Yea, the wound of shame, that Israel, challenged, is dumb. Israel has no champion! What wound of shame for the woman!

JONATHAN: Why risk the nation in a fight between champions? We are all champions, and we all fight the Philistine.

MICHAL: Only not this big one.

JONATHAN: In single combat, with the fate of the nation hanging in the issue, no! But if Goliath mingle in the battle ranks, then every man of Benjamin will have at him.

MICHAL: And mingles he not in the battle ranks?

JONATHAN: Ah no! He saves himself for the single combat, for this bawling of the challenge and the rattling of the oversized shield.

MICHAL: Some man should think of a way.

JONATHAN: Think thou! I must rest, and recover, and return to the field of battle.

CURTAIN

SCENE VII

The camp of the Israelites at Elah. In the background, black tents of worsted. Morning. Men assembling in arms, to battle. Much shouting of war-cries—much noise of war-like anticipation. DAVID entering, carrying a staff.

DAVID: Is yon the tent of Eliab of Bethlehem?

SOLDIER: The tent of the sons of Jesse.

SHAMMAH *(coming armed from the tent)*: Is not this our brother David? *(calling.)* Ho! David is here! *(embracing* DAVID.*)* And art thou also come to the fight?

ELIAB *(also armed)*: What, David! Hast thou left the sheep to come among the men-at-arms? *(They embrace.)*

DAVID: My father sent me here to inquire of you, and to bring you bread, and the cheeses for the captain of your thousand. The loaves and the parched corn and the cheeses have I left with the keeper of the victuals. But where is Abinadab?

ELIAB: With the host, where we must form to battle.

> *The men are forming in loose array,* ABINADAB *comes and embraces* DAVID.

ABINADAB: Hast thou come from Bethlehem? And how is our father, and all the homestead?

DAVID: Yea, all are well. My father sent me with victual, and to see how you fare, and to take your pledge.

ELIAB: The pledge we will give you after the fight. And how fares my young son at home?

CAPTAIN *(calling)*: The thousand of Judah, get you to your hundreds: get you to your places. *(Bustle of men falling into rank.)*

DAVID *(following his brothers)*: Your son was bitten by a hound, but all is well.

ELIAB: What hound, forsooth? And lives the dog yet?

SAUL *(passing)*: Five hundred of Benjamin, lead into the valley!

SOLDIERS: Ah! Ah! The five hundred are moving forth! *(Loud shouting of* SOLDIERS.*)*

DAVID: And how goes the fight?

SHAMMAH: Wellah, this way and that, as wind bloweth!

DAVID: The days are many, that you are afield. My father grew uneasy, and could stay no longer. Long days and no news are ill to live, said he.

ELIAB: Tell my father, this is no folding of sheep, out here.

DAVID: And has no weighty blow been struck, on either side?

SOLDIERS *(calling)*: Ha! Ha! The five hundred are near the brook! And behold, the Philistine champion cometh forth from the ranks, to meet them. *(Hush in the camp.)*

MIGHTY VOICE OF GOLIATH: Ho! Ho, there! Israel! Why are ye come to set your battle array? Am I not a Philistine, and ye

servants to Saul? Choose you a man for you, and let him come
down to me.

DAVID *(in the hush)*: But who is this?

SOLDIERS: Ha! Ha! The five hundred are fleeing back from him!
They are sore afraid.

    A hush.

SHAMMAH: This is Goliath, their champion.

VOICE OF GOLIATH: Ha! ha! Why run ye? Choose you a man
for you, and let him come down to me. If he can fight with me,
and kill me, then will we be your servants. But if I prevail against
him, and kill him, then shall ye be our servants, and serve us. It
is fairly said. Choose you a man for you!

DAVID *(in the hush)*: Surely he is a huge man! Goeth no man
forth to meet him?

SOLDIER: Have you seen this man! Surely, forty days has he come
up to defy Israel. And it shall be, that the man who killeth him,
the King will enrich him with great riches, and will give him his
daughter, and make his father's house free in Israel.

DAVID: What will the King do to the man that killeth this Philistine and taketh away the reproach from Israel? Will he surely
give him his daughter? The daughter of his house in Gilgal?

SOLDIER: Ay, surely he will. And much riches. And make his
father's house free in Israel.

DAVID: Who is this uncircumcised Philistine, that he should defy
the armies of the living God?

SOLDIERS: Ah! He is what thou seest.

DAVID: As the Lord liveth, there shall be an end to him.

SOLDIERS: Would it were so! But who shall do it?

DAVID: Is the Lord naught in the reckoning? The Lord is with me,
and I will do it.

SOLDIERS: Thou? How canst thou kill this great giant?

DAVID: I can do it. I will kill him, as the Lord liveth in me, were
his name six times Goliath.

SOLDIER: Nay, but how?

DAVID: The Lord will show you how. I, I will kill him.

ELIAB *(coming forward)*: What art thou doing here? Why camest
thou hither, and with whom hast thou left those few sheep in
the wilderness? I know thy pride, and the naughtiness of thy
heart. For thou art come down that thou mightest see the battle.

DAVID: What have I now done? Was I not sent by my father, for a cause?

ELIAB *(turning away in anger)*: Thou didst persuade him, in the vanity of thy mind.

SOLDIER: Shall we say to Saul of thee, that thou art minded to kill the giant?

DAVID: Say so to him. For the Lord is with me.

ANOTHER SOLDIER: Verily, feelest thou in the power to kill this mighty man?

DAVID: Verily! And is it sooth the King will give his daughter to him that slayeth the roaring Philistine?

SOLDIER: Yea, it is sooth, for it is so proclaimed. But tell us how thou wilt come nigh him, to slay him.

DAVID: The Lord will show you.

SOLDIERS: Saul is coming.

SAUL *(approaching)*: Which is this man will go forth against the Philistine?

DAVID: Let no man's heart fail because of the giant, for thy servant will go out and fight with him.

SAUL: Thou? Thou art not able to go against this Philistine to fight with him, for thou art but a youth, and he is a man of war from his youth.

DAVID: Thy servant slew both the lion and the bear; and this uncircumcised Philistine shall be as one of them, seeing he hath defied the armies of the living God.

SAUL: But neither lion nor bear came against thee in greaves of brass nor armed with sword a man's length. How shallst thou fight with this giant in panoply?

DAVID: The Lord that delivered me out of the paw of the lion, and out of the paw of the bear, He will deliver me out of the hand of the Philistine.

SAUL: Thou shalt go. And the Lord be with thee. *(To* ARMOUR-BEARER.*)* Fetch hither my armour, and another sword. For we will put them on him.

        Exit ARMOUR-BEARER.

DAVID: Shall thy servant go in armour clad?

SAUL: How else canst thou keep thy life?

VOICE OF GOLIATH: Ho! men of Saul! Is there no man among you, to answer when a fighter calls? Are you all maidens, combing

your hair? Where is Saul, the slayer of foemen? Is he crying like
a quail to his God? Call to Baal, and call to Astaroth, for the God
of Israel is a pigeon in a box.

DAVID: Ha! Lord God! Deliver him into my hand this day!

SAUL: Yea!

  Enter ARMOUR-BEARER.

Put the coat of proof upon him, and the helmet of brass.

  They put the armour of the KING *on* DAVID.

DAVID: I am not used to it.

SAUL *(unbuckling his sword)*: Take thou my sword.

DAVID *(girding it on)*: Thy servant hath honour beyond his lot.
Lo! I am strange in this array! The Lord hath not intended it for
me. *(Takes shield.)*

SAUL: Now thou art ready. A man shall bear thy shield.

DAVID: Then let me go. But let me assay this sword and battle
harness that is on me. *(Sets forth. Tries his sword; goes a little
way. Turns suddenly back.)* I cannot go with these, for I have
not proved them.

  Drops his shield. Hastily unbuckles sword, and gives it to
  SAUL. *Unfastens the helmet. The* ARMOUR-BEARER *disarms*
  DAVID.

SAUL: Then thou goest not! Uncovered thou canst not go.

DAVID: As the Lord liveth, I will go with naught but God upon
me.

VOICE OF GOLIATH: The God of Israel is a blue pigeon in a box,
and the men of Israel are quails in the net of the Philistine. Baal
is laughing aloud, and Astarte smiles behind her sleeve, for Israel
is no more than worms in a dung-hill.

DAVID: I shall go. Sound the trumpet!

  *He picks up his staff, recrosses hastily to the back of the
  stage, downwards as to a valley. Stoops in the distance: meanwhile trumpet sounds and the voice of the* HERALD *is heard,
  crying:*

HERALD: Come down, Goliath! Come forward, Philistine! For
Israel sendeth a champion against thee. *(Noise of shouting in
both camps.)*

SHAMMAH: See, David is picking smooth stones from the brook
bed.

ABINADAB: He has put them in his leather pouch, and taken his sling in his hand. Surely he will go after the Philistine as after a wolf.

SAUL: The Philistine cometh down with his shield-bearer before him.—Yea, but the youth is naked and unafraid.

VOICE OF GOLIATH: Where art thou, champion of Israel? I see thee not. Hast thou already perished of thy dread?

VOICE OF DAVID (small): Yea, I am coming.

VOICE OF GOLIATH: Thou!

SAUL: How he disdains the youth! If we have lost all on this throw!

VOICE OF GOLIATH: Am I a dog, that thou comest to me with staves? Now shall Astaroth slay thee with spittle, and Baal shall break thy bones with a loud laugh.

VOICE OF DAVID: Thou comest to me with a sword, and with a spear, and with a shield: but I come to thee in the name of the Lord of Hosts, the God of the armies of Israel, Whom thou hast defied.

VOICE OF GOLIATH: Come! Ha-ha! Come to me, and I will give thy flesh to the fowls of the air, and to the wild beasts of the hills.

> Meanwhile the bystanders, SHAMMAH, ABINADAB, SOLDIERS, all save the ARMOUR-BEARER and SAUL, have been running to the far background, to look closer.

VOICE OF DAVID: This day will the Lord deliver thee into my hand; and I will smite thee, and take thy head from thee.

VOICE OF GOLIATH: Ha! Ha! Canst thou chirp? Come over, thou egg, that they see me swallow thee. (Loud yelling from Philistines.)

VOICE OF DAVID: I will give the carcass of the host of the Philistines this day to the fowls of the air, and to the beasts of the earth. That all the earth may know there is a God in Israel. (Loud yelling of Israel.)

VOICE OF GOLIATH: Come, thou whistling bird! Come! Seest thou this sword? (Loud yelling of Philistines.)

VOICE OF DAVID: Yea! and all this people shall know that the Lord saveth not with sword and spear: for the battle is the Lord's, and He will deliver you into our hands. (Great defiance heard in Israel.)

VOICE OF GOLIATH: Must we die of thy talking? And wilt thou not come forth? Then must I fetch thee. . . . (Tumult in Philistia.)

ARMOUR-BEARER : The Philistine is hastening down!—Oh, and behold, the youth is running at him fast! Ha-a-a!

    ARMOUR-BEARER *rushes away, leaving* SAUL *alone.*

SAUL *(in a pause)* : Ah! Ah!—Lord, my Lord!—Is he down? *(Great
shouting heard—men running.)* What? Yea, the Philistine has
fallen! The boy but slang a stone at him! It is the Lord! Nay,
he riseth not!—Ah God! was it so easy a thing? Why had I not
done it! See, see, Saul, see, thou King of Israel, see this nameless
boy who hath run upon the fallen Philistine, and seized his sword
from his hand, and stands upon his body hewing at the neck of
the giant! Ah, sight for the King of Israel, who stands alone, in
safety, far off, and watches this thing done for him! Yea, they
may shout! It is not for me. It is for that boy, whom I know not.
How should I know him, with his young beard on his lip! It is a
hard thing to hack off the head of such a giant, and he cannot
find the neck joint. I see him stooping! *(A great wild shout is
heard.)* Ah! Even so! Even so!

    ABNER *enters, running.*

ABNER : The youth hath slain the Philistine with a stone from a
sling, and even now has hewn his head loose, and is holding it
up before the armies.

SAUL : Even so!

ABNER : Yea! He stands upon the body of that which was Goliath,
and holds up the head to Israel! The Lord has prevailed. *(Loud
shouting.)*

SOLDIERS *(running past)* : The host of the Philistines is in flight!
After them! After them!

ABNER : Shall we not pursue? Will not the King lead the pursuit?
Lo! they flee in abandon, flinging away their spears in their haste.

SAUL : This needs no leader. Any man can strike in the back of
a running enemy. What of the youth?

ABNER : He hath stripped the Philistine of his gear. Yea, I can see
the body of the giant naked in blood upon the ground.

SAUL : Who is this youth? Whose son is he?

ABNER : As thy soul liveth, O King, I cannot tell.

SAUL : Enquire thou whose son the stripling is.

ABNER : He is coming towards the brook. I will bring him hither.
    Exit ABNER.

SAUL : Yea, he is coming! And alone up the slope, for the men have

gone like hounds after the Philistine, and to the stripping of the
tents. Yea, as bees swarm in upon the sweetmeats, when the
window is opened. This is a day to make songs for. But not in
the name of Saul. Whom will the maidens sing to? To him
yonder, coming up the hill slowly, with the swinging head, and
the bright brass armour of the Philistine. To that ruddy-faced fair
youth, with a young beard on his mouth. It seems I should know
him, if I would. Yea, I shall know him in my hour. Ah the blithe
thing! Ah the blithe boy! Ah God! God! was I not blithe?
Where is it gone? Yea, where! Blitheness in a man is the Lord in
his body. Nay, boy, boy! I would not envy thee the head of the
Philistine. Nay, I would not envy thee the Kingdom itself. But the
blitheness of thy body, that is thy Lord in thee, I envy it thee
with a sore envy. For once my body too was blithe. But it hath
left me. It hath left me. Not because I am old. And were I ancient
as Samuel is, I could still have the alertness of God in me, and the
blithe bearing of the living God upon me. I have lost the best. I
had it, and have let it go. Ha! whither is he going? He turns
aside, among the tents. Aha! Aha! So it is. Among the tents of
Judah, and to the booth of the Bethlehemite! So, he has gone in
to lay down his spoil, the helmet of brass, and the greaves of
brass, the coat, the great sword, and the shirt fringed with scarlet.
Lay them by, they are thine. Yea, they are thine, lay them in thy
tent. No need to bring them unto the King. They are no king's
spoil. Yea, lead him hither, Abner! Lead him hither! He is bringing the head in his hand. Oh yes, the champion, the victor! He is
bringing the head in his hand, to swing it under the nose of the
King. But the sword, the great sword, and the greaves of brass
and the body-spoil he has e'en laid by in his own tent, where no
man may lay hand on it. Oh! it is a shrewd youth, and a canny
youth, cunning as the Lord makes them.

    Enter DAVID, *with head of* GOLIATH—*and* ABNER.

SAUL: So! Comest thou again?

DAVID: Even so! To lay the head of thine enemy before thee, O
    King!

SAUL: Whose son art thou, thou young man?

DAVID: I am the son of thy servant Jesse the Bethlehemite.

SAUL: Art thou so! Ay, thou art David! And brother to Eliab, and
    Abinadab, and Shammah, three men of war!—Thou hast put

cunning in thy skill, and slain thine enemy as he were a hare
among the bushes.

ABNER: See! The place where the stone sunk in, in the side of the
forehead bone! It lies still there, the stone of David.

SAUL: Yea, that was death without weapons meeting, indeed.

ABNER: Surely the Lord was in that round stone, that digged the
pit in Goliath's head-bone!

DAVID: Except the Lord had been with me, I had not done it.

SOLDIERS (*standing round*): Yea, the Lord sped the hand of David.
The Lord is with this young man.

SAUL: Praise we must give to the Lord, and to David the promised
reward. Seekest thou thy reward at the King's hand, thou young
man?

DAVID: It is as the King willeth. Yet what should the reward be?

SAUL: Hast thou not heard it proclaimed?

DAVID: Nay, I arrived but in the dawn, with provender from my
father to my brethren.

SAUL: Didst thou not set forth even now against the Philistine,
hoping big for the reward?

DAVID: Not so, O King. But the Lord moved me to go, to take off
the shame and the reproach from the army of the living God.

SAUL: Thou hast done well! Yet claimest thou thy reward?

DAVID: Shall I not hear from the King's mouth, what the reward
should be?

SAUL: How was it said, Abner? Recallest thou?

ABNER: Yea, O King! Riches and the King's daughter, and freedom
for his father's house, to the man that should slay Goliath in the
single combat.

SAUL: Single-handed hath David slain Goliath, indeed! Even without any combat at all. But how likest thou thy reward, thou
young man?

DAVID: Were it mine, O King, I should rejoice for my father's sake
and fall to the ground beneath the honour put upon me, being
son-in-law to the King.

SAUL: Even so! Now thou shalt stay with me, and live in my house
and return no more to thy father's house. And all shall be done
to thee, as was said.—For surely thou hast brought much honour
upon Israel. And we will make much of thee. For thou art
champion of Israel in the sight of all the people. And thou shalt

sit at the King's right hand, that all men may delight in thee.
Yet, since thou art young, and fresh from the sheepfold, we will
not hasten thee to thy confusion. But thou shalt dwell as a son
among us, and rise in degree as a son rises, sitting at the King's
meat. And behold, my elder daughter Merab, her will I give thee
to wife. Only be thou valiant for me, and fight the Lord's battles
DAVID: Let but thy servant serve thee, O King, in the sight of the
Lord. And Saul will take the head of this Philistine to put it on
a pole?
SAUL: Nay! Thou thyself shalt bring it before the people, in Jerusalem of Judah.

CURTAIN

SCENE VIII

*The king's tent at Elah: a square tent of dark worsted, with the wide
front open. Heaps of panoply and spoil without. Within, in
the public part of the tent,* SAUL, *with* DAVID *on his right hand,*
JONATHAN *on his left, and sitting around, the* CAPTAINS *of the
armies of Israel.*

SAUL: We have numbered the armies in tens, in hundreds, and in
thousands. And now are all men returned from pursuing after
the Philistine, and the spoil is all brought in. And the wounded
of the Philistine have fallen by the way, even to the valley of
Ekron and the gates of Gath, their dead are more than their living.
Yet are their princes within the land, holding on to strong places.
Therefore we will rejoice not yet, nor go home to the feasting.
But while his heart is sunk low, we will follow up the Philistine
in every place where he holds out. Is it sooth?
CAPTAINS: It is good, O King.
ABNER: The blow that was struck with a pebble, we will follow up
with swords and spears, till in the Lord's name not one uncir-
cumcised remains in the land.
CAPTAINS: It is good! It is good! *(They strike their shields.)*
SAUL *(presenting* DAVID*)*: This is David, that slew Goliath the Philis-

tine, and delivered Israel from reproach. Sits not David high in
the heart of every man in Israel, this day?

CAPTAINS : Yea! David! David! *(Striking shields.)*

SAUL : Who is first among the men of war this day? Is it not David,
my son David?

CAPTAINS : David! David! It is David!

SAUL : Yea, Captains! Your King is but captain of the captains!
Whom shall we set over the men of war this day? Shall it not
be David? This time, shall not David lead the hosts? Is he not
the first against the Philistine? Yea, in this foray of triumph and
this campaign of victory, should any man lead but David?

CAPTAINS : It is good! David shall command, till we return home
this time from smiting the Philistine. *(They clash shields with
martial noise.)*

SAUL *(to* DAVID*)* : Hearest thou, David, son of my delight?

DAVID : O King, I am no leader of men of war. I have no skill in
arts of battle. Honour me not to my confusion.

SAUL : Nay, this time shalt thou take the charge. For in *this* fight
art thou the first man among the men of war in Israel. Answer,
Captains! Is it not so?

CAPTAINS : Verily! This time we will have David.

ABNER : Verily, save David lead us, we will not go.

>   The CAPTAINS *rise, and lift locked shields before* DAVID *as if
>   to raise him up.*

SAUL : If we go not now, we lose the golden hour. The choice is
upon thee, David.

DAVID : Thy servant will do according to thy will, O King, and
according to the will of Abner, and of the Captains. *(He rises
before the* CAPTAINS.*)* But I am young, and not brought up to
war. And the Captains and the strong men will laugh at me, seeing my inexperience and my presumption.

ABNER : Nay! No man shall find occasion to laugh at thee, for the
fight is in thee as in a young eagle. Leading to war shalt thou
learn war.

DAVID : It is as the King and the Captains shall bid me.

SAUL *(rising)* : We will make ready, and send out the news through
the camp : *In this is David our leader!* Then David shall choose
his men, and go forth. He shall give his orders, and the Captains
shall march at his bidding. David, the day is thine!

Salutes. The CAPTAINS *again salute* DAVID *with spear on shield, then they go out.*

CAPTAINS : To thee, David!

Exeunt CAPTAINS.

DAVID *(to* JONATHAN*)* : How shall I bring this to a pass?

JONATHAN : Thy soul will not fail thee. Thou art the young lion of Judah, thou art the young eagle of the Lord. O David, is it well between me and thee, and hast thou verily not forgotten me?

DAVID : Verily, thou hast not left my soul. But how shall I go before these men?

JONATHAN : We have sworn a covenant, is it not between us? Wilt thou not swear with me, that our souls shall be as brothers, closer even than the blood? O David, my heart hath no peace save all be well between thy soul and mine, and thy blood and mine.

DAVID : As the Lord liveth, the soul of Jonathan is dearer to me than a brother's.—O brother, if I were but come out of this pass, and we might live before the Lord, together!

JONATHAN : What fearest thou then?

DAVID : In the Lord, I fear nothing. But before the faces of men, my heart misgives me.

JONATHAN : Sittest thou not high in the hearts of Israel?

DAVID : Yea, but who am I, to be suddenly lifted up! Will they not throw me as suddenly down?

JONATHAN : Who would throw thee down, that art strong as a young eagle, and subtle as the leopard?

DAVID : I will rest in the Lord.

JONATHAN : And in me wilt thou not trust?

DAVID : I will trust thee, Jonathan, and cleave to thee till the sun sets on me. Thou art good to me as man never before was good to me, and I have not deserved it. Say thou wilt not repent of thy kindness towards me!

JONATHAN : O brother, give me the oath, that naught shall sunder our souls, for ever.

DAVID : As the Lord liveth, my soul shall not part for ever from the soul of my brother Jonathan; but shall go with him up the steeps of heaven, or down the sides of the pit. And between his house and my house the covenant shall be everlasting. For as the hearts of men are made on earth, the heart of Jonathan is gentlest and most great.

JONATHAN: The covenant is between us. *(Covers his face.)*

DAVID *(after a pause)*: But how shall I go before these captains, O my brother? Comest thou not with me? Wilt thou not stand by me? Oh, come!

JONATHAN: I am limping still in the knee, and how shall I lead a foray? But thou art mine and I am thine. And I will clothe thee in my clothes, and give thee my sword and my bow, and so shall my spirit be added to thy spirit, and thou shalt be as the King's son and the eagle of the Lord, in the eyes of the people.

Takes off striped coat, or wide-sleeved tunic.

DAVID: But can I do this thing?

JONATHAN: Yea! That all men know thou art as the King's son in the world. For the eagle hath gold in his feathers and the young lion is bright. So shall David be seen in Israel.

DAVID *slowly pulls off his loose robe, a herdsman's tunic cut off at the knee.* JONATHAN *takes off his sleeveless shirt, and is seen in his leather loin-strap. From his upper arm he takes a metal bracelet.*

JONATHAN: Even all my garments thou shalt take, even the armlet that should not leave me till I die. And thou shalt wear it for ever. And thy garments will I take upon me, so the honour shall be mine.

DAVID *pulls off his shirt, and is seen in the leather loin-strap,* JONATHAN *puts his bracelet on* DAVID'S *arm, then his own shirt over* DAVID'S *head, and holds up his coloured robe.* DAVID *robed,* JONATHAN *brings him a coloured head-kerchief and girdle, then his sword and his bow and quiver and shoes.* JONATHAN *puts on* DAVID'S *clothes.*

DAVID: How do I appear?

JONATHAN: Even as the eagle in his own plumage. It is said, David, that thou art anointed of Samuel, before the Lord. Is it so?

DAVID: Yea.

JONATHAN: Thou hast the sun within thee, who shall deny thee?

DAVID: Why speakest thou sadly, Jonathan, brother?

JONATHAN: Lest thou go beyond me, and be lost to me.

DAVID: Lord! Lord! Let not my soul part from the soul of Jonathan for ever, for all that man can be to man on earth, is he to me.

JONATHAN: Would I could give thee more!

SAUL *(entering)*: Yea! And which now is the King's son, and which the shepherd?

DAVID: Thy son would have it so, O King.

JONATHAN: It is well, Father! Shall not the leader shine forth?

SAUL: Even so. And the young King-bird shall moult his feathers in the same hour.

JONATHAN: The robe of David honours the shoulders of Jonathan.

SAUL: Art thou ready, thou brave young man?

DAVID: I am ready, O King.

SAUL: The host is in array, awaiting thy coming.

DAVID: I will come where the King leads me.

SAUL *(to* JONATHAN*)*: Put another robe upon thee, ere thou come forth.

JONATHAN: I will not come forth. *(Turns abruptly.)*

> DAVID *follows* SAUL *from the tent—loud shouting of the army.*

JONATHAN *(alone)*: If the Lord hath anointed him for the kingdom, Jonathan will not quarrel with the Lord. My father knoweth. Yet Saul will strain against God. The Lord hath not revealed Himself unto me: save that once I saw the glisten in my father that now I see in David. My life belongs to my father, but my soul is David's. I cannot help it. The Lord sees fit to split me between King and King-to-be, and already I am torn asunder as between two wild horses straining opposite ways. Yet my blood is my father's. And my soul is David's. And the right hand and the left hand are strangers on me.

CURTAIN

SCENE IX

Outside the courtyard of SAUL'S *house in Gilgal. Doorway of courtyard seen open.* MAIDENS *running forth with instruments of music. Men-servants gazing into the distance. People waiting.*

MAIDENS: Lu-lu-a-li-lu-lu-lu! Lu-lu-lu-li-a-li-lu-lu! A-li-lu-lu-lu-a-li-lu! Lu-al-li-lu! Lu-al-li-lu-a!

MERAB: Out of Judah Saul comes in!

MICHAL : David slew the Philistine.

MERAB AND HER MAIDENS : Out of Judah Saul comes in!

MICHAL AND HER MAIDENS : David slew the Philistine.

ALL *(repeat several times)*: A-li-lu-lu! A-li-lu-lu-lu! Lu! lu! lu!
   lu! li! lu! lu! a! li! lu! lu! lu! lu!

MERAB : All the Philistine has fled.

MICHAL : By the roadside fell their dead.

MERAB : Wounded fell down in the path.

MICHAL : Beyond Ekron unto Gath.

MERAB AND MAIDENS : All the Philistine has fled.

MICHAL AND MAIDENS : By the roadside fell their dead.

MERAB AND MAIDENS : Wounded fell down in the path.

MICHAL AND MAIDENS : Beyond Ekron unto Gath.

ALL *(repeat continuously)*: Lu-li-lu-lu-lu! Lu-lu-li-a-lu-lu! Li-a-li-lu-
   lu-lu! Lu! Lu! Lu! A! li! Lu! Lu! Lu! Lu! Li! A! Lu! Lu!
   Li! Lu! A! Li! Lu! Lu! Lu! Lu! u!

MERAB : Saul in thousands slew their men!

MICHAL : David slew his thousands ten!

MERAB AND MAIDENS : Saul in thousands slew their men!

MICHAL AND MAIDENS : David slew his thousands ten! Oh! Lu! Lu!
   Lu! Lu! Lu! Lu! A! Li! Lu! Lu! Lu!

ALL : Lu! Lu! Lu! Li! Lu! Lu! Lu!—A-li-lu-lu-a-li-lu-lu! Lu-a-li-lu-
   lu-lu! Lu-lu-lu!

MERAB : Out of Judah Saul comes in.

MICHAL : David slew the Philistine.

MERAB AND MAIDENS : Out of Judah Saul comes in.

MICHAL AND MAIDENS : David slew the Philistine.

ALL : Lu-li-lu-lu-lu-li-li-lu! Lu-lu-a-li-lu-lu-lu!

> *They continue the repetition of the simple rhymes, as* SAUL
> *draws near, followed by* DAVID, JONATHAN, ABNER *and the*
> *armed men. The* MAIDENS *keep up the singing, all the time*
> *dancing;* MERAB *with her* MAIDENS *on one side of the men,*
> MICHAL *and her* MAIDENS *on the other, singing loudly back and*
> *forth all the time. The men pass slowly into the gate, without*
> *response. The* MAIDENS *run peering at the spoil the servant-men*
> *are carrying in. All pass in at the gate.*

CURTAIN

SCENE X

Courtyard of SAUL'S *house in Gilgal. Confusion of people and men just come in—*MAIDENS *still singing outside.*

ABNER: The King is returned to his own house once more full of victory. When shall we slay the sacrifice?

SAUL: To-night I will slay a bull calf for my house, and an ox will I sacrifice for my household. And for the men will we slay oxen and sheep and goats.

ABNER: Yea! For this is a great day before the Lord in Israel! And we will sprinkle the spoil with the sacrifice.

SAUL: Hast thou heard the song of the women? Nay, hearest thou? Hark! *(In the distance is heard the singing.)*

MERAB: Saul in thousands slew their men.

MICHAL: David slew his thousands ten.

ALL: Lu-lu-lu-li-lu-lu-a! A-li-lu-lu-a-li-lu!

ABNER: Ay!

SAUL: May such mouths be bruisel!

ABNER: Nay! Nay! King Saul! In this hour!

SAUL: In this instant! They have ascribed to David ten thousands, and to me they have ascribed but thousands. And what can he have more, but the Kingdom?

ABNER: Nay, nay, O Saul! It is but the light words of women. Ay, let them sing! For as vain women they fancy naught but that head of Goliath, with the round stone sunken in. But the King is King.

SAUL: Shall that shepherd oust me, even from the mouths of the maidens?

ABNER: Nay, this is folly, and less than kingly.

MICHAL *(followed by* MERAB—*running round the* KING *with their tambourines)*: Lu-li-lu-lu-a-li-lu! A-li-lu-lu-a-li-lu-lu-lu!

SAUL: Away!

MERAB AND MICHAL: Lu-lu-lu-lu! Saul, the King! Lu-lu-lu-lu-al-li-lu-lu! Saul! Saul! Lu-lu-lu! Saul! Saul! Lu-lu-lu!

SAUL: Peace, I say!

Exit SAUL, *passing into house.*

MERAB AND MICHAL : Jonathan and David. Lu-lu-lu! Here they come, the friendly two! Lu-lu-lu-lu-a-li-lu! Lu-lu-a-li-lu-lu-lu!

MERAB : Jonathan is kingly bred.

MICHAL : David took Goliath's head.

BOTH : Jonathan and David! Lu-lu-lu!—a! Here they come, the loving two-a!

MICHAL *(to* DAVID*)* : Where is the giant's head?

DAVID : It is in Jerusalem of Judah, O Maiden.

MICHAL : Why did you not bring it here, that we might see it?

DAVID : I am of Judah, and they would have it there.

MICHAL : But Saul is King, and could have it where he would.

DAVID : Saul would leave it in Jerusalem.

MICHAL : And the armour, and the greaves of brass, and the shield, and the sword? The coat of brass that weighs five thousand shekels. Where are these? I want to see them, O David!

DAVID : The armour is in my father's house, and in Jerusalem. The sword lies before the Lord in Ramah, with Samuel, O Maiden!

MICHAL : Why take it to Samuel? Do you not know my name, O David!

DAVID : You are Michal.

MICHAL : I am she. And this is Merab! Look at him, Merab, and see if you like him. Is it true, O my brother Jonathan, that the King will give Merab his daughter to the slayer of the Philistine?

JONATHAN : He hath said so.

MICHAL : To us he has not said one word. O Merab! Look at thy man! How likest thou him?

MERAB : I will not look at him yet.

MICHAL : Oh, thou! Thou hast spied out every hair in his beard. Is he not fox-red? I think the beard of a man should be raven-black. O Merab, thy David is very ruddy.

MERAB : Nay! He is not yet mine, nor I his.

MICHAL : Thou wouldst it were so! Aiee! Thou art hasty and before-hand with the red youth! Shame on thee, that art a King's daughter.

MERAB : Nay, now, I have said naught.

MICHAL : Thou shouldst have said somewhat, to cover thy un-maidenly longing.—O David, this Merab sighs in her soul for you. How like you her?

DAVID : She is fair and a modest maiden.

MICHAL: As am not I! Oh, but I am Saul's very daughter, and a hawk that soars kinghigh. And what has David brought, to lay before Merab?

DAVID: All I have is laid before the King.

MICHAL: But naught of the Philistine Goliath! All that spoil you took home to your father's house, as the fox brings his prey to his own hole. Ah, David, the wary one!

MERAB: It was his own! Where should he take it, but to his father's house!

MICHAL: Is not the King his father! Why should he not bring it here? Is Merab not worth the bride-money?

JONATHAN: Oh, peace! Thou art all mischief, Michal. Thou shouldst be married to a Philistine, for his undoing.

MICHAL: Ayee! This David has come back to trouble us! Why didst not *thou* slay the Philistine, Jonathan?

JONATHAN: Peace! Let us go in, David! These maidens are too forward. My father did never succeed in ruling his household of women.

MICHAL: Ayee! His household of women! Thou, Jonathan! Go in, David! They shall not put poison in your meat.

　　　　As DAVID *and* JONATHAN *depart she sings:*
　　　　　　Empty-handed David came!
　　　　　　Merab saw him full of shame!
　　　　Lu-lu-lu-lu-lu-li-lu! A-li-lu-a! A-li-lu!
　　　　　　Empty-handed David came!
　　　　　　Merab saw him full of shame!
　　　　A-li-lu-lu! A-li-lu-li! Li-lu-li-lu-a!

(To MERAB.) So he has come!

MERAB: Even so! Yet his brow says: *Have a care!*

MICHAL: Have a care, Merab! Have a care, David! Have a care, Michal! Have a care, Jonathan! Have a care, King Saul! I do not like his brow, it is too studied.

MERAB: Nay, it is manly, and grave.

MICHAL: Ayee! Ayee! He did not laugh. He did not once laugh. It will not be well, Merab!

MERAB: What will not be well?

MICHAL: The King will not give thee to him.

MERAB: But the King hath spoken.

MICHAL: I have read the brow of Saul, and it was black. I have

looked at David's brow, and it was heavy and secret. The King
will not give thee to David, Merab. I know it, I know it.

MERAB : A King should keep his word!

MICHAL : What! Art thou hot with anger against thy father, lest
he give thee not to this shepherd boy! David hath cast a spell
on Merab! The ruddy herdsman out of Judah has thrown a net
over the King's daughter! Oh, poor quail! poor partridge!

MERAB : I am not caught! I am not!

MICHAL : Thou art caught! And not by some chieftain, nor by some
owner of great herds. But by a sheep-tending boy! Oh, fie!

MERAB : Nay, I do not want him.

MICHAL : Yea, thou dost. And if some man of great substance came,
and my father would give thee to him, thou wouldst cry : *Nay!*
Nay! Nay! I am David's!

MERAB : Never would I cry this and that thou sayest. For I am not
his.—And am I not first daughter of the King!

MICHAL : Thou waitest and pantest after that red David. And he will
climb high in the sight of Israel, upon the mound of Merab. I
tell thee, he is a climber who would climb above our heads.

MIAHAL : Above my head he shall not climb.

MICHAL :   Empty-handed David came!
          Merab saw him full of shame!
      Lu-li-lu-li! Lu-li-lu-lu-li! A-li-lu-lu!

CURTAIN

SCENE XI

Room in KING'S *house at Gilgal. Bare adobe room, mats on the floor.*
SAUL, ABNER *and* ADRIEL *reclining around a little open hearth.*

SAUL : And how is the slayer of Goliath looked upon, in Gilgal?

ABNER : Yea! he is a wise young man, he brings no disfavour upon
himself.

SAUL : May Baal finish him! And how looks he on the King's
daughter? Does he eye Merab as a fox eyes a young lamb?

ABNER : Nay, he is wise, a young man full of discretion, watching
well his steps.

SAUL: Ay is he! Smooth-faced and soft-footed, as Joseph in the house of Pharaoh! I tell you, I like not this weasel.

ABNER: Nay, he is no enemy of the King. His eyes are clear, with the light of the Lord God. But he is alone and shy, as a rude young shepherd.

SAUL: Thou art his uncle, surely. I tell you, I will send him back to Bethlehem, to the sheep-cotes.

ABNER: He is grown beyond the sheep-cotes, O King! And wilt thou send him back into Judah, while the giant's head still blackens above the gates of Jerusalem, and David is darling of all Judea, in the hearts of the men of Judah? Better keep him here, where the King alone can honour him.

SAUL: I know him! Should I send him away, he will have them name him King in Judah, and Samuel will give testimony. Yea, when he carried the sword of the giant before Samuel in Ramah, did not Samuel bless him in the sight of all men, saying: Thou art chosen of the Lord out of Israel!

ABNER: If it be so, O King, we cannot put back the sun in heaven. Yet is David faithful servant to the King, and full of love for Jonathan. I find in him no presumption.

SAUL: My household is against me. Ah, this is the curse upon me! My children love my chief enemy, him who hath supplanted me before the Lord. Yea, my children pay court to David, and my daughters languish for him. But he shall not rise upon me. I say he shall not! Nor shall he marry my elder daughter Merab. Wellah, and he shall not.

ABNER: Yet Saul has given his word.

SAUL: And Saul shall take it back. What man should keep his word with a supplanter? Abner, have we not appointed him captain over a thousand? Captain over a thousand in the army of Saul shall he be. Oh yes! And to-morrow I will say to him, I will even say it again: *Behold Merab, my elder daughter, her will I give thee to wife: only be thou valiant for me, and fight the Lord's battles.* And then he shall go forth with his thousand again, quickly, against the Philistine. Let not my hand be upon him, but let the hand of the Philistine be upon him.

ABNER: But if the Lord be with him, and he fall not, but come back once more with spoil, wilt thou then withhold the hand of thy daughter Merab from him?

SAUL: He shall not have her! Nay, I know not. When the day comes that he returns back to this house, then Saul will answer him. We will not tempt the Thunderer.

ADRIEL: I have it sure, from Eliab his brother, that David was anointed by Samuel to be King over Israel, secretly, in the house of his father Jesse. And Eliab liketh not the youngster, saying he was ever heady, naughty-hearted, full of a youngling's naughty pride, and the conceit of the father's favourite. Now the tale is out in Judah, and many would have him King, saying: Why should Judah look to a King out of Benjamin? Is there no horn-anointed among the men of Judah?

SAUL: So is it! So is it!—To-morrow he shall go forth with his men, and the hand of the Philistine shall be upon him. I will not lift my hand upon him, for fear of the Dark! Yet where is he now? What is he conniving at this moment, in the house of Saul? Go see what he is about, O Adriel!

　　　　Exit ADRIEL.

ABNER: It is a bad thing, O Saul, to let this jealous worm eat into a King's heart, that always was noble!

SAUL: I cannot help it. The worm is there. And since the women sang—nay, in all the cities they sang the same—*Saul hath slain his thousands, but David hath slain his tens of thousands*, it gnaws me, Abner, and I feel I am no longer King in the sight of the Lord.

ABNER: Canst thou not speak with the Morning Wind? And if the Lord of Days have chosen David to be king over Israel after thee, canst thou not answer the great Wish of the Heavens, saying: *It is well!*?

SAUL: I cannot! I cannot deny my house, and my blood! I cannot cast down my own seed, for the seed of Jesse to sprout. I cannot! Wellah, and I will not! Speak not to me of this!

ABNER: Yet wert *thou* chosen of God! And always hast thou been a man of the bright horn.

SAUL: Yea, and am I brought to this pass! Yea, and must I cut myself off? Almost will I rather be a man of Belial, and call on Baal. Surely Astaroth were better to me. For I have kept the faith, yet must I cut myself off! Wellah, is there no other strength?

ABNER: I know not. Thou knowest, who hast heard the thunder and hast felt the Thunderer.

SAUL: I hear It no more, for It hath closed Its lips to me. But other voices hear I in the night—other voices!

 Enter ADRIEL.

SAUL: Well, and where is he?

ADRIEL: He is sitting in the house of Jonathan, and they make music together, so the women listen.

SAUL: Ah! And sings the bird of Bethlehem? What songs now?

ADRIEL: Even to the Lord: *How excellent is thy name in all the earth*. And men and women listen diligently, to learn as it droppeth from his mouth. And Jonathan, for very love, writes it down.

SAUL: Nay, canst thou not remember?

ADRIEL: I cannot, O King. Hark!

 A man is heard in the courtyard, singing loud and manly, from Psalm viii.

Voice of singer: What is man, that thou art mindful of him? and the son of man, that thou visitest him?

For thou hast made him a little lower than the angels, and hast crowned him with glory and honour.

Thou madest him to have dominion over the works of thy hands; Thou hast put all things under his feet:

All sheep and oxen, yea, and the beasts of the field;

The fowl of the air, and the fish of the sea, and whatsoever passeth through the paths of the seas.

O Lord our Lord, how excellent is thy name in all the earth!

 SAUL *listens moodily.*

SAUL: I hear him! Yea, they sing after him! He will set all Israel singing after him, and all men in all lands. All the world will sing what he sings. And I shall be dumb. Yea, I shall be dumb, and the lips of my house will be dust! What, am I naught; and set at naught! What do I know? Shall I go down into the grave silenced, and like one mute with ignorance? Ha! Ha! There are wells in the desert that go deep. And even there we water the sheep, when our faces are blackened with drought. Hath Saul no sight into the unseen? Ha, look! look down the deep well, how the black water is troubled.—Yea, and I see death, death, death! I see a sword through my body, and the body of Jonathan gaping wounds, and my son Abinadab, and my son Melchishua, and my son Ishbosheth lying in blood. Nay, I see the small pale issue of my house creeping on broken feet, as a lamed worm. Yea, yea, what an end! And the seed of David rising up and covering the earth, many, with a glory about them, and the wind of the Lord in their hair. Nay, then they wheel against the sun, and are dark, like the locusts sweeping in heaven, like the pillars of locusts moving, yea, as a tall, dark cloud upon the land. Till they drop in drops of blood, like thunder-rain, and the land is red. Then they turn again into the glory of the Lord. Yea, as a flight of birds down all the ages, now shedding sun and the gleam of God, now shedding shadow and the fall of blood, now as quails chirping in the spring, now as the locust pillars of cloud, as death upon the land. And they thicken and thicken, till the world's air grates and clicks as with the wings of locusts. And man is his own devourer, and the Deep turns away, without wish to look on him further. So the earth is a desert, and manless, yet covered with houses and iron. Yea, David, the pits are digged even under the feet of thy God, and thy God shall fall in. Oh, their God shall fall into the pit, that the sons of David have digged. Oh, men can dig a pit for the most high God, and He falls in—as they say of the huge elephant in the lands beyond the desert. And the world shall be Godless, there shall no God walk on the mountains, no whirlwind shall stir like a heart in the deeps of the blue firmament. And God shall be gone from the world. Only men there shall be, in myriads, like locusts, clicking and grating upon one another, and crawling over one another. The smell of them shall be as smoke, but it shall rise up into the air, without finding the nostrils of God. For God shall be gone! gone! gone! And men shall inherit the earth! Yea, like locusts and whirring on wings like locusts. To this the seed of David shall come, and this is their triumph, when the house of Saul has been swept up, long, long ago into the body of God. Godless the world! Godless the men in myriads even like locusts. No God in the air! No God on the mountains! Even out of the deeps of the sky they lured Him, into their pit! So the world is empty of God, empty, empty, like a blown egg-shell bunged with wax and floating meaningless. God shall fall Himself into the pit these men shall dig for Him! Ha! Ha! O David's Almighty, even He knows not the depth of the dark wells in the desert, where men may still water their flocks! Ha! Ha! Lord God of Judah, thou peepest not down the

pit where the black water twinkles. Ha-ha! Saul peeps and sees
the fate that wells up from below! Ha! Lo! Death and blood,
what is this Almighty that sees not the pits digged for Him by
the children of men? Ha! Ha! saith Saul. Look in the black
mirror! Ha!

ABNER: It is not well, O King.

SAUL: Ha! It is very well! It is very well. Let them lay their trap
for his Lord. For his Lord will fall into it. Aha! Aha! Give them
length of days. I do not ask it.

ABNER: My lord, the darkness is over your heart.

SAUL: And over my eyes! Ha! And on the swim of the dark are
visions. What? Are the demons not under the works of God,
as worms are under the roots of the vine? Look! *(Stares transfixed.)*

ABNER *(to* ADRIEL*)*: Go quickly and bring Jonathan, and David,
for the Kings is prophesying with the spirit of the under-
earth.

     Exit ADRIEL.

SAUL: The room is full of demons! I have known it filled with
the breath of Might. The glisten of the dark, old movers that first
got the world into shape. They say the god was once as a beetle,
but vast and dark. And he rolled the earth into a ball, and laid
his seed in it. Then he crept clicking away to hide for ever, while
the earth brought forth after him. He went down a deep pit. The
gods do not die. They go down a deep pit, and live on at the
bottom of oblivion. And when a man staggers, he stumbles and
falls backwards down the pit—down the pit, down through
oblivion after oblivion, where the gods of the past live on. And
they laugh, and eat his soul. And the time will come when even
the God of David will fall down the endless pit, till He passes the
place where the serpent lies living under oblivion, on to where
the Beetle of the Beginning lives under many layers of dark. I see
it! Aha! I see the Beetle clambering upon Him, Who was the
Lord of Hosts.

ABNER: I cannot hear thee, O King. I would e'en be deaf in this
hour. Peace! I bid thee! Peace!

SAUL: What? Did someone speak within the shadow? Come thou
forth then from the shadow, if thou hast aught to say.

ABNER: I say Peace! Peace, thou! Say thou no more!

SAUL: What? Peace! saith the voice? And what is peace? Hath the Beetle of the Beginning peace, under many layers of oblivion? Or the great serpent coiled for ever, is he coiled upon his own peace?

Enter JONATHAN, DAVID, *and* MEN.

SAUL *(continuing)*: I tell you, till the end of time, unrest will come upon the serpent of serpents, and he will lift his head and hiss against the children of men—thus will he hiss! (SAUL *hisses.*) Hiss! Hiss! and he will strike the children of men—thus——

SAUL *strikes as a serpent, and with his javelin.*

JONATHAN: Father, shall we sound music?

SAUL: Father! Who is father? Know ye not, the vast, dark, shining beetle was the first father, who laid his eggs in a dead ball of the dust of forgotten gods? And out of the egg the serpent of gold, who was great Lord of Life, came forth.

JONATHAN *(to DAVID)*: Now sing, that peace may come back upon us.

DAVID: If he heed me. *(Sings Psalm viii.)*

SAUL *meanwhile raves—then sinks into gloom, staring fixedly.*

SAUL: And the serpent was golden with life. But he said to him-self: I will lay an egg. So he laid the egg of his own undoing. And the Great White Bird came forth. Some say a dove, some say an eagle, some say a swan, some say a goose—all say a bird. And the serpent of the sun's life turned dark, as all the gods turn dark. Yea, and the Great White Bird beat wings in the firma-ment, so the dragon slid into a hole, the serpent crawled out of sight, down to the oblivion of oblivion, yet above the oblivion of the Beetle.

DAVID *meanwhile sings.*

SAUL *(striking with his hands as if at a wasp)*: Na-a! But what is this sound that comes like a hornet at my ears, and will not let me prophesy! Away! Away!

JONATHAN: My Father, it is a new song to sing.

SAUL: What art thou, Jonathan, thy father's enemy?

JONATHAN: Listen to the new song, Father.

SAUL: What? *(Hearkens a moment.)* I will not hear it! What! I say I will not hear it! Trouble me not, nor stop the dark fountain of my prophecy! I will not hearken! *(Listens.)*

DAVID *(singing)*: When I consider thy heavens, the work of thy fingers, the moon and the stars, which thou hast ordained.

SAUL: What! art thou there, thou brown hornet, thou stealer of life's honey! What, shalt thou stay in my sight! *(Suddenly hurls his javelin at* DAVID. DAVID *leaps aside.)*

JONATHAN: My Father, this shall not be!

SAUL: What! art thou there? Bring me here my dart.

JONATHAN *(picking up the javelin)*: Look then at the hole in the wall! Is not that a reproach against the house of the King for ever? *(Gives the javelin to* SAUL.)

> SAUL *sinks into moody silence, staring.* DAVID *begins to sing very softly.*

DAVID *(singing)*: O Lord our Lord, how excellent is thy name in all the earth! Who has set thy glory above the heavens.

> SAUL *very softly, with the soft, swift suddenness of a great cat, leaps round and hurls the javelin again.* DAVID *as swiftly leaps aside.*

SAUL: I will smite David even to the wall.

ABNER: Go hence, David! Swiftly hence!

JONATHAN: Twice, Father!

> *Exit* DAVID.

ABNER *(seizing javelin)*: The evil spirits upon thee have done this. O Saul! They have not prevailed.

SAUL: Have I pierced him? Is he down with the dead? Can we lay him in the sides of the pit?

ABNER: He is not dead! He is gone forth.

SAUL *(wearily)*: Gone forth! Ay! He is gone forth!—What, did I seek to slay him?

JONATHAN: Yea, twice.

SAUL: I was out of myself. I was then beside myself.

ABNER: Yea, the evil spirits were upon thee.

SAUL: Tell him, O Jonathan, Saul seeks not his life. Nay! Nay! Do I not love him, even as thou dost, but more, even as a father! O David! David! I have loved thee. Oh, I have loved thee and the Lord in thee.—And now the evil days have come upon me, and I have thrown the dart against thee, and against the Lord. I am a man given over to trouble, and tossed between two winds. Lo, how can I walk before the faces of men! *(Covers his face with his mantle.)*

ABNER : The evil spirits have left him. Peace comes with sorrow.

JONATHAN : And only then.

SAUL : Bring David hither to me, for I will make my peace with
him, for my heart is very sore.

JONATHAN : Verily, shall it be peace?

SAUL : Yea! For I fear the Night.

    Exit JONATHAN.

  Surely now will David publish it in Judah: *Saul hath lifted
his hand to slay me.*

ABNER : He will not publish it in Judah.

SAUL : And wherefore not? Is he not as the apple of their eyes to
the men of Judah, who love not overmuch the tribe of Benjamin?

ABNER : But David is the King's man.

SAUL : Ah, would it were verily so.

    Enter JONATHAN *and* DAVID.

DAVID : The Lord strengthen the King!

SAUL : Ah, David, my son, come, and come in peace. For my hands
are bare and my heart is washed and my eyes are no longer
deluded. May the Lord be with thee, David, and hold it not
against me, what I have done. Spirits of the earth possess me,
and I am not my own. Thou shalt not cherish it in thy heart,
what Saul did against thee, in the season of his bewilderment?

DAVID : Naught has the King done against me. And the heart of
thy servant knoweth no ill.

SAUL : Hatest thou me not, David?

DAVID : Let the word be unspoken, my Father!

SAUL : Ah, David! David! Why can I not love thee untroubled?—
But I will right the wrong.—Thou shalt henceforth be captain
of the thousand of Hebron, and dwell in thine own house, by the
men. And behold, Merab, my elder daughter, I will give thee to
wife.

DAVID : Who am I, and what is my life, or my father's family in
Israel, that I should be son-in-law to the King?

SAUL : Nay, thou art of mine own heart, and the Lord is thy great
strength. Only be valiant for me, and fight the Lord's battles.

DAVID : All my life is the King's, and my strength is to serve.

SAUL : It shall be well. And with thy thousand shalt thou succour
Israel.

               CURTAIN

S C E N E   X I I

The well at Gilgal: MAIDENS *coming with water-jars. Two* HERDS-
MEN *filling the trough—one below, at the water, one on the*
steps. They swing the leathern bucket back and forth with a
rough chant: the lower shepherd swinging the load to the
upper, who swings it to the trough, and hands it back. DAVID
approaching.

1ST HERDSMAN: Ya! David missed her.
2ND HERDSMAN: Let him get her sister—Oh! Oh-oh-h!
1ST HERDSMAN: Ya! David missed her.
2ND HERDSMAN: Let him get her sister—Oh-h-h-h! *(Continue several*
times.)
1ST MAIDEN: How long, O Herdsman!
2ND HERDSMAN: Ho-o-o! Enough!
1ST HERDSMAN *(coming up)*: Ya! David missed her!
        MAIDENS *run away from him.*
1ST MAIDEN: Ho, thou! Seest thou not David?
1ST HERDSMAN: Yea, he is there! Ho! David! And hast thou missed
    her?
        MAIDENS *laugh.*
DAVID: What sayest thou, O Man?
1ST HERDSMAN: Thou hast missed her—say!—am I not right?
DAVID: And whom have I missed?
1ST HERDSMAN: Wellah! And knowest thou not?
DAVID: Nay!
1ST HERDSMAN: Wellah! But Merab, the King's elder daughter!
    Wellah! We feasted her week half a moon ago, whilst you and
    your men were gone forth against the Philistines. Wellah, man,
    and didst thou not know?
DAVID: Sayest thou so?
1ST HERDSMAN: Wellah! And is it not so? Say, Maidens, hath not
    Adriel the Meholathite got Merab, Saul's daughter, to wife? And
    hath he not spent his week with her? Wellah, thou art ousted
    from that bed, O David.
DAVID: And hath the King given his daughter Merab unto Adriel

the Meholathite! Wellah, shall he not do as he choose, with his own?

1ST HERDSMAN: Ay, wellah, shall he! But thou wert promised. And in thy stead, another hath gone in unto her. Is it not so, O Maidens? Sleeps not Merab in the tent of Adriel the Meholathite?

1ST MAIDEN: Yea, the King hath married her to the man.

DAVID: And sings she as she shakes his butter-skin?

1ST MAIDEN: Nay, as yet she sings not. But if David sits here beneath the tree, she will come with her jar. Nay, is that not Adriel the Meholathite himself, coming forth? O Herdsman, drive not the cattle as yet to the drinking troughs! *(Goes down and fills her pitcher.)*

2ND MAIDEN: Will David sit awhile beneath the tree?

DAVID: Yea!

2ND MAIDEN: Then shall Michal, daughter of Saul, come hither with her water-jar. Is it well, O David?

DAVID: Yea, it is very well.

     MAIDEN *goes down with her pitcher.*

ADRIEL: Ha, David! And art thou returned? I have not seen thee before the King.

DAVID: I returned but yesterday. And I saw the King at the dawn. Now art thou become a great man in Israel, O Adriel, and son-in-law to the King. How fareth Merab in the tents of the Meholathite?

ADRIEL: Yea, and blithely. And to-morrow even in the early day will I set her on an ass, and we will get us to my father's house. For he is old, and the charge of his possessions is heavy upon him, and he fain would see his daughter Merab, who shall bring him sons—sons to gladden him. And she shall have her hand-maidens about her, and her store-barns of wool, and corn, and clotted figs, and bunches of raisins, all her wealth she shall see in store!

DAVID: May she live content, and bring thee sons, even males of worth.

ADRIEL: The Lord grant it! And thou hast come home once more with spoil! How thou chastenest the Philistine! Yea, and behold, the King hath delight in thee, and all his servants love thee! Lo! I am the King's son-in-law, of Merab. Now, therefore, be thou also the King's son-in-law, for there is yet a daughter.

DAVID: Seemeth it to you a light thing, to be the King's son-in-law, seeing that I am a poor man, and lightly esteemed?

ADRIEL: By my beard, the King delighteth in thee, and all his servants love thee. There is no man in Israel more fit to take a daughter of the King.

DAVID: Yea, there be men of mighty substance such as thou, whose flocks have not been counted, and who send men-at-arms pricking with iron lance-points, to the King's service. But what have I, save the bare hands and heart of a faithful servant?

ADRIEL: Nay, thy name is high among men. But lo! here cometh Saul, as he hath promised. He is coming out to my tents. I will go forward to bring him in. Come thou?

DAVID: Nay! Leave me here.

    Exit ADRIEL.

1ST HERDSMAN: I have heard the mouth of Adriel, O David! Surely he is the King's listener.

DAVID: And thou! Who made *thee* a listener?

1ST HERDSMAN: Nay, I must guard the water-troughs till the cattle have drunk. Adriel hath flocks and men-servants, but David hath the Lord, and the hearts of all Israel! Better a brave and bright man, with a face that shines to the heart, than a great owner of troops and herds, who struts with arms akimbo. As I plant this driving-stick in the soft earth, so hath the Lord planted David in the heart of Israel. I say: Stick, may thou flourish! May thou bud and blossom and be a great tree. For thou art not as the javelin of Saul, levelled at David's bosom.

DAVID: Peace! Saul cometh.

1ST HERDSMAN: Wellah! And I will go down to the water. *(Goes to the well.)*

DAVID: The Lord strengthen the King.

SAUL: Art thou my son, David? Yea, David, have they told thee, I have married my daughter Merab unto Adriel the Meholathite, even to him who stands here?

DAVID: Yea, O Saul! They told me the King's pleasure. May the Lord bless thy house for ever!

SAUL: Have I not promised my daughter unto thee? But my servants tell me the heart of Michal goes forth wishful unto David. Say now, is she fair in thine eyes?

DAVID: Yea! Yea, O King, yea!

SAUL : When the new moon shows her tender horns above the west, thou shalt this day be my son-in-law in one of the twain.

DAVID : Let thy servant but serve the King!

SAUL : Yea, an thou serve me, it shall be on the day of the new moon.

DAVID : Yea, will I serve without fail.

SAUL : So be it!

    Exit with ADRIEL.

HERDSMAN *(coming up)*: Now is David the richest man in Israel— in promises! Wilt thou not sell me a King's promise, for this my camel-stick?

DAVID : It is well.

HERDSMAN : Sayest thou? Then it is a bargain? Wellah! Take my stick. It is worth the word of a King.

DAVID : Peace!

HERDSMAN : Thou meanest *war*!

DAVID : How?

HERDSMAN : If thou get her, it is war. If thou get her not, it is more war. Sayest thou peace?

MAIDENS *(running)*: Oh, master David, hath Saul passed with Adriel?

HERDSMAN : They have passed, letting fall promises as the goat droppeth pills.

DAVID : Peace, O Man!

MAIDEN : Oh, master David, shall Michal come forth to fill her water-jar? For Merab is setting meats before the King, in the booth of Adriel. Oh, David, shall Michal bring her jar to the well?

HERDSMAN : Ay, wellah, shall she! And I will hold back the cattle this little while, for I hear their voices.

    Exit HERDSMAN.

DAVID : Run back quickly and let her come.

    Exit MAIDEN.

DAVID *(alone)*: Lord! dost Thou send this maiden to me? My entrails strain in me, for Michal, daughter of Saul. Lord God of my Salvation, my wanting of this maiden is next to my wanting Thee. My body is a strung bow. Lord, let me shoot mine arrow unto this mark. Thou fillest me with desire as with thunder, Thy lightning is in my loins, and my breast like a cloud leans forward for her. Lord! Lord! Thy left hand is about her middle, and Thy

right hand grasps my life. So Thou bringest us together in Thy
secret self, that it may be fulfilled for Thee in us. Lord of the
Great Wish, I will not let her go.

MICHAL *(entering—covering her chin and throat with her kerchief)*:
Wilt thou let me pass to fill my jar, O thou stranger?

DAVID: Come, Michal, and I will fill thy jar.

> *She comes forward—he takes her jar and goes down the
> steps. Returning he sets it on the ground at his feet.*

MICHAL: Oh, David! And art thou still unslain?

DAVID: As the Lord wills, no man shall slay me. And livest thou in
thine house lonely, without thy sister Merab?

MICHAL: Is thy heart sore in thee, David, that thou hast lost Merab?
Her heart is gentle, and she sighed for thee. But e'en she obeyed.

DAVID: She hath a man of more substance than David. And my
heart is very glad on her account.

MICHAL: It is well.

DAVID: O Michal, didst thou come willingly to the well, when the
maiden told thee I waited here?

MICHAL: Yea, willingly.

DAVID: O Michal, my heart runs before me, when it sees thee far
off, like one eager to come to his own place. Oh, thou with the
great eyes of the wilderness, shall my heart leap to thee, and shall
thou not say Nay! to it?

MICHAL: What said my father, O David, when he passed?

DAVID: He said: when the new moon showeth her horns in the
west, on this day shalt thou surely be my son-in-law of one of
the twain.

MICHAL: Yea, and is thy heart uplifted, to be a King's son-in-law?

DAVID: So she be Michal, my body is uplifted like the sail of a ship
when the wind arouses.

MICHAL: Nay, thou art a seeker of honours! Merab had been just
as well to thy liking.

DAVID: Ah, no! Ah! Ah! Merab is gentle and good, and my heart
softened with kindness for her, as a man unto a woman. But thou
art like the rising moon, that maketh the limbs of the mountain
glisten. O Michal, we twain are upon the hillsides of the Lord,
and surely He will bring our strength together!

MICHAL: And if the Lord God say thee nay!

DAVID: He will not. He hath thy life in His left hand, and my life

He holdeth in His right hand. And surely He will lay us together in the secret of His desire, and I shall come unto thee by the Lord's doing.

MICHAL : But if He say thee nay, thou wilt let me go.

DAVID : Thou knowest not the Lord my God. The flame He kindles He will not blow out. He is not yea-and-nay! But my Lord my God loveth a bright desire and yearneth over a great Wish, for its fulfilment. Oh, the Lord my God is a glowing flame and He loveth all things that do glow. So loves He thee, Michal, O woman before me, for thou glowest like a young tree in full flower, with flowers of gold and scarlet, and dark leaves. O thou young pomegranate tree, flowers and fruit together show on thy body. And flame calleth to flame, for flame is the body of God, like flowers of flame. Oh, and God is a great Wish, and a great Desire, and a pure flame for ever. Thou art kindled of the Lord, O Michal, and He will not let thee go.

MICHAL : Yet the Lord Himself will not marry me.

DAVID : I will marry thee, for the Lord hath kindled me unto thee, and hath said : Go to her, for the fruits of the pomegranate are ripe.

MICHAL : Will thou not seek me for thyself?

DAVID : Yea, for my very self; and for my very self; and for the Lord's own self in me.

MICHAL : Ever thou puttest the Lord between me and thee.

DAVID : The Lord is a sweet wind that fills thy bosom and thy belly as the sail of a ship; so I see thee sailing delicately towards me, borne onwards by my Lord.

MICHAL : Oh, David, would the new moon were come! For I fear my father, and I misdoubt his hindrances.

DAVID : Thinkest thou, he would marry thee away, as Merab?

MICHAL : Nay, but thou must make a song, and sing it before all Israel, that Michal is thine by the King's promise, no man shall look on her but David.

DAVID : Yea! I will make a song. And yea, I will not let thee go. Thou shalt come to me as wife, and I will know thee, and thou shalt lie in my bosom. Yea! As the Lord liveth!

MICHAL : And as the Lord liveth, not even my father shall constrain me, to give me to another man, before the new moon showeth her horns.

DAVID: It is well, O Michal! O Michal, wife of David, thou shalt sleep in my tent! In the tent of the men of war, beside the sword of David, Michal sleeps, and the hand of David is upon her hip. He has sealed her with his seal, and Michal of David is her name, and kingdoms shall he bring down to her. Michael of David shall blossom in the land, her name shall blossom in the mouths of soldiers as the rose of Sharon after rain. And men-at-arms shall shout her name, like a victory cry it shall be heard. And she shall be known in the land but as Michal of David; blossom of God, keeper of David's nakedness.

MICHAL: They shall not reive me from thee.—I see men coming.

DAVID: Wilt thou go?

MICHAL: I shall call my maidens. So ho! So ho! *(Waves the end of her kerchief.)*

HERDSMAN *(entering)*: There are two captains, servants of Saul, coming even now from the booths of the Meholathite, where the King is.

MICHAL: Yea, let them come, and we will hear the words they put forth.

HERDSMAN: And the cattle are being driven round by the apricot garden. They will soon be here.

DAVID: In two words we shall have the mind of Saul from these captains.

MAIDENS *enter, running.*

MAIDENS: O Michal, men are approaching!

MICHAL: Fill you your jar, and with one ear let us listen. David stays under the tree.

1ST MAIDEN: Stars are in thine eyes, O Michal, like a love night!

2ND MAIDEN: Oh! and the perfume of a new-opened flower! What sweetness has she heard?

3RD MAIDEN: Oh, say! what words like honey, and like new sweet dates of the Oasis, hath David the singer said to Michal? Oh, that we might have heard!

1ST CAPTAIN *(entering)*: David is still at the well?

DAVID: Yea, after war and foray, happy is the homely passage at the well?

2ND CAPTAIN: Wilt thou return to the King's house with us, and we will tell thee what is toward: even the words of Saul concerning thee.

DAVID: Say on! For I must in the other way.

1ST CAPTAIN: The King delighteth in thee more than in any man of Israel. For no man layeth low the King's enemies like David, in the land.

DAVID: Sayest thou so?

1ST CAPTAIN: Yea! And when the new moon shows her horns shalt thou be son-in-law to Saul, in his daughter Michal.

DAVID: As the Lord, and the King, willeth. Saul hath said as much to me, even now. Yet I am a poor man, and how shall the King at last accept me?

2ND CAPTAIN: This too hath Saul considered. And he hath said: Tell my son David, the King desireth not any bride-money, nay, neither sheep nor oxen nor asses, nor any substance of his. But an hundred foreskins of the Philistines shall he bring to the King, to be avenged of his enemies.

1ST CAPTAIN: So said the King: Before the new moon, as she cometh, sets on her first night, shall David bring the foreskins of an hundred Philistines unto Saul. And that night shall Saul deliver Michal, his daughter, unto David, and she shall sleep in David's house.

2ND CAPTAIN: And Israel shall be avenged of her enemies.

DAVID: Hath the King verily sent this message to me?

1ST CAPTAIN: Yea, he hath sent it, and a ring from his own hand. Lo! here it is! For said Saul: Let David keep this for a pledge between me and him, in this matter. And when he returneth, he shall give me my ring again, and the foreskins of the Philistine, and I will give him my daughter Michal to wife.

DAVID: Yea! Then I must hence, and call my men, and go forth against the Philistine. For while the nights are yet moonless, and without point of moon, will I return with the tally.

 Exit DAVID.

2ND CAPTAIN: Yea, he is gone on the King's errand.

1ST CAPTAIN: Let him meet what the King wishes.

 Exeunt 1ST *and* 2ND CAPTAINS.

HERDSMAN: Yea, I know what ye would have. Ye would slay David with the sword of the Philistine. For who keeps promise with a dead man! (MICHAL *and* MAIDENS *edge in.*) Hast thou heard, O Michal? David is gone forth against the Philistine. For Saul asketh an hundred foreskins of the enemy as thy bride-money. Is it not a tall dowry?

MICHAL : Yea! hath my father done this!

HERDSMAN : Wellah, hath he! For dead men marry no king's daughters. And the spear of some Philistine shall beget death in the body of David. Thy father hath made thee dear!

MICHAL : Nay, he hath made my name cheap in all Israel.

2ND HERDSMAN *(entering)* : Run, Maidens! The cattle are coming round the wall, athirst!

MAIDENS *(shouldering their jars)* : Away! Away!

  Exeunt.

CURTAIN

S C E N E   X I I I

A room in DAVID'S *house in Gilgal. Almost dark.* DAVID *alone, speaking softly: an image in a corner.*

DAVID : Give ear to my words, O Lord, consider my meditation. Hearken unto the voice of my cry, my King, and my God : for unto thee will I pray.

My voice shalt thou hear in the morning, O Lord; in the morning will I direct my prayer unto thee, and will look up.

For thou art not a God that hast pleasure in wickednes : neither shall evil dwell with thee.

The foolish shall not stand in thy sight : thou hatest all workers of iniquity.

Thou shalt destroy them that speak leasing : the Lord will abhor the bloody and deceitful man.

But as for me, I will come into thy house in the multitude of thy mercy : and in thy fear will I worship toward thy holy temple.

Lead me, O Lord, in thy righteousness, because of mine enemies; make thy way straight before my face.

For there is no faithfulness in their mouth; their inward part is very wickedness; their throat is an open sepulchre : they flatter with their tongue.

Destroy thou them, O God; let them fall by their own counsels;
cast them out in the multitude of their transgressions; for
they have rebelled against thee.

But let all those that put their trust in thee rejoice : let them ever
shout for joy, because thou defendest them : let them also
that love thy name be joyful in thee.

For thou, Lord, wilt bless the righteous; with favour wilt thou
compass him, as with a shield.

Pause.

Nay Lord, I am Thy anointed, and Thy son. With the oil of anoint-
ment hast Thou begotten me. Oh, I am twice begotten : of Jesse,
and of God! I go forth as a son of God, and the Lord is with me.
Yet for this they hate me, and Saul seeks to destroy me. What
can I do, O Lord, in this pass?

Enter MICHAL, *through curtain at side, with tray and lamp.*

MICHAL : The dawn is at hand. Art thou not faint with this long
watching before the Lord? Oh! why wilt thou leave thy bed and
thy pleasure of the night, to speak out into the empty, chill hour
towards morning? Come then, eat of the food which I have
brought.

DAVID : I will not eat now, for my soul still yearns away from me.

MICHAL : Art thou sick?

DAVID : Yea! My soul is sick.

MICHAL : Why?

DAVID : Nay, thou knowest. Thy father hates me beyond measure.

MICHAL : But I love you.

DAVID *(takes her hand)* : Yea!

MICHAL : Is it nothing to you that Michal is your wife and loves
you?

DAVID : Verily, it is not nothing. But, Michal, what will come to me
at last? From moon to moon Saul's anger waxes. I shall lose my
life at last. And what good shall I be to thee then?

MICHAL : Ah, no! Ah, no! Never shall I see thee dead. First thou
shalt see me dead. Never, never shall I tear my hair for thee, as a
widow. It shall not be. If thou go hence, it shall not be into death.

DAVID : Yet death is near. From month to month, since I came back
with the foreskins of the Philistine, and got thee to wife, Saul has
hated me more. Michal loves David, and Saul's hate waxes
greater. Jonathan loves David, and the King commands Jonathan,

saying: There, where thou seest him, there shalt thou slay David.

MICHAL: My father is no more a man. He is given over entirely to evil spirits. But Jonathan will save thee through it all.

DAVID: The Lord will save me. And Jonathan is dearer to me than a heart's brother.

MICHAL: Think, O husband, if Saul hateth thee, how Michal and Jonathan, who are children of Saul, do love thee.

DAVID: Yea, verily! It is like the rainbow in the sky unto me. But, O Michal, how shall we win through? I have loved Saul. And I have not it in me to hate him. Only his perpetual anger puts on me a surpassing heaviness, and a weariness, so my flesh wearies upon my bones.

MICHAL: But why? Why? Why does it matter to thee? I love thee, all the time—Jonathan loves thee—thy men love thee. Why does the frenzy of one distracted man so trouble thee? Why? It is out of all measure.

DAVID: Nay, he is Saul, and the Lord's anointed. And he is King over all Israel.

MICHAL: And what then? He is no man among men any more. Evil possesses him. Why heed him, and wake in the night for him?

DAVID: Because he is the Lord's anointed, and one day he will kill me.

MICHAL: He will never kill thee. Thou sayest thyself the Lord will prevent him. And if not the Lord, then I will prevent him—for I am not yet nothing in Gilgal. And Jonathan will prevent him. And the captains will prevent him. And art thou not also the Lord's anointed? And will not the Lord set thee King on the hill of Zion, in thine own Judah?

DAVID: O Michal! O Michal! That the hand of the Lord's anointed should be lifted against the Lord's anointed! What can I do? For Saul is the Lord's, and I may not even see an enemy in him. I cannot verily! Yet he seeks to slay me. All these months since he gave thee to me, after I brought the foreskins of the Philistine for thy dowry, he has hated me more, and sought my life. Before the moon of our marriage was waned away thy father commanded his servants, and even Jonathan, to slay David on that spot where they should find him. So Jonathan came to me in haste and secret, and sent me away into the fields by night and hid me. Yea, before the month of our marriage was finished I had to flee from thee in the night, and leave my place cold.

MICHAL: But not for long. Not for long. Jonathan persuaded my father, so he took thee back. Even he loved thee again.

DAVID: Yea, he also loves me! But Saul is a man falling backward down a deep pit, that must e'en clutch what is nearest him, and drag it down along with him.

MICHAL: But Saul swore: As the Lord liveth, David shall not be slain.

DAVID: Ay, he swore. But before two moons were passed his brow was black again. And when the season of the year came, that the Kings of the Philistine go forth, I went up against them, and fought. The months of the fighting I fought with them, and all the people rejoiced. But I saw with a sinking heart the face of Saul blacken, blacken darker with greater hate! Yea, he hath loved me, as the Lord's anointed must love the Lord's anointed. But Saul is slipping backward down the pit of despair, away from God. And each time he strives to come forth, the loose earth yields beneath his feet, and he slides deeper. So the upreach of his love fails him, and the downslide of his hate is great and greater in weight. I cannot hate him—nor love him—but, O Michal, I am oppressed with a horror of him.

MICHAL: Nay, do not dwell on him.

DAVID: And the year went round its course, and once more there was war with the Philistine. And once more we prevailed, in the Lord. And once more the armies shouted my name. And once more I came home to thee—and thou didst sing. And my heart did sing above thee. But as a bird hushes when the shadow of the hawk dances upon him from heaven, my heart went hushed under the shadow of Saul. And my heart could not sing between thy breasts, as it wanted to, even the heart of a bridegroom. For the shadow of Saul was upon it.

MICHAL: Oh, why do you care? Why do you care? Why do you not love me and never care?

DAVID: It is not in me. I have been blithe of thy love and thy body. But now three days ago, even in the midst of my blitheness, Saul again threw his javelin at me—yea, even in the feast. And I am marked among all men. And the end draws nigh.—For scarce may I leave this house, lest at some corner they slay me.

MICHAL: What end, then? What end draws nigh?

DAVID: I must get me gone. I must go into the wilderness.

MICHAL *(weeping)*: Oh, bitter! Bitter! My joy has been torn from me, as an eagle tears a lamb from the ewe. I have no joy in my life, nor in the body of my lord and my husband. A serpent is hid in my marriage bed, my joy is venomed. Oh, that they had wed me to a man that moved me not, rather than be moved to so much hurt.

DAVID: Nay, nay! Oh, nay, nay! Between me and thee is no bitterness, and between my body and thy body there is constant joy! Nay, nay! Thou art a flame to me of man's forgetting, and God's presence. Nay, nay! Thou shalt not weep for me, for thou art a delight to me, even a delight and a forgetting.

MICHAL: No! No! Thou leavest me in the night, to make prayers and moaning before the Lord. Oh, that thou hadst never married in thy body the daughter of thine enemy!

DAVID: Say not so, it is a wrong thing; thou art sweet to me, and all my desire.

MICHAL: It is not true! Thou moanest, and leavest me in the night, to fall before the Lord.

DAVID: Yea, trouble is come upon me. And I must take my trouble to the Lord. But thy breasts are my bliss and my forgetting. Oh, do not remember my complaining! But let thyself be sweet to me, and let me sleep among the lilies.

MICHAL: Thou wilt reproach me again with my father.

DAVID: Ah, no! Ah, never I reproached thee! But now I can forget, I can forget all but thee, and the blossom of thy sweetness. Oh, come with me, and let me know thee. For thou art ever again as new to me.

MICHAL *(rising as he takes her hand)*: Nay, thou wilt turn the bitterness of thy spirit upon me again.

DAVID: Ah, no! I will not! But the gate of my life can I open to thee again, and the world of bitterness shall be gone under as in a flood.

MICHAL: And wilt thou not leave me?

DAVID: Nay, lift up thy voice no more, for the hour of speech has passed.

    Exeunt DAVID *and* MICHAL *through curtain at back.*

SCENE XIV

The same room, unchanged, an hour or so later: but the grey light
of day. A WOMAN-SERVANT *comes in. There is a wooden image*
in a corner.

WOMAN-SERVANT: Yea, the lighted lamp, and the food! My lord
David hath kept watch again before the Lord, and tears will fall
in Michal's bosom, and darken her heart! Aiee! Aiee! That Saul
should so hate the life of David! Surely the evil spirits are strong
upon the King.

BOY *(entering)*: Jonathan, the King's son, is below, knocking softly
at the door.

WOMAN-SERVANT: Go! Open swiftly, and make fast again. Aiee!
Aiee! My lord Jonathan comes too early for a pleasure visit. I
will see if they sleep.

    Exit WOMAN-SERVANT *through the curtain.*
    Enter JONATHAN. JONATHAN *stands silent, pensive. Goes to*
    window. Re-enter WOMAN-SERVANT. *She starts, seeing* JONATHAN
    —then puts her hand on her mouth.

WOMAN-SERVANT: O my lord Jonathan! Hush!

JONATHAN: They are sleeping still?

WOMAN-SERVANT: They are sleeping the marriage sleep. David hath
even watched before the Lord, in the night. But now with Michal
he sleeps the marriage sleep in the lands of peace. Now grant a
son shall come of it, to ease the gnawing of Michal's heart.

JONATHAN: What gnaws in Michal's heart?

WOMAN-SERVANT: Ah, my lord, her love even for David, that will
not be appeased. If the Giver gave her a son, so should her love
for David abate, and cease to gnaw in her.

JONATHAN: But why should it gnaw in her? Hath she not got him,
and the joy of him?

WOMAN-SERVANT: O Jonathan, she is even as the house of Saul.
What she hath cannot appease her.

JONATHAN: What then would she more?

WOMAN-SERVANT: She is of the house of Saul, and her very love is
pain to her. Each cloud that crosses her is another death of her

love. Ah, it is better to let love come and to let it go, even as the
winds of the hills blow along the heavens. The sun shines, and is
dulled, and shines again; it is the day, and its alterings; and after,
it is night.

JONATHAN: David and Michal are asleep?

WOMAN-SERVANT: In the marriage sleep. Oh, break it not!

JONATHAN: The sun will soon rise. Lo! this house is upon the wall
of the city, and the fields and the hills lie open.

WOMAN-SERVANT: Shall I bring food to Jonathan?

JONATHAN: Nay! Hark! Men are crying at the city's western gate,
to open. The day is beginning.

WOMAN-SERVANT: May it bring good to this house!

JONATHAN: It is like to bring evil.

WOMAN-SERVANT: Ah, my lord!

DAVID *(appearing through the curtain at the back)*: Jonathan!

JONATHAN: David! Thou art awake!

DAVID *(laughing)*: Yea! Am I not? Thou art my brother Jonathan,
art thou not? *(They embrace.)*

JONATHAN: O David, the darkness was upon my father in the night,
and he hath again bid slay thee. Leave not the house. Unbar not
the door! Watch! And be ready to flee! If armed men stand
round the door *(enter MICHAL)*, then let down the boy from the
window, and send instantly to me. I will come with thy men and
with mine, and we will withstand the hosts of Saul, if need be.

MICHAL: Is something new toward?

JONATHAN: My father bade his men take David, and slay him in the
dawn. I must away, lest they see that I have warned thee. Farewell, O David!

DAVID: Farewell, my brother Jonathan! But I will come down the
stair with thee.

Exeunt DAVID *and* JONATHAN.

MICHAL: Yea! Yea! So sure as it is well between me and him, so
sure as we have peace in one another, so sure as we are together
—comes this evil wind, and blows upon us! And oh, I am weary
of my life, because of it!

WOMAN-SERVANT: Aiee! Aiee! Say not so, O Michal! For thy days
are many before thee.

MICHAL: This time, an they take him, they will surely kill
him.

WOMAN-SERVANT: Sayest thou so! Oh, why, in the Lord's name!

MICHAL: I know it. If they take him this time, he is lost.

WOMAN-SERVANT: Oh, then shall they surely not take him! Oh, but what shall we do?

MICHAL: Creep thou on the roof! Let no man see thee. And there lie: watch if armed men approach the house.

Enter DAVID.

DAVID: There is no one there.

MICHAL: They will come as the sun comes. *(To* WOMAN.) Go thou and watch.

WOMAN-SERVANT: Verily I will!

Exit WOMAN-SERVANT.

MICHAL: O David! So sure as it is springtime in me, and my body blossoms like an almond-tree, comes this evil wind upon me, and withers my bud! Oh, how can I bring forth children to thee when the spear of this vexation each time pierces my womb?

DAVID: Trouble not thyself, my flower. No wind shall wither thee.

MICHAL: Oh, but I know. This time, an they take thee, thou shalt lose thy life.—And Jonathan will not save thee.

DAVID: Nay! Be not afraid for me.

MICHAL: Yes! I am afraid! I am afraid! Ho! Ho, there! *(Claps her hands. Enter* BOY. *To* BOY.) Bring the water-skin for thy master, filled with water. And his pouch with bread—for he goeth on a journey.—O David! David! Now take thy cloak, and thy bow, and thy spear, and put on thy shoes. For thou must go! Jonathan cannot avail thee this time.

DAVID: Nay! Why shall I flee, when the sun is rising?

MICHAL: Yea! If thou go not before the sun is here in the morning shalt thou be slain. Oh make ready! Thy shoes! Put them on! *(*DAVID *reluctantly obeys.)* Thy cloak, so they shall not know thee! *(He puts it on.)* Thy spear and bow!

Enter BOY.

BOY: Here is the pouch and the water-flask.

MICHAL: Run, bring figs and dry curds. Dost thou hear aught at the door?

BOY: Naught!

Exit BOY.

MICHAL: O David, art thou ready! Oh, that thou leavest me!

DAVID: I need not go! Yea, to comfort thee, I will go to the place

that Jonathan knoweth of, and thou shalt send thither for me.
Or wilt thou——

    Re-enter WOMAN-SERVANT.

WOMAN-SERVANT: O Michal! O David, master! There be men-at-
arms approaching, under the wall, and walking by stealth. Oh,
flee! Oh, flee! for they mean thy life.

MICHAL: Now must thou go by the window, into the fields. I see
the sun's first glitter. Even for this hour have I kept the new rope
ready. (*She fastens the rope to a stout stake, and flings the ends
from the window. To* DAVID.) Go! Go! Swiftly be gone!

DAVID: I will come again to thee. Sooner or later as the Lord liveth,
I will take thee again to me, unto my bed and my body.

MICHAL: Hark! They knock! Ha—a!

    Enter BOY.

BOY: There are men at the door!

MICHAL: Go! Call to them! Ask what they want! But touch thou
not the door!

    DAVID *meanwhile climbs through the window—the stake
holds the rope.*

WOMAN-SERVANT (*climbing with her hands*): So! So! So! My lord
David! So! So! Swing him not against the wall, O spiteful rope.
So! So! He kicks free! Yea! And God be praised, he is on the
ground, looking an instant at his hands. So he looks up and
departs! Lifts his hand and departs!

MICHAL: Is he gone? Draw in the rope, and hide it safe.

WOMAN-SERVANT: That I will!

    Meanwhile MICHAL *has flung back the curtain of the recess
where the low earthen bank of the bed is seen with skins and
covers. She takes the wooden image of a god and lays it in the
bed, puts a pillow at its head, and draws the bed-cover high
over it.*

MICHAL (*to herself*): Yea, and my house's god which is in my house,
shall lie in my husband's place, and the image of my family god,
which came of old from my mother's house, shall deceive them.
For my house has its own gods, yea, from of old, and shall they
forsake me?

    Enter BOY.

BOY: They demand to enter. The King asketh for David, that he go
before the King's presence.

MICHAL: Go thou, say to them: My lord and my master, David, is
sick in his bed.

BOY: I will say that.

   Exit BOY.

WOMAN-SERVANT: Sit thou nigh the bed. And if they still will come
up thou shalt say he sleepeth.

MICHAL: Yea, will I. *(Sits by bed.)* O god of my household, O god
of my mother's house, O god in the bed of David, save me now!
   Enter BOY.

BOY: They will e'en set eyes on my master.

MICHAL: Stay! Say to them, that their captains shall come up, two
only: but softly, for my lord David hath been sick these three
days, and at last sleepeth.

BOY: I will tell them.

   Exit BOY.

WOMAN-SERVANT: And I too will go bid them hush.

   Exit WOMAN-SERVANT. MICHAL *sits in silence. Enter two* CAP-
   TAINS *with the* WOMAN-SERVANT.

WOMAN-SERVANT: There he sleepeth in the bed.

MICHAL: Sh-h-h!

1ST CAPTAIN: I will go even now and tell the King.

   Exeunt the CAPTAINS *after a pause.*

                          CURTAIN

   Curtain rises after a short time on same scene.

WOMAN-SERVANT *(rushing in)*: They are coming again down the
street, but boldly now.

MICHAL: Yea! Let them come! By this time is David beyond their
reach, in the secret place.

WOMAN-SERVANT: Oh, and what shall befall thee! Oh!

MICHAL: I am the King's daughter. Even Saul shall not lift his hand
against me. Go down thou to the door, and hold the men whilst
thou mayst. Why should we admit them forthwith? Say that
Michal is performing her ablutions.

WOMAN-SERVANT: Will I not!

   Exit WOMAN-SERVANT.

MICHAL: And shall I strip the bed? They will search the house and
the fields. Nay, I will leave it, and they shall see how they were

fools. O teraphim, O my god of my own house, hinder them and help me. O thou my teraphim, watch for me!

> *Sound of knocking below.*

VOICE OF SERVANT : Ho, ye! Who knocks, in the Lord's name?

VOICE OF CAPTAIN : Open! Open ye! In the name of the King.

VOICE OF SERVANT : What would ye in this house of sickness?

VOICE OF CAPTAIN : Open, and thou shalt know.

VOICE OF SERVANT : I may not open, save Michal bid me.

VOICE OF CAPTAIN : Then bid Michal bid thee open forthwith.

VOICE OF SERVANT : O thou captain of the loud shout, surely thou wert here before! Know then, my master is sick, and my mistress performeth her ablutions in the sight of the Lord. At this moment may I not open.

VOICE OF CAPTAIN : An thou open not, it shall cost thee.

VOICE OF SERVANT : Nay, now, is not my mistress King's daughter, and is not her command laid on me? O Captain, wilt thou hold it against me, who tremble between two terrors?

VOICE OF CAPTAIN : Tremble shalt thou, when the terror nips thee. E'en open the door, lest we break it in.

VOICE OF SERVANT : Oh, what uncouth man is this, that will break down the door of the King's daughter, and she naked at her bath, before the Lord!

VOICE OF CAPTAIN : We do but the King's bidding.

VOICE OF SERVANT : How can that be? What, did the King indeed bid ye break down the door of his daughter's house, and she un-covered in the Lord's sight, at her ablutions?

VOICE OF CAPTAIN: Yea! The King bade us bring before him instantly the bed of David, and David upon the bed!

VOICE OF SERVANT : Oh, now, what unseemly thing is this! Hath not the King legs long enough? And can he not walk hither on his feet? Oh, send, fetch the King, I pray thee, thou Captain. Say, I pray thee, that Michal prays the King come hither.

VOICE OF CAPTAIN : Word shall be sent. Yet open now this door, that the bird escapes me not.

VOICE OF SERVANT : O Captain! And is my master then a bird? O would he were, even the young eagle, that he might spread wing! O man, hast thou no fear what may befall thee, that thou namest David a bird? O Israel, uncover now thine ear!

VOICE OF CAPTAIN : I name him not.

VOICE OF SERVANT: And what would ye, with this bird my master! Oh, the Lord forbid that any man should call him a bird!

VOICE OF CAPTAIN: We e'en must bring him upon his bed before the King.

VOICE OF SERVANT: Now what is this! Will the King heal him with mighty spells? Or is David on his sick-bed to be carried before the people, that they may know his plight? What new wonder is this?

VOICE OF CAPTAIN: I cannot say—— Yet I will wait no longer.

MICHAL: Open, Maiden! Let them come up.

VOICE OF SERVANT: Oh, my mistress crieth unto me, that I open. Yea, O Michal, I will e'en open to these men. For who dare look aslant at the King's daughter?

> *Enter* CAPTAIN, *followed by* SOLDIERS.

CAPTAIN: Is David still in the bed? An he cannot rise, will we carry him upon the bed, before the King.

MICHAL: Now what is this?

CAPTAIN: Sleeps he yet? Ho, David, sleepest thou?

2ND SOLDIER: We will take up the bed, and wake him.

3RD SOLDIER: He stirs not at all.

CAPTAIN *(to* MICHAL): Yea, rouse him and tell him the King's will.

MICHAL: I will not rouse him.

CAPTAIN *(going to the bed)*: Ho, thou! Ho! David! *(He suddenly pulls back the bed-cover.)* What is this? *(Sudden loud shrilling laughter from the* WOMAN-SERVANT, *who flees when the men look round.)*

SOLDIERS *(crowding)*: We are deceived. Ha-ha! It is a man of wood and a goats'-hair bolster! Ha-ha-ha! What husband is this of Michal's?

MICHAL: My teraphim, and the god of my house.

CAPTAIN: Where hast thou hidden David?

MICHAL: I have not hidden him.

> *Pause.*

VOICE OF SAUL *(on the stair)*: Why tarry ye here? What! Must the King come on his own errands? *(Enter* SAUL.) And are ye here?

MICHAL: The Lord strengthen thee, my Father.

SAUL: Ha! Michal! And can then David not rise from his bed, when the King sendeth for him?

CAPTAIN: Lo! O King! Behold the sick man on the bed! We are deceived of Michal.

SAUL: What is this? *(Flings the image across the room.)*

MICHAL: Oh, my teraphim! Oh, god of my house! Oh, alas, alas, now will misfortune fall on my house! Oh, woe is! woe is me! *(Kneels before teraphim.)*

SAUL: Where is David? Why hast thou deceived me?

MICHAL: O god of my house, god of my mother's house, visit it not upon me!

SAUL: Answer me, or I will slay thee!

MICHAL: God of my house, I am slain! I am slain!

SAUL: Where is David?

MICHAL: O my lord, he is gone; he is gone ere the sun made day.

SAUL: Yea, thou hast helped him against me.

MICHAL *(weeping)*: Oh! Oh! He said unto me: *Let me go; why shouldst thou make me slay thee, to trouble my face in the sight of men.* I could not hinder him, he would have slain me there!

SAUL: Why hast thou deceived me so, and sent away mine enemy, that he escaped?

MICHAL *(weeping)*: I could not prevent him.

SAUL: Even when did he go?

MICHAL: He rose up before the Lord, in the deep night. And then he would away, while no man saw.

SAUL: Whither is he gone?

MICHAL: Verily, and verily, I know not.
    Pause.

SAUL: So! He hath escaped me! And my flesh and my blood hath helped mine enemy. Woe to you, Michal! Woe to you! Who have helped your father's enemy, who would pull down thy father to the ground. Lo! my flesh and my blood rebel against me, and my seed lies in wait for me, to make me fall!

MICHAL: Oh, why must David be slain?

SAUL: Woe to you, Michal! And David shall bring woe to you, and woe upon you. David shall pull down Saul, and David shall pull down Jonathan; thee, Michal, he will pull down, yea, and all thy house. Oh, thou mayst call on the teraphim of thy house. But if thy teraphim love thy house, then would he smite David speedily to the death, for if David liveth I shall not live, and thou

shalt not live, and thy brother shall not live. For David will bring
us all down in blood.

MICHAL *(weeping)*: O my Father, prophesy not against him!

SAUL: It shall be so. What, have I no insight into the dark! And
thou art now a woman abandoned of her man, and thy father
castest thee off, because thou hast deceived him, and brought
about his hurt.

MICHAL: O my Father, forgive me! Hold it not against me!

SAUL: Nay, thou hast bent thy will against thy father, and called
destruction upon thy father's house.

MICHAL: Ah, no! Ah, no!

CURTAIN

S C E N E   X V

*Naioth in Ramah. A round, pyramid-like hill, with a stair-like way
to the top, where is a rude rock altar. Many* PROPHETS, *young
and old, wild and dressed in blue ephods without mantle, on
the summit of the hill and down the slope. Some have harps,
psalteries, pipes and tabrets. There is wild music and rough,
ragged chanting. They are expecting something. Below,* SAMUEL
and DAVID, *talking. Not far off a* PROPHET *in attendance.*

PROPHETS *(on hill—irregularly crying and chanting)*: This is the
place of the Lord! Upon us shines the Unseen! Yea, here is very
God! Who dare come into the glory! O thou, filled with the
Lord, sing with me on this high place. For the egg of the world
is filled with God.

SAMUEL *(speaking to* DAVID): It is time thou shouldst go. As a fox
with the dogs upon him, hast thou much fleeing to do.

DAVID: Must I always flee, my Father? I am already weary of
flight.

SAMUEL: Yea, to flee away is thy portion. Saul cometh hither to
seek thee. But surely shall he fall before the Lord. When he gets
him back to his own city, enquire thou what is his will towards
thee. And if it still be evil, then flee from him diligently, while
he lives.

DAVID: And shall there never be peace between Saul's house and mine?

SAMUEL: Who knows the Lord utterly! If there be not peace this time, then shall there never in life be peace between thee and him, nor thy house and his.

DAVID: Yet am I his son-in-law, in Michal my wife! And my flesh yearneth unto mine own.

SAMUEL: Is the house of Saul thine own?

DAVID: Yea, verily!

SAMUEL: Dost thou say, *Yea, verily?* Hark, now! If this time there be peace between thee and him, it should be peace. But if not, then think of naught but to flee, and save thyself, and keep on fleeing while Saul yet liveth. The Lord's choice is on thee, and thou shalt be King in thy day. As for me, I shall never see thy day.

DAVID: Would I could make my peace with Saul! Would I could return to mine own house, and to mine own wife, and to the men of my charge!

SAMUEL: My son, once the Lord chose Saul. Now hath He passed Saul over and chosen thee. Canst thou look guiltless into the face of Saul? Can he look guiltless into thy face? Can ye look into each other's faces, as men who are open and at peace with one another?

DAVID: Yet would I serve him faithfully.

SAMUEL: Yea, verily! And in thine heart, art thou King, and pullest the crown from his brow with thine eyes.

DAVID: O my Father, I would not!

SAMUEL: Wouldst thou not? Willst thou say to me here and now: *As the Lord liveth, I will not be King! But Saul and his house shall rule Israel for ever: and Jonathan my friend shall be King over me!* Wilt thou say that to me?

DAVID: Does Samuel bid me say this thing?

SAMUEL: He bids thee not. But for Saul's sake, and for Jonathan's, and for Michal's, and for peace, wilt thou say it? Answer me from thine own heart, for I know the smell of false words. Yea, I bid thee, speak!

DAVID: The Lord shall do unto me as He will.

SAMUEL: Yea, for the Lord hath anointed thee, and thou shalt rule Israel when Saul is dead, and I am dead, and the Judges of

Israel are passed away. For my day is nearly over, and thine is another day. Yea, Saul has lived in my day, but thou livest in thine own day, that I know not of.

DAVID : O my lord, is there naught but wrath and sorrow between me and Saul henceforth?

SAMUEL : The Lord will show! Knowest thou not?

DAVID : I would it were peace!

SAMUEL : Wouldst thou verily? When the wind changes, will it not push the clouds its own way? Will fire leap lively in wet rain? The Lord is all things. And Saul hath seen a tall and rushing flame and hath gone mad, for the flame rushed over him. Thou seest thy God in thine own likeness, afar off, or as a brother beyond thee, who fulfils thy desire. Saul yearneth for the flame : thou for thy to-morrow's glory. The God of Saul hath no face. But thou wilt bargain with thy God. So be it! I am old, and would have done. Flee thou, flee, and flee again, and once more, flee. So shalt thou at last have the kingdom and the glory in the sight of men. I anointed thee, but I would see thee no more, for my heart is weary of its end.

DAVID : Wilt thou not bless me?

SAMUEL : Yea, I will bless thee! Yea, I will bless thee, my son. Yea, for now thy way is the way of might; yea, and even for a long space of time it shall be so. But after many days, men shall come again to the faceless flame of my Strength, and of Saul's. Yea, I will bless thee! Thou art brave, and alone, and by cunning must thou live, and by cunning shall thy house live for ever. But hath not the Lord created the fox, and the weasel that boundeth and skippeth like a snake!

DAVID : O Samuel, I have but tried to be wise! What should I do, and how should I walk in the sight of men? Tell me, my Father, and I will do it.

SAMUEL : Thou wilt not. Thou walkest wisely, and thy Lord is with thee. Yea, each man's Lord is his own, though God be but one. I know not thy Lord. Yet walk thou with Him. Yea, thou shalt bring a new day for Israel. Yea, thou shalt be great, thou shalt fight as a flower fighteth upwards, through the stones and alone with God, to flower in the sun at last. For the yearning of the Lord streameth as a sun, even upon the stones. (*A tumult above among the* PROPHETS. SAMUEL *looks up—continues abstractedly.*)

Yea, and as a flower thou shalt fade. But Saul was once a burning bush, afire with God. Alas, that he saw his own image mirrored in the faces of men! *(A blare of music above.)*

SAMUEL *(to* PROPHET*)*: What see ye?

PROPHETS *(shouting)*: The sun on the arms of the King.

SAMUEL *(to* DAVID*)*: Now shalt thou go! For I, too, will not set mine eyes upon Saul the King.

DAVID: Bless me then, O my Father!

SAMUEL: The Lord fill thy heart and thy soul! The Lord quicken thee! The Lord kindle thy spirit, so thou fall into no snare! And now get thee gone! And when Saul is returned to his own place, enquire thou secretly his will towards thee. And then act wisely, as thou knowest.

DAVID: I go forth into the fields, as a hare when the hound gives mouth! But if the Lord go with me . . .

Exit DAVID.

SAMUEL *(to* PROPHET*)*: Is Saul surely in sight?

PROPHET: Verily, he is not far off. He has passed the well of Shecu.

SAMUEL: Has he company of men?

PROPHET: Ten armed men has he.

SAMUEL: Will he still bring armed men to the high place? Lo! Say thou to him: Samuel hath gone before the Lord, in the hidden places of the Hill.

PROPHET: I will e'en say it.

SAMUEL: Say also to him: David, the anointed, is gone, we know not whither. And let the company of the prophets come down towards the King.

PROPHET: It shall be so.

Exit SAMUEL.

PROPHET *(climbing hill and calling)*: O ye Prophets of the Lord, put yourselves in array, to meet Saul the King.

2ND PROPHET *(on hill with flute—sounds flute loudly with a strong tune—shouts)*: Oh, come, all ye that know our God! Oh, put yourselves in array, ye that know the Name. For that which is without name is lovelier than anything named! *(Sounds the tune strongly.)*

PROPHETS *gather in array—musicians in front; they chant slowly. As* SAUL *approaches they slowly descend.*

CHORUS OF PROPHETS: Armies there are, for the Lord our God!

Armies there are against the Lord!
Wilt thou shake spears in the face of Almighty God?
Lo! in thy face shakes the lightning. [*Bis.*
Countest thou thyself a strong man, sayest thou Ha-ha!
Lo! We are strong in the Lord! Our arrow seest thou not!
Yet with the unseen arrows of high heaven
Pierce we the wicked man's feet, pierce we his feet in the fight.
Lo! the bow of our body is strung by God.
Lo! how He taketh aim with arrow-heads of our wrath!
Prophet of God is an arrow in full flight
And he shall pierce thy shield, thou, thou Lord's enemy.
Long is the fight, yet the unseen arrows fly
Keen to a wound in the soul of the great Lord's enemy.
Slowly he bleeds, yet the red drops run away
Unseen and inwardly, as bleeds the wicked man.
Bleeding of God! Secretly of God.

  SAUL *enters with* ARMED MEN. PROPHETS *continue to chant.*

SAUL: Peace be with you!

PROPHET: Peace be with the King!

SAUL: Lo! ye prophets of God! Is not Samuel set over you?

PROPHET: Yea! O King!

SAUL (*beginning to come under the influence of the chant and to
take the rhythm in his voice*): Is Samuel not here?

PROPHET: He hath gone up before the Lord!

SAUL: Surely the Lord is in this place! Surely the great brightness
(*Looks round.*)—and the son of Jesse, is he among the prophets?

PROPHET: Nay, he has gone hence.

SAUL: Gone! Gone! What, has he fled from the high place! Surely
he feared the glory! Yea, the brightness! So he has fled before
the flame! Thus shall he flee before the flame! But gone? Whither
gone?

PROPHET: We know not whither.

SAUL: Even let him go! Even let him go whither he will! Yea,
even let him go! Yea! Come we forth after such as he? Let him
go! Is not the Lord here? Surely the brightness is upon the hill!
Surely it gleams upon this high place!

LEADER OF MEN-AT-ARMS: Tarry we here, O King? Where shall we
seek the son of Jesse?

SAUL: Even where ye will.

LEADER: Tarrieth the King here?

SAUL: Yea! I will know if the Lord is verily in this place.

PROPHET: Verily He is here.

    Company of PROPHETS *still chant.*

SAUL *(going slowly forward)*: Art Thou here, O Lord? What? Is this Thy brightness upon the hill? What? Art Thou here in Thy glory?

COMPANY OF PROPHETS: Fire within fire is the presence of the Lord!

Sun within the sun is our God!   [*Bis.*

Rises the sun among the hills of thy heart

Rising to shine in thy breast?   [*Bis.*

SAUL: Yea! O Prophets! Am I not King? Shall not the Sun of suns rise among the hills of my heart, and make dawn in my body? What! Shall these prophets know the glory of the Lord, and shall the son of Kish stay under a cloud? *(Sticks his spear into the ground, and unbuckles his sword-belt.)*

LEADER OF ARMED MEN: Wilt thou go up before the Lord, O King? Then camp we here, to await thy pleasure.

SAUL: I will go up. Camp an ye will.

LEADER: Even camp we here. *(They untackle.)*

SAUL: Ha! Ha! Is there a glory upon the prophets? Do their voices resound like rocks in the valley! Ha! Ha! Thou of the sudden fire! I am coming! Yea! I will come into the glory!*(Advancing, throws down his woollen mantle. The* 1ST PROPHET *takes it up.)*

CHORUS OF PROPHETS: Whiteness of wool helps thee not in the high place

Colours on thy coat avail thee naught.   [*Bis.*

Fire unto fire only speaks, and only flame

Beckons to flame of the Lord!   [*Bis.*

    The PROPHETS *divide and make way as* SAUL *comes up.*

SAUL: Is my heart a cold hearth? Is my heart fireless unto Thee? Kindler! it shall not be so! My heart shall shine to Thee, yea, unshadow itself. Yea, the fire in me shall mount to the fire of Thee, Thou Wave of Brightness!

SOLDIER *(below—with loud and sudden shout)*: The sun is in my heart. Lo! I shine forth!

SAUL *(with suddenness)*: I will come up! Oh! I will come up! Dip me in the flame of brightness, Thou Bright One, call up the

sun in my heart, out of the clouds of me. Lo! I have been
darkened and deadened with ashes! Blow a fierce flame on me,
from the middle of Thy glory, O Thou of the faceless flame. *(Goes
slowly forward.)* Oh, dip me in the ceaseless flame!

> *Throws down his coat, or wide-sleeved tunic, that came
> below the knee and was heavily embroidered at neck and
> sleeves in many colours: is seen in the sleeveless shirt that
> comes half-way down the thigh.*

SOLDIER *(below)*: Kings come and pass away, but the flame is
flame for ever. The Lord is here, like a tree of white fire! Yea,
and the white glory goes in my nostrils like a scent.

SAUL: Shall a soldier be more blessed than I? Lo! I am not dead,
thou Almighty! My flesh is still flame, still steady flame. Flame
to flame calleth, and that which is dead is cast away. *(Flings off
his shirt: is seen, a dark-skinned man in leathern loin-girdle.)* Nay,
I carry naught upon me, the long flame of my body leans to the
flame of all glory! I am no king, save in the Glory of God. I have
no kingdom, save my body and soul. I have no name. But as a
slow and dark flame leaneth to a great glory of flame, and is
sipped up, naked and nameless lean I to the glory of the Lord.

CHORUS OF PROPHETS: Standeth a man upon the stem of upright
knees

Openeth the navel's closed bud, unfoldeth the flower of the
breast!

Lo! Like the cup of a flower, with morning sun

Filled is thy breast with the Lord, filled is thy navel's wide flower!

SOLDIER: Oh, come! For a little while the glory of the Lord stands
upon the high place! Oh, come! before they build Him houses,
and enclose Him within a roof! Oh, it is good to live now, with
the light of the first day's sun upon the breast. For when the seed
of David have put the Lord inside a house, the glory will be gone,
and men will walk with no transfiguration! Oh, come to this
high place! Oh, come!

SAUL: Surely I feel my death upon me! Surely the sleep of sleeps
descends. *(Casts himself down.)* I cast myself down, night and
day; as in death, lie I naked before God. Ah, what is life to me!
Alas that a man must live till death visit him!—that he cannot
walk away into the cloud of Sun! Alas for my life! For my
children and my children's children, alas! For the son of Jesse

will wipe them out! Alas for Israel! For the fox will trap the lion of strength, and the weasel that is a virgin, and bringeth forth her young from her mouth, shall be at the throats of brave men! Yea, by cunning shall Israel prosper, in the days of the seed of David: and by cunning and lurking in holes of the earth shall the seed of Jesse fill the earth. Then the Lord of Glory will have drawn far off, and gods shall be pitiful, and men shall be as locusts. But I, I feel my death upon me, even in the glory of the Lord. Yea, leave me in peace before my death, let me retreat into the flame!

    A pause.

ANOTHER SOLDIER : Saul hath abandoned his kingdom and his men! Yea, he puts the Lord between him and his work!

PROPHET : E'en let him be! For his loss is greater than another's triumph.

SOLDIER : Yea! But wherefore shall a man leave his men leader-less—even for the Lord!

IST SOLDIER *(prophesying)* : When thou withdrawest Thy glory, let me go with Thee, O Brightest, even into the fire of Thee!

CHORUS OF PROPHETS : Cast thyself down, that the Lord may snatch
    thee up.
Fall before the Lord, and fall high.
All things come forth from the flame of Almighty God,
Some things shall never return!   [*Bis.*
Some have their way and their will, and pass at last
To the worm's waiting mouth.   [*Bis.*
But the high Lord He leans down upon the hill,
And wraps His own in His flame,
Wraps them as whirlwind from the world,
Leaves not one sigh for the grave. . . .

CURTAIN

SCENE XVI

Late afternoon. A rocky place outside Gilgal. DAVID *is hiding near the stone Ezel.*

DAVID *(alone)*: Now, if Jonathan comes not, I am lost. This is the fourth day, and evening is nigh. Lo! Saul seeketh my life. O Lord, look upon me, and hinder mine enemies! Frustrate them, make them stumble, O my God! So near am I to Gilgal, yet between me and mine own house lies the whole gap of death. Yea, Michal, thou art not far from me. Yet art thou distant even as death. I hide and have hidden. Three days have I hidden, and eaten scant bread. Lo! Is this to be the Lord's anointed! Saul will kill me, and I shall die! There! Someone moves across the field! Ah, watch! watch! Is it Jonathan? It is two men; yea, it is two men. And one walks before the other. Surely it is Jonathan and his lad! Surely he has kept his word! O Lord, save me now from mine enemies, for they compass me round. O Lord my God, put a rope round the neck of my enemy, lest he rush forward and seize me in the secret place. Yea, it is Jonathan, in a striped coat. And a man behind him carrieth the bow. Yea, now must I listen, and uncover my ears, for this is life or death. O that he may say: *Behold, the arrows are on this side of thee, take them!* For then I can come forth and go to my house, and the King will look kindly on me.—But he comes slowly, and sadly. And he will say: *The arrows are beyond thee*—and I shall have to flee away like a hunted dog, into the desert.—It will be so! Yea! And I must hide lest that lad who follows Jonathan should see me, and set Saul's soldiery upon me.

  Exit DAVID *after a pause.*
  Enter JONATHAN *with bow, and* LAD *with quiver.*

JONATHAN *(stringing his bow)*: Lo! this is the stone Ezel. Seest thou the dead bush, like a camel's head? That is a mark I have shot at, and now, before the light falls, will I put an arrow through his nose. *(Takes an arrow.)* Will this fly well? *(Balancing it.)*

LAD: It is well shafted, O Jonathan.

JONATHAN: Ay! Let us shoot. *(Takes aim—shoots.)* Yea, it touched the camel's ear, but not his nose! Give me another! *(Shoots.)* Ah! Hadst thou a throat, thou camel, thou wert dead. Yet is thy nose too cheerful! Let us try again! *(Takes another arrow— shoots.)* Surely there is a scratch upon thy nose-tip! Nay, I am not myself! Give me the quiver. And run thou, take up the arrows ere the shadows come.

LAD: I will find them.

> *He runs, as he goes* JONATHAN *shoots an arrow over his head. The* LAD *runs after it—stops.*

JONATHAN: Is not the arrow beyond thee?

LAD: One is here! Here, another!

JONATHAN: The arrow is beyond thee! Make speed! Haste! Stay not!

LAD: Three have I! But the fourth——

JONATHAN: The arrow is beyond thee! Run, make haste!

LAD: I see it not! I see it not! Yea, it is there within bush. I have it, and it is whole. O master, is this all?

JONATHAN: There is one more. Behold it is beyond thee.

LAD *(running)*: I see it not! I see it not! Yea, it is here!

JONATHAN: It is all. Come, then! Come! Nay, the light is fading and I cannot see. Take thou the bow and the arrows, and go home. For I will rest here awhile by the stone Ezel.

LAD: Will my master come home alone?

JONATHAN: Yea will I, with the peace of day's-end upon me. Go now, and wait me in the house. I shall soon come.

> *Exit* LAD. JONATHAN *sits down on a stone till he is gone.*

JONATHAN *(calling softly)*: David! David!

> DAVID *comes forth, weeping. Falls on his face to the ground and bows himself three times before* JONATHAN. JONATHAN *raises him. They kiss one another, and weep.*

DAVID: Ah, then it is death, it is death to me from Saul?

JONATHAN: Yea, he seeks thy life, and thou must flee far hence.

DAVID *(weeping)*: Ah, Jonathan! Thy servant thanks thee from his heart. But ah, Jonathan, it is bitter to go, to flee like a dog, to be houseless and homeless and wifeless, without a friend or helpmate! Oh, what have I done, what have I done! Tell me, what have I done! And slay me if I be in fault.

JONATHAN *(in tears)*: Thou art not in fault. Nay, thou art not! But thou art anointed, and thou shalt be King. Hath not Samuel

said it even now, in Naioth, when he would not look upon the
face of Saul! Yea, thou must flee until thy day come, and the
day of the death of Saul, and the day of the death of Jonathan.

DAVID *(weeping)* : Oh, I have not chosen this. This have I not taken
upon myself. This is put upon me, I have not chosen it! I do not
want to go! Yea, let me come to Gilgal and die, so I see thy face,
and the face of Michal, and the face of the King. Let me die!
Let me come to Gilgal and die! *(Flings himself on the ground in
a paroxysm of grief.)*

JONATHAN : Nay! Thou shalt not die. Thou shalt flee! And till Saul
be dead, thou shalt flee. But when Saul has fallen, and I have
fallen with my father—for even now my life follows my father—
then thou shalt be King.

DAVID : I cannot go!

JONATHAN : Yea! Thou shalt go now. For they will send forth men
to meet me, ere the dark. Rise now, and be comforted. (DAVID
rises.)

DAVID : Why shouldst thou save me! Why dost thou withhold thy
hand! Slay me now!

JONATHAN : I would not slay thee, nor now nor ever. But leave me
now, and go. And go in peace, forasmuch as we have sworn
both of us in the name of the Lord, saying : *The Lord be between
me and thee, and between my seed and thy seed for ever.*

DAVID : Yea, the covenant is between us! And I will go, and keep it.
    They embrace in silence, and in silence DAVID *goes out.*

JONATHAN *(alone in the twilight)* : Thou goest, David! And the
hope of Israel with thee! I remain, with my father, and the star-
stone falling to despair. Yet what is it to me! I would not see
thy new day, David. For thy wisdom is the wisdom of the subtle,
and behind thy passion lies prudence. And naked thou wilt not
go into the fire. Yea, go thou forth, and let me die. For thy virtue
is in thy wit, and thy shrewdness. But in Saul have I known the
magnanimity of a man. Yea, thou art a smiter down of giants,
with a smart stone! Great men and magnanimous, men of the faceless flame, shall fall from Strength, fall before thee, thou David,
shrewd whelp of the lion of Judah! Yet my heart yearns hot
over thee, as over a tender, quick child. And the heart of my
father yearns, even amid its dark wrath. But thou goest forth,
and knowest no depth of yearning, thou son of Jesse. Yet go!

For my twilight is more to me than thy day, and my death is dearer to me than thy life! Take it! Take thou the kingdom, and the days to come. In the flames of death where Strength is, I will wait and watch till the day of David at last shall be finished, and wisdom no more be fox-faced, and the blood gets back its flame. Yea, the flame dies not, though the sun's red dies! And I must get me to the city.

Rises and departs hastily.

CURTAIN

The Married Man

A PLAY IN FOUR ACTS

(1912 – revised 1926)

CHARACTERS

DR GEORGE GRAINGER
WILLIAM BRENTNALL
MRS PLUM
JACK MAGNEER
ANNIE CALLADINE
ADA CALLADINE   sisters
EMILY CALLADINE
SALLY MAGNEER, Jack's sister
MR MAGNEER, father of Jack and Sally
ELSA SMITH, Brentnall's fiancée
GLADYS
TOM, husband of Gladys
ETHEL, Grainger's wife

ACT I
A bedroom in Mrs Plum's cottage

ACT II
The dining-room in the house of the Misses Calladine

ACT III
Kitchen at Mr Magneer's farm

ACT IV
The same as Act I

ACT I

A bedroom shared by GRAINGER *and* BRENTNALL *in the cottage of* MRS PLUM. *Both men are dressing.* GRAINGER *goes to the door and calls to* MRS PLUM.

GRAINGER : Bring me some collars up.

BRENTNALL : And what are you going to do?

GRAINGER : God knows.

BRENTNALL : How much money have you got?

GRAINGER : Four damn quid.

BRENTNALL : Hm!—You're well off, considering. But what *do* you think of doing?

GRAINGER : I don't know.

BRENTNALL : Where do you think of going Saturday?

GRAINGER : Hell.

BRENTNALL : Too expensive, my boy—four quid won't carry you there.

GRAINGER : Oh chuck it, Billy.

BRENTNALL : What the Hanover's the good of chucking it? You're not a blooming cock robin, to take no thought for the morrow.
    Enter MRS PLUM *with the collars.*

MRS PLUM : Gee, I'm sorry I forgot 'em, Dr Grainger. I'm ever so sorry.

GRAINGER : Don't fret yourself about that, Mrs Plum. You're all right, you are.

MRS PLUM : Gee, but I can't get it out of my head, that there what you've just told me.

GRAINGER : You want to sneeze hard, Mrs Plum. That'll shift it.

MRS PLUM *(laughing)*: Hee-hee—hark you there now. And have you got rid of it off your mind, Dr Grainger?

GRAINGER : My head's as clear as a bell o' brass, Mrs Plum. Nothing ails me.

MRS PLUM : My word, it doesn't. My word, but you're looking well, you're a sight better than when you come. Isn't he, Mr Brentnall?

BRENTNALL : He's too healthy for anything, Mrs Plum—he's so

healthy, he'd walk slap into a brick wall, and never know he'd hurt himself.

MRS PLUM: Gee—I don't know. But that there as you told me, Dr Grainger——

GRAINGER: Here, you go and see if that's Jack Magneer, and if it is, let him come up.

MRS PLUM: You're a caution, you are that, Dr Grainger.

Exit MRS PLUM.

BRENTNALL: The girl is gone on you, the kid is yours. You are a married man, and you mean to abide by your family?

GRAINGER: What the devil else is there to do?

BRENTNALL: Very well. Have you bothered about another job?

GRAINGER: No—I did when I was in Wolverhampton. Look what a fiendish business it is, offering yourself and being refused like a dog.

BRENTNALL: So you've taken no steps.

GRAINGER: No.

BRENTNALL: And you've absolutely no idea what you're going to do on Saturday, when you've finished here?

GRAINGER: No.

BRENTNALL: And yet you mean to stick by your wife and kid?

GRAINGER: What else can I do?

BRENTNALL: Well, you're a beauty! You're just skulking, like a frightened rabbit.

GRAINGER: Am I, begad?

BRENTNALL: Are you fond of'the kid?

GRAINGER: I shouldn't like anything to happen to it.

BRENTNALL: Neither should I. But the feelings of your breast to-wards it——?

GRAINGER: Well, I'm a lot *fonder* of that youngster at my digs in Wolverhampton—you know——

BRENTNALL: Then you feel no paternal emotion?

GRAINGER: No. Don't talk rot.

BRENTNALL: How often have you been over to see your wife?

GRAINGER: Once.

BRENTNALL: Once since you were married?

GRAINGER: Yes.

BRENTNALL: And that when the baby was first born?

GRAINGER : Yes.

BRENTNALL : And you're living—which, a recluse, or a gay bachelor?

GRAINGER : You can imagine me a recluse.

BRENTNALL : You're a blossom, Georgie, you're a jewel of a muddler.

GRAINGER : How could I help it! I was careful enough with the girl —I never thought, to tell you the truth, that—here's Jack!

BRENTNALL : That what?

GRAINGER : Shut up. Jack's a fine fellow.

BRENTNALL : Needs to be, to match you.

GRAINGER : Now Bill Brentnall, none of your sark.

JACK'S VOICE : How long are you going to be?

GRAINGER : How-do Jack! Shan't be a sec. Come up.

> Enter JACK MAGNEER—*aged 33*—*very big, a farmer, something of a gentleman, wears leggings and breeches, and a black bow tie.*

JACK : Seem to be donning yourselves up—how are you?

GRAINGER : Mr Magneer—Mr Brentnall : Jack—Billy.

JACK : Yis, quite so. How are you, Billy?

BRENTNALL : I'm very well. You're Miss Magneer's brother?

GRAINGER : Sally's.

JACK : Yis, I am, and what of it?

BRENTNALL : Oh—only you are lucky.

> GRAINGER *whistles gaily.*

JACK : What you whistling for, George lad? Aren't I lucky?

GRAINGER : I wish Sally was *my* sister, Jack.

JACK : Yis, you do, an' so do I, George lad—then me an' you'd be brothers.—Oh, my good God, are you going to be all night titivating yourselves up?

GRAINGER : Jack's in a hurry.

JACK : No I'm not, but damn it all——

GRAINGER : Alright Jacko, alright. I know she's a very nice girl——

BRENTNALL : Where are you taking me?

GRAINGER : To see some real fine girls.

JACK : Not so much fine girls, Billy—some damn *nice* girls, *nice* girls, mind you.

GRAINGER : Quite right, Jacko. *(Seriously.)* No, but they are, Billy, real nice girls. Three sisters, orphans.

JACK : An' the oldest of them will happen to be Mrs Grainger—eh, what?

GRAINGER : Liar!

JACK : You see Billy, it's like this. I'm glad you've come, because it levels us up. I believe you're a nice chap. Don't you take me wrong. I mean you're not one of these damn sods as can see nowt in a girl but—you know.

BRENTNALL : Yes.

GRAINGER : Yes, Billy knows. Most moral young man.

JACK : Fooling apart, George, aren't they nice girls?

GRAINGER : *Really* nice girls, they are.

JACK : But you see, there's three of 'em—an' we've never been but two of us—d'you twig?

BRENTNALL : I twig.

JACK : But no fooling, mind you.

BRENTNALL : Thanks for your caution, Mr Magneer.

JACK : Oh no, no. Nothing of the sort : only they *are* nice girls—you see what I mean—oh no, Billy——

GRAINGER : And three of 'em.

BRENTNALL : And the odd one falls to me. Thanks, I was born to oblige.

JACK : Now Billy, no. I want you t'have a good time. You see what I mean. I'm willing to step aside. You're here only for a bit—I'm always here. So I want you——

GRAINGER : "I want all of you t'have a good time."

JACK : Yis, I do. I do that, George.

GRAINGER : That's always Jacko's cry—"I want you t'have it your own road. I'm willing any road. I want you t'have a good time." Self-effacing chap is Jack.

BRENTNALL : Do I put on a dinner jacket?

GRAINGER : Good God, no—have you brought one?

BRENTNALL : Well—I might have to dine at some people's down towards Ashbourne.

CURTAIN

ACT II

*A long, low dining-room—table laid for supper—bowls of crimson
and white flowers, a large lamp—an old-fashioned room,
furnished with taste.*
The oldest MISS CALLADINE—*aged 32, tall, slim, pale, dressed in
black, wearing Parma violets, looks ladylike, but rather yearning. She walks about restlessly.*
Enter DR GRAINGER.

ANNIE: Aren't you late?

GRAINGER: A little—waiting for my friend. He's gone round to "The
George" with Jack—some arrangement about farm stock. *(He
takes both her hands, which she offers him yearningly, and, after
glancing round, kisses her hastily, as if unwillingly.)* Where's
Emily?

ANNIE: Emily and Ada are both entertaining Mrs Wesson in the
drawing-room. I hope they'll get rid of her before Jack comes.
I'm afraid we are being talked about. I'm afraid I'm not doing
my duty by the girls.

GRAINGER: What do you mean?

ANNIE: You are here so often.

GRAINGER: I'm going away directly, so you'll be safe after Saturday.

ANNIE: Really going away on Saturday—really—really. *(Puts her
hands on his shoulders.)*

GRAINGER: That's right.

ANNIE: Then people will talk more than ever. I shall be considered
loose: and what's to become of the girls——

GRAINGER: *You* considered loose—oh Cæsar!

ANNIE: Where are you going?

GRAINGER: Don't know.

ANNIE: Why won't you tell me?

GRAINGER: Because I don't know. I am waiting for a letter—it will
come to-morrow. Either I shall be going to Scotland, or down to
London—one or the other, but I don't know which.

ANNIE: Scotland or London!

GRAINGER : I hope it's London.

ANNIE : Why do you?

GRAINGER : Well—more life, for one thing.

ANNIE : And is it "life" you want? That sort of life?

GRAINGER : Not that sort, exactly—but—oh, by the way, I told you
I was bringing my friend——

ANNIE : Mr Brentnall—yes.

GRAINGER : Well, don't be surprised if I seem rather different to-
night, will you? Billy's very circumspect, *very* circumspect—nice,
mind you, but *good*.

ANNIE : I see.

GRAINGER : You'll like him though.

ANNIE *(bitingly)* : In spite of his goodness.

GRAINGER : Yes, I know you like "life" better than "goodness"—
don't you now?

> *He puts his hand under her chin.*

ANNIE *(drawing away)* : You seem to know a great deal about me.

GRAINGER : I know what you want.

ANNIE : What?

GRAINGER *(glancing round to see if he is safe—taking her in his
arms, pressing her close, kissing her. She submits because she
can scarcely help herself—there is a sound of feet and voices—he
hastily releases her)* : That!

ANNIE *(struggling with herself)* : Indeed no, Dr Grainger.

GRAINGER : That's the ticket—keep it up, Annie.

> *Enter* EMILY *and* ADA CALLADINE—EMILY, *aged 27, quiet, self-
possessed, dressed all in black*—ADA, *aged 23—rather plump,
handsome, charmingly young and wicked-looking—dressed in
black and purple, with a crimson flower.*

ANNIE : Has Mrs Wesson gone?

ADA : Not before she heard a man's voice—I told her you were
engaged.

GRAINGER : You what?

ADA *(bursting with laughter)* : I told her Annie was engaged.

ANNIE *(severely)* : With a caller, you mean, Ada?

GRAINGER : Oh, I see.

ADA : Yes—oh yes—oh how *funny!*

GRAINGER : Not funny at all—Jack's doing some business round at
"The George", Emily.

EMILY: Is he?

GRAINGER *(discomfited)*: I think I'll go and hurry them up.

ADA: Do!

ANNIE: You think it is quite safe to bring your *good* friend here?

GRAINGER: Oh, quite safe, Annie—don't be alarmed. Ta-ta!

>   *Exit* GRAINGER. *He is heard running down the stairs.*

ANNIE: I don't think Dr Grainger improves on acquaintance.

ADA: *We've* never got any further with him, so *we* can't say.

EMILY: Why do you think so, Annie?

ANNIE *(rather haughtily)*: You would not guess what he said to me.

ADA: I think you've given him rather a long rope.

ANNIE *(with dignity)*: If I have, he's hit me across the face with it.

EMILY: What did he say, Annie?

ANNIE: He is bringing a friend—a school and college friend—in a bank in London now—rather genteel, I believe. Well, Dr Grainger said to me this evening: "You know my friend is *very* circumspect, *very* circumspect, so you won't be surprised if my behaviour is rather different this evening."

ADA: Oh indeed!

EMILY: You should have kept him more in his place, Annie.

ANNIE: I should, but I thought he was a gentleman. I don't know *how* we're going to receive them this evening.

EMILY: We need simply take no notice of him, and be just polite.

ANNIE: But we don't know what he may have told his friend about us.

EMILY: I never cared for him.

ADA: Oh, what ripping fun!

ANNIE: Ada, be careful what you do and say.

ADA: It's not I who've put my foot in it. It is you if anyone.

ANNIE: I have been too free, perhaps; but you cannot say I have put my foot in it. I wish I had never admitted Dr Grainger at all— but he came with Jack——

EMILY: We shall go through alright with it. Simply despise Dr Grainger.

ANNIE: He is despicable.

ADA: He is here.

ANNIE: Emily, will you go downstairs and receive them? Ada, you stay here.

>   *Exit* EMILY—*voices downstairs.*

ADA : They are all three here—I must go also.

Exit ADA.

ANNIE CALLADINE *straightens her hair before the mirror, rubs out her wrinkles, puts her flowers nicely, and seats herself with much composure. Enter* GRAINGER *and* BRENTNALL, *followed by* ADA CALLADINE.

GRAINGER *(stiffly)* : Miss Annie Calladine—Mr Brentnall.

BRENTNALL : What a nice smell of flowers.

ANNIE : It is the mezereon that Mr Magneer brought.

BRENTNALL: Did Mr Magneer bring flowers? I shouldn't have thought the idea could occur to him.

ANNIE : He always brings flowers from the *garden*. It would never occur to him to buy them for us.

BRENTNALL : I see—how nice of him.

GRAINGER : All country fellows cart handfuls of flowers that they've got out of their own gardens, to their girls.

ANNIE : Nevertheless, Mr Magneer does it nicely.

Enter MAGNEER *and* EMILY.

JACK : Now we seem as if we're going to be alright. What do you say, George?

GRAINGER : I say the same.

ANNIE : Do take a seat, all of you. Jack, you love the couch——

JACK : It's a very nice couch, this is. *(Sits down.)*

BRENTNALL : I should think it would be the easiest thing in life to write a poem about a couch. I wonder if the woman was giving Cowper a gentle hint——

ADA *(shrieking with laughter)* : Yes—yes—yes!

BRENTNALL : I never see a couch but my heart moves to poetry. The very buttons must be full of echoes——

JACK *(bending his ear)* : Can't hear 'em, Billy.

BRENTNALL : Will none of you tune his ear?

ADA : Yes—yes!

EMILY *(seating herself quietly beside* JACK*)* : What is it you are listening for, Jack?

JACK *(awkwardly)* : I've no idea.

ANNIE : Where will you sit, Mr Brentnall? Do choose a comfortable chair.

BRENTNALL *(seating himself beside her)*: Thanks very much.

JACK : Nay—nay—nay, Billy.

BRENTNALL *(rising suddenly)* : Er—there's a broken spring in that chair, Miss Calladine. *(He crosses the hearth.)*

ANNIE : I'm so sorry—have a cushion—do!

BRENTNALL : Will you allow me to sit here?

ADA : Let me give you some supper.

GRAINGER : Shall I administer the drinks?

>   GRAINGER *gives the women burgundy, the men whisky and soda.* ADA CALLADINE *hands round food.* GRAINGER *seats himself reluctantly beside* ANNIE CALLADINE—ADA CALLADINE *takes a low chair next to* BRENTNALL.

JACK : Now we are alright—at least I hope so.

BRENTNALL *(to* ADA) : You are quite alright?

ADA *(laughing)* : As far as I know.

BRENTNALL *(to* EMILY*)* : I can see you are perfectly at home. (EMILY *bows quietly, with a smile.*) And you, Miss Calladine?

ANNIE : Thank you!

BRENTNALL : Gentlemen—the ladies!

GRAINGER *(ironically)* : God bless 'em.

JACK : Amen! *(They drink.)*

ADA : Ladies—the gentlemen!

ANNIE : God help them.

EMILY : Amen! *(They drink.)*

BRENTNALL : Wherein must the Lord help us, Miss Calladine?

ANNIE : To run away, Mr Brentnall.

EMILY : Annie!

ADA : To come to the scratch, you mean.

BRENTNALL : Ha! Gentlemen—to marriage!

JACK : I don't think!

ANNIE : What is *your* comment, Dr Grainger?

GRAINGER : Mine!

BRENTNALL : Dr Grainger is a confirmed misogynist.

GRAINGER : Shut up, you fool.

ANNIE : Oh—we've not heard so before.

JACK : D'you mean George doesn't believe in marriage? Nay, you're wrong there. When th' time comes——

ANNIE : When *does* the time come for a man to marry, Jack?

JACK : When he can't help it, I s'd think. *(Silence.)*

BRENTNALL : You're very quiet, George.

GRAINGER : Don't you be a fool.

ANNIE: Your humour is not very complimentary this evening, Dr Grainger.

JACK: There's perhaps too many of us in th' room, eh?

ANNIE: Not too many for me, Jack.

ADA *(bursting into laughter)*: Do be complimentary, somebody, if only to cheer us up.

JACK *(putting his arm round* EMILY'S *waist)*: Yis, I will.

BRENTNALL *(putting his arm round* ADA'S *neck)*: May I kiss you, Ada?

ADA *(laughing)*: How *(laughs)*—how awfully nice *(laughs heartily)* of you. *(*BRENTNALL *kisses her.)*

JACK: Oh my God, now we're coming on. *(He kisses* EMILY *furtively.)*

BRENTNALL: Mind your own business.

> *Seizes a newspaper, and screens it before him and* ADA—*they put their heads together.*

JACK: I call that comin' on—eh what?

BRENTNALL *(to* ADA—*behind the newspaper)*: Well, I'll be damned!

ANNIE *(loudly and sarcastically)*: Do you like the flavour, Mr Brentnall?

BRENTNALL *(from behind the paper)*: Excellent! *(Sotto voce.)* You are awfully jolly.

JACK *(bouncing with surprise)*: Well strike me lucky!

BRENTNALL *(throwing him another newspaper)*: Here you are then!

JACK: Good God! *(He spreads the paper before him and* EMILY.)

GRAINGER: You damn fool, Billy Brentnall.

BRENTNALL: Dog in the manger. *(Softly to* ADA.) Do you think I'm a fool? No, you like me.

JACK *(from behind his paper)*: How're you going on, Billy?

BRENTNALL: Fine. How're you going on, George?

> *The four peep over their newspapers at* GRAINGER *and* ANNIE.

BRENTNALL: Temperature down at freezing point over there?

GRAINGER: I'll have it out of you for this, William.

ANNIE: Why, what has Mr Brentnall done amiss, Dr Grainger?

BRENTNALL *(from behind his paper)*: Oh, it's not I. It's George's sins finding him out. Be sure your sins will find you out.

ADA *(softly)*: You're not a bit what I thought you would be

BRENTNALL *(softly)*: Worse or better?

ADA *(laughing)*: Oh—better.

BRENTNALL : What did you think I should be?

ADA : Circumspect.

> GRAINGER *sends a cushion smashing through their paper.*

JACK : What the devil's up, George?

ANNIE : Oh, it annoys him to see other people enjoying themselves when he can't.

BRENTNALL *(spreading the paper for screen)* : The nail on the head, Miss—may I say Annie?

ANNIE : Yes, Mr Brentnall.

BRENTNALL : I wish I were two men, Annie.

> GRAINGER *sends the cushion again smashing through the newspaper.*

JACK : God help thee George, do settle down.

BRENTNALL *(spreading the paper again)* : It's high time he did— settle down, Georgie—it's good advice.

ADA *(softly)* : What makes him so cross to-night?

BRENTNALL *(softly)* : Don't know—unless he's shy.

ADA *(bursting with laughter)* : Shy!

BRENTNALL : Why, isn't he?

ADA : You should see the way he carries on——

BRENTNALL : With you?

ADA : Annie.

> *The cushion crashes through the paper.*

JACK : Damn thee George, take Annie downstairs a minute, if tha can't bide still.

GRAINGER : That fool there——!

BRENTNALL *(restoring the fragments of paper—softly—to* ADA) : You know there's a secret about Dr Grainger.

ADA : Oh! *(Laughs.)* Do tell me.

GRAINGER : Billy Brentnall!

BRENTNALL : I hear you calling me.

ADA : Do tell me the secret.

BRENTNALL : Kiss me then. *(They kiss—she laughs.)* You are awfully jolly. *(Kisses her under the ear.)*

ADA *(shaking with laughter)* : Don't, don't, oh don't!

BRENTNALL : Does my moustache tickle you? Sorry.

JACK : Nation seize me, did ever you hear?

GRAINGER : Such a fool? I'll bet you never did.

ADA : Tell me that secret.

BRENTNALL : George has got another girl.

ADA : Who? Where?

GRAINGER : Oh, cheese it, Billy.

BRENTNALL : Sally Magneer.

GRAINGER : Damn you.

ADA : No!

BRENTNALL : Fact! She told me herself.

JACK : What's that, George?

GRAINGER *(to* BRENTNALL*)* : Liar!

BRENTNALL : It's the truth—mine's pistols.

JACK : You're a devil, George, you're a devil.

GRAINGER *(bitterly)* : I am that!

EMILY : And what is Mr Brentnall?

JACK *(shaking his head)*: Nay, I'm not going to say. *(He rises heavily, draws* EMILY *after him, and goes out of the room.)*

BRENTNALL *(rising)* : Well, this newspaper's no more good.

ADA : There's a fire in the drawing-room—and real screens there.

BRENTNALL : And Jack *does* occupy *himself.* Right you are.

GRAINGER : Chuck it, Billy.

BRENTNALL : What?

GRAINGER : None o' that.

BRENTNALL : Well, I'll go to——-

GRAINGER : I've no doubt.

ANNIE : Dr Grainger is afraid of being left alone: he must have some-one to protect him.

BRENTNALL : What from?

ANNIE : Presumably from me. *(To* GRAINGER.*)* Will you go down with Ada to the drawing-room? Ada, do you mind?

ADA : Not at all. *(Exit* ADA.*)*

GRAINGER *(bitterly)*: Very nice of you, Annie, very nice of you. *(Exit* GRAINGER.*)*

BRENTNALL *and* ANNIE *seat themselves.*

ANNIE : What do you think of all this, Mr Brentnall?

BRENTNALL : Why, it's a mere lark. Jack is really courting Emily, and Ada is sheer mischief, and I'm quite decent, really.

ANNIE : Are you really?

BRENTNALL : Judge from your own instinct.

ANNIE : I think you are—and is Dr Grainger?

BRENTNALL : What do you think?

ANNIE : There is something not nice about him.

BRENTNALL : Has he been courting you?

ANNIE *(drawing herself up)* : Well——!

BRENTNALL : You see, it's a pity——

ANNIE : What is a pity?

BRENTNALL : Why—shall I say just what I think——?

ANNIE : I want you to.

BRENTNALL : Well then—it's a pity that girls like you—you are over thirty?

ANNIE : Yes.

BRENTNALL : It's a pity that so many of the best women let their youth slip by, because they don't find a man good enough—and then, when dissatisfaction becomes a torture—later on—you are dissatisfied with life, you *do* lack something big.

ANNIE : Yes.

BRENTNALL : When it comes to that stage, the want of a man is a torture to you. And since the common men make the advances——

ANNIE : Yes!

BRENTNALL *(putting his arm round her and kissing her)* : You are either driven to a kind of degradation, or you go nearly, slightly mad from want——

ANNIE : Yes!

BRENTNALL *(kissing her)* : If you want love from men like Grainger, take it for what it's worth—because we're made so that either we must have love, or starve and go slightly mad.

ANNIE : But I don't want that kind of love.

BRENTNALL : But do be honest with yourself. Don't cause a split between your conscious self and your unconscious—that is insanity. You *do* want love, almost any sort. Make up your mind what you'll accept, or what you won't, but keep your ideal intact. Whatever men you take, keep the idea of man intact : let your soul wait whether your body does or not. But don't drag the first down to the second. Do you understand?

ANNIE : I could love you.

BRENTNALL : But I am going away in a day or two, and most probably shall not be here again—and I am engaged. You see, so many women are too good for the men, that for every decent man, there are thirty decent women. And you decent women go and waste and wither away. Do think it out square, and make the best of it. Virginity and all that is no good to you.

ANNIE: And what would you advise?

BRENTNALL: Know men, and have men, if you must. But keep your soul virgin, wait and believe in the *good* man you may never have.

ANNIE: It is not very—what made Dr Grainger so queer to-night?

BRENTNALL: Because he's married.

ANNIE: I *felt* it—to whom?

BRENTNALL: A girl in Wolverhampton—married last January, a son in March, now it's June.

ANNIE: Oh, the liar!—And what sort of girl?

BRENTNALL: Decent, I believe.

ANNIE: Does she love him?

BRENTNALL: Yes.

ANNIE: The brute—the——

BRENTNALL: He doesn't love her, you see——

ANNIE: It makes it no better—and she doesn't know how he's——

BRENTNALL: Of course not.

ANNIE: I wonder if I know her—what's her name?

BRENTNALL: Marson—her people are tailors in Broad Street.

ANNIE: No, I don't know her!—But to think——

BRENTNALL: Don't be too ready to blame.

ANNIE: You men are all alike.

BRENTNALL: Not true—who is coming?

ANNIE: I don't know.

> Enter SALLY MAGNEER—*a very big, strapping farmer's daughter, evidently moderately well off.*

SALLY: Good evening—Jack here?

ANNIE: Good evening. Yes, I believe he's in the drawing-room with Dr Grainger.

SALLY: That's how you arrange it, is it? (*To* BRENTNALL.) Nice, isn't it?

BRENTNALL: Very nice.

SALLY: Who else is in the drawing-room?

ANNIE: My sisters. I believe they're having some music.

SALLY: They don't make much noise over it, anyway. Can I go and see?

ANNIE: Certainly.

BRENTNALL *opens the door for her, and whistles quickly a*
private call—repeats it. GRAINGER'S *whistle is heard in answer.*

SALLY: Alright, I won't drop in on you too sudden. *(Exit* SALLY.*)*

ANNIE: What impertinence!

BRENTNALL *(laughing)*: She's made a dead set at Grainger. If he
weren't married, she'd get him.

ANNIE: How disgusting!

BRENTNALL: Maybe—but a woman who determines soon enough to
get married, succeeds. Delay is fatal—and marriage is beastly, on
most occasions.

ANNIE: I will go to the drawing-room. Will you excuse me? *(Exit*
ANNIE. BRENTNALL *pours himself a drink. Enter* GRAINGER.*)*

GRAINGER: What the hell have you been up to?

BRENTNALL: What the hell have you been up to?

GRAINGER: What have you been stuffing into Annie?

BRENTNALL: What have you been stuffing into Ada?

GRAINGER: Nothing, you devil.

BRENTNALL: Nothing, you devil.

GRAINGER: What's Sally after?

BRENTNALL: You.

GRAINGER: She ought to be shot.

BRENTNALL: So ought you.

      Enter JACK.

JACK: What the hell's up to-night?

BRENTNALL: My tail, and George's dander, and your—but what's
Miss Magneer after?

JACK: That's what I want to know. You know George here, he's a
devil. He's been on wi' some little game with our Sally.

GRAINGER: You sweet liar, Jack.

JACK: Now George, what is it?

GRAINGER: Nothing, Jack. Sally's taken a fancy to me, an' gives me
no chance. Can't you see for yourself?

JACK: I can, George—an' tha shanner be pestered.

GRAINGER: There's Charlie Greenhalgh won't speak to me now—
thinks I'm running him off. *I've* no desire to run Charlie off.

JACK: Sally's as good as you, George.

GRAINGER: Maybe, and a thousand times better. But that doesn't
say as I want to marry her.

JACK: No, George, no, that is so, lad.

Enter SALLY *and the other ladies.*

SALLY: How would you arrange six folks in three chairs——?

GRAINGER: Couldn't do it.

SALLY: I don't think! What's your opinion, Ada?

ADA: Why am I asked for my opinion? I've never sat in a chair with Dr Grainger.

SALLY: Where have you sat then?

ADA: I may have sat on his knee while he sat in the chair.

SALLY: Here, young man, explain yourself.

GRAINGER: Well, I'll be damned!

BRENTNALL: Sooner or later.

JACK: Now look here, our Sally, we're havin' none o' this. Charlie Greenhalgh is your man; you stick to him, and leave other young fellows alone.

SALLY: Oh you *are* good, Jack! And what about the girl *you* took to Blackpool?

JACK: Say no more, Sally, now say no more.

SALLY: No, I won't. Do you want me to drive you up to Selson, because th' cart's at the door?

JACK: No, we'll walk up.

GRAINGER: I dunno, Jack. It's getting late, and I believe Billy's tired. He's a convalescent, you know.

JACK: Never thought of it, lad. Sorry—sorry.

They bid good night. Exeunt SALLY *and* GRAINGER, EMILY, JACK, *and* ADA.

ANNIE: Isn't he a thing!

BRENTNALL: He's not bad—*do* be honest.

ANNIE: Oh *but!*

BRENTNALL: Remember what I say—don't starve yourself, and don't degrade the idea of men.

ANNIE: And shall I never see you again?

BRENTNALL: If I can, I will come again.

ANNIE: Good-bye.

He kisses her rather sorrowfully, and departs. ANNIE CALLA-DINE *closes the door—drinks the last drain from his glass— weeps—dries her eyes as the girls come upstairs. There is a call- ing of good-bye from outside.*

ADA: What's amiss?

ANNIE: Plenty.

EMILY : What?

ANNIE : Dr Grainger is only married and got a child.

ADA and EMILY : No—where—is his wife living?

ANNIE : His wife is at her home, in Wolverhampton—Broad Street.

ADA : I'll write to her—I will—I will.

ANNIE : No, Ada—no.

ADA : I will—I will—I will : "Dear Mrs George Grainger, come and look after your husband. He is running the rig out here, and if you don't come quick——"

> *She has flung her writing case on to the table, and sits down to write. Vain cries of "Ada," "Ada," from* ANNIE CALLADINE.

CURTAIN

ACT III

The kitchen at MAGNEER'S *farm.* SALLY MAGNEER, EMILY CALLADINE, ADA CALLADINE. MR MAGNEER, *farmer, not fat, but well looking: grey hair, black moustache; at present rather maudlin.* JACK MAGNEER, *still in riding breeches and leggings.* GRAINGER *and* BRENTNALL, *both in tennis flannels.* JACK *and* EMILY *sit together on a large old couch,* GRAINGER *next to them.* SALLY *is in a chair, looking as if any moment she would take wing.* BRENTNALL *is flirting with* ADA CALLADINE.

MR MAGNEER : An' so you really goin' ter leave us, Dr Grainger.

GRAINGER : That is so, Mr Magneer.

MR MAGNEER : An' when might you be goin'?

GRAINGER : Saturday.

MR MAGNEER : To-morrow! My word, that's sharp. Well, I know *one* as'll be sorry you goin'.

SALLY : Shut up, Father. *(She giggles, and twists her handkerchief to* GRAINGER : We s'll be seeing you again, though?

GRAINGER : Well, I really can't say—I'm going to London.

SALLY : London! Whatever are you going there for?

BRENTNALL : Set up a wife and family.

SALLY : What, all at once?—Give us a chance.

BRENTNALL : Not a ghost of a chance, Sally.

    ADA CALLADINE *laughs uncontrollably.*

GRAINGER : Got a joke over there?

ADA *(laughing)* : Yes—yes—yes!

SALLY *(jumping up)* : Just look at your glass! *(Takes* GRAINGER'S *tumbler and proceeds to mix him rum.)* Why ever didn't you speak?

MR MAGNEER : Yes, you must shout up when you're emp'y.

SALLY *(to* GRAINGER) : Like it sweet?

GRAINGER *(ironically)* : Not too much.

SALLY *(taking the glass and standing in front of him)* : How's this for you?

GRAINGER *(sipping)* : Quite alright, thank you, Sally.

MR MAGNEER *(laughing)*: "Quite alright," hark ye! It's "quite alright." *(He gives a great wink at* BRENTNALL. SALLY *begins to giggle.)*

GRAINGER *(lugubriously)* : Sally's got 'em again.

JACK : Sit you down, Sally, an' don't look so long o' th' leg.

SALLY *giggles half hysterically, and sinks beside* GRAINGER, *who edges away. She leans towards him—laughs uncontrollably.*

MR MAGNEER : Now we're comin' on. What yer doin' at 'er, Doctor?

GRAINGER : Begad, I'm doing nothing, Mr Magneer. I dunno what's got her.

MR MAGNEER *(laughs)* : He dunno, doesn't know what's got her. *(To* BRENTNALL.) We don't, do we?

BRENTNALL : Not a bit.

GRAINGER : I'll have a drop more water. *(Rises and goes to table.)*

MR MAGNEER : Come Sally, my lass, come.

SALLY *dries her eyes, still giggles, rises.* GRAINGER *hastily takes an odd chair at the table. She stands beside him.*

JACK : Are ter goin' ter sit thysen down, Sally?

SALLY : Am I hurtin' *you* by standin'?

JACK : Yis, you are.

BRENTNALL : Fill me up, Sally, there's a dear. (SALLY *takes his glass.*)

MR MAGNEER : Sally Magneer, there's a dear.

GRAINGER : Isn't Charlie coming?

SALLY : No, did you want him?

GRAINGER : No—but I thought *you* did.

SALLY *(beginning to giggle)* : Did you? You happen thought wrong.

BRENTNALL : Poor Charlie.

SALLY : What do you know about him?

BRENTNALL : Now Sally! It's best to be on with the new love before you're off with the old.

SALLY *(giggling)* : I don't know what you mean.

JACK : Art thou going to sit down?

SALLY : Yes. *(Retires discomfited to the couch.)*

BRENTNALL *(rising)* : I'll get a light.

GRAINGER : Matches?

BRENTNALL *(going to fire)* : Never mind. *(Lights his cigarette with a spill.)*

ADA *(laughing)* : Good-bye, Billy.

BRENTNALL *(blowing her kisses)* : Farewell, farewell. *(Sinks on the couch beside* SALLY.*)*

SALLY : What have you come for?

BRENTNALL : Won't you have me, Sally?

SALLY : I don't know.

GRAINGER *(shuffling the cards)* : A hand of crib, Mr Magneer?

MR MAGNEER : I don't mind if I do. Fill up.

BRENTNALL *(taking* SALLY'S *hand)* : Hurt your finger?

SALLY : My thumb.

BRENTNALL : Shame! What did you do?

SALLY : Chopped it.

BRENTNALL : How rotten. Is it getting better?

MR MAGNEER : There's a bit o' proud flesh in it.

GRAINGER : Your crib, Mr Magneer.

SALLY *(unwinding the bandage)* : Yes, it's going on alright now.

BRENTNALL *(examining it closely)* : Yes, that's healing right enough, but a nasty gash! What did Charlie say to it?

SALLY : Charlie!

BRENTNALL : Yes, Charlie. He's your fellow, isn't he?

SALLY : I don't know so much about that.

BRENTNALL : I heard you were as good as engaged.

SALLY : Oh, did you—who's been telling you?

BRENTNALL : Mrs Plum.

SALLY : She knows so much, you see.

BRENTNALL : Let me wrap it up for you. *(Bandages her thumb.)* But isn't it right?

SALLY : Not as *I* know of.

BRENTNALL : Oh, I'm sorry.

SALLY : Who are you sorry for?

BRENTNALL : Charlie, of course, poor devil.

SALLY : You needn't be sorry for him. Take your sorrow where your love lies.

BRENTNALL : Then I s'll have to be sorry for you, Sally.

SALLY : I *don't* think.

BRENTNALL *(putting his arm round her waist)* : I'm sorry you've got a bad finger, Sally.

SALLY *(beginning to giggle)* : Are you?

BRENTNALL: You don't mind that I'm not Dr Grainger, do you, Sally?

SALLY: What do you mean?

BRENTNALL: You'd as leave have me as Dr Grainger?

SALLY: Yes, if you like.

BRENTNALL *(kissing her)*: That's right. *(She giggles.)*

MR MAGNEER: Whey! Whey—up! Sally, thou scawdrag!

SALLY *(giggling hysterically)*: What am I a scawdrag for?

MR MAGNEER: Hark ye, hark ye! Jack, art takin' notice over there?

JACK: Billy's alright, Dad.

MR MAGNEER: Billy? By gosh! Billy!

GRAINGER: Turn, Mr Magneer.

ADA *(pegging)*: Two for his knobs.

BRENTNALL: You'd as leave have me as Dr Grainger? *(Kisses her under the ear.)*

SALLY *(with suppressed shrieks)*: Oh, oh, don't tickle!

GRAINGER *(turning around—with contempt)*: She'll never stop, Billy, she's got gigglemania.

MR MAGNEER: Giggolo—what? That's a good 'un!

BRENTNALL: Yes, she will stop—take me seriously, Sally, do! *(Squeezes her—SALLY giggles wildly. Her head rolls.)*

MR MAGNEER: Hark at that—take him seriously!

SALLY *(exhausted)*: Don't! Don't! Oh don't!

BRENTNALL: Sally, my dear, you are too discouraging for anything. Sit with me nicely.

SALLY: Oh! *(Lays her head on his shoulder.)*

BRENTNALL: Now we're coming on. *(Kisses her.)* You've not chipped with Charlie, have you?

SALLY: What d'you want to know for?

BRENTNALL: Sally, my darling.

MR MAGNEER: Gosh, it's come to "darling"—"darling Sally"!

BRENTNALL: You haven't, have you?

SALLY: No.

BRENTNALL: Why hasn't he come to-night?

SALLY: Because he wasn't asked.

BRENTNALL: Has he cooled off lately?

SALLY: I don't care whether he has or not.

BRENTNALL: Neither do I. *(Kisses her under the ear. She squeals.)*

JACK: God love you, Sally!

ADA: Don't play cribbage any more, Mr Magneer. Do play the comb-band.

MR MAGNEER *(throwing away his cards)*: No, I won't play any more. Fill up an' let's have a dance.

ADA: Yes, yes, yes!

> *The men drink—*SALLY *and* GRAINGER *push aside the table.*

GRAINGER: Comb-band, Mr Magneer?

MR MAGNEER *(wrapping the comb in tissue paper)*: That's the very item. *(He staggers slightly—all the men are affected by drink.)*

SALLY *(to* GRAINGER*)*: You're going to have one with me?

GRAINGER *(awkwardly)*: Er—I'd promised Ada.

ADA: That doesn't matter. Mr Brentnall will dance with me.

MR MAGNEER *(sounding the comb)*: Now then, are you ready? Sally's the belle of the ball, and you, Doctor, it's your party—so lead off.

GRAINGER: Polka—plain polka.

BRENTNALL: We shan't have breath to speak a word.

SALLY: Oh my goodness!

> *The comb-band buzzes away—they start to dance in a prancing fashion.*

SALLY: You're not going to leave me?

GRAINGER: I s'll have to.

SALLY: But you can't.

GRAINGER: Why not?

SALLY: You can't leave me now.

GRAINGER: But I've got to go to London——

JACK: Do you reckon you're really fond of me?

EMILY: I know I am—I don't reckon.

JACK: Not so very good——

EMILY: Why not?

JACK: Do you reckon you've been nice to me all this while?

EMILY: All what while?

JACK: While I've been coming to see you.

EMILY: And have you been very nice to me, Jack?

JACK: Well, haven't I?

EMILY: No, Jack, you haven't.

JACK: What do you mean?

ADA: I posted her the letter yesterday.

BRENTNALL: Why, did you know the address?

ADA: Yes, you told Annie.

BRENTNALL: Did I? Oh Lord, you little imp.

ADA: It's our turn now.

BRENTNALL: Whose turn?

ADA: The women's.

BRENTNALL: Don't be a vixen——

GRAINGER: Well, you won't say anything, will you? You see how I'm fixed.

SALLY: I don't know.

GRAINGER: I'll see you to-morrow—keep it back till then.

SALLY: You'll see me to-morrow?

GRAINGER: Yes——

JACK: You think I ought to get engaged to you?

EMILY: Or else you ought never to have come as you have—you had the option.

JACK: I dunna want to get married, somehow, Emily.

EMILY: Is that final, Jack?

JACK: What do *you* say?

EMILY: You leave me nothing to say.

JACK: Good God, Emily, I'm not a brute.

EMILY: I've heard you say so often, Jack. But you don't think it's been very happy for me—our—our friendship?

JACK: Good God, Emily—have I been——?

EMILY: Afraid of me, Jack. It's rather humiliating.

JACK: You can have me if you like—I'm not good enough——

EMILY: You know I consider you good enough.

JACK: Yis—I know you do.

EMILY: Men lack honour nowadays.

JACK: Good God!

> They dance—SALLY *suddenly drops exhausted on a couch*— GRAINGER *moves to the other side of the room.* JACK MAGNEER *flings off his coat.*

JACK: By the Lord, it's hot work! Take your coat off, George.

> GRAINGER *and* BRENTNALL *take off their coats.*

MR MAGNEER: My word, you went well. Have a drink.

SALLY: Is th' door open? Set the back door open, Jack.

> *He goes out and returns.*

BRENTNALL: Have the next with me, Sally.

SALLY: I will if you like.

ADA: What shall it be?

BRENTNALL: Waltz Valeta.

GRAINGER: Try a tune, Mr Magneer.

MR MAGNEER, *having repapered his comb, tries a tune.*
GRAINGER instructs him. They start off, SALLY *with* BRENTNALL,
GRAINGER with ADA CALLADINE.

BRENTNALL: Why would you rather dance with Dr Grainger?

SALLY: I wouldn't.

BRENTNALL: Yes, you would. Don't forget the two shuffle steps—
one—two!

SALLY: I've never done that before.

BRENTNALL: Something I've taught you then. But why would you
rather dance with Grainger?

SALLY: I *wouldn't*.

BRENTNALL: You *would*.

SALLY: I *wouldn't*.

BRENTNALL: You *would*. You're in love with him.

SALLY: Me! That I never am!

BRENTNALL: You are!

SALLY: Well, I never did!

BRENTNALL: And you're a fool to be in love with him.

SALLY: Why?

BRENTNALL: For the best of all reasons.

SALLY: What's that?

BRENTNALL: Because he's married.

SALLY: He's not!

BRENTNALL: He is—and has got a son.

SALLY: Where?

BRENTNALL: In Wolverhampton, where he came from.

SALLY: Oh, let's sit down.

BRENTNALL: No, you must dance with me. Don't you like to dance
with me? It's too bad, Sally.

SALLY: I'm getting dizzy.

BRENTNALL: You can't, not in Valeta. Besides, we'll walk the waltz
steps. *(He puts his arm around her.)*

SALLY: It's not right about Dr Grainger, is it?

A LADY *in motor cloak and wrap appears in the doorway.*
The men, slightly tipsy, bend talking to their partners, who are
engrossed. No one notices the newcomer.

BRENTNALL: It is, on my honour. You believe me, Sally?

She looks him earnestly in the face, as they dance the forward step. When they come together for the waltz, he kisses her.

You believe me?

SALLY *(almost in tears)*: Yes.

BRENTNALL: It is true. Poor Sally. *(Kisses her again. They begin to laugh.)*

JACK: Alright, I niver looked at it in that light.

EMILY: I know you didn't.

JACK: We'll count as we're engaged from now, then?

EMILY: What will your father say?

JACK: He'll be just fussy.

EMILY: I want him to know—I am so fond of him.

ADA: Oh!

GRAINGER: What?

They break apart. JACK *and* BRENTNALL *keep on dancing, the latter kissing* SALLY. GRAINGER *goes unsteadily to the doorway.*

THE LADY: I called to see Mr Brentnall—but don't disturb him, he looks so happy.

GRAINGER: Does—does he know you?

THE LADY: A little. *(She laughs.)*

GRAINGER: Billy! Billy!

BRENTNALL *(looking up)*: What now? *(Sees the lady.)* No!

He leaves SALLY—*she sways, he catches her again, takes her to a seat, draws his fingers across her cheek caressingly, and goes to the doorway, reeling slightly.*

Quite giddy, don't you know! Space is so small.

THE LADY: Not much room for you to spread out, was there?

BRENTNALL: Was I hugging Sally?

THE LADY: Sally! How lovely, how perfectly lovely!

BRENTNALL: Did I kiss her?

THE LADY: "Did I kiss her?" No, no, you poor dear, you didn't kiss her.

BRENTNALL: You mean I am drunk.

THE LADY: Are you drunk? No!

BRENTNALL: I am slightly tipsy, more with dancing than drink. Shall I come away?

THE LADY: Shall he come away—oh, you dear! Why should I decide for you?

BRENTNALL: Are you cross?

THE LADY: Not in the least. Go and kiss Sally if you will.

BRENTNALL: Poor Sally—I don't want to kiss her now.

THE LADY: How perfectly lovely! Do introduce me.

BRENTNALL: Mr Magneer, Sally Magneer, Emily Calladine, Ada Calladine, Jack Magneer, Dr Grainger—all of you, Elsa Smith.

ELSA: How awfully nice! Can I come in?

MR MAGNEER (*springing up and bowing tipsily*): Make yourself at 'ome, you're very welcome, Miss, you're very welcome.

ELSA: Thank you so much! I should love to dance. I've got two friends in the motor car. May I fetch them?

MR MAGNEER: Anybody you like, they're *all* welcome here, and there's plenty to drink for all.

ELSA: So nice!

   Exit ELSA.

GRAINGER: Who the devil——

BRENTNALL: My betrothed, my fiancée, my girl.

CHORUS OF WOMEN: You don't mean it!

SALLY: Well! Men——!

ADA: *Men?*

EMILY: *Men!*

MR MAGNEER: Ooh—you're done this time, Billy!

GRAINGER: Well, you devil, Billy Brentnall!

JACK: It's a corker, Billy, it's a winder.

EMILY: Are *you* any better, Jack?

JACK (*fiercely*): Look here, Dad. I'm engaged to Emily here, fair and square.

MR MAGNEER: Come here, Em'ler my ducky, come hither. (EMILY *goes very reluctantly. He kisses her.*) I like thee, Em'ler, I like thee. (*Kisses her again.*)

JACK: Cheese it, Dad.

MR MAGNEER: It's a winder, it is an' all.—An' aren't *you* goin' to be engaged an' all, Dr Grainger?

GRAINGER: Not this time.

MR MAGNEER: Hm! 'Appen you are engaged!

GRAINGER: No, I'm not.

MR MAGNEER: Come then, come then, come then.

Re-enter ELSA SMITH, *with a lady and gentleman.*

ELSA : All of you—Gladys and Tom. Gladys—That's Will——

MR MAGNEER : Ay, ay, Billy! Billy! (*It amuses him highly.*)

BRENTNALL (*bowing*) : I was to come to dinner to-night, I clean forgot. Don't be angry.

TOM : Cheek, if no more.

ELSA : Oh, you don't know Will, you don't.

MR MAGNEER : An *you* don't know Billy, Miss, it strikes me. (*Laughter*)

BRENTNALL : Leave me alone—I say, Elsa, Jack (*pointing*) has just got engaged to Emily.

ELSA : How perfectly charming. I love it all so much.

BRENTNALL : What?

ELSA : You—this.

BRENTNALL : Take your cloak off.

	Helps her. She is a handsome woman, large, blonde, about 30—dressed for dinner. Tom and Gladys disrobe—they are in dinner dress also.

TOM (*cynically*) : I suppose these are adventures.

GLADYS : Don't be a fool, Tom.

ELSA : This is fun.

BRENTNALL : Will you dance with me, Elsa?

ELSA : No, I won't.

BRENTNALL : Angry with me?

ELSA : No. I can dance with you any day.

GRAINGER : May I have the pleasure?

ELSA : No—forgive me (*very kindly*)—but I do want to dance with Jack. (*To* EMILY.) May I?

EMILY : Certainly. (JACK *pulls a face.*)

ELSA : He doesn't want me—but I won't let him off—no.

JACK : I'm shy, as a matter of fact.

ELSA : How lovely!

MR MAGNEER (*to* GLADYS) : Now Miss, you choose.

GLADYS : Will, you must dance with me.

BRENTNALL (*going to her side*) : You are shy.

MR MAGNEER : Now Ada, your turn to pick.

	ADA *looks wickedly at* TOM—*he bows.*

TOM : Thank you.

ADA : Are you shy? (*She laughs wickedly.*)

MR MAGNEER : Now for Dr Grainger. *(He holds his fists to* EMILY.) Which of 'em? (EMILY *touches the right fist.)* Wrong! *(Showing a coin in his left.)* Sally gets him.

SALLY : Sally doesn't.

GRAINGER : Come on, Sally.

MR MAGNEER : Now then, what is it?

BRENTNALL : Waltz.

> *The comb begins to buzz—the partners set off dancing—*MR MAGNEER *breaks the time—they laugh—he beckons* EMILY, *holds the comb in one hand, her with the other, and dances prancingly, buzzing breathlessly.*

CURTAIN

ACT IV

The bedroom in the cottage, same as Act I. It is nine o'clock in the morning. GRAINGER *and* BRENTNALL *are in bed.*

GRAINGER: Billy! *(No answer.)* You mean to say you're at it yet? *(No answer.)* Well, I'll be damned; you're a better sleeper even than a liar. *(No answer.)* Oh strike! *(Shies a pillow at* BRENTNALL.)

BRENTNALL: What the——!

GRAINGER: I should say so.

BRENTNALL: Dog in the manger! Go to sleep. I loathe the small hours. Oh-h! *(Yawns.)*

GRAINGER: Small hours, begad! It's past nine o'clock.

BRENTNALL *(half asleep)*: Early, frostily early.

GRAINGER: You mean to say——! *(He shies the bolster, viciously.)*

BRENTNALL: Don't, George! *(Sleeps.)*

GRAINGER: Devil! *(Shies slippers, one after the other.)*

BRENTNALL *(sitting up suddenly—furious)*: Go to blazes! *(Lies down again.)*

GRAINGER: If you go to sleep again, Billy B., I'll empty the water bottle over you—I will.

BRENTNALL: *I'm* not asleep.

GRAINGER: Billy!

BRENTNALL: What?

GRAINGER: Did you square Sally?

BRENTNALL: Eh?

GRAINGER: No, look here, Billy——

BRENTNALL *(stretching his arms)*: Georgie, you ought to be dead.

GRAINGER: I've no doubt. Billy Brentnall!

BRENTNALL: What?

GRAINGER: Did you square Sally?

BRENTNALL: Sally—Sally—Sally——

GRAINGER: Chuck it, fool.

BRENTNALL: I don't know.

GRAINGER: What d'you mean?

BRENTNALL: I told her you were a married man with a family, and begad, you look it——

GRAINGER: That's not the point.

BRENTNALL: I apologize. I say to Sally: "He's a married man." Sally says to me: "He's not." I say: "He is." Sally says: "I'm dizzy." I say: "You might well be."

GRAINGER: Chuck it, do chuck it.

BRENTNALL: It's the solemn fact. And our confab ended there.

GRAINGER: It did!

BRENTNALL: It did.

GRAINGER: Hm!

BRENTNALL: You're going to London to my rooms, aren't you?

GRAINGER: You say so.

BRENTNALL: Very well then—there's an end of Sally.

GRAINGER: I'm not so sure.

BRENTNALL: Why?

GRAINGER: She said she was coming round here.

BRENTNALL: When?

GRAINGER: This morning.

BRENTNALL: Then don't get up till this afternoon, and then belt for the station.

GRAINGER: I've not settled up at the Surgery.

BRENTNALL: Thou bungler—has Sally really got a case against you?

GRAINGER: She's got a case against *some* man or other, and she'd prefer it to be me.

BRENTNALL: But she must see *you're* quite a cold egg. And has Charlie Greenhalgh really cried off?

GRAINGER: No—at least—poor old Charlie's in a bit of a mess.

BRENTNALL: How?

GRAINGER: He was secretary to the football club—and he falsified the balance sheet, and failed to produce about fifteen quid.

BRENTNALL: *He's* not in a very rosy condition for marriage. However, old Magneer's not short of money?

GRAINGER: He isn't, begad!

BRENTNALL: Alright—let him work the oracle. Sally's no fool—and she'll be just as well, married to Charlie. You say his farm is going to the dogs. Alright, she'll shoo the dogs off.

GRAINGER: Very nice.

BRENTNALL: I think so.

GRAINGER : Who's that?

BRENTNALL : Dunno—get under the bed-clothes.

　　　　Sound of footsteps—enter JACK MAGNEER.

JACK : Letting the day get well aired?

BRENTNALL : I don't believe in running risks through the chill, damp air of early morning.

JACK : I s'd think you don't.

BRENTNALL : Take a seat.

JACK : So you're going to-day, George?

GRAINGER : I am, Jack—and sorry to leave you.

JACK : What's this our Sally's been telling me?

GRAINGER : Couldn't say, Jack.

JACK : As you're married——

BRENTNALL : And got a kid, quite right.

JACK : *Is* it, George?

GRAINGER : I believe so.

JACK : Hm! *(A pause.)*

BRENTNALL : Well, Jack, say he has your sympathy.

JACK : Yis—yis—he has. But I'm not so sure——

BRENTNALL : Eh Jack, it's a hole we might any of us slip into.

JACK : Seemingly. But why didn't you tell me, George?

BRENTNALL : Don't, Jack. Don't you see, I could give the whole of that recitation. "We've been good friends, George, and you'd no need to keep me in the dark like that. It's a false position for me, as well as for you, etc., etc." That's what you want to say?

JACK : Yis—and besides——

BRENTNALL : Well, look here, Jack, you might have done it yourself. George was let in down at Wolverhampton—kicked out of the town because he owned up and married the girl—hadn't either a penny or a job—girl has a good home. Would *you* have wanted to tell the whole story to these prating fools round here?

JACK : No, I can't say as I should. But then——

BRENTNALL : Then what?

JACK : There's our Sally, and there's Annie——

BRENTNALL : What about 'em?

JACK : He's courted 'em both—they're both up to the eyes in love with him——

BRENTNALL : Not Annie. On the quiet, she's rather gone on *me*. I showed George up in his true light to her.

GRAINGER : Rotter—rotter!

BRENTNALL : And I stepped into the limelight, and the trick was done.

JACK : You're a devil, Billy.—But look here, George, our Sally——

GRAINGER : Yes——

JACK : She's—she's gone a long way——

BRENTNALL *(quietly)* : How do you mean, Jack?

JACK : Well, she's given up Charlie Greenhalgh——

BRENTNALL : Not quite. And you know, Jack, she really loves Charlie, at the bottom. There's something fascinating about George.

GRAINGER : Damn your eyes, shut up, Billy.

BRENTNALL : There's something fascinating about George. He can't help it. The women melt like wax before him. They're all over him. It's not his beauty, it's his manliness. He can't help it.

GRAINGER : I s'll smash you, Billy Brentnall, if you don't shut up

JACK : Yis, there's something in it, George.

BRENTNALL : There *is*, Jack. Well, he can't help himself, so you've got to help him. It's no good hitting him when he's down.

JACK : *I'm* not hitting him.

BRENTNALL : And what you've got to do, you've got to get Charlie Greenhalgh and your Sally together again.

JACK : Me!—It's nowt to do with me.

BRENTNALL : Yes, it has. Charlie's not been up to your place lately, has he?

JACK : No.

BRENTNALL : And do you know why?

JACK : Yis.

BRENTNALL : It's not so much because of George. Have you heard what low water he's getting into up at Newmanley? It appears he's fifteen quid out with the football club.

JACK : I've heard a whisper.

BRENTNALL : Well, you help him, Jack, for Sally's sake. She loves him, Jack, she does. And if she married him quick, she'll pull him through, for she seems to have a business head on her, and a farming head.

JACK : She has that.

BRENTNALL : Well, you'll do what you can for poor old Charlie, won't you?

JACK: I will, Billy. And what time are you going?

BRENTNALL: 2.50 train.

JACK: Well—me and you's been good pals, George. I must say I'd ha' done anything for you——

GRAINGER: I know you would, Jack.

JACK: Yis, an' I would—an' I would.

BRENTNALL: I'm going up to Blythe Hall against Ashbourne for a day or two, Jack. Shall you come up for tennis?

JACK: I hardly think so—we s'll be busy just now.

BRENTNALL: Sunday afternoon—yes you will.

JACK: Good-bye, Billy.

BRENTNALL: Au revoir, Jack.

JACK: Well—good-bye, George—lad. We've not done amiss while you've been here. I s'll miss thee.

GRAINGER: You've been alright to me, Jack.

JACK: Yis—I try to do what I can for folks.

 Exit JACK.

BRENTNALL: The atmosphere clears, George.

GRAINGER: Oh damn you, shut up.

BRENTNALL: "Oh, what a sin is base ingratitude!"

GRAINGER: What did you tell Annie about me?

BRENTNALL: I said you were quite manly, and couldn't help yourself; all the virtues of good nature and so on, but a bit of a libidinous goat.

GRAINGER: Thank you—very nice of you.

BRENTNALL: Add to this that you won't face a situation, but always funk it, and you understand why Annie suddenly transferred her affections to me. For I showed myself, by contrast, a paragon of all virtues.

GRAINGER: You would.

BRENTNALL: I did.

GRAINGER: I shan't go to London to your rooms.

BRENTNALL: Now George, my dear chap——

GRAINGER: I shall not, Billy.

BRENTNALL: Then where will you go?

GRAINGER: Hell!

BRENTNALL: My dear, dear fellow, you've neither the cash nor the ability.

GRAINGER: Well, you're a——

BRENTNALL : Shall we get up?

GRAINGER : I will, whether you will or not. *(Sits on the side of the bed whistling "On the Banks of Allan Water". Footsteps on the stairs—enter* GRAINGER'S *wife,* ETHEL—*rather thin, with a light costume.)*

ETHEL: George! *(She goes forward and kisses him, not noticing* BRENTNALL.) *George!* *(Sinks her head on his shoulder.)* George!

GRAINGER : Ethel—well I'm blessed! *(Kisses her.)*

ETHEL *(drawing away)*: I had to come.

GRAINGER : Yes.

ETHEL : Are you angry?

GRAINGER : Me angry! What should I be angry for?

ETHEL : I thought you might be.

GRAINGER : What made you come?

ETHEL : I heard you were going away—and your letters seemed so constrained. Are you——?

GRAINGER : What?

ETHEL : Going away?

GRAINGER : I s'll have to—this job's done.

ETHEL : You never told me.

GRAINGER : What was the good?

ETHEL : Where are you going?

GRAINGER : Dunno—I don't know in the least.

ETHEL : Oh George, you must come home. Mother says you must.

GRAINGER : Hm!

ETHEL : Won't you?

GRAINGER : I'd rather not.

ETHEL : What will you do, then?

GRAINGER : I may—I shall probably get a job in London.

ETHEL : Oh George, don't, don't go to London.

GRAINGER : What else can I do?

ETHEL : Come home to Mother with me.

GRAINGER : I'll be damned if I will.

ETHEL : No, you never will do anything I ask you.

GRAINGER : I shan't do that.

ETHEL : Don't you want to be with me?

GRAINGER : If I want ever so badly, I can't, with no money.

ETHEL : Then how are you going to live alone, with no money?

GRAINGER : I can manage for myself.

ETHEL : I know what you want, you want to run away. It is mean, mean of you.

GRAINGER : What's the good of my coming to *your* place, there, where they kicked me out?

ETHEL : And what if you've nowhere else to go? And what are you going to do in London?

GRAINGER : Look for a job.

ETHEL : And what when you've got one?

GRAINGER : Save up to get some things together.

ETHEL : How much have you saved here?

GRAINGER : Not a fat lot—but I *have* saved.

ETHEL : How much?

GRAINGER : Some—at any rate.

ETHEL : Have you been miserable? I know you like plenty of life. Has it made you miserable to be tied up?

GRAINGER : Not miserable—but it's been a bit of a devil.

ETHEL : We ought to live together.

GRAINGER : On what?

ETHEL : On what we can get.

GRAINGER : No, thank you.

ETHEL : We might as well not be married. I believe you hate me for having married you. Do you—do you?

GRAINGER : Now Ethel, drop it. Don't get excited. You know I don't feel anything of the sort.

ETHEL *(weeping)* : But you don't love me.

GRAINGER *(tenderly)* : Why, I do, Ethel, I do.

ETHEL : I love you, George, I love you.

GRAINGER : Poor old Ethel—and I love you. And whoever says I don't, is a liar.

ETHEL : You've been true to me, George?

GRAINGER : What do you mean?

ETHEL : Have you been true to me?

BRENTNALL : No, he hasn't.

GRAINGER *(fiercely)* : Now Billy!

BRENTNALL : I am your husband's old friend, Brentnall, and *your* friend, Mrs Grainger. *(Gets out of bed, shakes hands with* ETHEL.)

ETHEL : I didn't know you were there.

BRENTNALL : Never mind. *(Puts on a dressing-gown.)*

ETHEL : Do you say George hasn't been true to me?

BRENTNALL: I do. Do you really love him?

ETHEL: He is my husband.

BRENTNALL: You do love him, I can see. Then, look here, *keep* him. You can do it, I should think. *Keep* him. And you, George, be decent.

GRAINGER: Be decent yourself.

BRENTNALL: I am. *(Lights a cigarette.)* You don't mind if I smoke?

ETHEL: No. George, oh George! It's not true what he says, is it?

GRAINGER: No!

ETHEL *(weeping)*: I couldn't bear it. *(Embracing him.)* I couldn't bear it.

BRENTNALL *(aside)*: That's the ticket.

GRAINGER: Never mind, little girl—never mind.

ETHEL: You won't leave me again?

BRENTNALL *(aside)*: Good shot!

GRAINGER: What can I do?

ETHEL: I've got seventy pounds, George, I've got seventy pounds.

GRAINGER: I don't want *your money*, Ethel.

ETHEL: You don't mind making a fool of me, and neglecting me, but you won't have my money.

GRAINGER: Now Ethel——

ETHEL *(flashing)*: Isn't it so?

GRAINGER: No, Ethel.

ETHEL: Then we'll live together on seventy pounds, till you get a job?

GRAINGER: But you see——

ETHEL *(turning, flashing, to* BRENTNALL*)*: *Has* he been living straight —*do* they know here he's married?

BRENTNALL: I've told a few of them.

ETHEL *(turning slowly to* GRAINGER*)*: Now then——

GRAINGER: You can do what the hell you like.

ETHEL: Then I shall live with you, from this minute onwards.

BRENTNALL: Knocked out, George!

GRAINGER: Curse you, Brentnall.

BRENTNALL: You are a rotter, my dear fellow.

ETHEL *(weeping)*: There's baby crying.

> *Exit* ETHEL, *weeping.* BRENTNALL *smokes a cigarette—* GRAINGER *fumes.*

BRENTNALL *(throwing him a dressing-gown)*: You'd better clothe yourself—you'll feel stronger.

GRAINGER *(getting into the dressing-gown)*: What d'you reckon you're up to?

BRENTNALL: *Don't* be a fool, George, *don't* be a swine. If you're going to clear out, stand up and say so honourably! Say you'll not abide by your marriage. You *can* do that, with decency.

GRAINGER: How the devil can I?

BRENTNALL: *Will* you?

GRAINGER: No, damn it, how can I? I'm not a——

BRENTNALL: Very well then, you won't clear out, you won't renounce your marriage. Very well then, go and live with the girl, and be decent. Have a cigarette! (GRAINGER *takes a cigarette.)*

GRAINGER: It's a cursed rotten hole——

BRENTNALL: Then for the Lord's sake, make it as comfortable as possible, if you're going to stop in it.

GRAINGER: Hark!

BRENTNALL: Sally!

GRAINGER: It is, begad!

ETHEL *appears.*

ETHEL: There's a woman enquiring for you.

GRAINGER: What for—what does she want?

ETHEL: She wants you.

GRAINGER: Hm! Is it Sally? She's been running after me ever since I've been here, bless her.

BRENTNALL: Let's have her up. *(Calling.)* Do come upstairs, Miss Magneer. It's quite decent.

GRAINGER: It's a bit thick, Billy.

Enter SALLY.

BRENTNALL *(to* SALLY*)*: Excuse our appearance, won't you? How do you do? *(Shakes hands.)*

SALLY: How do you do?

BRENTNALL: Have you been introduced to Mrs Grainger? Mrs Doctor Grainger—Miss Magneer.

SALLY: I've been given to understand this is Mrs Doctor Grainger—and that the baby downstairs——

BRENTNALL: Is Master Jimmy Grainger. Quite so.

SALLY: I think it *is* quite so. It's happened quite so, but it's not quite the thing.

BRENTNALL : Don't let us quarrel, Sally. Don't be quarrelling with us the last half-hour we shall be here.

SALLY : Perhaps not. But what was he masquerading round as not married for, if he had a wife and a child?

ETHEL : You see, Miss Magneer, the fact that Dr Grainger chose to keep his marriage a secret wouldn't have hurt *you*, unless you'd rushed in to be hurt.

SALLY : Yes—meaning to say as I ran after him. *(To* GRAINGER.*)* Eh?

GRAINGER : Well—what else can you call it, Sally?

SALLY : And who wanted me to walk down the fields with him, the first time he saw me?

GRAINGER : I must say I think you wanted me quite as much, if not more, than I wanted you, Sally.

SALLY : Oh, did I?

ETHEL : I have no doubt of it.

SALLY : And did every single girl you met want you then, Dr Grainger?

GRAINGER : I never said so nor meant so.

SALLY : The one downstairs, for instance.

GRAINGER : Who d'you mean?

SALLY : Annie Calladine.

GRAINGER : What's she doing here?

ETHEL : She met me at the station. I left her holding baby.

SALLY : Let *her* come up, and say *her* share. No, you daren't and you know it.

GRAINGER : Daren't I? I say, Annie—Annie!

ANNIE'S VOICE : Yes!

GRAINGER : Would you mind coming upstairs a minute?

SALLY : Now you s'll hear *her* side, as well.

　　　Enter ANNIE.

BRENTNALL : You will excuse us—we were not expecting callers.

ANNIE : How do you do?

GRAINGER : Annie, Sally wants to say everything you can against me, in Ethel's hearing.

ANNIE : I don't wish to say everything I can against you, Dr Grainger. But I do wish to say this, that you are a danger to every unmarried girl, when you go about as you *have* gone, here. And Mrs Grainger had better look after you very closely, if she means to keep you.

GRAINGER : Thank you, Annie, very nice.

ANNIE : Almost as nice as you have been to me.

GRAINGER : I'm not aware that I've done you much damage.

ANNIE : If you haven't, it's not your fault.

    ETHEL *flings herself suddenly on the bed, weeping wildly.*

SALLY : I'm thankful I'm not his wife.

ANNIE : And I am more than thankful.

BRENTNALL : Don't cry, Mrs Grainger. George is alright, really.

ANNIE *(fiercely)* : He is *not*, Mr Brentnall.

SALLY : Neither is he.

BRENTNALL : Nay, don't cry, Mrs Grainger.

    ELSA SMITH'S VOICE, *calling in a jolly singsong:* "Knabe, Knabe, wo bist du?"

BRENTNALL : *Gott sei dank, du bist gekommen. Komm hinauf.*

ELSA SMITH'S VOICE : *Ja! (Runs upstairs—enter, chattering in German.)* Oh!

BRENTNALL *(shaking hands)* : Frightful muddle! Miss Annie Calladine—Mrs Grainger's awfully cut up because George has been flirting round.

ELSA : With you, Miss Magneer—and Miss Calladine?

SALLY : Not to mention the rest.

ELSA : Oh—oh! I'm sorry. But don't cry, Mrs Grainger, please. He's not a villain if he makes love to the other girls, surely. Perhaps it's not *nice*. But it was under trying circumstances.

BRENTNALL : That's what I say.

ELSA : Yes, yes. You're just as bad yourself. *I* know you.

BRENTNALL : Nay Elsa, I'm not the same.

ELSA : Oh, oh—now *don't* try to duck your head in the whitewash pail with me, no. I won't have it. Don't cry, Mrs Grainger, don't cry. He loves you, I'm sure he does, even if he makes love to the others. *(To* GRAINGER.*)* Don't you? *(No reply.)* Now you are sulking just like a great baby. And then that's your *little* baby downstairs? Ah, the dear! *(Sobbing from* ETHEL.*)* Never mind, never mind, cry out your cry, then let me talk to you.

BRENTNALL : Come by motor-car?

ELSA : Yes, Will Hobson drove me.

BRENTNALL : Ha!

ELSA : I like him, so you needn't say "Ha!"

BRENTNALL : Ha!

ELSA (*laughing—putting her hand on his shoulder*): Not had break-fast, and smoking, and talking to ladies. Aren't you ashamed, sir?

BRENTNALL: I've nothing to be ashamed of.

ELSA (*laughing*): No, no; hear him. (*Kisses him.*) You are a dear, but a dreadful liar.

BRENTNALL: Nay, I'll be damned—I beg your pardon.

ELSA: No, you *never* use bad language, do you?

BRENTNALL: Not in the presence of ladies.

ELSA: Well, now listen, I prefer to have you as you are with *men*. If you swear when you are with men, I prefer you to swear when you are with me. Will you promise me you will?

BRENTNALL: It wouldn't be a hard promise to keep.

ELSA: Promise me you won't have one philosophy when you are with men, in your smoke-room, and another when you are with me, in the drawing-room. Promise me you will be faithful to your philosophy that you have with other men, even before me, always.

BRENTNALL: Ha! Not so easy.

ELSA: Promise me. I want the real you, not your fiction.

BRENTNALL: I promise to do my best.

ELSA: Yes, and I trust you, you are so decent.

BRENTNALL: Nay, Elsa——

ELSA: Yes you are. Oh I see your faults, I do. But you are decent. (*To* ETHEL, *who has stopped crying, but who still lies on the bed.*) Don't be *too* cross with Dr Grainger, will you, Mrs Grainger? It's not *very* dreadful. Perhaps Miss Magneer loved him a little——

SALLY: That I never did——

ELSA (*laughing*): Yes, you did. And (*to* ANNIE) you were inclined to love him?

ANNIE: That is the worst part of it.

ELSA: Well, I, who am a woman, when I see other women who are sweet or handsome or charming, I look at them and think: "Well, how can a man help loving them, to some extent? Even if he loves *me*, if I am not there, how can he help loving them?"

ANNIE: But not a married man.

ELSA: I think a man ought to be fair. He ought to offer his love for just what it is—the love of a man married to another woman—and so on. And, if there is any strain, he ought to tell his wife—"I love this other woman."

SALLY: It's worse than Mormons.

BRENTNALL: But better than subterfuge, bestiality, or starvation and sterility.

ELSA: Yes, yes. If only men were decent enough.

BRENTNALL: And women.

ELSA: Yes. Don't fret, Mrs Grainger. By loving these two women, Dr Grainger has not lost any of his love for you. I would stay with him.

SALLY: He certainly never loved me—except for what he could get.

ELSA: Ha-ha! *(Very quaint and very earnest.)* That is rather dreadful. But yes, he must have loved you—something in you.

SALLY: It *was* something.

ELSA: Yes, I see what you mean—but I don't think you're quite right. No, it's *not quite* so brutal.

BRENTNALL: Shall I walk across to you after lunch?

ELSA: Yes, do that.

ANNIE: I think I will go. Good-bye, Dr Grainger. *(Shakes hands.)* Good-bye, Sally. Good-bye, Mr Brentnall.

BRENTNALL: Good-bye, Annie. Remember what I told you, and decide for the best. *Don't* be afraid. *(Kisses her.)*

ELSA: Yes. I think, with a little love, we can help each other so much.

ANNIE *(to* ELSA*)*: Good-bye. *(Crossing and putting her arms round* ETHEL.*)* He isn't bad, dear. You must bring out the best in him. The baby is a *dear.* And you'll write to me.

    Exit ANNIE.

SALLY: Well, good-bye all. And if I were your wife, Dr Grainger, I'd keep the bit between your teeth.

ELSA: No, no. No one should be driven like a horse between the shafts. Each should live his own life; you are there to *help* your husband, not to drive him.

SALLY: And to watch he doesn't help himself too often. Well, good-bye. Shall we be seeing you again, Mr Brentnall?

BRENTNALL: Next week.

SALLY: Right—*do* come. Good-bye.

    Exit SALLY.

ELSA *(crossing to* ETHEL*)*: Good-bye. Don't make sorrow and trouble in the world; try to make happiness. I think Satan is in hard judgment, even more than is sin. Try to exonerate.

ETHEL : It's such a shock.

ELSA *(kissing her)* : Ah yes, it is cruel. But don't let your own suffering blind you, try not to. Good-bye. *(Kisses her.)* Good-bye, Dr Grainger. *(Shakes hands.)*

BRENTNALL : I will see you downstairs—by the way, Grainger and Mrs Grainger are going to stay in my rooms.

ELSA : How perfectly delightful! Then I shall see you in London. How lovely! Good-bye.

BRENTNALL : I suppose I'm respectable enough to see you downstairs.

> *Exeunt* ELSA *and* BRENTNALL. GRAINGER *and his wife sit silent a while. They are afraid of each other.*

GRAINGER : Will you go to London to Billy's rooms?

ETHEL : Does he want us to?

GRAINGER : I suppose so.

> *Silence.*

GRAINGER : Will you?

ETHEL : Do you want me to?

GRAINGER : You please yourself. I'm not coming to Wolverhampton.

ETHEL *(trying not to cry)* : Well, we'll go to London.

GRAINGER : It's a damned mess.

ETHEL *(crying)* : You'd better do just as you like, then, and I'll go home.

GRAINGER : I didn't mean that.

ETHEL *(crying)* : I'll go home.

GRAINGER : Don't begin again, Ethel.

ETHEL : You hate the thought of being married to me. So you can be free of me.

GRAINGER : And what about the baby? Don't talk rot, Ethel. *(Puts his arm round her.)*

ETHEL : You don't care for that, either.

GRAINGER : Don't I—you don't know. They all make me look as black as I can——

ETHEL : Well, I don't know.

GRAINGER : Yes they do—and they always have done. I never have had anybody to stick up for me. *(Weeps a few tears.)* I've had a rotten time, a rotten time.

ETHEL : And so have I.

GRAINGER : You don't know what it is to be a man.

ETHEL : I know what it is to be your wife.

GRAINGER : Are you going to sling it in my teeth for ever?

ETHEL : No, I'm not. But what did you marry me for? *(Cries.)*

GRAINGER *(embracing her)*: You're the only girl I could have married, Ethel. I've been a rotter to you, I have.

ETHEL : Never mind, we *shall* get on together, we shall. Mind, somebody is coming.

> *A knock—enter* MRS PLUM *with the baby.*

MRS PLUM : He wants you, the precious little lad, he does. Oh Dr Grainger, let me see you hold him! *(Gives the baby to* GRAINGER.)

> *Enter* BRENTNALL.

BRENTNALL : That's the way, George.

GRAINGER : Shut up, fool.

CURTAIN

The Daughter-in-Law

A PLAY IN FOUR ACTS

(1912)

CHARACTERS

MRS GASCOIGNE
JOE
MRS PURDY
MINNIE
LUTHER
CABMAN

The action of the play takes place in the kitchen of Luther Gascoigne's new home.

ACT I

SCENE I

A collier's kitchen—not poor. Windsor chairs, deal table, dresser of painted wood, sofa covered with red cotton stuff. Time: About half-past two of a winter's afternoon.

A large, stoutish woman of sixty-five, with smooth black hair parted down the middle of her head: MRS GASCOIGNE.

Enter a young man, about twenty-six, dark, good-looking; has his right arm in a sling; does not take off cap: JOE GASCOIGNE.

MRS GASCOIGNE : Well, I s'd ha' thought thy belly 'ud a browt thee whoam afore this.

JOE *sits on sofa without answering.*

Doesn't ter want no dinner?

JOE *(looking up)* : I want it if the' is ony.

MRS GASCOIGNE : An' if the' isna, tha can go be out? Tha talks large, my fine jockey! *(She puts a newspaper on the table; on it a plate and his dinner.)* Wheer dost reckon ter's bin?

JOE : I've bin ter th' office for my munny.

MRS GASCOIGNE : Tha's niver bin a' this while at th' office.

JOE : They kep' me ower an hour, an' then gen me nowt.

MRS GASCOIGNE : Gen thee nowt! Why, how do they ma'e that out? It's a wik sin' tha got hurt, an' if a man wi' a broken arm canna ha' his fourteen shillin' a week accident pay, who can, I s'd like to know?

JOE : They'll gie me nowt, whether or not.

MRS GASCOIGNE : An' for why, prithee?

JOE *(does not answer for some time; then, sullenly)* : They reckon I niver got it while I wor at work.

MRS GASCOIGNE : Then where did ter get it, might I ax? I'd think they'd like to lay it onto me.

JOE : Tha talks like a fool, Mother.

MRS GASCOIGNE : Tha looks like one, me lad.

She has given him his dinner; he begins to eat with a fork.

Here, hutch up, gammy-leg—gammy-arm.

He makes room; she sits by him on the sofa and cuts up his meat for him.

It's a rum un as I should start ha'in' babies again, an' feedin' 'em wi' spoon-meat. *(Gives him a spoon.)* An' now let's hear why they winna gi'e thee thy pay. Another o' Macintyre's dirty knivey dodges, I s'd think.

JOE : They reckon I did it wi' foolery, an' not wi' work.

MRS GASCOIGNE : Oh indeed! An' what by that?

JOE *(eating)* : They wunna gie me nowt, that's a'.

MRS GASCOIGNE : It's a nice thing! An' what did ter say?

JOE : I said nowt.

MRS GASCOIGNE : Tha wouldna'! Tha stood like a stuffed duck, an' said thank-yer.

JOE : Well, it wor raight.

MRS GASCOIGNE : How raight?

JOE : I did do it wi' foolery.

MRS GASCOIGNE : Then what did ter go axin' fer pay fer?

JOE : I did it at work, didna I? An' a man as gets accident at work's titled ter disability pay, isna he?

MRS GASCOIGNE : Tha said a minnit sin' as tha got it wi' foolery.

JOE : An' so I did.

MRS GASCOIGNE : I niver 'eered such talk i' my life.

JOE : I dunna care what ter's 'eered an' what t'asna. I wor foolin' wi' a wringer an' a pick-heft—ta's it as ter's a mind.

MRS GASCOIGNE : What, down pit?

JOE : I' th' stall, at snap time.

MRS GASCOIGNE : Showin' off a bit, like?

JOE : Ye'.

MRS GASCOIGNE : An' what then?

JOE : Th' wringer gen me a rap ower th'arm, an' that's a'.

MRS GASCOIGNE : An' tha reported it as a accident?

JOE : It wor accident, worn't it? I niver did it a'purpose.

MRS GASCOIGNE : But a pit accident.

JOE : Well, an' what else wor't? It wor a h'accident I got i' th' pit, i' th' sta' wheer I wor workin'.

MRS GASCOIGNE : But not *while* tha wor workin'.

JOE : What by that?—it wor a pit accident as I got i' th' stall.

MRS GASCOIGNE: But tha didna tell 'em how it happened.

JOE: I said some stuff fell on my arm, an' brok' it. An' worna that trew?

MRS GASCOIGNE: It wor very likely trew enough, lad, if on'y they'd ha' believed it.

JOE: An they would ha' believed it, but for Hewett bully-raggin' Bettesworth 'cos he knowed he was a chappil man. *(He imitates the underground manager, Hewett, and Bettesworth, a butty.)* "About this accident, Bettesworth. How exactly did it occur?" "I couldn't exactly say for certing, sir, because I wasn't linkin'." "Then tell me as near as you can." "Well, Mester, I'm sure I don't know." "That's curious, Bettesworth—I must have a report. Do you know anything about it, or don't you? It happened in your stall; you're responsible for it, and I'm responsible for you." "Well, Gaffer, what's right's right, I suppose, ter th' mesters or th' men. An' 'e wor conjurin' a' snap-time wi' a pick-heft an' a wringer, an' the wringer catched 'im ower th' arm." "I thought you didn't know!" "I said *for certain*—I didn't see exactly how 'twas done."

MRS GASCOIGNE: Hm.

JOE: Bettesworth 'ud non ha' clat-fasted but for nosy Hewett. He says, "Yo know, Joseph, when he says to me, 'Do you know anything about that haccident?'—then I says to myself, 'Take not the word of truth hutterly outer thy mouth.' "

MRS GASCOIGNE: If he took a bit o' slaver outen's mouth, it 'ud do.

JOE: So this mornin' when I went ter th' office, Mester Salmon he com out an' said: " 'Ow did this haccident occur, Joseph?" and I said, "Some stuff fell on't." So he says, "Stuff fell on't, stuff fell on't! You mean coal or rock or what?" So I says, "Well, it worn't a thipenny bit." "No," he says, "but what was it?" "It wor a piece o' clunch," I says. "You don't use clunch for wringers," he says, "do you?" "The wringin' of the nose bringeth forth blood," I says——

MRS GASCOIGNE: Why, you know you never did. *(She begins making a pudding.)*

JOE: No—b'r I'd ha' meant t'r'a done.

MRS GASCOIGNE: We know thee! Tha's done thysen one i' th' eye this time. When dost think tha'll iver get ter be a butty, at this rate? There's Luther nowt b'r a day man yet.

JOE: I'd as lief be a day man as a butty, i' pits that rat-gnawed there's hardly a stall worth havin'; an' a company as 'ud like yer ter scrape yer tabs afore you went home, for fear you took a grain o' coal.

MRS GASCOIGNE: Maybe—but tha's got ter get thy livin' by 'em.

JOE: I hanna. I s'll go to Australia.

MRS GASCOIGNE: Tha'lt do no such thing, while I'm o' this earth.

JOE: Ah, but though, I shall—else get married, like our Luther.

MRS GASCOIGNE: A fat sight better off tha'lt be for that.

JOE: You niver know, Mother, dun yer?

MRS GASCOIGNE: You dunna, me lad—not till yer find yerself let in. Marriage is like a mouse-trap, for either man or woman. You've soon come to th' end o' th' cheese.

JOE: Well, ha'ef a loaf's better nor no bread.

MRS GASCOIGNE: Why, wheer's th' loaf as tha'd like ter gnawg a' thy life?

JOE: Nay, nowhere yet.

MRS GASCOIGNE: Well, dunna thee talk, then. Tha's done thysen harm enow for one day, wi' thy tongue.

JOE: An' good as well, Mother—I've aten my dinner, a'most.

MRS GASCOIGNE: An' swilled thy belly afore that, methinks.

JOE: Niver i' this world!

MRS GASCOIGNE: And I've got thee to keep on ten shillin's a wik club-money, han I?

JOE: Tha needna, if ter doesna want. Besides, we s'll be out on strike afore we know wheer we are.

MRS GASCOIGNE: I'm sure. You've on'y bin in——

JOE: Now, Mother, spit on thy hands an' ta'e fresh hold. We s'll be out on strike in a wik or a fortnit——

MRS GASCOIGNE: Strike's a' they're fit for—a pack o' slutherers as . . .

    Her words tail off as she goes into pantry.

JOE *(to himself)*: Tha goes chunterin' i' th' pantry when somebody's at th' door. *(Rises, goes to door.)*

MRS PURDY'S VOICE: Is your mother in?

JOE: Yi, 'er's in right enough.

MRS PURDY: Well, then, can I speak to her?

JOE *(calling)*: Mrs Purdy wants ter speak to thee, Mother.

MRS GASCOIGNE *crosses the kitchen heavily, with a dripping-pan; stands in doorway.*

MRS GASCOIGNE: Good afternoon.

MRS PURDY: Good afternoon.

MRS GASCOIGNE: Er—what is it?

MRS PURDY *enters. She is a little fat, red-faced body in bonnet and black cape.*

MRS PURDY: I wanted to speak to yer rather pertickler.

MRS GASCOIGNE *(giving way)*: Oh, yes?

ALL THREE *enter the kitchen.* MRS PURDY *stands near the door.*

MRS PURDY *(nodding at* JOE*)*: Has he had a haccident?

MRS GASCOIGNE: Broke his arm.

MRS PURDY: Oh my! that's nasty. When did 'e do that?

MRS GASCOIGNE: A wik sin' to-day.

MRS PURDY: In th' pit?

MRS GASCOIGNE: Yes—an's not goin' to get any accident pay—says as 'e worn't workin'; he wor foolin' about.

MRS PURDY: T-t-t-t! Did iver you know! I tell you what, missis, it's a wonder they let us live on the face o' the earth at all—it's a wonder we don't have to fly up i' th' air like birds.

JOE: There'd be a squark i' th' sky then!

MRS PURDY: But it is indeed. It's somethink awful. They've gave my mester a dirty job o' nights, at a guinea a week, an' he's worked fifty years for th' company, an' isn't but sixty-two now—said he wasn't equal to stall-workin', whereas he has to slave on th' roads an' comes whoam that tired he can't put's food in's mouth.

JOE: He's about like me.

MRS PURDY: Yis. But it's no nice thing, a guinea a week.

MRS GASCOIGNE: Well, that's how they're servin' 'em a' round—widders' coals stopped—leadin' raised to four-an'-eight—an' ivry man niggled down to nothink.

MRS PURDY: I wish I'd got that Fraser strung up by th' heels—I'd ma'e *his* sides o' bacon rowdy.

MRS GASCOIGNE: He's put a new manager to ivry pit, an' ivry one a nigger-driver.

MRS PURDY: Says he's got to economise—says the company's not a philanthropic concern——

MRS GASCOIGNE: But ta'es twelve hundred a year for hissen.

MRS PURDY: A mangy bachelor wi' 'is iron-men.

JOE: But they wunna work.

MRS PURDY: They say how he did but coss an' swear about them American Cutters. I should like to see one set outer 'im—they'd work hard enough rippin's guts out—even iron's got enough sense for that. *(She suddenly subsides.)*
> *There is a pause.*

MRS GASCOIGNE: How do you like living down Nethergreen?

MRS PURDY: Well—we're very comfortable. It's small, but it's handy, an' sin' the mester's gone down t'a guinea——

MRS GASCOIGNE: It'll do for you three.

MRS PURDY: Yes.
> *Another pause.*

MRS GASCOIGNE: The men are comin' out again, they say.

MRS PURDY: Isn't it summat sickenin'? Well, I've werritted an' werritted till I'm soul-sick——

JOE: It sends yer that thin an' threadbare, y'have ter stop sometime.

MRS PURDY: There can be as much ache in a motherly body as in bones an' gristle, I'm sure o' that.

JOE: Nay, I'm more than bones an' gristle.

MRS PURDY: That's true as the day.
> *Another long pause.*

MRS GASCOIGNE: An' how have yer all bin keepin'?

MRS PURDY: Oh, very nicely—except our Bertha.

MRS GASCOIGNE: Is she poorly, then?

MRS PURDY: That's what I com ter tell yer. I niver knowed a word on't till a Sat'day, nor niver noticed a thing. Then she says to me, as white as a sheet, "I've been sick every morning, Mother," an' it com across me like a shot from a gun. I sunk down i' that chair an' couldna fetch a breath.—An' me as prided myself! I've often laughed about it, an' said I was thankful my children had all turned out so well, lads an' wenches as well, an' said it was a'cause they was all got of a Sunday—their father was too drunk a' Saturday, an' too tired o' wik-days. An' it's a fact, they've all turned out well, for I'd allers bin to chappil. Well, I've said it for a joke, but now it's turned on me. I'd better ha' kep' my tongue still.

JOE: It's not me, though, missis. I wish it wor.

MRS PURDY: There's no occasions to ma'e gam' of it neither, as far as I can see. The youngest an' the last of 'em as I've got, an' a lass as I liked, for she's simple, but she's good-natured, an' him a married man. Thinks I to myself, "I'd better go to's mother, she'll ha'e more about 'er than's new wife—for she's a stuck-up piece o' goods as ever trod."

MRS GASCOIGNE: Why, what d'yer mean?

MRS PURDY: I mean what I say—an' there's no denyin' it. That girl —well, it's nigh on breakin' my heart, for I'm that short o' breath. *(Sighs.)* I'm sure!

MRS GASCOIGNE: Why don't yer say what yer mean?

MRS PURDY: I've said it, haven't I? There's my gal gone four month wi' childt to your Luther.

MRS GASCOIGNE: Nay, nay, nay, missis! You'll never ma'e me believe it.

MRS PURDY: Glad would I be if I nedna. But I've gone through it all since Sat'day on. I've wanted to break every bone in 'er body —an' I've said I should on'y be happy if I was scraightin' at 'er funeral—an' I've said I'd wring his neck for 'im. But it doesn't alter it—there it is—an' there it will be. An' I s'll be a grandmother where my heart heaves, an' maun drag a wastrel baby through my old age. An' it's neither a cryin' nor a laughin' matter, but it's a matter of a girl wi' child, an' a man six week married.

MRS GASCOIGNE: But our Luther never went wi' your Bertha. How d'you make it out?

MRS PURDY: Yea, yea, missis—yea indeed.

JOE: Yi, Mother, he's bin out wi' 'er. She wor pals wi' Liza Ann Varley, as went out wi' Jim Horrocks. So Jim he passed Bertha onter our Luther. Why, I've had many a glass wi' the four of 'em, i' "Th' Ram".

MRS GASCOIGNE: I niver knowed nowt o' *this* afore.

JOE: Tha doesna know ivrythink, Mother.

MRS GASCOIGNE: An' it's well I don't, methinks.

JOE: Tha doesna want, neither.

MRS GASCOIGNE: Well, I dunno what we're goin' to do, missis. He's a young married man.

MRS PURDY: An' she's a girl o' mine.

MRS GASCOIGNE: How old is she?

MRS PURDY: She wor twenty-three last September.

MRS GASCOIGNE: Well then, I sh'd 'a thought she'd ha' known better.

MRS PURDY: An' what about him, missis, as goes and gets married t'r another fine madam d'rectly after he's been wi' my long lass?

JOE: But he never knowed owt about.

MRS PURDY: He'd seen th' blossom i' flower, if he hadna spotted the fruit a-comin'.

JOE: Yi—but——

MRS GASCOIGNE: Yi but what?

JOE: Well—you dunna expect—ivry time yer cast yer bread on th' wathers, as it'll come whoam to you like.

MRS GASCOIGNE: Well, I dunno what we're goin' to do.

MRS PURDY: I thought I'd better come to you, rather than——

JOE: Ah, you non want it gettin' about—an' *she'd* best not know—if it can be helped.

MRS GASCOIGNE: I can't see for why.

MRS PURDY: No indeed—a man as plays fast an' loose first wi' one an' then goes an' marries another stuck-up piece . . .

MRS GASCOIGNE: An' a wench as goes sittin' i' "Th' Ram" wi' th' fellers mun expect what she gets, missis.

MRS PURDY: 'Appen so, 'appen so. An' th' man maun abide by what he's gi'en.

MRS GASCOIGNE: I dunno *what* we're goin' to do!

JOE: We'd best keep it as quiet as we can.

MRS PURDY: I thinks to mysen, "It'll non become *me* to go an' jack up a married couple, for if *he's* at fault, it's her as 'ud ha'e ter suffer." An' though she's haughty, I knowed her mother, as nice a body as ever stept, an' treated scandylos by Jim Hetherington. An', thinks I, she's a horphan, if she's got money, an' nobbut her husband i' th' world. Thinks I to mysen it's no good visitin' it on 'er head, if he's a villain. For whatever th' men does, th' women maun ma'e up for. An' though I do consider as it's nowt b'r a dirty trick o' his'n to ta'e a poor lass like my long thing, an' go an' marry a woman wi' money——

MRS GASCOIGNE: Woman wi' money, an' peace go wi' 'er, 'er an' 'er money! What she's got, she'll keep, you take my word for it, missis.

MRS PURDY: Yes, an' she's right of it.

JOE: Nay, Mother, she's non close.

MRS GASCOIGNE: Isn't she?—oh, isn't she? An' what is she then?
All she wanted was as much for her money as she could get.
An' when she fun as nob'dy was for sale but our Luther, she says,
"Well, I'll take it."

JOE: Nay, it worna like that—it wor him as wor that come-day-
go-day——

MRS PURDY: God send Sunday.

MRS GASCOIGNE: An' what more canna man do, think yer, but ax
a woman? When has *thee* ever done as much?

JOE: No, I hanna, 'cos I've niver seen th' woman as I wanted to
say "snap"—but he slormed an' she——

MRS GASCOIGNE: Slormed! Thee slorm but one fiftieth part to any
lass thee likes, an' see if 'er's not all over thee afore tha's said
six words. Slormed! 'Er wor that high an' mighty, 'er wanted
summat bett'nor 'im.

JOE: Nay—I reckon he niver showed the spunk of a sprat-herring
to 'er.

MRS GASCOIGNE: Did *thee* show any more? Hast iver done? Yet
onybody 'ud think tha wor for marryin' 'er thysen.

JOE: If I'd ha' *bin* for marryin' 'er, I'd ha' gone wholesale, not ha'
fudged and haffled.

MRS GASCOIGNE: But tha *worna* for marryin' neither 'er nor nobody.

JOE: No, I worna.

MRS GASCOIGNE: No, tha worna.

> *There is a long pause. The mother turns half apologetically,*
> *half explanatorily, to* MRS PURDY.

It's like this 'ere, missis, if you'll not say nothink about it—sin'
it's got to come out atween us. He courted Minnie Hetherington
when she wor at her uncle's, at th' "Bell o' Brass", an' he wor
nowt bu'r a lad o' twenty-two, an' she twenty-one. An' he wor
gone on 'er right enow. Then she had that row wi' 'er uncle, for
she wor iver overbearin' an' chancy. Then our Luther says to me,
"I s'll ax 'er to marry me, Mother," an' I says: "Tha pleases
thysen, but ter my thinkin' tha'rt a sight too young an' doesna
know thy own mind." Howsoever, much notice 'e takes o' me.

JOE: He took a lot o' notice on thee, tha knows well enough.

MRS GASCOIGNE: An' for what shouldn't he? Hadn't I bin a good
mother to 'im i' ivry shape an' form? Let *her* make him as good
a wife as I made him a mother! Well—we'll see. You'll see *him*

repent the day. But they're not to be bidden. An' so, missis, he did ax 'er, as 'e'd said 'e should. But hoity-toity an' no thank yer, she wasna for havin' him, but mun go an' be a nursery governess up i' Manchester. Thinks I to myself, she's after a town johnny, a Bertie-Willie an' a yard o' cuffs. But he kep' on writin' to 'er, now an' again—an' she answered—as if she wor standin' at top of a flight of steps——

JOE: An' 'appen on'y wanted fetchin' down.

MRS GASCOIGNE: Wi' a kick from behint, if I'd ha' had th' doin' o't. So they go mornin' on. He sees 'er once i' a blew moon. If he goes ter Manchester, she condescends to see him for a couple of hours. If she comes here, she ca's i' this house wi' a "how-do-you-do, Mrs Gascoigne", an' off again. If they go f'r a walk . . .

JOE: He's whoam again at nine o'clock.

MRS GASCOIGNE: If they go for a walk it's "Thank you, I mustn't be very late. Good night, Luther." I thought it ud niver come ter nothink. Then 'er uncle dies an' leaves her a hundred pounds, which considerin' th' way she'd been with 'im, was more than I'd ha' gen her—an' she was a bit nicer. She writes ter Luther ter come an' see 'er an' stop a couple o' days. He ta'es her to the the-etter, an's for goin' i' th' pit at a shillin', when she says: "It's my treat, Luther, and five shillin' seats apiece, if you please."

JOE: An' he couldna luik at th' performance, for fear as the folks was luikin' at 'im.

MRS GASCOIGNE: An' after th' the-etter, it must be supper wi' a man i' a tail-coat an' silver forks, an' she pays. "Yes," says I when he told me, "that's the tricks of servants, showin' off afore decent folk."

JOE: She could do what she liked, couldn't she?

MRS GASCOIGNE: Well, an' after that, he didna write, 'cept to say thank yer. For it put 'im in a horkard position. That wor four years ago, an' she's nobbut seen him three times sin' that. If she could but ha' snapped up somebody else, it 'ud bin good-bye to Luther——

JOE: As tha told him many a time.

MRS GASCOIGNE: As I told him many a time, for am I to sit an' see my own lad bitted an' bobbed, tasted an' spit out by a madam i' service? Then all of a suddin, three months back, come a letter: "Dear Luther, I have been thinking it over, an' have come to the opinion that we'd better get married now, if we are ever goin' to. We've been dallying on all these years, and we seem to get no further. So we'd better make the plunge, if ever we're going to. Of course you will say exactly what you think. Don't agree to anything unless you want to. I only want to say that I think, if we're ever going to be married, we'd better do it without waiting any longer." Well, missis, he got that letter when he com whoam fra work. I seed him porin' an' porin', but I says nowt. Then he ate some o's dinner, and went out. When he com in, it wor about haef past ten, an' 'e wor white as a sheet. He gen me that letter, an' says: "What's think o' that, Mother?" Well, you could ha' knocked me down wi' a feather when I'd read it. I says: "I think it's tidy cheek, my lad." He took it back an' puts 's pocket, an' after a bit, 'e says: "What should ter say, Mother?" "Tha says what's a mind, my lad," I says. So he begins unlacin' 's boots. Sudden he stops, an' wi's boot-tags rattlin', goes rummagin' for th' pen an' ink. "What art goin' to say?" I says. "I'm goin' ter say, 'er can do as 'er's a mind. If 'er wants ter be married, 'er can, an' if 'er doesna, 'er nedna." So I thinks we could leave it at that. He sits him down, an' doesna write more nor a side an' a haef. I thinks: "That's done it, it'll be an end between them two now." He niver gen th' letter to me to read.

JOE: He did to me. He says: "I'm ready an' willin' to do what you want, whenever yer want. I'm earnin' about thirty-five bob a week, an' haven't got any money because my mother gi'es me what I ax for ter spend. But I can have what I ask for to set up house with. Your loving—Luther." He says to me: "Dost think it's a'right?" I says: "I s'd think so; 'er maun ma'e what 'er likes out on't."

MRS GASCOIGNE: On th' Monday after, she wor here livin' at 'er A'nt's an' th' notice was in at th' registrar. I says: "What money dost want?" He says: "Thee buy what tha thinks we s'll want." So he tells Minnie, an' she says: "Not bi-out I'm theer." Well, we goes ter Nottingham, an' she will ha'e nowt b'r old-fashioned stuff. I says: "That's niver *my* mind, Minnie." She says: "Well, I like it, an' yo'll see it'll look nice. I'll pay for it." Which to be sure I never let her. For she'd had a mester as made a fool of her, tellin' her this an' that, what wor good taste, what wor bad.

JOE: An' it *does* look nice, Mother, their house.

MRS GASCOIGNE: We'll see how it looks i' ten years' time, my lad, wi' th' racket an' tacket o' children. For it's not serviceable, missis.

MRS PURDY *(who has been a sympathetic and exclamative listener):* Then it's no good.

MRS GASCOIGNE: An' that's how they got married.

JOE: An' he went about wi's tail atween his legs, scared outer's life.

MRS GASCOIGNE: For I said no more. If he axed me owt, I did it; if he wanted owt, I got it. But it wasn't for me to go interferin' where I wasn't wanted.

JOE: If ever I get married, Mother, I s'll go i' lodgin's six month aforehand.

MRS GASCOIGNE: Tha'd better—ter get thysen a bit case-hardened.

JOE: Yi. But I'm goin' t'r Australia.

MRS GASCOIGNE: I come withee, then.

JOE: Tha doesna.

MRS GASCOIGNE: I dunna fret—tha'lt non go.

MRS PURDY: Well, it was what I should call a bit off-hand, I must say.

MRS GASCOIGNE: You can see now how he got married, an' who's to blame.

JOE: Nay, yo' canna ma'e 'er to blame for Bertha. Liza Ann Varley's ter blame for th' lass goin' out o' nights.

MRS PURDY: An' there I thought they wor both i' Varley's—not gallivantin'.

JOE: They often was. An' Jim Horrocks is ter blame fer couplin' 'er onter our Luther, an' him an' her's ter blame for the rest. I dunno how you can lay it on Minnie. You might as well lay it on 'er if th' childt wor mine.

MRS GASCOIGNE *(sharply):* Tha'd ha'e more sense!

JOE: I'd try.

MRS GASCOIGNE: But now she's played fast an' loose wi' him— twice I *know* he axed 'er to ha'e him—now she's asked for what she's got. She's put her puddin' in her mouth, an' if she's burnt herself, serve her right.

MRS PURDY: Well, I didn't want to go to court. I thought, his mother'll be th' best one to go to——

MRS GASCOIGNE: No—you mun go to him hisself—go an' tell him

i' front of her—an' if she wants anythink, she mun ma'e arrangements herself.

JOE: What was you thinkin' of, Missis Purdy?

MRS PURDY: Well, I was thinkin', she's a poor lass—an' I didn't want 'er to go to court, for they ax such questions—an' I thought it was such a *thing*, him six wik married—though to be sure I'd no notions of how it was—I thought, we might happen say, it was one o' them electricians as was along when they laid th' wires under th' road down to Batsford—and——

JOE: And arrange for a lump sum, like?

MRS PURDY: Yes—we're poor, an' she's poor—an' if she had a bit o' money of 'er own—for we should niver touch it—it might be a inducement to some other young feller—for, poor long thing, she's that simple——

MRS GASCOIGNE: Well, ter my knowledge, them as has had a childt seems to get off i' marriage better nor many as hasn't. I'm sure, there's a lot o' men likes it, if they think a woman's had a baby by another man.

MRS PURDY: That's nothing to trust by, missis; you'll say so yourself.

JOE: An' about how much do you want? Thirty pounds?

MRS PURDY: We want what's fair. I got it fra Emma Stapleton; they had forty wi' their Lucy.

JOE: Forty pound?

MRS PURDY: Yes.

MRS GASCOIGNE: Well, then, let *her* find it. She's paid for nothing but the wedding. She's got money enough, if he's none. Let *her* find it. She made the bargain, she maun stick by it. It was her dip i' th' bran-tub—if there's a mouse nips hold of her finger, she maun suck it better, for nobody axed her to dip.

MRS PURDY: You think I'd better go to him? Eh, missis, it's a nasty business. But right's right.

MRS GASCOIGNE: Right *is* right, Mrs Purdy. And you go tell him a-front of her—that's the best thing you can do. Then iverything's straight.

MRS PURDY: But for her he might ha' married our Bertha.

MRS GASCOIGNE: To be sure, to be sure.

MRS PURDY: What right had she to snatch when it pleased her?

MRS GASCOIGNE: That's what I say. If th' woman ca's for th' piper, th' woman maun pay th' tune.

MRS PURDY: Not but what——

JOE: It's a nasty business.

MRS GASCOIGNE: Nasty or not, it's hers now, not mine. He's *her* husband. "My son's my son till he takes him a wife," an' no longer. Now let her answer for it.

MRS PURDY: An' you think I'd better go when they're both in?

MRS GASCOIGNE: I should go to-night, atween six an' seven, that's what I should do.

JOE: I never should. If I was you, I'd settle it wi'out Minnie's knowin'—it's bad enough.

MRS GASCOIGNE: What's bad enough?

JOE: Why, that.

MRS GASCOIGNE: What?

JOE: Him an' 'er—it's bad enough as it is.

MRS GASCOIGNE (*with great bitterness*): Then let it be a bit worse, let it be a bit worse. Let her have it, then; it'll do her good. Who is she, to trample eggs that another hen would sit warm? No— Mrs Purdy, *give* it her. It'll take her down a peg or two, and, my sirs, she wants it, my sirs, she needs it!

JOE (*muttering*): A fat lot o' good it'll do.

MRS GASCOIGNE: What has thee ter say, I should like to know? Fed an' clothed an' coddled, tha art, an' not a thing tha lacks. But wait till I'm gone, my lad; tha'lt know what I've done for thee, then, tha will.

JOE: For a' that, it's no good 'er knowin'.

MRS GASCOIGNE: Isna it?—isna it? If it's not good for 'er, it's good for 'im.

JOE: I dunna believe it.

MRS GASCOIGNE: Who asked *thee* to believe it? Tha's showed thysen a wise man *this* day, hasn't ter? Wheer should ter be terday but for me? Wheer should ter iver ha' bin? An' then *tha* sits up for to talk. It ud look better o' thee not to spit i' th' hand as holds thy bread an' butter.

JOE: Neither do I.

MRS GASCOIGNE: Doesn't ter! Tha has a bit too much chelp an' chunter. It doesna go well, my lad. Tha wor blortin' an' bletherin' down at th' office a bit sin', an' a mighty fool tha made o' thysen. How should thee like to go home wi' *thy* tale o' to-day, to Minnie, might I ax thee?

JOE: If she didna like it, she could lump it.

MRS GASCOIGNE: It 'ud be thee as 'ud lump, my lad. But what does thee know about it? 'Er's rip th' guts out on thee like a tiger, an' stan' grinnin' at thee when tha shrivelled up 'cause tha'd no inside left.

MRS PURDY: She looks it, I must admit—every bit of it.

JOE: For a' that, it's no good her knowing.

MRS GASCOIGNE: Well, I say it *is*—an' thee, tha shiftly little know-all, as blorts at one minute like a suckin' calf an' th' next blethers like a hass, dunna thee come layin' th' law down to me, for I know better. No, Mrs Purdy, it's no good comin' to me. You've a right to some compensation, an' that lass o' yours has; but let them as cooked the goose eat it, that's all. Let him arrange it hisself—an' if he does nothink, put him i' court, that's all.

MRS PURDY: He's not goin' scot-free, you may back your life o' that.

MRS GASCOIGNE: You go down to-night atween six an' seven, an' let 'em have it straight. You know where they live?

MRS PURDY: I' Simson Street?

MRS GASCOIGNE: About four houses up—next Holbrooks.

MRS PURDY *(rising)*: Yes.

JOE: An' it'll do no good. Gie me th' money, Mother; I'll pay it.

MRS GASCOIGNE: Tha wunna!

JOE: I've a right to th' money—I've addled it.

MRS GASCOIGNE: A' right—an' I've saved it for thee. But tha has none on't till tha knocks me down an' ta'es it out o' my pocket.

MRS PURDY: No—let them pay themselves. It's not thy childt, is it?

JOE: It isna—but the money is.

MRS GASCOIGNE: We'll see.

MRS PURDY: Well, I mun get back. Thank yer, missis.

MRS GASCOIGNE: And thank *you*! I'll come down to-morrow—at dark hour.

MRS PURDY: Thank yer.—I hope yer arm'll soon be better.

JOE: Thank yer.

MRS GASCOIGNE: I'll come down to-morrow. You'll go to-night—atween six an' seven?

MRS PURDY: Yes—if it mun be done, it mun. He took his own way, she took hers, now I mun take mine. Well, good afternoon. I mun see about th' mester's dinner.

JOE: And you haven't said nothink to nobody?

MRS PURDY: I haven't—I shouldn't be flig, should I?

JOE: No—I should keep it quiet as long's you can.

MRS GASCOIGNE: There's no need for a' th' world to know—but them as is concerned maun abide by it.

MRS PURDY: Well, good afternoon.

MRS GASCOIGNE: Good afternoon.

JOE: Good afternoon.

> *Exit* MRS PURDY.

Well, that's a winder!

MRS GASCOIGNE: Serve her right, for tip-callin' wi'm all those years.

JOE: She niver ought to know.

MRS GASCOIGNE: I—I could fetch thee a wipe ower th' face, I could!

> *He sulks. She is in a rage.*

SCENE II

The kitchen of LUTHER GASCOIGNE'S *new home.*

> *It is pretty—in "cottage" style; rush-bottomed chairs, black oak-bureau, brass candlesticks, delft, etc. Green cushions in chairs. Towards five o'clock. Firelight. It is growing dark.*
>
> MINNIE GASCOIGNE *is busy about the fire: a tall, good-looking young woman, in a shirt-blouse and dark skirt, and apron. She lifts lids of saucepans, etc., hovers impatiently, looks at clock, begins to trim lamp.*

MINNIE: I wish he'd come. If I didn't want him, he'd be here half-an-hour since. But just because I've got a pudding that wants eating on the tick . . . ! He—he's *never* up to the cratch; he never is. As if the day wasn't long enough!

> *Sound of footsteps. She seizes a saucepan, and is rushing towards the door. The latch has clacked.* LUTHER *appears in the doorway, in his pit-dirt—a collier of medium height, with*

fair moustache. He has a red scarf knotted round his throat, and a cap with a Union medal. The two almost collide.

LUTHER: My word, you're on the hop!

MINNIE *(disappearing into scullery)*: You *nearly* made me drop the saucepan. Why are you so late?

LUTHER: I'm non late, am I?

MINNIE: You're twenty minutes later than yesterday.

LUTHER: Oh ah, I stopped finishing a stint, an' com up wi' a'most th' last batch.

He takes a tin bottle and a dirty calico snap-bag out of his pocket, puts them on the bureau; goes into the scullery.

MINNIE'S VOICE: No!

She comes hurrying out with the saucepan. In a moment, LUTHER *follows. He has taken off his coat and cap, his heavy trousers are belted round his hips, his arms are bare to above the elbow, because the pit-singlet of thick flannel is almost sleeveless.*

LUTHER: Tha *art* throng!

MINNIE *(at the fire, flushed)*: Yes, and everything's ready, and will be spoiled.

LUTHER: Then we'd better eat it afore I wash me.

MINNIE: No—no—it's not nice——

LUTHER: Just as ter's a mind—but there's scarce a collier in a thousand washes hissen afore he has his dinner. We niver did a-whoam.

MINNIE: But it doesn't look nice.

LUTHER: Eh, wench, tha'lt soon get used ter th' looks on me. A bit o' dirt's like a veil on my face—I shine through th' 'andsomer. What hast got? *(He peers over her range.)*

MINNIE *(waving a fork)*: You're not to look.

LUTHER: It smells good.

MINNIE: Are you *going* to have your dinner like that?

LUTHER: Ay, lass—just for once.

He spreads a newspaper in one of the green-cushioned arm-chairs and sits down. She disappears into the scullery with a saucepan. He takes off his great pit-boots. She sets a soup-tureen on the table, and lights the lamp. He watches her face in the glow.

Tha'rt non bad-luikin' when ter's a mind.

MINNIE: *When* have I a mind?

LUTHER: Tha's allers a mind—but when ter lights th' lamp tha'rt i' luck's way.

MINNIE: Come on, then.

He drags his chair to the table.

LUTHER: I s'll ha'e ter ha'e a newspaper afront on me, or thy cloth'll be a blackymoor. *(Begins disarranging the pots.)*

MINNIE: Oh, you *are* a nuisance! *(Jumps up.)*

LUTHER: I can put 'em a' back again.

MINNIE: I know your puttings back.

LUTHER: Tha couldna get married by thysen, could ter?—so tha'lt ha'e ter ma'e th' best on me.

MINNIE: But you're such a bother—never here at the right time—never doing the right thing——

LUTHER: An' my mouth's ter wide an' my head's ter narrow. Shalt iver ha' come ter th' end of my faults an' failin's?

MINNIE *(giving him soup)*: I wish I could.

LUTHER: An' now tha'lt snap mu head off 'cos I slobber, shanna tha?

MINNIE: Then don't slobber.

LUTHER: I'll try my luck. What hast bin doin' a' day?

MINNIE: Working.

LUTHER: Has our Joe bin in?

MINNIE: No. I rather thought he might, but he hasn't.

LUTHER: You've not been up home?

MINNIE: To your mother's? No, what should I go there for?

LUTHER: Eh, I dunno what ter should go for—I thought tha 'appen might.

MINNIE: But what for?

LUTHER: Nay—I niver thowt nowt about what for.

MINNIE: Then why did you ask me?

LUTHER: I dunno. *(A pause.)*

MINNIE: Your mother can come here, can't she?

LUTHER: Ay, she can come. Tha'll be goin' up wi' me to-night—I want ter go an' see about our Joe.

MINNIE: What about him?

LUTHER: How he went on about's club money. Shall ter come wi' me?

MINNIE: I wanted to do my curtains.

LUTHER : But tha's got a' day to do them in.

MINNIE : But I want to do them to-night—I feel like it.

LUTHER : A' right.—I shanna be long, at any rate.

(*A pause.*)

What dost keep lookin' at?

MINNIE : How?

LUTHER : Tha keeps thy eye on me rarely.

MINNIE *(laughing)* : It's your mouth—it looks *so* red and bright, in your black face.

LUTHER : Does it look nasty to thee?

MINNIE : No—no-o.

LUTHER *(pushing his moustache, laughing)* : It ma'es you look like a nigger, i' your pit-dirt—th' whites o' your eyes!

MINNIE : Just.

She gets up to take his plate; goes and stands beside him. He lifts his face to her.

I want to see if I can see you; you look so different.

LUTHER : Tha can see me well enough. Why dost want to?

MINNIE : It's almost like having a stranger.

LUTHER : Would ter rather?

MINNIE : What?

LUTHER : Ha'e a stranger?

MINNIE : What for?

LUTHER : Hao—I dunno.

MINNIE *(touching his hair)* : You look rather nice—an' your hair's so dirty.

LUTHER : Gi'e me a kiss.

MINNIE : But where? You're all grime.

LUTHER : I'm sure I've licked my mouth clean.

MINNIE *(stooping suddenly, and kissing him)* : You don't look nearly such a tame rabbit, in your pit-dirt.

LUTHER *(catching her in his arms)* : Dunna I? *(Kisses her.)* What colour is my eyes?

MINNIE : Bluey-grey.

LUTHER : An' thine's grey an' black.

MINNIE : Mind! *(She looks at her blouse when he releases her.)*

LUTHER *(timid)* : Have I blacked it?

MINNIE : A bit.

She goes to the scullery; returns with another dish.

LUTHER: They talkin' about comin' out again

MINNIE *(returning)*: Good laws!—they've no need.

LUTHER: They are, though.

MINNIE: It's a holiday they want.

LUTHER: Nay, it isna. They want th' proper scale here, just as they ha'e it ivrywhere else.

MINNIE: But if the seams are thin, and the company can't afford.

LUTHER: They can afford a' this gret new electric plant; they can afford to build new houses for managers, an' ter give blo— ter give Frazer twelve hundred a year.

MINNIE: If they want a good manager to make the pits pay, they have to give him a good salary.

LUTHER: So's he can clip down our wages.

MINNIE: Why, what are yours clipped down?

LUTHER: Mine isn't, but there's plenty as is.

MINNIE: And will this strike make a butty of you?

LUTHER: You don't strike to get made a butty on.

MINNIE: Then how *do* you do it? You're thirty-one.

LUTHER: An' there's many as owd as me as is day-men yet.

MINNIE: But there's more that aren't, that are butties.

LUTHER: Ay, they've had luck.

MINNIE: Luck! You mean they've had some *go* in them.

LUTHER: Why, what can I do more than I am doin'?

MINNIE: It isn't what you do, it's how you do it. Sluther through any job; get to th' end of it, no matter how. That's you.

LUTHER: I hole a stint as well as any man.

MINNIE: Then I back it takes you twice as long.

LUTHER: Nay, nor that neither.

MINNIE: I *know* you're not much of a workman—I've heard it from other butties, that you never put your heart into anything.

LUTHER: Who hast heard it fra?

MINNIE: From those that know. And I could ha' told it *them*, for I know you. You'll be a day-man at seven shillings a day till the end of your life—and you'll be satisfied, so long as you can shilly-shally through. That's what your mother did for you— mardin' you up till you were all mard-soft.

LUTHER: Tha's got a lot ter say a' of a suddin. Thee shut thy mouth.

MINNIE: You've been dragged round at your mother's apron-strings, all the lot of you, till there isn't half a man among you.

LUTHER : Tha seems fond enough of our Joe.

MINNIE : He is th' best in the bunch.

LUTHER : Tha should ha' married him, then.

MINNIE : I shouldn't have had to ask *him*, if he was ready.

LUTHER : I'd axed thee twice afore—tha knowed tha could ha'e it when ter wanted.

MINNIE : *Axed* me! It was like asking me to pull out a tooth for you.

LUTHER : Yi, an' it felt like it

MINNIE : What?

LUTHER : Axin' thee to marry me. I'm blessed if it didna feel like axin' the doctor to pull ten teeth out of a stroke.

MINNIE : And then you expect me to have you!

LUTHER : Well, tha *has* done, whether or not.

MINNIE : I—yes, I had to fetch you, like a mother fetches a kid from school. A pretty sight you looked. Didn't your mother give you a ha'penny to spend, to get you to go?

LUTHER : No; she spent it for me.

MINNIE : She would! She wouldn't even let you spend your own ha'penny. You'd have lost it, or let somebody take it from you.

LUTHER : Yi. Thee.

MINNIE : Me!—me take anything from you! Why, you've got nothing worth having.

LUTHER : I dunno—tha seems ter think so sometimes.

MINNIE : Oh! Shilly-shally and crawl, that's all you can do. You ought to have stopped with your mother.

LUTHER : I should ha' done, if tha hadna hawksed me out.

MINNIE : You aren't *fit* for a woman to have married, you're not.

LUTHER : Then why did thee marry me? It wor thy doin's.

MINNIE : Because I could get nobody better.

LUTHER : I'm more class than I thought for, then.

MINNIE : Are you! Are you!

    JOE'S *voice is heard.*

JOE : I'm comin' in, you two, so stop snaggin' an' snarlin'.

LUTHER : Come in; 'er'll 'appen turn 'er tap on thee.

    JOE *enters.*

JOE : Are you eatin' yet?

LUTHER : Ay—it ta'es 'er that long ter tell my sins. Tha's just come right for puddin'. Get thee a plate outer t'cupboard—an' a spoon outer t'basket.

JOE *(at the cupboard)*: You've got ivrythink tip-top. What should ter do if I broke thee a plate, Minnie?

MINNIE: I should break another over your head.

He deliberately drops and smashes a plate. She flushes crimson.

LUTHER: Well, I'm glad it worna me.

JOE: I'm that clumsy wi' my left 'and, Minnie! Why doesna ter break another ower my head?

LUTHER *(rising and putting pudding on a plate)*: Here, ta'e this an' sit thee down.

His brother seats himself.

Hold thy knees straight, an' for God's sake dunna thee break this. Can ter manage?

JOE: I reckon so. If I canna, Minnie'll feed me wi' a spoon. Shonna ter?

MINNIE: Why did you break my plate?

JOE: Nay, I didna break it—it wor the floor.

MINNIE: You did it on purpose.

JOE: How could I? I didn't say ter th' floor: "Break thou this plate, O floor!"

MINNIE: You have no right.

JOE *(addressing the floor)*: Tha'd no right to break that plate—dost hear? I'd a good mind ter drop a bit o' puddin' on thy face.

He balances the spoon; the plate slides down from his knee, smash into the fender.

MINNIE *(screams)*: It's my best service! *(Begins to sob.)*

LUTHER: Nay, our Joe!

JOE: 'Er's no occasions ter scraight. I bought th' service an' I can get th' plates matched. What's her grizzlin' about?

MINNIE: I shan't ask you to get them matched.

JOE: Dunna thee, an' then tha runs no risk o' bein' denied.

MINNIE: What have you come here like this for?

JOE: I haena come here like this. I come ter tell yer our Harriet says, would yer mind goin' an' tellin' 'er what she can do with that childt's coat, as she's made a' wrong. If you'd looked slippy, I'd ha' ta'en yer ter th' Cinematograph after. But, dearly-beloved

brethren, let us weep; these our dear departed dinner-plates . . .
Come, Minnie, drop a tear as you pass by.

LUTHER *(to* MINNIE) : Tha needna fret, Minnie, they can easy be
matched again.

MINNIE : You're just pleased to see him make a fool of me, aren't
you?

LUTHER : He's non made a fool o' thee—tha's made a fool o' thysen, scraightin' an' carryin' on.

JOE : It's a fact, Minnie. Nay, let me kiss thee better.

> *She has risen, with shut face.*
>
> *He approaches with outstretched left arm. She swings round,
> fetches him a blow over his upper right arm. He bites his
> lip with pain.*

LUTHER *(rising)* : Has it hurt thee, lad? Tha shouldna fool wi' her.

> MINNIE *watches the two brothers with tears of mortification
> in her eyes. Then she throws off her apron, pins on her hat,
> puts on her coat, and is marching out of the house.*

LUTHER : Are you going to Harriet's?

JOE : I'll come and fetch you in time for th' Cinematograph.

> *The door is heard to bang.*

JOE *(picking up broken fragments of plates)* : That's done it.

LUTHER : It's bad luck—ne'er mind. How art goin' on?

JOE : Oh, alright.

LUTHER : What about thy club money?

JOE : They wunna gi'e't me. But, I say, sorry—tha'rt for it.

LUTHER : Ay—I dunno what 'er married me for, f'r it's nowt bu'
fault she finds wi' me, from th' minnit I come i' th' house to th'
minnit I leave it.

JOE : Dost wish tha'd niver done it?—niver got married?

LUTHER *(sulky)* : I dunno—sometimes.

JOE *(with tragic emphasis)* : Then it's the blasted devil!

LUTHER: I dunno—I'm married to 'er, an' she's married to me, so
she can pick holes i' me as much as she likes——

JOE : As a rule, she's nice enough wi' me.

LUTHER : She's nice wi' ivrybody but me.

JOE : An' dost ter care?

LUTHER : Ay—I do.

JOE : Why doesn't ter go out an' leave her?

LUTHER : I dunno.

JOE: By the Lord, she'd cop it if I had 'er.
    Pause.
LUTHER: I wor comin' up to-night.
JOE: I thought tha would be. But there's Mrs Purdy comin' ter see thee.
LUTHER: There's who?
JOE: Mrs Purdy. Didna ter ha'e a bit of a go wi' their Bertha, just afore Minnie wrote thee?
LUTHER: Ay. Why?
JOE: 'Er mother says she's wi' childt by thee. She come up ter my mother this afternoon, an' said she wor comin' here to-night.
LUTHER: Says what?
JOE: Says as their Bertha's goin' ter ha'e a child, an' 'er lays it on ter thee.
LUTHER: Oh, my good God!
JOE: Isna it right?
LUTHER: It's right if 'er says so.
JOE: Then it's the blasted devil! *(A pause.)* So I come on here ter see if I could get Minnie to go up to our Harriet.
LUTHER: Oh, my good God!
JOE: I thought, if we could keep it from 'er, we might settle summat, an' 'er niver know.
LUTHER *(slowly)*: My God alive!
JOE: She said she'd hush it up, an' lay it ont'r a electrician as laid th' cable, an' is gone goodness knows where—make an arrangement, for forty pound.
LUTHER *(thoughtfully)*: I wish I wor struck dead.
JOE: Well, tha arena', an' so tha'd better think about it. My mother said as Minnie ought to know, but I say diff'rent, an' if Mrs Purdy doesna tell her, nobody need.
LUTHER: I wish I wor struck dead. I wish a ton o' rock 'ud fa' on me to-morrer.
JOE: It wunna for wishin'.
LUTHER: My good God!
JOE: An' so—I'll get thee forty quid, an' lend it thee. When Mrs Purdy comes, tell her she shall ha'e twenty quid this day week, an' twenty quid a year from now, if thy name's niver been mentioned. I believe 'er's a clat-fart.

LUTHER : Me a childt by Bertha Purdy! But—but what's that for—
now there's Minnie?

JOE : I dunno what it's for, but theer it is, as I'm tellin' thee. I'll
stop for another haef an hour, an' if 'er doesna come, than mun
see to 'er by thysen.

LUTHER : 'Er'll be back afore ha'ef an hour's up. Tha mun go an'
stop 'er . . . I—I niver meant—— Look here, our Joe, I—if I—
if she—if she—— My God, what have I done now!

JOE : We can stop her from knowin'.

LUTHER *(looking round)* : She'll be comin' back any minnit. Nay, I
niver meant t'r ha'. Joe . . .

JOE : What?

LUTHER : She—she——

JOE : 'Er niver ned know.

LUTHER : Ah, but though . . .

JOE : What?

LUTHER : I—I—I've *done* it.

JOE : Well, it might ha' happened t'r anybody.

LUTHER : But when 'er knows—an' it's *me* as has done it . . .

JOE : It wouldn't ha' mattered o' anyhow, if it had bin sumb'dy else.
But tha knows what ter's got ter say. Arena' ter goin' ter wesh
thee? Go an' get th' panchion.

LUTHER *(rising)* : 'Er'll be comin' in any minnit.

JOE : Get thee weshed, man.

LUTHER *(fetching a bucket and lading-can from the scullery, and
emptying water from the boiler)* : Go an' ta'e 'er somewhere,
while Mrs Purdy goes, sholl ter?

JOE : D'rectly. Tha heered what I telled thee?

> *There is a noise of splashing in the scullery. Then a knock.*
> JOE *goes to the door. He is heard saying "Come in."*
> *Enter* MRS PURDY.

MRS PURDY : I hope I've not come a-mealtimes.

JOE : No, they've finished. Minnie's gone up t'r our Harriet's.

MRS PURDY : Thank the Lord for small mercies—for I didn't fancy
sittin' an' tellin' her about our Bertha.

JOE : We dunna want 'er ter know. Sit thee down.

MRS PURDY : I'm of that mind, mester, I am. As I said, what's th'
good o' jackin' up a young married couple? For it won't unmarry

'em nor ma'e things right. An' yet, my long lass oughtner ter bear a' th' brunt.

JOE: Well, an' 'er isna goin' to.

MRS PURDY: Is that Mester weshin'?

JOE: Ah.

MRS PURDY: 'As ter towd him?

JOE: Ah.

MRS PURDY: Well, it's none o' my wishin's, I'm sure o' that. Eh, dear, you've bin breakin' th' crockery a'ready!

JOE: Yes, that's me, bein' wallit.

MRS PURDY: T-t-t! So this is 'ow she fancied it?

JOE: Ah, an' it non luiks bad, does it?

MRS PURDY: Very natty. Very nice an' natty.

JOE *(taking up the lamp)*: Come an' look at th' parlour.

> JOE *and* MRS PURDY *exit R.*

MRS PURDY'S VOICE: Yis—yis—it's nice an' plain. But a bit o' red plush is 'andsomer, to my mind. It's th'old-fashioned style, like! My word, but them three ornyments is gaudy-lookin'.

JOE: An' they reckon they're worth five pound. 'Er mester gen 'em 'er.

MRS PURDY: I'd rather had th' money.

JOE: Ah, me an' a'.

> *During this time,* LUTHER *has come hurrying out of the scullery into the kitchen, rubbing his face with a big roller-towel. He is naked to the waist. He kneels with his knees on the fender, sitting on his heels, rubbing himself. His back is not washed. He rubs his hair dry.*

> *Enter* JOE, *with the lamp, followed by* MRS PURDY.

MRS PURDY: It's uncommon, very uncommon, Mester Gaskin—and looks well, too, for them as likes it. But it hardly goes wi' my fancy, somehow, startin' wi' second-hand, owd-fashioned stuff. You dunno *who's* sotten themselves on these 'ere chairs, now, do you?

LUTHER: It ma'es no diff'rence to me who's sot on 'em an' who 'asna.

MRS PURDY: No—you get used to'm.

LUTHER *(to* JOE): Shall thee go up t'r our Harriet's?

JOE: If ter's a mind. *(Takes up his cap. To* MRS PURDY): An' you two can settle as best you can.

MRS PURDY: Yes—yes. I'm not one for baulkin' mysen an' cuttin'
off my nose ter spite my face.

> LUTHER *has finished wiping himself. He takes a shifting shirt
> from the bureau, and struggles into it; then goes into the
> scullery.*

JOE: An' you sure you'll keep it quiet, missis?

MRS PURDY: Am I goin' bletherin' up street an' down street, think
yer?

JOE: An' dunna tell your Bob.

MRS PURDY: I've more sense. There's not a word 'e 'ears a-whoam
as is of any count, for out it 'ud leak when he wor canned. Yes,
my guyney—we know what our mester is.

> *Re-enter* LUTHER, *in shirt and black trousers. He drops his
> pit-trousers and singlet beside the hearth.*

> MRS PURDY *bends down and opens his pit-trousers.*

MRS PURDY: Nay, if ter drops 'em of a heap, they niver goin' ter
get dry an' cosy. Tha sweats o' th' hips, as my lads did.

LUTHER: Well, go thy ways, Joe.

JOE: Ay—well—good luck. An' good night, Mrs Purdy.

MRS PURDY: Good night.

> *Exit* JOE.

> *There are several moments of silence.*

> LUTHER *puts the broken pots on the table.*

MRS PURDY: It's sad work, Mester Gaskin, f'r a' on us.

LUTHER: Ay.

MRS PURDY: I left that long lass o' mine fair gaunt, fair chalked
of a line, I did, poor thing. Not bu' what 'er should 'a 'ad more
sense.

LUTHER: Ah!

MRS PURDY: But it's no use throwin' good words after bad deeds.
Not but what it's a nasty thing for yer t'r 'a done, it is—an' yer
can scarce look your missis i' th' face again, I should think.
(Pause.) But I says t'r our Bertha, "It's his'n, an' he mun pay!"
Eh, but how 'er did but scraight an' cry. It fair turned me ower.
"Dunna go to 'm, Mother," 'er says, "dunna go to 'm for to tell
him!" "Yi," I says, "right's right—tha doesna get off wi' nowt,
nor shall 'e neither. 'E wor but a scamp to do such a thing," I
says, yes, I did. For you was older nor 'er. Not but what she was
old enough ter ha'e more sense. But 'er wor allers one o' th' come-

day go-day sort, as 'ud gi'e th' clothes off 'er back an' niver know 'er wor nek'd—a gra't soft looney as she is, an' serves 'er right for bein' such a gaby. Yi, an' I believe 'er wor fond on thee—if a wench can be fond of a married man. For one blessing, 'er doesna know what 'er wor an' what 'er worn't. For they mau talk o' bein' i' love—but you non in love wi' onybody, wi'out they's a chance o' their marryin' you—howiver much you may like 'em. An' I'm thinkin', th' childt'll set 'er up again when it comes, for 'er's gone that wezzel-brained an' doited, I'm sure! An' it's a mort o' trouble for me, mester, a sight o' trouble it is. Not as I s'll be hard on 'er. She knowed I wor comin' 'ere to-night, an's not spoke a word for hours. I left 'er sittin' on th' sofey hangin' 'er 'ead. But it's a weary business, mester, an' nowt ter be proud on. I s'd think tha wishes tha'd niver clapt eyes on our Bertha.

LUTHER *(thinking hard)*: I dunna—I dunna. An' I dunna wish as I'd niver seen 'er, no, I dunna. 'Er liked me, an' I liked 'er.

MRS PURDY: An' 'appen, but for this 'ere marriage o' thine, tha'd 'a married 'er.

LUTHER: Ah, I should. F'r 'er liked me, an' 'er worna neither nice nor near, nor owt else, an' 'er'd bin fond o' me.

MRS PURDY: 'Er would, an' it's a thousand pities. But what's done's done.

LUTHER: Ah, I know that.

MRS PURDY: An' as for yer missis——

LUTHER: 'Er mun do as 'er likes.

MRS PURDY: But tha'rt not for tellin' 'er?

LUTHER: 'Er—'er'll know some time or other.

MRS PURDY: Nay, nay, 'er nedna. You married now, lad, an' you canna please yoursen.

LUTHER: It's a fact.

MRS PURDY: An' Lizzy Stapleton, she had forty pound wi' 'er lad, an' it's not as if you hadn't got money. An' to be sure, we've none.

LUTHER: No, an' I've none.

MRS PURDY: Yes, you've some atween you—an'—well . . .

LUTHER: I can get some.

MRS PURDY: Then what do you say?

LUTHER: I say as Bertha's welcome t'r any forty pounds, if I'd got

it. For—for—missis, she wor better to me than iver my wife's
bin.

MRS PURDY *(frightened by his rage)*: Niver, lad!

LUTHER: She wor—ah but though she wor. She thought a lot on me.

MRS PURDY: An' so I'm sure your missis does. She naggles thy heart
out, maybe. But that's just the wrigglin' a place out for hersen.
She'll settle down comfortable, lad,

LUTHER *(bitterly)*: Will she!

MRS PURDY: Yi—yi. An' tha's done 'er a crewel wrong, my lad.
An' tha's done my gel one as well. For, though she was old
enough to know better, yet she's good-hearted and trusting, an'
'ud gi'e 'er shoes off 'er feet. An' tha's landed 'er, tha knows. For
it's not th' bad women as 'as bastards nowadays—they've a sight
too much gumption. It's fools like our'n—poor thing.

LUTHER: I've done everything that was bad, I know that.

MRS PURDY: Nay—nay—young fellers, they are like that. But it's
wrong, for look at my long lass sittin' theer on that sofey, as if
'er back wor broke.

LUTHER *(loudly)*: But I dunna wish I'd niver seen 'er, I dunna. It
wor—it wor—she wor good to me, she wor, an' I dunna wish
I'd niver done it.

MRS PURDY: Then tha ought, that's a'. For I do—an' 'er does.

LUTHER: Does 'er say 'er wishes 'er'd niver seen me?

MRS PURDY: 'Er says nowt o' nohow.

LUTHER: Then 'er doesna wish it. An' I wish I'd ha' married 'er.

MRS PURDY: Come, my lad, come. Married tha art——

LUTHER *(bitterly)*: Married I am, an' I wish I worna. Your Bertha
'er'd 'a thought a thousand times more on me than *she* does. But
I'm wrong, wrong, wrong, i' ivry breath I take. An' I will be
wrong, yi, an' I *will* be wrong.

MRS PURDY: Hush thee—there's somebody comin'.

    They wait.

    Enter JOE *and* MINNIE, JOE *talking loudly.*

MINNIE: No, you've not, you've no right at all. *(To* LUTHER*)*:
Haven't you even cleared away? *(To* MRS PURDY*)*: Good evening.

MRS PURDY: Good evenin', missis. I was just goin'—I've bin sayin'
it looks very nice, th' 'ouse.

MINNIE: Do you think so?

MRS PURDY: I do, indeed.

MINNIE : Don't notice of the mess we're in, shall you? *He (pointing to* JOE) broke the plates—and then I had to rush off up to Mrs Preston's afore I could clear away. And he hasn't even mended the fire.

LUTHER : I can do—I niver noticed.

MINNIE *(to* MRS PURDY): Have a piece of cake? *(Goes to cupboard.)*

MRS PURDY : No, thanks, no, thanks. I mun get off afore th' Co-op shuts up. Thank yer very much. Well—good night, all.

JOE *opens the door;* MRS PURDY *goes out.*

MINNIE *(bustling, clearing away as* LUTHER *comes in with coals):* Did you settle it?

LUTHER : What?

MINNIE : What she'd come about.

LUTHER : Ah.

MINNIE : An' I bet you'll go and forget.

LUTHER : Oh ah!

MINNIE : And poor old Bob Purdy will go on just the same.

LUTHER : Very likely.

MINNIE : Don't let the dust all go on the hearth. Why didn't you clear away? The house was like a pigsty for her to come into.

LUTHER : Then I wor the pig.

MINNIE *(halting)*: Why—who's trod on your tail now?

LUTHER : There'd be nobody to tread on it if tha wor out.

MINNIE : Oh—oh, dearo' me. *(To* JOE): I think we'd better go to· the Cinematograph, and leave him to nurse his sore tail.

JOE : We better had.

LUTHER : An' joy go with yer.

MINNIE : We certainly shan't leave it at home. *(To* JOE): What time does it begin?

JOE : Seven o'clock.

MINNIE : And I want to call in Sisson's shop. Shall you go with me, or wouldn't you condescend to go shopping with me? *(She has cleared the table, brought a tray and a bowl, and is washing up the pots.)*

JOE : Dost think I'm daunted by Polly Sisson?

MINNIE : You're braver than most men if you dare go in a shop. Here, take a towel and wipe these pots.

JOE : How can I?

MINNIE: If you were a gentleman, you'd hold the plates in your teeth to wipe them.

JOE: Tha wouldna look very ladylike at th' end on't.

MINNIE: Why?

JOE: Why, hast forgot a'ready what a shine tha kicked up when I broke them two other plates? *(He has got a towel, and wedging a plate against his thighs, is laboriously wiping it.)*

MINNIE: I never kicked up a shine. It *is* nice of you!

JOE: What?

MINNIE: To do this for me.

    LUTHER *has begun sweeping the hearth.*

JOE: Tha's got two servants.

MINNIE: But I'm sure you want to smoke while you're doing it—don't you now?

JOE: Sin' tha says so. *(Fumbles in his pocket.)*

MINNIE *(hastily wiping her hands, puts a cigarette between his lips—gets matches from the mantelpiece, ignoring her husband, who is kneeling sweeping the hearth—lights his cigarette)*: It's so nice to have a lamed man. You feel you've got an excuse for making a fuss of him. You've got awfully nice eyes and eyebrows. I like dark eyes.

JOE: Oh ah!

    LUTHER *rises hastily, goes in the passage, crosses the room quietly. He wears his coat, a red scarf and a cap.*

MINNIE: There's more go in them than in blue. *(Watches her husband go out. There is silence between the two.)*

JOE: He'll come round again.

MINNIE: He'll have to. He'll go on sulking now. *(Her face breaks.)* You—you don't know how hard it is.

JOE: What?

MINNIE *(crying a few fierce tears)*: This . . .

JOE *(aghast)*: What?

MINNIE: Why—you don't know. You don't know how hard it is, with a man as—as leaves you alone all the time.

JOE: But—he niver hardly goes out.

MINNIE: No, but—you don't know—he leaves me alone, he always has done—and there's nobody . . .

JOE: But he . . .

MINNIE: He never trusts me—he leaves me so alone—and—*(a little*

burst of tears) it *is* hard! *(She changes suddenly.)* You've wiped
your plates; my word, you are a champion.

JOE: I think so an' a'.

MINNIE: I hope the pictures will be jolly—but the sad ones make
me laugh more, don't they you?

JOE: I canna do wi' 'em.

CURTAIN

ACT II

The same evening—eleven o'clock. LUTHER'S *house.*

> MINNIE, *alone, weeping. She gets up, fills the kettle, puts it on the hob, sits down, weeps again; then hears somebody coming, dries her eyes swiftly, turns the lamp low.*
> Enter LUTHER. *He stands in the doorway—is rather tipsy; flings his cap down, sits in his chair, lurching it slightly. Neither speaks for some moments.*

LUTHER: Well, did yer like yer pictures?

MINNIE: Where have you been?

LUTHER: What does it matter where I've been?

MINNIE: Have you been drinking?

LUTHER: What's it matter if I have?

MINNIE: It matters a lot to me

LUTHER: Oh ah!

MINNIE: Do you think I'm going to sleep with a man who is half-drunk?

LUTHER: Nay, I non know who tha'rt goin' ter sleep wi'.

MINNIE *(rising)*: I shall make the bed in the other room.

LUTHER: Tha's no 'casions. I s'll do very nicely on t' sofa; it's warmer.

MINNIE: Oh, you can have your own bed.

LUTHER: If tha doesna sleep in it, I dunna.

MINNIE: And if *you do*, I don't.

LUTHER: Tha pleases thysen. Tha can sleep by thysen for iver, if ter's a mind to't.

MINNIE *(who has stood hesitating)*: Oh, very well!

> *She goes upstairs, returns immediately with a pillow and two blankets, which she throws on the sofa.*

LUTHER: Thank yer kindly.

MINNIE: Shall you rake?

LUTHER: I'll rake.

> *She moves about; lays table for his morning's breakfast: a newspaper, cup, plate, etc.—no food, because it would go dry;*

rinses his tin pit-bottle, puts it and his snap-bag on the table.
I could do it for mysen. Tha ned do nowt for me.

MINNIE: Why this sudden fit of unselfishness?

LUTHER: I niver want thee to do nowt for me, niver no more. No, not so much as lift a finger for me—not if I wor dyin'.

MINNIE: You're not dying; you're only tipsy.

LUTHER: Well, it's no matter to thee what I am.

MINNIE: It's very comfortable for you to think so.

LUTHER: I know nowt about that.

MINNIE *(after a pause)*: Where have you been to-night?

LUTHER: There an' back, to see how far it is.

MINNIE *(making an effort)*: Have you been up to your mother's?

LUTHER: Where I've bin, I've bin, and where I haven't, I haven't.

MINNIE: Pah!—you needn't try to magnify it and make a mountain. You've been to your mother's, and then to "The Ram".

LUTHER: All right—if tha knows, tha knows, an' theer's an end on't.

MINNIE: You talk like a fool.

LUTHER: That comes o' bein' a fool.

MINNIE: When were you a fool?

LUTHER: Ivry day o' my life, an' ivry breath I've ta'en.

MINNIE *(having finished work, sits down again)*: I suppose you haven't got it in you to say anything fresh.

LUTHER: Why, what dost want me ter say? *(He looks at her for the first time.)*

MINNIE *(with a queer catch)*: You might be more of a man if you said you were sorry.

LUTHER: Sorry! Sorry for what?

MINNIE: You've nothing to be sorry *for*, have you?

LUTHER *(looking at her, quickly)*: What art goin' ter say?

MINNIE: It's what are *you* going to say. *(A silence.)*

LUTHER *(doggedly)*: I'm goin' ter say nowt.

MINNIE *(bitterly)*: No, you're not *man* enough to say anything—you can only slobber. You do a woman a wrong, but you're never man enough to say you're sorry for it. You're *not* a man, you're not—you're something crawling!

LUTHER: I'm glad! I'm glad! I'm glad! No, an' I wouldna ta'e't back, no. 'Er wor nice wi' me, which is a thing tha's niver bin. An' so tha's got it, an' mun keep it.

MINNIE: Who was nice with you?

LUTHER: *She* was—an' would ha'e bin at this minnit, but for thee.

MINNIE: Pah!—you're not fit to have a wife. You only want your mother to rock you to sleep.

LUTHER: Neither mother, nor wife, neither thee nor onybody do I want—no—no.

MINNIE: No—you've had three cans of beer.

LUTHER: An' if ter niver sleeps i' th' bed wi' me again, an' if ter niver does a hand's turn for me niver no more, I'm glad, I'm glad. I non want thee. I non want ter see thee.

MINNIE: You mean coward. Good God! I never thought you were such a mean coward as this.

LUTHER: An' as for thy money—yi, I wouldna smell on't. An' neither thine, nor our Joe's, nor my mother's will I ha'e. What I addle's my own. What I gi'e thee, I gie thee. An' she maun ha'e ten shillin's a month, an' tha maun abide by't.

MINNIE: What are you talking about?

LUTHER: My mother wouldna gi'e me th' money. She says she's done her share. An' tha's done thine. An' I've done mine, begod. An' what yer canna chew yer maun swaller.

MINNIE: You must be quite drunk.

LUTHER: Must I? Alright, it's Dutch courage then. A'right, then Dutch courage it is. But I tell thee, tha does as ter's a mind. Tha can leave me, an' go back inter service, if ter wants. What's it ter me, if I'm but a lump o' suck i' th' 'ouse wheer tha art? Tha should ha' had our Joe—he's got more go than me. An' I should ha' had 'er. I'd got go enough for *her*; 'appen a bit too much.

MINNIE: Her? Who?

LUTHER: Her! An' I'm glad 'er's wi' my childt. I'm glad I did it. I'm glad! For tha's wiped tha feet on me enough. Yi, tha's wiped thy feet on me till what's it to me if tha does it or not? It isna! An' now—tha maun abide by what ter's got, tha maun. I s'll ha'e to—an' by plenty I hadna got I've abided. An' so—an' so— yi.

MINNIE: But who is it you—who is she?

LUTHER: Tha knowed a' along.

MINNIE: Who is it?

They are both silent.

Aren't you going to speak?

LUTHER: What's the good?

MINNIE *(coldly)*: But I must know.

LUTHER: Tha does know.

MINNIE: I can assure you I don't.

LUTHER: Then assure thysen an' find out.

    Another silence.

MINNIE: Do you mean somebody is going to have a baby by you?

LUTHER: I mean what I've said, an' I mean nowt else.

MINNIE: But you must tell me.

LUTHER: I've boiled my cabbage twice a'ready, hanna I?

MINNIE: Do you mean somebody is going to have a child by you?

LUTHER: Tha can chew it ower, if ter's a mind.

MINNIE *(helpless)*: But . . . *(She struggles with herself, then goes calm.)*

LUTHER: That's what I say—but . . . !

    A silence.

MINNIE: And who is she?

LUTHER: Thee, for a' I know.

MINNIE *(calmly, patiently)*: I asked you a question.

LUTHER: Ah—an' I 'eered thee.

MINNIE: Then answer me—who is she?

LUTHER: Tha knows well enow—tha knowed afore they'd towd, thee——

MINNIE: Nobody has told me. Who is she?

LUTHER: Well, tha's seed 'er mother.

MINNIE *(numb)*: Mrs Purdy?

LUTHER: Yi.

MINNIE: Their Bertha?

LUTHER: Yi.

    A silence.

MINNIE: Why didn't you tell me?

LUTHER: Tell thee what?

MINNIE: This.

LUTHER: Tha knowed afore I did.

MINNIE: I know *now*.

LUTHER: Me an' a'.

    A pause.

MINNIE: Didn't you know till to-night?

LUTHER: Our Joe told me when tha'd just gone—I niver dreamt afore—an' then 'er mother . . .

MINNIE: What did her mother come for?

LUTHER: Ter see if we could hush it up a'cause o' thee, an' gi'e 'er a lump sum.

MINNIE: Hush it up because of me?

LUTHER: Ah—lay it ont'r an electrician as wor wi' th' gang as laid th' cable down to Balford—he's gone God knows where.

MINNIE: But it's yours.

LUTHER: I know that.

MINNIE: Then why lay it onto somebody else?

LUTHER: Because o' thee.

MINNIE: But why because of me?

LUTHER: To stop thee knowin', I s'd think.

MINNIE: And why shouldn't I know?

LUTHER: Eh, I dunno.

   A pause.

MINNIE: And what were you going to do to stop me knowing?

LUTHER: 'Er axed for forty pounds down.

MINNIE: And if you paid forty pounds, you got off scot-free?

LUTHER: Summat so.

MINNIE: And where were the forty pounds coming from?

LUTHER: Our Joe said 'e'd lend 'em me. I thought my mother would, but 'er said 'er wouldna—neither would she gi'e't our Joe ter lend me, she said. For I wor a married man now, an' it behoved my wife to look after me. An' I thought tha knowed. I thought tha'd twigged, else bin telled. An' I didna care, an' dunna care.

MINNIE: And this is what you married me to!

LUTHER: This is what tha married me to. But I'll niver ax thee for, no, not so much as the liftin' of a finger—no——

MINNIE: But when you wrote and told me you were willing to marry me, why didn't you tell me this?

LUTHER: Because—as I've telled thee—I didna know till this very mortal night.

MINNIE: But you knew you'd been with her.

LUTHER: Ay, I knowed that.

   A pause.

MINNIE: And why didn't you tell me?

LUTHER : What for should I tell thee? What good would it ha' done thee? Tha niver towd *me* nowt.

MINNIE : So that is how you look at it?

LUTHER : I non care how I look at it.

A pause.

MINNIE : And was there anybody else?

LUTHER : How dost mean?

MINNIE : Have you been with any other woman?

LUTHER : I dunno—I might—I dunno.

MINNIE : That means you have.

LUTHER : I'm thirty.

MINNIE : And who *were* they?

LUTHER : I dunno. I've niver bin much wi' anybody—little, very little—an' then it wor an off-chance. Our Joe wor more that way than me—I worn't that way.

A pause.

MINNIE : So—this was what I waited for you for!

LUTHER : Yha niver waited for me. Tha had me a'cause tha couldna get nobody better.

MINNIE : And so——

LUTHER *(after a moment)* : Yi, an' so. An' so, I non care what ter does. If ter leaves me——

MINNIE *(in a flash)* : What's the good of me leaving you? Aren't I married to you—tied to you?

LUTHER : Tha could leave me whether or not. I should go t'r Australia wi' our Joe.

MINNIE : And what about that girl?

LUTHER : I should send 'er th' money.

MINNIE : And what about me?

LUTHER : Tha'd please thysen.

MINNIE : Should you *like* me to leave you, and let you go to Australia?

LUTHER : 'Appen I should.

MINNIE : What did you marry me for?

LUTHER : 'Cos tha axed me.

MINNIE : Did you never care for me?

He does not answer.

Didn't you?

He does not answer.

Didn't you?

LUTHER *(slowly)*: You niver wanted me—you thought me dirt.

MINNIE: Ha! *(A pause.)* You can have the forty pounds.

LUTHER *(very doggedly)*: I shanna.

MINNIE: She's got to be paid.

LUTHER: Tha keeps thy money.

MINNIE: Then where shall you get it from?

LUTHER: I s'll pay 'er month by month.

MINNIE: But you can't. Think!

LUTHER: Then I'll borrow forty quid somewhere else, an' pay it back i' instalments. Tha keeps thy money.

MINNIE: You can borrow it from me.

LUTHER: I shall not.

MINNIE: Very well. I only wanted not to have the bother of paying month by month. I think I shall go back to my old place.

LUTHER: Tha pleases thysen.

MINNIE: And you can go and live with your mother again.

LUTHER: That I should niver do—but tha pleases thysen. We've bin married seven wik come Tuesday.

MINNIE: I niver ought to ha' done it.

LUTHER: What?

MINNIE: Married you.

LUTHER: No.

MINNIE: For you never cared enough.

LUTHER: Yi—it's my fault.

MINNIE: Yes.

LUTHER: It would be. Tha's niver made a fault i' thy life.

MINNIE: Who are you, to talk about my faults!

LUTHER: Well——

    A pause.

MINNIE: I shall write to Mr Westlake to-morrow.

LUTHER: Tha does as pleases thee.

MINNIE: And if they can't take me back straight away, I shall ask him if he knows another place.

LUTHER: A'right. An' we'll sell th' furniture.

MINNIE *(looking round at her home)*: Yes.

LUTHER: It'll non bring ha'ef tha giv for't—but it'll bring enough ter ta'e me out theer.

MINNIE: I'll make up what you lose by it, since I chose it.

LUTHER : Tha can give ter them as'll ha'e.

MINNIE : But I shall feel I owe it you.

LUTHER : I've had six weeks o' married life wi' thee. I mun pay for that.

MINNIE : You are mean, mean.

LUTHER : I know—though tha'rt first as has told me so. When dost reckon tha'lt go?

MINNIE : I'll go to-morrow if you want to get rid of me.

LUTHER : Nay—tha does just as pleases thysen. I non want ter get rid on thee. Nay, nay, it's not that. It's thee as wants ter go.

MINNIE : At any rate, I s'll have a place inside a fortnight.

LUTHER *(dully)*: Alright.

MINNIE : So I shall have to trouble you till then.

LUTHER : But I dunna want thee ter do owt for me—no, I dunna.

MINNIE : I shall keep the house, in payment for my board and lodgings. And I'll make the bed up in the back room, and I'll sleep there, because it's not furnished, and the house is yours.

LUTHER : Th'art—tha'rt—I wish I might strike thee down!

MINNIE : And I shall keep the account of every penny I spend, and you must just pay the bills.

LUTHER *(rising suddenly)*: I'll murder thee afore tha does.

> *He goes out. She sits twisting her apron. He returns with a large lump of coal in his hands, and rakes the fire.*

MINNIE : You cared more for her than for me.

LUTHER : For who?

MINNIE : For her. She was the sort of sawney you ought to have had. Did she think you perfect?

LUTHER *(with grim satisfaction)*: She liked me.

MINNIE : And you could do just as you wanted with her?

LUTHER : She'd ha' done owt for me.

MINNIE : And it flattered you, did it? Because a long stalk wi' no flower was at your service, it flattered you, did it? My word, it ought—— As for your Joe, he's not a fool like you, and that's why women think more of him. He wouldn't want a Bertha Purdy. He'd get a woman who was something—and because he knew how to appreciate her. You—what good are you?

LUTHER : I'm no good, but to fetch an' carry.

MINNIE : And a tuppenny scullery-girl could do that as well.

LUTHER : Alright.

MINNIE: I'll bet even Bertha Purdy thinks what a clown you are. She never wanted you to marry her, did she?

LUTHER: She knowed I wouldn't.

MINNIE: You flatter yourself. I'll bet she never wanted you. I shouldn't be surprised if the child isn't somebody else's, that she just foists on you because you're so soft.

LUTHER: Oh ah!

MINNIE: It even flatters you to think it's yours.

LUTHER: Oh ah!

MINNIE: And quite right too—for it's the only thing you could have to be proud of. And then really it's not you . . .

LUTHER: Oh ah!

MINNIE: If a woman has a child, and you think you're the cause, do you think it's *your* doings?

LUTHER: If tha has one, it will be.

MINNIE: And is *that* anything for you to be proud of? Me whom you've insulted and deceived and treated as no snail would treat a woman! And then you expect me to bear your children!

LUTHER: I dunna expect thee. If tha does tha does.

MINNIE: And you gloat over it and feel proud of it!

LUTHER: Yi, I do.

MINNIE: No—no! I'd rather have married a tramp off the streets than you. And—and I don't believe you *can* have children.

LUTHER: Theer tha knows tha'rt a liar.

MINNIE: I hate you.

LUTHER: Alright.

MINNIE: And I *will* leave you, I *will*.

LUTHER: Tha's said so afore.

MINNIE: And I mean it.

LUTHER: Alright.

MINNIE: But it's your mother's doing. *She* mollycoddled and marded you till you weren't a man—and now—I have to pay for it.

LUTHER: Oh ah!

MINNIE: No, you're not a man!

LUTHER: Alright. They's plenty of women as would say I am.

MINNIE: They'd be lying to get something out of you.

LUTHER: Why, what could they get outer me?

MINNIE: Yes—yes—what could they . . . *(She stutters to a close.)*

He begins to take off his boots.

LUTHER : If tha'rt goin', tha'd better go afore th' strike begins. We should be on short commons then—ten bob a wik.

MINNIE : There's one thing, you'd be on short commons without me. For nobody would keep you for ten shillings a week, unless you went to your mother's.

LUTHER : I could live at our Harriet's, an' pay 'er off after. An' there'd be th' furniture sold.

MINNIE : And you'd be delighted if there *was* a strike, so you could loaf about. You don't even get drunk. You only loaf. You're lazy, lazy, and without the stomach of a louse. You *want* a strike.

LUTHER : Alright.

MINNIE : And I hope you'll get what you deserve, I do.

LUTHER : Tha'rt gi'en it me.

MINNIE *(lifting her hand suddenly)*: How *dare* you say so—how *dare* you! I'm too good for you.

LUTHER *(sullenly)*: I know.

MINNIE : Yes.

She gets a candle, lights it, and goes to bed. He flings off his scarf and coat and waistcoat, throws the pillow on the hearth-rug, wraps himself in the blankets, blows the lamp out, and lies down.

CURTAIN

ACT III

A fortnight later—afternoon. The kitchen of LUTHER GASCOIGNE'S *house.*

MRS GASCOIGNE, *senior, alone. Enter* MINNIE GASCOIGNE, *dressed from travelling. She is followed by a* CABMAN *carrying a bag.*

MRS GASCOIGNE: What—is it you!

MINNIE: Yes. Didn't you get my wire?

MRS GASCOIGNE: Thy wire! Dost mean a tallygram? No, we'n had nowt though th' house 'as bin shut up.

MINNIE *(to the* CABMAN*)*: Thank you. How much?

CABMAN: Ha'ef-a-crown.

MRS GASCOIGNE: Ha'ef-a-crown for commin' from th' Midland station! Why, tha non know what's talkin' about.

MINNIE *(paying him)*: Thank you.

CABMAN: Thank yer. Good afternoon.

The CABMAN *goes out.*

MRS GASCOIGNE: My word, tha knows how ter ma'e th' money fly.

MINNIE: I couldn't carry a bag.

MRS GASCOIGNE: Tha could ha' come i' th' 'bus ter Eastwood an' then a man 'ud 'a browt it on.

MINNIE: It is raining.

MRS GASCOIGNE: Tha'rt neither sugar nor salt.

MINNIE: I wonder you didn't get my telegram.

MRS GASCOIGNE: I tell thee, th' 'ouse wor shut up last night.

MINNIE: Oh!

MRS GASCOIGNE: I dunno wheer 'e slep'—wi' some o's pals I should think.

MINNIE: Oh!

MRS GASCOIGNE: Thinks I to mysen, I'd better go an' get some dinner ready down theer. So I told our Joe ter come 'ere for's dinner as well, but they'm neither on 'em bin in yet. That's allers t'road when it's strike. They stop mornin' about, bletherin' and boomin' an' meals, bless yer, they don't count. Tha's bin i' Manchester four days then?

MINNIE: Yes.

MRS GASCOIGNE: Ay.—Our Luther's niver bin up ter tell me. If I hadna ha' met Mrs Pervin fra next door here, I should niver ha' knowed a word. That wor yisterday. So I sent our Joe down. But it seems 'e's neither bin a-whoam yesterday nor th' day afore. He slep' i' th' 'ouse by hissen for two nights. So Mrs Sharley said. He said tha'd gone ter Manchester on business.

MINNIE: Yes.

MRS GASCOIGNE: But he niver come ter tell *me* nowt on't.

MINNIE: Didn't he?

MRS GASCOIGNE: It's trew what they say:

"My son's my son till he ta'es him a wife,

But my daughter's my daughter the whole of her life."

MINNIE: Do you think so?

MRS GASCOIGNE: I'm sure. An' th' men's been out ten days now, an' such carryin's-on.

MINNIE: Oh! Why—what?

MRS GASCOIGNE: Meetin's ivry mornin'—crier for ever down th' street wi's bell—an' agitators. They say as Fraser dursn't venture out o' th' door. Watna' pit-top's bin afire, and there's a rigiment o' soldiers drillin' i' th' statutes ground—bits o' things they are, an' a', like a lot o' little monkeys i' their red coats—Staffordshire men. But wiry, so they say. Same as marched wi' Lord Roberts to Candyhar. But not a man among 'em. If you watch out fra th' gardin end, you'll see 'em i' th' colliers' train goin' up th' line ter Watna'—wi' their red coats jammed i' th' winders. They say as Fraser's got ten on 'em in's house ter guard him—an' they's sentinels at pit top, standin' wi' their guns, an' th' men crackin' their sides wi' laughing at 'em.

MINNIE: What for?

MRS GASCOIGNE: Nay, that I canna tell thee. They've got the Black Watch up at Heanor—so they says—great big Scotchmen i' kilts. They look well, ha'en them i' Heanor, wi' a' them lasses.

MINNIE: And what is all the fuss about?

MRS GASCOIGNE: Riotin'. I thought tha'd bobbled off ter Manchester ter be i' safety.

MINNIE: Oh, no—I never knew there was any danger.

MRS GASCOIGNE: No more there is, as far as that goes. What's up atween you an' our Luther?

MINNIE: Oh, nothing particular.

MRS GASCOIGNE: I knowed summat wor amiss, when 'e niver come up. It's a fortnight last Tuesday, sin' 'e's set foot i' my house—an' I've niver clapt eyes on him. I axed our Joe, but he's as stubborn as a jackass, an' you canna get a word out on 'im, not for love nor money.

MINNIE: Oh!

MRS GASCOIGNE: Talks o' goin' t'r Australay. But not if I can help it. An' hints as if our Luther—you not thinkin' of it, are you?

MINNIE: No, I'm not—not that I know of.

MRS GASCOIGNE: H'm! It's a rum go, when nobody seems ter know where they are, nor what they're goin' ter do. But there's more blort than bustle, i' this world. What took thee to Manchester?

MINNIE: Oh, I just wanted to go, on business.

MRS GASCOIGNE: Summat about thy money, like?

MINNIE: Yes.

MRS GASCOIGNE: Our Luther wor axin' me for forty pound, th' last time 'e wor up—but I didna see it. No—I fun' him a' as 'e wanted for's marriage, and gen 'im ten pound i' hand, an' I thought it 'ud suffice. An' as for forty pound—it's ter much, that's what I think.

MINNIE: I don't.

MRS GASCOIGNE: Oh, well, if tha doesna, a' well an' good. 'Appen he's paid it, then?

MINNIE: Paid it! Why, wheer was he to get it from?

MRS GASCOIGNE: I thought you had it atween you.

MINNIE: We haven't.

MRS GASCOIGNE: Why, how dost mean?

MINNIE: I mean we've neither of us got as much as forty pounds.

MRS GASCOIGNE: Dost mean *tha* hasna?

MINNIE: No, I haven't.

MRS GASCOIGNE: What's a-gait now?

MINNIE: Nothing.

MRS GASCOIGNE: What hast bin up to?

MINNIE: I? Nothing. I went to Manchester to settle a little business, that's all.

MRS GASCOIGNE: And wheer did ter stop?

MINNIE: I stayed with my old master.

MRS GASCOIGNE: Wor there no missis, then?

MINNIE : No—his wife is dead. You know I was governess for his grandchildren, who were born in India.

MRS GASCOIGNE : H'm! So tha went to see *him*?

MINNIE : Yes—I've always told him everything.

MRS GASCOIGNE : So tha went clat-fartin' ter 'im about our Luther, did ter?

MINNIE : Well—he's the only soul in the world that I *can* go to.

MRS GASCOIGNE : H'm! It doesna become thee, methinks.

MINNIE : Well!

Footsteps are heard.

MRS GASCOIGNE : Here's them lads, I s'd think.

Enter LUTHER *and* JOE.

JOE *(to* MINNIE*)* : Hello! has thee come?

MINNIE : Yes. I sent a wire, and thought someone might come to meet me.

JOE : Nay, there wor no wire. We thought tha'd gone for good.

MINNIE : Who thought so?

JOE : Well—didna tha say so?

MINNIE : Say what?

JOE : As tha'd go, an' he could do what he liked?

MINNIE : I've said many things.

MRS GASCOIGNE : So that was how it stood! Tha'rt a fool, our Luther. If ter ta'es a woman at 'er word, well, tha deserves what ter gets.

LUTHER : What am I to do, might I ax?

MRS GASCOIGNE : Nay, that thy wits should tell thee. Wheer hast bin these two days?

LUTHER : I walked ower wi' Jim Horrocks ter their Annie's i' Mansfield.

MRS GASCOIGNE : I'm sure she'd got enough to do, without two men planting themselves on her. An' how did ter get back?

LUTHER : Walked.

MRS GASCOIGNE : Trapsein' thy shoe-leather off thee feet, walkin' twenty miles. Hast had thy dinner?

JOE : We've both had free dinners at th' Methodist Chapel.

LUTHER : I met Tom Heseldine i' "Th' Badger Box", Mother.

MRS GASCOIGNE : Oh ay! Wide-mouthed as iver, I reckon.

JOE : Just same. But what dost think, Mother? It's leaked out as Fraser's got a lot o' chaps to go to-morrer mornin', ter see after th' roads an' a' that.

MRS GASCOIGNE : Th' roads wants keepin' safe, dunna they?

JOE : Yi—but if th' mesters wunna ha'e th' union men, let 'em do it theirselves.

MRS GASCOIGNE : Tha talks like a fool.

LUTHER : What right ha' they ter get a lot of scrawdrags an' black-legs in ter do our work? A' th' pit maun fa' in, if they wunna settle it fair wi' us.

JOE : Then workin's is ours, an' th' mesters'. If th' mesters wunna treat us fair, then they mun keep 'em right theirselves. They non goin' ter ha'e no third body in.

MINNIE : But even when it's settled, how are you going back, if the roof has come in, and the roads are gone?

JOE : Tha mun ax th' mesters that. If we canna go back ter th' rotten owd pits no more, we mun look elsewhere. An' th' mesters can sit atop o' their pits an' stroke 'em.

LUTHER *(to* MINNIE): If I got a woman in to do th' housework as tha wunna do for me, tha'd sit smilin', shouldn't ter?

MINNIE : She could do as she liked.

LUTHER : Alright. Then, Mother, 'appen tha'lt boss this house. She run off ter Manchester, an' left me ter starve. So 'appen tha'lt come an' do for me.

MRS GASCOIGNE : Nay—if ter wants owt tha mun come ter *me.*

JOE : That's right. Dunna thee play blackleg i' this establishment.

MRS GASCOIGNE : I s'll mind my own business.

JOE *(to* MINNIE): Now, does *thee* think it right, Minnie, as th' mesters should get a lot o' crawlin' buggers in ter keep their pits i' order, when th' keepin' o' them pits i' order belongs by right to us?

MINNIE : It belongs to whosoever the masters pay to do it.

LUTHER : A' right. Then it belongs to me to ha'e any woman in ter do for me, as I've a mind. Tha's gone on strike, so I ha'e the right ter get anybody else.

MINNIE : When have I gone on strike? I have always done your housework.

LUTHER : Housework—yi! But we dunna on'y keep th' roof from comin' in. We *get* as well. An' even th' housework tha went on strike wi'. Tha skedaddled off ter Manchester, an' left me to't.

MINNIE : I went on business.

LUTHER : An' we've come out on strike "on business".

MINNIE : You've not; it's a game.

LUTHER : An' the mesters'll ta'e us back when they're ready, or when they're forced to. An' same wi' thee by me.

MINNIE : Oh!

JOE : We got it fr' Tom Rooke—'e wor goin' ter turn 'em down. At four to-morrer mornin', there's ower twenty men goin' down.

MRS GASCOIGNE : What a lot of fools men are! As if th' pits didn't need ter be kep' tidy, ready for you to go back to'm.

JOE : They'll be kep' tidy by us, then an' when we've a mind—an' by nobody else.

MRS GASCOIGNE : Tha talks very high an' mighty. That's because I ha'e th' feedin' on thee.

JOE : You put it like our Luther says, then. He stands for t'mesters, an' Minnie stands for t'men—cos 'er's gone on strike. Now becos she's went ter Manchester, had he got ony right ter ha'e Lizzie Charley in for a couple o' nights an' days?

MRS GASCOIGNE : Tha talks like a fool!

JOE : I dunna.

MINNIE : He's welcome to Lizzie Charley.

JOE : Alright.—She's a nice gel. We'll ax 'er to come in an' manage th' 'ouse—he can pay 'er.

MINNIE : What with?

JOE : Niver you mind. Should yer like it?

MINNIE : He can do just as he likes.

JOE : Then should I fetch her?—should I, Luther?

LUTHER : If ter's a mind.

JOE : Should I, then, Minnie?

MINNIE : If he wants her.

LUTHER : I want somebody ter look after me.

JOE : Right tha art. *(Puts his cap on.)* I'll say as Minnie canna look after th' house, will 'er come. That it?

LUTHER : Ah.

MRS GASCOIGNE : Dunna be a fool. Tha's had a can or two.

JOE : Well—'er'll be glad o' the job.

MRS GASCOIGNE : You'd better stop him, one of you.

LUTHER : I want somebody ter look after me—an' tha wunna.

MRS GASCOIGNE : Eh dear o' me! Dunna thee be a fool, our Joe.

    Exit JOE.

What wor this job about goin' ter Manchester?

LUTHER: She said she wouldna live wi' me, an' so 'er went. I thought 'er'd gone for good.

MINNIE: You didn't—you *knew*.

LUTHER: I knowed what tha'd towd me—as tha'd live wi' me no longer. Tha's come back o' thy own accord.

MINNIE: I never said I shouldn't come back.

LUTHER: Tha said as tha wouldna live wi' me. An' tha *didna*, neither,—not for——

MRS GASCOIGNE: Well, Minnie, you've brought it on your own head. You put him off, an' you put him off, as if 'e was of no account, an' then all of a sudden you invited him to marry you——

MINNIE: Put him off! He didn't need much putting off. He never came any faster than a snail.

MRS GASCOIGNE: Twice, to my knowledge, he axed thee—an' what can a man do more?

MINNIE: Yes, what! A gramophone in breeches could do as much.

MRS GASCOIGNE: Oh, indeed! What ailed him was, he wor in collier's britches, i'stead o' a stool-arsed Jack's.

MINNIE: No—what ailed him was that *you* kept him like a kid hanging on to you.

MRS GASCOIGNE: An' tha bit thy own nose off, when ter said him nay. For had ter married him at twenty-three, there'd ha' been none of this trouble.

MINNIE: And why didn't I? Why didn't I? Because he came in his half-hearted "I will if you like" fashion, and I despised him, yes I did.

MRS GASCOIGNE: And who are *you* to be despising him, I should like to know?

MINNIE: I'm a woman, and that's enough. But I know now, it was your fault. You held him, and persuaded him that what he wanted was *you*. You kept him, like a child, you even gave him what money he wanted, like a child. He never roughed it—he never faced out anything. You did all that for him.

MRS GASCOIGNE: And what if I did! If you made as good a wife to him as I made a mother, you'd do.

MINNIE: Should I? You didn't care what women your sons went with, so long as they didn't love them. What do you care really about this affair of Bertha Purdy? You don't. All you cared about was to keep your sons for yourself. You kept the solid meal, and the orts and slarts any other woman could have. But I tell you, I'm *not* for having the orts and slarts, and your leavings from your sons. I'll have a man, or nothing, I will.

MRS GASCOIGNE: It's rare to be some folks, ter pick and choose.

MINNIE: I can't pick and choose, no. But what I won't have, I won't have, and that is all.

MRS GASCOIGNE *(to* LUTHER): Have I ever kept thee from doin' as tha wanted? Have I iver marded and coddled thee?

LUTHER: Tha hasna, beguy!

MINNIE: No, you haven't, perhaps, not by the look of things. But you've bossed him. You've decided everything for him, really. He's depended on you as much when he was thirty as when he was three. You told him what to do, and he did it.

MRS GASCOIGNE: My word, I've never known all he did.

MINNIE: You have—everything that mattered. You maybe didn't know it was Bertha Purdy, but you knew it was some woman like her, and what did you care? *She* had the orts and slarts, you kept your son. And you want to keep him, even now. Yes—and you do keep him.

MRS GASCOIGNE: We're learnin' a thing or two, Luther.

LUTHER: Ay.

> *Enter* JOE.

MINNIE: Yes! What did you care about the woman who would have to take some after you? Nothing! You left her with just the slarts of a man. Yes.

MRS GASCOIGNE: Indeed! I canna see as you're so badly off. You've got a husband as doesn't drink, as waits on you hand and foot, as gives you a free hand in everything. It's you as doesn't know when you're well off, madam.

MINNIE: I'd rather have had a husband who knocked me about than a husband who was good to me because he belonged to his mother. He doesn't and can't *really* care for me. You stand before him. His *real* caring goes to *you*. Me he only wants sometimes.

JOE: She'll be in in a minute.

MRS GASCOIGNE: Tha'rt the biggest fool an' jackanapes, our Joe, as iver God made.

MINNIE: If she crosses that doorstep, then I go for good.

MRS GASCOIGNE *(bursting into fury—to* JOE): Tha see what thy bobby interferin' has done.

JOE: Nay—that's how it stood.

MRS GASCOIGNE: Tha mun go an' stop her, our Luther. Tell 'er it wor our Joe's foolery. An' look sharp.

LUTHER: What should *I* go for?

> LUTHER *goes out, furious.*

MINNIE: You see—you see! His mother's word is law to him. He'd do what I told him, but his *feel* would be for you. He's got no *feeling* for me. You keep all that.

MRS GASCOIGNE: You talk like a jealous woman.

MINNIE: I do! And for that matter, why doesn't Joe marry, either? Because you keep him too. You know, in spite of his bluster, he cares more for your little finger than he does for all the women in the world—or ever will. And it's wrong—it's wrong. How is a woman ever to have a husband, when the men all belong to their mothers? It's wrong.

MRS GASCOIGNE: Oh, indeed!—is it? You know, don't you? You know everything.

MINNIE: I know this, because I've suffered from it. Your elder sons you let go, and they *are* husbands. But your young sons you've kept. And Luther is your son, and the man that lives with me. But first, he's your son. And Joe ought never to marry, for he'd break a woman's heart.

MRS GASCOIGNE: Tha hears, lad! We're bein' told off.

JOE: Ah, I hear. An' what's more, it's true, Mother.

MINNIE: It is—it is. He only likes playing round me and getting some pleasure out of teasing me, because he knows I'm safely married to Luther, and can never look to him to marry me and belong to me. He's safe, so he likes me. If I were single, he'd be frightened to death of me.

JOE: Happen I should.

MRS GASCOIGNE: Tha'rt a fool.

MINNIE: And that's what you've done to me—that's my life spoiled —spoiled—ay, worse than if I'd had a drunken husband that knocked me about. For it's dead.

MRS GASCOIGNE: Tha'rt shoutin' because nowt ails thee—that's what tha art.

JOE: Nay, Mother, tha knows it's right. Tha knows tha's got me—an'll ha'e me till ter dies—an' after that—yi.

MRS GASCOIGNE: Tha talks like a fool.

JOE: And sometimes, Mother, I wish I wor dead, I do.

MINNIE: You see, you see! You see what you've done to them. It's strong women like you, who were too much for their husbands—ah!

JOE: Tha knows I couldna leave thee, Mother—tha knows I couldna. An' me, a young man, belongs to thy owd age. An' there's nowheer for me to go, Mother. For tha'rt gettin' nearer to death an' yet I canna leave thee to go my own road. An' I wish, yi, often, as I wor dead.

MRS GASCOIGNE: Dunna, lad—dunna let 'er put these ideas i' thy head.

JOE: An' I can but fritter my days away. There's no goin' forrard for me.

MRS GASCOIGNE: Nay, lad, nay—what lad's better off than thee, dost reckon?

JOE: If I went t'r Australia, th' best part on me wouldna go wi' me.

MRS GASCOIGNE: Tha wunna go t'r Australia!

JOE: If I went, I should be a husk of a man. I'm allers a husk of a man, Mother. There's nowt solid about me. The' isna.

MRS GASCOIGNE: Whativer dost mean? You've a' set on me at once.

JOE: I'm nowt, Mother, an' I count for nowt. Yi, an' I know it.

MRS GASCOIGNE: Tha does. Tha sounds as if tha counts for nowt, as a rule, doesn't ter?

JOE: There's not much of a man about me. T'other chaps is more of fools, but they more of men an' a'—an' they know it.

MRS GASCOIGNE: That's thy fault.

JOE: Yi—an' will be—ter th' end o' th' chapter.

Enter LUTHER.

MINNIE: Did you tell her?

LUTHER: Yes.

MINNIE: We'll have some tea, should we?

JOE: Ay, let's. For it's bin dry work.

She sets the kettle on.

MRS GASCOIGNE: I mun be goin'.

MINNIE: Wait and have a cup of tea. I brought a cake.

JOE: But we non goin' ter ha'e it, are we, Luther, these 'ere blacklegs goin' down interferin'.

LUTHER: We arena.

MRS GASCOIGNE: But how are you going to stop them?

JOE: We s'll manage it, one road or t'other.

MRS GASCOIGNE: You'll non go gettin' yourselves into trouble.

LUTHER: We in trouble enow.

MINNIE: If you'd have had Lizzie Charley in, what should you have paid her with?

LUTHER: We should ha' found the money somewhere.

MINNIE: Do you know what I had to keep house on this week, Mother?

MRS GASCOIGNE: Not much, sin' there wor nowt but ten shillin' strike pay.

MINNIE: He gave me five shillings.

LUTHER: Tha could ha' had what things ter wanted on strap.

MINNIE: No—but why should you keep, to drink on, as much as you give me to keep house on? Five shillings!

JOE: Five bob's non a whackin' sight o' pocket money for a man's week.

MINNIE: It is, if he earns nothing. It was that as finished me off.

JOE: Well, *tha* niver ned go short—tha can let *him*.

MINNIE: I knew that was what *he* thought. But if he wouldna have my money for one thing, he wasn't going to for another.

MRS GASCOIGNE: Why, what wouldn't he have it for?

MINNIE: He wouldn't have that forty pounds, when I went on my knees to beg and beseech him to.

LUTHER: Tha did! Tha throwed it at me as if I wor a beggar as stank.

MINNIE: And you wouldn't have it when I asked you.

LUTHER: No—an' wouldna ha'e it now.

MINNIE: You can't.

LUTHER: I dunna want it.

MINNIE: And if you don't find money to keep the house on, we shall both of us starve. For you've got to keep me. And I've got no money of my own now.

LUTHER: Why, what dost mean?

MINNIE: I mean what I say.

MRS GASCOIGNE: Why, what?

MINNIE: I was sick of having it between us. It was but a hundred and twenty. So I went ·to Manchester and spent it.

MRS GASCOIGNE: Tha's bin an' spent a hundred and twenty pound i' four days?

MINNIE: Yes, I have.

MRS GASCOIGNE: Whativer are we comin' to!

JOE: That wor a stroke worth two. Tell us what tha bought.

MINNIE: I bought myself a ring, for one thing. I thought if I ever had any children, and they asked me where was my engagement ring, I should have to show them something, for their father's sake. Do you like it? *(Holds out her hand to* JOE.*)*

JOE: My word, but that's a bobby-dazzler. Look, Mother.

MRS GASCOIGNE: H'm.

　　　JOE *takes the ring off.*

JOE: My word, but that's a diamond, if you like. How much did it cost?

MINNIE: Thirty pounds. I've got the bill in my pocket.

MRS GASCOIGNE: I only hope you'll niver come to want some day.

MINNIE: Luther must see to that.

JOE: And what else did ter buy?

MINNIE: I'll show you. *(Gets her bag, unlocks it, takes out three prints.)*

JOE: I dunna reckon much ter these.

MRS GASCOIGNE: Nor me neither. An' how much has ter gen for them apiece?

MINNIE: That was twenty-five pounds. They're beautiful prints.

MRS GASCOIGNE: I dunna believe a word tha says.

MINNIE: I'll show you the bill. My master's a collector, and he picked them for me. He says they're well worth the money. And I like them.

MRS GASCOIGNE: Well, I niver seed such a job in my life. T-t-t-t! Well, a' I can say is, I hope tha'll niver come ter want. Throwin' good money i' th' gutter like this. Nay, I feel fair bad. Nay! T-t-t-t! Such tricks! And such bits o' dirty paper!

JOE: I'd rather ha'e the Co-op almanack.

MRS GASCOIGNE: So would I, any day! What dost say to't, our Luther?

LUTHER: 'Er does as 'er likes.

MINNIE: I had a lovely time with Mr Westlake, choosing them at the dealer's. He *is* clever.

MRS GASCOIGNE: Tha towd him tha wanted to get rid o' thy money, did ter?

MINNIE: No—I said I wanted some pictures for the parlour, and asked him if he'd help me choose.

MRS GASCOIGNE: Good money thrown away. Maybe the very bread of your children.

MINNIE: Nay, that's Luther's duty to provide.

MRS GASCOIGNE: Well, a' I can say is, I hope you may never come ter want. If our Luther died . . .

MINNIE: I should go back to work.

MRS GASCOIGNE: But what if tha'd three or four children?

MINNIE: A hundred and twenty pounds wouldn't make much odds then.

MRS GASCOIGNE: Well, a' I can say, I hope tha'lt niver live ter rue the day.

JOE: What dost think on 'er, Luther?

LUTHER: Nay, she's done as she liked with her own.

MINNIE *(emptying her purse in her lap)*: I've got just seventeen shillings. You drew your strike pay yesterday. How much have you got of that, Luther?

LUTHER: Three bob.

MINNIE: And do you want to keep it?

LUTHER: Ah.

MINNIE: Very well . . . I shall spend this seventeen shillings till it's gone, and then we shall have to live on soup-tickets.

MRS GASCOIGNE: I'll back my life!

JOE: And who'll fetch the soup?

MINNIE: Oh, I shall. I've been thinking, that big jug will do nicely. I'm in the same boat as other men's wives now, and so I must do the same.

JOE: They'll gi'e you strap at West's.

MINNIE: I'm not going to run up bills, no, I'm not. I'll go to the free teas, and fetch soup, an' with ten shillings a week we shall manage.

MRS GASCOIGNE: Well, that's one road, lass.

MINNIE: It's the only one. And now, if he can provide, he must, and if he can't, he must tell me so, and I'll go back into service, and not be a burden to him.

MRS GASCOIGNE: High and mighty, high and mighty! We'll see, my lass; we'll see.

MINNIE: That's all we can do.

MRS GASCOIGNE: Tha doesna care how he takes it.

MINNIE: The prints belong to both of us. *(Hands them to* LUTHER.) You haven't said if you like them yet.

LUTHER *(taking them, suddenly rams them in the fire)*: Tha can go to hell.

MINNIE *(with a cry)*: Ah!—that's my ninety pounds gone. *(Tries to snatch them out.)*

MRS GASCOIGNE *(beginning to cry)*: Come, Joe, let's go; let's go, my lad. I've seen as much this day as ever my eyes want to see. Let's go, my lad. *(Gets up, beginning to tie on her bonnet.)*

MINNIE *(white and intense, to* LUTHER*)*: Should you like to throw my ring after them? It's all I've got left. *(She holds out her hand—he flings it from him.)*

LUTHER: Yi, what do I care what I do! *(Clenching his fists as if he would strike her.)*—what do I!—what do I——!

MRS GASCOIGNE *(putting on her shawl)*: A day's work—a day's work! Ninety pound! Nay—nay, oh, nay—nay, oh, nay—nay! Let's go, Joe, my lad. Eh, our Luther, our Luther! Let's go, Joe. Come.

JOE: Ah, I'll come, Mother.

MRS GASCOIGNE: Luther!

LUTHER: What?

MRS GASCOIGNE: It's a day's work, it is, wi' thee. Eh dear! Come, let's go, Joe. Let's go whoam.

LUTHER: An' I'll go.

MRS GASCOIGNE: Dunna thee do nowt as ter'll repent of, Luther— dunna thee. It's thy mother axes thee. Come, Joe.

> MRS GASCOIGNE *goes out, followed by* JOE. LUTHER *stands with face averted from his wife; mutters something, reaches for his cap, goes out.* MINNIE *stands with her hand on the mantelpiece.*

CURTAIN

ACT IV

The following morning—about 5 a.m. A candle is burning.
MINNIE *sits by the fire in a dressing-gown. She is weeping. A*
knock, and MRS GASCOIGNE'S *voice.* MINNIE *goes to open the*
door; re-enters with her mother-in-law, the latter with a big
brown shawl over her head.

MRS GASCOIGNE: Is Luther a-whoam?

MINNIE: No—he's not been in all night.

MRS GASCOIGNE: T-t-t-t! Now whereiver can they be? Joe's not
in neither.

MINNIE: Isn't he?

MRS GASCOIGNE: No. He said he might be late, so I went to bed,
and slept a bit uneasy-like till about four o'clock. Then I wakes
up a' of a sudden, an' says: "I'm by mysen i' th' house!" It gave
me such a turn I daresn't shout. So I gets me up an' goes ter his
room, an' he'd niver bin i' bed a' night. Well, I went down, but
no signs nowhere. An' 'im wi' a broken arm. An' I listened an'
I listened—an' then methinks I heered a gun go off. I felt as if I
should die if I stopped by mysen another minute. So I on's wi'
my shawl an' nips down here. There's not a soul astir nowhere.
I a'most dropped when I seed your light. Hasn't Luther bin in a'
night, dost say?

MINNIE: He went out with you, and he never came in again. I
went to bed, thinking perhaps he'd be sleeping on the sofa. And
then I came down, and he wasn't here.

MRS GASCOIGNE: Well, I've seen nowt of him, for he never come
up to our house.—Now I wonder what's afoot wi' th' silly fools?

MINNIE: I thought he'd gone and left me.

MRS GASCOIGNE: It's more like some o' this strike work. When I
heered that gun, I said: "Theer goes one o' my lads!"

MINNIE: You don't think they're killed?

MRS GASCOIGNE: Heaven knows what they are. But I niver thought
he'd ha' served me this trick—left me by myself without telling
me, and gone cutting off a' th' night through—an' him wi' a
broken arm.

MINNIE: Where do you think they've gone?

MRS GASCOIGNE: The Lord above alone knows—but I'se warrant it's one o' these riotin' tricks—stopping them blacklegs as wor goin' down to see to th' roads.

MINNIE: Do you think——?

MRS GASCOIGNE: I'll back anything. For I heered th' winding engines plain as anything. Hark!

They listen.

MINNIE: I believe I can hear them.

MRS GASCOIGNE: Th' ingines?

MINNIE: Yes.

MRS GASCOIGNE: They're winding something down. Eh dear, what a dead world it seems, wi' none o' th' pits chuffin' an' no steam wavin' by day, an' no lights shinin' by night. You may back your life there was a gang of 'em going to stop that lot of blacklegs. And there'd be soldiers for a certainty. If I didn't hear a shot, I heered summat much like one.

MINNIE: But they'd never shoot, would they?

MRS GASCOIGNE: Haven't they shot men up an' down th' country? Didn't I know them lads was pining to go an' be shot at? I did. Methinks when I heard that gun, "They'd niver rest till this had happened."

MINNIE: But they're not shot, Mother. You exaggerate.

MRS GASCOIGNE: I niver said they wor. But if anything happens to a man, my lass, you may back your life, nine cases out o' ten, it's a spit on th' women.

MINNIE: Oh, what a thing to say! Why, there are accidents.

MRS GASCOIGNE: Yes, an' men verily gets accidents, to pay us out, I do believe. They get huffed up, they bend down their faces, and they say to theirselves: "Now I'll get myself hurt, an' she'll be sorry," else: "Now I'll get myself killed, an' she'll ha'e nobody to sleep wi' 'er, an' nobody to nag at." Oh, my lass, I've had a husband an' six sons. Children they are, these men, but, my word, they're revengeful children. Children men is a' the days o' their lives. But they're master of us women when their dander's up, an' they pay us back double an' treble—they do—an' you mun allers expect it.

MINNIE: But if they went to stop the blacklegs, they wouldn't be doing it to spite us.

MRS GASCOIGNE: Wouldn't they! Yi, but they would. My lads 'ud do it to spite me, an' our Luther 'ud do it to spite thee. Yes— and it's trew. For they'd run theirselves into danger and lick their lips for joy, thinking, if I'm killed, then *she* maun lay me out. Yi—I seed it in our mester. He got killed a' pit. An' when I laid him out, his face wor that grim, an' his body that stiff, an' it said as plain as plain: "Nowthen, you've done for me." For it's risky work, handlin' men, my lass, an' niver thee pray for sons—— Not but what daughters is any good. Th' world is made o' men, for me, lass—there's only the men for me. An' tha'rt similar. An' so, tha'lt reap trouble by the peck, an' sorrow by the bushel. For when a woman builds her life on men, either husbands or sons, she builds on summat as sooner or later brings the house down crash on her head—yi, she does.

MINNIE: But it depends how and what she builds.

MRS GASCOIGNE: It depends, it depends. An' tha thinks tha can steer clear o' what I've done. An' perhaps tha can. But steer clear the whole length o' th' road, tha canna, an' tha'lt see. Nay, a childt is a troublesome pleasure to a woman, but a man's a trouble pure and simple.

MINNIE: I'm sure it depends what you make of him.

MRS GASCOIGNE: Maybe—maybe. But I've allers tried to do my best, i' spite o' what tha said against me this afternoon.

MINNIE: I didn't mean it—I was in a rage.

MRS GASCOIGNE: Yi, tha meant it plain enow. But I've tried an' tried my best for my lads, I have—an' this is what owd age brings me—wi' 'em.

MINNIE: Nay, Mother—nay. See how fond they are of you.

MRS GASCOIGNE: Yi—an' they go now i' their mischief, yes, tryin' to get killed, to spite me. Yi!

MINNIE: Nay. Nay.

MRS GASCOIGNE: It's true. An' tha can ha'e Luther. Tha'lt get him, an' tha can ha'e him.

MINNIE: Do you think I shall?

MRS GASCOIGNE: I can see. Tha'lt get him—but tha'lt get sorrow wi' 'em, an' wi' th' sons tha has. See if tha doesna.

MINNIE: But I don't care. Only don't keep him from me. It leaves me so—with nothing—not even trouble.

MRS GASCOIGNE: He'll come to thee—an' he'll think no more o' me as is his mother than he will o' that poker.

MINNIE: Oh, no—oh, no.

MRS GASCOIGNE: Yi—I know well—an' then that other.

There is a silence—the two women listening.

MINNIE: If they'd been hurt, we should ha' known by now.

MRS GASCOIGNE: Happen we should. If they come, they'll come together. An' they'll come to this house first.

A silence. MINNIE *starts.*

Did ter hear owt?

MINNIE: Somebody got over the stile.

MRS GASCOIGNE *(listening)*: Yi.

MINNIE *(listening)*: It *is* somebody.

MRS GASCOIGNE: I' t'street.

MINNIE *(starting up)*: Yes.

MRS GASCOIGNE: Comin'? It's Luther. *(Goes to the door.)* An' it's on'y Luther.

Both women stand, the mother nearer the door. The door opens—a slight sluther. Enter LUTHER, *with blood on his face—rather shaky and dishevelled.*

My boy! my boy!

LUTHER: Mother! *(He goes blindly.)* Where's Minnie?

MINNIE *(with a cry)*: Oh!

MRS GASCOIGNE: Wheer's Joe?—wheer's our Joe?

LUTHER *(to* MINNIE, *queer, stunned, almost polite)*: It worn't 'cause I wor mad wi' thee I didna come whoam.

MRS GASCOIGNE *(clutching him sternly)*: Where's Joe?

LUTHER: He's gone up street—he thought tha might ha' wakkened.

MRS GASCOIGNE: Wakkened enow.

MRS GASCOIGNE *goes out.*

MINNIE: Oh, what have you done?

LUTHER: We'd promised not to tell nobody—else I should. We stopped them blacklegs—leastways—but it worn't because I— I—— *(He stops to think.)* I wor mad wi' thee, as I didna come whoam.

MINNIE: What have you done to your head?

LUTHER: It wor a stone or summat catched it. It's gev me a head-ache. Tha mun—tha mun tie a rag round it—if ter will *(He sways as he takes his cap off.)*

She catches him in her arms. He leans on her as if he were tipsy.

Minnie——

MINNIE: My love—my love!

LUTHER: Minnie—I want thee ter ma'e what tha can o' me. *(He sounds almost sleepy.)*

MINNIE *(crying)*: My love—my love!

LUTHER: I know what tha says is true.

MINNIE: No, my love—it isn't—it isn't.

LUTHER: But if ter'lt ma'e what ter can o' me—an' then if ter has a childt—tha'lt happen ha'e enow.

MINNIE: No—no—it's you. It's you I want. It's you.

LUTHER: But tha's allers had me.

MINNIE: No, never—and it hurt so.

LUTHER: I thowt tha despised me.

MINNIE: Ah—my love!

LUTHER: Dunna say I'm mean, to me—an' got no go.

MINNIE: I only said it because you wouldn't let me love you.

LUTHER: Tha didna love me.

MINNIE: Ha!—it was *you*.

LUTHER: Yi. *(He looses himself and sits down heavily.)* I'll ta'e my boots off. *(He bends forward.)*

MINNIE: Let me do them. *(He sits up again.)*

LUTHER: It's started bleedin'. I'll do 'em i' ha'ef a minute.

MINNIE: No—trust me—trust yourself to me. Let me have you now for my own. *(She begins to undo his boots.)*

LUTHER: Dost want me?

MINNIE *(she kisses his hands)*: Oh, my love! *(She takes him in her arms.)*

He suddenly begins to cry.

CURTAIN

The Fight for Barbara

A COMEDY IN FOUR ACTS

(1912)

CHARACTERS

FRANCESCA
WESSON
BARBARA
DR FREDERIC TRESSIDER
LADY CHARLCOTE
SIR WILLIAM CHARLCOTE
BUTCHER

Scene: A Villa in Italy

ACT I

8.30 in the morning. The kitchen of an Italian villa—a big open fire-place of stone, with a little charcoal grate—fornello—on either side—cupboards, table, rush-bottom chairs with high backs—many bright copper pans of all sizes hanging up.

The door-bell rings in the kitchen—rings hard—after a minute a door is heard to bang.

Enter WESSON, *in dressing-gown and pyjamas: a young man of about twenty-six, with thick hair ruffled from sleep. He crosses and goes through door R. Sounds of voices. Re-enter* WESSON, *followed by Italian maid-servant,* FRANCESCA, *young, fair, pretty—wears a black lace scarf over her head. She carries a saucepan full of milk. On the table stand a soup-tureen and an enamel jug.*

FRANCESCA: *Questa? (Puts her hand on the jug.)*

WESSON: No, in the other. *(She pours the milk into the tureen.)*

FRANCESCA *(smiling)*: *Abondante misura!*

WESSON: What's that? *Come?*

FRANCESCA: *Abondante misura latte!*

WESSON: Oh—full measure. *Si!*—running over!

FRANCESCA: Ranning ova. *(Both laugh.)*

WESSON: Right you are—you're learning English.

FRANCESCA: *Come?*

WESSON: *Vous apprenez anglais—voi—inglese!*

FRANCESCAH O—*non—niente inglese!*

WESSON: Nothing English? Oh yes! Er—*fa tempo cattivo!*

FRANCESCA: *Tempo cattivo—si.*

WESSON: Rotten weather——

FRANCESCA: *Come?*

WESSON: It's all the same. *(She puts the lid on her saucepan and turns away.)* Er—what day is it?—er—*giorno che giorno?*

FRANCESCA: *Oggi? Domenica.*

WESSON: *Domenica!—dimanche—Sonntag—*Sunday.

FRANCESCA: *Come?*

WESSON : Sunday!

FRANCESCA : Sendy!

WESSON : That's it. *(Both laugh—she blushes and turns away—bows.)*

FRANCESCA : *Buon giorno, Signore.*

WESSON : *Buon giorno.*

> *Exit* FRANCESCA R. *He drinks some milk, wipes his mouth and begins to whistle: "Put me among the girls!"—takes some branches of olive and ilex from a box near the fire—puts them in the fireplace. As he is so doing, enter Left—*BARBARA*—age about twenty-six—fair—rather a fine young woman, holding her blue silk dressing-gown about her. She stands in the doorway L., holding up her finger.*

BARBARA : Yes, you may well whistle that! *I* heard you, Giacometti.

WESSON *(turning round)* : And did it fetch you out of bed?

BARBARA : Yes, it did. *I* heard your dulcet tones.

WESSON : They were no dulcetter than usual.

BARBARA : And, pray, what right had they to be *as dulcet!*—*(draws herself up)*—to a little servant-maid, indeed!

WESSON : She's awfully nice, and quite a lady.

BARBARA : Yes—yes—I know you! She's pretty, is she?

WESSON : Awfully pretty! *(Lighting the heap of branches in the fire.)* These matches are the stinking devil.

BARBARA : Aren't they! I tried to light a cigarette with them, and I thought I should have died!

WESSON : You should have waited till the sulphur had burned away *(laughing)*. And the pretty maid had got a mantilla on this morning.

BARBARA : Ah! I suppose the poor thing had been to church.

WESSON : It took my breath away when I opened the door, and I said "Oh!"

BARBARA : *Giacomo!*

WESSON : *Do* call me Jimmy—I hate to be Italianized!—and she blushed like fury.

BARBARA : Poor thing! Really, Giacometti, really, you are impossible.

WESSON : What for?

BARBARA : Fancy saying "Oh!" to the young maid! Remember, you're a gentleman in her eyes.

WESSON : And what's wrong with saying "Oh!" when she's got a fascinating mantilla on? I can't say delicate things in Italian—and —"Oh!"—who can't say "Oh!"—after all, what is there in it?

BARBARA: What could have been more expressive! Think of the poor thing, how embarrassed she must feel.

The fire blazes up in the big chimney.

Oh, how beautiful! Now that makes me *perfectly* happy. How *gorgeous*! How adorable! No, but, Wesson, I don't like it.

WESSON: What's that, the fire?

BARBARA: No, the little servant-maid. And you made her feel *so* uncomfortable.

WESSON: I didn't.

BARBARA: You must have done! Think—to her, at any rate, you're a gentleman.

WESSON: A thundering lot of a gentleman, when she finds me lighting the fire and grinding the coffee——

BARBARA: Yes, but no doubt she thinks that's an eccentricity.

WESSON: There's a lot of eccentricity about living on a hundred-and-twenty a year, the pair of us.

BARBARA: And you must remember how fearfully poor these Italians are——

WESSON: It's enough for me how fearfully poor we are ourselves— you in your silk dressing-gown! It'll be some time before you get such a one out of our purse.

BARBARA: Well, it doesn't matter—you *are* a gentleman here. Look, this flat is quite grand.

WESSON: It will be when you have to clean it.

BARBARA: *I* don't mind cleaning it; don't be horrid! This adorable fire! But you won't do it, will you?

WESSON: What?

BARBARA: Say "Oh!" to the little maid. It's not nice, really.

WESSON: Well, you see, it popped out when I saw the mantilla. I s'll be used to it another time.

BARBARA: And you won't say it?

WESSON: I won't say "Oh!"; oh dear, oh no, never no more, I won't. *(Sings.)*

BARBARA *(kissing him)*: Dear!

WESSON *(kissing her)*: What d'yer want?

BARBARA: I love you.

WESSON: So you ought.

BARBARA: Why ought I?

WESSON *(at the fire)*: There you are, you see, that's how to set a fornello going.

BARBARA *(teasing)*: Oh—oh, is it? And now you're going to make coffee l'Italienne, aren't you? Oh, you wonderful person!

WESSON: I am.

> Gets the coffee-mill from cupboard—grinds coffee on the
> table, singing:
>> Johnny used to grind the coffee-mill,
>> Mix the sugar with the sand;
>> But he got run in and all through mixing
>> His master's money with his own.

BARBARA: What is that beautiful and classic song?

> WESSON *sings it again.*

BARBARA *(laughing)*: Oh, you common, common brat! Anybody could tell your father was a coal-miner.

WESSON: A butty collier—and I wish yours had been ditto—you'd ha' been more use. Think of me, Lord of Creation, getting the breakfast ready. *(She takes his head between her hands, and ruffles his hair.)* While you stand messing about.

BARBARA: Oh, your lovely hair!—it makes waves just like the Apollo Belvedere.

WESSON: And come again to-morrer.

BARBARA: Don't—don't laugh at yourself—or at me when I say it's nice hair. It *is*, Giacomo, it's really beautiful.

WESSON: I know; it's the Apollo Belvedere, and my beautiful nose is Antinous, and my lovely chin is Endymion—clear out.

BARBARA: You are horrid to yourself! Why won't you let me say you're nice?

WESSON: Because the water's boiling.

BARBARA: You're not a bit nice.

WESSON: Mind!—my water's boiling! *(Breaks away—making coffee in a brass jug.)* If this was Pimlico or Bloomsbury, and this was a London kitchen, you wouldn't love me, would you?

BARBARA: If you could do anything so horrid as to stifle me in a poor part of London, I would *not* love you—I would hate you for ever. Think of me!

WESSON: But because we come careering to Italy, and the pans are of copper and brass, you adore me, don't you?

BARBARA: Yes—on the whole.

WESSON: That is, for the first month or two. We've been here six
weeks.

BARBARA: Think of it—Giacomo mio, it seems like six minutes—
it frightens me.

WESSON *(hesitating)*: It doesn't seem three months since we left
England, does it?

BARBARA: I can't believe we're here yet. Giacomo, Giacomo, why
is it so new, every day? Giacomo, why is it always more? It's
always more, isn't it?

WESSON *(putting his arms round her)*: You're a Judy! *(Kisses her.)*

BARBARA: Do you love me?

WESSON: Not a bit.

BARBARA: Not a teenty bit?

WESSON: Not a seroddy atom. *(Laughs—tightens her in his arms—
kisses her.)*

BARBARA: You're a *common* thing!

WESSON: Am I no gentleman, as Frederick said?

BARBARA: No, no one could ever accuse you of being a gentleman.

WESSON: Am I a lout?

BARBARA: Oh—*did* it call him a lout!

WESSON: Am I a clodhopper?

BARBARA: Now—that makes me happy! That Frederick should call
you a clodhopper—no, that is too much joy!

WESSON: Have they called me any more names?

BARBARA: You forget the clumsy clown——

WESSON: That your papa would have kicked downstairs—think of
the poor old winded baronet——

BARBARA: Who's had his Selma all his life! And then says you're
a degraded scoundrel for running away with me.

WESSON: Yes—his rotten old cheek.

BARBARA: He's a failure, too, you know—Papa's a failure! Why
are all people failures?

WESSON: Couldn't say.

BARBARA: It's because their women have been so rotten to them.
Mama treated my father badly, she did, just because of his
Selma.

WESSON: You'd let *me* have a Selma, wouldn't you?

BARBARA: What! *I'd* show you—I'll show you if you try any of your little games on me. But poor Papa—everything he has done has gone wrong—his money—he had no son——

WESSON: So there'll be no fifth baronet—how sad—what an awful loss to society!

BARBARA: And here am I, his favourite daughter, have run away with the son of a coal-miner, from my good and loving husband.

WESSON: The right worthy Frederick Tressider, doctor of medicine. Gentleman of means. Worth a dozen of me.

BARBARA: Oh, how I hated his wooden face!

WESSON: Well, you knocked spots off it pretty roughly.

BARBARA: How common, how inexpressibly common your language is.

WESSON: There goes the milk. *(Dashes to the fire.)* Are you going to have bregger in the kitchen, or in the bedroom?

BARBARA: We'll have it here for once. Should we—because of this lovely fire—put some more sticks on.

WESSON: Put 'em on yourself—or, wait a minute—want eggs, or don't you?

BARBARA: Yes, let's have eggs.

WESSON: You're a lazy little devil.

BARBARA: Think—think how I worked yesterday!

WESSON: Yes—it nearly killed you, didn't it!

Silence for a moment.

BARBARA: Poor Frederick. He *does* love me! If I'd seen it before I'd left him—I don't think I could have done it. Why did he always hide it from me?

WESSON: He didn't. You merely never saw it.

BARBARA: Oh, but it never came out!

WESSON: What did you *want* him to do! He loved you right enough; you merely didn't love him—and there it stands.

BARBARA: But—I knew he was in love with me—but—why could I never *feel* his love? Why could I never feel it *warm* me?

WESSON: Because you never wanted to. You were non-conductive to this particular form of love, that's all.

BARBARA: Think, I was married to him for three years, and I was no nearer to him than I am to that fornello.

WESSON: Poor devil—it wasn't his fault.

BARBARA: Yes, I have treated him badly.

WESSON: You might have done worse by staying with him.

BARBARA: But think—how he adored me! Why did it never seem anything to me, his love? But think, Giacomo, how he must suffer—such a highly esteemed man, and so proud and sensitive——

WESSON: And we'd only known each other three weeks.

BARBARA: Oh, Giacomo; it makes me tremble! Do you think we shall bring it off?

WESSON: We shall—if we make up our minds to. But if you keep footling with the idea of Frederick, and your people, and duty—then we shan't.

BARBARA: But, Giacomo—they loved me so.

WESSON: So do I.

BARBARA: Yes, but they needed me more. And I belonged to them! And they say love wears off—and if it does!

WESSON: You were saying only a minute since it was always more.

BARBARA: Giacomo, I'm frightened.

WESSON: What of?

BARBARA: Of everything—and sometimes I wonder—don't be cross if I say it, will you?

WESSON: Say what you like.

BARBARA: Sometimes I wonder—it seems horrid—I wonder if I can trust you.

WESSON: Why?

BARBARA: You are so queer—and I am so all alone—and if you weren't good to me——

WESSON: I think you needn't be mean——

BARBARA: But look—you seem to want to take me away from everything and everybody. I feel as if you wanted to swallow me, and take my will away. You won't do it, will you, Giacomo?

WESSON: You're fatter than I am—ask a cat not to swallow a camel.

BARBARA: But do you think Frederick will divorce me?

WESSON: You'll have to insist on it.

BARBARA: No—I can't—it seems so cruel. I can't, dear. He's so cut up. You know, he says he can't publicly accuse me.

WESSON: If he'd hate you and have done with it, it would be easier. Or if he loved you, he would offer you divorce. But no, he messes about between one thing and another, and sentimentalizes.

BARBARA: But he *does* love me, Giacomo.

WESSON: And a fat lot of use it is to you. But he sees you don't clearly want a divorce and so he hangs on. Now he talks about your going to live with your mother, and repenting, then he'll have you back. But you like to leave a loophole by which you could creep out and go back, don't you? Ah, you do.

BARBARA: No—no—don't say it—don't say it. Only I'm frightened.

WESSON: You know your people have given out you've gone into a convent in France, for a little while, because you had got religious ideas or something like that. And I know they think you'll come crawling back at last—and Frederick is waiting for you—he's waiting—and you like to have it so—you do.

BARBARA *(putting her arms round his neck)*: No, it's not true, Giacometti, it's not true. I *do* love you, don't I?

WESSON: You only don't want to belong to me.

BARBARA: But I do belong to you.

WESSON: You don't—you tamper with the idea of Frederick.

BARBARA: He'd never do to me what you want to do.

WESSON: What?

BARBARA: Humble me, and make me nothing—and then swallow me. And it's *wrong*. It's *wrong* for you to want to swallow me. I am myself—and you ought to leave me free.

WESSON: Well, so I do.

BARBARA: You don't. All the time you're at me. Oh, and I hate you so sometimes, Giacomo. Now you're cross with me.

WESSON: I should think the eggs are done.

BARBARA *(seating herself)*: I'm hungry, Giacomo—are you?

WESSON: No—it makes me sick, the way you're always bleeding my self-respect.

BARBARA: *I! I!* Why it's I who've given you your self-respect. Think of the crumpled up, despairing, hating creature that came into Mrs Kelly's drawing-room—and now look at yourself.

WESSON: But you *won't* love me—you want to keep upper hand.

BARBARA *(laughing with scorn)*: There you are quite mistaken. *I* want there to be *no* upper hand. I only want both of us to be free to be ourselves—and you seem as if you *can't* have it—you want to bully me, you want to bully me inside.

WESSON: All right—eat your breakfast then.

BARBARA: And it makes me feel as if I want to run—I want to run from you.

WESSON: Back to Frederick.

BARBARA: Yes—poor Frederick—he never made me feel like this. I was always a free woman with him.

WESSON: And mightily you regretted it.

BARBARA: No—no! Not that! Your idea of marriage is like the old savages: hit a woman on the head and run off with her.

WESSON: Very well.

> *The bell rings noisily.*

There's the butcher.

> *Goes out door R—voices—re-enter* WESSON.

What do you want?

BARBARA: I don't know—what do we?

WESSON: I!——

> *He turns round. The butcher, a handsome young fellow of about twenty, has followed him and stands in the doorway.*

BARBARA: Oh!—Buon giorno!

BUTCHER: Buon giorno, signora.

BARBARA: Piove?

BUTCHER: Si.

BARBARA: Ah!—e il lago——?

BUTCHER: È burrascoso.

BARBARA: Ah—tempo cattivo per voi

> *The butcher laughs.*

WESSON: What do you want?

BARBARA: Er—ha vitello?

BUTCHER: Si—Si—quanto?

BARBARA: How much do we want?

WESSON: Mezzo chilo.

BARBARA: Mezzo chilo.

BUTCHER *(touching his hood)*: Grazia—buon giorno.

> *The door is heard to close.*

BARBARA: Oh, I like him, I like him—you said he wasn't nice.

WESSON: He's not—look at the way he comes in.

BARBARA: I like it. It's so decided, at any rate. I hate English people for the way they always hang fire.

WESSON: Do you?

BARBARA: Yes! I like him as he stands there—he looks like a wild young bull or something, peering out of his hood.

WESSON: And you flirt with him.

BARBARA: *Wesson!*

WESSON: I know it's a great insult to say so. But he *is* good-look-ing—and see the way you stretch out your arm, and show your throat.

BARBARA: But Wesson, how *can* you. I simply spoke to him. And when you think of yourself with the servant maid——

WESSON: I only laugh—you sort of show yourself.

BARBARA: Well, really, this is too much!

WESSON: True, whether or not. And you're always doing it. You always want men to think I don't *keep* you. You write to your mother like that, you write to Frederick like that—always as if I didn't keep you, as if you were rather undecided, you would make up your mind to walk away from me in a little while, probably.

BARBARA: How *can* you be so false? It would serve you right if I *did* leave you.

WESSON: I know that, you've said it before.

BARBARA: Really—no one but a common man would say I flirted with that butcher——

WESSON: Well, I *am* common—what's the odds? You've lived with me for three months.

BARBARA: That doesn't say I shall live with you for ever.

WESSON: You can go the minute you want to go.

BARBARA: Ha, could I! It's easy for you to talk. You'd see, when it came to it, how you would let me go.

WESSON: I wouldn't try to stop you, if you really, really wanted to leave me. But you've got to convince me of that first.

BARBARA: You think there's not another like you, don't you?

WESSON: For you, there isn't.

BARBARA: I'm not so sure.

WESSON: I am! But try, only try. Only try, and make your mis-take. But it'll be too late, once you've done it.

BARBARA: Pooh! you needn't think you'll threaten me.

WESSON: I only tell you. Can I give you anything?

BARBARA: The honey.

He rises and gets it from the cupboard.

WESSON: I wait on you, yet I want to bully you.

BARBARA: Yes, it's subtler than that.

WESSON: If you let me wait on you, you leave yourself in my hands.

BARBARA: Not a bit of it—not a bit of it! Do you think it makes any difference to me? Frederick would have waited on me on his knees.

WESSON: Then it's time somebody taught you you're not as great as you think. You imagine you're the one and only phœnix.

BARBARA *(laughing)*: And I am, aren't I, Giacometti? Say I am.

WESSON: I say you're a pecky, scratchy one, at that rate.

BARBARA: No—no! Say I'm nice—say I'm ever so nice.

WESSON: On rare occasions.

BARBARA: Always—say always.

WESSON: It wouldn't be true.

BARBARA: Yes—yes, it would, Giacomo. See, I'm ever so nice, aren't I? I'm ever so nice! Look at my nice arms, how they love you.

WESSON: Better than you do.

BARBARA: No—not better than I do. Come and kiss them. Come and give them a little kiss.

WESSON *(going and kissing her arms)*: You're cruel, if you're nothing else.

BARBARA: No, I'm not. Say I'm not. Kiss me!

  WESSON, *laughing shakily, kisses her—A voice is heard outside. "La posta."*

WESSON: Oh, Lord, there's the postman—he's the serpent in my Eden.

VOICE: La posta!

  WESSON *goes to the door, re-enters with letters.*

WESSON *(tearing open an envelope)*: The serpent's left his venom.

BARBARA *(making a frightened face)*: Is it Frederick?

WESSON: And your mother.

BARBARA: Oh dear! Gia, I can't stand it.

WESSON: Why not?

BARBARA: I can't stand it—I can't—poor Frederick. If he was ill, Giacomo?

WESSON: He'd have to get better.

BARBARA: He might die.

WESSON: He wouldn't be such a fool. What's up in your letter?

BARBARA *(wiping her eyes)*: It seems so cruel!

WESSON: Your father's ill.

BARBARA *(starting and snatching the letter from his hand)*: Papa!
   She reads, crying quietly. WESSON *sits waiting—he has read
   Frederick's letter.*
BARBARA *(looking up)*: Is he very ill, Giacomo?
WESSON: No.
BARBARA: They'll say it's me.
WESSON: Let 'em. It's the whisky, as a matter of fact.
BARBARA: Look how cruel mama is, "Your father is very ill, but he
   does not wish to see you while you continue your present mode
   of life. The doctor says he is to be spared all strain and anxiety."
WESSON: And they're thinking of going to Harrogate, so he's not
   at death's door.
BARBARA: And look at Frederick's letter—"Ever since you drove a
   spike into my brain, on February the 24th, I have been mad." Do
   you think he *is* mad, Giacomo?
WESSON: A bit, perhaps—but so were you when you lived with
   him—going clean cracked.
BARBARA: He won't commit suicide, will he?
WESSON: No—no more than I shall.
BARBARA *(reading)*: "There are some nights when I never sleep at
   all—I try to work, but my brain has gone." *(Shudders.)*
WESSON: It *is* vile—but I can't help it. Think of the hell if you
   went back to him.
BARBARA *(reading—laughs)*: "Do not speak of Wesson. I do not
   wish to hear of his existence, or to know that he exists. Only,
   if ever he crosses my path, I will crush him like a beetle." How
   strong his feelings are!
WESSON: His words, you mean.
BARBARA: No, he *is* passionate—you don't know. And he *can* hate.
WESSON: He can sound like it.
BARBARA: But if he came here and killed you?
WESSON: I should offer myself to the knife, of course. I must
   practise being "daggerous" in readiness. *(Puts a pointed kitchen
   knife between his teeth.)* So!
BARBARA: Oh, you are lovely! *(Laughs.)* Let me kiss you. *(He takes
   the knife from between his teeth—she kisses him.)* Oh, the way
   he submits! Doesn't he like it, then?
WESSON: He likes it all right—but he's sick of this tragedy.
BARBARA: Are you tired of me, Giacomo?

WESSON: Tired of the mess we're in, that's all.

BARBARA: Do you want to be rid of me?

WESSON: I want to be sure of you.

BARBARA: Well, and you are. *Do* you think Frederick will ever let me go?

WESSON: You must insist on his divorcing you.

BARBARA: But I daren't, Giacomo, I daren't.

WESSON: You'd rather remain as we are?

BARBARA: No—no! Only he seems something so sure—you know—like when he said: "You have dishonoured our marriage vow, but I never will."

WESSON: That's as he pleases.

BARBARA: But it's rather fine.

WESSON: He *is* fine, in a thousand ways where I'm not. But you never loved him.

BARBARA: No—I never loved him. Poor Frederick, it doesn't seem fair, does it?

WESSON: It does not. You were rottenly unfair to him.

BARBARA: In what way?

WESSON: Holding him cheap. Holding his love for you lightly, when it was the biggest thing about him.

BARBARA: *Why* did it never seem so much to me, till I'd left him?

WESSON: You hated him. While he could keep you, he felt a man—but you didn't mean to be kept—you tortured him—you fought against him—you undermined him—you were killing him.

BARBARA: Oh no—oh no! I never hated him. I did a lot for him.

WESSON: You, perhaps, had plenty of good-will towards him—but you tortured him like hell. You, with your kindness, are one of the cruellest things going.

BARBARA: How *can* you say so, Giacomo! Am I cruel to you?

WESSON: You are.

BARBARA *(laughing)*: It seems to me only funny when you say I'm cruel—I, who wouldn't hurt a fly.

WESSON: Then I wish I was a fly, and not a man.

BARBARA: Aw, did it be a man!—did it be a little man in trousers, then, did it!

WESSON: It did!—I think they're getting a bit impatient, your people. You'll see they'll combine forces just now to get you back.

BARBARA: Even if they did, I'd be gone again in three weeks.

WESSON: But if they got hold of the right handle, they'd get you back and keep you.

BARBARA: What handle?

WESSON: Oh, I dunno. Your pity, your self-sacrifice, your desire to be straight.

BARBARA: Self-sacrifice! There's a lot of self-sacrifice about me. *(Laughs.)* They'd find I don't work well with *that* handle.

WESSON: You don't know yourself. *You* keep them dangling.

BARBARA: Why do you hate me?

WESSON: Go to hell.

BARBARA *(plaintive)*: Are you cross with me? But you *are*! *(very plaintive)*. *Why* are you cross with me, Giacomo, when I love you?

WESSON: You—you only love yourself.

BARBARA: No, Giacometti, no, I don't. See how loving I am, really —see how unselfish I am——

WESSON: So unselfish you'd rob Peter to pay Paul, then go back to Peter to console him.

BARBARA: You're horrid to me.

WESSON: And you are worse to me.

BARBARA: But I'm not.

WESSON: Hm.

BARBARA *(mocking him)*: "Hm!"—what common grunts! Kiss me *(pleading)*: Don't you want to kiss me?

WESSON: No.

BARBARA *(sadly)*: Aw!

WESSON *(turning and taking her in his arms)*: You're a baggage.

BARBARA: Do you *want* to kiss me? *(She draws back.)*

WESSON: Resigned, I kiss the rod.

BARBARA: And am I the rod? Oh, Giacomo, think of *me* as a rod.

WESSON: *You* see if Frederick and your mother aren't up to some little trick just now.

BARBARA: I'm frightened, Giacomo.

WESSON: Then you're frightened of yourself, of your own hesitating, half-and-half, neither-fish-flesh-fowl—nor—good-red-herring self.

CURTAIN

ACT II

Evening, several days after the first act. The dining-room of the same villa—a rather large room, with piano, writing-desk and old furniture. In the big bay window, which looks over a garden on to the lake, is a large couch. BARBARA *is lying on the couch* WESSON, *without his collar and tie, sits beside her.*

WESSON: You've got a nice chin.

BARBARA: Frederick used to adore it.

WESSON: Then he'd no business to.

BARBARA *(putting her arms round his neck)*: Dear!

WESSON: Don't you wish there'd never been any Frederick—or anybody else——

BARBARA: Well, *you* haven't much room to talk; look what a mess your women had got you into.

WESSON: But don't you wish we could have come straight to each other, and been married simply, before we'd knocked about?

BARBARA: I don't trust marriage.

WESSON: Because you were stupid and married wrong—that's not the fault of marriage.

BARBARA: No—but I don't trust it.

WESSON: Folk are such fools, they should marry the right people.

BARBARA: Even when the right people are *married*, they go wrong.

WESSON: No—I don't believe it—and I don't believe you love me— and whether you do or not, I *do* love you.

BARBARA: Because you've decided to.

WESSON: Yes, because I know. I may hate you, I may rage against you, I may sneer at you—very well! It doesn't alter the fact that I love you.

BARBARA: It seems to me so queer, to make up your mind that you love anybody.

WESSON: You poke holes in me—well, I'll patch 'em up—I won't give in.

BARBARA: Oh—oh—the dear! He's on his nice little high horse, is he? Oh!—he should be on the roundabouts, on his wooden prancer!

WESSON: Or on a round-about chicken.

BARBARA: And he looks so pathetic on his chicken—the dear. *(Kisses him.)*

WESSON: Will you stick to me, Barbara?

BARBARA: Oh, did it want to be stuck to? It shall then—Oh, it's nice hair!

WESSON: Till death do us part——

BARBARA: Aw, is it talking about death, is it—aw!

WESSON: It's ten-past-six. What train did your mother say—the five-to-six?

BARBARA *(starting)*: No, half-past seven.

WESSON: The six train has just gone.

BARBARA: Are you frightened?

WESSON: No—no—I'm not frightened. Only we're rather raw, really, about the business. It seems funny that we're a scandal.

BARBARA: Doesn't it!

WESSON: I'll go and look if I can see anybody, shall I?

BARBARA: Yes! Kiss me first. *(He kisses her.)*

> Exit WESSON. BARBARA *sits up straightening her hair. She is in Bavarian peasant dress, with bare arms and throat.* WESSON *comes running in.*

WESSON: I don't think it's she—but there *is* a woman——

BARBARA: Good gracious—and look at us! *(She flies out—her voice is heard, excited)*: yes—it's she. Quick!

WESSON: Well, I must get my collar on first.

> *In a great flurry, he ties his tie, then runs out. The stage is empty. Then voices are heard.*

VOICE OF BARBARA: Poor Mama!

> *They both laugh—there is silence. The door-bell rings loudly.* BARBARA *rushes in and stands near the door.* WESSON *is heard outside.*

VOICE OF WESSON: Oh, how do you do! This is earlier than we thought.

VOICE OF LADY CHARLCOTE: How do you do, Mr Wesson?

> *Enter* LADY CHARLCOTE—*about sixty—white hair, shortish, stout, rather handsome—looks resentful—uglily dressed.*

BARBARA : Oh—Mama!

Runs forward, laughing shakily—does not kiss—takes her mother's hand—then stands embarrassed.

LADY CHARLCOTE *(looking round)* : Yes——

BARBARA : Take your things off——

LADY CHARLCOTE : But I mustn't stay—I mustn't stay. *(Taking off her gloves—nervous.)* I want to say to you, Mr Wesson, why don't you do something for Barbara?

WESSON *(astonished)* : But I do.

LADY CHARLCOTE : But you don't. A married woman, and you keep her here with you as she is. It is wrong, quite wrong.

WESSON : But you don't know—you don't understand.

LADY CHARLCOTE : Yes, yes, I do understand. It is you who don't understand. What right have you to do it? Barbara has a husband in England, a good honest gentleman, who is going mad because of her. She is here, but she can go back.

BARBARA : But, Mama, what I do, I do of myself. *(She is crocheting nervously.)*

LADY CHARLCOTE : Yes. *(Turning to* WESSON.*)* You have not got even enough money to keep her. She has to have money from her sister, from her friends. She is the daughter of a high-born and highly cultured gentleman.

BARBARA : But if I choose to do it, Mama, it is my own affair.

LADY CHARLCOTE : No, it isn't. Think of your father—think of Frederick. *(Turning to* WESSON.*)* And do you expect to build up happiness on the ruins of this life? You cannot. Think of your future. You can do nothing with my daughter. You can't put her in her own station, you can't even give her an honest name. Is she to live with you, and take money from her husband and her friends?

WESSON : She needn't take any money from anybody.

LADY CHARLCOTE : And you say you will live here. You try it for six months, Mr Wesson, and you will wish yourself dead, you will find it so dull. And Barbara is to be the servant, and she is to have no friends, no, not a friend in the world, but is to live buried here among these common Italians. Another man's wedding ring and engagement ring on her finger at this minute. The very bills of her last dresses left for her husband to pay.

BARBARA: But, Mama, I'm not a horse that is to be kept. You don't consider me.

LADY CHARLCOTE: Yes, it is you I consider. How can any man say he loves you, when he brings you into this shame. Where will you live?

WESSON: But if there were a divorce——

LADY CHARLCOTE *(to him)*: You think only of yourself. Think of her father. He is getting old now. Where will he go, that he can hold his head up. It is a shame that will kill him. It will kill everybody. *(Beginning to cry—looking in her handbag for a hanky.)* We are old, and hoped to live at last in peace. Haven't we had trouble enough in our lives? And how can I sleep at night, thinking of my daughter, and what is to become of her. Her father does not want to see her again. *(Cries.)* There is no rest, and no peace. Her husband comes, and it nearly kills me to see the state he is in. A woman—what is to become of her, what is to become of her. And you keep her here.

WESSON: No—I don't keep her.

LADY CHARLCOTE: Yes, you keep her here—the daughter of a highly cultured gentleman, as your mistress. It is impossible. And her husband is so good. He will have her back in spite of all, and everything can be hushed up——

BARBARA: I don't want things to be hushed up. What I do I want to be done openly——

LADY CHARLCOTE: Don't be a fool—you can't live on ideas.

WESSON: No—I don't want people to talk——

LADY CHARLCOTE: But they *will* talk. Sir William and I have come out here because they've started—and his heart so bad! We expect to be considered by our children, but they turn on us. It's not natural that we should have all this trouble now, when we're not expecting it. Everything begins to look comfortable, and Barbara so well settled, when this happens. As her mother, as a woman older than yourself, I've *got* to tell you it's wrong, absolutely wrong, and can only end in sorrow. You will see in a few years' time where you will be. It is my duty to warn you. And you must let Barbara go back with me.

> WESSON *shakes his head*—BARBARA *crochets nervously— there is silence.*

BARBARA: Has Papa come with you, then?

LADY CHARLCOTE: Yes—we're staying a month with Laura in Gardone.

WESSON *(rising)*: Let me give you something to eat.

LADY CHARLCOTE: No—no—I must be going at once. I must be going. It's such a long way to the station.

WESSON: Excuse me.

> *Exit* WESSON.

BARBARA *(quietly)*: How does Frederick look?

LADY CHARLCOTE: Oh, poor fellow! If you saw him, you could never do it.

BARBARA *(bending her head over her work)*: Is he ill?

LADY CHARLCOTE: Ill!—poor fellow! He is three parts mad! And he loves you, Barbara, he loves you! How can you throw away the love of a man like that?

BARBARA: Does he really want *me*, or does he want his reputation— or rather mine.

LADY CHARLCOTE: Poor fellow—such a position to leave him in. And has he ever been anything but good to you? You have had every-thing you wanted——

BARBARA: I haven't. He *has* been good to me—I wish he hadn't, it would have been easier. He has been good to me, and he's given me everything he could. But I haven't had what I wanted, no, and he couldn't give it me.

LADY CHARLCOTE: And do you mean that this man can?

> BARBARA *crochets in silence—they wait for each other.*

BARBARA: Will it kill him?

LADY CHARLCOTE: I tell him, at this rate he won't live long.

> *Enter* WESSON *with a tray, wine, biscuits, bread and butter.*

WESSON: Will you have a glass of wine—it's "vin de pays", but it's —at any rate, it's all right for me, though I'm no connoisseur.

LADY CHARLCOTE: No, thank you.

WESSON: Could I make you a cup of tea?

LADY CHARLCOTE: Oh no, thank you very much.

BARBARA: Is Papa in Gardone?

LADY CHARLCOTE: In Brescia—but he doesn't want to see you. Oh, thank you—But he expects you to come back in a proper state of mind—I think it's all you can do, to make the best of it now. This *is* impossible. *(Neither of them answers.)* And we are staying at the Monte Baldo. You will write to me, Barbara.

BARBARA: Yes. Good-bye, Mama. *(They shake hands.)*

LADY CHARLCOTE: Good-bye. *(To* WESSON*)*: Oh, don't you trouble to come out.

WESSON: I think it is no good for Barbara to go back to Frederick. It would only be misery for them both. They can't——

> *Exit talking.* BARBARA *remains alone. Her hands fall in her lap, and she broods. There is sound of a carriage—re-enter* WESSON—*he flings his cap on the table. When* BARBARA *hears him coming she picks up her crocheting. When he enters she looks up with a laugh.*

BARBARA: Poor Mama—always full of commonsense. She was always a good one at showing the sensible side of the affair. But didn't it seem common to you—like any of the women of the common people you've told me about?

WESSON: Just. Only it's natural. At any rate she wasn't lofty.

BARBARA: Oh no—Mama would never have been that. She would have said just the same to a Grand Duke.

WESSON: She wouldn't—look at the money business. You *don't* need any of their money—we *can* live on what I earn.

BARBARA: And *I* don't mind making your bed. I wouldn't do it for any man—no, I wouldn't. But I don't mind.

WESSON: If I can't give you much money, well, I give you everything I've got.

BARBARA: Yes, it was mean of her, bringing that up—it's like kicking a man when he's down.

WESSON: But I suppose anybody would do it. She doesn't seem superior, that's one thing. But I hate them! Why can't they leave us alone! What do I care what the old Mrs Baronet says.

BARBARA *(laughing)*: You looked as if you didn't care—the way you sat in that chair. *(Imitates him, half crouching.)*

WESSON: Well—that coming all at once——

BARBARA: When we'd been so happy—yes, it *was* a bit overwhelming!

WESSON: I thought the heavens had opened and the last day come.

BARBARA: You looked it—the way you sat crumpled up in that chair. *(Laughs.)*

WESSON: What could I do?

BARBARA *(laughing)*: You looked so frightened, so crumpled up! I expected you every minute to wither away into nothing. *(Laughs uncontrollably)* I thought there'd be nothing left of you *(interrupted by her laughter)*. You—you seemed to get less and less—till—*(helpless with laughter)* I thought you'd be gone. *(laughing)* I was frightened—I wanted to get hold of your coat-tails *(laugh)* to keep you.

WESSON: Well, what could I *do*?

BARBARA: I thought you were going to creep under that desk. *(Shaking and helpless with laughter, she points to the hole under the writing desk, by which he sits.)* I thought you were going to crawl inside like a dog into a kennel *(helpless laughter)* and pop your head out, and look sideways at her, and say "Yap—yap" in a little, frightened voice—then rush inside.

WESSON: Well—if she'd been a man, I might have shouted—but what else could I do?

BARBARA: You looked so crumpled up, with your little tail between your legs. *(Laughs.)* You *did* want to get into that corner. *(Laughs helplessly—then rises.)* Mind, let me show you. *(Laughing, she almost falls to the floor, then creeps inside the space under the desk—pokes out her head—falls face forward on the floor with laughter—lifts up her face, peering sideways.)* Yap—yapyap! Yap!—the little dog! *(She shrieks with laughter—he giggles from time to time—she rises again.)*

WESSON: No—I wasn't as bad as that.

BARBARA *(shrieking)*: You were, you were! I thought I should have died. And every minute I had visions of you collapsing under the desk and barking at Mama. *(Laughing.)* Poor Mama, what would she have done if you had?

WESSON: I wish I had.

BARBARA: I wish you had, I wish you had! *(Drying her eyes.)* But no, you sat there getting less and less. You can go so little, like a dying pig.

WESSON: Well, *you* were impressed, you know you were.

BARBARA: I wasn't—I wanted to scream. Why didn't you suddenly get up and flap your arms like a cockerel and crow?

WESSON: But what good would it have done?

BARBARA: It would have been so beautiful. Or you might have got astride on a chair and gone riding round the room, shouting.

WESSON: I might have done a lot of things.

BARBARA: Oh, you might, and you did nothing but crumple up!

What a pity! *(Beginning to laugh again.)* You looked anything but a hero that time.

WESSON: I didn't feel a hero. And if I'd crowed like a cock I shouldn't have looked a hero.

BARBARA: Mama little thought what havoc she'd work in our little ménage. *(Laughing.)* But why do you take it so seriously?

WESSON: I don't take it seriously, but I reckon it's rather rotten of her. We thought she was coming friendlily, to help. . . . What will you eat?

BARBARA: I don't mind a bit.

WESSON *(drinking wine)*: Drink?

BARBARA: Thank you. *(She drinks a little.)*

WESSON: I told her the only thing possible was a divorce.

BARBARA: You know what a muddler she is. She blows with every wind.

WESSON: I don't care how she blows, so long as we can get that divorce.

BARBARA: If she goes and gets Frederick's back up now, God knows when you'll get it, I tell you.

WESSON: I don't care—they can all go to hell! But until you stand up in front of me and say, "I want definitely to go back to Frederick—you're no good to me", I shall tell them to go to blazes.

BARBARA: It looks as if you'll tell them a lot. Poor little dog, is his tail coming up again? Come here and be kissed.

WESSON: I don't want to be kissed. Will you eat now?

BARBARA: Just as you like.

WESSON: A tray is ready.

> *Goes out—returns immediately with the supper tray.*

BARBARA: Poor Frederick—it does twist my inside to think about him.

WESSON: And a lot of good may it do you.

BARBARA: Do you think he really might go mad?

WESSON: Not unless he's weak-minded to start with.

BARBARA: Well, he isn't—his mind is stronger than yours, if it came to it.

WESSON *(rather ashamed)*: I know he's not—and he won't go mad.

BARBARA: But he loves me so. *(Plaintively.)*

WESSON: He should have more sense, then, for you don't love *him*.

BARBARA : But I do, Giacomo.

WESSON : Very well, you *do*, then.

BARBARA : And I can't bear him to suffer.

WESSON : You made him suffer worse underneath, twisting your spear in his secret wound, before you left him, than you do now that it's open. He can doctor an open wound. A secret one drives him mad.

BARBARA : But I didn't torture him. I was a joy to him. And think of it, Giacomo, I was the only joy he'd ever had in his life.

WESSON : And the only sorrow.

BARBARA : Why do you want to say horrid things about me?

WESSON : I don't.

BARBARA : But you do! Look, you say I tortured Frederick.

WESSON : So you did. So you torture me.

BARBARA : But how?—tell me *how*, Giacomo.

WESSON : You needn't laugh at me when I'm feeling a fool.

BARBARA : You hate me, Giacomo.

WESSON : Does it please you?

BARBARA : Why should it please me? Why *should* it please me, Giacomo?

WESSON : It appears to. You seem to exult.

BARBARA : I exult because you wither away when Mama scolds you! I assure you I don't exult in your heroic appearance *then*.

WESSON : I don't ask you to.

BARBARA : What does he want then—does he want me to fall at his feet and worship him, does he then? *(She does so—goes on her knees at his feet, puts her forehead to the ground—raises it up and down—in a consoling, mocking voice.)* La—di-da—di-da! —did it want to be worshipped?

WESSON *(seizing her by the arm)* : Get up, you lunatic.

BARBARA : But don't you like to be worshipped?

WESSON *(gripping her arm)* : Get up.

> *She rises slowly—he grips both her arms.*

You love! You love only *yourself*!

BARBARA *(putting her tongue out at him)* : Tra—la-la—la!

WESSON : Yes.

BARBARA: Tra—la-la—la! *(He remains holding her—she says, almost pleading)* : Let me go.

WESSON : I won't.

BARBARA: I'll make you.

WESSON: Try!

BARBARA: I *will*!

WESSON: Try! *(A moment of silence.)*

BARBARA *(subduedly)*: You hurt my arms.

WESSON *(through his teeth)*: And why shouldn't I?

BARBARA: Don't be horrid.

   WESSON *puts his arms round her, fastens her close.*

WESSON: Oh, you're not faithful to me!

   His voice is like a cry. He reaches forward, his mouth to her throat.

BARBARA *(thickly)*: I am.

CURTAIN

ACT III

SCENE I

Morning, the next day. BARBARA *in walking-out dress,* WESSON *in an old jacket.*

BARBARA: What time did the man say Mama would be here?

WESSON: I understood she would come for you in a carriage at ten o'clock.

BARBARA: And did she really say you mustn't come?

WESSON: She said she wished to drive alone with you.

BARBARA: Put your coat on and come, too.

WESSON: No—perhaps she wants to talk to you, and to have you to herself a bit. It's natural. You needn't do anything that you don't want to do.

BARBARA: Why *should* she ask me for a drive without *you*? It's like her impudence—I *won't* go!

WESSON: Yes, you'd better.

BARBARA: You'd say I'd better do any miserable thing they liked to ask me.

WESSON: Alright.

BARBARA: Why don't you say I *oughtn't* to go for a drive with Mama without you?

WESSON: Because I don't care—your mother can use all her persuasions and reasons till she's sick of it.

BARBARA: But why should she?

WESSON: It's probably the shortest way, if we stick to ourselves all through.

BARBARA: A fine lot of sticking to yourself *you* do, don't you? Think of the shrivelling creature whom Mama scolded yesterday.

WESSON: I *was* true to myself, then—and to you.

BARBARA: Were you—were you! Then I'll have another kind of fidelity, thank you.

WESSON: You won't. And now you'd better go.

BARBARA: Go!

WESSON: For your drive. You'll find Lady Charlcote before you get to the Piazza.

BARBARA: And if I don't choose to?

WESSON (*shrugging*): You'll please yourself.

BARBARA: Tra—la-la—la!

WESSON: I wish you'd go.

BARBARA: Why do you wish I'd go? I will, then.

Exit—the door is heard to bang. WESSON *watches her.*

WESSON: There goes the carriage, and the old lady. I should like to murder the twopence-ha'penny lot of them, with their grizzling and whining and chuffing. If they'd leave us alone we should be alright—damn them! Miserable bits of shouters! My mother was worth a million of 'em, for they've none of 'em the backbone of a flea—She doesn't *want* to stick to me—she doesn't *want* to love me—she won't *let* herself love me. She wants to save some rotten rag of independence—she's afraid to let herself go and to belong to me.

He goes to the sideboard, drinks wine, looks at a book, throws it down, plays a dozen chords on the piano, gets up, drinks more wine, sits down to write, and remains perfectly still, as if transfixed—all the time he has moved quietly—the door-bell rings—he does not hear—it rings louder—he starts up and goes to the door—is heard saying, "How do you do? Will you come in?" Enter SIR WILLIAM CHARLCOTE—*short, stout, a gentleman—grey bristling moustache.*

WESSON: Will you sit down?

SIR WILLIAM (*taking a seat near the door*): Thank you.

WESSON (*offering cigarettes in a threepenny packet*): Excuse the packet.

SIR WILLIAM: Thank you, I have some of my own.

WESSON *throws the packet on the table and sits on the couch.*

WESSON: It's a nice day.

SIR WILLIAM: Yes. (*Clearing his throat.*) I called to hear from yourself an account of what you intend to do.

WESSON (*knitting his fingers*): I intend to do nothing but what I am doing.

SIR WILLIAM: And what is that?

WESSON: Living here—working——

SIR WILLIAM: And keeping my daughter under the present conditions?

WESSON: Barbara stays as long as she will. I am here for her while she wants me.

SIR WILLIAM: But you have no right to be here for her to want.

WESSON: But I say, while ever she wants me, I am here for her.

SIR WILLIAM: Don't you see that is cowardly and base.

WESSON: Is it the morality of it you want to discuss?

SIR WILLIAM: Yes—yes—it is the *right* of it. You may perhaps think I have no room to talk. That is like your damned impudence.

WESSON: But that's not the point.

SIR WILLIAM: A man has a right to any woman whom he can get, so long as she's not a married woman. Go with all the unmarried women you like. But touch a married woman, and you are a scoundrel.

WESSON: So!

SIR WILLIAM: It destroys the whole family system, and strikes at the whole of society. A man who does it is as much a criminal as a thief, a burglar, or even a murderer. You see my point?

WESSON: Your point of view.

SIR WILLIAM: You see so much. Then you see what you are doing: a criminal act against the State, against the rights of man altogether, against Dr Tressider, and against my daughter.

WESSON: So!

SIR WILLIAM: And seeing *that*, only an—only a criminal by conviction can continue in what he is doing—a fellow who deserves to be locked up.

WESSON: If life went according to deserts.

SIR WILLIAM: If you intend to behave in the least like a man, you will clear out of this place——

WESSON: I've got the house on a six months' lease.

SIR WILLIAM: I will pay the lease.

WESSON: It is paid—but I like the place, and prefer to stay.

SIR WILLIAM: That is, you will continue to keep my daughter in—in—in this shame and scandal——

WESSON: She chooses to stay.

SIR WILLIAM: If plain reasoning will not convince you, we must try other methods.

WESSON: Very well.

SIR WILLIAM : You—whom I thought to be doing a service by asking you to my house——

    The bell rings.

WESSON *(rising)* : Excuse me a moment.

    Exit—voices—enter BARBARA, *followed by* LADY CHARLCOTE *and* WESSON.

BARBARA : Papa!

SIR WILLIAM : I came to speak with this man.

BARBARA : But why behind my back?

SIR WILLIAM : I will come when I like. I will not have women, and especially women like you, about me when I have anything to say.

BARBARA : Nor more will I have men like you interfering with my affairs behind my back, Papa!

LADY CHARLCOTE : For shame, Barbara.

BARBARA *(turning, flashing)* : What right has he to come bullying Wesson behind my back. *I* came away with him—it was *I* who suggested he should come to Italy with me when I was coming to see Laura. So when you have anything to say, Papa, say it to me—if you dare.

SIR WILLIAM : Dare! Dare!

BARBARA : Whom are you talking to, Papa—and you of all people! I did not love Frederick, and I won't live with him—so there—and you may go.

SIR WILLIAM *(picking up his hat)* : I never want to see you again.

LADY CHARLCOTE : Barbara, you should respect your father.

BARBARA : Mama—you—you—then let him respect *me*, and the man I live with.

    Exit SIR WILLIAM.

LADY CHARLCOTE : What has he said?

WESSON : It does not matter.

LADY CHARLCOTE : Well—now you must make the best of your own affairs—for you've cut off all your own people from you, Barbara.

BARBARA : I have *not* cut myself off—it's you who have left me in the lurch. I was miserable with Frederick. I felt I couldn't stand it. *You* would have helped me to have had lovers, Mama. But because I come away decently and openly you all turn on me.

LADY CHARLCOTE : You know it is impossible——

BARBARA: Very well, I will *be* impossible!

LADY CHARLCOTE: I shall never leave you in the lurch. *(Crying.)* You are my daughter, whatever happens.

> *Exit*—WESSON *hurries to the door after her—it is heard to close—he returns.*

BARBARA: Why do you let them trample on you? *Why* do you play the poor worm? It drives me *mad*!

WESSON: But you don't want me to insult your father.

BARBARA: But why do you let yourself be bullied and treated like dirt?

WESSON: I don't.

BARBARA: You do—you do—and I *hate* you for it.

WESSON: Very well. *(She sits down on the couch, twisting her handkerchief. He seats himself beside her and takes her hand.)* Never mind, they'll get over it.

BARBARA: Papa won't—and I have loved him so.

WESSON: He will.

BARBARA: He won't! Oh, but I hate him—a mean funker! But he always was a funker. He had his Selma on the sly, and when Mama found him out—it positively broke him. What did he say to you?

WESSON: He explained his point of view, which seems to me perfectly logical.

BARBARA: And I suppose you agreed with him?

WESSON: No; I didn't agree with him—only I understood.

BARBARA: And you cringed to him, I know you did.

WESSON: I don't think so.

BARBARA: And now they've left me.

WESSON: Never mind—they can slam at us, but we can stand it.

BARBARA: But it's so horrible—and I have to fight for you, as if you weren't a man.

WESSON: I don't think you have any need.

BARBARA: Yes, but I have—and all the burden falls on me—you don't take your share.

WESSON: Surely I do! Never mind, I know it's horrid for you. But you will stick to me, won't you?

BARBARA: I didn't think it would be so hard—I have to fight you, and them, and everybody. Not a soul in the world gives me the tiniest bit of help.

WESSON : That's only because you feel rotten. I love you, Barbara.

BARBARA : Doesn't it make you hate me, all this horridness?

WESSON : Why should it? I don't care what comes, so that we get a little closer.

BARBARA : But it's worth it, isn't it, Giacomo?—say I'm worth it.

WESSON *(putting his arms round her and kissing her)* : You're the only thing in life and in the world that I've got—you are.

BARBARA : Are you sure?

WESSON : I've got my work, which isn't life. Then there's nothing else but you—not a thing—and if you leave me—well, I've done.

BARBARA : How do you mean, done?

WESSON : Only my effort at life. I shall feel as if I had made my big effort—put all my money down—and lost. The only thing remaining would be to go on and make the best of it.

BARBARA : I suppose that's how Frederick feels.

WESSON : I suppose it is—if only he would get a grip on and try to make the best of it.

BARBARA : But it's not so easy.

WESSON : No, it isn't, poor devil. But if he's got to do it, he may as well.

BARBARA : Oh, do you love me enough, Giacomo?

WESSON : I love you enough for whatever you want me for.

BARBARA : Sure?

WESSON : Sure! The question is, do you love *me* enough?

BARBARA : I love you better than you love me.

WESSON : Take your hat off, I can't kiss you.

BARBARA *(obediently removing her hat)* : Mama told me Papa was coming—I was furious, it seemed such a mean dodge. They *are* mean, though, and sordid. Did he say horrid things to you?

WESSON : He said he'd thrash me.

BARBARA *(laughing)* : Fancy little Papa!

WESSON : Are you miserable? Are you sorry you're done out of your drive?

BARBARA : No, I'm thankful to be back with you. If *only* they left us in peace, we could be so happy.

WESSON : They seem to grudge it us, don't they?

BARBARA : Yes! And Mama says perhaps Frederick's coming.

WESSON : At any rate we s'll have had 'em all, then.

BARBARA : But I couldn't bear to see him, Giacomo!

WESSON: Then don't see him.

BARBARA: But he might do something mad.

WESSON: Let him.

BARBARA: No—I couldn't bear it. I couldn't bear it if anything happened to him.

WESSON: Why *should* anything happen to him?

BARBARA: And what would he do if he saw me? Would he go quite mad?

WESSON: You're not such a magical person as all that.

BARBARA: But you don't know him.

WESSON: Quite sufficiently.

BARBARA: Isn't it funny—when I was first engaged to him, and was reading Othello, I thought what a good Othello he'd make, better than the real one.

WESSON: You feel sure he'll slay you, poor Desdemona.

BARBARA *(laughing)*: Yes—he's so Othelloish.

WESSON: And you so Desdemoniacal, aren't you?

BARBARA *(laughing)*: What does that mean?

WESSON: It means you sit sighing by a sycamore tree, you poor soul.

BARBARA *(kissing him)*: O, I love you!

WESSON: Do you?

CURTAIN

SCENE II

Evening of the same day, WESSON *sits alone, writing. Enter* BARBARA, *resplendent in an evening dress, with ornament in her hair. She stands in the doorway, looking across at herself in a mirror.*

BARBARA: You've never seen me in this before. *(He looks up—puts his pen between his teeth—she preens herself.)*

WESSON *(after a moment)*: I hate it.

BARBARA *(hurt)*: But why?—I look nice. Don't I look nice?

WESSON: I hate it—I hate it—you belong to those others in it.

BARBARA: But how nasty of you, Giacometti! It's only the dress— the woman is just the same.

WESSON: She's not. She's according to her frock, which is Frederick's. You put it on for Frederick, not for me.

BARBARA: I didn't. I want you to see how grand I can look. Don't you really think I look nice?

WESSON: No—I'd rather see you in your kitchen pinafore.

BARBARA: See how you want to drag me down. But you've got an evening suit. *(Laughing)*: Does it really hurt you? *(Sits down and begins to play a dance on the piano—it is the "Blue Danube" —she breaks off.)* It's the dearest dress I ever had.

WESSON: Take it off, Barbara.

BARBARA *(slowing down—she is very quiet)*: Yes.

> *Rises—exit slowly. He sits chewing his pen—in a moment she rushes back, lays her hands on his shoulder.*

BARBARA: There's Frederick!

WESSON: Rubbish!—Where?

BARBARA: At the gate—with Mama—I saw them from the bed-room window.

> LADY CHARLCOTE'S *voice is heard calling "Barbara!"*

BARBARA: Quick! I'll call to them from the window *I'm* coming— I will—*(Moves to the window.)*

WESSON: What's the good? Let them go away again.

BARBARA: I'll call now——

WESSON: Damn!

> *He moves grudgingly to the door.* BARBARA *stands with her hands clasped over her bare breast, terrified—listening. The gate is heard to bang open—voices—enter* FREDERICK, *alone— a haggard, handsome man of forty, brown moustache, dark brown eyes, greying at the temples. He hesitates at the door.*

FREDERICK *(ironically)*: May I come in?

BARBARA *(frightened)*: What do you want?

FREDERICK: Merely permission to speak to you.

BARBARA: You know you may speak to me.

> *They hesitate—enter* WESSON, *followed by* LADY CHARLCOTE.

WESSON: Barbara, do you want me to go with Lady Charlcote to the Hotel Cervo for half an hour?

BARBARA: I don't know. *(Sinks on to the couch.)*

WESSON: You must *tell* me to go.

> DR TRESSIDER *looks at him sideways and shows his teeth, but does not speak—*BARBARA *watches the two men in terror.*

BARBARA: Perhaps you'd better go—Mama can stay with me.

LADY CHARLCOTE: I think Frederick has the right to speak to you alone, Barbara.

BARBARA *(almost whispering)*: But why——?

FREDERICK: Are you afraid that I may abduct you?

LADY CHARLCOTE: No, Frederick, I don't think it is fair to leave her alone with you.

FREDERICK *(nastily)*: Don't you? Perhaps it isn't safe——

LADY CHARLCOTE: You might not be responsible for what you did.

FREDERICK: So the only place for me is the lunatic asylum.

BARBARA: If you are like that, Frederick, I don't know what you can want to speak to me at all for.

FREDERICK: It *is* a question for surprise.

BARBARA: I'd much rather you *did* treat me as dirt, and left me alone.

WESSON: Will you sit down, Lady Charlcote?

FREDERICK *(to WESSON)*: Will you please take yourself away, while I speak to my wife?

BARBARA: Yes, go, Wesson.

LADY CHARLCOTE: I would go for a few minutes, Mr Wesson. It can't do you any harm. Things will settle themselves then.

WESSON *(to BARBARA)*: Must I?

BARBARA: Only to the—to one of the other rooms.

WESSON: I'll go to the bedroom, then.

          Exit sullenly.

FREDERICK *(taking a seat)*: I'm glad you look so well, Barbara.

LADY CHARLCOTE: You won't do any good that way, Frederick.

FREDERICK *(turning slowly to her)*: Perhaps you'll tell me what to say!

LADY CHARLCOTE: You needn't behave like a fool, at any rate.

BARBARA: I'm afraid you've been ill, Frederick.

FREDERICK: Yes—I am ill! I am glad to see you are so well.

BARBARA: Don't, Frederick—what *is* the good of this—what *is* the good of it? Let us make the best we can now——

FREDERICK: Exactly!

BARBARA: Then the only sane thing would be to say what you came to say and let us get it over.

FREDERICK: I came for your instructions, of course.

BARBARA: It seems rather stupid, don't you think?

FREDERICK: I've no doubt I always was stupid—a trusting fool——

BARBARA: You know it wasn't like that. Do you really wish to speak to me?

FREDERICK: Yes, I think I can honestly say I do. It, no doubt, surprises you.

BARBARA: Then for God's sake don't torture me any longer.

FREDERICK: It *would* be a pity! But what I have to say I have to say to my wife, not to the world at large, or even to my mother-in-law, or your paramour.

BARBARA: Perhaps you *had* better leave us alone, Mama.

FREDERICK: Hadn't you better consider again, Barbara? Wouldn't that be giving me too much encouragement? I might take a liberty. I might even ask you to gallivant with me, like a seductive footman, or dustman. *(There is silence.)*

LADY CHARLCOTE: I can go into another room. *(Making signs to* BARBARA.*)* Where can I go, Barbara?

  BARBARA *rises—they go out together—*FREDERICK *looks round—gnaws the ends of his moustache. Re-enter* BARBARA— *she leaves the door open—he glances, sees it, but makes no remark.*

BARBARA *(taking her former seat)*: Mama is in my bedroom.

FREDERICK: Anything to say to me?

BARBARA: Don't be horrid with me, Frederick. I *know* I deserve it——

FREDERICK: I'll try not to be. *(He sits devouring her with his eyes.)* You're in full-dress to-night, madam! Was it a great occasion?

BARBARA: No—I put it on—it's the first time.

FREDERICK: You look the thing in it. I turned up to see you on your mettle, by good luck.

BARBARA: Don't.

FREDERICK: Beautiful good luck. War-paint, I suppose!

BARBARA: You told me once you'd never be hard on a woman.

FREDERICK: I'm sorry if I'm hard on you—that *would* be unjust!

BARBARA: Don't talk like that—Frederick.

FREDERICK: What shall we talk about—you or me?

BARBARA: Tell me about yourself——

FREDERICK: Ha!—how I suffered, you mean?

BARBARA: I know it's been awful for you.

FREDERICK: Do you really—I shouldn't have thought it.

BARBARA: Oh, but I do! It's nearly driven me cracked sometimes.

FREDERICK: Ha! It was kind of you.

BARBARA (*going forward impulsively and putting her hand on his knee*): Don't——

FREDERICK: I won't—but tell me what—I must——

BARBARA: Don't be like this—I can't bear it.

FREDERICK: You might tell me what you can bear.

BARBARA: Why can't you cast me off—why can't you find some other woman—there's Annabel, who adores you—or Lizzie Burroughs——

FREDERICK: You think they'd make good successors to you?

BARBARA: You might love them better than me—you might! See, I was not faithful to you.

FREDERICK (*laughing*): I wouldn't rub it in, if I were you.

BARBARA (*frightened*): But I'm not!

FREDERICK: So you think I might do well to marry again?

BARBARA: I thought—I can't bear—to think of you being lonely.

FREDERICK: And you'd give me a wedding present, I dare say, and give the woman advice how to fool me.

BARBARA: No—no—I won't let you say these things——

FREDERICK: I dare say. You were wasted on me, weren't you?

BARBARA: You were *good* to me—but you never understood me——

FREDERICK: I'm sorry! I understood you wanted a decent life, and I worked hard for you. I understood you wanted some amusement—you did exactly as you liked—you had everything I had—and had your own way. I was faithful to you from the day I saw you—and before that. You might have called me a model husband. I suppose that was my fault.

BARBARA (*crying*): No—it wasn't your fault to be a good husband—that's why I love you still—in a way—you were so good to me—but—you weren't near to me——

FREDERICK: I think I was as near as ever you'd let me come.

BARBARA: No—no—can't you remember—when we were first married—I thought marriage would be a jolly thing—I thought I could have lovely games with the man. Can you remember, when I climbed to the top of the cupboard, in Lucerne? I thought you'd look for me, and laugh, and fetch me down. No, you were terrified. You daren't even come in the room. You stood in the door looking frightened to death. And I climbed down. And that's how it always was. I had to climb down.

FREDERICK: And so you left me?

BARBARA: Yes! I couldn't live with you.

FREDERICK: Because I didn't drag you by the ankle from the cupboard tops!

BARBARA: Yes—that's it.

FREDERICK: And how long did it take you to find this out?

BARBARA: You know very well that I was only introduced to Wesson about a month before—you knew all about it.

FREDERICK: And may I inquire after the predecessors of this clown?

BARBARA: Yourself.

FREDERICK: I enjoy that honour alone, do I—with the miserable clown——

BARBARA: You were not going to speak of him.

FREDERICK: And pray, when did you find out then that I had not—not found the real *you*.

BARBARA: The first night of our marriage—when I stood on that balcony and wanted to drown myself—and you were asleep.

FREDERICK: And afterwards—I suppose you forgot it?

BARBARA: Sometimes. You were good to me—and I didn't think then there *could* be anything else.

FREDERICK: Than what?

BARBARA: Than going on as I was—as your wife.

FREDERICK: And you *never* loved me?

BARBARA: Sometimes—when you were so nice to me——

FREDERICK: Out of gratitude, as it were, and feeling you *ought* to love me.

BARBARA: I always felt I ought to love you.

FREDERICK: But could never bring it off. Ha!—thank you for the try, at any rate.

BARBARA: And of course sometimes I hated you.

FREDERICK: Naturally.

BARBARA: And now it's over.

FREDERICK: As you say—it's over.

There is a long silence.

FREDERICK *(in a sudden outburst)*: Woman, do you know I've given my life to you? Do you know, everything I did, everything I thought, everywhere I went, was for you? I have worked till I reeled, I was so tired. I have been your slave——

BARBARA: That's it—I didn't want you to be my slave——

FREDERICK: I—I—I have done everything. How often have I asked you, "What do you want of me?" Why didn't you tell me then? Why didn't you say? Why have you deceived me all this while, letting me think you loved me?

BARBARA: I didn't deceive you; *(crying)* I didn't know myself.

FREDERICK: How many times have you had your arms round my neck, and said, "Do you love me?"—I might well answer, "Malheureusement." What was that but deceit——

BARBARA: It wasn't lying to you, Frederick—you *did* love me, and I wanted you to love me——

FREDERICK: What right had you to want me to love you, when you cared not a couple of straws about me?

BARBARA: I *did* want you to love me—you were all I had——

FREDERICK: Until another came along, and then you threw my love away like a piece of dirty paper wrapping.

BARBARA: No—no—I didn't!

FREDERICK: What else have you done? You have thrown me away like a bit of paper off a parcel. You got all the goods out of the packet, and threw me away—I gave you everything, my life, everything, and it is not worth the stump of a cigarette, when it comes to—I tell you, this is the end of me. I could work then, but now my brain has gone.

BARBARA: No, Frederick, no—you will work again.

FREDERICK: I tell you I can no more work now than you can row a boat when you have lost the oars. I am done for—as a man you see me here a ruin. Some nights I sleep, some nights I never close my eyes. I force myself to keep sane. But in the end my brain will go—and then I shall make an end——

BARBARA *(going over to him, kneeling with her hand on his knee, crying)*: No—no, Frederick—no—no!

FREDERICK: Then I shall go to Wood Norton—do you remember, where I saw you first—a girl of eighteen with a sash? I shall go to that pine wood where the little grove of larches is, and I shall make an end.

BARBARA *(her head on his knee—weeping)*: Oh, what can I do— what can I do?

FREDERICK: I've no doubt it all sounds very melodramatic—but it's the truth for me. Then your work will be finished. I have loved you. I would have spilt my blood on every paving stone in Bromley for you, if you had wanted me to——

BARBARA: But I didn't want you to. I wanted you to come near to me and make me yours and you be mine. But you went on worshipping me instead of loving me—kissing my feet instead of helping me. You put me on a pedestal, and I was miserable.

FREDERICK: And you never loved me all the time!

BARBARA: I did love you—I did love you!

FREDERICK *(his fists clenched—shuddering)*: I could strangle you!

BARBARA *(terrified)*: Don't—don't—I shall scream! *(She gets up afraid and draws back. He gets hold of one of her arms.)*

FREDERICK: You devil—you devil—you devil! But you belong to me, do you hear?—you belong to me!

BARBARA *(pushing him away)*: Don't—don't—let me go—I shall call Mama—oh——

> He releases her—she flings herself face down on the sofa—he sits crouching, glaring. Silence for some time.

FREDERICK: Well, have you been there long enough?

BARBARA *(sitting up)*: Yes—long enough to know that it never was any good, and it never would be any good.

FREDERICK: "It never was any good, and never would be any good"—what?

BARBARA: You and me.

FREDERICK: You and me! Do you mean to tell me that my life has been a lie and a falsity?

BARBARA: Why?

FREDERICK: *You* were my life—you—and you say it was never any good between us.

BARBARA: But you had your work. Think, if you had to choose between me and your work.

FREDERICK: You might as well ask an apple-tree to choose between enjoying the sunshine and growing its own apples: the one depends on the other and is the result of the other.

BARBARA: No, Frederick. Why, look how happy you could be with your work when I was miserable.

FREDERICK: But you had no reason to be. I gave you everything you asked for. What did you want?

BARBARA : I suppose I wanted something you could not give.

FREDERICK *(glaring at her—after a silence, suddenly)* : I had a good mind to murder you.

BARBARA *(frightened)* : Why?

FREDERICK : I had a good mind to murder you as you sit there.

BARBARA *(frightened)* : See—see how you loved me!

FREDERICK : How I loved you! Yes—*you* see! You see how I loved you, you callous devil! Haven't I loved you with every breath I've fetched—haven't I?

BARBARA : But what was the good of loving me if you had all the fun out of it? It didn't seem anything to me because I didn't realize—I didn't know——

FREDERICK : You didn't *love* me!

BARBARA : No—well—you should have seen that I did. It doesn't do me any good, if a man *dies* for love of me, unless there is some answer in me, so that it lives in me.

FREDERICK : I ought to have killed myself rather than marry you.

BARBARA : But I couldn't help that, could I?

FREDERICK : No, you could help nothing. You could only throw me away like waste-paper that had wrapped up a few years of your life.

BARBARA : I'm sorry, Frederick. I'll do what I can; I will, really.

FREDERICK : *What* will you do?

BARBARA : Don't you trust me?

FREDERICK : Trust you, yes! You can go on doing as you like with me.

BARBARA : There you are, you see, resigned. Resigned from the very start—resigned to lose. You are, and you always were.

FREDERICK : Very well, you little devil—it seems you were determined——

BARBARA : What?

FREDERICK : To destroy me.

BARBARA *(going and putting her arms round his neck)* : No—no, Frederick. I'd do an awful lot for you—I really would—I have loved you.

FREDERICK : What, for example?

BARBARA : I'd help you with the people in Chislehurst—come and live for a time in the same house.

FREDERICK *(holding her by the arms and looking in her eyes)*: Will you give up this man and come back to me?

BARBARA: Oh—what's the good of promising, Frederick—I might only break it again. Don't force me.

FREDERICK: Will you try? Will you try *me* again for three months?

BARBARA: Come and live with you again?

FREDERICK: Yes.

BARBARA: As your wife?

FREDERICK: Yes.

BARBARA: Altogether as your wife?

FREDERICK: Yes—or even—at first——

BARBARA *(piteously)*: I don't know, Frederick.

FREDERICK: Will you think about it?

BARBARA: But I don't know! What is the good of thinking about it? But I don't know, Frederick.

FREDERICK: You can make up your mind.

BARBARA: But I can't—I can't—it pulls both ways. I don't know, Frederick.

FREDERICK: Will you know better to-morrow—will you come, then, and tell me—will you?

BARBARA: But I shan't know any better to-morrow. It's now! And I can't tell. Don't make me decide, Frederick!

FREDERICK: What?

BARBARA: Which way. Don't make me decide! *(She goes and sits on the couch, hiding her face in a cushion.)*

FREDERICK *(suddenly flings his arms on the table and sobs)*: Oh, good God—I can't bear it!

BARBARA *(looks at him, goes and puts her hand on his shoulder)*: Don't, Frederick—don't! I *will* make up my mind, I will!

FREDERICK *(his face muffled)*: I can't stand it.

BARBARA: No, dear. *(He sobs—she touches his hair.)* Don't! Don't! You shall—I will do—what I can.

FREDERICK *(his face still hidden)*: It will kill me, Barbara.

BARBARA: No, dear—no, it won't. I must think of something. I will tell you to-morrow. I will come and tell you——

FREDERICK *(his face still hidden)*: What?

BARBARA: I don't know, dear—but I will see—I will come. Look at me—look at me. *(He lifts his face.)* Dear! *(He folds her in his*

arms—she puts her head back as he kisses her.) There's Mama!
        He listens—hears a sound, snatches his hat and dashes out—
        BARBARA *turns to the piano—straightens her hair—stands wait-*
        ing. Enter LADY CHARLCOTE.

LADY CHARLCOTE : Has Frederick gone?

BARBARA : Yes.

        Enter WESSON.

LADY CHARLCOTE : What have you decided?

BARBARA : I don't know.

LADY CHARLCOTE : That's no answer. Have you decided nothing?

BARBARA : No.

LADY CHARLCOTE : I hope he won't go and jump in the lake.

BARBARA : I said I'd see him to-morrow.

LADY CHARLCOTE : Then he won't be such a fool. How did he be-
        have?

BARBARA : Oh, don't talk about it, Mama!

LADY CHARLCOTE : And are you coming to the Monte Baldo to-
        morrow then?

BARBARA : Yes.

LADY CHARLCOTE : What time?

BARBARA : In the morning—about eleven.

LADY CHARLCOTE : And you'll bring him your answer then?

BARBARA : Yes.

LADY CHARLCOTE : Well, you must decide for the best for yourself.
        Only don't go and make a double mess of it, that's all.

BARBARA : How do you mean, a double mess?

LADY CHARLCOTE : You'll have to stick to one or the other now, at
        any rate—so you'd better stick to the one you can live with, and
        not to the one you can do without—for if you get the wrong one,
        you might as well drown two people then instead of one.

BARBARA : I don't know—I shall know to-morrow, Mama. Good
        night.

LADY CHARLCOTE *(kissing her—crying)* : Well—all you can do now
        is to make the bed for yourself. Good night! Oh, don't trouble
        to come out, Mr Wesson, don't.

        WESSON *follows her. Exit both.* BARBARA *sits down and begins*
        to play a waltz on the piano. Re-enter WESSON.

WESSON : Frederick wasn't far off—he hadn't drowned himself.

        BARBARA *goes on playing.*

WESSON : I don't particularly want to hear that piano, Barbara.

BARBARA : Don't you? *(Plays a few more bars, then stops.)* What *do* you want?

WESSON : So you are going to see him to-morrow.

BARBARA : I am.

WESSON : What for?

BARBARA *(hesitating)* : To tell him I'll go back to him.

> *She remains with her back to* WESSON—*he sits at the table. There is dead silence.*

WESSON : Did you tell him that tonight?

BARBARA : No.

WESSON : Why not?

BARBARA : Because I didn't want to.

WESSON : Did you give him hopes of that answer?

BARBARA : I don't know.

WESSON : You do! Tell me.

BARBARA : I say I don't know.

WESSON : Then you're lying. I don't believe you intended to tell him that. I believe you say it to make me wild.

BARBARA : I don't.

WESSON : Then go now.

BARBARA : I said I'd go to-morrow.

WESSON : If you're going back to Frederick in the morning, you're not going to spend a night under this roof—hear that?

BARBARA : Why not? I've spent a good many nights under this roof —what does one more or less matter?

WESSON : While you've been with me here I considered you as a woman who wanted to stick to me as a wife—and as anything else I *don't want you.*

BARBARA : Very much as a wife you considered me at first—you were as unsure of us as ever I was.

WESSON : That was at the very first.

BARBARA : Was it—was it?

WESSON : Whether or not—that's what I say now.

BARBARA : "Whether or not!"—you *would* say that. At any rate, Frederick wouldn't say "whether or not".

WESSON : And you want to go back to him?

BARBARA : All men are alike. They don't care what a woman wants. They try to get hold of what they want themselves, as if it were a pipe. As for the woman, she's not considered—and so—that's where you make your mistake, gentlemen.

WESSON: Want? What *do* you want?

BARBARA: That's for you to find out.

WESSON: What you want is some of the conceit knocking out of you.

BARBARA: You do it, Mr Tuppeny-ha'penny.

WESSON: If Frederick hadn't been such a damn fool he'd have taken you down a peg or two. Now, you think yourself so blighted high and mighty that nobody's good enough to dangle after you.

BARBARA: Only a little puppy-dog that barks at my skirts.

WESSON: Very well, then the little puppy-dog *will* bark. Are you going to see Frederick in the morning?

BARBARA: Yes.

WESSON: And are you going to tell him, then, that you're going back to him?

BARBARA: I don't know.

WESSON: You must know then, because if you are, you're not going to stop the night in this house.

BARBARA: Pooh! What do I care about your house?

WESSON: You know it was really *you* who wanted it, and whose it is.

BARBARA: As if *I* care for this house—I'd leave it any minute. I'll leave it now.

WESSON: If you're going to go back to Frederick, *leave* it now. I ask you to.

BARBARA: Oh, very well—that is soon done.

She goes out quickly.

CURTAIN

ACT IV

Ten minutes later. WESSON *is smoking. Enter* BARBARA, *dressed, with her hat on.*

BARBARA : Here I am, then!

WESSON : Are you going straight to Gardone, to the Monte Baldo?

BARBARA : No—I'm going to the Hotel Cervo.

WESSON: But you can't—she knows us, the landlady—and thinks we're man and wife. You can't make that mess. If you're going, go straight to Frederick to-night—I'll see you there.

BARBARA : I'm *not* going to Frederick to-night—I'm not going to Gardone—I'm going to. the Hotel Cervo.

WESSON: How much money have you got?

BARBARA : None.

WESSON : Then I won't give you any.

BARBARA : Don't you trouble—I wouldn't take any of your money.

WESSON : Have you got your night-things in the handbag?

BARBARA : Yes.

WESSON : Some soap—some hankies?

BARBARA : No—forgotten 'em.

WESSON : You would.

    Exit—comes running back in a moment, puts the things in her bag.

BARBARA : Thank you.

WESSON: And your box I'll pack to-morrow. The things you said were mine I shall put in.

BARBARA : You needn't.

WESSON: I shall. I've never given you anything, so you've nothing to return.

BARBARA : No—you were always stingy.

WESSON : Very well—Frederick isn't.

BARBARA : I suppose it's having been brought up so poor, you can't help it.

WESSON : We won't discuss me now, nor my bringing-up.

BARBARA : Oh, alright!

WESSON: I consider I owe you, of money you had, about eleven pounds. I'll be stingy and keep one of them. Here's ten out of the forty we'd got.

BARBARA: I shan't have them.

WESSON: You can't go without any money.

BARBARA: Yes, I can.

WESSON: No, you can't. If you don't have these ten pounds, I'll post them to Frederick to you.

BARBARA: Alright.

WESSON *(feeling in his pocket)*: Well, have ten lire, at any rate.

BARBARA: No, I won't have anything.

WESSON: You ought to be murdered for your obstinacy.

BARBARA: Not twice in one night.

WESSON: Very well, then—I will come with you down the village, since you're frightened of the men.

BARBARA: You needn't—I'm not frightened.

WESSON: No—you're too damned high and mighty to possess a single one of the human virtues or vices, you are! *(A silence.)* Do you want to go, really?

BARBARA: Yes.

WESSON: Liar!—Liar!—you are showing off! *(Snatches the handbag and flings it into the kitchen.)* Fool's idiotic theatrical game. Take that hat off.

BARBARA: You're giving your orders.

WESSON: Alright. *(Seizes the hat, flings it through the door.)*

BARBARA *(flashing)*: What are you doing?

WESSON: Stopping you being a fool. Take your coat off.

BARBARA: I shall take my coat off when I please. Indeed, *you* needn't show off, for the minute I want to walk out of this house I shall walk out, and you nor anybody else will prevent me.

WESSON *(taking up his position with his back to the door)*: Alright —you want to walk out now, and see!

BARBARA: If I want to——

WESSON: Want to, then——

BARBARA *(with a laugh of scorn)*: Ha—you stop me! *(Marches up to him with her breast high. He stands immovable.)* Come out! *(He shakes his head.)* Come out!

WESSON: I told you I wouldn't.

BARBARA: Won't you?.

Seizes him. He grapples with her. They struggle. He forces her backward, flings her with a smash on to the couch.

WESSON: You shan't! *(Goes and locks the door—stands at a loss.)*

BARBARA *(recovering)*: It's very heroic—but I go to-morrow, whether or not.

WESSON: You'll pass the night in this room then. *(He sits down— there is silence for some minutes—at last he looks up, speaks falteringly.)* You *don't* want to leave me, do you, Barbara? *(No answer.)* You *don't* want to? *(Silence.)* Well, whether you think you do or not, I shall never believe you want to leave me, not really—so there! *(A silence.)*

BARBARA: A woman couldn't want to leave such a wonder as you, you think.

WESSON: You can't want to leave *me*.

BARBARA: Why not?

WESSON *(sulkily)*: Because I don't believe you can. *(There is a silence.)*

BARBARA *(with difficulty)*: A sort of faith performance!

He looks at her steadily, rises, goes and sits beside her.

WESSON: Barbican!

BARBARA *(dropping her head on his shoulder with a cry)*: It's so hard on him, Giacomo.

WESSON *(putting his arms round her)*: Never mind, he'll suffer at first, then he'll get better.

BARBARA *(crying)*: He won't.

WESSON: He will—he shall—he shall! And you'll see he will. He'll be alright in the end. You were too big a mouthful for him to swallow, and he was choking.

BARBARA: But I make him suffer so.

WESSON *(kissing and kissing her)*: No—it's my fault. You don't want to leave me, do you?

BARBARA: I don't know what to do.

WESSON: Stay with me, Barbican, my darling, and we'll manage that he's alright.

BARBARA: It's not fair when a man goes loving you so much when you don't love him—it makes you feel as if you'd have to go back to him.

WESSON: You can't go back to him—it would be wrong. His love isn't living for you.

BARBARA: It isn't, is it, Giacomo?

WESSON: No—kiss me, Barbara, will you? *(She kisses him.)* I love you, Barbara.

BARBARA: Do you really love me?

WESSON: Malheureusement.

BARBARA: He says that.

WESSON: And I don't mean it. I'm glad I love you, even if you torture me into hell.

BARBARA: But do you love me an awful lot?

WESSON: More than enough.

BARBARA: Really?

WESSON: Truly.

BARBARA: But if he dies, I shall torment the life out of you.

WESSON: You'll do that anyway.

BARBARA *(looking up—taking his face between her hands)*: Shall I? —No!—Say no—say I am a joy to you.

WESSON: You are a living joy to me, you are—especially this evening.

BARBARA *(laughs)*: No—but am I really?

WESSON: Yes.

BARBARA: Kiss me—kiss me—and love me—love me a fearful lot— love me a fearful lot.

WESSON: I do. And to-morrow you'll just say to Frederick, "I can't come back—divorce me if you love me." You'll say it, won't you? *(kissing her.)*

BARBARA: Yes.

WESSON: If it kills him—it won't kill him—but you'll say it?

BARBARA *(hiding her face)*: Must I, Giacomo?

WESSON: Yes.

BARBARA: Then I s'll have to—oh dear! But you'll love me—love me a lot. *(She clings to him wildly.)*

WESSON: I do—and I will.

BARBARA: Love me a fearful lot!

CURTAIN

Touch and Go

A PLAY IN THREE ACTS

(1920)

CHARACTERS

GERALD BARLOW
MR BARLOW (his father)
OLIVER TURTON
JOB ARTHUR FREER
WILLIE HOUGHTON
ALFRED BREFFITT
WILLIAM (a butler)
CLERKS, MINERS, etc.
ANABEL WRATH
MRS BARLOW
WINIFRED BARLOW
EVA (a maid)

ACT I

SCENE I: *Market-place of a Midland mining village*
SCENE II: *Winifred's studio at Lilley Close*

ACT II

Drawing-room at Lilley Close

ACT III

SCENE I: *An old park*
SCENE II: *Same as Act I Scene I*

ACT I

SCENE I

Sunday morning. Market-place of a large mining village in the Mid-
lands. A man addressing a small gang of colliers from the foot
of a stumpy memorial obelisk. Church bells heard. Churchgoers
passing along the outer pavements.

WILLIE HOUGHTON: What's the matter with you folks, as I've told
you before, and as I shall keep on telling you every now and
again, though it doesn't make a bit of difference, is that you've
got no idea of freedom whatsoever. I've lived in this blessed place
for fifty years, and I've never seen the spark of an idea, nor of
any response to an idea, come out of a single one of you, all the
time. I don't know what it is with colliers—whether it's spending
so much time in the bowels of the earth—but they never seem to
be able to get their thoughts above their bellies. If you've got
plenty to eat and drink, and a bit over to keep the missis quiet,
you're satisfied. I never saw such a satisfied bloomin' lot in my
life as you Barlow and Walsall's men are, really. Of course you
can growse as well as anybody, and you do growse. But you don't
do anything else. You're stuck in a sort of mud of contentment,
and you feel yourselves sinking, but you make no efforts to get
out. You bleat a bit, like sheep in a bog—but you like it, you
know. You like sinking in—you don't have to stand on your own
feet then.

I'll tell you what'll happen to you chaps. I'll give you a little
picture of what you'll be like in the future. Barlow and Walsall's
'll make a number of compounds, such as they keep niggers in in
South Africa, and there you'll be kept. And every one of you'll
have a little brass collar round his neck, with a number on it.
You won't have names any more. And you'll go from the compound to the pit, and from the pit back again to the compound.
You won't be allowed to go outside the gates, except at week-
ends. They'll let you go home to your wives on Saturday nights,

to stop over Sunday. But you'll have to be in again by half-past nine on Sunday night; and if you're late, you'll have your next week-end knocked off. And there you'll be—and you'll be quite happy. They'll give you plenty to eat, and a can of beer a day, and a bit of bacca—and they'll provide dominoes and skittles for you to play with. And you'll be the most contented set of men alive.—But you won't be men. You won't even be animals. You'll go from number one to number three thousand, a lot of numbered slaves—a new sort of slaves——

VOICE : An' wheer shall thee be, Willie?

WILLIE : Oh, I shall be outside the palings, laughing at you. I shall have to laugh, because it'll be your own faults. You'll have nobody but yourself to thank for it. You don't *want* to be men. You'd rather *not* be free—much rather. You're like those people spoken of in Shakespeare : "Oh, how eager these men are to be slaves!" I believe it's Shakespeare—or the Bible—one or the other—it mostly is——

ANABEL WRATH *(passing to church)* : It was Tiberius.

WILLIE : Eh?

ANABEL : Tiberius said it.

WILLIE : Tiberius!—Oh, did he? *(Laughs.)* Thanks! Well, if Tiberius said it, there must be something in it. And he only just missed being in the Bible, anyway. He was a day late, or they'd have had him in. "Oh, how eager these men are to be slaves!"—It's evident the Romans deserved all they got from Tiberius—and you'll deserve all you get, every bit of it. But don't you bother, you'll get it. You.won't be at the mercy of Tiberius, you'll be at the mercy of something a jolly sight worse. Tiberius took the skin off a few Romans, apparently. But you'll have the soul taken out of you—every one of you. And I'd rather lose my skin than my soul, any day. But perhaps you wouldn't.

VOICE : What art makin' for, Willie? Tha seems to say a lot, but tha goes round it. Tha'rt like a donkey on a gin. Tha gets ravelled.

WILLIE : Yes, that's just it. I am precisely like a donkey on a gin—a donkey that's trying to wind a lot of colliers up to the surface. There's many a donkey that's brought more colliers than you up to see daylight, by trotting round.—But do you want to know what I'm making for? I can soon tell you that. You Barlow and Walsall's men, you haven't a soul to call your own. Barlow and

Walsall's have only to say to one of you, Come, and he cometh;
Go, and he goeth, Lie down and be kicked, and he lieth down
and he *is* kicked—and serve him jolly well right.

VOICE: Ay—an' what about it? Tha's got a behind o' thy own,
hasn't ter?

WILLIE: Do you stand there and ask me what about it, and haven't
the sense to alter it? Couldn't you set up a proper Government
to-morrow, if you liked? Couldn't you contrive that the pits belonged to you, instead of you belonging to the pits, like so many
old pit-ponies that stop down till they are blind, and take to eating coal-slack for meadow-grass, not knowing the difference? If
only you'd learn to think, I'd respect you. As you are, I can't, not
if I try my hardest. All you can think of is to ask for another
shilling a day. That's as far as your imagination carries you. And
perhaps you get sevenpence ha'penny, but pay for it with half a
crown's worth of sweat. The masters aren't fools—as you are.
They'll give you two-thirds of what you ask for, but they'll get
five-thirds of it back again—and they'll get it out of your flesh
and blood, too, in jolly hard work. Shylock wasn't in it with
them. He only wanted a pound of flesh. But you cheerfully give
up a pound a week, each one of you, and keep on giving it
up.—But you don't seem to see these things. You can't think
beyond your dinners and your 'lowance. You think if you can
get another shilling a day you're set up. You make me tired, I
tell you.

JOB ARTHUR FREER: We think of others besides ourselves.

WILLIE: Hello, Job Arthur—are you there? I didn't recognise you
without your frock-coat and silk hat—on the Sabbath.—What
was that you said? You think of something else, besides yourselves?—Oh ay—I'm glad to hear it. Did you mean your own
importance?

> *A motor car*, GERALD BARLOW *driving*, OLIVER TURTON *with*
> *him, has pulled up.*

JOB ARTHUR (*glancing at the car*): No, I didn't.

WILLIE: Didn't you, though?—Come, speak up, let us have it. The
more the merrier. You were going to say something.

JOB ARTHUR: Nay, you were doing the talking.

WILLIE: Yes, so I was, till you interrupted, with a great idea on the
tip of your tongue. Come, spit it out. No matter if Mr Barlow

hears you. You know how sorry for you we feel, that you've always got to make your speeches twice—once to those above, and once to us here below. I didn't mean the angels and the devils, but never mind. Speak up, Job Arthur.

JOB ARTHUR: It's not everybody as has as much to say as you, Mr Houghton.

WILLIE: No, not in the open—that's a fact. Some folks says a great deal more, in semi-private. You were just going to explain to me, on behalf of the men, whom you so ably represent and so wisely lead, Job Arthur—we won't say by the nose—you were just going to tell me—on behalf of the men, of course, not of the masters— that you think of others, besides yourself. Do you mind explaining *what* others?

JOB ARTHUR: Everybody's used to your talk, Mr Houghton, and for that reason it doesn't make much impression. What I meant to say, in plain words, was that we have to think of what's best for everybody, not only for ourselves.

WILLIE: Oh, I see. What's best for everybody! I see! Well, for myself, I'm much obliged—there's nothing for us to do, gentlemen, but for all of us to bow acknowledgments to Mr Job Arthur Freer, who so kindly has *all* our interests at heart.

JOB ARTHUR: I don't profess to be a red-rag Socialist. I don't pretend to think that if the Government had the pits it would be any better for us. No. What I mean is, that the pits are there, and every man on this place depends on them, one way or another. They're the cow that gives the milk. And what I mean is, how every man shall have a proper share of the milk, which is food and living. I don't want to kill the cow and share up the meat. It's like killing the goose that laid the golden egg. I want to keep the cow healthy and strong. And the cow is the pits, and we're the men that depend on the pits.

WILLIE: Who's the cat that's going to lick the cream?

JOB ARTHUR: My position is this—and I state it before masters and men—that it's our business to strike such a balance between the interests of the men and the interests of the masters that the pits remain healthy, and everybody profits.

WILLIE: You're out for the millennium, I can see—with Mr Job Arthur Freer striking the balance. We all see you, Job Arthur, one foot on either side of the fence, balancing the see-saw, with masters at one end and men at the other. You'll have to give one side a lot of pudding.—But go back a bit, to where we were before the motor car took your breath away. When you said, Job Arthur, that you think of others besides yourself, didn't you mean, as a matter of fact, the office men? Didn't you mean that the colliers, led—we won't mention noses—by you, were going to come out in sympathy with the office clerks, supposing they didn't get the rise in wages which they've asked for—the office clerks? Wasn't that it?

JOB ARTHUR : There's been some talk among the men of standing by the office. I don't know what they'll do. But they'll do it of their own decision, whatever it is.

WILLIE : There's not a shadow of doubt about it, Job Arthur. But it's a funny thing the decisions all have the same foxy smell about them, Job Arthur.

OLIVER TURTON *(calling from the car)* : What was the speech about, in the first place?

WILLIE : I beg pardon?

OLIVER : What was the address about, to begin with?

WILLIE : Oh, the same old hat—Freedom. But partly it's given to annoy the Unco Guid, as they pass to their Sabbath banquet of self-complacency.

OLIVER : What *about* Freedom?

WILLIE : Very much as usual, I believe. But you should have been here ten minutes sooner, before we began to read the lessons. *(Laughs.)*

ANABEL W. *(moving forward, and holding out her hand)* : You'd merely have been told what Freedom *isn't* : and you know that already. How are you, Oliver?

OLIVER : Good God, Anabel!—are you part of the meeting? How long have you been back in England?

ANABEL : Some months, now. My family have moved here, you know.

OLIVER : Your family! Where have they moved from?—from the moon?

ANABEL : No, only from Derby.—How are you, Gerald?

GERALD *twists in his seat to give her his hand.*

GERALD : I saw you before.

ANABEL : Yes, I know you did.

JOB ARTHUR *has disappeared. The men disperse sheepishly into groups, to stand and sit on their heels by the walls and the causeway edge.* WILLIE HOUGHTON *begins to talk to individuals.*

OLIVER : Won't you get in and drive on with us a little way?

ANABEL : No, I was going to church.

OLIVER : Going to church! Is that a new habit?

ANABEL : Not a habit. But I've been twice since I saw you last.

OLIVER: I see. And that's nearly two years ago. It's an annual thing, like a birthday?

ANABEL : No. I'll go on, then.

OLIVER : You'll be late now.

ANABEL : Shall I? It doesn't matter.

OLIVER : We are going to see you again, aren't we?

ANABEL *(after a pause)* : Yes, I hope so, Oliver.

OLIVER : How have you been these two years—well?—happy?

ANABEL : No, neither. How have you?

OLIVER : Yes, fairly happy. Have you been ill?

ANABEL : Yes, in France I was very ill.

OLIVER : Your old neuritis?

ANABEL : No. My chest. Pneumonia—oh, a complication.

OLIVER : How sickening! Who looked after you? Is it better?

ANABEL : Yes, it's a great deal better.

OLIVER : And what are you doing in England—working?

ANABEL : No, not much.—I won't keep the car here : good-bye.

GERALD : Oh, it's alright.

OLIVER: But, Anabel—we must fix a meeting. I say, wait just a moment. Could I call on your people? Go into town with me one day. I don't know whether Gerald intends to see you— whether he intends to ask you to Lilley Close.

GERALD : I——

ANABEL : He's no need. I'm fixed up there already.

GERALD : What do you mean?

ANABEL : I am at Lilley Close every day—or most days—to work with your sister Winifred in the studio.

GERALD : What?—why, how's that?

ANABEL : Your father asked me. My father was already giving her some lessons.

GERALD : And you're at our house every day?

ANABEL : Most days.

GERALD: Well, I'm—well, I'll be—you managed it very sharp, didn't you? I've only been away a fortnight.

ANABEL: Your father asked me—he offered me twelve pounds a month—I wanted to do something.

GERALD: Oh yes, but you didn't hire yourself out at Lilley Close as a sort of upper servant just for twelve pounds a month.

ANABEL: You're wrong—you're wrong. I'm not a sort of upper servant at all—not at all.

GERALD: Oh yes, you are, if you're paid twelve pounds a month—three pounds a week. That's about what Father's sick-nurse gets, I believe. You're a kind of upper servant, like a nurse. You don't do it for twelve pounds a month. You can make twelve pounds in a day, if you like to work at your little models: I know you can sell your little statuette things as soon as you make them.

ANABEL: But I *can't* make them. I *can't* make them. I've lost the spirit—the *joie de vivre*—I don't know what, since I've been ill. I tell you I've *got* to earn something.

GERALD: Nevertheless, you won't make me believe, Anabel, that you've come and buried yourself in the provinces—*such* provinces—just to earn Father's three pounds a week. Why don't you admit it, that you came back to try and take up the old threads?

OLIVER: Why not, Gerald? Don't you think we ought to take up the old threads?

GERALD: I don't think we ought to be left without choice. I don't think Anabel ought to come back and thrust herself on me—for that's what it amounts to, after all—when one remembers what's gone before.

ANABEL: I *don't* thrust myself on you at all. I know I'm a fool, a fool, to come back. But I wanted to. I wanted to see you again. Now I know I've presumed. I've made myself *cheap* to you. I wanted to—I wanted to. And now I've done it, I won't come to Lilley Close again, nor anywhere where you are. Tell your father I have gone to France again—it will be true.

GERALD: You play tricks on me—and on yourself. You know you do. You do it for the pure enjoyment of it. You're making a scene here in this filthy market-place, just for the fun of it. You like to see these accursed colliers standing eyeing you, and squatting on their heels. You like to catch me out, here where I'm known, where I've been the object of their eyes since I was born. This is a great *coup de main* for you. I knew it the moment I saw you here.

OLIVER : After all, we *are* making a scene in the market-place. Get in, Anabel, and we'll settle the dispute more privately. I'm glad you came back, anyhow. I'm glad you came right down on us. Get in, and let us run down to Whatmore.

ANABEL : No, Oliver. I don't want to run down to Whatmore. I wanted to see you—I wanted to see Gerald—and I've seen him—and I've heard him. That will suffice me. We'll make an end of the scene in the market-place. *(She turns away.)*

OLIVER : I knew it wasn't ended. I knew she would come back and tell us she'd come. But she's done her bit—now she'll go again. My God, what a fool of a world!—You go on, Gerald—I'll just go after her and see it out. *(Calls.)* One moment, Anabel.

ANABEL *(calling)* : Don't come, Oliver. *(Turns.)*

GERALD : Anabel! *(Blows the horn of the motor car violently and agitatedly—she looks round—turns again as if frightened.)* God damn the woman! *(Gets down from the car.)* Drive home for me, Oliver.

CURTAIN

SCENE II

WINIFRED'S *studio at Lilley Close.* ANABEL *and* WINIFRED *working at a model in clay.*

WINIFRED : But isn't it lovely to be in Paris, and to have exhibitions, and to be famous?

ANABEL : Paris *was* a good place. But I was never famous.

WINIFRED : But your little animals and birds were famous. Jack said so. You know he brought us that bronze thrush that is singing, that is in his room. He has only let me see it twice. It's the loveliest thing I've ever seen. Oh, if I can do anything like that!—I've worshipped it, I have. Is it your best thing?

ANABEL : One of the best.

WINIFRED: It must be. When I see it, with its beak lifted, singing, something comes loose in my heart, and I feel as if I should cry, and fly up to heaven. Do you know what I mean? Oh, I'm sure you do, or you could never have made that thrush. Father is so glad you've come to show me how to work. He says now I shall have a life-work, and I shall be happy. It's true, too.

ANABEL: Yes, till the life-work collapses.

WINIFRED: Oh, it can't collapse. I can't believe it could collapse. Do tell me about something else you made, which you loved—something you sculpted. Oh, it makes my heart burn to hear you!—Do you think I might call you Anabel? I should love to. You do call me Winifred already.

ANABEL: Yes, do.

WINIFRED: Won't you tell me about something else you made—something lovely?

ANABEL: Well, I did a small kitten—asleep—with its paws crossed. You know, Winifred, that wonderful look that kittens have, as if they were blown along like a bit of fluff—as if they weighed nothing at all—just wafted about—and yet so *alive*—do you know——?

WINIFRED: Darlings—darlings—I love them!

ANABEL: Well, my kitten really came off—it had that quality. It looked as if it had just wafted there.

WINIFRED: Oh, yes!—oh, I know! And was it in clay?

ANABEL: I cut it in soft grey stone as well. I loved my kitten. An Armenian bought her.

WINIFRED: And where is she now?

ANABEL: I don't know—in Armenia, I suppose, if there is such a place. It would have to be kept under glass, because the stone wouldn't polish—and I didn't want it polished. But I dislike things under glass—don't you?

WINIFRED: Yes, I do. We had a golden clock, but Gerald wouldn't have the glass cover, and Daddy wouldn't have it without. So now the clock is in Father's room. Gerald often went to Paris. Oliver used to have a studio there. I don't care much for painting —do you?

ANABEL: No. I want something I can touch, if it's something outside me.

WINIFRED: Yes, isn't it wonderful, when things are substantial.

Gerald and Oliver came back yesterday from Yorkshire. You know we have a colliery there.

ANABEL: Yes, I believe I've heard.

WINIFRED: I want to introduce you to Gerald, to see if you like him. He's good at the bottom, but he's very overbearing and definite.

ANABEL: Is he?

WINIFRED: Terribly clever in business. He'll get awfully rich.

ANABEL: Isn't he rich enough already?

WINIFRED: Oh yes, because Daddy is rich enough, really. I think if Gerald was a bit different, he'd be really nice. Now he's so *managing*. It's sickening. Do you dislike managing people, Anabel?

ANABEL: I dislike them extremely, Winifred.

WINIFRED: They're such a bore.

ANABEL: What does Gerald manage?

WINIFRED: Everything. You know he's revolutionized the collieries and the whole Company. He's made a whole new thing of it, so *modern*. Father says he almost wishes he'd let it die out—let the pits be closed. But I suppose things *must* be modernized, don't you think? Though it's very unpeaceful, you know, really.

ANABEL: Decidedly unpeaceful, I should say.

WINIFRED: The colliers work awfully hard. The pits are quite wonderful now. Father says it's against nature—all this electricity and so on. Gerald adores electricity. Isn't it curious?

ANABEL: Very. How are you getting on?

WINIFRED: I don't know. It's so hard to make things *balance* as if they were alive. Where *is* the balance in a thing that's alive?

ANABEL: The poise? Yes, Winifred—to me, all the secret of life is in that—just the—the inexpressible poise of a living thing, that makes it so different from a dead thing. To me it's the soul, you know—all living things have it—flowers, trees as well. It makes life always marvellous.

WINIFRED: Ah, yes!—ah, yes! If only I could put it in my model.

ANABEL: I think you will. You are a sculptor, Winifred.—Isn't there someone there?

WINIFRED (*running to the door*): Oh, Oliver!

OLIVER: Hello, Winnie! Can I come in? This is your sanctum: you can keep us out if you like.

WINIFRED: Oh, no. Do you know Miss Wrath, Oliver? She's a famous sculptress.

OLIVER : Is she? We have met.—Is Winifred going to make a sculptress, do you think?

ANABEL : I do.

OLIVER : Good! I like your studio, Winnie. Awfully nice up here
over the out-buildings. Are you happy in it?

WINIFRED : Yes, I'm perfectly happy—only I shall *never* be able to
make real models, Oliver—it's so difficult.

OLIVER : Fine room for a party—give us a studio party one day,
Win, and we'll dance.

WINIFRED (*flying to him*) : Yes, Oliver, do let us dance. What shall
we dance to?

OLIVER : Dance?—Dance *Vigni-vignons*—we all know that. Ready?

WINIFRED : Yes.

> *They begin to sing, dancing meanwhile, in a free little ballet-*
> *manner, a wine-dance, dancing separate and then together.*

> *De terre en vigne*
> *La voilà la jolie vigne,*
> *Vigni-vignons—vignons le vin,*
> *La voilà la jolie vigne au vin,*
> *La voilà la jolie vigne.*

OLIVER : Join in—join in, all.

> ANABEL *joins in; the three dance and move in rhythm.*

WINIFRED : I love it—I love it! Do *Ma capote à trois boutons*—you
know it, don't you, Anabel? Ready—now——

> *They begin to dance to a quick little march-rhythm, all sing-*
> *ing and dancing till they are out of breath.*

OLIVER : Oh!—tired!—let us sit down.

WINIFRED : Oliver!—oh, Oliver!—I *love* you and Anabel.

OLIVER : Oh, Winifred, I brought you a present—you'll love me
more now.

WINIFRED : Yes, I shall. Do give it me.

OLIVER : I left it in the morning-room. I put it on the mantelpiece
for you.

WINIFRED : Shall I go for it?

OLIVER : There it is, if you want it.

WINIFRED : Yes—do you mind? I won't be long.

> WINIFRED *goes out.*

OLIVER : She's a nice child.

ANABEL : A *very* nice child.

OLIVER : Why did you come back, Anabel?

ANABEL : Why does the moon rise, Oliver?

OLIVER : For some mischief or other, so they say.

ANABEL : You think I came back for mischief's sake?

OLIVER : Did you?

ANABEL : No.

OLIVER : Ah!

ANABEL : Tell me, Oliver, how is everything now?—how is it with you?—how is it between us all?

OLIVER : How is it between us all?—How *isn't* it, is more the mark.

ANABEL : Why?

OLIVER : You made a fool of us.

ANABEL : Of whom?

OLIVER : Well—of Gerald particularly—and of me.

ANABEL : How did I make a fool of you, Oliver?

OLIVER : That you know best, Anabel.

ANABEL : No, I don't know. Was it ever right between Gerald and me, all the three years we knew each other—we were together?

OLIVER : Was it all wrong?

ANABEL: No, not all. But it was terrible. It was terrible, Oliver. You don't realize. You don't realize how awful passion can be, when it never resolves, when it never becomes anything else. It is hate, really.

OLIVER : What did you want the passion to resolve into?

ANABEL : I was blinded—maddened. Gerald stung me and stung me till I was mad. I left him for reason's sake, for sanity's sake. We should have killed one another.

OLIVER : You stung him too, you know—and pretty badly, at the last: you dehumanized him.

ANABEL : When? When I left him, you mean?

OLIVER : Yes, when you went away with that Norwegian—playing your game a little too far.

ANABEL : Yes, I knew you'd blame me. I knew you'd be against me. But don't you see, Oliver, you helped to make it impossible for us.

OLIVER : Did I? I didn't intend to.

ANABEL : Ha, ha, Oliver! Your good intentions! They are too good to bear investigation, my friend. Ah, but for your good and friendly intentions——

OLIVER : You might have been alright?

ANABEL : No, no, I don't mean that. But we were a vicious triangle, Oliver—you must admit it.

OLIVER : You mean my friendship with Gerald went against you?

ANABEL : Yes. And your friendship with me went against Gerald.

OLIVER : So I am the devil in the piece.

ANABEL : You see, Oliver, Gerald loved you far too well ever to love me altogether. He loved us both. But the Gerald that loved you so dearly, old, old friends as you were, and *trusted* you, he turned a terrible face of contempt on me. You don't know, Oliver, the cold edge of Gerald's contempt for me—because he was so secure and strong in his old friendship with you. You don't know his sneering attitude to me in the deepest things—because he shared the deepest things with you. He had a passion for me. But he loved you.

OLIVER : Well, he doesn't any more. We went apart after you had gone. The friendship has become almost casual.

ANABEL : You see how bitterly you speak.

OLIVER : Yet you didn't hate me, Anabel.

ANABEL : No, Oliver—I was *awfully* fond of you. I trusted you—and I trust you still. You see I knew how fond Gerald was of you. And I had to respect this feeling. So I *had* to be aware of you : I *had* to be conscious of you : in a way, I had to love you. You understand how I mean? Not with the same fearful love with which I loved Gerald. You seemed to me warm and protecting—like a brother, you know—but a brother one *loves*.

OLIVER : And then you hated me?

ANABEL : Yes, I had to hate you.

OLIVER : And you hated Gerald?

ANABEL : Almost to madness—almost to madness.

OLIVER : Then you went away with that Norwegian. What of him?

ANABEL : What of him? Well, he's dead.

OLIVER : Ah! That's why you came back?

ANABEL : No, no. I came back because my only hope in life was in coming back. Baard was beautiful—and awful. You know how glisteningly blond he was. Oliver, have you ever watched the polar bears? He was cold as iron when it is so cold that it burns you. Coldness wasn't negative with him. It was positive—and awful beyond expression—like the aurora borealis.

OLIVER: I wonder you ever got back.

ANABEL: Yes, so do I. I feel as if I'd fallen down a fissure in the ice. Yet I have come back, haven't I?

OLIVER: God knows! At least, Anabel, we've gone through too much ever to start the old game again. There'll be no more sticky love between us.

ANABEL: No, I think there won't, either.

OLIVER: And what of Gerald?

ANABEL: I don't know. What do you think of him?

OLIVER: I can't think any more. I can only blindly go from day to day, now.

ANABEL: So can I. Do you think I was wrong to come back? Do you think I wrong Gerald?

OLIVER: No. I'm glad you came. But I feel I can't *know* anything. We must just go on.

ANABEL: Sometimes I feel I ought never to have come to Gerald again—never—never—never.

OLIVER: Just left the gap?—Perhaps, if everything has to come asunder. But I think, if ever there is to be life—hope,—then you had to come back. I always knew it. There is something eternal between you and him; and if there is to be any happiness, it depends on that. But perhaps there is to *be* no more happiness— for our part of the world.

ANABEL *(after a pause)*: Yet I feel hope—don't you?

OLIVER: Yes, sometimes.

ANABEL: It seemed to me, especially that winter in Norway,—I can hardly express it,—as if any moment life might give way under one, like thin ice, and one would be more than dead. And then I knew my only hope was here—the only hope.

OLIVER: Yes, I believe it. And I believe——

    Enter MRS BARLOW.

MRS BARLOW: Oh, I wanted to speak to you, Oliver.

OLIVER: Shall I come across?

MRS BARLOW: No, not now. I believe Father is coming here with Gerald.

OLIVER: Is he going to walk so far?

MRS BARLOW: He will do it.—I suppose you know Oliver?

ANABEL: Yes, we have met before.

MRS BARLOW *(to* OLIVER*)*: You didn't mention it. Where have you met Miss Wrath? She's been about the world, I believe.

ANABEL: About the world?—no, Mrs Barlow. If one happens to know Paris and London——

MRS BARLOW: Paris and London! Well, I don't say you are altogether an adventuress. My husband seems very pleased with you —for Winifred's sake, I suppose—and he's wrapped up in Winifred.

ANABEL: Winifred is an artist.

MRS BARLOW: All my children have the artist in them. They get it from my family. My father went mad in Rome. My family is born with a black fate—they all inherit it.

OLIVER: I believe one is master of one's fate sometimes, Mrs Barlow. There are moments of pure choice.

MRS BARLOW: Between two ways to the same end, no doubt. There's no changing the end.

OLIVER: I think there is.

MRS BARLOW: Yes, you have a *parvenu's* presumptuousness somewhere about you.

OLIVER: Well, better than a blue-blooded fatalism.

MRS BARLOW: The fate is in the blood: you can't change the blood.

Enter WINIFRED.

WINIFRED: Oh, thank you, Oliver, for the wolf and the goat, thank you so much!—The wolf has sprung on the goat, Miss Wrath, and has her by the throat.

ANABEL: The wolf?

OLIVER: It's a little marble group—Italian—in hard marble.

WINIFRED: The wolf—I love the wolf—he pounces so beautifully. His backbone is so terribly fierce. I don't feel a bit sorry for the goat, somehow.

OLIVER: I didn't. She is too much like the wrong sort of clergyman.

WINIFRED: Yes—such a stiff, long face. I wish he'd kill her.

MRS BARLOW: There's a wish!

WINIFRED: Father and Gerald are coming. That's them, I suppose.

Enter MR BARLOW *and* GERALD.

MR BARLOW: Ah, good morning—good morning—quite a little gathering! Ah——

OLIVER: The steps tire you, Mr Barlow.

MR BARLOW: A little—a little—thank you.—Well, Miss Wrath, are you quite comfortable here?

ANABEL: Very comfortable, thanks.

GERALD: It was clever of you, Father, to turn this place into a studio.

MR BARLOW: Yes, Gerald. You make the worldly schemes and I the homely. Yes, it's a delightful place. I shall come here often if the two young ladies will allow me.—By the way, Miss Wrath, I don't know if you have been introduced to my son Gerald. I beg your pardon. Miss Wrath, Gerald—my son, Miss Wrath. *(They bow.)* Well, we are quite a gathering, quite a pleasant little gathering. We never expected anything so delightful a month ago, did we, Winifred, darling?

WINIFRED: No, Daddy, it's much nicer than expectations.

MR BARLOW: So it is, dear—to have such exceptional companionship and such a pleasant retreat. We are very happy to have Miss Wrath with us—very happy.

GERALD: A studio's awfully nice, you know; it is such a retreat. A newspaper has no effect in it—falls quite flat, no matter what the headlines are.

MR BARLOW: Quite true, Gerald, dear. It is a sanctum the world cannot invade—unlike all other sanctuaries, I am afraid.

GERALD: By the way, Oliver—to go back to profanities—the colliers really are coming out in support of the poor, ill-used clerks.

MR BARLOW: No, no, Gerald—no, no! Don't be such an alarmist. Let us leave these subjects before the ladies. No, no: the clerks will have their increase quite peacefully.

GERALD: Yes, dear father—but they can't have it peacefully now. We've been threatened already by the colliers—we've already received an ultimatum.

MR BARLOW: Nonsense, my boy—nonsense! Don't let us split words. You won't go against the clerks in such a small matter. Always avoid trouble over small matters. Don't make bad feeling—don't make bad blood.

MRS BARLOW: The blood is already rotten in this neighbourhood. What it needs is letting out. We need a few veins opening, or we shall have mortification setting in. The blood is black.

MR BARLOW: We won't accept your figure of speech literally, dear. No, Gerald, don't go to war over trifles.

GERALD: It's just over trifles that one must make war, Father. One can yield gracefully over big matters. But to be bullied over trifles is a sign of criminal weakness.

MR BARLOW: Ah, not so, not so, my boy. When you are as old as I am, you will know the comparative insignificance of these trifles.

GERALD: The older *I* get, Father, the more such trifles stick in my throat.

MR BARLOW: Ah, it is an increasingly irritable disposition in you, my child. Nothing costs so bitterly, in the end, as a stubborn pride.

MRS BARLOW: Except a stubborn humility—and that will cost you more. Avoid humility, beware of stubborn humility: it degrades. Hark, Gerald—fight! When the occasion comes, fight! If it's one against five thousand, fight! Don't give them your heart on a dish! Never! If they want to eat your heart out, make them fight for it, and then give it them poisoned at last, poisoned with your own blood.—What do you say, young woman?

ANABEL: Is it for me to speak, Mrs Barlow?

MRS BARLOW: Weren't you asked?

ANABEL: Certainly I would *never* give the world my heart on a dish. But can't there ever be peace—real peace?

MRS BARLOW: No—not while there is devilish enmity.

MR BARLOW: You are wrong, dear, you are wrong. The peace can come, the peace that passeth all understanding.

MRS BARLOW: That there is already between me and Almighty God. I am at peace with the God that made me, and made me proud. With men who humiliate me I am at war. Between me and the shameful humble there is war to the end, though they are millions and I am one. I hate the people. Between my race and them there is war—between them and me, between them and my children—for ever war, for ever and ever.

MR BARLOW: Ah, Henrietta—you have said all this before.

MRS BARLOW: And say it again. Fight, Gerald. You have my blood in you, thank God. Fight for it, Gerald. Spend it as if it were costly, Gerald, drop by drop. Let no dogs lap it.—Look at your father. He set his heart on a plate at the door, for the poorest

mongrel to eat up. See him now, wasted and crossed out like a
mistake—and swear, Gerald, swear to be true to my blood in
you. Never lie down before the mob, Gerald. Fight it and stab it,
and die fighting. It's a lost hope—but fight!

GERALD: Don't say these things here, Mother.

MRS BARLOW: Yes, I will—I will. I'll say them before you, and the
child Winifred—she knows. And before Oliver and the young
woman—they know, too.

MR BARLOW: You see, dear, you can never understand that, although
I am weak and wasted, although I may be crossed out from the
world like a mistake, I still have peace in my soul, dear, the peace
that passeth all understanding.

MRS BARLOW: And what right have you to it? All very well for
you to take peace with you into the other world. What do you
leave for your sons to inherit?

MR BARLOW: The peace of God, Henrietta, if there is no peace
among men.

MRS BARLOW: Then why did you have children? Why weren't you
celibate? They have to live among men. If they have no place
among men, why have you put them there? If the peace of God
is no more than the peace of death, why are your sons born of
you? How can you have peace with God, if you leave no peace
for your sons—no peace, no pride, no place on earth?

GERALD: Nay, Mother, nay. You shall never blame Father on my
behalf.

MRS BARLOW: Don't trouble—he is blameless—I, a hulking, half-
demented woman, I am *glad* when you blame me. But don't blame
me when I tell you to fight. Don't do that, or you will regret it
when you must die. Ah, your father was stiff and proud enough
before men of better rank than himself. He was overbearing
enough with his equals and his betters. But he humbled himself
before the poor, he made me ashamed. He must hear it—he must
hear it! Better he should hear it than die coddling himself with
peace. His humility, and my pride, they have made a nice ruin
of each other. Yet he is the man I wanted to marry—he is the
man I would marry again. But never, never again would I give
way before his goodness. Gerald, if you must be true to your
father, be true to me as well. Don't set me down at nothing because I haven't a humble case.

GERALD : No, Mother—no, dear Mother. You see, dear Mother, I have rather a job between the two halves of myself. When you come to have the wild horses in your own soul, Mother, it makes it difficult.

MRS BARLOW : Never mind, you'll have help.

GERALD : Thank you for the assurance, darling.—Father, you don't mind what Mother says, I hope. I believe there's some truth in it—don't you?

MR BARLOW : I have nothing to say.

WINIFRED : *I* think there's some truth in it, Daddy. You were always worrying about those horrid colliers, and they didn't care a bit about you. And they *ought* to have cared a million pounds.

MR BARLOW : You don't understand, my child.

CURTAIN

SCENE: *Evening of the same day. Drawing-room at Lilley Close.*
MR BARLOW, GERALD, WINIFRED, ANABEL, OLIVER *present.*
BUTLER *pours coffee.*

MR BARLOW: And you are quite a stranger in these parts, Miss Wrath?

ANABEL: Practically. But I was born at Derby.

MR BARLOW: I was born in this house—but it was a different affair then: my father was a farmer, you know. The coal has brought us what moderate wealth we have. Of course, we were never poor or needy—farmers, substantial farmers. And I think we were happier so—yes.—Winnie, dear, hand Miss Wrath the sweets. I hope they're good. I ordered them from London for you.—Oliver, my boy, have you everything you like? That's right.—It gives me such pleasure to see a little festive gathering in this room again. I wish Bertie and Elinor might be here. What time is it, Gerald?

GERALD: A quarter to nine, Father.

MR BARLOW: Not late yet. I can sit with you another half-hour. I am feeling better to-day. Winifred, sing something to us.

WINIFRED: Something jolly, Father?

MR BARLOW: Very jolly, darling.

WINIFRED: I'll sing "The Lincolnshire Poacher", shall I?

MR BARLOW: Do, darling, and we'll all join in the chorus.—Will you join in the chorus, Miss Wrath?

ANABEL: I will. It is a good song.

MR BARLOW: Yes, isn't it!

WINIFRED: All dance for the chorus, as well as singing.

They sing; some pirouette a little for the chorus.

MR BARLOW: Ah, splendid, splendid! There is nothing like gaiety.

WINIFRED: I do love to dance about. I know: let us do a little ballet—four of us—oh, do!

GERALD: What ballet, Winifred?

WINIFRED: Any. Eva can play for us. She plays well.

MR BARLOW: You won't disturb your mother? Don't disturb Eva if she is busy with your mother.

Exit WINIFRED.

If only I can see Winifred happy, my heart is at rest: if only I can hope for her to be happy in her life.

GERALD: Oh, Winnie's alright, Father—especially now she has Miss Wrath to initiate her into the mysteries of life and labour.

ANABEL: Why are you ironical?

MR BARLOW: Oh, Miss Wrath, believe me, we all feel that—it is the greatest possible pleasure to me that you have come.

GERALD: I wasn't ironical, I assure you.

MR BARLOW: No, indeed—no, indeed! We have every belief in you.

ANABEL: But why should you have?

MR BARLOW: Ah, my dear child, allow us the credit of our own discernment. And don't take offence at my familiarity. I am afraid I am spoilt since I am an invalid.

Re-enter WINIFRED, *with* EVA.

MR BARLOW: Come, Eva, you will excuse us for upsetting your evening. Will you be so good as to play something for us to dance to?

EVA: Yes, sir. What shall I play?

WINIFRED: Mozart—I'll find you the piece. Mozart's the saddest musician in the world—but he's the best to dance to.

MR BARLOW: Why, how is it you are such a connoisseur in sadness, darling?

GERALD: She isn't. She's a flagrant amateur.

EVA *plays; they dance a little ballet.*

MR BARLOW: Charming—charming, Miss Wrath: will you allow me to say *Anabel*, we shall all feel so much more at home? Yes—thank you—er—you enter into the spirit of it wonderfully, Anabel, dear. The others are accustomed to play together. But it is not so easy to come in on occasion as you do.

GERALD: Oh, Anabel's a genius!—I beg your pardon, Miss Wrath—familiarity is catching.

MR BARLOW: Gerald, my boy, don't forget that you are virtually host here.

EVA: Did you want any more music, sir?

GERALD: No, don't stay, Eva. We mustn't tire Father.

Exit EVA.

MR BARLOW: I am afraid, Anabel, you will have a great deal to excuse in us, in the way of manners. We have never been a formal household. But you have lived in the world of artists: you will understand, I hope.

ANABEL: Oh, surely——

MR BARLOW: Yes, I know. We have been a turbulent family, and we have had our share of sorrow, even more, perhaps, than of joys. And sorrow makes one indifferent to the conventionalities of life.

GERALD: Excuse me, Father: do you mind if I go and write a letter I have on my conscience?

MR BARLOW: No, my boy. *(Exit* GERALD.) We have had our share of sorrow and of conflict, Miss Wrath, as you may have gathered

ANABEL: Yes—a little.

MR BARLOW: The mines were opened when my father was a boy— the first—and I was born late, when he was nearly fifty. So that all my life has been involved with coal and colliers. As a young man, I was gay and thoughtless. But I married young, and we lost our first child through a terrible accident. Two children we have lost through sudden and violent death. (WINIFRED *goes out unnoticed.*) It made me reflect. And when I came to reflect, Anabel, I could not justify my position in life. If I believed in the teachings of the New Testament—which I did, and do—how could I keep two or three thousand men employed underground in the mines, at a wage, let us say, of two pounds a week, whilst I lived in this comfortable house, and took something like two thousand pounds a year—let us name any figure——

ANABEL: Yes, of course. But is it money that really matters, Mr Barlow?

MR BARLOW: My dear, if you are a working man, it matters. When I went into the homes of my poor fellows, when they were ill or had had accidents—then I knew it mattered. I knew that the great disparity was wrong—even as we are taught that it is wrong.

ANABEL: Yes, I believe that the great disparity is a mistake. But take their lives, Mr Barlow. Do you think they would *live* more, if they had more money? Do you think the poor live less than the rich?—is their life emptier?

MR BARLOW: Surely their lives would be better, Anabel.

OLIVER: All our lives would be better, if we hadn't to hang on in the perpetual tug-of-war, like two donkeys pulling at one carrot. The ghastly tension of possessions, and struggling for possession, spoils life for everybody.

MR BARLOW: Yes, I know now, as I knew then, that it was wrong. But how to avoid the wrong? If I gave away the whole of my income, it would merely be an arbitrary dispensation of charity. The money would still be mine to give, and those that received it would probably only be weakened instead of strengthened. And then my wife was accustomed to a certain way of living, a certain establishment. Had I any right to sacrifice her, without her consent?

ANABEL: Why, no!

MR BARLOW: Again, if I withdrew from the Company, if I retired on a small income, I knew that another man would automatically take my place, and make it probably harder for the men.

ANABEL: Of course—while the system stands, if one makes self-sacrifice one only panders to the system, makes it fatter.

MR BARLOW: One panders to the system—one panders to the system. And so, you see, the problem is too much. One man cannot alter or affect the system; he can only sacrifice himself to it. Which is the worst thing probably that he can do.

OLIVER: Quite. But why feel guilty for the system?—everybody supports it, the poor as much as the rich. If every rich man withdrew from the system, the working classes and socialists would keep it going, every man in the hope of getting rich himself at last. It's the people that are wrong. They want the system much more than the rich do—because they are much more anxious to be rich—never having been rich, poor devils.

MR BARLOW: Just the system. So I decided at last that the best way was to give every private help that lay in my power. I would help my men individually and personally, wherever I could. Not one of them came to me and went away unheard; and there was no distress which could be alleviated that I did not try to alleviate. Yet I am afraid that the greatest distress I never heard of, the most distressed never came to me. They hid their trouble.

ANABEL: Yes, the decent ones.

MR BARLOW: But I wished to help—it was my duty. Still, I think that, on the whole, we were a comfortable and happy community. Barlow and Walsall's men were not unhappy in those days, I believe. We were liberal; the men lived.

OLIVER: Yes, that is true. Even twenty years ago the place was still jolly.

MR BARLOW: And then, when Gerald was a lad of thirteen, came the great lock-out. We belonged to the Masters' Federation—I was but one man on the Board. We had to abide by the decision. The mines were closed till the men would accept the reduction.— Well, that cut my life across. We were shutting the men out from work, starving their families, in order to force them to accept a reduction. It may be the condition of trade made it imperative. But, for myself, I would rather have lost everything. —Of course, we did what we could. Food was very cheap— practically given away. We had open kitchen here. And it was mercifully warm summer-time. Nevertheless, there was privation and suffering, and trouble and bitterness. We had the redcoats down—even to guard this house. And from this window I saw Whatmore head-stocks ablaze, and before I could get to the spot the soldiers had shot two poor fellows. They were not killed, thank God——

OLIVER: Ah, but they enjoyed it—they enjoyed it immensely. I remember what grand old sporting weeks they were. It was like a fox-hunt, so lively and gay—bands and tea-parties and excitement everywhere, pit-ponies loose, men all over the countryside——

MR BARLOW: There was a great deal of suffering which you were too young to appreciate. However, since that year I have had to acknowledge a new situation—a radical if unspoken opposition between masters and men. Since that year we have been split into opposite camps. Whatever I might privately feel, I was one of the owners, one of the masters, and therefore in the opposite camp. To my men I was an oppressor, a representative of injustice and greed. Privately, I like to think that even to this day they bear me no malice, that they have some lingering regard for me. But the master stands before the human being, and the condition of war overrides individuals—they hate the master, even whilst, as a human being, he would be their friend. I recognize the inevitable justice. It is the price one has to pay.

ANABEL : Yes, it is difficult—very.

MR BARLOW : Perhaps I weary you?

ANABEL : Oh, no—no.

MR BARLOW : Well—then the mines began to pay badly. The seams ran thin and unprofitable, work was short. Either we must close down or introduce a new system, American methods, which I dislike so extremely. Now it really became a case of men working against machines, flesh and blood working against iron, for a livelihood. Still, it had to be done—the whole system revolutionized. Gerald took it in hand—and now I hardly know my own pits, with the great electric plants and strange machinery, and the new coal-cutters—iron men, as the colliers call them—everything running at top speed, utterly dehumanized, inhuman. Well, it had to be done; it was the only alternative to closing down and throwing three thousand men out of work. And Gerald has done it. But I can't bear to see it. The men of this generation are not like my men. They are worn and gloomy; they have a hollow look that I can't bear to see. They are a great grief to me. I remember my men even twenty years ago—a noisy, lively, careless set, who kept the place ringing. Now it is too quiet—too quiet. There is something wrong in the quietness, something unnatural. I feel it is unnatural; I feel afraid of it. And I cannot help feeling guilty.

ANABEL : Yes—I understand. It terrifies me.

MR BARLOW : Does it?—does it?—Yes.—And as my wife says, I leave it all to Gerald—this terrible situation. But I appeal to God, if anything in my power could have averted it, I would have averted it. I would have made any sacrifice. For it is a great and bitter trouble to me.

ANABEL : Ah, well, in death there is no industrial situation. Something must be different there.

MR BARLOW : Yes—yes.

OLIVER : And you see sacrifice isn't the slightest use. If only people would be sane and decent.

MR BARLOW : Yes, indeed.—Would you be so good as to ring, Oliver? I think I must go to bed.

ANABEL : Ah, you have over-tired yourself.

MR BARLOW : No, my dear—not over-tired. Excuse me if I have burdened you with all this. It relieves me to speak of it.

ANABEL: I realize *how* terrible it is, Mr Barlow—and how helpless one is.

MR BARLOW: Thank you, my dear, for your sympathy.

OLIVER: If the people for one minute pulled themselves up and conquered their mania for money and machine excitement, the whole thing would be solved.—Would you like me to find Winnie and tell her to say good night to you?

MR BARLOW: If you would be so kind. *(Exit* OLIVER.*)* Can't you find a sweet that you would like, my dear? Won't you take a little cherry brandy?

Enter BUTLER.

ANABEL: Thank you.

WILLIAM: You will go up, sir?

MR BARLOW: Yes, William.

WILLIAM: You are tired to-night, sir.

MR BARLOW: It has come over me just now.

WILLIAM: I wish you went up before you became so over-tired, sir. Would you like Nurse?

MR BARLOW: No, I'll go with you, William. Good night, my dear.

ANABEL: Good night, Mr Barlow. I am so sorry if you are over-tired.

Exit BUTLER *and* MR BARLOW. ANABEL *takes a drink and goes to the fire. Enter* GERALD.

GERALD: Father gone up?

ANABEL: Yes.

GERALD: I thought I heard him. Has he been talking too much?— Poor Father, he will take things to heart.

ANABEL: Tragic, really.

GERALD: Yes, I suppose it is. But one can get beyond tragedy— beyond the state of feeling tragical, I mean. Father himself is tragical. One feels he is mistaken—and yet he wouldn't be any different, and be himself, I suppose. He's sort of crucified on an idea of the working people. It's rather horrible when he's one father.—However, apart from tragedy, how do you like being here, in this house?

ANABEL: I like the house. It's rather too comfortable.

GERALD: Yes. But how do you like being here?

ANABEL: How do you like my being in your home?

GERALD: Oh, I think you're very decorative.

ANABEL : More decorative than comfortable?

GERALD : Perhaps. But perhaps you give the necessary finish to the establishment.

ANABEL : Like the correct window-curtains?

GERALD : Yes, something like that. I say, why did you come, Anabel? Why did you come slap-bang into the middle of us?—It's not expostulation—I want to know.

ANABEL : You mean you want to be told.

GERALD : Yes, I want to be told.

ANABEL : That's rather mean of you. You should savvy, and let it go without saying.

GERALD : Yes, but I don't savvy.

ANABEL : Then wait till you do.

GERALD : No, I want to be told. There's a difference in you, Anabel, that puts me out, rather. You're sort of softer and sweeter—I'm not sure whether it isn't a touch of Father in you. There's a little sanctified smudge on your face. Are you really a bit sanctified?

ANABEL : No, not sanctified. It's true I feel different. I feel I want a new way of life—something more dignified, more religious, if you like—anyhow, something *positive*.

GERALD : Is it the change of heart, Anabel?

ANABEL : Perhaps it is, Gerald.

GERALD : I'm not sure that I like it. Isn't it like a berry that decides to get very sweet, and goes soft?

ANABEL : I don't think so.

GERALD : Slightly sanctimonious. I think I liked you better before. I don't think I like you with this touch of aureole. People seem to me so horribly self-satisfied when they get a change of heart— they take such a fearful lot of credit to themselves on the strength of it.

ANABEL : I don't think I do.—Do you feel no different, Gerald?

GERALD : Radically, I can't say I do.—I feel very much more *in*different.

ANABEL : What to?

GERALD : Everything.

ANABEL : You're still angry—that's what it is.

GERALD : Oh yes, I'm angry. But that is part of my normal state.

ANABEL : Why are you angry?

GERALD : Is there any reason why I shouldn't be angry? I'm angry because you treated me—well, so impudently, really—clearing out and leaving one to whistle to the empty walls.

ANABEL: Don't you think it was time I cleared out, when you became so violent, and really dangerous, really like a madman?

GERALD: Time or not time, you went—you disappeared and left us high and dry—and I am still angry.—But I'm not only angry about that. I'm angry with the colliers, with Labour for its low-down impudence—and I'm angry with Father for being so ill—and I'm angry with Mother for looking such a hopeless thing—and I'm angry with Oliver because he thinks so much——

ANABEL: And what are you angry with yourself for?

GERALD: I'm angry with myself for being myself—I always was that. I was always a curse to myself.

ANABEL: And that's why you curse others so much?

GERALD: You talk as if butter wouldn't melt in your mouth.

ANABEL: You see, Gerald, there has to be a change. You'll have to change.

GERALD: Change of heart?—Well, it won't be to get softer, Anabel.

ANABEL: You needn't be softer. But you can be quieter, more sane even. There ought to be some part of you that can be quiet and apart from the world, some part that can be happy and gentle.

GERALD: Well, there isn't. I don't pretend to be able to extricate a soft sort of John Halifax, Gentleman, out of the machine I'm mixed up in, and keep him to gladden the connubial hearth. I'm angry, and I'm angry right through, and I'm not going to play bo-peep with myself, pretending I'm not.

ANABEL: Nobody asks you to. But is there no part of you that can be a bit gentle and peaceful and happy with a woman?

GERALD: No, there isn't.—I'm not going to smug with you—no, not I. You're smug in your coming back. You feel virtuous, and expect me to rise to it. I won't.

ANABEL: Then I'd better have stayed away.

GERALD: If you want me to virtue-ize and smug with you, you had.

ANABEL: What *do* you want, then?

GERALD: I don't know. I know I don't want *that*.

ANABEL: Oh, very well. *(Goes to the piano; begins to play.)*

    Enter MRS BARLOW.

GERALD : Hello, Mother! Father *has* gone to bed.

MRS BARLOW : Oh, I thought he was down here talking. You two alone?

GERALD : With the piano for chaperone, Mother.

MRS BARLOW : That's more than I gave you credit for. I haven't come to chaperone you either, Gerald.

GERALD : Chaperone *me*, Mother! Do you think I need it?

MRS BARLOW : If you do, you won't get it. I've come too late to be of any use in that way, as far as I hear.

GERALD : What have you heard, Mother?

MRS BARLOW : I heard Oliver and this young woman talking.

GERALD : Oh, did you? When? What did they say?

MRS BARLOW : Something about married in the sight of heaven, but couldn't keep it up on earth.

GERALD : I don't understand.

MRS BARLOW : That you and this young woman were married in the sight of heaven, or through eternity, or something similar, but that you couldn't make up your minds to it on earth.

GERALD : Really! That's very curious, Mother.

MRS BARLOW : Very common occurrence, I believe.

GERALD : Yes, so it is. But I don't think you heard quite right, dear. There seems to be some lingering uneasiness in heaven as a matter of fact. We'd quite made up our minds to live apart on earth. But where did you hear this, Mother?

MRS BARLOW : I heard it outside the studio door this morning.

GERALD : You mean you happened to be on one side of the door while Oliver and Anabel were talking on the other?

MRS BARLOW : You'd make a detective, Gerald—you're so good at putting two and two together. I listened till I'd heard as much as I wanted. I'm not sure I didn't come down here hoping to hear another conversation going on.

GERALD : Listen outside the door, darling?

MRS BARLOW : There'd be nothing to listen to if I were inside.

GERALD : It isn't usually done, you know.

MRS BARLOW : I listen outside doors when I have occasion to be interested—which isn't often, unfortunately for me.

GERALD : But I've a queer feeling that you have a permanent occasion to be interested in me. I only half like it.

MRS BARLOW : It's surprising how uninteresting you are, Gerald, for a man of your years. I have not had occasion to listen outside a door, for you, no, not for a great while, believe me.

GERALD : I believe you implicitly, darling. But do you happen to know me through and through, and in and out, all my past and present doings, Mother? Have you a secret access to my room, and a spy-hole, and all those things? This is uncomfortably thrilling. You take on a new lustre.

MRS BARLOW : Your memoirs wouldn't make you famous, my son.

GERALD : Infamous, dear?

MRS BARLOW : Good heavens, no! What a lot you expect from your very mild sins! You and this young woman have lived together, then?

GERALD : Don't say "this young woman", Mother dear—it's slightly vulgar. It isn't for me to compromise Anabel by admitting such a thing, you know.

MRS BARLOW : Do you ask me to call her Anabel? I won't.

GERALD : Then say "this person", Mother. It's more becoming.

MRS BARLOW : I didn't come to speak to you, Gerald. I know you. I came to speak to this young woman.

GERALD : "Person", Mother.—Will you curtsey, Anabel? And I'll twist my handkerchief. We shall make a Cruikshank drawing, if Mother makes her hair a little more slovenly.

MRS BARLOW : You and 'Gerald were together for some time?

GERALD : Three years, off and on, Mother.

MRS BARLOW : And then you suddenly dropped my son, and went away?

GERALD : To Norway, Mother—so I have gathered.

MRS BARLOW : And now you have come back because that last one died?

GERALD : Is he dead, Anabel? How did he die?

ANABEL : He was killed on the ice.

GERALD : Oh, God!

MRS BARLOW : Now, having had your fill of tragedy, you have come back to be demure and to marry Gerald. Does he thank you?

GERALD : You must listen outside the door, Mother, to find that out.

MRS BARLOW : Well, it's your own affair.

GERALD : What a lame summing up, Mother!—quite unworthy of you.

ANABEL : What did you wish to say to me, Mrs Barlow? Please
say it.

MRS BARLOW : What did I wish to say! Ay, what did I wish to say!
What is the use of my saying anything? What am I but a buffoon
and a slovenly caricature in the family?

GERALD : No, Mother dear, don't climb down—please don't. Tell
Anabel what you wanted to say.

MRS BARLOW : Yes—yes—yes. I came to say—don't be good to my
son—don't be good to him.

GERALD : Sounds weak, dear—mere contrariness.

MRS BARLOW : Don't presume to be good to my son, young woman.
I won't have it, even if he will. You hear me?

ANABEL : Yes. I won't presume, then.

GERALD : May she presume to be bad to me, Mother?

MRS BARLOW : For that you may look after yourself.—But a woman
who was good to him would ruin him in six months, take the
manhood out of him. He has a tendency, a secret hankering, to
make a gift of himself to somebody. He shan't do it. I warn you.
I am not a woman to be despised.

ANABEL : No—I understand.

MRS BARLOW : Only one other thing I ask. If he must fight—and
fight he must—let him alone : don't you try to shield him or save
him. *Don't interfere*—do you hear?

ANABEL : Not till I must.

MRS BARLOW : *Never.* Learn your place, and keep it. Keep away
from him, if you are going to be a wife to him. Don't go too near.
And don't let him come too near. Beat him off if he tries. Keep a
solitude in your heart even when you love him best. Keep it. If
you lose it, you lose everything.

GERALD : But that isn't love, Mother.

MRS BARLOW : What?

GERALD : That isn't love.

MRS BARLOW : *What?* What do you know of love, you ninny? You
only know the feeding-bottle. It's what you want, all of you—to
be brought up by hand, and mew about love. Ah, God!—Ah,
God!—that you should none of you know the only thing which
would make you worth having.

GERALD : I don't believe in your only thing, Mother. But what is it?

MRS BARLOW : What you haven't got—the power to be alone.

GERALD: Sort of megalomania, you mean?

MRS BARLOW: What? Megalomania! What is your *love* but a megalomania, flowing over everybody, and everything like spilt water? Megalomania! I hate you, you softy! I would *beat* you *(suddenly advancing on him and beating him fiercely)*—beat you into some manhood—beat you——

GERALD: Stop, Mother—keep off.

MRS BARLOW: It's the men who need beating nowadays, not the children. Beat the softness out of him, young woman. It's the only way, if you love him enough—if you love him enough.

GERALD: You hear, Anabel?

> *Speak roughly to your little boy,*
> *And beat him when he sneezes.*

MRS BARLOW *(catching up a large old fan, and smashing it about his head)*: You softy—you piffler—you will never have had enough! Ah, you should be thrust in the fire, you should, to have the softness and the brittleness burnt out of you!

> *The door opens*—OLIVER TURTON *enters, followed by* JOB ARTHUR FREER. MRS BARLOW *is still attacking* GERALD. *She turns, infuriated.*

Go out! Go out! What do you mean by coming in unannounced? Take him upstairs—take that fellow into the library, Oliver Turton.

GERALD: Mother, you improve our already pretty reputation. Already they say you are mad.

MRS BARLOW *(ringing violently)*: Let me be mad then. I am mad—driven mad. One day I shall kill you, Gerald.

GERALD: You won't, Mother, because I shan't let you.

MRS BARLOW: Let me!—let me! As if I should wait for you to let me!

GERALD: I am a match for you even in violence, come to that.

MRS BARLOW: A match! A damp match. A wet match.

> *Enter* BUTLER.

WILLIAM: You rang, madam?

MRS BARLOW: Clear up those bits.—Where are you going to see that white-faced fellow? Here?

GERALD: I think so.

MRS BARLOW: You will *still* have them coming to the house, will you? You will still let them trample in our private rooms, will you? Bah! I ought to leave you to your own devices.

Exit MRS BARLOW.

GERALD: When you've done that, William, ask Mr Freer to come down here.

WILLIAM: Yes, sir.

A pause. Exit WILLIAM.

GERALD: So—o—o. You've had another glimpse of the family life.

ANABEL: Yes. Rather—disturbing.

GERALD: Not at all, when you're used to it. Mother isn't as mad as she pretends to be.

ANABEL: I don't think she's mad at all. I think she has most desperate courage.

GERALD: "Courage" is good. That's a new term for it.

ANABEL: Yes, courage. When a man says "courage" he means the courage to die. A woman means the courage to live. That's what women hate men most for; that they haven't the courage to live.

GERALD: Mother takes her courage into both hands rather late.

ANABEL: We're a little late ourselves.

GERALD: We are, rather. By the way, you seem to have had plenty of the courage of death—you've played a pretty deathly game, it seems to me—both when I knew you and afterwards, you've had your finger pretty deep in the death-pie.

ANABEL: That's why I want a change of—of——

GERALD: Of heart?—Better take Mother's tip, and try the poker.

ANABEL: I will.

GERALD: Ha—corraggio!

ANABEL: Yes—corraggio!

GERALD: Corraggiaccio!

ANABEL: Corraggione!

GERALD: Cock-a-doodle-doo!

Enter OLIVER *and* FREER.

Oh, come in. Don't be afraid; it's a charade. (ANABEL *rises.*) No, don't go, Anabel. Corraggio! Take a seat, Mr Freer.

JOB ARTHUR: Sounds like a sneezing game, doesn't it?

GERALD: It is. Do you know the famous rhyme:

> *Speak roughly to your little boy,*
> *And beat him when he sneezes?*

JOB ARTHUR : No, I can't say I do.

GERALD : My mother does. Will you have anything to drink? Will you help yourself?

JOB ARTHUR : Well—no—I don't think I'll have anything, thanks.

GERALD : A cherry brandy?—Yes?—Anabel, what's yours.

ANABEL : Did I see Kümmel?

GERALD : You did. *(They all take drinks.)* What's the latest, Mr Freer?

JOB ARTHUR : The latest? Well, I don't know, I'm sure——

GERALD : Oh, yes. Trot it out. We're quite private.

JOB ARTHUR : Well—I don't know. There's several things.

GERALD : The more the merrier.

JOB ARTHUR : I'm not so sure. The men are in a very funny temper, Mr Barlow—very funny.

GERALD : Coincidence—so am I. Not surprising, is it?

JOB ARTHUR : The men, perhaps not.

GERALD : What else, Job Arthur?

JOB ARTHUR : You know the men have decided to stand by the office men?

GERALD : Yes.

JOB ARTHUR : They've agreed to come out next Monday.

GERALD : Have they?

JOB ARTHUR : Yes; there was no stopping them. They decided for it like one man.

GERALD : How was that?

JOB ARTHUR : That's what surprises me. They're a jolly sight more certain over this than they've ever been over their own interests.

GERALD : All their love for the office clerks coming out in a rush?

JOB ARTHUR : Well, I don't know about love; but that's how it is.

GERALD : What is it, if it isn't love?

JOB ARTHUR : I can't say. They're in a funny temper. It's hard to make out.

GERALD : A funny temper, are they? Then I suppose we ought to laugh.

JOB ARTHUR : No, I don't think it's a laughing matter. They're coming out on Monday for certain.

GERALD : Yes—so are daffodils.

JOB ARTHUR : Beg pardon?

GERALD : Daffodils.

JOB ARTHUR : No, I don't follow what you mean.

GERALD : Don't you? But I thought Alfred Breffitt and William Straw were not very popular.

JOB ARTHUR : No, they aren't—not in themselves. But it's the principle of the thing—so it seems.

GERALD : What principle?

JOB ARTHUR : Why, all sticking together, for one thing—all Barlow and Walsall's men holding by one another.

GERALD : United we stand?

JOB ARTHUR : That's it. And then it's the strong defending the weak as well. There's three thousand colliers standing up for thirty-odd office men. I must say I think it's sporting myself.

GERALD : You do, do you? United we stand, divided we fall. What do they stand for, really? What is it?

JOB ARTHUR : Well—for their right to a living wage. That's how I see it.

GERALD : For their right to a living wage! Just that?

JOB ARTHUR : Yes, sir—that's how I see it.

GERALD : Well, that doesn't seem so preposterously difficult, does it?

JOB ARTHUR : Why, that's what I think myself, Mr Gerald. It's such a little thing.

GERALD : Quite. I suppose the men themselves are to judge what is a living wage?

JOB ARTHUR : Oh, I think they're quite reasonable, you know.

GERALD : Oh, yes, eminently reasonable. Reason's their strong point. —And if they get their increase, they'll be quite contented?

JOB ARTHUR : Yes, as far as I know, they will.

GERALD : As far as you know? Why, is there something you don't know?—something you're not sure about?

JOB ARTHUR : No—I don't think so. I think they'll be quite satisfied this time.

GERALD : Why this time? Is there going to be a next time—every-day-has-its-to-morrow kind of thing?

JOB ARTHUR : I don't know about that. It's a funny world, Mr Barlow.

GERALD : Yes, I quite believe it. How do you see it funny?

JOB ARTHUR : Oh, I don't know. Everything's in a funny state.

GERALD : What do you mean by everything?

JOB ARTHUR : Well—I mean things in general—Labour, for example.

GERALD : You think Labour's in a funny state, do you? What do you
think it wants? What do you think, personally?

JOB ARTHUR : Well, in my own mind, I think it wants a bit of its
own back.

GERALD : And how does it mean to get it?

JOB ARTHUR : Ha! that's not so easy to say. But it means to have
it, in the long run.

GERALD : You mean by increasing demands for higher wages?

JOB ARTHUR : Yes, perhaps that's one road.

GERALD : Do you see any other?

JOB ARTHUR : Not just for the present.

GERALD: But later on?

JOB ARTHUR : I can't say about that. The men will be quiet enough
for a bit, if it's alright about the office men, you know.

GERALD : Probably. But have Barlow and Walsall's men any special
grievance apart from the rest of the miners?

JOB ARTHUR : I don't know. They've no liking for you, you know,
sir.

GERALD : Why?

JOB ARTHUR : They think you've got a down on them.

GERALD : Why should they?

JOB ARTHUR : I don't know, sir; but they do.

GERALD : So they have a personal feeling against me? You don't
think all the colliers are the same, all over the country?

JOB ARTHUR : I think there's a good deal of feeling——

GERALD : Of wanting their own back?

JOB ARTHUR : That's it.

GERALD : But what can they do? I don't see what they can do. They
can go out on strike—but they've done that before, and the
owners, at a pinch, can stand it better than they can. As for the
ruin of the industry, if they do ruin it, it falls heaviest on them.
In fact, it leaves them destitute. There's nothing they can do, you
know, that doesn't hit them worse than it hits us.

JOB ARTHUR : I know there's something in that. But if they had a
strong man to head them, you see——

GERALD : Yes, I've heard a lot about that strong man—but I've
never come across any signs of him, you know. I don't believe
in one strong man appearing out of so many little men. All men

are pretty big in an age, or in a movement, which produces a really big man. And Labour is a great swarm of hopelessly little men. That's how I see it.

JOB ARTHUR: I'm not so sure about that.

GERALD: I am. Labour is a thing that can't have a head. It's a sort of unwieldy monster that's bound to run its skull against the wall sooner or later, and knock out what bit of brain it's got. You see, you need wit and courage and real understanding if you're going to do anything positive. And Labour has none of these things—certainly it shows no sign of them.

JOB ARTHUR: Yes, when it has a chance, I think you'll see plenty of courage and plenty of understanding.

GERALD: It always has a chance. And where one sees a bit of courage, there's no understanding; and where there's some understanding, there's absolutely no courage. It's hopeless, you know—it would be far best if they'd all give it up, and try a new line.

JOB ARTHUR: I don't think they will.

GERALD: No, I don't either. They'll make a mess, and when they've made it, they'll never get out of it. They can't—they're too stupid.

JOB ARTHUR: They've never had a try yet.

GERALD: They're trying every day. They just simply couldn't control modern industry—they haven't the intelligence. They've no *life* intelligence. The owners may have little enough, but Labour has none. They're just mechanical little things that can make one or two motions, and they're done. They've no more idea of life than a lawn-mower has.

JOB ARTHUR: It remains to be seen.

GERALD: No, it doesn't. It's perfectly obvious—there's nothing remains to be seen. All that Labour is capable of, is smashing things up. And even for that I don't believe it has either energy or the courage or the bit of necessary passion, or slap-dash—call it whatever you will. However, we'll see.

JOB ARTHUR: Yes, sir. Perhaps you see now why you're not so very popular, Mr Gerald.

GERALD: We can't all be popular, Job Arthur. You're very high up in popularity, I believe.

JOB ARTHUR: Not so very. They listen to me a bit. But you never know when they'll let you down. I know they'll let me down one day—so it won't be a surprise.

GERALD: I should think not.

JOB ARTHUR: But about the office men, Mr Gerald. You think it'll be alright?

GERALD: Oh, yes, that'll be alright.

JOB ARTHUR: Easiest for this time, anyhow, sir. We don't want bloodshed, do we?

GERALD: I shouldn't mind at all. It might clear the way to something. But I have absolutely no belief in the power of Labour even to bring about anything so positive as bloodshed.

JOB ARTHUR: I don't know about that—I don't know.—Well.

GERALD: Have another drink before you go.—Yes, do. Help yourself.

JOB ARTHUR: Well—if you're so pressing. *(Helps himself.)* Here's luck, all!

ALL: Thanks.

GERALD: Take a cigar—there's the box. Go on—take a handful— fill your case.

JOB ARTHUR: They're a great luxury nowadays, aren't they? Almost beyond a man like me.

GERALD: Yes, that's the worst of not being a bloated capitalist. Never mind, you'll be a Cabinet Minister some day.—Oh, alright —I'll open the door for you.

JOB ARTHUR: Oh, don't trouble. Good night—good night.

Exeunt JOB ARTHUR *and* GERALD.

OLIVER: Oh God, what a world to live in!

ANABEL: I rather liked him. What is he?

OLIVER: Checkweighman—local secretary for the Miners' Federation—plays the violin well, although he was a collier, and it spoilt his hands. They're a musical family.

ANABEL: But isn't he rather nice?

OLIVER: I don't like him. But I confess he's a study. He's the modern Judas.

ANABEL: Don't you think he likes Gerald?

OLIVER: I'm sure he does. The way he suns himself here—like a cat purring in his luxuriation.

ANABEL: Yes, I don't mind it. It shows a certain sensitiveness and a certain taste.

OLIVER: Yes, he has both—touch of the artist, as Mrs Barlow says. He loves refinement, culture, breeding, all those things—loves them—and a presence, a fine free manner.

ANABEL: But that is nice in him.

OLIVER: Quite. But what he loves, and what he admires, and what he aspires to, he *must* betray. It's his fatality. He lives for the moment when he can kiss Gerald in the Garden of Olives, or wherever it was.

ANABEL: But Gerald shouldn't be kissed.

OLIVER: That's what I say.

ANABEL: And that's what his mother means as well, I suppose.

    Enter GERALD.

GERALD: Well—you've heard the voice of the people.

ANABEL: He isn't the people.

GERALD: I think he is, myself—the epitome.

OLIVER: No, he's a special type.

GERALD: Ineffectual, don't you think?

ANABEL: How pleased you are, Gerald! How pleased you are with yourself! You love the turn with him.

GERALD: It's rather stimulating, you know.

ANABEL: It oughtn't to be, then.

OLIVER: He's your Judas, and you love him.

GERALD: Nothing so deep. He's just a sort of Æolian harp that sings to the temper of the wind. I find him amusing.

ANABEL: I think it's boring.

OLIVER: And I think it's nasty.

GERALD: I believe you're both jealous of him. What do you think of the British working man, Oliver?

OLIVER: It seems to me he's in nearly as bad a way as the British employer: he's nearly as much beside the point.

GERALD: What point?

OLIVER: Oh, just life.

GERALD: That's too vague, my boy. Do you think they'll ever make a bust-up?

OLIVER: I can't tell. I don't see any good in it, if they do.

GERALD: It might clear the way—and it might block the way for ever: depends what comes through. But, sincerely, I don't think they've got it in them.

ANABEL: They may have something better.

GERALD: That suggestion doesn't interest me, Anabel. Ah well, we shall see what we shall see. Have a whisky and soda with me, Oliver, and let the troubled course of this evening run to a smooth close. It's quite like old times. Aren't you smoking, Anabel?

ANABEL: No, thanks.

GERALD: I believe you're a reformed character. So it won't be like old times, after all.

ANABEL: I don't want old times. I want new ones.

GERALD: Wait till Job Arthur has risen like Antichrist, and proclaimed the resurrection of the gods.—Do you see Job Arthur proclaiming Dionysus and Aphrodite?

ANABEL: It bores me. I don't like your mood. Good night.

GERALD: Oh, don't go.

ANABEL: Yes, good night.

Exit ANABEL.

OLIVER: She's *not* reformed, Gerald. She's the same old moral character—moral to the last bit of her, really—as she always was.

GERALD: Is that what it is?—But one must be moral.

OLIVER: Oh, yes. Oliver Cromwell wasn't as moral as Anabel is— nor such an iconoclast.

GERALD: Poor old Anabel!

OLIVER: How she hates the dark gods!

GERALD: And yet they cast a spell over her. Poor old Anabel! Well, Oliver, is Bacchus the father of whisky?

OLIVER: I don't know.—I don't like you either. You seem to smile all over yourself. It's objectionable. Good night.

GERALD: Oh, look here, this is censorious.

OLIVER: You smile to yourself.

Exit OLIVER.

CURTAIN

ACT III

SCENE I

An old park. Early evening. In the background a low Georgian hall, which has been turned into offices for the Company, shows windows already lighted. GERALD *and* ANABEL *walk along the path.*

ANABEL: How beautiful this old park is!

GERALD: Yes, it is beautiful—seems so far away from everywhere, if one doesn't remember that the hall is turned into offices.— No one has lived here since I was a little boy. I remember going to a Christmas party at the Walsalls'.

ANABEL: Has it been shut up so long?

GERALD: The Walsalls didn't like it—too near the ugliness. They were county, you know—we never were: Father never gave Mother a chance, there. And besides, the place is damp, cellars full of water.

ANABEL: Even now?

GERALD: No, not now—they've been drained. But the place would be too damp for a dwelling-house. It's alright as offices. They burn enormous fires. The rooms are quite charming. This is what happens to the stately homes of England—they buzz with inky clerks, or their equivalent. Stateliness is on its last legs.

ANABEL: Yes, it grieves me—though I should be bored if I had to be stately, I think.—Isn't it beautiful in this light, like an eighteenth-century aquatint? I'm sure no age was as ugly as this, since the world began.

GERALD: For pure ugliness, certainly not. And I believe none has been so filthy to live in.—Let us sit down a minute, shall we? and watch the rooks fly home. It always stirs sad, sentimental feelings in me.

ANABEL: So it does in me.—Listen! one can hear the coal-carts on the road—and the brook—and the dull noise of the town—and the beating of New London pit—and voices—and the rooks— and yet it is so still. We seem so still here, don't we?

GERALD: Yes.

ANABEL: Don't you think we've been wrong?

GERALD: How?

ANABEL: In the way we've lived—and the way we've loved.

GERALD: It hasn't been heaven, has it? Yet, I don't know that we've been wrong, Anabel. We had it to go through.

ANABEL: Perhaps.—And, yes, we've been wrong too.

GERALD: Probably. Only, I don't feel it like that.

ANABEL: Then I think you ought. You ought to feel you've been wrong.

GERALD: Yes, probably. Only, I don't. I can't help it. I think we've gone the way we had to go, following our own natures.

ANABEL: And where has it landed us?

GERALD: Here.

ANABEL: And where is that?

GERALD: Just on this bench in the park, looking at the evening.

ANABEL: But what next?

GERALD: God knows! Why trouble?

ANABEL: One must trouble. I want to feel sure.

GERALD: What of?

ANABEL: Of you—and of myself.

GERALD: Then *be* sure.

ANABEL: But I can't. Think of the past—what it's been.

GERALD: This isn't the past.

ANABEL: But what is it? Is there anything sure in it? Is there any real happiness?

GERALD: Why not?

ANABEL: But how can you ask? Think of what our life has been.

GERALD: I don't want to.

ANABEL: No, you don't. But what *do* you want?

GERALD: I'm alright, you know, sitting here like this.

ANABEL: But one can't sit here for ever, can one?

GERALD: I don't want to.

ANABEL: And what will you do when we leave here?

GERALD: God knows! Don't worry me. Be still a bit.

ANABEL: But *I'm* worried. You don't love me.

GERALD: I won't argue it.

ANABEL: And I'm not happy.

GERALD: Why not, Anabel?

ANABEL: Because you don't love me—and I can't forget.

GERALD: I do love you—and to-night I've forgotten.

ANABEL: Then make me forget, too. Make me happy.

GERALD: I *can't* make you—and you know it.

ANABEL: Yes, you can. It's your business to make me happy. I've made you happy.

GERALD: You want to make me unhappy.

ANABEL: I *do* think you're the last word in selfishness. If I say I can't forget, you merely say, "*I've* forgotten"; and if I say I'm unhappy, all *you* can answer is that I want to make *you* unhappy. I don't in the least. I want to be happy myself. But you don't help me.

GERALD: There is no help for it, you see. If you *were* happy with me here you'd be happy. As you aren't, nothing will make you—not genuinely.

ANABEL: And that's all you care.

GERALD: No—I wish we could both be happy at the same moment. But apparently we can't.

ANABEL: And why not?—Because you're selfish, and think of nothing but yourself and your own feelings.

GERALD: If it is so, it is so.

ANABEL: Then we shall never be happy.

GERALD: Then we shan't. *(A pause.)*

ANABEL: Then what are we going to do?

GERALD: Do?

ANABEL: Do you want me to be with you?

GERALD: Yes.

ANABEL: Are you sure?

GERALD: Yes.

ANABEL: Then why don't you want me to be happy?

GERALD: If you'd only *be* happy, here and now——

ANABEL: How can I?

GERALD: How can't you?—You've got a devil inside you.

ANABEL: Then make me not have a devil.

GERALD: I've known you long enough—and known myself long enough—to know I can make you nothing at all, Anabel: neither can you make me. If the happiness isn't there—well, we shall have to wait for it, like a dispensation. It probably means we shall have to hate each other a little more.—I suppose hate is a real process.

ANABEL: Yes, I know you believe more in hate than in love.

GERALD: Nobody is more weary of hate than I am—and yet we can't fix our own hour, when we shall leave off hating and fighting. It has to work itself out in us.

ANABEL: But I don't *want* to hate and fight with you any more. I don't *believe* in it—not any more.

GERALD: It's a cleansing process—like Aristotle's Katharsis. We shall hate ourselves clean at last, I suppose.

ANABEL: Why aren't you clean now? Why can't you love? *(He laughs.)* Do you love me?

GERALD: Yes.

ANABEL: Do you want to be with me for ever?

GERALD: Yes.

ANABEL: Sure?

GERALD: Quite sure.

ANABEL: Why are you so cool about it?

GERALD: I'm not. I'm only sure—which you are not.

ANABEL: Yes, I am—I *want* to be married to you.

GERALD: I know you want me to want you to be married to me. But whether off your own bat you have a positive desire that way, I'm not sure. You keep something back—some sort of female reservation—like a dagger up your sleeve. You want to see me in transports of love for you.

ANABEL: How can you say so? There—you see—there—this is the man that pretends to love me, and then says I keep a dagger up my sleeve. You liar!

GERALD: I do love you—and you do keep a dagger up your sleeve —some devilish little female reservation which spies at me from a distance, in your soul, all the time, as if I were an enemy.

ANABEL: How *can* you say so?—Doesn't it show what you must be yourself? Doesn't it show?—What is there in your soul?

GERALD: I don't know.

ANABEL: Love, pure love?—Do you pretend it's love?

GERALD: I'm so tired of this.

ANABEL: So am I, dead tired: you self-deceiving, self-complacent thing. Ha!—aren't you just the same. You haven't altered one scrap, not a scrap.

GERALD: Alright—you are always free to change yourself.

ANABEL: I *have* changed, I *am* better, I *do* love you—I love you wholly and unselfishly—I do—and I want a good new life with you.

GERALD: You're terribly wrapped up in your new goodness. I wish you'd make up your mind to be downright bad.

ANABEL: Ha!—Do you?—You'd soon see. You'd soon see where you'd be if—— There's somebody coming. (*Rises.*)

GERALD: Never mind; it's the clerks leaving work, I suppose. Sit still.

ANABEL: Won't you go?

GERALD: No. (*A man draws near, followed by another.*) Good evening.

CLERK: Good evening, sir. (*Passes on.*) Good evening, Mr Barlow.

ANABEL: They are afraid.

GERALD: I suppose their consciences are uneasy about this strike.

ANABEL: Did you come to sit here just to catch them, like a spider waiting for them?

GERALD: No. I wanted to speak to Breffitt.

ANABEL: I believe you're capable of any horridness.

GERALD: Alright, you believe it. (*Two more figures approach.*) Good evening.

CLERKS: Good night, sir. (*One passes, one stops.*) Good evening, Mr Barlow. Er—did you want to see Mr Breffitt, sir?

GERALD: Not particularly.

CLERK: Oh! He'll be out directly, sir—if you'd like me to go back and tell him you wanted him.

GERALD: No, thank you.

CLERK: Good night, sir. Excuse me asking.

GERALD: Good night.

ANABEL: Who is Mr Breffitt?

GERALD: He is the chief clerk—and cashier—one of Father's old pillars of society.

ANABEL: Don't you like him?

GERALD: Not much.

ANABEL: Why?—You seem to dislike very easily.

GERALD: Oh, they all used to try to snub me, these old buffers. They detest me like poison, because I am different from Father.

ANABEL: I believe you enjoy being detested.

GERALD: I do. *(Another clerk approaches—hesitates—stops.)*

CLERK: Good evening, sir. Good evening, Mr Barlow. Er—did you want anybody at the office, sir? We're just closing.

GERALD: No, I didn't want anybody.

CLERK: Oh, no, sir. I see. Er—by the way, sir—er—I hope you don't think this—er—bother about an increase—this strike threat—started in the office.

GERALD: Where did it start?

CLERK: I should think it started—where it usually starts, Mr Barlow—among a few loud-mouthed people who think they can do as they like with the men. They're only using the office men as a cry—that's all. They've no interest in us. They want to show their power.—That's how it is, sir.

GERALD: Oh, yes.

CLERK: We're powerless, if they like to make a cry out of us.

GERALD: Quite.

CLERK: We're as much put out about it as anybody.

GERALD: Of course.

CLERK: Yes—well—good night, sir. *(Clerks draw near—there is a sound of loud young voices and bicycle bells. Bicycles sweep past.)*

CLERKS: Good night, sir.—Good night, sir.

GERALD: Good night.—They're very bucked to see me sitting here with a woman—a young lady as they'll say. I guess your name will be flying round to-morrow. They stop partly to have a good look at you. Do they know you, do you think?

ANABEL: Sure.

CLERKS: Mr Breffitt's just coming, sir.—Good night, sir.—Good night, sir. *(Another bicycle passes.)*

ANABEL: The bicycles don't see us.—Isn't it rather hateful to be a master? The attitude of them all is so ugly. I can quite see that it makes you rather a bully.

GERALD: I suppose it does. *(Figure of a large man approaches.)*

BREFFITT: Oh—ah—it's Mr Gerald!—I couldn't make out who it was.—Were you coming up to the office, sir? Do you want me to go back with you?

GERALD: No, thank you—I just wanted a word with you about this agitation. It'll do just as well here. It's a pity it started—that the office should have set it going, Breffitt.

BREFFITT: It's none of the office's doing, I think you'll find, Mr Gerald. The office men did nothing but ask for a just advance—at any rate, times and prices being what they are, I consider it a fair advance. If the men took it up, it's because they've got a set of loud-mouthed blatherers and agitators among them like Job Arthur Freer, who deserve to be hung—and hanging they'd get, if I could have the judging of them.

GERALD: Well—it's very unfortunate—because we can't give the clerks their increase now, you know.

BREFFITT: Can't you?—can't you? I can't see that it would be anything out of the way, if I say what I think.

GERALD: No. They won't get any increase now. It shouldn't have been allowed to become a public cry with the colliers. We can't give in now.

BREFFITT: Have the Board decided that?

GERALD: They have—on my advice.

BREFFITT: Hm! then the men will come out.

GERALD: We will see.

BREFFITT: It's trouble for nothing—it's trouble that could be avoided. The clerks could have their advance, and it would hurt nobody.

GERALD: Too late now.—I suppose if the men come out, the clerks will come out with them?

BREFFITT: They'll have to—they'll have to.

GERALD: If they do, we may then make certain alterations in the office staff which have needed making for some time.

BREFFITT: Very good—very good. I know what you mean.—I don't know how your father bears all this, Mr Gerald.

GERALD: We keep it from him as much as possible.—You'll let the clerks know the decision. And if they stay out with the men, I'll go over the list of the staff with you. It has needed revising for a long time.

BREFFITT: I know what you mean—I know what you mean—I believe I understand the firm's interest in my department. I ought, after forty years studying it. I've studied the firm's interests for forty years, Mr Gerald. I'm not likely to forget them now.

GERALD: Of course.

BREFFITT: But I think it's a mistake—I think it's a mistake, and I'm bound to say it, to let a great deal of trouble rise for a very

small cause. The clerks might have had what they reasonably
asked for.

GERALD : Well, it's too late now.

BREFFITT : I suppose it is—I suppose it is. I hope you'll remember,
sir, that I've put the interest of the firm before everything—
before every consideration.

GERALD : Of course, Breffitt.

BREFFITT : But you've not had any liking for the office staff, I'm
afraid, sir—not since your father put you amongst us for a few
months.—Well, sir, we shall weather this gale, I hope, as we've
weathered those in the past. Times don't become better, do they?
Men are an ungrateful lot, and these agitators should be lynched.
They would, if I had my way.

GERALD : Yes, of course. Don't wait.

BREFFITT : Good night to you.

        Exit BREFFITT.

GERALD : Good night.

ANABEL : He's the last, apparently.

GERALD : We'll hope so.

ANABEL : He puts you in a fury.

GERALD : It's his manner. My father spoilt them—abominable old
limpets. And they're so self-righteous. They think I'm a sort of
criminal who has instigated this new devilish system which runs
everything so close and cuts it so fine—as if they hadn't made
this inevitable by their shameless carelessness and wastefulness
in the past. He may well boast of his forty years—forty years'
crass, stupid wastefulness.

        *Two or three more clerks pass, talking till they approach the
        seat, then becoming silent after bidding good night.*

ANABEL : But aren't you a bit sorry for them?

GERALD : Why? If they're poor, what does it matter in a world
of chaos?

ANABEL : And aren't you an obstinate ass not to give them the bit
they want. It's mere stupid obstinacy.

GERALD : It may be. I call it policy.

ANABEL : Men always do call their obstinacy policy.

GERALD : Well, I don't care what happens. I wish things would
come to a head. I only fear they won't.

ANABEL : Aren't you rather wicked?—*Asking* for strife?

GERALD: I hope I am. It's quite a relief to me to feel that I may be wicked. I fear I'm not. I can see them all anticipating victory, in their low-down fashion wanting to crow their low-down crowings. I'm afraid I feel it's a righteous cause, to cut a lot of little combs before I die.

ANABEL: But if they're in the right in what they want?

GERALD: In the right—in the right!—They're just greedy, incompetent, stupid, gloating in a sense of the worst sort of power. They're like vicious children, who would like to kill their parents so that they could have the run of the larder. The rest is just cant.

ANABEL: If you're the parent in the case, I must say you flow over with loving-kindness for them.

GERALD: I don't—I detest them. I only hope they will fight. If they would, I'd have some respect for them. But you'll see what it will be.

ANABEL: I wish I needn't, for it's very sickening.

GERALD: Sickening beyond expression.

ANABEL: I wish we could go right away.

GERALD: So do I—if one could get oneself out of this. But one can't. It's the same wherever you have industrialism—and you have industrialism everywhere, whether it's Timbuctoo or Paraguay or Antananarivo.

ANABEL: No, it isn't: you exaggerate.

JOB ARTHUR (*suddenly approaching from the other side*): Good evening, Mr Barlow. I heard you were in here. Could I have a word with you?

GERALD: Get on with it, then.

JOB ARTHUR: Is it right that you won't meet the clerks?

GERALD: Yes.

JOB ARTHUR: Not in any way?

GERALD: Not in any way whatsoever.

JOB ARTHUR: But—I thought I understood from you the other night——

GERALD: It's all the same what you understood.

JOB ARTHUR: Then you take it back, sir?

GERALD: I take nothing back, because I gave nothing.

JOB ARTHUR: Oh, excuse me, excuse me, sir. You said it would be alright about the clerks. This lady heard you say it.

GERALD: Don't you call witnesses against me.—Besides, what does it matter to you? What in the name of——

JOB ARTHUR: Well, sir, you said it would be alright, and I went on that——

GERALD: You went on that! Where did you go to?

JOB ARTHUR: The men'll be out on Monday.

GERALD: So shall I.

JOB ARTHUR: Oh, yes, but—where's it going to end?

GERALD: Do you want me to prophesy? When did I set up for a public prophet?

JOB ARTHUR: I don't know, sir. But perhaps you're doing more than you know. There's a funny feeling just now among the men.

GERALD: So I've heard before. Why should I concern myself with their feelings? Am I to cry when every collier bumps his funny-bone—or to laugh?

JOB ARTHUR: It's no laughing matter, you see.

GERALD: And I'm sure it's no crying matter—unless you want to cry, do you see?

JOB ARTHUR: Ah, but, very likely, it wouldn't be me who would cry.—You don't know what might happen, now.

GERALD: I'm waiting for something to happen. I should like something to happen—very much—very much indeed.

JOB ARTHUR: Yes, but perhaps you'd be sorry if it did happen.

GERALD: Is that a warning or a threat?

JOB ARTHUR: I don't know—it might be a bit of both. What I mean to say——

GERALD (*suddenly seizing him by the scruff of the neck and shaking him*): What do you mean to say?—I mean you to say less, do you see?—a great deal less—do you see? You've run on with your saying long enough: that clock had better run down. So stop your sayings—stop your sayings, I tell you—or you'll have them shaken out of you—shaken out of you—shaken out of you, do you see? (*Suddenly flings him aside.*)

JOB ARTHUR, *staggering, falls.*

ANABEL: Oh no!—oh, no!

GERALD: Now get up, Job Arthur; and get up wiser than you went down. You've played your little game and your little tricks and made your little sayings long enough. You're going to stop now.

We've had quite enough of strong men of your stamp, Job Arthur—quite enough—such Labour leaders as you.

JOB ARTHUR: You'll be sorry, Mr Barlow—you'll be sorry. You'll wish you'd not attacked me.

GERALD: Don't you trouble about me and my sorrow. Mind your own.

JOB ARTHUR: You will—you'll be sorry. You'll be sorry for what you've done. You'll wish you'd never begun this.

GERALD: Begun—begun?—I'd like to finish, too, that I would. I'd like to finish with you, too—I warn *you*.

JOB ARTHUR: I warn you—I warn you. You won't go on much longer. Every parish has its own vermin.

GERALD: Vermin?

JOB ARTHUR: Every parish has its own vermin; it lies with every parish to destroy its own. We shan't have a clean parish till we've destroyed the vermin we've got.

GERALD: Vermin? The fool's raving. Vermin!—Another phrase-maker, by God! Another phrase-maker to lead the people.—Vermin? What vermin? I know quite well what *I* mean by vermin, Job Arthur. But what do you mean? Vermin? Explain yourself.

JOB ARTHUR: Yes, vermin. Vermin is what lives on other people's lives, living on their lives and profiting by it. We've got 'em in every parish—vermin, I say—that live on the sweat and blood of the people—live on it, and get rich on it—get rich through living on other people's lives, the lives of the working men— living on the bodies of the working men—that's vermin—if it isn't, what is it? And every parish must destroy its own—every parish must destroy its own vermin.

GERALD: The phrase, my God! the phrase.

JOB ARTHUR: Phrase or no phrase, there it is, and face it out if you can. There it is—there's not one in every parish—there's more than one—there's a number——

GERALD (*suddenly kicking him*): Go! (*Kicks him.*) Go! (*Kicks him.*) Go! (JOB ARTHUR *falls.*) Get out! (*Kicks him.*) Get out, I say! Get out, I tell you! Get out! Get out!—Vermin!—Vermin!— I'll vermin you! I'll put my foot through your phrases. Get up, I say, get up and go—*go!*

JOB ARTHUR: It'll be you as'll go, this time.

GERALD: What? What?—By God! I'll kick you out of this park like a rotten bundle if you don't get up and go.

ANABEL: No, Gerald, no. Don't forget yourself. It's enough now. It's enough now.—Come away. Do come away. Come away—leave him——

JOB ARTHUR *(still on the ground)*: It's your turn to go. It's you as'll go, this time.

GERALD *(looking at him)*: One can't even tread on you.

ANABEL: Don't, Gerald, don't—don't look at him.—Don't say any more, you, Job Arthur.—Come away, Gerald. Come away—come —do come.

GERALD *(turning)*: *That* a human being! My God!—But he's right —it's I who go. It's we who go, Anabel. He's still there.—My God! a human being!

CURTAIN

S C E N E I I

Market-place as in Act I. WILLIE HOUGHTON, *addressing a large crowd of men from the foot of the obelisk.*

WILLIE: And now you're out on strike—now you've been out for a week pretty nearly, what further are you? I heard a great deal of talk about what you were going to do. Well, what *are* you going to do? You don't know. You've not the smallest idea. You haven't any idea whatsoever. You've got your leaders. Now then, Job Arthur, throw a little light on the way in front, will you: for it seems to me we're lost in a bog. Which way are we to steer? Come—give the word, and let's gee-up.

JOB ARTHUR: You ask me which way we are to go. I say we can't go our own way, because of the obstacles that lie in front. You've got to remove the obstacles from the way.

WILLIE: So said Balaam's ass. But you're not an ass—beg pardon; and you're not Balaam—you're Job. And we've all got to be little Jobs, learning how to spell patience backwards. We've lost our jobs and we've found a Job. It's picking up a scorpion when

you're looking for an egg.—Tell us what you propose doing. . . .
Remove an obstacle from the way! What obstacle? And whose
way?

JOB ARTHUR : I think it's pretty plain what the obstacle is.

WILLIE : Oh ay. Tell us then.

JOB ARTHUR : The obstacle to Labour is Capital.

WILLIE : And how are we going to put salt on Capital's tail?

JOB ARTHUR : By Labour we mean us working men; and by Capital
we mean those that derive benefit from us, take the cream off us
and leave us the skim.

WILLIE : Oh yes.

JOB ARTHUR : So that, if you're going to remove the obstacle, you've
got to remove the masters, and all that belongs to them. Does
everybody agree with me?

VOICES *(loud)* : Ah, we do—yes—we do that—we do an' a'—yi—
yi—that's it!

WILLIE : Agreed unanimously. But how are we going to do it? Do
you propose to send for Williamson's furniture van, to pack them
in? I should think one pantechnicon would do, just for this parish.
I'll drive. Who'll be the vanmen to lift and carry?

JOB ARTHUR : It's no use fooling. You've fooled for thirty years, and
we're no further. What's got to be done will have to be begun.
It's for every man to sweep in front of his own doorstep. You
can't call your neighbours dirty till you've washed your own face.
Every parish has got its own vermin, and it's the business of every
parish to get rid of its own.

VOICES : That's it—that's it—that's the ticket—that's the style!

WILLIE : And are you going to comb 'em out, or do you propose to
use Keating's?

VOICES : Shut it! Shut it up! Stop thy face! Hold thy gab!—Go on,
Job Arthur.

JOB ARTHUR : How it's got to be done is for us all to decide. I'm not
one for violence, except it's a force-put. But it's like this. We've
been travelling for years to where we stand now—and here the
road stops. There's only room for one at a time on this path.
There's a precipice below and a rock-face above. And in front of
us stand the masters. Now there's three things we can do. We
can either throw ourselves over the precipice; or we can lie
down and let the masters walk over us; or we can *get on.*

WILLIE: Yes. That's alright. But how are you going to get on?

JOB ARTHUR: Well—we've either got to throw the obstacle down the cliff—or walk over it.

VOICES: Ay—ay—ay—yes—that's a fact.

WILLIE: I quite follow you, Job Arthur. You've either got to do for the masters—or else just remove them, and put them somewhere else.

VOICES: Ged rid on 'em—drop 'em down the shaft—sink 'em—ha' done wi' 'em—drop 'em down the shaft—bust the beggars—what do you do wi' vermin?

WILLIE: Supposing you begin. Supposing you take Gerald Barlow, and hang him up from this lamp-post, with a piece of coal in his mouth for a sacrament——

VOICES: Ay—serve him right—serve the beggar right! Shove it down 's throttle—ay!

WILLIE: Supposing you do it—supposing you've done it—and supposing you aren't caught and punished—even supposing that— what are you going to do next? *that's* the point.

JOB ARTHUR: We know what we're going to do. Once we can get our hands free, we know what we're going to do.

WILLIE: Yes, so do I. You're either going to make *such* a mess that we shall never get out of it—which I don't think you will do, for the English working man is the soul of obedience and order, and he'd behave himself to-morrow as if he was at Sunday school, no matter what he does to-day.—No, what you'll do, Job Arthur, you'll set up another lot of masters, such a jolly sight worse than what we've got now. I'd rather be mastered by Gerald Barlow, if it comes to mastering, than by Job Arthur Freer—oh, *such* a lot! You'll be far less free with Job Arthur for your boss than ever you were with Gerald Barlow. You'll be far more degraded.—In fact, though I've preached socialism in the market-place for thirty years—if you're going to start killing the masters to set yourselves up for bosses—why, kill me along with the masters. For I'd rather die with somebody who has one tiny little spark of decency left—though it *is* a little tiny spark—than live to triumph with those that have none.

VOICES: Shut thy face, Houghton—shut it up—shut him up—hustle the beggar! Hoi!—hoi-ee!—whoo!—whoam-it, whoam-it!— whoo!—bow-wow!—wet-whiskers!——

WILLIE: And it's no use you making fools of yourselves—— *(His words are heard through an ugly, jeering, cold commotion.)*

VOICE *(loudly)*: He's comin'.

VOICES: Who?

VOICE: Barlow.—See 's motor?—comin' up—sithee?

WILLIE: If you've any sense left—— *(Suddenly and violently disappears.)*

VOICES: Sorry!—he's comin'—'s comin'—sorry, ah! Who's in?— That's Turton drivin'—yi, he's behind wi' a woman—ah, he's comin'—he'll non go back—hold on. Sorry!—wheer's 'e comin'? —up from Loddo—ay—— *(The cries die down—the motor car slowly comes into sight, OLIVER driving, GERALD and ANABEL behind. The men stand in a mass in the way.)*

OLIVER: Mind yourself, there. *(Laughter.)*

GERALD: Go ahead, Oliver.

VOICE: What's yer 'urry?

Crowd sways and surges on the car. OLIVER is suddenly dragged out. GERALD stands up—he, too, is seized from behind —he wrestles—is torn out of his great-coat—then falls—disappears. Loud cries—"Hi!—hoi!—hoi-ee!" all the while. The car shakes and presses uneasily.

VOICE: Stop the blazin' motor, somebody.

VOICE: Here y'are!—hold a minute. *(A man jumps in and stops the engine—he drops in the driver's seat.)*

COLLIER *(outside the car)*: Step down, miss.

ANABEL: I am Mrs Barlow.

COLLIER: Missis, then. *(Laugh.)* Step down—lead 'er forrard. Take 'em forrard—take 'em forrard.

JOB ARTHUR: Ay, make a road.

GERALD: You're makin' a proper fool of yourself now, Freer.

JOB ARTHUR: You've brought it on yourself. *You've* made fools of plenty of men.

COLLIERS: Come on, now—come on! Whoa!—whoa!—he's a jibber—go pretty now, go pretty!

VOICES *(suddenly)*: Lay hold o' Houghton—nab 'im—seize 'im— rats!—rats!—bring 'im forrard!

ANABEL *(in a loud, clear voice)*: I never knew anything so *ridiculous*.

VOICES *(falsetto)*: Ridiculous! Oh, ridiculous! Mind the step, dear! —I'm Mrs Barlow!—Oh, are you?—Tweet—tweet!

JOB ARTHUR: Make a space, boys, make a space. *(He stands with prisoners in a cleared space before the obelisk.)* Now—now—quiet a minute—we want to ask a few questions of these gentlemen.

VOICES: Quiet!—quiet—Sh-h-h! Sh-h-h!—Answer pretty—answer pretty now!—Quiet!—Shh-h-h!

JOB ARTHUR: We want to ask you, Mr Gerald Barlow, why you have given occasion for this present trouble?

GERALD: You are a fool.

VOICES: Oh!—oh!—naughty Barlow!—naughty baa-lamb—answer pretty—answer pretty—be good baa-lamb—baa—baa!—answer pretty when gentleman asks you.

JOB ARTHUR: Quiet a bit. Sh-h-h!—We put this plain question to you, Mr Barlow. Why did you refuse to give the clerks this just and fair advance, when you knew that by refusing you would throw three thousand men out of employment?

GERALD: You are a fool, I say.

VOICES: Oh!—oh!—won't do—won't do, Barlow—wrong answer —wrong answer—be good baa-lamb—naughty boy—naughty boy!

JOB ARTHUR: Quiet a bit—now!—If three thousand men ask you a just, straightforward question, do you consider they've no right to an answer?

GERALD: I would answer you with my foot.

VOICES *(amid a threatening scuffle)*: Da-di-da! Hark ye—hark ye! Oh—whoa—whoa a bit!—won't do!—won't do!—naughty—naughty—say you're sorry—say you're sorry—kneel and say you're sorry—kneel and beg pardon!

JOB ARTHUR: Hold on a bit—keep clear!

VOICES: Make him kneel—make him kneel—on his knees with him!

JOB ARTHUR: I think you'd better kneel down.

> The crowd press on GERALD—*he struggles—they hit him behind the knees, force him down.*

OLIVER: This is shameful and unnecessary.

VOICES: All of 'em—on your knees—all of 'em—on their knees!

> *They seize* OLIVER *and* WILLIE *and* ANABEL, *hustling.* ANABEL *kneels quietly—the others struggle.*

WILLIE: Well, of all the damned, dirty, cowardly——

VOICES : Shut up, Houghton—shut him up—squeeze him!

OLIVER : Get off me—let me alone—I'll kneel.

VOICES : Good little doggies—nice doggies—kneel and beg pardon
—yap-yap—answer—make him answer!

JOB ARTHUR *(holding up his hand for silence)* : It would be better
if you answered straight off, Barlow. We want to know why you
prevented that advance?

VOICES *(after a pause)* : Nip his neck! Make him yelp!

OLIVER : Let me answer, then.—Because it's worse, perhaps, to be
bullied by three thousand men than by one man.

VOICES : Oh!—oh!—dog keeps barking—stuff his mouth—stop him
up—here's a bit of paper—answer, Barlow—nip his neck—stuff
his mug—make him yelp—cork the bottle!

    They press a lump of newspaper into OLIVER'S *mouth, and
bear down on* GERALD.

JOB ARTHUR : Quiet—quiet—quiet—a minute, everybody. We give
him a minute—we give him a minute to answer.

VOICES : Give him a minute—a holy minute—say your prayers,
Barlow—you've got a minute—tick-tick, says the clock—time
him!

JOB ARTHUR : Keep quiet.

WILLIE : Of all the damned, cowardly——

VOICES : Sh-h-h!—Squeeze him—throttle him! Silence is golden,
Houghton.—Close the shutters, Willie's dead.—Dry up, wet-
whiskers!

JOB ARTHUR : You've fifteen seconds.

VOICES : There's a long, long trail a-winding——

JOB ARTHUR : The minute's up.—We ask you again, Gerald Barlow,
why you refused a just and fair demand, when you know it was
against the wishes of three thousand men all as good as yourself?

VOICES : And a sight better—I don't think—we're not all vermin—
we're not all crawlers, living off the sweat of other folks—we're
not all parish vermin—parish vermin.

JOB ARTHUR: And on what grounds you think you have no occasion
to answer the straightforward question we put you here?

ANABEL *(after a pause)* : Answer them, Gerald. What's the use of
prolonging this?

GERALD : I've nothing to answer.

VOICES : Nothing to answer—Gerald, darling—Gerald, duckie—oh, lovey-dovey—I've nothing to answer—no, by God—no, by God, he hasna—nowt to answer—ma'e him find summat, then—answer for him—gi'e him 's answer—let him ha'e it—go on—mum—mum—lovey-dovey—rub his nose in it—kiss the dirt, ducky—bend him down—rub his nose in—he's saying something—oh no, he isn't—sorry I spoke—bend him down!

JOB ARTHUR : Quiet a bit—quiet, everybody—he's got to answer—keep quiet.—Now—— *(A silence.)* Now then, Barlow, will you answer, or won't you? *(Silence.)*

ANABEL : Answer them, Gerald—never mind.

VOICES : Sh-h-h! Sh-h-h! *(Silence.)*

JOB ARTHUR : You won't answer, Barlow?

VOICE : Down the beggar!

VOICES : Down him—put his nose down—flatten him!

> *The crowd surges and begins to howl—they sway dangerously—*GERALD *is spread-eagled on the ground, face down.*

JOB ARTHUR : Back—back—back a minute—back—back! *(They recoil.)*

WILLIE : I *hope* there's a God in heaven.

VOICES : Put him down—flatten him!

> WILLIE *is flattened on the ground.*

JOB ARTHUR : Now then—now then—if you won't answer, Barlow, I can't stand here for you any more.—Take your feet off him, boys, and turn him over. Turn him over—let us look at him. Let us see if he *can* speak. *(They turn him over, with another scuffle.)* Now then, Barlow—you can see the sky above you. Now do you think you're going to play with three thousand men, with their lives and with their souls?—now do you think you're going to answer them with your foot?—do you—do you?

> *The crowd has begun to sway and heave dangerously, with a low, muffled roar, above which is heard* JOB ARTHUR's *voice. As he ceases, the roar breaks into a yell—the crowd heaves.*

VOICES : Down him—crack the vermin—on top of him—put your foot on the vermin!

ANABEL *(with a loud, piercing cry, suddenly starting up)*: Ah no! Ah no! Ah-h-h-h no-o-o-o! Ah-h-h-h no-o-o-o! Ah-h-h-h no-o-o-o! No-o-o-o! No-o-o-o! No-o! No-o-o!—Ah-h-h-h!—it's enough, it's

enough, it's enough! It's enough—he's a man as you are. He's a
man as you are. He's a man as you are. He's a man as you are.
(Weeps—a breath of silence.)

OLIVER: Let us stop now—let us stop now. Let me stand up.
(Silence.) I want to stand up. *(A muffled noise.)*

VOICE: Let him get up. (OLIVER *rises.*)

OLIVER: Be quiet. Be quiet.—Now—choose! Choose! Choose!
Choose what you will do! Only choose! Choose!—it will be
irrevocable. *(A moment's pause.)* Thank God we haven't gone
too far.—Gerald, get up. *(Men still hold him down.)*

JOB ARTHUR: Isn't he to answer us? Isn't he going to answer
us?

OLIVER: Yes, he shall answer you. He shall answer you. But let him
stand up. No more of this. Let him stand up. He must stand up.
(Men still hold GERALD down.) (OLIVER *takes hold of their hands
and removes them.)* Let go—let go now. Yes, let go—yes—I ask
you to let go. *(Slowly, sullenly, the men let go.* GERALD *is free,
but he does not move.)* There—get up, Gerald! Get up! You
aren't hurt, are you? You must get up—it's no use. We're doing
our best—you must do yours. When things are like this, we have
to put up with what we get. (GERALD *rises slowly and faces the
mob. They roar dully.)* You ask why the clerks didn't get this
increase? Wait! Wait! Do you still wish for any answer, Mr
Freer?

JOB ARTHUR: Yes, that's what we've been waiting for.

OLIVER: Then answer, Gerald.

GERALD: They've trodden on my face.

OLIVER: No matter. Job Arthur will easily answer that you've
trodden on their souls. Don't start an altercation. *(The crowd is
beginning to roar.)*

GERALD: You want to know why the clerks didn't get their rise?—
Because you interfered and attempted to bully about it, do you
see. That's why.

VOICES: You want bullying.—You'll get bullying, you will.

OLIVER: Can't you see it's no good, either side? It's no mortal use.
We might as well all die to-morrow, or to-day, or this minute,
as go on bullying one another, one side bullying the other side,
and the other side bullying back. We'd *better* all die.

WILLIE: And a great deal better. I'm damned if I'll take sides with anybody against anything, after this. If I'm to die, I'll die by myself. As for living, it seems impossible.

JOB ARTHUR : Have the men nothing to be said for their side?

OLIVER : They have a great deal—but not *everything*, you see.

JOB ARTHUR : Haven't they been wronged? And *aren't* they wronged?

OLIVER : They have—and they are. But haven't they been wrong themselves, too?—and aren't they wrong now?

JOB ARTHUR : How?

OLIVER : What about this affair? Do you call it right?

JOB ARTHUR : Haven't we been driven to it?

OLIVER : Partly. And haven't you driven the masters to it, as well?

JOB ARTHUR : I don't see that.

OLIVER : Can't you see that it takes two to make a quarrel? And as long as each party hangs on to its own end of the stick, and struggles to get full hold of the stick, the quarrel will continue. It will continue till you've killed one another. And even then, what better shall you be? What better would you be, really, if you'd killed Gerald Barlow just now? You wouldn't, you know. We're all human beings, after all. And why can't we try really to leave off struggling against one another, and set up a new state of things?

JOB ARTHUR : That's all very well, you see, while you've got the goods.

OLIVER : I've got very little, I assure you.

JOB ARTHUR : Well, if you haven't, those you mix with have. They've got the money, and the power, and they intend to keep it.

OLIVER : As for power, somebody must have it, you know. It only rests with you to put it into the hands of the best men, the men you *really* believe in.—And as for money, it's life, it's living that matters, not simply having money.

JOB ARTHUR : You can't live without money.

OLIVER : I know that. And therefore why can't we have the decency to agree simply about money—just agree to dispose of it so that all men could live their own lives.

JOB ARTHUR : That's what we want to do. But the others, such as Gerald Barlow, they keep the money—*and* the power.

OLIVER : You see, if you wanted to arrange things so that money flowed more naturally, so that it flowed naturally to every man, according to his needs, I think we could all soon agree. But you don't. What you want is to take it away from one set and give it to another—or keep it yourselves.

JOB ARTHUR: We want every man to have his proper share.

OLIVER: I'm sure *I* do. I want every man to be able to live and be free. But we shall never manage it by fighting over the money. If you want what is natural and good, I'm sure the owners would soon agree with you.

JOB ARTHUR: What? Gerald Barlow agree with us?

OLIVER: Why not? I believe so.

JOB ARTHUR: You ask him.

OLIVER: Do you think, Gerald, that if the men really wanted a whole, better way, you would agree with them?

GERALD: I want a better way myself—but not their way.

JOB ARTHUR: There, you see!

VOICES: Ah-h! look you!—That's him—that's him all over.

OLIVER: You want a better way,—but not his way: he wants a better way—but not your way. Why can't you both drop your buts, and simply say you want a better way, and believe yourselves and one another when you say it? Why can't you?

GERALD: Look here! I'm quite as tired of my way of life as you are of yours. If you make me believe you want something better, then I assure you I do: I want what you want. But Job Arthur Freer's not the man to lead you to anything better. You can tell what people want by the leaders they choose, do you see? You choose leaders whom I respect, and I'll respect you, do you see? As it is, I don't. And now I'm going.

VOICES: Who says?—Oh ay!—Who says goin'?

GERALD: Yes, I'm going. About this affair here we'll cry quits; no more said about it. About a new way of life, a better way all round—I tell you I want it and need it as much as ever you do. I don't care about money really. But I'm never going to be bullied.

VOICE: Who doesn't care about money?

GERALD: I don't. I think we ought to be able to alter the whole system—but not by bullying, not because one lot wants what the other has got.

VOICE : No, because you've got everything.
GERALD : Where's my coat? Now then, step out of the way.
They move towards the car.

CURTAIN

The Merry-Go-Round

A PLAY IN FIVE ACTS
(1912)

CHARACTERS

MRS HEMSTOCK
NURSE BROADBANKS
MR HEMSTOCK
HARRY HEMSTOCK
BARON RUDOLF VON RUGE
THE BAKER, JOB ARTHUR BOWERS
MRS SUSY SMALLEY
DR FOULES
RACHEL WILCOX
BARONESS VON RUGE
MR WILCOX

ACT I

SCENE I: *Downstairs front room of the Hemstocks' cottage*
SCENE II: *Kitchen of the Hemstocks' house*

ACT II

SCENE I: *The same*
SCENE II: *The road outside the Hemstocks' house*
SCENE III: *Kitchen of the Hemstocks' house*

ACT III

SCENE I: *The dining-room at the vicarage*
SCENE II: *Nurse's room at the miner's cottage*

ACT IV

SCENE I: *Kitchen of the Hemstocks' house*

ACT V

SCENE I: *Porch of the Grunston church*
SCENE II: *Beside the vicarage garden walk*
SCENE III: *Porch of the Grunston church*

ACT I

SCENE I

The downstairs front room of a moderate-sized cottage. There is a wide fireplace, with a heaped-up ashy fire. The parlour is used as a bedroom, and contains a heavy old-fashioned mahogany dressing-table, a washstand, and a bedstead whose canopy is missing, so that the handsome posts stand like ruined columns. The room is in an untidy, neglected condition, medicine bottles and sickroom paraphernalia littered about. In the bed, a woman between sixty and seventy, with a large-boned face, and a long plait of fine dark hair. Enter the parish NURSE, *in uniform, but without cloak and bonnet. She is a well-built woman of some thirty years, smooth-haired, pale, soothing in manner.*

MRS HEMSTOCK: Eh, Nurse, I'm glad to see thee. I *han* been motherless while thou's been away.

NURSE: Haven't they looked after you, Mrs Hemstock?

MRS HEMSTOCK: They hanna, Nurse. Here I lie, day in, day out, like a beetle on my back, an' not a soul comes nigh me, saving th' Mester, when 'e's forced. An' 'im. *(She points to mirror of dressing-table.)*

NURSE: Who is that, Mrs Hemstock?

MRS HEMSTOCK: Canna ter see 'im? That little fat chap as stands there laughing at me.

NURSE: There's no little fat chap, Mrs Hemstock.

MRS HEMSTOCK: There is an' a'. He's bobbing a' thee now.

NURSE, *who has been rolling up her sleeves, showing a fine white arm, throws her rolled cuffs at the mirror.*

NURSE: Then we'll send him away.

MRS HEMSTOCK: Nay, dunna thee hurt him. 'E's nowt but a little chap!

NURSE: I'll wash you, shall I?

MRS HEMSTOCK: Tha nedna but gi' me a catlick. I'm as snug as a bug in a rug.

NURSE *(laughing)*: Very well.

    She goes into the kitchen.

MRS HEMSTOCK *(calling)*: Who's in there, Nurse?

NURSE: There's nobody, Mrs Hemstock.

MRS HEMSTOCK: I bet he's gallivanting off after some woman.

NURSE *(calling)*: Who?

MRS HEMSTOCK: Why, our Mester. 'E's a ronk 'un, I can tell you. 'As our Harry done it?

NURSE: Done what, Mrs Hemstock?

MRS HEMSTOCK: Cut 'is throat. 'E's allers threatenin'!

NURSE *(entering with a jug of hot water)*: What! You're not serious, Mrs Hemstock.

MRS HEMSTOCK: Aren't I? But I am. An' 'e'll do it one o' these days, if 'e's not a'ready. I 'avena clapped eyes on him for five days.

NURSE: How is that?

MRS HEMSTOCK: Eh, dunna ax me. 'E niver comes in if 'e can 'elp it.

NURSE: How strange! Why is it, do you think?

MRS HEMSTOCK: Summat's gen 'im mulligurles. 'E'll not live long.

NURSE: What! Harry? He's quite young, and has nothing the matter, has he?

MRS HEMSTOCK: You know, Nurse, I 'as a fish inside me. I wor like Jonah back'ards. I used ter feel it floppin' about in my inside like a good 'un, an' nobody'd get it out——

NURSE: But Harry hasn't got a fish in his inside——

MRS HEMSTOCK: 'E 'asna—but I believe 'e's got a leech.

NURSE: Oh!

MRS HEMSTOCK: Dunna thee wet my 'air, Nurse—it ma'es it go grey.

NURSE *(smiling)*: Very well, I'll be careful. But what makes you say Harry has a leech in his inside?

MRS HEMSTOCK: On 'is 'eart. 'Asn't ter noticed 'e gets as white-faced as a flat fish? It's that.

NURSE: Oh, and did he swallow it?

MRS HEMSTOCK: 'E didna. 'E bred it like a mackerel's head breeds maggots.

NURSE: How dreadful!

MRS HEMSTOCK: When you've owt up with you, you allers breed summat.

NURSE: And what was up with Mr Hemstock?

MRS HEMSTOCK: With our Mester?

NURSE: With Harry.

MRS HEMSTOCK: You knowed, didna you, as 'e'd had ructions wi' Rachel Wilcox?

NURSE: No.

MRS HEMSTOCK: Oh, yes. 'E fell off 'is bike eighteen month sin', a'most into her lap, an' 'er's been sick for 'im ever sin'.

NURSE: But he didn't care for her?

MRS HEMSTOCK: I dunno. 'E went out wi' 'er for about twelve month—but 'e never wanted 'er. 'E's funny, an' allers 'as been.

NURSE: Rather churlish?

MRS HEMSTOCK: No—'e wor allers one o' the' lovin' sor' when 'e wor but a lad, 'd follow me about, and "mammy" me.

NURSE: But he got into bad ways——

MRS HEMSTOCK: Well, I got sick of him stormin' about like a cat lookin' for her kittens, so I hustled him out. 'E began drinkin' a bit, an' carryin' on. I thought 'e wor goin' to be like his father for women. But 'e wor allers a mother's lad—an' Rachel Wilcox cured him o' women.

NURSE: She's not a nice girl.

MRS HEMSTOCK: 'E'd only ter stick 'is 'ead out of the door an' 'er'd run like a pig as 'ears the bucket. 'Er wor like a cat foriver slidin', rubbin' 'erself against him.

NURSE: How dreadful!

MRS HEMSTOCK: But I encouraged 'er. I thought 'e wor such a soft 'un, at 'is age, a man of thirty!

NURSE: Was he always quiet?

MRS HEMSTOCK: Eh, bless you. 'E'd talk the leg off an iron pot, once on a day. But now, it's like pottering to get a penny out of a money box afore you can get a word from 'im edgeways.

NURSE: And he won't come to see you.

MRS HEMSTOCK: Not him! 'E once had a rabbit what got consumption, an' 'e wouldn't kill it, nor let me, neither would he go near it, so it died of starvation, an' 'e throwed a hammer at me for telling him so. You see—harsh! That's our Mester.

NURSE: Yes. Do I hurt you? They've let your hair get very cottered.

MRS HEMSTOCK: Get it out, Nurse—never mind me.

Enter MR HEMSTOCK, *a very white-haired old man, clean-shaven, with brown eyes. There is a certain courtliness in his quiet bearing.*

MR HEMSTOCK: I'm glad to see you back, Nurse—very glad. *(He bows by instinct.)*

NURSE: Thank you, Mr Hemstock. I'm pleased to see you again.

MRS HEMSTOCK *(to her husband)*: Tha'rt not 'alf as glad to see her as I am. 'Ere I lie from hour to hour, an' niver a sound but cows rumblin' and cocks shoutin'. An' where dost reckon tha's been? Tha's been slivin' somewhere like a tomcat, ever sin' breakfast.

MR HEMSTOCK *(to NURSE)*: I've been gone ten minutes. *(To his wife.)* I've on'y been for a penn'orth of barm ter ma'e thee some barm dumplings.

MRS HEMSTOCK: An' wheer's our Harry?

MR HEMSTOCK: He's in garden, diggin'.

MRS HEMSTOCK: What are ter out o' breath wi'?

MR HEMSTOCK: I've been runnin' our Susy's kids. They was drivin' our fowls again.

MRS HEMSTOCK: Tha shouldna ha' wanted ter come here, a mile away from anybody but our Susy.

NURSE: It is rather lonely—only Mrs Smalley's farm and your cottage. And the children *are* rather wild.

MRS HEMSTOCK: Let me live in a street. What does colliers want livin' in country cottages, wi' nowt but fowls an' things shoutin' at you or takin' no notice of you, as if you was not there?

MR HEMSTOCK *(to NURSE)*: We came for the garden.

NURSE: I suppose you are still on strike.

MR HEMSTOCK: There's talk of settlement. I see they're opening some of the pits. But I've done, you know.

NURSE: Of course you have, Mr Hemstock. Harry will be glad to begin, though.

MR HEMSTOCK: I'm afraid whether 'e'll get a job. You see——

MRS HEMSTOCK: What hast got for dinner?

MR HEMSTOCK: Roast pork, rushes, barm dumplings.

MRS HEMSTOCK: Then look slippy about gettin' it ready. I'm clammin'. Ha' thy heels crack.

MR HEMSTOCK *(to NURSE)*: You wouldn't think she'd been bed-fast thirteen month, would you?

MRS HEMSTOCK: Tha nedna ha'e none o' thy palaver wi' Nurse.

Nurse, ta'e no notice o' a word 'e says. (HEMSTOCK *goes out.*)

MRS HEMSTOCK: He's a good cook, and that's all you can say for him.

NURSE: I think he's very good to you, Mrs Hemstock.

MRS HEMSTOCK: He's too busy runnin' after a parcel o' women to be good to me.

NURSE: If all men were as good——

MRS HEMSTOCK: Tha's niver had him to put up wi'. Tha's niver been married, 'as ter?

NURSE: No, Mrs Hemstock.

MRS HEMSTOCK: A man's fair enough to you' face—if 'e's not as fow as a jackass; but let you' back be turned, an' you no more know what's in his breeches an' waistcoat than if 'e wor another man.

NURSE: Oh, Mrs Hemstock!

MRS HEMSTOCK: Yes, an' tha'll "oh" when tha knows.

NURSE: I'm sure you're getting tired. Won't you have your bed made?

MRS HEMSTOCK: Sin' it's gone that long, it might easy go a bit longer.

NURSE: Why, when was it made last?

MRS HEMSTOCK: How long has thee been gone away?

NURSE: Three weeks.

MRS HEMSTOCK: Then it's that long.

NURSE: Oh, what a shame! Wouldn't Mrs Smalley do it?

MRS HEMSTOCK: Our Susy! 'Er'd better not show 'er face inside that door.

NURSE: What a pity she's so quarrelsome! But you will have it made?

MRS HEMSTOCK: I know tha'll whittle me to death if I dunna. Does tha like roast pork?

NURSE: Fairly. Now, shall I lift you onto the couch?

MRS HEMSTOCK: No, tha wunna. I want na droppin' an' smashin' like a pot. I'm nowt but noggins o' bone, like iron bars in a paper bag. Eh, if I wor but the staunch fourteen stone I used to be.

NURSE: You've been a big woman.

MRS HEMSTOCK: I could ha' shadowed thee an' left plenty to spare. How heavy are ter, Nurse?

NURSE: I don't know—about ten and a half stone. Will Mr Hemstock lift you, then?

MRS HEMSTOCK: I say, Nurse—just look under the bed, atween th' bed slats at th' bottom corner, an' see if tha can see th' will.

NURSE *(doubtful)*: What! *(She stoops dubiously.)*

MRS HEMSTOCK: Right hand corner. I told the doctor to put it there. Canna ter see it?

NURSE: Oh, yes, here it is. *(She reappears with an envelope.)*

MRS HEMSTOCK: That's it—it's fastened safe. It's a new will, Nurse. I made 'em do it while tha wor away—doctor and Mr Leahy.

NURSE: Oh, yes——

MRS HEMSTOCK: An' I'm not goin' ter ha'e none on 'em gleggin' at it. I know our Susy often has a bit of a rummage, but I'm sharper than 'er thinks for.

NURSE: And what shall I do with it, Mrs Hemstock?

MRS HEMSTOCK: Why, get upon th' table, an' look if there isna a hole in top o' the bedpost, at th' head there, where a peg used ter fit in.

NURSE *(climbing up)*: Yes, there is.

MRS HEMSTOCK: Then roll it up, an' shove it in. On'y leave a scroddy bit out.

NURSE: That's done it, then.

MRS HEMSTOCK: Tha'll know where it is, then. Tha ought, tha's been more to me than any of my own for these twelve month.

NURSE: Oh, Mrs Hemstock, I hope——

MRS HEMSTOCK: Nay, tha nedna—tha'rt knowin' nowt, I tell thee. How much dost reckon I've got, Nurse?

NURSE: I don't know, Mrs Hemstock.

MRS HEMSTOCK: Over five hundred, I can tell thee. I made 'em in a little shop as I had in Northrop when the colleries hadna started long—an' I did well—an' so did our Mester—an' so 'as th' lads done——

NURSE: It is a good thing, for now they're both out of work they'd have nothing.

MRS HEMSTOCK: Oh, our Harry's got a bit of his own, an' our Mester's got about a hundred. It'll keep 'em goin' for a bit, wi'out mine.

NURSE: You *are* queer, Mrs Hemstock.

MRS HEMSTOCK: Ha, that's what they say about th' Almighty—

they canna ma'e Him out. But I'll warrant He knows His own
business, as I do.

NURSE: Oh, Mrs Hemstock.

MRS HEMSTOCK: Yes, an' I want my bed makin', dunna I? Shout
our Harry. Harry! Harry!

After a moment, HARRY *enters: a man of moderate stature,
rather strongly built: dark hair, heavy, dark moustache, pale,
rather hollow cheeks, dangerous-looking brown eyes. A certain
furious shrinking from contact makes him seem young, in
spite of a hangdog, heavy slouch.*

HARRY *(to his mother—in broad dialect)*: What's want?

MRS HEMSTOCK: I s'd think it is "What's want" an' I hanna set
eyes on thee for pretty nigh a week. Tha'll happen come to lie
thyself, my lad, an' then tha can think o' me hours an' hours by
mysen.

HARRY: What's want?

MRS HEMSTOCK: An' why art paddlin' about in thy stockin' feet
for? Tha 'asna gumption enough ter put thy slippers on, if ter's
been i' th' garden. Nurse, gi' me a drop o' brandy. *(She lies back
exhausted.* NURSE *administers.)*

NURSE: Your mother wants lifting onto the couch, Mr Hemstock.
(He comes forward.) Perhaps you will wash your hands in this
water, will you—*(He obeys sullenly.)*

MRS HEMSTOCK: Tha'd better wesh 'em for 'im, Nurse, 'e's nowt
but a baby. 'As 'er catched thee yet? *(He does not answer.)* 'E
dursna go round th' corner, Nurse, for fear of a bogey—durst
ter, eh? 'E's scared to death of a wench, so 'e goes about wi' a
goose.

A goose comes paddling into the room and wanders up to
HARRY.

NURSE: Hullo, Patty! You dear old silly.

MRS HEMSTOCK: Dost like 'er, Nurse?

NURSE: She's a dear old thing.

MRS HEMSTOCK: Then tha'll like *him*. He's just the same: soft,
canna say a word, thinks a mighty lot of himself, an's scared to
death o' nowt.

NURSE: Oh, Mrs Hemstock!

MRS HEMSTOCK: I canna abide a sawney.

NURSE: Are you ready, Mr Hemstock?

He comes forward. NURSE *wraps Mrs Hemstock in a quilt.*

MRS HEMSTOCK: To think as I should be crippled like this!

NURSE: Yes, it is dreadful.

HARRY *lifts his mother*—NURSE *showing him how.*

MRS HEMSTOCK: Tha's got fingers like gre't tree-roots.

NURSE *shows him how to place his hands. Then she lifts the trailing quilt and follows him to the couch.*

MRS HEMSTOCK (*rather faintly*): I canna abide to feel a man's arms shiverin' agen me. It ma'es me feel like a tallywag post hummin'.

NURSE: There, be still—you are upset. I'm sure Mr Hemstock did it gently.

She stoops and strokes Patty, who is crouched near the bed. HARRY *moves as if to go.*

Will you fetch clean sheets and pillow slips—be quick, will you?

HARRY *goes out.* NURSE *begins to make the bed.*

MRS HEMSTOCK: Isna 'e like that there goose, now?

NURSE: Well, I'm sure Patty's a very lovable creature.

MRS HEMSTOCK: I'm glad tha thinks so. It's not many as can find in their heart to love a gaby like that.

NURSE: Poor Patty!

MRS HEMSTOCK: An' that other hussy on'y wants him cause she canna get him.

NURSE: It's often the case.

MRS HEMSTOCK: It is wi' a woman who's that cunning at kissin' an' cuddlin' that a man 'ud run after 'er a hundred miles for the same again.

NURSE: Is she clever, then?

MRS HEMSTOCK: She melts herself into a man like butter in a hot tater. She ma'es him feel like a pearl button swimmin' away in hot vinegar. That's what I made out from 'im.

NURSE: She's not a nice girl.

MRS HEMSTOCK: An' 'e hated her cause I shoved him at her.

NURSE: But you don't care for her, surely.

MRS HEMSTOCK: Canna bear her. A pussy cat always rubbin' 'erself agen a man's legs—an' one o' the quiet sort. But for all that, I should like to see him married afore I die. I dunna like, Nurse, leavin' 'im like 'e is. 'E wor my darlin'.

NURSE (*softly*): Yes.

MRS HEMSTOCK : An' 'e niver wor a drunkard, but 'e's the makin's of one.

NURSE : Surely not—oh, how dreadful!

Enter HARRY *with bedding. He helps* NURSE *shake up and make the bed.*

NURSE : How sweet the sheets are! They were aired on the currant bushes. Did Mrs Smalley wash them?

MRS HEMSTOCK : Our Susy! Not likely. She'd never do a hand's turn. I expect our Harry there weshed 'em—an' 'is father. Dunna look so; canna ter answer a bit of a question? *(He does not answer.)* 'E looks as if 'e'd swallowed a year o' foul weather.

NURSE : Hem at the top. *(She stumbles over Patty.)* Oh, poor Patty —poor old bird! Come here then, you dear old thing—did I hurt you?

MRS HEMSTOCK : Tha's more fondness for that goose than I han, Nurse. It's too much like him. Birds of a feather flock together.

NURSE : You include me.

MRS HEMSTOCK : If tha likes.

NURSE : It's not a compliment.

MRS HEMSTOCK : It isna. Tha'rt a lady, an' han a lady's time, an' tha'rt a fool if tha changes.

NURSE : I am not so sure——

MRS HEMSTOCK : Tha gets a good wage, an' th' minute tha enters a house everybody gets up to run about after thee. What more dost want?

NURSE : I don't know.

MRS HEMSTOCK : No, I s'd think tha doesna.

NURSE : Sometimes I get tired, and then—I wish—I wish I'd somebody to fad after me a bit. I nurse so many people, and——

MRS HEMSTOCK : Tha'd like nursin' thysen. Eh, bless you, a man's knee's a chair as is soon worn out.

NURSE : It's not that—I should like a home of my own, where I could be private. There's a lonely corner in most of us that not all the *friends* in the world can fill up——

MRS HEMSTOCK : And a husband only changes a lonely corner into a lonely house.

NURSE : Perhaps so. But I should like to be able to shut my own doors, and shut all the world out, and be at home, quiet, comfortable.

MRS HEMSTOCK: You'd find you shut the door to stop folks hearing you crying.

NURSE *(bending down and stroking Patty)*: Perhaps so.

MRS HEMSTOCK: Tha art fond o' that bird.

NURSE *(flushing)*: I am.

MRS HEMSTOCK: If I wor thee, our Harry, I wouldna let Patty beat me, even.

HARRY: What dost mean?

MRS HEMSTOCK: Stroke him, Nurse—and say "Poor old Harry".

NURSE: Mr Hemstock will have a grudge against me if you slate him so in my presence.

MRS HEMSTOCK: And would it grieve thee?

NURSE: I should be sorry.

MRS HEMSTOCK *(after a pause—vehemently)*: Ha, if he worn't such a slow fool! Can thee lift me back, Nurse?

NURSE: Won't you let Mr Hemstock——?

MRS HEMSTOCK: No—thee do it.

> *Exit* HARRY.

Did ter niver ha'e a sweetheart, Nurse?

NURSE: Yes—when I was in the hospital. He was a doctor.

MRS HEMSTOCK: An' where is he?

NURSE: He was too good for me, his mother said, and so——

MRS HEMSTOCK: Tha'rt well rid o' such a draggletail. How long is it since?

NURSE: Eight years.

MRS HEMSTOCK: Oh, so tha'rt none heartbroken. We'n got a new assistant. I like him better than the owd doctor. His name's Foules.

NURSE: What!

CURTAIN

SCENE II

Time: the same. The kitchen of HEMSTOCK'S *house, a large, low, old-fashioned room. Fowls are pecking on the floor.* HARRY, *in a coarse apron, is washing the floor.* MR HEMSTOCK, *at the table, is mixing flour in a bowl.*

MR HEMSTOCK: Who wor that scraightin' a bit sin'?

HARRY: Our Susy's kid.

MR HEMSTOCK: What for?

HARRY: I fetched him a wipe across th' mouth.

MR HEMSTOCK: There's more bother then——

HARRY: He was settin' that dog on th' fowls again.

MR HEMSTOCK: We s'll be having her round in a tear, directly, then.

HARRY: Well, I'm not——

There is a knock: and in the open doorway at the back a little, withered, old clergyman, the BARON, *is seen.*

BARON: How is the sick woman this morning? *(He speaks with a very foreign German accent.)*

MR HEMSTOCK: I think she's middlin', thank you.

BARON: I will go and see her, and speak to her.

HARRY: We've told you a dozen times 'er na wants you.

BARON: It is my duty that I shall go——

HARRY *(rising from his knees)*: Tha are na——!

BARON: I am the vicar of this parish. I am the Baron von Ruge. I will do my duty——

HARRY *(confronting him)*: Tha'rt na goin' to bother her. Her na wants thee.

BARON: Stand clear of my way, sir—I *will* go, I will not be barred, I will go to her, I will remind her——

HARRY *(frustrating his efforts)*: 'Er na wants thee——

He suddenly moves: the BARON *rushes into Patty. The goose flaps and squawks and attacks him. The* BARON *retreats hastily. Enter* NURSE.

NURSE: Whatever is the matter?

MR HEMSTOCK: It's Patty haulin' the Baron out——

NURSE: Oh dear—how dreadful!

MR HEMSTOCK: 'E's bin plenty of times, an' every time our Harry tells 'im as Missis won't be bothered wi' him——

NURSE: What a pity she won't see him. Don't you think if you let him go——

HARRY: Ask 'er thysen if 'er wants 'im—an' if 'er doesna want 'im, 'e's na goin'——

NURSE: But what a pity——!

MR HEMSTOCK: You can't make heads or tails of what 'e says. I

can't think what they want wi' a bit of a German Baron bein'
a vicar in England—in *this* country an' a', where there wants a
bluff man.

NURSE: He's a Polish nobleman, Mr Hemstock, exiled after fighting for his country. He's a brave man, and a good gentleman.
I like him very much.

MR HEMSTOCK: He treats you as if you was dirt, an' talks like a
chokin' cock——

HARRY: An' 'e's na goin' pesterin' 'er when 'er doesna want 'im.

NURSE: Well, of course you know best—but don't you think Mrs
Hemstock ought to see a minister? I think——

Enter the BAKER, *a big, stout, pale man of about forty.*

BAKER: Been havin' a shindy with the Baron?

MR HEMSTOCK: He wants to see the Missis, an' we not let him.

BAKER: You'd best keep th' right side of 'im. *(He swings his large
basket, which he carries sackwise on his shoulder, down to a
chair.)* The strike is settled, an' th' men's goin' back on the old
terms.

NURSE: Oh, I'm so glad.

BAKER: Fisher's a deep 'un. The Company'll know yet as they've
got a manager.

NURSE *(to* HARRY*)*: So you'll be going back to work soon, Mr Hemstock. You will be glad.

MR HEMSTOCK: Me—I s'll never work again. An' it's doubtful as
our Harry won't get on——

BAKER: They gave you a place before the strike, didn't they, where
you had to work you inside out for about fifteen shillings a
week?

HARRY: Ha.

He goes out.

MR HEMSTOCK: Yes, they treated him very shabbily.

BAKER: I bet it was th' owd Baron. He's a good hand at having
your eye for a word, an' your tooth for a look. I bet Harry'll
get no job——

MR HEMSTOCK: No, I'm afraid 'e wunna. The Baron will go down
to Fisher——

BAKER: And Harry can go down to—his godfather, eh, Nurse?

NURSE: I don't understand.

BAKER: *Old* Harry.

MR HEMSTOCK: I hope to goodness 'e will get something to do, else 'e'll mope himself into the cut, or the 'sylum, afore long.

BAKER: Oh, it's love what's upset him, isn't it? Rachel Wilcox was too much for his stomach——

MR HEMSTOCK: I dunno what it is.

BAKER: She's a bit of a ronk 'un. She was his first cigar, an' it's left him sick yet. She's not half bad, you know, if you can stand 'em strong.

NURSE *goes out.*

I've scared Nurse off.—But Harry's got a bit of a thin stomach, hasn't he? Rachel's not a half bad little ha-p'orth.

MR HEMSTOCK: Some's got a stomach for tan-tafflins, an' some 'ud rather ha'e bread an' butter——

BAKER: And Rachel's creamy—she's a cream horn of plenty—eh, what?

MR HEMSTOCK: A bit sickly.

BAKER: I dunno—it 'ud take a lot o' rich food to turn me. How many——?

MR HEMSTOCK: One of yesterday's bakin', please.

BAKER *sets the loaf on the table.*

BAKER: Your Susy wa'nt in—I wonder what she wants. Where is she, do you know?

MR HEMSTOCK: She'll be somewhere lookin' after th' land.

BAKER: I reckon she makes a rare farmer.

MR HEMSTOCK: Yes.

BAKER: Bill left the place in a bit of a mess——

MR HEMSTOCK: A man as drinks himself to death——

BAKER: Ay! She wishes she'd had me astead of him, she says. I tell her it's never too late to mend. He's made the hole, I'll be the patch. But it's not much of a place, Smalley's farm——?

MR HEMSTOCK: It takes her all her time to manage an' pay off Bill's debts.

BAKER: Debts—why, I thought from what she said——

Enter SUSY SMALLEY, *a buxom, ruddy, bold woman of thirty-five, wearing thick boots and a dark blue milkmaid bonnet.*

MRS SMALLEY: Wheer's our Harry?

MR HEMSTOCK: I dunno. 'E went out a bit sin'——

MRS SMALLEY: An' wheer is 'e? I'll let him know whether he's——

    Enter HARRY.

Oh, I've foun' thee, have I? What dost reckon tha's been doin' to my lad?

HARRY: Tha nedna ha' hunted for me. I wor nobbut i' th' garden.

BAKER: You should ha' looked in th' parsley bed, Susy.

MRS SMALLEY: That's wheer to find *babies*—an' I'll baby him. What did thee hit my lad for?

HARRY: Ask thysen.

MRS SMALLEY: I'm axin' thee. Tha thinks because I hanna a man to stand up for me, tha can——

HARRY: There's a lot o' helpless widder about thee!

MRS SMALLEY: No, an' it's a good thing I'm not helpless, else I should be trod underfoot like straw, by a parcel of——

HARRY: It's tha as does th' treadin'. Tha's trod your Bill a long way underfoot—six foot or more.

BAKER: It's a fat sight deeper than that afore you get to blazes.

MRS SMALLEY: Whatever our Bill was or wan't, 'e was not a' idle skilk livin' on two old folks, devourin' 'em.

NURSE *(entering)*: Oh, think of your mother, Mrs Smalley.

MRS SMALLEY: I s'll think of who I like——

BAKER: An' who *do* you like, Susy?

MRS SMALLEY: You keep your "Susy" to yourself——

BAKER: Only too glad, when I get her——

MRS SMALLEY: An' we don't thank Nurse Broadbanks for inter-ferin'. *She* only comes carneyin' round for what she gets. Our Harry an' her's matched; a pair of mealy-mouthed creeps, deep as they make 'em. An' my father's not much better. What all of 'em's after's my mother's money.

NURSE: Oh, for shame, for shame!

HARRY: Shut thy mouth, or I'll shut it for thee.

MRS SMALLEY: Oh, shall you? I should like to see you. It's as much as you durst do to hit a child, you great coward, you kid.

MR HEMSTOCK: Shut it up, now, shut it up!

MRS SMALLEY: But I'll let him know, if he touches my child again; I'll give him what for. I'll thrash him myself——

BAKER: That's your brother, not your husband.

MRS SMALLEY: I will an' a'. Him an' his blessed fowls! 'E's nobbut

a chuck himself, as dursn't say boh to a goose, an' as hides in th'
water-butt if his girl comes to see him——

>   HARRY *dashes forward as if to strike her. The* BAKER *interposes.*

BAKER : Here, none o' that, none o' that!

MRS SMALLEY : A great coward! He thinks he'll show Nurse Broadbanks what he is, does he? I hope she'll storm round him after this bit.

HARRY *(in a fury)* : If tha doesn't——

MR HEMSTOCK : Let's have no more of it, let's have no more of it——

BAKER : How much bread, Mrs Smalley? I reckon your Bill bettered himself when he flitted—what? I *don't* think. How many loaves? I saved you a crusty one.

MR HEMSTOCK : She's crust enough on her——

BAKER : Oh, I like 'em a bit brown. Good morning, everybody.

>   *He swings up his basket and follows* MRS SMALLEY *out.*

NURSE : How shameful to make a disturbance like that!

MR HEMSTOCK : We never have a bit of peace. She won't do a hand's turn in the house, and seems as if she can't bear herself because we manage without her.

HARRY : She's after the money.

NURSE : How dreadful! You are a strange family.

>   *She goes into the parlour again, and keeps coming in and out with water ewer and so on.* MR HEMSTOCK *flourishes his balls of dough.* HARRY *puts on the saucepan.*

MR HEMSTOCK : Dost think Job Arthur will marry our Susy?

HARRY : No.

MR HEMSTOCK : He seems to hang round her a good bit. Your mother often says he lets his bread get stale stoppin' there.

HARRY : If 'e married 'er, 'e'll settle her.

MR HEMSTOCK : Yes—he's all there.

HARRY : All but what he's short to pay his debts.

>   *He goes out.*

NURSE : I think I've done everything, Mr Hemstock.

>   *She begins packing her black bag.*

MR HEMSTOCK : Could you wait half a minute while I go—to Goddard's?

NURSE : Well—ten minutes.

*The old man takes a jar from the cupboard, and puts on his
hat. At the door he meets the doctor, a clean-shaven fair man
rather full at the stomach and low at the chest.*

DR FOULES: Good morning, Mr Hemstock—you are going out?

MR HEMSTOCK: For a second, Doctor, just to the shop.

DR FOULES: I see. Then shall I go in?

MR HEMSTOCK: Oh, yes, Doctor.

DR FOULES: Thank you.

    He enters. NURSE *is just putting on her bonnet. The doctor
stands confused.*

NURSE *(low and purring)*: Good morning.

DR FOULES: Nurse Broadbanks!

NURSE *(low)*: Yes—just fancy.

DR FOULES: Well. I am surprised. Who ever——

NURSE: I knew it was you. No other doctor would have been so
polite about entering the house.

DR FOULES: Well—I can hardly find words—I am sure——

NURSE: Fancy your keeping your old shyness.

DR FOULES *(flushing)*: I don't know that I do——

NURSE: I should have thought it would have worn off—all the
experience you have had.

DR FOULES: Have I had so much experience?

NURSE: Eight years.

DR FOULES: Ah, Nurse, we don't measure experience by years.

NURSE: Surely, you have a quotation!

DR FOULES *(smiling)*: No, I have not—for a wonder. Indeed I'm
growing out of touch with literature.

NURSE: I shall not know you. You used to be——

DR FOULES: *Vox, et præterea nihil.* "A voice, and nothing more."

NURSE: You are yourself. But you have not had much experience,
in eight years?

DR FOULES: Not much has happened to me.

NURSE: And you a doctor!

DR FOULES: And I a doctor!

NURSE: But you have lost your old æsthetic look—wistful, I nearly
said.

DR FOULES: *Damnosa quid non imminuit dies?* "Whom has not
pernicious time impaired?"

NURSE: Not your stock of learning, evidently.

DR FOULES *(bowing)*: Nor your wit, Nurse. *Suum cuique.* You have not——?

NURSE: What?

DR FOULES: You have not—married?

NURSE: Nurse Broadbanks.

DR FOULES: Of course—ha ha—how slow of me. *Verbum sat sapienti.*

NURSE: And you——?

DR FOULES: What, Nurse?

NURSE: Married?

DR FOULES: No, Nurse, I am not. Nor, if it is anything to your satisfaction, likely to be.

NURSE: Your *mother* is still alive?

DR FOULES *(bowing)*: *Rem acu tetigisti.* "You have pricked the point with your needle."

NURSE: I beg your pardon.

DR FOULES: Do not, I beg, do not.

NURSE: *Semper idem*—I know so much Latin.

DR FOULES: In what am I always the same, Nurse?

NURSE: Well—your politeness.

DR FOULES: *Suaviter in modo, fortiter in re.* My old motto, you remember.

NURSE: I do not know the English for it.

DR FOULES: "Gentle in manner, resolute in deed."

NURSE: In what deed, may I ask, Doctor?

DR FOULES: You may ask, Nurse. I am afraid I cannot tell you. And I, may I ask what *you* have done?

NURSE: Worked enough to be rather tired, Doctor—and found the world full of friends.

DR FOULES: *Non multa sed multum.* "Not many things, but much," Nurse. I could not say so much.

NURSE *(laughing)*: No?

DR FOULES: *Quid rides?* "Wherefore do you laugh?"

NURSE: She lives with you here?

DR FOULES: My mother? Yes.

NURSE: It will always be said of you—"He was a good son."

DR FOULES: I hope so, Nurse.

NURSE: Yes—it is the best.

DR FOULES *(softly)*: You look sad.

NURSE : Not on my own behalf, Doctor.

DR FOULES : On mine, Nurse?

NURSE *(reluctantly)* : No, not quite that.

DR FOULES : *Tædium vitæ*—all unresolved emotions and sicknesses go under that "weariness of life".

NURSE : Life? Doctor—do we get enough life to be weary of it? Work, perhaps.

DR FOULES : It may be—but——

NURSE : You don't *want* life.

DR FOULES *(smiling)* : Not much. I *see* too much of it to want it.

NURSE : Your mother will, I hope, live long enough to save you from experience.

DR FOULES : I hope it is a good wish, Nurse.

NURSE : Do you doubt it?

DR FOULES : Will you come and see us, Nurse?

NURSE : And see your mother?

DR FOULES : And see my mother, Nurse. *(He bows.)*

NURSE *(smiling)* : Thank you—I will.

    Enter HARRY—*he stands rather confused in the doorway.*

DR FOULES : Good morning, Mr Hemstock. How is Mrs Hemstock this morning?

HARRY : 'Er's pretty middlin', I believe.

    Enter MR HEMSTOCK.

DR FOULES : I have just discovered that Nurse and I are old friends.

MR HEMSTOCK : I am glad of that——

DR FOULES : Thank you.

NURSE : Dr Foules used to be my sweetheart.

MR HEMSTOCK : You don't mean it!

DR FOULES : Is it so long ago, Nurse, that you jest about it?

NURSE : I do not jest, Doctor. You are always to be taken very seriously.

DR FOULES *(bowing)* : Thank you.

NURSE *(to* HARRY*)* : Where did I leave my galoshes, Mr Hemstock?

HARRY : I'll fetch 'em.

    He brings them in.

NURSE : How good of you to clean them for me!

    They all stand watching while NURSE *pulls them on.*

DR FOULES : "A world full of friends," Nurse.

NURSE: Mr Hemstock and I are very good friends—are we not, Mr Hemstock?

HARRY: I dinna know—you know best—'appen we are.

DR FOULES: You are repudiated, Nurse.

NURSE: Twice! You shouldn't have begun it.

DR FOULES: I am very sorry. It is never too late to mend.

NURSE: We've heard that before this morning. I must go.

DR FOULES: You will come and see us—soon.

NURSE: I am at your disposal, Doctor. Good day, everybody.

ALL: Good day, Nurse.

DR FOULES: Well, I will see how Mrs Hemstock is.

    He goes out.

MR HEMSTOCK: He's a nice fellow.

HARRY: Hm!

MR HEMSTOCK: Fancy he used ter court Nurse! I shouldna be surprised if they got together again.

HARRY: It doesna matter to me whether 'er does or not.

MR HEMSTOCK: No, it na matters to us—on'y I should like to see her settled wi' a decent chap. She's a good woman for any man. If I'd a been thy age——

HARRY: Wi' that other hangin' round—an' no work to do—tha's ha' done wonders.

MR HEMSTOCK: T'other—tha's gin 'er the sack—an' tha can get work elsewhere.

HARRY: Dost think 'er'd ha'e me! *(He laughs contemptuously.)*

    There is a noise of yelping and crying. The men stand and listen.

MR HEMSTOCK: It's that dog!—An' Nurse!

    HARRY *rushes out. There is a great yelping and ki-yi-ing, a scream from* NURSE. *Immediately* NURSE *enters, carrying Patty, who flaps in a torn and gory state.* HARRY *follows.* NURSE, *panting, sets down Patty.*

MR HEMSTOCK: Whatever——

HARRY *(flushing in fury)*: Has it hurt thee—did it touch thee?

NURSE: Me!

HARRY: I'll break its neck.

NURSE: Oh—don't be——

HARRY: Where did it touch thee? There's blood on thee.

NURSE: It's not me, it's Patty.

HARRY: 'Appen tha non knows—'appen it catched thee. Look at thy arm—look there!

NURSE: No—I'm not hurt, I'm sure I'm not.

HARRY: I'll break its neck, the brute.

NURSE: It had got hold of poor Patty by the wing—poor old bird.

HARRY: Look at thy cuffs. I'll break its neck.

NURSE: No—oh no, don't go out—no—get me some warm water, will you—and I'll see to Patty.

> HARRY *brings a bowl of warm water.* NURSE *takes bandaging from her bag.*

MR HEMSTOCK: It's been at her before.

NURSE *(to* HARRY*)*: You look after her other wing—keep her still—poor old bird—*(She proceeds to dress the wounded wing.)*

MR HEMSTOCK: She'd be alright, Nurse, without you bothering.

NURSE: The idea—poor old thing!

MR HEMSTOCK: We've been many time worse hurt at pit, an' not half that attention.

NURSE: But—you see, you're not geese.

HARRY: We're not of as much count.

NURSE: Hand me the scissors, please—you don't know what you are——

> DR FOULES *enters and stands in doorway.*

MR HEMSTOCK: I keep telling him, if he set more stock by himself other folks 'ud think better of him.

NURSE: They might *know* him a little better if he'd let them.

DR FOULES: I see my help is superfluous.

NURSE: Yes, Doctor—it's one of the lower animals.

DR FOULES: Ah——

CURTAIN

ACT II

SCENE I

The same evening. The HEMSTOCKS' *kitchen, with the lamp lighted.*
The BAKER *and* HARRY *sit with glasses of whisky.*

BAKER: An' tha doesn't want 'er?

HARRY: I heave at the sight of her.

BAKER: She'll ha'e a bit o' money, I reckon.

HARRY: She's got to wait till old Hezekiah cops out, first.

BAKER: Hm! That'll be a long time yet—if he doesn't get married again. They say he's hankerin' after Nurse.

HARRY: 'Er'll niver ha'e 'im.

BAKER: Too old. But what hast got against Rachel?

HARRY: Nowt—but I heave wi' sickness at the thought of 'er.

BAKER: Hm! I like one as'll give as much as she takes.

HARRY: Sight more.

BAKER: It depends who's who.

HARRY: I can never make out why she went in service at the vicarage.

BAKER: Can't you? I've had many a nice evening up there. Baron an' Baroness go to bed at nine o'clock and then—— Oh, all the girls know the advantage of being at the vicarage.

HARRY: Oh—an' does she ha'e thee up in the kitchen?

BAKER: Does she not half.

HARRY: I thought she wor so much struck on me!

BAKER: You wait a minute. If she can't feed i' th' paddock she'll feed at th' roadside. Not but what she's all right, you know.

HARRY: I do know.

BAKER: She's not got the spirit of your Susy. By Jove, *she's* a terror. No liberties there.

HARRY: Not likely.

BAKER: They say Bill left 'er in debt.

HARRY: He did.

BAKER: Hm! She'll have a long pull, then, to get it paid off.

HARRY : She's a-waitin' for my mother's money.

BAKER : Is she likely to get much?

HARRY : Happen a couple o' hundred—happen nowt.

BAKER : Depends on the will?

HARRY : Yes.

BAKER : A couple of hundred. . . .

HARRY : About that apiece, we should ha'e.

BAKER : Hm! You've seen the will?

HARRY : No—my mother takes good care o' that.

BAKER : Then none of you know? But you've some idea.

HARRY: We hanna. My mother's funny—there's no tellin' what 'er might do.

BAKER : Hm! She might leave the money away from her own children?

HARRY : I shouldna be a bit surprised.

BAKER : Hm! An' your Susy——

MRS SMALLEY *(entering)* : What about your Susy?

BAKER : Hello!

MRS SMALLEY : You're stoppin' a precious long time. Where might you be bound to-night?

BAKER : Not far.

MRS SMALLEY : No further than the vicarage, an' that's two closes off. But Rachel'll be givin' you up.

BAKER : 'Appen so.

MRS SMALLEY : Then she'll be tryin' her chances down here.

BAKER : I wish her luck.

HARRY *(going out)* : I'll go an' get a bit o' bacca.

MRS SMALLEY : An' what do you call luck?

BAKER : Which do you reckon is a lucky-bag, me or your Harry?

MRS SMALLEY : You're both about as good : he's only got a little bunged-up whistle in him, an' many a hand's ferreted in you an' fetched out what's worth havin'.

BAKER : So I'm not worth havin'?

MRS SMALLEY : No, you're not, that's flat.

BAKER : So you wouldn't have me?

MRS SMALLEY : You're giving yourself away, are you?

BAKER *(incisively)* : No, I'm not.

MRS SMALLEY : Indeed. And what's your figure, may I ask?

BAKER : A couple of hundred, to *you*; to anyone else, *more*.

MRS SMALLEY : Thank you for the offer—very kind of you, I'm sure. And how much is it to Rachel?

BAKER : Two hundred an' fifty.

MRS SMALLEY : Oh! So I'm worth fifty pound to you, am I—*after* I've put my two hundred down. Ready money?

BAKER : Six months bill.

MRS SMALLEY : You are a swine.

BAKER : Do you accept?

MRS SMALLEY : You *are* a pig! You'd eat cinders if you could get nowt else.

BAKER : I should. I'd rather have you than any of the boiling; but I must, I must, have——

MRS SMALLEY : Two hundred?

BAKER : Not less.

MRS SMALLEY : Six months bill.

BAKER : Six months bill.

MRS SMALLEY : I hope you'll get it.

BAKER : I intend to.

MRS SMALLEY (*after a speechless moment*) : You are a devil when you've had a drop.

BAKER : Am I a dear one?

MRS SMALLEY : Do you call yourself cheap?

BAKER : What do *you* think? I was always one of the "take it or leave it" sellers.

MRS SMALLEY : I think you imagine yourself worth a great sight more than you are.

BAKER : Hm! I should have thought you'd have found the figure easy. And I've always said I'd rather it was you than anybody.

MRS SMALLEY : You was mighty slow, then, once on a day.

BAKER : I was a young cock-sparrow then—common—but wouldn't die in a cage.

MRS SMALLEY : An' what do you reckon you are now?

BAKER : I'm an old duck that knows "dilly-dilly"!

MRS SMALLEY : "Come and be killed."

BAKER : Scatter me a bit of golden corn—two hundred—and you may wring my neck.

MRS SMALLEY : You must have an empty crop.

BAKER : A few pebbles that'll digest *me* if I don't——

MRS SMALLEY : Debts?

BAKER : I said pebbles.

MRS SMALLEY : You're a positive fiend in drink.

BAKER : But what about——?

> *Enter* RACHEL, *a tall, pale girl, with dark circles under her eyes. She has a consumed look, as if her quiet pallor smothered a fire. She wears a servant's cap and apron covered by a large dark shawl. She enters softly.*

RACHEL : I thought I heard you two.

MRS SMALLEY *(startled)* : You *might* knock!

RACHEL : Were you talking secrets?

BAKER : Have you come to look for me, Rachel?

RACHEL *(cuttingly)* : You think a mighty lot of yourself.

BAKER : Have a drop of Scotch? No? How's that? There's Harry's glass—drink out of that.

RACHEL : You're very clever at giving away what's not your own. Give me yours.

BAKER : I've not finished with it—but you can drink with me. Here!

RACHEL : No, thank you.

BAKER *(softly, smiling)* : Why, what has offended you?

RACHEL : Nothing, indeed.

BAKER : That's alright. I don't like you to be offended. As a sign of good luck. *(She sips.)* Thanks. I'm sorry I'm late.

RACHEL : You're not there yet, so you can't be late.

BAKER : Yes, I am there. What farther have I to go?

RACHEL *(singing)* :

> "You've got a long way to go,
> You've got a long way to go,"

MRS SMALLEY *(singing in a masculine voice)* :

> "Before you get hold of the donkey's tether
> You've got a long way to go."

BAKER *(singing in a fine bass)* :

> "If I had an ass and he wouldn't go,
> Would I wallop him? Oh, dear no!
> I'd give him some corn and say 'Gee whow,
> Neddy, stand still while I mount, oh ho!' "

MRS SMALLEY : He's the donkey.

BAKER : Who doesn't make an ass of himself sometimes?

MRS SMALLEY : And we've got to give him some corn.

BAKER : For you'll never catch him to get hold of his tail—salt's no good.

MRS SMALLEY : How much corn? Tell her.

BAKER : Two hundred—and fifty—golden grains. No more.

RACHEL : What's up with him to-night?

MRS SMALLEY : Oh, he's had a drop, an' it always sets him on edge. He's like a razor. When he's had a drop, if you stroke him you cut yourself a-two.

RACHEL : Goodness!

BAKER : Rachel, I'd sell my immortal soul for two hundred—and fifty—golden sovereigns.

RACHEL : I'm not buying immortal souls, thanks.

BAKER : With this *(He spreads out his hands.)*—this paper and string to wrap it in.

RACHEL : An' a nice parcel of goods you are!

BAKER : I'm a lucky bag, Rachel. You don't know all that's in me, yet.

RACHEL : And what is that, pray?

BAKER : I don't know myself. But you shall have leave to rummage me. *(He throws open his arms.)* Look! *(He rises from his chair, as it were superbly. He is a fine, portly, not unhandsome man. He strikes a "superb" attitude.)* Look, Rachel. For two hundred and fifty pounds, three months bill, I am *(He bows.)* your slave. You shall *(He speaks with cynical sincerity.)* bring down my head as low as you like *(He bows low.)*, I swear it, and I never swore a lie.

RACHEL : But what do you want two hundred and fifty pounds for?

HARRY *(entering)* : Has Nurse come?

BAKER : Not yet. Are you going to finish your glass? It has taken me all my time to stop the women sipping from it.

RACHEL : Story! You know I wouldn't——

BAKER : Hush! Don't be rash *now*, or you'll hate me to-morrow.

RACHEL : And should you care?

BAKER : I am willing to give you full rights over my immortal soul and this paper and string——

MRS SMALLEY : For two hundred down——

BAKER *(bowing—then looking to* RACHEL *)*: And fifty, Mrs Smalley.

RACHEL : What do you think of it, Susy? Is it a bargain?

BAKER *(setting his cap on the back of his head and pulling on a large overcoat—he is well dressed)* : We have not struck hands yet.

MRS SMALLEY *(to* RACHEL*)* : What do *you* say?

RACHEL : Nay, I want to hear what *you* say.

MRS SMALLEY : I'm going to say nowt, yet a while——

RACHEL : Well, we'll see. *(She pulls her shawl over her head to follow him.)*

BAKER : Nay—I'm going down Northrop—on business.

RACHEL : Wasn't you coming up?

BAKER : To the vicarage? I had this to tell you; that is all.

RACHEL : Well, I must say—but come up just for——

BAKER : Not for a moment, Rachel. I am going down Northrop.

MRS SMALLEY : It's no good you saying nothing, Rachel. You might as well save your breath.

BAKER *(smiling to* RACHEL*)* : You hear? I'll see you in the morning. Good night all.

 Exit BAKER.

RACHEL *(looking after him)* : I hate him.

MRS SMALLEY : I'm going home.

 She hurries out. There is an awkward pause. HARRY *sits bending over the fire.*

RACHEL : How is your mother?

HARRY : Same.

RACHEL : Who's with her?

HARRY : Dad.

RACHEL : Where's Patty?

HARRY : Cupboard.

RACHEL : When do you expect Nurse?

HARRY : Dunno.

RACHEL : Have you been drinking whisky? *(No answer.)* Are you going to leave these glasses for Nurse to see? *(No answer.)* Are you going to let her see you drinking? *(No answer.)* Well, I do reckon you might speak to a body. I've not spoke to you for a week—hardly seen you. I can see you in your garden from the vicarage front bedrooms. I often watch you. Do you want your glass?

HARRY : Gi'e's it here!

RACHEL : You might say thank you. Job Arthur Bowers wants me to marry him. And I shouldn't be surprised if I did. *(She cries.)*

HARRY : Well, tha nedna scraight.

RACHEL:No—I mun only cry when I'm by myself. *(Sobs.)* I'm sure I'm sobbing half the night. *(She cries.)* Do you sleep bad? You do get up early—I can see your candle at half-past three, and you don't know how it frightens me.

HARRY: What's it frighten thee for?

RACHEL: I don't know. I feel frightened, for you seem so funny nowadays.

HARRY: 'As ter on'y just foun' it out?

RACHEL: You know I've told you about it many a time.

HARRY: A sight too often.

RACHEL: You *are* horrid. What have I done? Tell me.

HARRY: I'm non goin' to be made shift of. Tha'rt non goin' ter ma'e a spitton of me, ter spit the taste of somebody else out of thy mouth into.

RACHEL:Well, if I've been hateful, you've drove me to it—haven't you?

HARRY: I've told thee, I dunna want thee.

RACHEL: An' I went into service, so's I'd have something to do—an' so's I should be near—when——

HARRY: Go on—an' so's—an' so's an' so's—I'm thy spitton, tha can spit owt inter me.

RACHEL: You're right, you're full o' sawdust.

HARRY *(showing his teeth)*: What?

RACHEL: Sawdust, like a dummy. You've no more life in you.

HARRY *(in a passion)*: What! What!

RACHEL: Sawdust.

HARRY *(springing and seizing her by the shoulders)*: I'll settle thee!

RACHEL: You've been drinking.

HARRY *(shouting)*: I'll settle thee, if I hang for it!

RACHEL: You're hurting me!

HARRY *(quietly)*: Come here. *(He binds her in her large shawl.)*

RACHEL: Oh! What are you doing?

HARRY: I'll ha'e thee now, I will. *(He seats her in the big arm-chair, strapping her with a leather belt he takes from his waist.)*

RACHEL *(quietly)*: Have you gone mad?

HARRY: Now then—answer me! Did ter court Bill Naylor a' the time as thou wert goin' wi' me?

RACHEL: No.

HARRY *(his fist close to her eyes—loudly)*: Trewth!

RACHEL: Yes.

HARRY: Did ter tell him I used ter shout out that somebody wor coming if thou wanted to kiss me?

RACHEL: Yes.

HARRY: An' as I was allers swallerin' my spittle for fright?

RACHEL: Yes.

HARRY: An' I wor like a girl, as dursn't look thee atween the eyes, for all I was worth?

RACHEL: Yes.

HARRY: An' dursn't I?

RACHEL: Yes—an' don't. *(She closes her eyes.)*

HARRY: What! An' all t'other things about me as the pit was full of?

RACHEL: Oh, no! Oh, no!

HARRY: Yes, tha did!

RACHEL: No, oh no, Harry!

HARRY: An' are ter courtin' Job Arthur Bowers?

RACHEL: Oh!

HARRY: Scream, an' I'll squeeze thy head again' that chair-back till it cracks like a nut.

RACHEL *(whimpering)*: Oh dear, oh dear.

HARRY: It is "oh dear"—an' it 'as been for me "oh dear". Listen 'ere, tha brazend hussy. Tha keeps thy face shut when tha comes near me. Dost hear?

RACHEL: Yes.

HARRY: None o' thy cheek, not another word, in future—or I'll— what?

RACHEL: No.

HARRY: An' dunna touch me till tha'rt axed. Not so much as wi' thy frock. Dost hear?

RACHEL: Yes.

HARRY: What dost hear?

RACHEL: I mustn't touch you.

HARRY: Not till thou'rt axed. An' lu' thee here, my lady—I s'll brain thee if tha says a word to me—sithee? *(He thrusts his fist in her face.)*

RACHEL: Somebody will come—let me go, let me go!

HARRY: An' what I've said, I mean—drunk or sover. Sithee?

RACHEL: Yes, Harry! Oh, let me go.

HARRY: I'll let thee go. *(He does so, slowly.)* An' tha can go wi' who tha likes, an' marry who tha likes, but if tha says a word about me, I'll come for thee. There! *(He unbinds her. She lays her hand on his sleeve.)* No! *(He shakes her off. She rises and stands dejectedly before him.)* I hate thee now enough to strangle thee.

RACHEL *(bursting into tears)*: Oh, you are——

HARRY: Now go wi' who tha likes—get off.

RACHEL: You are——

HARRY: I want none o' thee—go!

> *She is departing.*

An' ta'e thy shawl wi' thee.

> *She, weeping, picks up her shawl.*

An' lap it round thee—it's a raw night.

> *She does so. He speaks gently now.*

Now go.

> *Exit* RACHEL. HARRY *pours himself another glass of whisky. He goes to the cupboard.*

Patty! Pat!

> *He puts his face caressingly among the bird's feathers.*

We'll settle her Pat—eh? We'll stop her gallop. Hey, Pat!

> *He tosses the bird into the air wildly.*

CURTAIN

SCENE II

> *A few moments later. The road just outside the* HEMSTOCKS'. *Deep darkness: two cottage lights in the background. In the foreground, a large white swing gate leading from the farmyard into the road, a stile beside the gate.* MRS SMALLEY *leans against the big white gatepost. Enter* RACHEL, *drying her tears, from the background. She steps through the stile.* SUSY *moves.*

RACHEL: Oh! Oh! Oh Harry!

MRS SMALLEY: It's only me; shut up.

RACHEL: Oh, you did give me a turn, Susy!

MRS SMALLEY: Whatever's up?

RACHEL: Nothing. Who are you looking for?

MRS SMALLEY: Nobody.

RACHEL: Has Job Arthur gone?

MRS SMALLEY: You saw him go.

RACHEL: Not that *I* care.

MRS SMALLEY: I bet you don't. You carry on as if you don't care. You do. You needn't pretend to be so mighty struck on our Harry, you know it's all sham.

RACHEL: It's not, Susy. There's no sham about it; I wish there was. He's got his eye on Nurse, it's my belief.

MRS SMALLEY: An' she's got her eye on my mother's money, I know. She's sniffing like a cat over a mouse hole, an' cottoning on to our Harry.

RACHEL: She's deep, she is—an' he'd be as big as a lord for at the bottom he's that stuck-up he doesn't know what to do with himself.

MRS SMALLEY: I believe she knows something about the will.

RACHEL: Well, surely——

MRS SMALLEY: An' from summat as my mother let drop, I'd be bound she's in it, wi' our Harry.

RACHEL: His mother always made me cheap in his eyes.

MRS SMALLEY: If I could get to know——

RACHEL: Doesn't your Harry know?

MRS SMALLEY: How should I know what he knows?

RACHEL: My father's pining for Nurse, the old fool. I wish he'd get her. His money might get her. I'll buck him up.

MRS SMALLEY: I'll get in her way wi' our Harry as much as I can.

RACHEL: Alright. You are a bit gone on Job Arthur, aren't you?

MRS SMALLEY: He should ha' married me, by rights, twelve years back.

RACHEL: There's something fascinating about him. Does he really want £250?

MRS SMALLEY: Yes.

RACHEL: I believe my father would give it me, if I got married to please him.

MRS SMALLEY: Alright, there's your chance then.

RACHEL: You needn't be nasty, Susy. I don't want the chance.

MRS SMALLEY: You dodge round too many corners, like a ferret, you do.

RACHEL: At any rate, I'm not waiting for somebody to die and leave me bait to chuck to a fat fist of a fellow.

MRS SMALLEY: You'd better mind what you're saying, Rachel Wilcox.

RACHEL: I don't care about *you*. So there.

MRS SMALLEY: Doesn't 'er though? What about our Harry? I'll let him know a thing or two.

RACHEL: It's you as has been saying things, I know. You've been telling him about Job Arthur Bowers.

MRS SMALLEY: Oh, have I? You're mighty clever.

RACHEL: You don't need to be clever to see through you. But I'll make you pay for it, my lady.

MRS SMALLEY: What? Come out here——

RACHEL: There's the Baron—an' they don't know I'm out!

She runs into hiding as a lantern appears down the lane. SUSY *draws after her.*

SUSY: What's he after?

RACHEL: Lovers. They hunt 'em out every Monday night. Shut up now. *(In a whisper.)* Does my white apron show?

BARON: We haf done good work this night.

BARONESS *(tall and spare, in an antique cloak and bonnet):* Seven couples, Baron—and we have only been out an hour. Isn't it terrible!

BARON: These miners are not men—they are animals that prowl by night.

BARONESS: The girls are worse, with their faces of brass. It is they who entice the young men into these naughty holes and crannies.

BARON: But if a man haf honour, will he not woo a maiden in her father's house, in the presence of her family?

BARONESS: This is a parish of sin, Baron, the people love sin.

BARON: Defiant in sin, they are! But I will overthrow them. I will drive them before me into the pit.

BARONESS: To think of that brazen besom telling us to go home and go to bed——

BARON: And the man—ah, infamous, gross insult! And coward, to revile me that I have no child.

BARONESS: If they had a few less—and they born of sin—the low women! That is the house of the woman Hemstock. Have you seen her?

BARON: Not yet. I will not bury her, heathen and blasphemous woman. She shall not soil my graveyard of good dead. And those, her men folk, obstreperous and enemies of God, I will bow low their necks——

BARONESS: Hush, there are some—I believe there are—behind the gate——

BARON: More? Ah, misery, more than linked worms! Where? My dull eyes!

BARONESS: There—behind the gatepost——

BARON *(holding aloft the candle)*: Lovers, if you be there, why do you suck at sin? Is this honour, you man? There is no one there, Baroness.

BARONESS: Yes, Baron, yes. I can see her apron. Who are you? Come out of there. You, girl, I see you. Come out, for shame. You do not know what you are doing; or, if you do, you are the depth of wickedness. *(A titter is heard.)*

BARON: Where is the man? Show yourself, sir. Let me see the man. You lurk, sir, in a hole like a rat. Ah, the disgrace of mankind.

BARONESS: What is going to become of you, girl? Go home, before it is too late. Go home and learn to do your housework.

BARON: You press into the boughs of the trees, but the boughs are the little arms of God. You hide youselves deep in the darkness, which is but the pupil of the eye of God. Ah, like a hot spark you fret the eye of God with your lust.

BARONESS: You will rue it this time next year, I tell you.

BARON: The face of the man is full of shame, it is afraid lest it fall under my eye.

He holds the lantern peering at the woman. The BARONESS *hovers close behind.* RACHEL *pushes* SUSY *out upon the little man. The lantern is extinguished.*

BARONESS: Oh, oh, come away, Baron, come away!

BARON: Ha! Ha! *(His voice is screaming.)* It is the attack! Stand behind me, Baroness, I defend you. *(He ends on a high note, flourishing a stick he carries.)* I have hit him! Ha! Come on!

MRS SMALLEY: You've hit me, you little swine.

BARON: Stand behind me, Baroness. I defeat this man—I—*(He chokes with gutturals and consonants.)*

MRS SMALLEY: Would you, you *little* swine!

BARON: I will thrash you—I will thrash you—low-bred knave, I will—*(He sputters into German.)*

MRS SMALLEY: Let me get hold on thee, I'll crack thy little yed for thee.

BARONESS: Baron, Baron, they are murdering you!

BARON: Ah, my sword, my sword! Baroness, my sword! I keep him at bay with this stick.

MRS SMALLEY: I'll show thee, the little nuisance, whether tha'rt ter hit *me* on the shoulder.

BARON: I have not my strength of old, if I had my sword he were killed.

BARONESS: Thy are murdering the Baron! Help! Help! Oh Baron——

RACHEL *(suddenly rushing at her)*:Shut up, you old chuck! Shoo!

BARONESS *(screaming)*: Baron! Rudolf, Rudolf! Oh-h——!

BARON *(groaning)*: Ah, Baroness!

    He turns. SUSY *rushes through his guard and seizes his wrist.*

MRS SMALLEY: I'll have that stick!

BARON: The lady—the Baroness von Ruge, my wife, let me go to her!

MRS SMALLEY: Drop that stick, tha little——!

BARON:Little, little again! Ah, my sword to thee. Let go my wrists, foul one, base one, fight thus! *(He lapses into a foreign fizzle.)*

BARONESS *(fleeing)*: Help, help, help!

RACHEL *(catching her by the end of her long cloak and pulling her round backwards)*: Whoa, you're going a bit too fast!

BARONESS: Whose voice is that? What? Oh-h——!

    Enter NURSE.

NURSE *(breathless)*: Whatever is the matter? Who is it?

MRS SMALLEY: Drop that stick, little lizard——

BARON: My wife! God, think of my wife!

BARONESS: Baron—they're killing me—Baron!

NURSE: Baroness! Oh, for shame—oh, how dreadful!

    She runs to RACHEL, *who flees.*

HARRY *(rushing up)*: What's goin' off?

NURSE: The poor Baron—an old man! Oh, how dreadful!

BARONESS: Rudolf, Rudolf! Where am I—what—where?

BARON: I will *kill* you.

HARRY *(to his sister)*: Has ter no more sense, gre't hound?

MRS SMALLEY: What's tha got ter do wi' it? *(to the* BARON*)* Drop that stick!

BARON: I will certainly——

HARRY: Come off! *(He wrenches loose her wrists.)*

BARON: Ha! *(In triumph.)* Thief! *(He rushes forward.* SUSY *avoids him quickly. He attacks* HARRY, *fetching him a smart whack.)*

HARRY: The little wasp——

NURSE: Don't, Mr Hemstock—don't hurt him!

BARON: Ha! *(He rushes again.* HARRY *dodges to avoid him, stumbles, the* BARON *gets in a blow.* HARRY *goes down.)* Ha, I have smitten him—Ha!

BARONESS *(fleeing)*: Baron—help! Help! Baron——

BARON *(pursuing)*: My wife——

NURSE *(to* BARONESS*)*: Come away, Baroness, come away quickly. The Baron is alright.

BARONESS: I have lost a galosher, he has lost his hat, and the lantern—oh!

BARON: Ah, Baroness, safe! God be glorified. What—oh, only Nurse. We haf been ambushed by a band of ruffians.

NURSE: You had better hurry to the vicarage, Baron, you will take cold.

BARON: Speak not to me of cold. We haf narrowly escaped. Are you wounded, Baroness?

BARONESS: Where is your hat, and the lantern, and my galosher?

BARON: What matter——

NURSE: You had better take the Baroness home, Baron. She will be ill.

BARONESS: We can't afford to lose them—the lantern and your hat and a pair of galoshes.

BARON: Speak not of such——

They leave.

HARRY *(rising slowly)*: The little snipe!

MRS SMALLEY: It serves thee right.

CURTAIN

SCENE III

The kitchen of the HEMSTOCKS' *house.* MR HEMSTOCK *is stirring a saucepan over the fire.*

NURSE *(entering)*: I am late. Are you making the food? I'm sorry.

MR HEMSTOCK: I hardly liked leavin' her—she's funny to-night. What's a' th' row been about?

NURSE: Somebody buffeting the Baron and Baroness. I've just seen them safely on the path. Has Harry come in?

MR HEMSTOCK: No—hark—here he is! Whatever!

The door opens. Enter HARRY, *very muddy, blood running down his cheek.*

Whatever 'as ter done to thysen?

HARRY: Fell down.

NURSE: Oh dear—how dreadful! Come and let me look! What a gash! I must bind it up. It is not serious.

MR HEMSTOCK: Tha'd better ta'e thy jacket off, afore Nurse touches thee.

HARRY does so. MR HEMSTOCK *continues making the food.* NURSE *sets the kettle on the fire and gets a bowl.*

NURSE *(to* HARRY*)*: You feel faint—would you like to lie down?

HARRY: I'm a' right.

NURSE: Yes, you *are* all right, I think. Sit here. What a house of calamities! However did it happen?

HARRY: The Baron hit me, and I fell over the lantern.

NURSE: Dear me—how dreadful!

HARRY: I feel fair dizzy, Nurse—as soft as grease.

NURSE: You are sure to do.

Exit MR HEMSTOCK *with basin.*

HARRY: Drunk, like. Tha'rt as good as a mother to me, Nurse.

NURSE: Am I?

HARRY: My mother worna one ter handle you very tender. 'Er wor rough, not like thee.

NURSE: You see, she hadn't my practice.

HARRY: She 'adna thy hands. 'Er's rayther bad to-day, Nurse. I s'll be glad when 'er's gone. It ma'es yer feel as if you was screwed in a tight jacket—as if you'd burst innerds.

NURSE: I understand—it has been so long.

HARRY: It has. I feel as if I should burst. *Tha* has got a nice touch wi' thee, Nurse. 'Appen 'er'll leave me a bit of money——

NURSE: Oh, Mr Hemstock!

HARRY: An' if I could get some work—dost think I ought to get married, Nurse?

NURSE: Certainly, when you've found the right woman.

HARRY: If I was in steady work—Nurse, dost think I'm a kid?

NURSE: No—why?

HARRY: I want motherin', Nurse. I feel as if I could scraight. I've been that worked-up this last eight month——

NURSE: I know, it has been dreadful for you.

HARRY: I dunna want huggin' an' kissin', Nurse. I want—thar't a nurse, aren't ter?

NURSE: Yes, I'm a nurse.

HARRY: I s'll reckon I'm badly, an' then tha can nurse me.

NURSE: You *are* sick——

HARRY: I am, Nurse, I'm heartsick of everything.

NURSE: I know you are——

HARRY: An' after my mother's gone—what am I to do?

NURSE: What creatures you are, you men. You all live by a woman.

HARRY: I've lived by my mother. What am I to do, Nurse?

NURSE: You must get married——

HARRY: If I was in steady work——

NURSE: You'll get work, I'm sure.

HARRY: And if my mother leaves me some money——

NURSE: I must tell you where the will is, for fear anything should happen.

HARRY: Then I can ax—is it done, Nurse?

NURSE: Just finished.

HARRY: Should I lie down?

NURSE: Let me straighten the sofa for you; don't get up yet. Then I must see to Mrs Hemstock, and I'll speak to you about the Baroness's things, and about the will, when I come back. How does the head feel?

HARRY: Swimming, like—like a puff o' steam wafflin'.

NURSE: Come along—come and lie down—there, I'll cover you up.

MR HEMSTOCK *(entering)*: Is he badly?

NURSE: I think he'll be fairly by to-morrow.

MR HEMSTOCK: Tha'rt cading him a bit, Nurse.

NURSE: It is what will do him good—to be spoiled a while.

MR HEMSTOCK: 'Appen so—but it'll be a wonder.

NURSE: Why?

MR HEMSTOCK: Spoilin' is spoilin', Nurse, especially for a man.

NURSE: Oh, I don't know. How is Mrs Hemstock?

MR HEMSTOCK: Funny. I canna ma'e heads or tails of her.

CURTAIN

ACT III

SCENE I

The morning after the previous scene. The dining-room at the vicarage, a spacious but sparsely furnished apartment, the BARON *considering himself in all circumstances a soldier. The* BARON, *in martial-looking smoking jacket, is seated at a desk, writing, saying the words aloud. The clock shows eleven. Enter* BARONESS, *in tight-sleeved paisley dressing-gown, ruched at neck and down the front. She wears a mobcap.*

BARON *(rising hastily and leading her to her chair)*: You are sure, Baroness, you are sufficiently recovered to do this?

BARONESS: I am only pinned together, Baron. I shall collapse if the least thing happens.

BARON: It shall not happen.

BARONESS: My head has threshed round like a windmill all night.

BARON: Did I sleep?

BARONESS: No, Baron, no, no! How do you find yourself this morning?

BARON: Younger, Baroness. I have heard the clash of battle.

BARONESS: I was so afraid you had felt it.

BARON: I—I—but I shall fall to no sickness. I shall receive the thrust when I am in the pulpit, I shall hear the cry, "Rudolf von Ruge"! I fling up my hand, and my spirit stands at attention before the Commander.

BARONESS: Oh Baron, don't. I shall dread Sunday.

BARON: Dread it, Baroness! Ah, when it comes, what glory! Baroness, I have fought obscurely. I have fought the small, inconspicuous fight, wounded with many little wounds of ignominy. But then—what glory!

BARONESS: Has Nurse come yet?

BARON: She has not, Baroness.

BARONESS: I wish she would.

BARON: You feel ill—hide nothing from me.

BARONESS: She promised to try and get the things. I know the hat will be ruined, but if we recover the galosh and the lantern, 'twill be a salvation.

BARON : 'Tis nothing.

BARONESS : 'Tis, Baron, your hat cost 15/— —and my pair of galoshes, 3/6, and the lantern, 2/11. What is that, Baron? Reckon it up.

BARON : I cannot—I have not—*(a pause)* it is twenty-one shillings and one penny.

BARONESS : 15/– and 3/6—15, 16, 17, 18—that's 18/6 and 2/11— 18—19, 20. *(Counting.)* And *five* pence, Baron. Twenty-one shillings and *five* pence.

BARON : 'Tis nothing, Baroness.

BARONESS : 'Tis a great deal, Baron. Hark! Who is that called?

BARON : I cannot hear.

BARONESS : I will go and see.

BARON : No, Baroness—*I* go.

BARONESS : To the kitchen, Baron?

> *Exit. The* BARON, *at the window, cries on the Lord, in German.*

NURSE *(at the door)* : Good morning.

BARONESS *(hastily turning back)* : Have you got them?

NURSE : The hat and the galosh—we couldn't find the lantern.

BARONESS : Those wicked Hemstocks have appropriated it.

NURSE : No, Baroness, I think not.

BARONESS : Your hat is not ruined, Baron—a miracle. Put it on— it looks as good as new. What a blessing. Just a little brushing— and my galosh is not hurt. But to think those wretches should secrete my lantern. I will show them——

BARON : Baroness!

BARONESS : I was going to the kitchen. I hear a man's voice.

NURSE : The Baker's cart is there.

BARONESS : Ah! *(Exit* BARONESS.*)*

NURSE : I am very glad the Baroness is not ill this morning.

BARON : Ah Nurse, the villainy of this world. Believe that a number of miners, ruffians, should ambush and attack the Baroness and me, out of wrath at our good work. The power of evil is strong, Nurse.

NURSE : It is, Baron, I'm sorry to say.

BARON : I think those people Hemstock instigated this, Nurse.

NURSE: No, Baron, I am sure not.

BARON: Will you say why you are sure, Nurse?

NURSE: I saw, Baron. It was not Harry Hemstock, nor his father.

BARON: Then who, Nurse? They are criminals. It is wickedness to cover their sin. Then who, Nurse?

NURSE: Some people from Northrop. I cannot say whom. You know, Baron, you are an aristocrat, and these people hate you for it.

BARON: The mob issues from its lair like a plague of rats. Shall it put us down and devour the land? Ah, its appetite is base, each for his several stomach. You knew them, Nurse?

NURSE: No, Baron.

BARON: You heard them—what they said—their voices.

NURSE: I heard one say "Catch hold of Throttle-ha'penny!"

BARON: "Catch hold of Trottle-ha'penny"—Throttle-ha'penny, what is that?

NURSE: I think it means the Baroness. They are so broad, these people, I can't understand them.

BARON: I will punish them. Under the sword they shall find wisdom.

BARONESS'S VOICE: Oh, shameless! Shameless!

RACHEL'S VOICE: He was looking at my brooch.

BARONESS'S VOICE: Come here, Baker, come back.

BAKER'S VOICE: A stale loaf to change, Baroness?

BARONESS'S VOICE: You shall go before the Baron this time. Go in the dining-room, Rachel.

BAKER'S VOICE: Me too?

    Enter RACHEL, *in cap and apron, the* BAKER, *and the* BARONESS.

BAKER *(entering)*: Thank you, Missis. Good morning, Nurse. Expect to find the Baroness in bed? I did.

BARONESS *(to* RACHEL*)*: Stand there!

BARON *(sternly to* BAKER*)*: Stand there! Take a seat, Nurse. Pray be seated, Baroness.

BAKER *(seating himself in the armchair)*: Hope I haven't got your chair, Baron.

BARON: Stand, sir.

BAKER *(to* NURSE, *as he rises)*: Nearly like my father said to the curate: "They're a' mine!"

BARON: Baroness!

BARONESS: He was, Baron, he was——

RACHEL: He was bending down to look at my new brooch. *(She shows it.)*

BARONESS: With his arm——

BAKER: On her apron strings——

BARONESS: He was stooping——

BAKER: To look at her new brooch.

BARON: Silence!

BARONESS: He kissed her.

BARON: Coward! Coward! Coward, *sir*!

BAKER: Ditto to you, Mister.

BARON: What! *Sir!* Do you know——?

BAKER: That you are the "Baron von Ruge"? No, I've only your bare word for it.

NURSE: For shame, Mr Bowers.

BAKER: When a little old man, Nurse, calls a big young man a coward, he's presuming on his years and size to bully, and I say, a bully's a coward.

BARON: You contaminate my maid.

BAKER: I contaminate your maid?

BARONESS: The shameless baggage. What have I always said of her!

BARON: Baroness von Ruge! *(to* BAKER*)* You are going to marry her?

BAKER: It's a question generally put to the woman.

BARON: Answer me, sir.

BAKER: I couldn't say which she's going to marry, out of her one or two fellows.

BARONESS: Shameless! Ah, the slut!

BARON: I repeat, sir—do you intend to marry this maid?

BAKER: I hadn't fully made up my mind——

BARON: Then, sir, you are a villain——

BAKER: You've got the muscle of your years up, Mister——

BARON: You threaten me!

BARONESS: Baron!

RACHEL: I sh'd have thought you'd more about you, Job Arthur Bowers.

NURSE *(deprecating)*: Oh, Mr Bowers!

BAKER: Right you are, Nurse!

BARON : I say, sir, a man who kisses a maid——

BAKER : Ought to be hanged for it—so say I.

BARON : Sir, your facetiousness is untimely. I say, a man who kisses a maid——

BARONESS : Baron, such people do not understand——

BARON *(kissing her hand)* : Baroness!

RACHEL *(melting)* : We're not given the chance.

BARON : Sir, is there no reverence in a kiss? If you strike a match against the box, even, you wonder at the outburst of fire. Then, sir—but do you wonder at nothing?

BAKER : Nothing's surprising—but everything is comical, Baron, that's how I find it.

BARON *(puzzled and distressed)* : So! So! Ah, but a woman *is*, according to her image in the eye of the men.

BAKER *(looking at the* BARONESS*)* : Some of us must have fancy eyes.

NURSE : How can you be so flippant?

BARONESS : A woman is what a man makes her.

BAKER : By gum, there's no tellin' what you might manufacture in time, then. It's a big job to begin of.

RACHEL *(laughing)* : For shame, Job Arthur.

BARONESS : What have you to say? You bad creature! What wonder men are as they are?

BAKER : When the women make them.

BARON : You are of my parish?

BAKER : Yes—but I'm in Northrop Church choir.

BARON : You are a chorister? You *wish* to marry Rachel?

BAKER : As I say, I haven't decided.

BARON : But what are you doing? What of this maid?

BARONESS : What does he care! Are you a married man, Baker?

BAKER : Not that I know to, Missis.

BARON : Sir, I am an old man, you remind me——

BAKER : Beg pardon, Baron.

BARON : And—a powerless—and I will say it, I will—a useless——

BARONESS : Baron!

BARON : Sir—I shall soon be called in—and, sir, you are of my parish, Rachel is of my house. What have I done, who am responsible?

BAKER : Nay, Baron, I can't see as you're to fault.

BARON: My fault, sir, is failure, and failure without honour. In three campaigns, which are my life, I have been miserably beaten.

BARONESS: No, Baron, no. How are you to blame?

NURSE: No, Baron, you have not failed.

BARON: In Poland, in London, and in my parish of Greenway. Baroness, we retire to a cottage; I sit still and contain myself, under sentence—Baroness, your pardon!

BARONESS: You shall not retire, Baron. Before God, I witness, you are no failure. Ah, Rachel, see now what you've done.

RACHEL *(weeping)*: It's not me.

BAKER: Nay, for that matter—would you marry me, Rachel, eh?

RACHEL: Opportunity's a fine thing, you mean.

BAKER: Will you marry me, Rachel?

RACHEL: I—yes, I will, Job Arthur.

BARON: She loves you, she let you kiss her. But you, sir, do you honour her?

BAKER: I do.

BARON: Then will you leave me?

BAKER: Good morning, sir—and thank you.

        He and RACHEL *leave.*

BARONESS: You are not ill, Baron?

BARON: No, Baroness. Nurse, who is this man?

NURSE: The Baker? Oh, he's Job Arthur Bowers—a bit rackety. He lives down Greenhill with his old mother. She's as deaf as a post, and a little bit crazed. But she's very fond of her son.

BARON: Ah! She is mad? She is old? Will Rachel be good to her?

BARONESS: I very much doubt it.

NURSE: Rachel will be afraid of Job Arthur Bowers. He is too big for her ever to get her apron strings round him.

BARON *(smiling slightly)*: I began to be afraid, Nurse——

BARONESS *(at the window)*: He is bringing my lantern.

NURSE: Who? Ah, that's right.

BARONESS: Will you ring, Baron? I will question that young man. We must get to the bottom of last night's affair, Baron.

BARON: Those ruffians shall not go unpunished. Still I have power for that.

BARONESS *(to* RACHEL*)*: Show that young man in here. Nurse, you

will help us. We must hold our own against these ungodly creatures. Must we not, Baron?

BARON : Ah, Baroness, still we fight.

RACHEL : Harry Hemstock.

HARRY *(entering, his head bound up)* : I've brought this 'ere hurri-
cane-lamp.

BARONESS : Thank you. And where did you find it?

HARRY : Where you'd lost it.

BARONESS : What have you done to your head?

HARRY *(after a silence)* : You should know.

BARONESS : There, Baron. I was right. And you would have stolen
the lantern if Nurse had not——

BARON : Leave the lantern, Baroness. Sir, who were your accom-
plices in this nightly attack?

HARRY : What's 'e mean, Nurse?

NURSE : The Baron means what men were those that attacked the
Baroness and him last night. I say they were some men out of
Northrop—that you could not recognize them. Mr Hemstock
came to your assistance, Baron.

BARON : Is that so?

HARRY : I pulled 'er off'n thee.

BARON : What is it he says, Nurse?

NURSE : He says he pulled the man away who was trying to hold
you.

BARON : Ah! Tell me, sir—who was this ruffian?

HARRY : I non know, no.

BARON : Who struck you that blow? That you must know, and
that must be told to me.

HARRY : Tha ought ter know thysen.

BARONESS : You are speaking to the Baron, remember.

HARRY : An't wor him as gin me a crack ower th' yed.

BARON : Then you were with the enemy. Now I behold you, sir. I
will cause you, sir, I will make you to confess. I will see you
punished. You shall suffer this course.

NURSE : You are mistaken, Baron.

BARON : Nurse, I will conduct this inquiry of myself. It is not of
myself. But your cowardice, yours and those others', to attack
a lady, by night. There is a penalty for such, sir; I say you are
vile, and you shall name me the other villains.

HARRY : There was no other villains—without you call a couple of women villains.

BARON : What mean you by a couple of women?

BARONESS : He doesn't know what he is talking about.

NURSE : There were some men, Mr Hemstock—from Northrop.

HARRY : Well, if there wan, I didna see 'em. All I see'd was two women draggin' at th' old Baron.

BARON : You mean to say we were attacked only by two women—Baroness?

NURSE : He must be mistaken.

BARONESS : These people would say anything.

BARON : Tell me, sir, tell me the truth at once.

HARRY : I've told you the truth.

BARON : It was some men, Baroness? At least, Baroness, one man there was——

BARONESS : There *was* one man—how many more I can't say.

BARON : The throat of these people is fuller of untruth than a bird's gizzard——

HARRY : It is the truth I've told you.

BARON : Nurse—speak—was it two women?

NURSE : It certainly was men, Baron.

HARRY : Well, it certainly wan't, an' I'm not a liar.

BARON : Then it was two women?

HARRY : It *was*.

BARON : And a woman has smitten your head?

HARRY : No, you did that youself, with your thick stick, when I'd pulled our Susy off'n you. An' I fell over your lantern and it cut me.

BARONESS : A likely tale.

HARRY : Is it true, Nurse Broadbanks?

NURSE : I think you are mistaken, Mr Hemstock. Oh, do not be so persistent.

HARRY : I'll not be made a liar of. Wheer's Rachel?

BARONESS : Why Rachel? She has nothing to do with it.

HARRY : Fetch her in then.

NURSE : She has just been in. She is engaged to Job Arthur Bowers——

HARRY : I don't care what she is.

BARON : I will ring.

BARONESS : Do not, Baron, do not trouble.

BARON : Sir, it was not two women—I defy you, sir. You make me a silly thing; it is your spleen.

BARONESS : You had better go, you.

HARRY : I'm not going to be made a liar of.

Enter RACHEL.

Rachel, who was it knocked the Baron's hat off an' shook him last night?

NURSE : Do you know the names of those men from Northrop, Rachel?

RACHEL : It wan't him, Baron, he helped you.

BARON : He would patch me with shame. You saw this attack?

RACHEL : I was just slipping down to get some milk from Mrs Smalley, there was none for supper——

BARON : And what did you see?

RACHEL : I saw some men, an' I heard some shouting, and I saw somebody hit him on the head. Then I ran home, and I'd just got in when you came.

HARRY : Why, wan't it you and our Susy as was raggin' the Baron an' Baroness, an' I come up an' stopped you?

RACHEL : Me! Me an' your Susy?

HARRY : You shammer!

RACHEL : I know you went up an' stopped the men, whoever they was——

HARRY : So I'm a liar? So I'm a liar?

BARONESS : Yes—and you may go.

HARRY : So I'm a liar, Nurse Broadbanks?

He goes out.

BARON : God help us, we begin to believe in the plots they imagine against us. *(He looks at his hands.)* It was *not* two women, Baroness?

BARONESS : No, Baron, no.

BARON : You saw several men, Nurse?

NURSE : Yes, Baron.

BARON : Rachel—but why weep! Rachel—he defended me against men?

RACHEL *(sobbing)* : Yes, Baron.

BARONESS : Rachel, leave the room.

RACHEL *leaves.*

BARON : Nurse, I am a soldier.

NURSE : You are, Baron.

BARON : I must reward that—fellow—although——

NURSE : It is good of you, Baron.

BARONESS : And you called yourself a failure, Rudolf.

BARON : I can—I must speak for him at the colliery. There I still have some influence.

NURSE : It is so good of you.

BARON : He has suffered already for his opposition. It is not good for the enemies of God to prosper. But I will write to my nephew.

NURSE : I could leave a letter, Baron—I am going past the colliery.

BARON : I will write now—then my honour is free. *(Seats himself at the desk.)* "My dear Nephew, I am placed under an obligation to that man of whom I have spoken to you before, Henry Hemstock, of the cottage at the end of the glebe close. It is within the bounds of your generosity to relieve me of this burden of gratitude contracted to one of such order. You will, of your fullness of spirit, lap over the confine of my debt with bounty. Your Aunt salutes you, and I reach you my right hand. Rudolf von Ruge."
—The manager of the collieries is as my own son to me, Nurse.

BARONESS : And he is a good son. He is *my* nephew.

NURSE : I will leave the letter.

CURTAIN

SCENE II

Evening of the same day. NURSE'S *room, the sitting-room of a miner's cottage: comfortable, warm, pleasant.* NURSE *in the armchair on one side of the fire.* MR WILCOX *on the other. He is a stout, elderly miner, with grey round whiskers and a face like a spaniel.*

MR WILCOX : No, Nurse, I've not a bit of comfort.

NURSE : Why shouldn't Rachel stay and look after you?

MR WILCOX : Nay, don't ask me—an ungrateful hussy. And I can't seem to get a housekeeper as'll manage for me.

NURSE: It is difficult.

MR WILCOX: I've been trying this last ten years, an' I've not had a good one yet. Either they eat you up, or waste, or drink. What do you think to-day? You know how it was raining. I got home from pit soaked. No breeches an' waistcoat put to warm—fire nearly out.

NURSE: Oh, it *is* too bad.

MR WILCOX: An' in the fender, a great row of roast potatoes, hard as nag-nails—not done a bit——

NURSE: What a shame——

MR WILCOX: An' not a morsel of meat to eat to them. She'd aten the great piece of cold mutton left from yesterday, an' then said I hadn't left 'er no money for no meat.

NURSE: How stupid!

MR WILCOX: So it was taters—you had to chomp 'em like raw turnip—an' drippin'—an' a bit of a batter puddin' tough as whit-leather.

NURSE: Poor man.

MR WILCOX: An' no fire—there never is when I come home. I believe she sells the coal.

NURSE: Isn't it dreadful?

MR WILCOX: An' they're all alike.

NURSE: I suppose they are.

MR WILCOX: They are. You know I'm an easy man to live with, Nurse.

NURSE: I'm sure you are.

MR WILCOX: One as gives very little trouble. Nay, I can fettle for myself—an' does so.

NURSE: I have seen you.

MR WILCOX: And I think I deserve a bit better treatment, Nurse.

NURSE: I'm sure you do.

MR WILCOX: An' I ought to be able to get it. If I was drunken or thriftless I should say nothing.

NURSE: But you're not.

MR WILCOX: No, I'm not. I've been a steady and careful man all my life. A Chapel-going man, whereas you're Church—but that's a detail.

NURSE: It *ought* not to matter.

MR WILCOX: You know, Nurse, I've got four *good* houses—lets at six shillings each.

NURSE: Yes, I know you have.

MR WILCOX: Besides a tidy bit in the bank.

NURSE: And you have saved it all?

MR WILCOX: Every penny.

NURSE: Ha!

MR WILCOX: An' there's on'y Rachel. I'd give her a couple of houses straight off, an' then we should be alright *there*: nobody could grumble.

NURSE: You *could* do that, of course.

MR WILCOX: Nurse, do you know how old I am?

NURSE: No, Mr Wilcox.

MR WILCOX: I'm just fifty-eight.

NURSE: Hm! I should have thought you were more.

MR WILCOX: I'm not.

NURSE: It is comparatively young.

MR WILCOX: It's not *old*, is it? And though I've been a widower these ten years—I'm not—I'm not good for nowt, d'yer see?

NURSE: Of course you're not.

MR WILCOX: An' you know, Nurse, you're just the one for me.

NURSE *(laughing)*: Am I, Mr Wilcox?

MR WILCOX: Nurse, will you tell me your name?

NURSE: Broadbanks.

MR WILCOX: You know I meant your Christian name. Don't torment me, Nurse, I can't stand it.

NURSE: I was baptized Millicent Emily.

MR WILCOX: "Millicent Emily"—it's like the "Song of Solomon". Can I say it again?

NURSE: If you will say it only to yourself.

MR WILCOX: My name is James—Jim for short.

NURSE: I thought it was Hezekiah—or Ezekiel.

MR WILCOX: Hezekiah's my second name—James Hezekiah.

NURSE: I like Hezekiah better.

MR WILCOX: Do you—I thought you didn't. Oh, I'm glad you like it. But yours is lovely.

NURSE: I prefer Nurse.

MR WILCOX: So do I—nice and short. *(A pause.)* Shall I sing to you, Nurse?

NURSE: Do you sing?

MR WILCOX: Oh, yes—I used to be a great one at "Ora pro Nobis". Should I sing you "Gentle Annie"? I used to sing that forty years since.

NURSE: When you were courting, Mr Wilcox?

MR WILCOX: Afore that.

He hesitates—goes to the piano and, after fumbling, begins to vamp to "What Are the Wild Waves Saying". He begins to sing, "lamentoso".

NURSE: There's someone at the door!

Not hearing, or observing, he continues to play. She opens to DR FOULES: they stand smiling. MR WILCOX stops playing and wheels round.

DR FOULES: "Music, when soft voices die, vibrates in the memory."

NURSE: Mr Wilcox was enlivening my leisure. Do you know Mr Wilcox, Dr Foules?

DR FOULES: I have not had the pleasure till now.

He bows.

MR WILCOX: Good even'—I wasn't aware as anybody was here.

DR FOULES: "By rapture's blaze impelled he swelled the artless lay."

NURSE: I think Mr Wilcox sings very well indeed. Will you finish, Mr Wilcox?

MR WILCOX: No, thanks, I must be going.

DR FOULES: Pray do not let me hasten you away.

MR WILCOX: Oh, I was just going. Well—happen you'll call at our house, Nurse?

NURSE: I will, Mr Wilcox.

He leaves.

DR FOULES: Did I interrupt you?

NURSE: You did not interrupt *me*.

DR FOULES: Then I incur no disfavour?

NURSE: Not for stopping poor Mr Wilcox at "Brother, I hear no singing"—Poor man!

DR FOULES: You pity him?

NURSE: I do.

DR FOULES: Ah! Is it of the mind-melting sort?

NURSE: I do not understand.

DR FOULES: "For pity melts the mind to love"——

NURSE: No—poor man. I can just imagine my mother, if I took him down to Kent. Well, you've done a nice thing for yourself——

DR FOULES: You daren't face family criticism?

NURSE: I daren't.

DR FOULES: Ah! Then he *does* aspire?

NURSE: Poor old fellow!

DR FOULES: I do not like your pity, Nurse—however near akin it may be to something better.

NURSE: You have often incurred it, Doctor.

DR FOULES: Which of the two, Nurse?

NURSE: The pity, of course. I have said "poor boy".

DR FOULES: Why?

NURSE: Why? *(She laughs.)* Because, I suppose, you were pitiable

DR FOULES *(blushing)*: You mean I was to be pitied. Why?

NURSE: Because you were not like the Pears' Soapy baby—"He won't be happy till he gets it," but you went on washing yourself without soap, good as gold.

DR FOULES: I cannot apply your simile.

NURSE: Perhaps not. I never was literary.

DR FOULES: You have grown brilliant—and caustic, if I may say so.

NURSE: It is the first time I have been accused of brilliance.

DR FOULES: Then perhaps I am the steel which sheds the sparks from your flint.

NURSE: Oh, the sparks may come, but they're not noticed. Perhaps you are only the literary man who catches them on his tinder and blows them into notice. You love a phrase beyond everything.

DR FOULES: Really—I hardly recognize you, Nurse.

NURSE: And what did your mother say of me?

DR FOULES: I thank you for calling so soon. Did she seem changed, to you?

NURSE: She looks very ill.

DR FOULES: Yes, I am worried.

NURSE: You are afraid it is something serious?

DR FOULES: Yes.

NURSE: I hope not. But it put me about to see her looking so frail. She was very kind to me.

DR FOULES: You are very good, Nurse.

NURSE : It is my duty to be sympathetic, Doctor.

DR FOULES : And use is second nature. I will take courage, Nurse.

NURSE : Will it not be a complete disguise?

DR FOULES : Your duty does not extend to *me*, Nurse.

NURSE : No, Doctor.

DR FOULES : You wish me to see you in *your* new guise, Nurse. You stick daw's feathers among your dove's plumage.

NURSE *(laughing)* : What, am I a dove then? It is a silly bird.

DR FOULES : You have had a hard time, Nurse?

NURSE : I have got over the hardness, thank you. It is all moderate, now.

DR FOULES : Might it not be *more* than moderate?

NURSE : I hope it will be some day.

DR FOULES : Could I help it, do you think?

NURSE : Everybody helps it, by being amiable——

DR FOULES : But might I not help it—more particularly? You used to——

NURSE : Say you are in love with me, Doctor——

DR FOULES : I have always been——

NURSE : Then the light has been under a bushel.

DR FOULES : "Blown to a core of ardour by the awful breath of——" *(He smiles very confusedly.)* I may hope then, Nurse.

NURSE *(smiling)* : Along with Mr Wilcox.

DR FOULES : Thank you for the company.

NURSE : Look here, Arthur, you have lived like a smug little candle in a corner, with your mother to shelter you from every draught. Now you can get blown a bit. I do not feel inclined to shelter you for the rest of your life.

DR FOULES : Thank you.

NURSE : I am sorry if I am nasty. But I am angry with you.

DR FOULES : It is evident.

NURSE : And I will still come and see your mother, if I may. She is a woman to respect.

DR FOULES : I do not order my mother's comings and goings. The case is the reverse, you remember.

NURSE : Very well. On your high horse, you are more like the nursery than ever.

DR FOULES : Thank you.

NURSE *(mimicking)* : Thank you.

DR FOULES : I am surprised——

NURSE : I am surprised—but—was that someone at the door?

DR FOULES : I could not tell you.

NURSE : Excuse me, I will see.

DR FOULES : Let me go, first. *(Catching his hat to depart.)*

NURSE *(opening the door)* : You, Mr Hemstock. Will you come in?
    Enter HARRY.

DR FOULES : Good evening, Mr Hemstock. I will make way for you.

NURSE : "Applications considered Tuesday, between seven and nine
    p.m." That is your meaning, Doctor?

DR FOULES : With your usual astuteness, you have it.

NURSE : With my usual astuteness, I have avoided so far the
    "Matrimonial Post". This is the irony of fate, Doctor. It never
    rains but it pours.

DR FOULES *(bowing to* NURSE *and* HARRY) : The third time pays for
    all, they say.

NURSE *(laughing)* : I will tell you to-morrow.

DR FOULES : It will not be too late to drop me a post card.

NURSE : I will see. Good night, Dr Foules.

DR FOULES : Good night, Nurse Broadbanks. I wish you luck.

NURSE : And lifelong happiness.

DR FOULES : Good night!
    Exit DR FOULES.

NURSE : He is very pleasant, isn't he?

HARRY : They say so.

NURSE : How is Mrs Hemstock?

HARRY : She's worse. She's not speakin'.

NURSE : Oh, I'm sorry to hear that. Did you want me to do any-
    thing? Poor thing, it will be a relief when she's gone.

HARRY : The 'owd doctor's bin. He told us to ax you to see her
    settled down——

NURSE : Shall I come now?

HARRY : Or in about half an hour's time—when you're ready.

NURSE : I may as well come now—when I've just tidied the room.
    Are you going to sit up with her?

HARRY : No—my father is, an' our Susy. I'm going to work.

NURSE : Going to work? I thought you hadn't a place.

HARRY : They sent me word as I wor to go to-morrow—buttyin' wi'
    Joe Birkin.

NURSE: And will it be a good place?

HARRY: Ha! It's a sight better than ever I expected.

NURSE: Oh, that *is* nice, isn't it?

HARRY: It's better nor mormin' about at home.

NURSE: It is. I'm so glad, Mr Hemstock. Then you'll stop at Green-way?

HARRY: I'm reckonin' so. There's nowt else, is there?

NURSE: No—why should there be? You'll have to begin afresh after Mrs Hemstock has gone——

HARRY: I s'll make a start o' some sort.

NURSE: You will? Do you know, I've had old Mr Wilcox here to-night.

HARRY: Oh—ah?

NURSE: He's so comical. He was singing to me. *(She laughs into her hand.)*

HARRY: He must ha' wanted summat to do——

NURSE: I think so. You never heard anything like it in your life.

HARRY: 'E never wor but dosy-baked.

NURSE *(purring)*: What does that mean?

HARRY: Soft, batchy, sawney.

NURSE: Poor old chap. It's no use being angry with him, is it?

HARRY: What for?

NURSE: For thinking I would accept him.

HARRY: No, it's not good bein' mad wi' *him*.

NURSE: He looked so crestfallen.

HARRY: He'll be just as game by to-morrow.

NURSE: Of course he will. Men only pretend to be so heartbroken. By supper-time they've forgotten.

HARRY: An' what's a woman do?

NURSE: I don't know. You see it means more to a woman. It's her life. To a man it's only a pleasant change.

HARRY: To all appearances, you'd think it worn't such a life-an'-death affair to her.

NURSE: Why?

HARRY: Woman is reckoned to be pinin' for you, goes an' makes a liar an' a fool of you in front of other folks.

NURSE: You mean Rachel Wilcox.

HARRY: Ah—'appen I do.

NURSE: But, poor old Baron, it would have killed him.

HARRY: Then let him die. What good is he, here or anywhere else?

NURSE: Oh, Mr Hemstock!

HARRY: Besides, she did it to spite me, because 'er wor mad wi' me.

NURSE: But she is engaged to Mr Bowers.

HARRY: 'Appen so. 'Er bites 'er nose off to spite her face.

NURSE: But poor old Baron—it would have been so cruel.

HARRY: Would he have stopped tellin' everybody else the truth?

NURSE: But you can't judge in that way——

HARRY: Why canna I? You make a liar an' a swine of *me*, an' a dam' fool of him——

NURSE: Oh, come, Mr Hemstock.

HARRY: He is a little fool—an' wants to boss everybody else wi' it, an' a'——

NURSE: You ought not to speak of the Baron like that.

HARRY: No, it's all palaver, an' smooth talk. I'll see anybody in hell before I'm fed wi' mealy-mouthed words like a young pigeon.

NURSE: I think you don't know what you're talking about.

HARRY: Dunna I though, but I do. I'm not going to be made a convenience of, an' then buttered up, like a trussed fowl.

NURSE: There is no one wants to butter you up, to my knowledge.

HARRY: Alright, then—then there isn't.

NURSE: And all this, I think, has been very uncalled for—and unnecessary.

HARRY: Alright, then—an' it has. But I'm not a kid, nor to be treated like one——

NURSE: It's there you make your mistake.

HARRY: Nay, it's somebody else as had made a mistake.

NURSE: Yes—we do think the quiet vessels are the full ones. But it seems they only want shaking to rattle worse than any.

HARRY: Alright. Say what you like.

NURSE: Thank you, I don't wish to say any more, except that I pity whoever has you, for you seem to be in a state of chronic bad temper.

HARRY: Alright—I'll be going.

NURSE *(who has been tidying the room)*: I will be at your house
   in ten minutes.

HARRY: There's no occasion to hurry—am I to wait for you?

NURSE: No, thank you—I would rather come alone.

CURTAIN

ACT IV

The evening after the last scene. It is the third day of the play. The kitchen at the HEMSTOCKS'.

NURSE: And what about the fire in the room?

SUSY: I'll let it go out and take the ashes up by daylight. It's falling dusk, an' I don't like being in by myself.

NURSE: Poor Mrs Hemstock—she went away quickly at the last.

SUSY *(red-eyed—sniffing)*: She did that. Eh, but wan't she wasted? A fair skeleton! I'm glad you laid her out, Nurse.

NURSE: I shall miss her. I've been coming here over a year now.

SUSY: I hope I don't lie like that. She used to be as strong as a horse. But she *was* hard, you know.

NURSE: Perhaps she had enough to make her.

SUSY: She had—wi' my father an' the lads. She was easiest wi' our Harry. He was always mother's lad.

NURSE: Yet they have been so indifferent——

SUSY: At the bottom they haven't. She never forgave him for going with Rachel Wilcox—an' he was always funny-tempered, would rool up like a pea-bug, at a word.

NURSE: I thought she favoured Rachel Wilcox.

SUSY: No, hated her; but she used her to make game of him.

NURSE: She is engaged to the Baker now.

SUSY: Yes. He's only having her for her money—an' she'll hate him when she's rubbed the fur off a bit. But she's one would fuss round a pair of breeches on a clothesline, rather than have no man.

NURSE: I don't like her.

SUSY: Not many does. She fair pines for our Harry, yet she'd have Job Arthur for fear of getting nobody.

NURSE: How dreadful! *(She goes for her cloak.)*

SUSY: Nay, dunna go. Stop an' ha'e a cup o' tea. I durstn't stop in by mysen. The kettle'll boil in a minute. *(She lays the table.)*

NURSE: I really ought to go.

SUSY: Don't, I should be scared to death. You'll stop five minutes, Nurse.

NURSE: A quarter of an hour.

SUSY *(staring)*: What's that?

NURSE *(going to the door)*: It's only Patty.

SUSY: She's been that lost a' day without our Harry.

NURSE: Poor old Patty!

    Enter HARRY.

SUSY: Tha'rt a bit sooner than I thought fer.

HARRY *(surly)*: Am I?

SUSY: I hanna been able to get thee no dinner.

HARRY: Why?

SUSY: She on'y died at two o'clock—an' we've been busy ever sin', haven't we, Nurse?

NURSE: We have, Mrs Smalley.

SUSY: Shall ter ha'e tea wi' me an' Nurse?

HARRY: No.

SUSY: What then?

HARRY: Nowt.

SUSY: Shall ter wesh thysen?

HARRY: Ha.

SUSY: Pump wor frozen this mornin'——

HARRY: I know.

    SUSY *fetches a large red pancheon from outside, puts in cold water, brings towel and soap, setting all on a stool on hearth-rug.* HARRY *sets tin bottle and knotted snap-bag on table, takes off his cap, red wool scarf, coat, and waistcoat. He pours hot water from boiler into pancheon, strips off his singlet or vest—he wears no shirt—and kneels down to wash.* NURSE *and* SUSY *sit down to tea.*

NURSE *(to* HARRY*)*: You must be tired to-day. *(No answer.)*

SUSY: I bet his hands is sore—are they? *(No answer.)* Best leave him alone—they always grumble about their hands, first day.

HARRY: Wheer's my Dad?

SUSY: Gone to registrar's.

NURSE: Yes, they must take some time to harden.

SUSY: Shall you sit there, Nurse? I'd better light the lamp, you can't see.

HARRY: Tha nedna.

SUSY: What's thaigh to stop me for?

NURSE: No—I like the twilight—really.

SUSY: There's a lot o' dirt wi' a collier—an' mess.

NURSE: Yes.

SUSY: I allers said I'd not marry one. I'd had enough wi' my father an' th' lads.

NURSE: They say it's clean dirt.

SUSY: Is it? Muck an' mess, to my thinkin'.

NURSE: Yes, I suppose so. I used to think it would be dreadful.

SUSY: But you've altered.

NURSE: Well, I've thought about it—I'm afraid I should never fit in.

SUSY: No—you're too much of a lady—you like a lady's ways.

NURSE: I don't know. Perhaps one does get a bit finicky after a certain time.

SUSY *(to* HARRY*)*: Dost want thy back doin'?

He grunts assent. She washes his back with a flannel, and wipes it as she talks.

NURSE: It's the thought of it day after day, day after day—it is rather appalling.

SUSY: The thought of any man, like that, is.

NURSE *(smiling)*: It was not the man—it was the life—the company one would have to keep.

SUSY: Yes. So you wouldn't marry a collier, Nurse?

NURSE: Yes, I would—for all that. If I cared for him.

SUSY: That makes the difference.

NURSE: It does.

SUSY: I can't imagine you married to a collier.

NURSE: Sometimes it seems mad, to me; sometimes it doesn't.

SUSY: I shouldn't ha' thought, though, Nurse, you'd ha' had one——

NURSE: No? I might.

SUSY: Not an old one?

NURSE: Certainly not an old one. Not Mr Wilcox.

SUSY: Ha. Have another cup? I wish Patty would keep still. She fair worrits me. I'm sure I'd like to drop your cup, she made me jump that much.

NURSE: I am surprised you are nervous.

SUSY: We all are. I wonder, Nurse, where my mother's will is?

NURSE: Oh—I meant to have told you. In the socket of the bed-post nearest the drawers, at the top.

SUSY: Would you believe it!

NURSE: She was very quaint sometimes. Poor Mrs Hemstock.

SUSY: Do you think she was in her right mind?

NURSE: Oh, yes—and Doctor does, too.

SUSY: Well—I used to have my doubts.

NURSE: Poor Mrs Hemstock.

   A knock.

SUSY: Oh!

RACHEL *(entering)*: I thought there was nobody in, seeing no light. Is Nurse here?

NURSE: Yes.

RACHEL: The Baroness wants you to go up, she's got a pain. I've been to your place for you.

NURSE: Poor Baroness! What is the matter?

RACHEL: She's got a pain in her shoulder.

NURSE: Rheumatism?

RACHEL: She says she believes it's pleurisy.

NURSE *(smiling)*: Poor old Baroness; she *does* fancy.

RACHEL: But she won't pay for a doctor, fancy or no fancy, not if she can help it. Her fancy mustn't *cost* her anything.

NURSE: She knows I can treat her. I can go straight there.

RACHEL: Oh, an' will you go an' see what's up with my father? He's not been to work—been in bed all day—can't eat—won't have the doctor—fading away——

NURSE: That is sad! What ails him?

RACHEL: I don't know—Minnie's been up for me. Says he feels hot inside, an' believes he's got an inflammation.

NURSE: I'll call if I have time. I must go.

RACHEL: He's done nothing but ask were his eyes bloodshot, and would Minnie be frightened if he turned delirious. She's frit—an' *I* can't go down——

NURSE: I will call. Good night, everybody.

   Exit NURSE.

SUSY: I must light the lamp.

RACHEL: I didn't hear till four o'clock as she'd gone. Was she unconscious?

SUSY: Yes, all day.

RACHEL *(to* HARRY—*who is struggling into his shirt)*: And was you at work? Fancy, you been at home all this time, then it to happen the first day you was away. Things do happen cruel.

SUSY: Shall you give him his tea, while I go an' see to my lad?

RACHEL: I mustn't be long.

> SUSY *goes out.*

What shall you have?

HARRY: Nowt.

RACHEL: Oh, you must 'ave somethink. Just a cup of tea, if nothing else. Come on—come an' sit here. See, it's waiting. You must be fair sinkin' after bein' at work all day. I've thought of you every minute, I'm sure. I've heard the driving engines shudder-ing every time, an' I've thought of you. *(She cuts bread and toasts it.)* They say you're hard, but they don't know. *(Suspicion of tears.)* I used to think myself as you was a kid, a frightened bit of a rabbit—but I know different now. *(She cries.)* I know what you've had to go through—an' I've been a cat to you, I have. I know what you've felt—as if you was pushed up against a wall, an' all the breath squeezed out of you—her dyin' by inches—an' I've been a cat to you. *(She butters the toast.)*

HARRY: Tha needna do that for me.

RACHEL: Yes, do eat a bit—you'll be sinkin'. I've had no tea—I'll eat a bit with you, if you will. *(She sits down, drinks tea, and eats a little.)* You know I've fair hated myself—I've wished I was dead. But I needn't talk about myself. Are your hands sore?

HARRY: A bit.

RACHEL: I knew they must be—because you've worked like a horse, I know you have, to stop thinking. I can see you're dog-tired. Let me look. *(She takes his hand.)* Fair raw! *(Melting into tears.)* You don't care a bit about yourself, you don't, an' it's not fair.

HARRY: Tha hasna bothered thysen above thy boot-tops.

RACHEL: I know I haven't. Oh, I was jealous of your mother, 'cause I knowed you was fonder of her——

HARRY: Tha nedna—*(She weeps—he hides his face.)*

RACHEL: I s'll never forgive myself——

HARRY: Dunna——

> RACHEL, *sobbing, goes to him, takes his head on her bosom, and rocks it.*

RACHEL: An' I've been such a cat to thee, Harry.

HARRY *(putting his arms round her waist)*: I've not seen her for two days.

RACHEL: Never mind, never mind. She's been wandering—never mind.

HARRY: Now 'er's gone.

RACHEL: Never mind, we s'll die ourselves someday, we shall. I know tha loved her, better than me—tha allers would—I know. But let me be wi' thee. *(She sits down on his knee.)* Let me stop wi' thee, tha wants somebody. An' I care for nowt but thee—tha knows I do.

HARRY: Should we go an' look at her?

RACHEL *(kissing him)*: We will. *(She kisses him again.)* Tha's been like a bird on a frozen pond, tha has. Tha's been frozen out——

HARRY: Rachel?

RACHEL: What?

HARRY: Dunna kiss me yet——

RACHEL: No—I won't—I won't.

HARRY: Afterwards——

RACHEL: Yes, I know—I know. *(Silence a moment.)* Come then, we'll go an' look at her.

> *She lights a candle, takes his hand. They go into the front room.*
>
> *Enter* SUSY.

SUSY: Where are they? I'd think they've carted off an' left th' house empty. *(Calls.)* Rachel! Oh my goodness! Harry!

> *Enter* RACHEL *and* HARRY, *both with red eyes, from the sick-room.*

Oh, here you are.

RACHEL: Yes. Did you think I'd gone?

> HARRY *pulls on his coat and goes out.*

SUSY: Yes—you said you was in a hurry.

RACHEL: I *shall* have to be goin'.

SUSY: I wish my father would come. Is he grumpy yet?

RACHEL: Harry? No, he's not grumpy, no.

SUSY: What? Have you made it up?

RACHEL: There was nothing to make.

SUSY: I'm glad to hear it. What about Job Arthur?

RACHEL: I never did care a bit about him or anybody else——

SUSY: No, but——

RACHEL: Well, but what?

SUSY: Has he asked you? Has he promised you? Our Harry?

RACHEL: Yes, not in words—but I know.

SUSY: You don't. Nurse wants him, an' Nurse'll get him.

RACHEL: She won't.

SUSY: You see.

RACHEL: Don't you fret your fat. He's not that easy to grab.

SUSY: But he's got a fancy for Nurse. He's as proud as they make 'em, an' it would just suit him to crow over us, marryin' a lady.

RACHEL: A lady!

SUSY: Well, you know what I mean. An' I believe there's summat in the will for her. My mother harped on her an' our Harry——

RACHEL: An' does she know?

SUSY: She's not far off o' guessin', I'll be bound. She is a deep one, Nurse is.

RACHEL: She is. Oh, she'd soon know everything if she got a sniff. An' has your father got the will?

SUSY: No, it's in the front room.

RACHEL: Well—you should get it, an' see what it says. *You* should come in for something, and then——

SUSY: Durst you come with me?

RACHEL: Yes, I durst come.

SUSY: Should us then?

RACHEL: Yes, let us. You could burn it if there was owt you didn't like.

SUSY: Durst you get it? *(She lights a candle.)*

RACHEL: Yes, if you'll show me.

   They go into the next room.

SUSY'S VOICE: Doesn't it smell cold a'ready. Oh!

RACHEL'S VOICE: It does.

SUSY'S VOICE: Look, you want to get on this table. This blessed candle does jump.

RACHEL'S VOICE: I could ha' sworn tha sheet moved.

   A shriek from SUSY—*shrieks from* RACHEL—*a bump—more shrieks.* SUSY *rushes across the kitchen out of doors. In a moment* HARRY *appears in the outer doorway.* RACHEL *flies blindly into him.*

HARRY: Whatever's up?

RACHEL: Oh Harry! Oh Harry!

HARRY: Well—what's up? What's ter got in thy hand?

RACHEL: Oh, whatever was it? Let's go.

HARRY: What wor that? What!

> *He starts as Patty walks mildly from the front room.*

It wor nowt but our Patty.

RACHEL: I thought I should have died.

HARRY: What wor ther doin'?

RACHEL: I fell off that table. Oh, and I have bruised my arm.

HARRY: What wor you doin'? What's this?

SUSY *(entering)*: Oh Rachel!

RACHEL: It was only Patty.

SUSY: Did you get it? Oh, look at our Harry opening it!

HARRY: Why, it's th' will. I sh'd ha' thought you'd have more about you—— *(He reads.)*

SUSY: What's it say?

HARRY: Look for thysen, if tha'rt in such a mighty hurry.

SUSY *(reading)*: Five hundred and fifty pounds for him and Nurse Broadbanks if they marry—an' if not, to be divided between me an' him. What did I say! Would you credit, now? But there's one thing, Nurse won't *have* him.

RACHEL: He doesn't want her.

HARRY: She's worth a million such as you, cats as wants nowt but to lap at a full saucer. You couldna let her lie quiet for five minutes, but must be after her bit of money.

RACHEL: Indeed, I didn't want the money.

SUSY: He wants it himself, an' that's what he's been contrivin' for all along—him an' that slivin' Nurse. There's a pair of 'em.

HARRY: There's a pair of you, more like it—a couple of slitherin' cats, nowt else. No more you think of her, than if she wor a dead fish wi' the money in her mouth. But you shan't have it, you shan't, if I can scotch you.

RACHEL: Oh, Mr Sharp-shins, you think you know everything, do you? You're mistaken. It's not fair, it isn't. I only——

HARRY: Tha needs to tell me nowt.

NURSE *(entering)*: Oh, you are here! The Baroness asked me to call and see where you were, Rachel.

RACHEL: And now you've seen, you can go back an' tell her you've been.

HARRY: They've been after th' will, couldna let her rest still in her own room, but what must they do, go ferretin' for her money——

SUSY: Shut thy mouth, tha's said enough.

HARRY: That I hanna. They'd claw the stuff out of her hand, if it wor there——

SUSY: Hadn't we a right to see the will?

HARRY: There's a lot of right about you. Here, come here. Give us hold of it.

SUSY: I shan't.

HARRY: What! Now, Nurse, thee read it. We'n all read. Now thee read it. (NURSE *reads*.) Hast got it all? Tha sees?

NURSE: Yes, I understand it.

HARRY: An' what dost say?

NURSE: I say nothing.

SUSY: This is what she's been working for.

HARRY: Then let them as has worked be paid. What? I say "snip", Nurse, will tha say "snap"? Come on—"snap" me, Nurse. Say "snap". Snip?

NURSE: This is hardly the occasion.

RACHEL: He doesn't love you, Nurse. This is only his temper.

NURSE: I think, out of respect to the dead, we ought not to go on like this.

SUSY: You'll be precise and proper—all lardy-da. Oh yes—but you've got what you've been aiming at, haven't you? You've worked it round very clever. You see what carneyin' 'll do for you, Rachel. If you'd ha' buttered your words, you might ha' been alright.

RACHEL: I couldn't creep.

HARRY: No; you could slither, though.

NURSE: I'm afraid I must be going.

SUSY: Yes, you can smile to yourself, and hug yourself under your cloak in the dark. It's worth marryin' him for, five hundred and fifty pounds.

NURSE *goes out*.

HARRY: She's a lady, she is, an' she makes you two look small.

RACHEL: Well, Harry, you can think what you like about me: and you always have thought me as bad as you could imagine. But I only did it to help Susy—and all I've done I've done with you sleering at me. An' I shan't marry Job Arthur; I s'll go in service in Derby. An' you needn't sleer at me no more—because it's your fault, even more than mine.

HARRY: A' right, ma'e it my fault.

RACHEL: As much as mine, I said.

HARRY: Dunna let me stop thee from ha'ein' Job Arthur.

RACHEL: Job Arthur's a man as can play his own tune on any mortal woman, brazen as brass, or cuddlin' as a fiddle——

HARRY: Or as ronk as an old mouth organ.

RACHEL: Or like a bagpipe as wants squeezin', or a mandolin as wants tickling. He gets a tune out of the whole job lot, the whole band——

HARRY: Shut up.

RACHEL: But I'll buy you a cuckoo-clock to keep you company.

HARRY: I'll buy my own.

RACHEL (*flapping her arms suddenly at him*): Cuckoo! Cuckoo! Cuckoo!

CURTAIN

ACT V

SCENE I

The Sunday following the last scene. The porch of Grunstom Church. The HEMSTOCKS *have attended the post-funeral service. Mourners are leaving the church.*

1ST MOURNER : Well, I niver knowed the likes——

2ND MOURNER : What?

1ST MOURNER : Nurse Broadbanks to be axed wi' old Hezekiah Wilcox, an' Job Arthur Bowers wi' Rachel Wilcox.

3RD MOURNER : An' what about it?

1ST MOURNER : Well, I never thought Nurse would have him an' everybody said Job Arthur would never marry now.

2ND MOURNER : I'm not surprised at neither of 'em.

1ST MOURNER : I was never more taken in in my life.

Exit 1ST *and* 2ND MOURNERS.

SUSY : No.

3RD MOURNER : I don't call it decent—two sets of banns put up at a funeral Sunday. They might ha' waited till next week.

SUSY : I'm going to see about this.

3RD MOURNER : Yes, th' old Baron wants telling, the old nuisance, for he's nothing else.

Exit SUSY *and* 3RD MOURNER.

4TH MOURNER *(sighing)* : That did me good. I'm sure I've fair cried my eyes up.

5TH MOURNER : You can't make out half the old Baron says, but he makes you feel funny.

4TH MOURNER : As if you'd got ghosts in your bowels. An' when he said—what was it?

5TH MOURNER : Was it Hezekiah Wilcox wi' Nurse Broadbanks?

4TH MOURNER : Yes—fancy 'em both bein' there to hear it. What a come-down for her.

5TH MOURNER : I dunno. The old chap's tidy well off——

4TH MOURNER : But he's mushy—he slavers like a slobbering spaniel——

5TH MOURNER: Well, women like that sort.

Exit 4TH *and* 5TH MOURNERS.

MR HEMSTOCK: I allers thought 'er'd a worn widow's weeds for me——

HARRY: Dost wish it wor that road about?

MR HEMSTOCK: Nay, I non know——

HARRY: Are ter stoppin'?

MR HEMSTOCK: I want ter speak ter Nurse.

HARRY: I'm goin' then.

MR HEMSTOCK: Dunna thee—tha wait a bit.

HARRY: Nay.

Exit HARRY.

BAKER *(in very genteel black)*: Good morning, Mr Hemstock.

MR HEMSTOCK: Good morning.

BAKER: We got more than we bargained for.

MR HEMSTOCK: Yes, a bit surprisin'.

BAKER: I'm going to strike—Nurse for a mother-in-law is too much for a good thing. Why, bless me, you want to be careful what relatives you have—some you can't help—but a mother-in-law, you can.

MR HEMSTOCK: I want to speak to Nurse.

MR WILCOX *(frock-coated)*: You've 'ad a big loss, Mr Hemstock—I've been through it myself, so I know what it is.

BAKER: Here, I say, Hezekiah—I don't mind you for a father-in-law——

MR WILCOX: Hello, Job Arthur! Well, I never! I am surprised, I can tell you.

BAKER: So'm I.

MR WILCOX: But it's a glad surprise—I'd rather say "My son" to you, Job Arthur——

BAKER: Hold on a bit, Hezekiah; you've always stood me as a good uncle, let's leave it at that.

MR WILCOX: I'll make you a wedding present of it, Job Arthur—that little thing, you know.

BAKER: I do, worse luck! I've pledged my soul and my honour to you, uncle, my uncle on the pop-shop side, but my body's my ewe lamb—I don't sell. Good morning, Dr Foules.

DR FOULES: Good morning. Er—excuse me—but Nurse Broadbanks has not gone yet?

BAKER : Not yet, Doctor. Here's her husband-that-is-to-be waiting for her.

DR FOULES : Ha!

MR WILCOX : Nurse has not gone yet, Doctor.

DR FOULES : Thank you.

BAKER : Let's have a look! *(He peeps into the church.)* Oh—oh Baron, may I speak to you?

Enter BARON, *in surplice, with* BARONESS *and* NURSE.

BARON : And you, what have you to say?

BAKER : Not much. Only there's a bit of an alteration wants makin'. Rachel's given me the sack.

BARON : I do not understand, sir.

BARONESS : He wishes to escape from his promise. He wishes to dodge Rachel.

BARON : You, sir, have you not given your word?

BAKER : And you're welcome keep it, for what it's worth. But you can't cork a woman's promise, Baroness. In short, Baron—and Mr Wilcox—Rachel has asked to be released from her engagement—hem!—with me—and I have felt it my duty to release her. *(He bows.)*

BARON : It is an indignity to the Church. It is insult to the Holy Church.

BARONESS : I do not believe this man. It is his ruse to escape from a bond.

MR WILCOX : Yes, my lady, that's what it is—my poor girl—Nurse! Nurse?

NURSE : Let Rachel come herself.

BARONESS : She shall.

BARON *(to* MR HEMSTOCK*)* : Go and bring Rachel here.

MR HEMSTOCK *(shrugging)* : Where am I to go?

NURSE : Please, Mr Hemstock.

He goes.

BARON : Sir, I believe you are a scoundrel.

BAKER : I wouldn't deny it, Baron.

MR WILCOX : No—we know him too well—he'd better not begin denyin'.

NURSE : This is the man, Baron—the—the—the *Wilcox*.

BARON : What! What!

BARONESS: What do you mean, you old wicked man, insulting Nurse in this fashion?

BARON: You—*you*—you, sir! If you speak I will cut you down. The double shame, the double blasphemy! Ah! Leave from my sight—go—don't stir, sir, till you answer.

DR FOULES: May I ask, Nurse, if I am to congratulate you on your banns?

NURSE: I should think you have no need to ask. I am ready to die. I am so mortified and ashamed.

BAKER: Hello—I am only the mote in the eye of the Church, am I? Oh uncle, uncle!

DR FOULES: Then it is a mistake?

NURSE: Worse. It is a mean, base contrivance to trap me. I knew nothing of these banns—I could have dropped. He knows I wouldn't marry him—no, not if—not if——

BAKER: You died in a ditch with your shoes on. I'm undone this time, curse it. Uncle, have a pound of flesh, will you, instead? I could spare a pound and a half, cut judiciously.

BARON: What do you say, sir?

BAKER: I'm inviting him to have his pound of flesh, instead of his two hundred pounds of money. Though it's dear meat, I own.

NURSE: What do you mean, Mr Bowers?

BAKER: I owe him £180, and he'll foreclose on our house in a couple of months. Then goodbye my bakery, and they cart my old mother to a lunatic asylum, though she's no more mad than I am.

BARONESS: And what have you done with the money?

BAKER: Paid some of my debts, Baroness—and some of it I have—as it were, eaten. So in a pound of flesh he'd get his money glorified.

BARON: What do you say, sir?

MR WILCOX: I say nothing.

CURTAIN

SCENE II

The vicarage garden wall, under which runs the path. RACHEL *looks over the wall; enter* HARRY.

RACHEL: All by yourself? Where's the others?

HARRY: Stopping.

RACHEL: Did they give my father's banns out?

HARRY: His'n an' thine.

RACHEL: What! Mine! Why, I told Job Arthur as I wouldn't have him.

HARRY: 'Appen so.

RACHEL: I did. An' he's never told the Baron. Whatever shall I do?

HARRY: What?

RACHEL: You don't believe as I told him.

HARRY: I believe nowt.

RACHEL: But I did, an' he's agreed. And did they ask my father and Nurse?

HARRY: Yes.

RACHEL: Oh—but I shan't have him—I shan't. The Baron'll give it me—but I shan't have him. You needn't believe me, if you don't want to.

HARRY: When did ter tell Job Arthur?

RACHEL: Yesterday. An' he was glad. He doesn't really care for me.

HARRY: Are ter having me on?

RACHEL: May I be struck dead this minute if I am.

HARRY: An' what shall ter do?

RACHEL: I don't know—go to Derby. Perhaps I'll learn to be a nurse.

HARRY: She's marryin' thy father.

RACHEL *(melting into tears)*: Don't—tha's hurt me enough. *(Dashing away her tears.)* Well, I must go in and see to the dinner. Then I'll tell the Baron, and have my head bitten off. *(She turns to go.)*

HARRY: Are ter sure tha told Job Arthur?

RACHEL: Go and ask him.

HARRY : There's no tellin' what tha does.

RACHEL : No—there isn't—for the simple reason that I've built my house on the sand.

HARRY : How dost mean?

RACHEL : You know right enough. Well, I'll go an' warm th' rice pudding up.

HARRY : Rachel—dost care for me?

RACHEL : You'll make me wild in a minute.

HARRY : Rachel—dunna go—it's that lonely.

RACHEL : I s'll have to go and put that pudding in.

HARRY : Come down here first—a minute.

RACHEL : Come you up here.

HARRY *(climbing up)* : Rachel.

RACHEL : What?

HARRY : It seems that quiet-like—dunna go an' leave me. I go rummagin' down i' the loose ground, to look at th' coffin.

RACHEL : Do you?

HARRY : I do. I feel as if I should have to get at her an' mak' her speak. I canna stand this dead o'night quiet.

RACHEL : No.

HARRY : Comin' out of church into this sunshine's like goin' in a cinematograph show. Things jumps about in a flare of light, an' you expect it every minute to go out an' be pitch dark. All the shoutin' an' singin', an' yet there's a sort of quiet, Rachel.

RACHEL : Never mind—it will be so for a bit.

HARRY : I canna be by myself, though, I canna.

RACHEL : There are plenty of people.

HARRY : Nay, I non want 'em.

RACHEL : Only Nurse.

HARRY : Nor her neither—never.

RACHEL : 'Appen so.

HARRY : Tha doesna believe me?

RACHEL : "I believe nowt."

HARRY : I wish I may drop dead this minute if I ever did care for her.

RACHEL *(smiling)* : You *thought* you did?

HARRY : 'Appen I did think so.

RACHEL : I know you did.

HARRY : But 'er knows nowt about me, like thee.

RACHEL: No.

HARRY: Shall ter ha'e me, Rachel?

RACHEL: You want me?

HARRY: Let us be married afore the week's out, Rachel. Dunna leave me by mysen.

RACHEL: Are you in a hurry now, at the last pinch?

HARRY: Shall ter, Rachel?

RACHEL: Yes. *(He kisses her.)*

MR HEMSTOCK *(entering)*: I should ha thought you'd more about you than to be kissin' there where everybody can see you—an' to-day.

RACHEL: There's nobody but you.

MR HEMSTOCK: You don't know who there is.

RACHEL: And I don't care. We're going to be married directly.

MR HEMSTOCK: It'll look nice, that will—his mother buried yester-day.

HARRY: It ma'es no difference to her, does it?

MR HEMSTOCK: Tha'rt a fawce un, Rachel. Tha's contrived it, after a'. Tha'rt a fawce un, an' no mistake. But tha's got to come to the Baron.

RACHEL: What for?

MR HEMSTOCK: Nay, dunna ask me. Tha'd better look sharp. Ma'e thy heels crack.

RACHEL. What's up now, I wonder?

They go out.

CURTAIN

S C E N E   I I I

The church porch.

BARON: Do not speak, sir. You have vilified me, you have held up the Church to ridicule.

MR WILCOX: I can speak, can't I?

BARON: Do not speak, you shall not, do not speak. We will not hear your voice. You are a blasphemer.

MR WILCOX: I can't see but what a Methodist's as good as a Church, whatever. What have I done, what have I done?

BARONESS : What have you done!

MR WILCOX : Whatever anybody says, there's nobody can say I've never done anything as wan't right.

BARON : What, sir, what——

BAKER : Here's Rachel.

SUSY : I'll bet it's her doin's. She's the deepest I ever met, bar none.

BARON : Rachel?

RACHEL : Yes, Baron.

BARON : Who wrote to see the letter of the banns for your father and Nurse?

MR WILCOX : I did.

BARON : Scoundrel! Impostor!

NURSE : You had not the slightest justification for it.

DR FOULES : Surely, Nurse, you are flattered. A woman loves a peremptory wooing.

MR WILCOX : You accepted me on Friday night, Nurse, you know you did.

NURSE : I did no such thing.

BAKER : Now, Rachel, speak up. I say you've refused me——

RACHEL : So I have.

BAKER : Of course. And I forgot to take the banns back.

RACHEL : That's your lookout.

BARON : Rachel! Ah, insolent!

BAKER : Now, my case settled—did Nurse accept your father? Of course not.

RACHEL : She did.

MR WILCOX : There you are.

NURSE : I did not. I would not demean myself. I did not.

BARONESS : This is very funny, Nurse.

BARON : I have spoken the banns.

MR WILCOX : Come now, Nurse.

NURSE : You horrid, hateful old man. You know you worked yourself into a state, I thought you were delirious, and I had to promise anything.

MR WILCOX : A promise is a promise.

SUSY : Of all the deep-uns, Rachel, you cap all.

RACHEL : What's it to do with me?

NURSE : You pestered and pestered and pestered me.

DR FOULES : All's fair in love and war, Nurse.

BARON : What were the exact words?

RACHEL : "Yes, yes. I'll marry you—if you'll settle down now and go to sleep."

NURSE : Why! What! You are an underhand thing.

RACHEL : What if I did happen to hear?

NURSE : You were listening!

RACHEL : I could hear it all.

NURSE : How hateful, how hateful!

BARON : I do not understand—explain.

NURSE : He was shamming——

MR WILCOX : She's had me on a string——

RACHEL : She's sniffed at him for months, wondering whether or not to lick him up.

DR FOULES : The debatable tit-bit.

BARON : I will understand this matter. Speak, Nurse.

NURSE : He shammed fever, delirium—and to comfort him, to soothe him, I said I would marry him. I thought he was raving. And I would not marry him—I'd rather beg in the streets.

MR WILCOX : Oh, but Nurse, Nurse, look here.

BARON : Silence, sir, silence. You are a base, malingering pulamiting wretch.

RACHEL : Well, she came to see him often enough, and stopped long enough——

BARONESS : You cannot, Baron, blame the man for everything.

DR FOULES : A man who was delirious in fever on Friday night would hardly be disporting himself at church on Sunday morning——

MR WILCOX : I'm not disporting myself.

BARONESS : I don't know. It's not much, and there are still miracles.

DR FOULES : Surely miracles are not wasted on—Methodists, Baroness?

BARONESS : I do not know—I do not know. Rachel, did you put the pudding to warm?

RACHEL : Yes'm.

BARONESS : Then it's burnt to a cinder.

BARON : You, sir, you Wilcox, are a base scoundrel.

MR WILCOX : She shall pay for this.

NURSE : I must have it contradicted—I must.

BAKER : I will contradict it, Nurse.

DR FOULES : And I.

MR HEMSTOCK : And me.

HARRY : An' me.

BARONESS : But I'm not so sure——

BARON : Enough, enough. I am again a disgrace and a laughing stock. You, sir, you Wilcox——

MR WILCOX : What, Baron von Ruge?

BARON : You—you—you are a scoundrel.

BAKER : It's old news.

BARON : I withdraw and refute these double banns next Sunday.

MR WILCOX : Not with my consent.

BARON : Do not speak. And in the public paper must be refutation.

NURSE : Oh, isn't it dreadful!

SUSY : Folks shouldn't shilly-shally.

BARON : And then—I have done.

DR FOULES : Perhaps you can say there was a mistake. Substitute my name for that of Mr Wilcox.

BAKER : All's fair in love and war. Substitute Mrs Smalley's name for Rachel's.

RACHEL : A change for the better is always welcome. Substitute Harry Hemstock for Job Arthur Bowers.

BARON : This is madness and insult.

DR FOULES : It is deadly earnest, Baron. Nurse, will you be asked in church with me next Sunday?

BAKER : Susy, will you be asked in church with me next Sunday?

HARRY : Rachel, shall you be axed in church with me next Sunday?

BARON : Enough, enough! Go away, I will suffer no more of this!

BARONESS : Such wicked frivolity! Rachel, go home at once to see to that pudding.

DR FOULES : We are most deeply serious, Nurse, are we not?

BAKER : Susy, are we not?

HARRY : Rachel, are we not?

RACHEL : Chorus of ladies, "Yes"!

NURSE AND SUSY : Chorus of ladies, "Yes"!

DR FOULES : Millicent Broadbanks—Arthur William Foules.

BAKER : Job Arthur Bowers—Susan Smalley, née Hemstock, widow.

HARRY : Rachel Wilcox—Harry Hemstock.

BARON : Away! Away!

DR FOULES : Baron, you should play Duke to our "As You Like It"

BARON : I do not like it, I will not.

SUSY : Then lump it.

MR WILCOX : I call it scandalous, going on like this.

RACHEL : Like it or lump it, Father, like it or lump it.

DR FOULES : You accept me, Nurse?

NURSE : I do, Doctor. *(He kisses her hand.)*

BAKER : You accept me, Susan?

SUSY : This once, Job Arthur. *(He kisses her cheek.)*

RACHEL *(after a moment)* : Come on here, Harry. *(They kiss on the mouth.)*

BARON : Go away from here. You shall not pollute my church.

BARONESS : It is disgraceful.

MR WILCOX : They want horsewhipping, every one of them.

MR HEMSTOCK : Well—I must say——

DR FOULES : It's "As You Like It"

BAKER : It's "As You *Lump* It", Hezekiah.

CURTAIN

A Collier's Friday Night

A PLAY IN THREE ACTS

(About 1909 – first published 1934)

CHARACTERS

MRS LAMBERT
LAMBERT
NELLIE LAMBERT
ERNEST LAMBERT
MAGGIE PEARSON
GERTIE COOMBER
BEATRICE WYLD
BARKER
CARLIN

The action of the play takes place in the kitchen of the Lamberts'
house.

ACT I

*The kitchen or living-room of a working-man's house. At the back
the fireplace, with a large fire burning. On the left, on the oven
side of the stove, a* WOMAN *of some fifty-five years sits in a
wooden rocking-chair, reading. Behind her and above her, in
the recess made by the fireplace, four shelves of books, the
shelf-covers being of green serge, with woollen ball fringe, and
the books being ill-assorted school books, with an edition of
Lessing, florid in green and gilt, but tarnished. On the left, a
window looking on a garden where the rain is dripping
through the first twilight. Under the window, a sofa, the bed
covered with red chintz. By the side of the window, on the
wall near the ceiling, a quiver clothes-horse is outspread with
the cotton articles which have been ironed, hanging to air.
Under the outspread clothes is the door which communicates
with the scullery and with the yard. On the right side of the
fireplace, in the recess equivalent to that where the bookshelves stand, a long narrow window, and below it, a low,
brown, fixed cupboard, whose top forms a little sideboard, on
which stand a large black enamel box of oil-colours, and a
similar japanned box of water-colours, with Reeve's silver
trade-mark. There is also on the cupboard top a tall glass jar
containing ragged pink chrysanthemums. On the right is a
bookcase upon a chest of drawers. This piece of furniture is of
stained polished wood in imitation of mahogany. The upper
case is full of books, seen through the two flimsy glass doors: a
large set of the* World's Famous Literature *in dark green at the
top—then on the next shelf prize-books in calf and gold, and
imitation soft leather poetry-books, and a Nuttall's dictionary
and Cassell's French, German and Latin dictionaries. On each
side of the bookcase are prints from water-colours, large,
pleasing and well framed in oak. Between the little brown
cupboard and the bookcase, an arm-chair, small, round, with
many little staves; a comfortable chair such as is seen in many
working-class kitchens; it has a red chintz cushion. There is*

*another Windsor chair on the other side of the bookcase. Over
the mantelpiece, which is high, with brass candlesticks and
two "Coronation" tumblers in enamel, hangs a picture of
Venice, from one of Stead's Christmas Numbers—nevertheless,
satisfactory enough.*

The WOMAN *in the rocking-chair is dressed in black, and wears
a black sateen apron. She wears spectacles, and is reading*
The New Age. *Now and again she looks over her paper at
a piece of bread which stands on a hanging bar before the fire,
propped up by a fork, toasting. There is a little pile of toast on
a plate on the boiler hob beside a large saucepan; the kettle
and a brown teapot are occupying the oven-top near the*
WOMAN. *The table is laid for tea, with four large breakfast-
cups in dark-blue willow-pattern, and plates similar. It is an
oval mahogany table, large enough to seat eight comfortably.
The* WOMAN *sees the piece of bread smoking, and takes it from
the fire. She butters it and places it on the plate on the hob,
after which she looks out of the window, then, taking her
paper, sits down again in her place.*

SOMEONE *passes the long narrow window, only the head
being seen, then quite close to the large window on the left.
There is a noise as the outer door opens and is shut, then the
kitchen door opens, and a* GIRL *enters. She is tall and thin, and
wears a long grey coat and a large blue hat, quite plain. After
glancing at the table, she crosses the room, drops her two
exercise-books on the wooden chair by the bookcase, saying:*

NELLIE LAMBERT : Oh! I am weary.

MOTHER : You are late.

NELLIE: I know I am. It's Agatha Karton—she is a great gaby.
There's always something wrong with her register, and old
Tommy gets in such a fever, the great kid.

　　　*She takes off her hat, and going to the door on right, stands
in the doorway, hanging it up with her coat on the pegs in
the passage, just by the doorway.*

And I'm sure the youngsters have been regular little demons; I
could have killed them.

MOTHER : I've no doubt they felt the same towards you, poor little
wretches.

NELLIE *(with a short laugh)*: I'll bet they did, for I spanked one or two of 'em well.

MOTHER: Trust you, trust you! You'll be getting the mothers if you're not careful.

NELLIE *(contemptuously)*: I had one old cat this afternoon. But I told her straight. I said: "If your Johnny, or Sammy, or whatever he is, is a nuisance, he'll be smacked, and there's an end of it." She was mad, but I told her straight; I didn't care. She can go to Tommy if she likes: I know he'll fuss her round, but I'll tell *him* too. Pah! he fusses the creatures up!—I *would*!

She comes towards the table, pushing up her hair with her fingers. It is heavy and brown, and has been flattened by her hat. She glances at herself in the little square mirror which hangs from a nail under the right end of the mantelpiece, a mere unconscious glance which betrays no feeling, and is just enough to make her negligently touch her hair again. She turns a trifle fretfully to the table.

NELLIE: Is there only potted meat? You know I can't bear it.

MOTHER *(conciliatorily)*: Why, I thought you'd like it, a raw day like this—and with toast.

NELLIE: You know I don't. Why didn't you get some fruit?—a little tin of apricots——

MOTHER: I thought you'd be sick of apricots—I know Ernest is.

NELLIE: Well, I'm not—you know I'm not. Pappy potted meat!

She sits down on the sofa wearily. Her MOTHER pours out two cups of tea, and replaces the pot on the hob.

MOTHER: Won't you have some, then?

NELLIE *(petulantly)*: No, I don't want it.

The MOTHER stands irresolute a moment, then she goes out. NELLIE reaches over to the bookshelves and takes a copy of The Scarlet Pimpernel, *which she opens on the table, and reads, sipping her tea but not eating. In a moment or two she glances up, as the MOTHER passes the window and enters the scullery. There is the sound of the opening of a tin.*

NELLIE: Have you fetched some?—Oh, you are a sweetling!

The MOTHER enters, with a little glass dish of small tinned apricots. They begin tea.

MOTHER: Polly Goddard says her young man got hurt in the pit this morning.

NELLIE : Oh—is it much? *(She looks up from her book.)*

MOTHER : One of his feet crushed. Poor Polly's very sad. What made her tell me was Ben Goddard going by. I didn't know he was at work again, but he was just coming home, and I asked her about him, and then she went on to tell me of her young man. They're all coming home from Selson, so I expect your father won't be long.

NELLIE : Goodness!—I hope he'll let us get our tea first.

MOTHER : Well, you were late. If he once gets seated in the Miner's Arms there's no telling when he comes.

NELLIE : I don't care when he does, so long as he doesn't come yet.

MOTHER : Oh, it's all very well!

They both begin to read as they eat. After a moment another girl runs past the window and enters. She is a plump, fair girl, pink and white. She has just run across from the next house

GERTIE COOMBER : Hello, my duck, and how are you?

NELLIE *(looking up)* : Oh, alright, my bird.

GERTIE : Friday to-night. No Eddie for you! Oh, poor Nellie! Aren't I glad, though! *(She snaps her fingers quaintly.)*

The MOTHER *laughs.*

NELLIE : Mean cat!

GERTIE *(giggling)* : No, I'm not a mean cat. But I like Friday night; we can go jinking off up town and wink at the boys. I like market night. *(She puts her head on one side in a peculiar, quaint, simple fashion.)*

The MOTHER *laughs.*

NELLIE : *You* wink! If she so much as sees a fellow who'd speak to her, she gets behind me and stands on one foot and then another.

GERTIE : I don't! No, I don't, Nellie Lambert. I go like this : "Oh, good evening, *how* are you? I'm sure I'm very pleased——" *(She says this in a very quaint "prunes-and-prisms" manner, with her chin in the air and her hand extended. At the end she giggles.)*

The MOTHER, *with her cup in her hand, leans back and laughs.* NELLIE, *amused in spite of herself, smiles shortly.*

NELLIE : You are a daft object! What about last week, when David Thompson——

GERTIE *puts her hand up and flips the air with affected contempt.*

GERTIE : David Thompson! A bacon sawyer! Ph!

NELLIE : What a name! Not likely. Mrs Grocock! *(She giggles.)* Oh dear no, nothing short of Mrs Carooso.

> *She holds back the skirts of her long pinafore with one hand and affects the Gibson bend.*

MOTHER *(laughing heartily)*: Caruso! Caruso! A great fat fellow——!

GERTIE : Besides, a collier! I'm not going to wash stinking pit-things.

NELLIE : You don't know what you'll do yet, my girl. I never knew such cheek! I should think you want somebody grand, you do.

GERTIE : I do that. Somebody who'll say, "Yes, dear. Oh *yes*, dear! Certainly, certainly!"

> *She simpers across the room, then giggles.*

NELLIE : You soft cat, you! But look here, Gert, you'll get paid out, treating Bernard Hufton as you do.

GERTIE *(suddenly irritated)*: Oh, I can't abide him. I always feel as if I could smack his face. He thinks himself slikey. He always makes my——

> *A head passes the narrow side window.*

Oh, glory! there's Mr Lambert. I'm off!

> *She draws back against the bookcase. A man passes the large window. The door opens and he enters. He is a man of middling stature, a miner, black from the pit. His shoulders are pushed up because he is cold. He has a bushy iron-grey beard. He takes from his pocket a tin bottle and a knotted "snap" bag—his food bag of dirty calico—and puts them with a bang on the table. Then he drags his heavily-shod feet to the door on right; he limps slightly, one leg being shorter than the other. He hangs up his coat and cap in the passage and comes back into the living-room. No one speaks. He wears a grey-and-black neckerchief and, being coatless, his black arms are bare to the elbows, where end the loose dirty sleeves of his flannel singlet. The MOTHER rises and goes to the scullery, carrying the heavy saucepan. The man gets hold of the table and pulls it nearer the fire, away from his daughter.*

NELLIE : Why can't you leave the table where it was! We don't *want* it stuck on top of the fire.

FATHER : Ah dun, if you dunna.

He drags up his arm-chair and sits down at the table full in front of the fire.

'An yer got a drink for me?

The MOTHER *comes and pours out a cup of tea, then goes back to the scullery.*

It's a nice thing as a man as comes home from th' pit parched up canna ha'e a drink got 'im. *(He speaks disagreeably.)*

MOTHER: Oh, you needn't begin! I know you've been stopping, drinking.

FATHER: Dun yer?—Well, yer know too much, then. You wiser than them as knows, you are!

There is a general silence, as if the three listeners were shrugging their shoulders in contempt and anger. The FATHER *pours out his tea into his saucer, blows it and sucks it up.* NELLIE *looks up from her book and glowers at him with ferocity.* GERTIE *puts her hand before her mouth and giggles behind his back at the noise. He does not drink much, but sets the cup back in the saucer and lays his grimed arms wearily along the table. The* MOTHER *enters with a plate of cabbage.*

MOTHER: Here, that's a clean cloth.

She does not speak unkindly.

FATHER *(brutally)*: You should put a dotty (dirty) 'un on, then.

The MOTHER *takes a newspaper and spreads it over the cloth before him. She kneels at the oven, takes out a stew-jar, and puts meat and gravy on the plate with the cabbage, and sets it before him. He does not begin at once to eat. The* MOTHER *puts back her chair against the wall and sits down.*

MOTHER: Are your trousers wet?

FATHER *(as he eats)*: A bit.

MOTHER: Then why don't you take them off?

FATHER *(in a tone of brutal authority)*: Fetch my breeches an' wa's'coat down, Nellie.

NELLIE *(continuing to read, her hands pushed in among her hair)*: You can ask me properly.

The FATHER *pushes his beard forward and glares at her with futile ferocity. She reads on.* GERTIE COOMBER, *at the back, shifts from one foot to the other, then coughs behind her hand as if she had a little cold. The* MOTHER *rises and goes out by door on right.*

FATHER: You lazy, idle bitch, you let your mother go!

NELLIE *(shrugging her shoulders)*: You can shut up. *(She speaks with cold contempt.)*

> GERTIE *sighs audibly. The tension of the scene will not let her run home.* NELLIE *looks up, flushed, carefully avoiding her father.*

NELLIE: Aren't you going to sit down, Gert?

GERTIE: No, I'm off.

NELLIE: Wait a bit and I'll come across with you. I don't want to stop *here*.

> The FATHER *stirs in his chair with rage at the implication. The* MOTHER *comes downstairs and enters with a pair of black trousers, from which the braces are trailing, and a black waist-coat lined with cream and red lining. She drops them against her husband's chair.*

MOTHER *(kindly, trying to restore the atmosphere)*: Aren't you going to sit down, Gertie? Go on the stool.

> GERTIE *takes a small stool on the right side of fireplace, and sits toying with the bright brass tap of the boiler. The* MOTHER *goes out again on right, and enters immediately with five bread tins and a piece of lard paper. She stands on the hearth-rug greasing the tins. The* FATHER *kicks off his great boots and stands warming his trousers before the fire, turning them and warming them thoroughly.*

GERTIE: Are they cold, Mr Lambert?

FATHER: They are that! Look you, they steaming like a sweating hoss.

MOTHER: Get away, man! The driest thing in the house would smoke if you held it in front of the fire like that.

FATHER *(shortly)*: Ah, I know I'm a liar. I knowed it to begin wi'.

NELLIE *(much irritated)*: Isn't he a nasty-tempered kid!

GERTIE: But those front bedrooms are clammy.

FATHER *(gratified)*: They h'are, Gertie, they h'are.

GERTIE *(turning to avoid* NELLIE'S *contempt and pottering the fire)*: I know the things I bring down from ours, they fair damp in a day.

FATHER: They h'are, Gertie, I know it. And I wonder how 'er'd like to clap 'er arse into wet breeches.

> He goes scrambling off to door on right, trailing his breeches.

NELLIE *(fiercely)* : Father!

    GERTIE *puts her face into her hands and laughs with a half-audible laugh that shakes her body.*

I can't think what you've got to laugh at, Gertie Coomber.

    The MOTHER, *glancing at her irate daughter, laughs also. She moves aside the small wooden rocking-chair, and, drawing forth a great panchion of dough from the corner under the book-shelves, begins to fill the bread tins. She sets them on the hearth—which has no fender, the day being Friday, when the steel fender is put away, after having been carefully cleaned to be saved for Saturday afternoon. The* FATHER *enters, the braces of his trousers dangling, and drops the heavy moleskin pit breeches in corner on right.*

NELLIE : I wonder why you can't put them in the scullery; the smell of them's hateful.

FATHER : You mun put up wi' it, then. If you were i' th' pit you'd niver put your nose up at them again.

    He sits down and recommences eating. The sound further irritates his daughter, who again pushes her fingers into her hair, covering her ears with her palms. Her father notices, and his manners become coarser. NELLIE *rises, leaving her book open on the table.*

NELLIE : Come on, Gert! *(She speaks with contemptuous impatience.)*

    The FATHER *watches them go out. He lays his arms along the newspaper, wearily.*

FATHER : I'm too tired ter h'eat.

MOTHER *(sniffing, and hardening a little)* : I wonder why you always have to go and set her off in a tantrum as soon as you come in.

FATHER : A cheeky bitch; 'er wants a good slap at th' side o' th' mouth!

MOTHER *(incensed)* : If you've no more sense than that, I don't wonder——

FATHER : You don't wonder—you don't wonder! No, I know you don't wonder. It's you as eggs 'em on against me, both on em.

MOTHER *(scornfully)* : You set them against yourself. You do your best for it, every time they come in.

FATHER : Do I, do I! I set 'em against me, do I? I'm going to stand 'em orderin' me about, an' turnin' their noses up, am I?

MOTHER : You shouldn't make them turn their noses up, then. If you do your best for it, what do you expect?

FATHER : A jumped-up monkey! An' it's you as 'as made 'em like it, the pair on 'em. There's neither of 'em but what treats me like a dog. I'm not daft! I'm not blind! I can see it.

MOTHER : If you're so clever at seeing it, I should have thought you'd have sense enough not to begin it and carry it on as you do.

FATHER : Me begin it! When do I begin it? You niver hear me say a word to 'em, till they've snapped at me as if I was a—as if I was a—— No, it's you as puts 'em on in. It's you, you blasted——

He bangs the table with his fist. The MOTHER *puts the bread in the oven, from which she takes a rice pudding; then she sits down to read. He glares across the table, then goes on eating. After a little while he pushes the plate from him. The* MOTHER *affects not to notice for a moment.*

'An yer got any puddin'?

MOTHER : Have you finished?

She rises, takes a plate and, crouching on the hearth, gives him his pudding. She glances at the clock, and clears the tea-things from her daughter's place. She puts another piece of toast down, there remaining only two pieces on the plate.

FATHER *(looking at the rice pudding)* : Is this what you'n had?

MOTHER : No; we had nothing.

FATHER : No, I'll bet you non 'ad this baby pap.

MOTHER : No, I had nothing for a change, and Nellie took her dinner.

FATHER *(eating unwillingly)* : Is there no other puddin' as you could 'a made?

MOTHER : Goodness, man, are you so mightily particular about your belly? This is the first rice pudding you've had for goodness knows how long, and—— No, I couldn't make any other. In the first place, it's Friday, and in the second, I'd nothing to make it with.

FATHER : You wouldna ha'e, not for me. But if you 'a wanted——

MOTHER *(interrupting)* : You needn't say any more. The fact of the matter is, somebody's put you out at the pit, and you come home to vent your spleen on us.

FATHER *(shouting)*: You're a liar, you're a liar! A man comes home after a hard day's work to folks as 'as never a word to say to 'im, 'as shuts up the minute 'e enters the house, as 'ates the sight of 'im as soon as 'e comes in th' room——!

MOTHER *(with fierceness)*: We've had quite enough, we've had quite enough! Our Ernest'll be in in a minute and we're not going to have this row going on; he's coming home all the way from Derby, trailing from college to a house like this, tired out with study and all this journey: we're not going to have it, I tell you.

> *Her husband stares at her dumbly, betwixt anger and shame and sorrow, of which an undignified rage is predominant. The* MOTHER *carries out some pots to the scullery, re-enters, takes the slice of toast and butters it.*

FATHER: It's about time as we had a light on it; I canna see what I'm eatin'.

> *The* MOTHER *puts down the toast on the hob, and having fetched a dustpan from the scullery, goes out on right to the cellar to turn on the gas and to bring coals. She is heard coming up the steps heavily. She mends the fire, and then lights the gas at a brass pendant hanging over the table. Directly after there enters a young man of twenty-one, tall and broad, pale, clean-shaven, with the brownish hair of the "ginger" class, which is all ruffled when he has taken off his cap, after having pulled various books from his pockets and put them on the little cupboard top. He takes off his coat at door right as his sister has done.*

ERNEST *(blowing slightly through pursed lips)*: Phew! It is hot in here!

FATHER *(bluntly, but amiably)*: Hot! It's non hot! I could do wi' it ten times hotter.

MOTHER: Oh, you! You've got, as I've always said, a hide like a hippopotamus. You ought to have been a salamander.

FATHER: Oh ah, I know tha'll ha'e summat ter say.

MOTHER: Is it raining now, Ernest?

ERNEST: Just a drizzle in the air, like a thick mist.

MOTHER: Ay, isn't it sickening? You'd better take your boots off.

ERNEST *(sitting in his sister's place on the sofa)*: Oh, they're not wet.

MOTHER: They must be damp.

ERNEST: No, they're not. There's a pavement all the way. Here, look at my rose! One of the girls in Coll. gave it me, and the tan-yard girls tried to beg it. They are brazen hussies! "Gi'e's thy flower, Sorry; gi'e's thy buttonhole"—and one of them tried to snatch it. They have a bobby down by the tan-yard brook every night now. Their talk used to be awful, and it's so dark down there, under the trees. Where's Nellie?

MOTHER: In Coombers'.

ERNEST: Give me a bit of my paper, Father. You know the leaf I want: that with the reviews of books on.

FATHER: Nay, I know nowt about reviews o' books. Here t'art. Ta'e it.

    FATHER *hands the newspaper to his son, who takes out two leaves and hands the rest back.*

ERNEST: Here you are; I only want this.

FATHER: Nay, I non want it. I mun get me washed. We s'll ha'e th' men here directly.

ERNEST: I say, Mater, another seven-and-six up your sleeve?

MOTHER: I'm sure! And in the middle of the term, too! What's it for *this* time?

ERNEST: *Piers the Ploughman*, that piffle, and two books of Horace: Quintus Horatius Flaccus, dear old chap.

MOTHER: And when have you to pay for them?

ERNEST: Well, I've ordered them, and they'll come on Tuesday. I'm sure I don't know what we wanted that Piers Ploughman for—it's sheer rot, and old Beasley could have gassed on it without making us buy it, if he'd liked. Yes, I did feel wild. Seven-and-sixpence!

FATHER: I should non get tem, then. You needna buy 'em unless you like. Dunna get 'em, then.

ERNEST: Well, I've ordered them.

FATHER: If you 'anna the money you canna 'a'e 'em, whether or not.

MOTHER: Don't talk nonsense. If he has to have them, he has. But the money you have to pay for books, and they're no good when you've done with them!—I'm sure it's really sickening, it is!

ERNEST: Oh, never mind, Little; I s'll get 'em for six shillings. Is it a worry, Mütterchen?

MOTHER: It is, but I suppose if it has to be, it has.

ERNEST: Old Beasley is an old chough. While he was lecturing this afternoon Arnold and Hinrich were playing nap; and the girls always write letters, and I went fast asleep.

FATHER: So that's what you go'n to Collige for, is it?

ERNEST (*nettled*): No, it isn't. Only old Beasley's such a dry old ass, with his lectures on Burke. He's a mumbling parson, so what do you expect?

> *The* FATHER *grunts, rises and fetches a clean new bucket from the scullery. He hangs this on the top of the boiler, and turns on the water. Then he pulls off his flannel singlet and stands stripped to the waist, watching the hot water dribble into the bucket. The pail half-filled, he goes out to the scullery on left.*

Do you know what Professor Staynes said this morning, Mother? He said I'd got an instinct for Latin—and you know he's one of the best fellows in England on the classics: edits Ovid and what-not. An instinct for Latin, he said.

MOTHER (*smiling, gratified*): Well, it's a funny thing to have an instinct for.

ERNEST: I generally get an alpha plus. That's the highest, you know, Mater. Prof. Staynes generally gives me that.

MOTHER: Your grandfather was always fond of dry reading: economics and history. But I don't know where an instinct for Latin comes from—not from the Lamberts, that's a certainty. Your Aunt Ellen would say, from the Vernons.

> *She smiles ironically as she rises to pour him another cup of tea, taking the teapot from the hob and standing it, empty, on the father's plate.*

ERNEST: Who are the Vernons?

MOTHER (*smiling*): It's a wonder your Aunt Ellen or your Aunt Eunice has never told you. . . .

ERNEST: Well, they haven't. What is it, Mütter?

MOTHER (*sniffing*): A parcel of nonsense. . . .

ERNEST: Oh, go on, Ma, you are tantalizing! You hug it like any blessed girl.

MOTHER: Yes, your Aunt Ellen always said she would claim the peacock and thistle for her crest, if ever . . .

ERNEST *(delighted)*: The Peacock and Thistle! It sounds like the name of a pub.

MOTHER: My great-great-grandfather married a Lady Vernon—so they say. As if it made any matter—a mere tale!

ERNEST: Is it a fact though, Matoushka? Why didn't you tell us before?

MOTHER *(sniffing)*: What should I repeat such——

FATHER *(shouting from the scullery, whence has come the noise of his washing)*: 'An yer put that towil ter dry?

MOTHER *(muttering)*: The towel's dry enough.

> *She goes out and is heard taking the roller towel from behind the outer door. She returns, and stands before the fire, holding the towel to dry.* ERNEST LAMBERT, *having frowned and shrugged his shoulders, is reading.*

MOTHER: I suppose you won't have that bit of rice pudding?

> *Her son looks up, reaches over and takes the brown dish from the hearth. He begins to eat from the dish.*

ERNEST: I went to the "Savoy" to-day.

MOTHER: I shouldn't go to that vegetable place. I don't believe there's any substance in it.

ERNEST: Substance! Oh, lord! I had an asparagus omelette, I believe they called it; it was too much for me! A great stodgy thing! But I like the Savoy, generally. It was——

> *Somebody comes running across the yard.* NELLIE LAMBERT *enters with a rush.*

NELLIE: Hello! have you done?

FATHER *(from the scullery)*: Are you going to shut that doo-ar! *(Shouting.)*

NELLIE *(with a quick shrug of the shoulders)*: It *is* shut. *(brightly, to her brother)* Who brought this rose? It'll just do for me. Who gave it you?—Lois?

ERNEST *(flushing)*: What do you want to know for? You're always saying "Lois". I don't care a button about Lois.

NELLIE: Keep cool, dear boy, keep cool.

> *She goes flying lightly round, clearing the table. The* FATHER, *dripping, bending forward almost double, comes hurrying from the scullery to the fire.* NELLIE *whisks by him, her long pinafore rustling.*

FATHER *(taking the towel)*: Ow (she) goes rushin' about, draughtin'

(Rubs his head, sitting on his heels very close to the fire.)

NELLIE *(smiling contemptuously, to herself)*: Poor kid!

FATHER *(having wiped his face)*: An' there isn't another man in th' kingdom as 'ud stan' i' that scullery stark naked. It's like standin' i' t'cowd watter.

MOTHER *(calmly)*: Many a man stands in a colder.

FATHER *(shortly)*: Ah, I'll back; I'll back there is! Other men's wives brings th' puncheon on to th' 'earthstone, an' gets the watter for 'em, an'——

MOTHER: Other men's wives may do: more fools them: you won't catch me.

FATHER: No, you wunna; you may back your life o' that! An' what if you 'ad to?

MOTHER: Who'd make me?

FATHER *(blustering)*: Me.

MOTHER *(laughing shortly)*: Not half a dozen such.

> *The* FATHER *grunts.* NELLIE, *having cleared the table, pushes him aside a little and lets the crumbs fall into hearth.*

FATHER: A lazy, idle, stinkin' trick!

> *She whisks the tablecloth away without speaking.*

An' tha doesna come waftin' in again when I'm washin' me, tha remembers.

ERNEST *(to his mother, who is turning the bread)*: Fancy! Swinburne's dead.

MOTHER: Yes, so I saw. But he was getting on.

FATHER *(to* NELLIE, *who has come to the boiler and is kneeling, getting a lading-can full of water)*: Here, Nellie, gie my back a wash.

> *She goes out, and comes immediately with flannel and soap. She claps the flannel on his back.*

(Wincing) Ooo! The nasty bitch!

> NELLIE *bubbles with laughter. The* MOTHER *turns aside to laugh.*

NELLIE: You great baby, afraid of a cold flannel!

> *She finishes washing his back and goes into the scullery to wash the pots. The* FATHER *takes his flannel shirt from the bookcase cupboard and puts it on, letting it hang over his trousers. Then he takes a little blue-striped cotton bag from his pit trousers' pocket and throws it on the table to his wife.*

FATHER : Count it. *(He shuffles upstairs.)*

The MOTHER *counts the money, putting it in little piles, checking it from two white papers. She leaves it on the table.* ERNEST *goes into the scullery to wash his hands and is heard talking to his sister, who is wiping the pots. A knock at the outer door.*

ERNEST : Good evening, Mr Barker.

A VOICE : Good evenin', Ernest.

A miner enters: pale, short, but well-made. He has a hard-looking head with short black hair. He lays his cap on a chair. Good evenin', Missis. 'Asn't Carlin come? Mester upstairs?

MOTHER : Yes, he'll be down in a minute. I don't expect Mr Carlin will be many minutes. Sit down, Mr Barker. How's that lad of yours?

BARKER : Well, 'e seems to be goin' on nicely, thank yer. Dixon took th' splints off last wik.

MOTHER : Oh, well, that's better. He'll be alright directly. I should think he doesn't want to go in the pit again.

BARKER: 'E doesna. 'E says 'e shall go farmin' wi' Jakes; but I shanna let 'im. It's nowt o' a sort o' job, that.

MOTHER : No, it isn't. *(Lowering her voice.)* And how's missis?

BARKER *(also lowering his voice)* : Well, I don't know. I want ter get back as soon as I'n got a few groceries an' stuff in. I sent for Mrs Smalley afore I com'n out. An' I'm come an' forgot th' market bag.

MOTHER *(going into the scullery)* : Have mine, have mine. Nay, I've got another. *(Brings him a large carpet bag with leather handles.)*

BARKER : Thank yer, Missis. I can bring it back next wik. You sure you wunna want it?

Another knock. Enter another man, fair, pale, smiling, an inconsiderable man.

CARLIN : Hgh! Tha's bested me then? Good evenin', Missis.

BARKER : Yes, I'n bet thee.

Enter the FATHER. *He has put on a turn-down collar and a black tie, and his black waistcoat is buttoned, but he wears no coat. The other men take off the large neckerchiefs, grey and white silk, in fine check, and show similar collars. The* FATHER *assumes a slight tone of superiority.*

FATHER : Well, you've arrived, then! An' 'ow's the missis by now, Joe?

BARKER : Well, I dun know, Walter. It might be any minnit.

FATHER *(sympathetically)*: Hu! We may as well set to, then, an' get it done.

> *They sit at the table, on the side of the fire.* ERNEST LAMBERT *comes in and takes an exercise-book from the shelves and begins to do algebra, using a text-book. He writes with a fountain-pen.*

CARLIN : They gran' things, them fountain-pens.

BARKER: They are that!

CARLIN : What's th' mak on it, Ernest?

ERNEST : It's an Onoto.

BARKER : Oh-ah! An' 'ow *dun* yer fill it? They says as it hold wi' a vacum.

ERNEST : It's like this: you push this down, put the nib in th' ink, and then pull it out. It's a sort of a pump.

BARKER : Um! It's a canny thing, that!

CARLIN : It is an' a'.

FATHER : Yes, it's a very good idea. *(He is slightly condescending.)*

MOTHER : Look at the bread, Ernest.

ERNEST : Alright, Mater.

> *She goes upstairs, it being tacitly understood that she shall not know how much money falls to her husband's share as chief "butty" in the weekly reckoning.*

BARKER : Is it counted?

FATHER : Yes. It's alright, Ernest?

ERNEST *(not looking up)*: Yes.

> *They begin to reckon, first putting aside the wages of their day men; then the* FATHER *and* BARKER *take four-and-three-pence, as equivalent to* CARLIN'S *rent, which has been stopped; then the* FATHER *gives a coin each, dividing the money in that way. It is occasionally a puzzling process and needs the Ready Reckoner from the shelf behind.*

END OF ACT I

ACT II

Scene, as before: the men are just finishing reckoning.
BARKER and CARLIN, talking in a mutter, put their money in their pockets. ERNEST LAMBERT is drawing a circle with a pair of compasses. CARLIN rises.

CARLIN: Well, I might as well be shiftin'.
BARKER: Ay, I mun get off.
Enter NELLIE, who has finished washing the pots, drying her hands on a small towel. She crosses to the mirror hanging at the right extremity of the mantelpiece.
CARLIN: Well, Nellie!
NELLIE *(very amiably, even gaily)*: Good evening, Mr Carlin. Just off?
CARLIN: Yes—ah mun goo.
BARKER: An' 'ow's th' instrument by now, Nellie?
NELLIE: The instrument? Oh, the piano! Ours is a tinny old thing. Oh, yes, you're learning. How are you getting on?
BARKER: Oh, we keep goin' on, like. 'Ave you got any fresh music?
FATHER: Ah, I bet 'er 'as. Ow's gerrin' some iv'ry day or tow.
NELLIE: I've got some Grieg—lovely! Hard, though. It is funny— ever so funny.
BARKER: An' yer iver 'eared that piece "The Maiden's Prayer"?
NELLIE *(turning aside and laughing)*: Yes. Do you like it? It is pretty, isn't it?
BARKER: I 'ad that for my last piece.
NELLIE: Did you? Can you play it?
BARKER *(with some satisfaction)*: Yes, I can do it pretty fair. 'An yer got th' piece?
NELLIE: Yes. Will you play it for us? Half a minute.
She finishes stroking her hair up with her side-combs, and, taking the matches from the mantelpiece, leads the way to the door.
Come on.
FATHER: Yes, step forward, Joe.

BARKER *goes out after* NELLIE. *Through the open door comes the crashing sound of the miner's banging through* The Maiden's Prayer *on an old sharp-toned piano.* CARLIN *stands listening, and shakes his head at the* FATHER, *who smiles back, glancing at the same time nervously at his son, who has buried his hands in his hair.*

CARLIN: Well, are ter comin' down, George? *(He moves towards the door.)*

FATHER *(lighting his pipe—between the puffs)*: In about quarter of an hour, Fred.

CARLIN: Good night, then. Good night, Ernest. *(He goes out.)*

The MOTHER *is heard coming downstairs. She glances at her son, and shuts the passage door. Then she hurries to the oven and turns the bread. As she moves away again her husband thrusts out his hand and gives her something.*

FATHER *(going towards the passage door)*: I know it's a bad wik. *(He goes out.)*

MOTHER *(counts the money he has given her, gives a little rapid clicking with her tongue on the roof of her mouth, tossing her head up once)*: Twenty-eight shillings! *(Counts again.)* Twenty-eight shillings! *(To her son.)* And what was the cheque?

ERNEST *(looking up, with a frown of irritation)*: Eight pounds one and six, and stoppages.

MOTHER: And he gives me a frowsty twenty-eight . . . and I've got his club to pay, and you a pair of boots. . . . Twenty-eight! . . . I wonder if he thinks the house is kept on nothing. . . . I'll take good care he gets nothing extra, I will, too. . . . I knew it, though—I knew he'd been running up a nice score at the Tunns'—that's what it is. There's rent, six-and-six, and clubs seven shillings, besides insurance and gas and everything else. I wonder how he thinks it's done—I wonder if he thinks we live on air?

ERNEST *(looking up with pain and irritation)*: Oh, Mater, don't bother! What's the good? If you worry for ever it won't make it any more.

MOTHER *(softened, conquering her distress)*: Oh, yes, it's all very well for you, but if I didn't worry what would become of us I should like to know?

GERTIE COOMBER *runs in. She is wearing a large blue felt*

hat and a Norfolk costume; she is carrying a round basket. From the parlour comes the sound of Grieg's Anitra's Tanz, *and then* Ase's Tod, *played well, with real sympathy.*

GERTIE *(with a little shy apprehension)*: Who's in the parlour?

MOTHER: It's only Mr Barker. *(Smiling slightly.)* He wanted to show Nellie how well he could play "The Maiden's Prayer".

    GERTIE *suddenly covers her mouth and laughs.*

GERTIE *(still laughing)*: He, he! I'll bet it was a thump! Pomp! Pomp! *(Makes a piano-thumping gesture.)* Did you hear it, Ernest?

ERNEST *(not looking up)*: Infernal shindy.

    GERTIE *puts up her shoulders and giggles, looking askance at the student who, she knows, is getting tired of interruptions.*

MOTHER: Yes, I wish he'd go—*(almost whispering)*—and his wife is expecting to go to bed any minute.

    GERTIE *puts her lower lip between her teeth and looks serious. The music stops.* BARKER *and* NELLIE *are heard talking, then the* FATHER. *There is a click of boots on the tiled passage and they enter.*

NELLIE: What did you think of Mr Barker, Mother?—don't you think it's good? I think it's wonderful—don't you, Ernest?

ERNEST *(grunting)*: Um—it is.

    GERTIE COOMBER *suddenly hides behind her friend and laughs.*

MOTHER *(to* BARKER*)*: Yes, I'm sure you get on wonderfully—wonderfully—considering.

BARKER: Yes, ah's non done so bad, I think.

FATHER: Tha 'asna, Joe, tha 'asna, indeed!

MOTHER: Don't forget the bag, Mr Barker—I know you'll want it.

BARKER: Oh, thank yer. Well, I mun goo. Tha'rt comin' down, George?

FATHER: Yes, I'm comin' down, Joe. I'll just get my top-coat on, an' then—— *(He struggles awkwardly into his overcoat.)*

    BARKER *resumes his grey muffler.*

BARKER: Well, good night, everybody; good night, Ernest—an' thank yer, Missis.

MOTHER: I hope things will be—*(She nods significantly.)*—alright.

BARKER: Ah, thank yer, I hope it will. I expect so: there's no reason why it shouldn't. Good night.

ALL : Good night, Mr Barker.

The FATHER *and* BARKER *go out. Immediately* NELLIE *flings her arms round* GERTIE'S *neck.*

NELLIE : Save me, Gert, save me! I thought I was done for that time. . . . I gave myself up! The poor piano! Mother, it'll want tuning now, if it never did before.

MOTHER *(with slight asperity, half-amused)* : It may want at it, then.

GERTIE *(laughing)* : You're done, Nellie, you're done brown! If it's like dropping a saucepan-lid—no—you've got to put up with it!

NELLIE : I don't care. It couldn't be much worse than it is, rotten old thing. *(She pulls off her pinafore and hangs it over the back of a chair, then goes to the mirror, once more to arrange her hair.)*

GERTIE : Oh, come on, Nellie, Cornell's will be crammed.

NELLIE : Don't worry, my dear. What are you going to fetch? Anything nice?

GERTIE : No, I'm not—only bacon and cheese; they send you any stuff: cat and candles—any muck!

The MOTHER *takes the little stool and sits down on it on the hearthrug, lacing up her boots.*

MOTHER : I suppose you're not going out, Ernest?

ERNEST : No.

MOTHER : Oh—so you can look after the bread. There are two brown loaves at the top; they'll be about half an hour; the white one's nearly done. Put the other in as soon as they come out. Don't go and forget them, now.

ERNEST : No.

MOTHER : He says "No!" *(She shakes her head at him with indulgent, proud affection.)*

NELLIE *(as if casually, yet at once putting tension into the atmosphere)* : Is Mag coming down?

He does not answer immediately.

MOTHER : I should think not. a night like this, and all the mud there is.

ERNEST : She said she'd come and do some French. Why?

NELLIE *(with a half-smile, off-handedly)* : Nothing.

MOTHER : You'd never think she'd trapse through all this mud. . . .

NELLIE: Don't bother. She'd come if she had to have water-wings to flop through.

> GERTIE *begins to giggle at the idea. The* MOTHER *sniffs.*

ERNEST *(satirically)*: Just as you'd flounder to your Eddie.

> GERTIE *lifts her hands with a little sharp gesture as if to say, "Now the fun's begun!"*

NELLIE *(turning suddenly, afire with scorn)*: Oh, should I? You'd catch me running after anybody!

MOTHER *(rising)*: There, that'll do. Why don't you go up town, if you're going?

> NELLIE LAMBERT *haughtily marches off and puts on a dark coat and a blue hat.*

NELLIE: Is it raining, Gert?

GERTIE: No, it's quite fine.

NELLIE: I'll bet it's fine!

GERTIE: Well, you asked me. It *is* fine; it's not raining.

> The MOTHER *re-enters from the passage, bringing a bonnet and a black coat.*

NELLIE: Want me to bring anything, Mater?

MOTHER: I shall leave the meat for you.

NELLIE: Alright. Come on, Gert.

> *They go out.*

MOTHER *(She dreads that her son is angry with her and, affecting carelessness, puts the question to him, to find out)*: Should we be getting a few Christmas-tree things for little Margaret? I expect Emma and Joe will be here for Christmas: it seems nothing but right, and it's only six weeks now.

ERNEST *(coldly)*: Alright.

> *He gets up and takes another book from the shelf without looking at her. She stands a moment suspended in the act of putting a pin through her bonnet.*

MOTHER: Well, I think we ought to make a bit of Christmas for the little thing, don't you?

ERNEST: Ay. You gave our things to the lads, didn't you? *(He still does not look up from his books.)*

MOTHER *(with a sound of failure in her voice)*: Yes. And they've kept them better than ever I thought they would. They've only broken your blue bird—the one you bought when you were quite little.

There is a noise of footsteps and a knock at the door. The
MOTHER *answers.*
(Trying to be affable, but diffident, her gorge having risen a little.)
Oh, is it you, Maggie? Come in. How ever have you got down, a
night like this? Didn't you get over the ankles in mud?
*She re-enters, followed by a ruddy girl of twenty, a full-
bosomed, heavily-built girl, of medium stature and handsome
appearance, ruddy and black. She is wearing a crimson tam-o'-
shanter and a long grey coat. She keeps her head lowered, and
glancing only once splendidly at* ERNEST, *replies with a
strange, humble defiance:*
MAGGIE: No—oh, it's not so bad: besides, I came all round by
the road.
MOTHER: I should think you're tired, after school.
MAGGIE: No; it's a relief to walk in the open; and I rather like a
black night; you can wrap yourself up in it. Is Nellie out?
MOTHER *(stiffly)*: Yes; she's gone up town.
MAGGIE *(non-significantly)*: Ah, I thought I passed her. I wasn't
sure. She wouldn't notice me; it *is* dark over the fields.
MOTHER: Yes, it is. I'm sure *I'm* awful at recognizing people.
MAGGIE: Yes—and so am I, generally. But it's no good bothering.
If they like to take offence, they have to. . . . I can't help it.
The MOTHER *sniffs slightly. She goes into the passage and
returns with a string net bag. She is ready to go out.*
MOTHER *(still distantly)*: Won't you take your things off? *(Looks
at the bread once more before going.)*
MAGGIE: Ah, thanks, I will.
*She takes off her hat and coat and hangs them in the passage.
She is wearing a dark blue cloth "pinafore-dress", and beneath
the blue straps and shoulder pieces a blouse of fine woollen
stuff with a small intricate pattern of brown and red. She is
flushed and handsome; her features are large, her eyes dark,
and her hair falls in loose profusion of black tendrils about
her face. The coil at the back is coming undone; it is short
and not heavy. She glances supremely at* ERNEST, *feeling him
watching her.*
MOTHER *(at the oven)*: You hear, Ernest? This white cake will be
done in about five minutes, and the brown loaves in about
twenty.

ERNEST : Alright, my dear.

This time it is she who will not look at him.

MAGGIE *(laughing a low, short laugh)*: My hair!—is it a sight? I
have to keep my coat collar up, or it would drop right down—
what bit of it there is.

*She stands away from the mirror, pinning it up; but she
cannot refrain from just one glance at herself.*

ERNEST LAMBERT *watches her, and then turns to his* MOTHER,
who is pulling on a pair of shabby black gloves. MRS LAMBERT,
*however, keeps her eyes consciously averted; she is offended,
and is a woman of fierce pride.*

MOTHER : Well, I expect I shall see you again, Maggie.

MAGGIE *(with a faint, grave triumph)*: It depends what time you
come back. I shan't have to be late.

MOTHER : Oh, you'll be here when I get back.

MAGGIE *(submissive, but with minute irony)*: Very well.

MOTHER : And don't forget that bread, Ernest.

*She picks her bag off the table and goes out, without having
looked at either of them.*

ERNEST *(affectionately)*: No, Little, I won't.

There is a pause for a moment. MAGGIE PEARSON *sits in the
arm-chair opposite him, who is on the sofa, and looks straight
at him. He raises his head after a moment and smiles at her.*

MAGGIE : Did you expect me?

ERNEST *(nodding)*: I knew you'd come. You know, when you feel
as certain as if you couldn't possibly be mistaken. But I *did*
swear when I came out of Coll. and found it raining.

MAGGIE : So did I. Well, not swear, but I was mad. Hasn't it been
a horrid week?

ERNEST : Hasn't it?—and I've been so sick of things.

MAGGIE : Of what?

ERNEST : Oh, of fooling about at College—and everything.

MAGGIE *(grimly)*: You'd be sicker of school.

ERNEST : I don't know. At any rate I should be doing something
real, whereas, as it is—oh, Coll.'s all foolery and flummery.

MAGGIE : I wish I had a chance of going. I feel as if they'd been
pulling things away from me all week—like a baby that has had
everything taken from it.

ERNEST *(laughing)*: Well, if school pulls all your playthings and pretty things away from you, College does worse: it makes them all silly and idiotic, and you hate them—and—what then——!

MAGGIE *(seriously)*: Why? How?

ERNEST: Oh, I don't know. You have to fool about so much, and listen when you're not interested, and see old professors like old dogs walking round as large as life with ancient bones they've buried and scratched up again a hundred times; and they're just as proud as ever. It's such a farce! And when you see that farce, you see all the rest: all the waddling tribe of old dogs with their fossil bones—parsons and professors and councillors—wagging their tails and putting their paws on the bones and barking their important old barks—and all the puppies yelping loud applause.

MAGGIE *(accepting him with earnestness)*: Ay! But are they all alike?

ERNEST: Pretty well. It makes you a bit sick. I used to think men in great places were great——

MAGGIE *(fervently)*: I know you did.

ERNEST: ——and then to find they're no better than yourself—not a bit——

MAGGIE: Well, I don't see why they should be.

ERNEST *(ignoring her)*: ——it takes the wind out of your sails. What's the good of anything if that's a farce?

MAGGIE: What?

ERNEST: The folks at the top. By Jove, if you once lose your illusion of "great men", you're pretty well disillusioned of everything—religion and everything.

MAGGIE *sits absorbedly, sadly biting her forefinger: an act which irritates him.*

(Suddenly): What time did Mother go out?

MAGGIE *(starting)*: I don't know—I never noticed the time.

ERNEST *(rising and going to the oven, picking up the oven-cloth from the hearth)*: At any rate I should think it's five minutes.

He goes to the oven door, and takes from the lower shelf a "cake" loaf, baked in a dripping-pan, and, turning it over, taps it with his knuckles.

ERNEST: I should think it's done. I'll give it five minutes to soak.

He puts the bread in the oven shelf, turns the brown loaves, and shuts the oven door. Then he rises and takes a little notebook from the shelf.

Guess what I've been doing.

MAGGIE *(rising, dilating, reaching towards him)*: I don't know. What?

ERNEST *(smiling)*: Verses.

MAGGIE *(putting out her hand to him, supplicating)*: Give them to me!

ERNEST *(still smiling)*: They're such piffle.

MAGGIE *(betwixt supplication and command)*: Give them to me.

> *He hands her the little volume, and goes out to the scullery. She sits down and reads with absorption.*

> *He returns in a moment, his hands dripping with clear water, and, pulling forward the panchion from the corner, takes out the last piece of white dough, scrapes the little pieces together, and begins to work the mass into a flattish ball, passing it from hand to hand. Then he drops the dough into the dripping-pan, and leaves it standing on the hearth. When he rises and looks at her, she looks up at him swiftly, with wide, brown, glowing eyes, her lips parted. He stands a moment smiling down at her.*

ERNEST: Well, do you like them?

MAGGIE *(nodding several times, does not reply for a second)*: Yes, I do.

ERNEST: They're not up to much, though.

MAGGIE *(softly)*: Why not?

ERNEST *(slightly crestfallen at her readiness to accept him again)*: Well, are they?

MAGGIE *(nodding again)*: Yes, they are! What makes you say they're not? I think they're splendid.

ERNEST *(smiling, gratified, but not thinking the same himself)*: Which do you like best?

MAGGIE *(softly and thoughtfully)*: I don't know. I think this is so lovely, this about the almond tree.

ERNEST *(smiling)*: And you under it.

> *She laughs up at him a moment, splendidly.*

But that's not the best.

MAGGIE *(looking at him expectantly)*: No?

ERNEST: That one, "A Life History", is the best.

MAGGIE *(wondering)*: Yes?

ERNEST *(smiling)*: It is. It means more. Look how full of significance it is, when you think of it. The profs. would make a great long essay out of the idea. Then the rhythm is finer: it's more complicated.

MAGGIE *(seizing the word to vindicate herself when no vindication is required)*: Yes, it is more complicated: it is more complicated in every way. You see, I didn't understand it at first. It is best. Yes, it is. *(She reads it again.)*

    He takes the loaf from the oven and puts the fresh one in.

ERNEST: What have *you* been doing?

MAGGIE *(faltering, smiling)*: I? Only—only some French.

ERNEST: What, your diary?

MAGGIE *(laughing, confused)*: Ah—but I don't think I want you to see it.

ERNEST: Now, you know you wrote it for me! Don't you think it was a good idea, to get you to write your diary in French? You'd never have done any French at all but for that, and you'd certainly never have told me. . . . You never tell me *your* side.

MAGGIE: There's nothing to tell.

ERNEST *(shaking his finger excitedly)*: That's just what you say, that's just what you say! As many things happen for you as for me.

MAGGIE: Oh, but you go to Derby every day, and you see folks, and I——

ERNEST *(flinging his hand at her)*: Piffle! I tell you—do I tell you the train was late? Do I——?

MAGGIE *(interrupting, laughing in confusion and humility)*: Yes, you do—ah!

    He has stopped suddenly with tremendous seriousness and excitement.

ERNEST: When?

MAGGIE *(nervous, apologizing, laughing)*: On Sunday—when you told me you'd have——

ERNEST *(flinging her words aside with excited gesture)*: There you are!—you're raking up a trifle to save you from the main issue. Just like a woman! What I said was *(He becomes suddenly slow and fierce.)* you never tell me about you, and you drink me up, get me up like a cup with both hands and drink yourself breathless—and—and there you are—you, you never pour me any wine of yourself——

MAGGIE *(watching him, fascinated and a little bit terror-struck)*: But isn't it your fault?

He turns on her with a fierce gesture. She starts.

ERNEST: How can it be, when I'm always asking you——? *(He scratches his head with wild exasperation.)*

MAGGIE *(almost inaudibly)*: Well——

He blazes at her so fiercely, she does not continue, but drops her head and looks at her knee, biting her finger.

ERNEST *(abruptly)*: Come on—let's see what hundreds of mistakes . . .

She looks at him; dilates, laughs nervously, and goes to her coat, returning with a school exercise-book, doubled up.

He sits on the sofa, brings her beside him with a swift gesture. Then he looks up at the fire, and starts away round the table.

ERNEST *(going into the scullery and crossing the room with dustpan)*: I must mend the fire. There's a book of French verse with my books. Be looking at that while I . . .

His voice descends to the cellar, where he is heard hammering the coal. He returns directly.

She stands at the little cupboard, with her face in a book. She is very short-sighted.

He mends the fire without speaking to her, and goes out to wash his hands.

ERNEST *(returning)*: Well, what do you think of it? I got it for fourpence.

MAGGIE: I like it ever so much.

ERNEST: You've hardly seen it yet. Come on.

They sit together on the sofa and read from the exercise-book, she nervously.

(Suddenly): Now, look here—Oh, the poor verbs! I don't think anybody dare treat them as you do! Look here!

She puts her head closer.

He jerks back his head, rubbing his nose frantically, laughing. Your hair did tickle me!

She turns her face to his, laughing, with open mouth. He breaks the spell.

Well, have you seen it?

MAGGIE *(hesitating, peering across the lines)*: No-o-o.

ERNEST *(suddenly thrusting his finger before her)*: There! I wonder
it doesn't peck your nose off. You *are* a——
> *She has discovered her mistake and draws back with a little
> vibrating laugh of shame and conviction.*

You hussy, what should it have been?

MAGGIE *(hesitating)*: "Eurent?"

ERNEST *(sitting suddenly erect and startling her up too)*: What!
The *preterite*? The *preterite*? And you're talking about going to
school!
> *She laughs at him with nervous shame; when he glares at
> her, she dilates with fine terror.*

(Ominously): Well——?

MAGGIE *(in the depths of laughing despair, very softly and timidly)*:
I don't know.

ERNEST *(relaxing into pathetic patience)*: Verbs of motion take
être, and if you do a thing frequently, use the imperfect. You
are—— Well, you're inexpressible!
> *They turn to the diary: she covered with humiliation, he
> aggrieved. They read for a while, he shaking his head when her
> light springing hair tickles him again.*

(Softly): What makes you say that?

MAGGIE *(softly)*: What?

ERNEST: That you are "un enfant de Samedi"—a Saturday
child?

MAGGIE *(mistrusting herself so soon)*: Why—it's what they say,
you know.

ERNEST *(gently)*: How?

MAGGIE: Oh—when a child is serious; when it doesn't play except
on Saturdays, when it is quite free.

ERNEST: And you mean you don't play?
> *She looks at him seriously.*

No, you haven't got much play in you, have you?—I fool about
so much.

MAGGIE *(nodding)*: That's it. You can forget things and play about.
I always think of Francis Thompson's *Shelley*, you know—how
he made paper boats. . . .

ERNEST *(flattered at the comparison)*: But I don't make paper
boats. I tell you, you think too much about me. I tell you I have
got nothing but a gift of coloured words. And do I teach you to

play?—not to hold everything so serious and earnest? *(He is very serious.)*

She nods at him again. He looks back at the paper. It is finished. Then they look at one another, and laugh a little laugh, not of amusement.

ERNEST : Ah, your poor diary! *(He speaks very gently.)*

She hides her head and is confused.

I haven't marked the rest of the mistakes. Never mind—we won't bother, shall we? You'd make them again, just the same.

She laughs. They are silent a moment or two; it is very still. You know *(He begins sadly, and she does not answer.)*—you think too much of me—you do, you know.

She looks at him with a proud, sceptical smile.

(Suddenly wroth) : You are such a flat, you won't believe me! But *I* know—if I don't, who does? It's just like a woman, always aching to believe in somebody or other, or something or other

She smiles.

I say, what will you have? Baudelaire?

MAGGIE *(not understanding)* : What?

ERNEST : Baudelaire.

MAGGIE *(nervous, faltering)* : But who's——?

ERNEST : Do you mean to say you don't know who Baudelaire is?

MAGGIE *(defensively)* : How should I?

ERNEST : Why, I gassed to you for half an hour about him, a month back—and now he might be a Maori——!

MAGGIE : It's the names—being foreign.

ERNEST : Baudelaire—Baudelaire—it's no different from Pearson!

MAGGIE *(laughing)* : It sounds a lot better.

ERNEST *(laughing, also, and opening the book)* : Come on! Here, let's have *Maîtresse des Maîtresses*; should we?

MAGGIE *(with gentle persuasiveness)* : Yes. You'll read it?

ERNEST : *You* can have a go, if you like.

They both laugh. He begins to read Le Balcon *in tolerably bad French, but with some genuine feeling. She watches him all the time. At the end, he turns to her in triumph, and she looks back in ecstasy.*

There! isn't that fine?

She nods repeatedly.

That's what they can do in France. It's so heavy and full and

voluptuous : like oranges falling and rolling a little way along a
dark-blue carpet; like twilight outside when the lamp's lighted;
you get a sense of rich, heavy things, as if you smelt them, and
felt them about you in the dusk : isn't it?
>   *She nods again.*
Ah, let me read you *The Albatross.* This is one of the best—anybody would say so—you see, fine, as good as anything in the
world. *(Begins to read.)*
>   *There is a light, quick step outside, and a light tap at the
>   door, which opens.*
>   *They frown at each other, and he whispers:*
ERNEST : Damn! *(Aloud.)* Hell, Beat!
>   *There enters a girl of twenty-three or four; short, slight,
>   pale, with dark circles under her rather large blue eyes, and
>   with dust-coloured hair. She wears a large brown beaver hat
>   and a long grey-green waterproof-coat.*
BEATRICE WYLD : Hello, Ernest, how are ter? Hello, Mag! Are they
all out?
ERNEST *(shutting up the book and drawing away from* MAGGIE. *The
action is reciprocal—*BEATRICE WYLD *seats herself in the arm-
chair opposite)* : They've gone up town. I don't suppose Nellie
will be long.
BEATRICE *(coughing, speaking demurely)* : No, she won't see Eddie
to-night.
ERNEST *(leaning back)* : Not till after ten.
BEATRICE *(rather loudly, sitting up)* : What! Does he come round
after they shut up shop?
ERNEST *(smiling ironically)* : Ay, if it's getting on for eleven——!
BEATRICE *(turning in her chair)* : Good lawk!—are they that bad?
Isn't it fair sickenin'?
ERNEST : He gets a bit wild sometimes.
BEATRICE : I should think so, at that price. Shall you ever get like
that, Mag?
MAGGIE : Like what, Beatrice?
BEATRICE : Now, Maggie Pearson, don't pretend to be 'ormin'. She
knows as well as I do, doesn't she, Ernest?
MAGGIE : Indeed I don't. *(She is rather high-and-mighty, but not
impressive.)*
BEATRICE : Garn! We know you, don't we, Ernie? She's as bad as

anybody at the bottom, but she pretends to be mighty 'ormin'.

MAGGIE : I'm sure you're mistaken, Beatrice.

BEATRICE : Not much of it, old girl. We're not often mistaken, are we, Ernie? Get out; we're the "dead certs"—aren't we, Willie? *(She laughs with mischievous exultance, her tongue between her teeth.)*

MAGGIE *(with great but ineffectual irony)*: Oh, I'm glad somebody is a "dead cert". I'm very glad indeed! I shall know where to find one now.

BEATRICE : You will, Maggie.

> *There is a slight, dangerous pause.*

BEATRICE *(demurely)*: I met Nellie and Gertie, coming.

ERNEST : Ay, you would.

MAGGIE *(bitterly)*: Oh, yes.

BEATRICE *(still innocently)*: She had got a lovely rose. I won-dered——

ERNEST : Yes, she thought Eddie would be peeping over the mouse-traps and bird-cages. I bet she examines those drowning-mouse engines every time she goes past.

BEATRICE *(with vivacity)*: Not likely, not likely! She marches by as if there was nothing but a blank in the atmosphere. You watch her. Eyes *Right!*—but she nudges Gert to make her see if he's there.

ERNEST *(laughing)*: And then she turns in great surprise.

BEATRICE : No, she doesn't. She keeps "Eyes Front", and smiles like a young pup—and the blushes!—Oh, William, too lov'ly f'r any-fing!

ERNEST : I'll bet the dear boy enjoys that blush.

BEATRICE : Ra-ther! *(Artlessly revenant à son mouton.)* And he'll have the rose and all, to rejoice the cockles of his heart this time.

ERNEST *(trying to ward it off)*: Ay. I suppose you'll see him with it on Sunday.

BEATRICE *(still innocently)*: It *was* a beauty, William! Did you bring it for her?

ERNEST : I got it in Derby.

BEATRICE *(unmasking)*: Did you? Who *gave* it you, Willie?

ERNEST *(evasively, pretending to laugh)*: Nay, it wouldn't do to tell.

BEATRICE : Oh, William, *do* tell us! Was it the Dark, or the Athletics?

ERNEST : What if it was neither?

BEATRICE : Oh, Willie, *another!* Oh, it *is* shameful! Think of the poor things, what damage you may do them.

ERNEST *(uneasily)* : Yes, they are delicate pieces of goods, women. Men have to handle them gently; like a man selling millinery.

BEATRICE *(hesitating, then refraining from answering this attack fully)* : It's the hat-pins, Willie dear. But *do* tell us. Was it the Gypsy?—let's see, you generally call it her in German, don't you? —What's the German for gypsy, Maggie?—But was it the Gypsy, or the Athletic Girl that does Botany?

ERNEST *(shaking his head)* : No. It was an Erewhonian.

BEATRICE *(knitting her brows)* : Is that the German for another? Don't say so, William! *(Sighs heavily.)* "Sigh no more, ladies"— Oh, William! And these two are quite fresh ones, and all. Do you *like* being a mutton-bone, William?—one bitch at one end and one at the other? Do *you* think he's such a juicy bone to squabble for, Maggie?

MAGGIE *(red and mortified)* : I'm sure I don't think anything at all about it, Beatrice.

BEATRICE : No; we've got more sense, we have, Maggie. We know him too well—he's not worth it, is he?

　　MAGGIE PEARSON *does not reply.*

　　BEATRICE WYLD *looks at her dress, carefully rubbing off some spot or other; then she resumes:*

BEATRICE : But surely it's not another, Willie?

ERNEST : What does it matter who it is? Hang me, I've not spoken to—— I've hardly said ten words—you said yourself, I've only just known them.

BEATRICE : Oh, Willie, I'm sure I thought it was most desperate— from what you told me.

　　There is another deadly silence. BEATRICE *resumes innocently, quite unperturbed.*

Has he told *you*, Maggie?

MAGGIE *(very coldly)* : I'm sure I don't know.

BEATRICE *(simply)* : Oh, he can't have done, then. You'd never have forgot. There's one like a Spaniard—or was it like an Amazon, Willie?

ERNEST : Go on. Either'll do.

BEATRICE : A Spanish Amazon, Maggie—olive-coloured, like the

colour of a young clear bit of sea-weed, he said—and, oh, I
know! "great free gestures"—a cool clear colour, not red. Don't
you think she'd be lovely?

MAGGIE: I do indeed.

BEATRICE: Too lovely f'r anyfing?—And the other. Oh, yes: "You
should see her run up the college stairs! She can go three at a
time, like a hare running uphill."—And she was top of the Inter.
list for Maths and Botany. Don't you wish you were at college,
Maggie?

MAGGIE: For some things.

BEATRICE: *I* do. We don't know what he's up to when he's there,
do we?

MAGGIE: I don't know that we're so very anxious——

BEATRICE *(convincingly)*: We're not, but he thinks we are, and I
believe he makes it all up. I bet the girls just think: "H'm. Here's
a ginger-and-white fellow; let's take a bit of the conceit out of
him"—and he thinks they're gone on him, doesn't he?

MAGGIE: Very likely.

BEATRICE: He *does*, Maggie; that's what he does. And I'll bet, if
we could hear him—the things he says about us! I'll bet he says
there's a girl with great brown eyes——

ERNEST: Shut up, Beat! you little devil—you don't know when
to stop.

BEATRICE *(affecting great surprise)*: William! Maggie! Just *fancy!!*
  *There is another silence, not ominous this time, but charged
  with suspense.*
What am I a devil for? *(Half timidly.)*

ERNEST *(flushing up at the sound of her ill-assurance)*: Look here;
you may just as well drop it. It's stale, it's flat. It makes no mark,
don't flatter yourself—we're sick of it, that's all. It's a case of
*ennui. Vous m'agacez les nerfs. Il faut aller au diable. (He rises,
half laughing, and goes for the dust-pan.)*

BEATRICE *(her nose a trifle out of joint)*: Translate for us, Maggie.
  MAGGIE *shakes her head, without replying. She has a slight
  advantage now.*
  ERNEST *crosses the room to go to coal-cellar.*
  BEATRICE *coughs slightly, adjusts her tone to a casual, dis-
  interested conversation, and then says, from sheer inability to
  conquer her spite:*

You *do* look well, Maggie. I don't think I've seen anybody with such a colour. It's fair fine.

MAGGIE *laughs and pulls a book towards her. There is silence.*

ERNEST'S *steps are heard descending to the cellar and hammering the coal. Presently he re-mounts. The girls are silent,* MAGGIE *pretending to read;* BEATRICE *staring across the room, half smiling, tapping her feet.*

ERNEST *(hurrying in and putting the coal on the hob)*: Begum, what about the bread?

MAGGIE *(starting up and dilating towards him with her old brilliance)*: Oh, what have we——? Is it——? Oh!

ERNEST *has forestalled her at the oven. There issues a great puff of hot smoke. He draws back a little, and* MAGGIE *utters a quick, tremulous "Oh!"*

BEATRICE *(with concern)*: Hel-lo, Ernest! that smells a bit thick!

He pulls out the loaves one after another. There is one brown loaf much blackened, one in tolerable condition, and the white "cake" very much scorched on one side.

BEATRICE *begins to laugh, in spite of her sympathy at the dismay; he is kneeling on the hearth, the oven door open, the oven-cloth in his hand, and the burnt bread toppled out of its tins on the hearth before him.* MAGGIE *is bending over his shoulder, in great concern.* BEATRICE *sputters with more laughter.* ERNEST *looks up at her, and the dismay and chagrin on his face change also to an irresistible troubled amusement at the mishap, and he laughs heartily.* MAGGIE *joins in, strainedly at first, then with natural shaking, and all three laugh with abandonment,* BEATRICE *putting her hand up over her face, and again doubling over till her head touches her knees.*

ERNEST: No—no! Won't Ma be wild, though!—What a beastly shame!

BEATRICE *breaks out afresh, and he, though grieved, bubbles again into grudging laughter.*

Another day and the rotten fire would burn slow, but to-night it's ramped like——

BEATRICE: Hell, Ernie!

She goes off again into a wild tossing of laugher, hesitating

*a moment to watch him as he lugubriously picks up the worst
loaf and eyes it over.*

ERNEST *(grimly)* : It's black bread now, that they talk about. *(He
sniffs the loaf.)*

> BEATRICE *resumes her mad, interrupted laughter.* MAGGIE *sits
> down on the sofa and laughs till the tears come.*
> ERNEST *taps the loaf with his finger.*

BEATRICE : Are you trying to see if it's done, William? *(From naïve
irony she departs into laughter.)*

ERNEST *(answers, his lugubrious soul struggling with laughter, the
girls laughing the while)*: No; I was listening if it sounded hollow.
Hark!

> *They listen. Laughter.*

It sounds cindery. I wonder how deep it goes. *(In a spirit of
curiosity, he rises and fetches a knife, and, pulling a newspaper
over the hearth, begins to cut away the burnt crust. The bread-
charcoal falls freely on the paper. He looks at the loaf.)* By Jove,
there is a lot! It's like a sort of fine coke.

> *The girls laugh their final burst, and pant with exhaustion,
> their hands pressed in their sides.*

It's about done for, at any rate. *(Puts it down and takes another
brown loaf; taps it.)* This is not so bad, really, is it? *(Sadly.)* It
sounds a bit desiccated, though. Poor Ma! *(He laughs.)* She'll say
it's your fault, Mag.

MAGGIE *(with astonished, incredulous laughter)* : Me?

BEATRICE : She will, Mag, she will! She'll say if you hadn't been
here making a fuss of him——

MAGGIE *(still laughing)* : I'd better go before she comes.

BEATRICE : You want to scrape that with the nutmeg-grater, Ernest.
Where is it? Here, give it me.

> *She takes the loaf, and* ERNEST *goes out and returns with
> the grater. She begins to grate the loaf.*
> MAGGIE *takes up the white "cake" and feels the pale side,
> tapping the bottom.*

MAGGIE *(with decision)* : This isn't done. It's no good cutting it off
till it's all finished. I may as well put it in again. *(She feels the
heat of the two shelves, and puts the loaf on the upper.)*

> ERNEST *picks up the ruined loaf.*

ERNEST : What will she say when she sees this?

MAGGIE: Put it on the fire and have done with it.

> *They look at her in some astonishment at the vandalism of the remark.*

ERNEST: But . . . *(He looks at the loaf on all sides.)*

MAGGIE: It's no good, and it'll only grieve their poor hearts if they see it. "What the heart doesn't . . ."

BEATRICE: Ay, put it on, William. What's it matter? Tell 'em the cat ate it.

ERNEST *(hesitating)*: Should I?

BEATRICE *(nudging his elbow)*: Ay, go on.

> *He puts the loaf on the fire, which is not yet mended, and they stand watching the transparent flames lick it up.*

ERNEST *(half sad, whimsically, repentant)*: The Staff of Life——!

MAGGIE: It's a faggot now, not a staff.

ERNEST: Ah, well! *(He slides all the cinders and* BEATRICE'S *scrapings together in the newspaper and pours them in the fire.)*

BEATRICE *(holding up her scraped loaf)*: It doesn't show, being brown. You want to wrap it in a damp cloth now. Have you got a cloth?

ERNEST: What?—a clean tea-towel?

BEATRICE: Ay, that'll do. Come here; let's go and wet it.

> *She goes out, and re-enters directly with the towel screwed up. She folds it round the loaf, the others watching. She sets the shrouded loaf on the table, and they all sit down. There is a little pause.*

Have you given over coming down to chapel now, Maggie?

MAGGIE: N-no. I don't know that I have. Why?

BEATRICE: You don't often put in an appearance now.

MAGGIE *(a trifle petulantly)*: Don't I? Well, I don't feel like it, I suppose.

BEATRICE: William, you have something to answer for, my boy. *(She speaks portentously.)*

ERNEST: Shall I? Ne'er mind; I'll say "adsum" every time. Recording Angel: "Ernest Lambert."—"Adsum!"

BEATRICE: But you don't know what the little Mas say about you, my lad.

ERNEST: The dear little Mas! They will be gossiping about——

BEATRICE *(springing from her chair)*: Look out! there's Nellie. Take that in th' pantry, William. Come out!

She thrusts the towelled loaf into ERNEST'S *hands, and he hurries away with it, while she hastily shoots the coal on the fire, and, putting down the dust-pan by the boiler, sits in her chair and looks " 'ormin'."*

Enter NELLIE LAMBERT *and* GERTIE COOMBER, *blinking.*

NELLIE *(bending her head to shield her eyes)*: Hasn't Ma come? I never saw her. Hullo, Maggie, you've not gone yet, you see. *(She sniffs and goes straight to the oven.)* Goodness, what a smell of burning! Have you been and forgotten the bread? *(She kneels and looks in the oven.)*

BEATRICE *(very quietly and negligently)*: Ernest forgot that one. It's only a bit caught.

NELLIE *peeps in the panchion where the other loaves are— those baked by the mother.*

NELLIE: He generally forgets if Maggie's here.

BEATRICE *bursts out laughing.*

MAGGIE *(rising, indignant)*: Why, Nellie, when has it ever been burnt before?

NELLIE *(smiling a careless smile)*: Many a time.

MAGGIE: Not when I've been here.

NELLIE: Aren't you going to sit down a bit, Gert?

GERTIE: No, I'm off. Our Frances'll be wanting her ducks. *(She laughs, but does not go.)*

MAGGIE, *her head hanging, goes to put on her hat and coat. The other girls smile, meaningly, at one another.*

Are you going, then, Maggie?

MAGGIE *(distantly)*: Yes, it's getting late. I've a long walk, you see.

GERTIE: You have! I'm glad I've not got it. I often wonder how you dare go through those woods on a pitch-dark night.

BEATRICE: I daresn't. *(She laughs at herself.)*

MAGGIE: I'd rather go through our wood than through Nottingham Road, with the people——!

BEATRICE: I'm glad you would, for I wouldn't.

ERNEST LAMBERT *pulls on his overcoat and his cap. He gathers certain books. He looks at* MAGGIE, *and she at him.*

MAGGIE: Well, good night, everybody. I shall have to go. *(She hesitates, finding it difficult to break away.)*

BEATRICE AND NELLIE: Good night.

GERTIE : Good night, Maggie. I hope it won't be too muddy for you.

MAGGIE *laughs slightly.*

NELLIE *(as the two go through the door, loudly)* : And don't be ever so late back, our Ernest!

They do not reply. As their steps are heard passing the wide window, BEATRICE *flings up her arms and her feet in an ungraceful, exultant glee, flicking her fingers with noiseless venom.*

BEATRICE *(in an undertone)* : I gave her beans!

NELLIE *(turning, with a smile, and lighting up)* : Did you? What did you say?

GERTIE *(amused, giggling, but shamefaced)* : Did you?

BEATRICE *(exultant)* : Oh, lum! I'll bet her cheeks are warm!

END OF ACT II

ACT III

The same room, half an hour later.

BEATRICE WYLD sits in the arm-chair, and NELLIE LAMBERT on the sofa, the latter doing drawn-thread work on a white tray-cloth, part of which is fixed in a ring: at this part NELLIE is stitching.

BEATRICE: Ah, it makes you grin! the way she used to talk before she had him!

NELLIE: She did. She thought nobody was as good as her Arthur. She's found her mistake out.

BEATRICE: She *has* an' all! He wanted some chips for his supper the other night, when I was there. "Well," I said, "it's not far to Fretwell's, Arthur." He did look mad at me. "I'm not going to fetch chips," he said, a cocky little fool; and he crossed his little legs till I should 'a liked to have smacked his mouth. I said to her, "Well, Mabel, if *you* do, you're a fool!"—in her state, and all the men that were about! He's not a bit of consideration. You never saw anybody as fagged as she looks.

NELLIE: She does. I felt fair sorry for her when I saw her last Sunday but one. She doesn't look like she used.

BEATRICE: By Jove, she doesn't! He's brought her down a good many pegs. I shouldn't wonder if she wasn't quite safe, either. She told me she had awful shooting pains up her side, and they last for five minutes.

NELLIE *(looking up)*: Oh?

BEATRICE: Ay! I'm glad I'm not in her shoes. They may talk about getting married as they like! Not this child!

NELLIE: Not to a thing like him.

BEATRICE: I asked her if she didn't feel frightened, an' she said she didn't care a scrap. I should care, though—and I'll bet she does, at the bottom.

The latch clicks. The MOTHER enters, carrying a large net full of puchases, and a brown-paper parcel. She lets these fall heavily on the table, and sits on the nearest chair, panting a little, with evident labour of the heart.

MOTHER: Yes, my lady!—you called for that meat, didn't you?

NELLIE *(rising and going to look in the parcels)*: Well, my duck, I looked for you downtown; then when I was coming back, I forgot all about it.

MOTHER: And I—was silly enough—to lug it myself——

NELLIE *(crossing to her mother, all repentant)*: Well, what *did* you for?—you *knew* I could fetch it again! You do do such ridiculous things! *(She begins to take off her mother's bonnet.)*

MOTHER: Yes! We know your fetching it—again. If I hadn't met little Abel Gibson—I really don't think I should have got home.

BEATRICE *(leaning forward)*: If Nellie forgets it, you should forget it, Mrs Lambert. I'm sure you ought not to go lugging all those things.

MOTHER: But I met young Abel Gibson just when I was thinking I should have to drop them—and I said: "Here, Abel, my lad, are you going home?" and he said he was, so I told him he could carry my bag. He's a nice little lad. He says his father hasn't got much work, poor fellow. I believe that woman's a bad manager. She'd let that child clean up when he got home—and he said his Dad always made the beds. She's not a nice woman, I'm sure. *(She shakes her head and begins to unfasten her coat.)*

> NELLIE, *seeing her mother launched into easy gossip, is at ease on her score, and returns to the bags.*

You needn't go looking; there's nothing for you.

NELLIE *(petulantly)*: You always used to bring us something——

MOTHER: Ay, I've no doubt I did. . . . *(She sniffs and looks at* BEATRICE WYLD.*)*

NELLIE *(still looking, unconvinced)*: Hello! Have a grape, Beatrice. *(She offers* BEATRICE *a white-paper bag of very small black grapes.)*

MOTHER: They want washing first, to get the sawdust out. Our Ernest likes those little grapes, and they *are* cheap: only four-pence.

BEATRICE *(looking up from the bag)*: Oh, they are cheap. No, I won't have any, Nellie, thanks.

NELLIE: I'll wash them.

MOTHER: Just let the tap run on them—and get a plate.

NELLIE: Well, as if I shouldn't get a plate! The little Ma thinks we're all daft.

MOTHER *(sniffing—it is her manner of winking)*: Is all the bread done?

NELLIE: Yes. I took the last out about a quarter of an hour ago.

MOTHER *(to BEATRICE)*: Was Maggie Pearson gone when you came?

BEATRICE: No—she's only been gone about three-quarters of an hour.

MOTHER *(tossing her head and lowering her tone confidentially)*: Well, really! I stopped looking at a man selling curtains a bit longer than I should, thinking she'd be gone.

BEATRICE: Pah!—it makes you sick, doesn't it?

MOTHER: It does. You wouldn't think she'd want to come trailing down here in weather like this, would you?

BEATRICE: You wouldn't. I'll bet you'd not catch me!—and she knows what you think, alright.

MOTHER: Of course she does.

BEATRICE: She wouldn't care if the old Dad was here, scowling at her; she'd come.

MOTHER: If that lad was at home.

BEATRICE *(scornfully)*: Ay!

> The MOTHER *rises and goes out with her coat.*
> NELLIE *enters, with a plate of wet black grapes.*

NELLIE: Now, Beat! *(Offering the grapes.)*

BEATRICE: No, Nellie, I don't think I'll have any.

NELLIE: Go on—have some! Have some—go on! *(Speaks rather imperatively.)*

> BEATRICE *takes a few grapes in her hand.*

What a scroddy few! Here, have some more.

BEATRICE *(quietly)*: No, Nellie, thanks, I won't have any more. I don't think they'd suit me.

> NELLIE *sits down and begins to eat the grapes, putting the skins on a piece of paper.*
> The MOTHER *re-enters. She looks very tired. She begins carrying away the little parcels.*

NELLIE: Don't you put those away, Mother; I'll do it in a minute.

> The MOTHER *continues.* NELLIE *rises in a moment or two, frowning.*

You *are* a persistent little woman! Why don't you wait a bit and let me do it?

MOTHER : Because your father will be in in a minute, and I don't want him peeking and prying into everything, thinking I'm a millionaire. *(She comes and sits down in her rocking-chair by the oven.)*

NELLIE *continues to carry away the goods, which have littered the table, looking into every parcel.*

NELLIE : Hello! what are these little things?

MOTHER : Never you mind.

NELLIE : Now, little woman, don't you try to hug yourself and be secretive. What are they?

MOTHER : They're pine-kernels. *(Turning to BEATRICE.)* Our Ernest's always talking about the nut-cakes he gets at Mrs Dacre's; I thought I'd see what they were like. Put them away; don't let him see them. I shan't let him know at all, if they're not up to much. I'm not going to have him saying Mother Dacre's things are better than mine.

BEATRICE : I wouldn't—for I'm sure they're not.

MOTHER : Still, I rather like the idea of nuts. Here, give me one; I'll try it.

They each eat a pine-kernel with the air of a connoisseur in flavours.

(smiling to herself) : Um—aren't they oily!

BEATRICE : They *are*! But I rather like them.

NELLIE : So do I. *(Takes another.)*

MOTHER *(gratified)* : Here, put them away, miss!

NELLIE *takes another. The* MOTHER *rises and snatches them away from her, really very pleased.*

There won't be one left, I know, if I leave them with *her*. *(She puts them away.)*

NELLIE *(smiling and nodding her head after her mother; in a whisper)* : Isn't she fussy?

BEATRICE *puts out her tongue and laughs.*

MOTHER *(returning)* : I tried a gelatine sponge last week. He likes it much better than cornflour. Mrs Dacre puts them in mince-meat, instead of suet—the pine-kernels. I must try a bit.

BEATRICE : Oh! it *sounds* better.

MOTHER *(seating herself)* : It does. *(She looks down at the bread.)*

BEATRICE *puts up her shoulders in suspense.*

I think you let this one dry up.

NELLIE: No, I didn't. It was our Ernest who let it burn.

MOTHER: Trust him! And what's he done? *(She begins to look round.)*

> BEATRICE *pulls a very wry face, straightens it quickly and says calmly:*

BEATRICE: Is your clock right, Mrs Lambert?

MOTHER *(looking round at the clock)*: Ten minutes—ten minutes fast. Why, what time is it?

BEATRICE: Good lack! *(Rising suddenly.)* It's half-past ten! Won't our Pa rave! "Yes, my gel—it's turning-out time again. We're going to have a stop put to it." And our mother will recite! Oh, the recitations!—there's no shutting her up when she begins. But at any rate, she shuts our Pa up, and he's a nuisance when he thinks he's got just cause to be wrath.—Where did I put my things?

MOTHER: I should think that Nellie's put hers on top. *(She looks at NELLIE.)* Don't sit there eating every one of those grapes. You know our Ernest likes them.

NELLIE *(suddenly incensed)*: Good gracious! I don't believe I've had more than half a dozen of the things!

MOTHER *(laughing and scornful)*: Half a dozen!

NELLIE: Yes, half a dozen.—Beatrice, we can't have a thing in this house—everything's for our Ernest.

MOTHER: What a story! What a story! But he *does* like those little grapes.

NELLIE: And everything else.

MOTHER *(quietly, with emphasis)*: He gets a good deal less than you.

NELLIE *(withdrawing from dangerous ground)*: I'll bet.

> GERTIE COOMBER *runs in.*

BEATRICE: Hello, Gert, haven't you seen John?

GERTIE *(putting up her chin)*: No.

BEATRICE: A little nuisance!—fancy!

GERTIE: Eh, I don't care—not me.

NELLIE: No, it's her fault. She never does want to see him. I wonder any fellow comes to her.

GERTIE *(nonchalantly)*: Um—so do I.

BEATRICE: Get out, Gert; you know you're fretting your heart out 'cause he's not come.

GERTIE *(with great scorn)*: Am I? Oh, *am* I? Not me! If I heard him whistling this moment, I wouldn't go out to him.

NELLIE: Wouldn't you! I'd shove you out, you little cat!

GERTIE *(with great assumption of amusing dignity)*: Oh, would you, indeed!

> *They all laugh.*

> BEATRICE *pins on her hat before the mirror.*

You haven't got Ernest to take you home to-night, Beat. Where is he? With Maggie Pearson? Hasn't he come back yet?

MOTHER *(with some bitterness)*: He hasn't. An' he's got to go to college to-morrow. Then he reckons he can get no work done.

GERTIE: Ha!—they're all alike when it suits them.

MOTHER: I should thank her not to come down here messing every Friday and Sunday.

NELLIE: Ah, she's always here. I should be ashamed of *myself*.

BEATRICE: Well—our Pa! I must get off. Good night, everybody. See you to-morrow, Nell.

NELLIE: I'll just come with you across the field.

> *She fetches a large white cashmere shawl and puts it over her head. She disposes it round her face at the mirror.*

> BEATRICE *winks at the* MOTHER.

GERTIE: She's going to look for Eddie.

NELLIE *(blushing)*: Well, what if I am? Shan't be many minutes, Ma.

MOTHER *(rather coldly)*: I should think not! I don't know what you want at all going out at this time o' night.

> NELLIE *shrugs her shoulders, and goes out with* BEATRICE WYLD, *who laughs and bids another good night.*

MOTHER *(when they have gone)*: A silly young hussy, gadding to look for *him*. As if she couldn't sleep without seeing him.

GERTIE: Oh, he always says, "Come and look for me about eleven." I bet he's longing to shut that shop up.

MOTHER *(shortly)*: Ha! he's softer than she is, and I'm sure that's not necessary. I can't understand myself how folks can be such looneys. I'm sure I was never like it.

GERTIE: And I'm sure I never should be. I often think, when John's coming, "Oh, hang it, I wish he'd stay away!"

MOTHER: Ah, but that's too bad, Gertie. If you feel like that you'd better not keep it on any longer.—Yet I used to be about the same myself. *I* was born with too much sense for that sort of slobber.

GERTIE : Yes, isn't it hateful? I often think, "Oh, get off with you!" I'm sure I should never be like Nellie.—Isn't Ernest late? You'll have Mr Lambert in first.

MOTHER *(bitterly)*: He *is* late. He must have gone every bit of the way.

GERTIE : Nay, I bet he's not—that.

There is silence a moment.

The MOTHER *remembers the bread.*

MOTHER *(turning round and looking in the panchion)*: Well, there ought to be two more brown loaves. What have they done with them, now? *(Turns over the loaves, and looks about.)*

GERTIE *(laughing)*: I should think they've gone and eaten them, between them.

MOTHER : That's very funny. *(She rises, and is going to look round the room.)*

There is a whistle outside.

GERTIE *(turning her head sharply aside)*: Oh, *hang* it! I'm not going—I'm not!

MOTHER : Who is it? John?

GERTIE : It is, and I'm *not* going.

The whistle is heard again.

He can shut up, 'cause I'm not going!

MOTHER *(smiling)*: You'll have to just go and speak to him, if he's waiting for you.

The whistle is heard louder.

GERTIE : Isn't it hateful! I don't care. I'll tell him I was in bed. I should be if my father wasn't at the "Ram".

MOTHER *(sighing)*: Ay! But you may guess he's seen Nellie, and she's been saying something to him.

GERTIE : Well, she needn't, then!

The whistle goes again.

GERTIE *cannot resist the will of the other, especially as the* MOTHER *bids her go. She flings her hand, and turns with great impatience.*

He can shut up! What's he want to come at this time for? Oh, *hang* him!

*She goes out slowly and unwillingly, her lips closed angrily.
The* MOTHER *smiles, sighs, and looks sad and tired again.*

MOTHER *(to herself)*: It's a very funny thing!

*She wanders round the room, looking for the bread. She
lights a taper and goes into the scullery.*

(re-passing, she repeats): A very remarkable thing!

*She goes into the pantry on right, and after a moment
returns with the loaf in the damp cloth, which she has un-
folded. She stands looking at the loaf, repeating a sharp little
sound against her palate with her tongue, quickly vibrating
her head up and down.*

(to herself): So this is it, is it? It's a nice thing!—And they put
it down there, thinking I shouldn't see it. It's a nice thing! *(Goes
and looks in the oven, then says bitterly)*: I always said she was
a deep one. And he thinks he'll stop out till his father comes!—
And what have they done with the other?—Burnt it, I should
think. That's what they've done. It's a nice thing—a nice thing!
*(She sits down in the rocking-chair, perfectly rigid, still overdone
with weariness and anger and pain.)*

*After a moment, the garden gate is heard to bang back, and
a heavy step comes up the path, halting, punctuated with the
scratch and thrust of a walking-stick, rather jarring on the
bricked yard.*

The FATHER *enters. He also bends his head a little from the
light, peering under his hat-brim.*

The MOTHER *has quickly taken the withered loaf and
dropped it in among the others in the panchion.*

The FATHER *does not speak, but goes straight to the passage,
and hangs up his hat, overcoat, and jacket, then returns and
stands very near the fire, holding his hands close down to the
open ruddy grate. He sways slightly when he turns, after a
moment or two, and stands with his hands spread behind his
back, very near the fire.*

The MOTHER *turns away her head from him.*

*He remains thus for a minute or so, then he takes a step
forward, and, leaning heavily on the table, begins to pick the
grapes from the plate, spitting out the skins into his right hand
and flinging them at random towards the fire behind his back,
leaning all the time heavily with the left hand on the table.*

After a while this irritates the MOTHER *exceedingly.*

MOTHER : You needn't eat all those grapes. There's somebody else!

FATHER *(speaking with an exaggerated imitation of his son's English)*: "Somebody else!" Yes, there *is* "somebody else"! *(He pushes the plate away and the grapes roll on the table.)* I know they was not bought for me! I know it! I know it! *(His voice is rising.)* Somebody else! Yes, there *is* somebody else! I'm not daft! I'm not a fool.

Nothing's got for me. No-o. You can get things for them, you can,
     The MOTHER *turns away her head, with a gesture of contempt.*
(Continues with maddening tipsy, ironic snarl): I'm not a fool! I can see it! I can see it! I'm not daft! There's nothing for me. but you begrudge me every bit I put in my mouth.

MOTHER *(with cold contempt)*: You put enough down your own throat. There's no need for anybody else. You take good care you have your share.

FATHER : I have my share. Yes, I do, I do!

MOTHER *(contemptuously)*: Yes, you do.

FATHER : Yes, I do. But I shouldn't if you could help it, you begrudging bitch. What did you put away when I came in, so that I shouldn't see it? Something! Yes! Something you'd got for them! Nobody else. Yes! *I* know you'd got it for somebody else!

MOTHER *(quietly, with bitter scorn)*: As it happens, it was nothing.

FATHER *(his accent is becoming still more urban. His O's are A's, so that "nothing" is "nathing")*: Nathing! Nathing! You're a liar, you're a liar. I heard the scuffle. You don't think I'm a fool, do you, woman?
     She curls her lips in a deadly smile.

FATHER : I know, I know! Do *you* have what you give me for dinner? No, you don't. You take good care of it!

MOTHER : Look here, you get your good share. Don't think *you* keep the house. Do you think I manage on the few lousy shillings you give me? No, you get as much as you deserve, if any man did. And if *you* had a rice pudding, it was because *we* had *none*. Don't come here talking. *You* look after *yourself*, there's no mistake.

FATHER : An' I mean to, an' I mean to!

MOTHER : Very well, then!

FATHER *(suddenly flaring)*: But I'm not going to be treated like a dog in my own house! I'm *not*, so don't think it! I'm master in this house, an' I'm *going* to be. I tell you, I'm master of this house.

MOTHER: You're the only one who thinks so.

FATHER: I'll stop it! I'll put a stop to it. They can go—they can go!

MOTHER: You'd be on short commons if they did.

FATHER: What? What? Me! You saucy bitch, I can keep myself, an' you as well, an' him an' all as holds his head above me—am doing—an' I'll stop it, I'll stop it—or they can go.

MOTHER: Don't make any mistake—*you* don't keep us. You hardly keep yourself.

FATHER: Do I?—do I? And who does keep 'em, then?

MOTHER: I do—and the girl.

FATHER: You do, do you, you snappy little bitch! You do, do you? Well, keep 'em yourself, then. Keep that lad in his idleness yourself, then.

MOTHER: Very willingly, very willingly. And that lad works ten times as hard as you do.

FATHER: Does he? I should like to see him go down th' pit every day! I should like to see him working every day in th' hole. No, he won't dirty his fingers.

MOTHER: Yes, you wanted to drag all the lads into the pit, and you only begrudge them because I wouldn't let them.

FATHER *(shouting)*: You're a liar—you're a liar! I never wanted 'em in th' pit.

MOTHER *(interrupting)*: You did your best to get the other two there, anyway.

FATHER *(still shouting)*: You're a liar—I never did anything of the sort. What other man would keep his sons doing nothing till they're twenty-two? Where would you find another? Not that I begrudge it him—I don't, bless him. . . .

MOTHER: Sounds like it.

FATHER: I don't. I begrudge 'em nothing. I'm willing to do everything I can for 'em, and 'ow do they treat me? Like a dog, I say, like a dog!

MOTHER: And whose fault is it?

FATHER: Yours, you stinking hussy! It's you as makes 'em like it.

They're like you. You teach 'em to hate me. You make me like
dirt for 'em : you set 'em against me . . .

MOTHER : You set them yourself.

FATHER *(shouting)*: You're a liar! *(He jumps from his chair and
stands bending towards her, his fist clenched and ready and
threatening.)* It's you. It always 'as been you. You've done it——

   Enter ERNEST LAMBERT.

ERNEST *(pulling off his cap and flashing with anger)*: It's a fine row
you're kicking up. I should bring the neighbours in!

FATHER : I don't care a damn what I do, you sneering devil, you!
*(He turns to his son, but remains in the same crouching, threaten-
ing attitude.)*

ERNEST *(flaring)*: You needn't swear at me, either.

FATHER : I shall swear at who the devil I like. Who are you, you
young hound—who are you, you measley little——

ERNEST : At any rate, I'm not a foul-mouthed drunken fool.

FATHER *(springing towards him)*: What! I'll smite you to the
ground if you say it again, I will, I *will*!

ERNEST : Pah!

   *He turns his face aside in contempt from the fist brandished
   near his mouth.*

FATHER *(shouting)*: What! Say it! I'll drive my fist through you!

ERNEST *(suddenly tightening with rage as the fist is pushed near
his face)*: Get away, you spitting old fool!

   The FATHER *jerks nearer and trembles his fist so near the
   other's nose that he draws his head back, quivering with
   intense passion and loathing, and lifts his hands.*

MOTHER : Ernest, Ernest, don't!

   There is a slight relaxation.

(Lamentable, pleading): Don't say any more, Ernest! Let him
say what he likes. What should I do if . . .

   There is a pause.

   ERNEST *continues rigidly to glare into space beyond his
   father.*

   The FATHER *turns to the* MOTHER *with a snarling movement,
   which is nevertheless a movement of defeat. He withdraws,
   sits down in the arm-chair, and begins, fumbling, to get off his
   collar and tie, and afterwards his boots.*

   ERNEST *has taken a book, and stands quite motionless, look-*

ing at it. There is heard only the slash of the FATHER'S *boot-laces. Then he drags off the boot, and it falls with a loud noise.*

ERNEST, *very tense, puts down the book, takes off his over-coat, hangs it up, and returns to the side of the sofa nearest the door, where he sits, pretending to read.*

There is silence for some moments, and again the whip of boot-laces. Suddenly a snarl breaks the silence.

FATHER : But don't think I'm going to be put down in my own house! It would take a better man than you, you white-faced jockey—or your mother either—or all the lot of you put together! *(He waits awhile.)* I'm not daft—I can see what she's driving at. *(Silence.)* I'm not a fool, if you think so. I can pay you yet, you sliving bitch! *(He sticks out his chin at his wife.)*

ERNEST *lifts his head and looks at him.*

(Turns with renewing ferocity on his son) : Yes, and you either. I'll stand no more of your chelp. I'll stand no *more*! Do you hear me?

MOTHER : Ernest!

ERNEST *looks down at his book.*

The FATHER *turns to the* MOTHER.

FATHER : Ernest! Ay, prompt him! Set him on—you know how to do it—you know how to do it!

There is a persistent silence.

I know it! I know it! I'm not daft, I'm not a fool! *(The other boot falls to the floor.)*

He rises, pulling himself up with the arms of the chair, and, turning round, takes a Waterbury watch with a brass chain from the wall beside the bookcase: his pit watch that the MOTHER *hung there when she put his pit-trousers in the cup-board—and winds it up, swaying on his feet as he does so. Then he puts it back on the nail, and a key swings at the end of the chain. Then he takes a silver watch from his pocket, and, fumbling, missing the keyhole, winds that up also with a key, and, swaying forward, hangs it up over the cupboard. Then he lurches round, and, limping pitiably, goes off upstairs.*

There is a heavy silence. The Waterbury watch can be heard ticking.

ERNEST : I would kill him, if it weren't that I shiver at the thought of touching him.

MOTHER : Oh, you mustn't! Think how awful it would be if there were anything like that. I couldn't bear it.

ERNEST : He is a damned, accursed fool!

    The MOTHER *sighs.* ERNEST *begins to read.*

    There is a quick patter of feet, and GERTIE COOMBER *comes running in.*

GERTIE : Has Mr Lambert come?

MOTHER : Ay—in bed.

GERTIE : My father hasn't come yet. Isn't it sickening?

MOTHER : It is, child. They want horsewhipping, and those that serve them, more.

GERTIE : I'm sure we haven't a bit of peace of our lives. I'm sure when Mother was alive, she used to say her life was a burden, for she never knew when he'd come home, or how.

MOTHER : And it is so.

GERTIE : Did you go far, Ernest?

ERNEST *(not looking up)* : I don't know. Middling.

MOTHER : He must have gone about home, for he's not been back many minutes.

GERTIE : There's our Frances shouting!

    She runs off.

MOTHER *(quietly)* : What did you do with that other loaf?

ERNEST *(looking up, smiling)* : Why, we forgot it, and it got all burned.

MOTHER *(rather bitterly)*: Of course you forgot it. And where is it?

ERNEST : Well, it was no good keeping it. I thought it would only grieve your heart, the sight of it, so I put it on the fire.

MOTHER : Yes, I'm sure! That was a nice thing to do, I must say! . . . Put a brown loaf on the fire, and dry the only other one up to a cinder!

    The smile dies from his face, and he begins to frown.

(She speaks bitterly): It's always alike, though. If Maggie Pearson's here, nobody else matters. It's only a laughing matter if the bread gets burnt to cinders and put on the fire. *(Suddenly bursts into a glow of bitterness.)* It's all very well, my son—you may talk about caring for me, but when it comes to Maggie Pearson it's very little you care for me—or Nellie—or anybody else.

ERNEST *(dashing his fingers through his hair)*: You talk *just* like a woman! As if it makes any difference! As if it makes the least difference!

MOTHER *(folding her hands in her lap and turning her face from him)*: Yes, it does.

ERNEST *(frowning fiercely)*: It doesn't. Why should it? If I like apples, does it mean I don't like—bread? You know, Ma, it doesn't make any difference.

MOTHER *(doggedly)*: *I* know it does.

ERNEST *(shaking his finger at her)*: But why should it, why should it? You know you wouldn't be interested in the things we talk about: you know you wouldn't.

MOTHER: Why shouldn't I?

ERNEST: Should you, now? Look here: we talked about French poetry. Should you care about that?

No answer.

You know you wouldn't! And then we talked about those pictures at the Exhibition—about Frank Brangwyn—about Impressionism—for ever such a long time. You would only be bored by that——

MOTHER: Why should I? You never tried.

ERNEST: But you wouldn't. You wouldn't care whether it's Impressionism or pre-Raphaelism. *(Pathetically.)*

MOTHER: I don't see why I shouldn't.

ERNEST *(ruffling his hair in despair; after a pause)*: And, besides, there are lots of things you can't talk to your own folks about, that you would tell a stranger.

MOTHER *(bitterly)*: Yes, I know there are.

ERNEST *(wildly)*: Well, I can't help it—can I, now?

MOTHER *(reluctantly)*: No—I suppose not—if you say so.

ERNEST: But you know——!

MOTHER *(turning aside again; with some bitterness and passion)*: I do know, my boy—I *do* know!

ERNEST: But I can't help it.

His MOTHER does not reply, but sits with her face averted.
Can I, now? Can I?

MOTHER: You say not.

ERNEST *(changing the position again)*: And you wouldn't care if it was Alice, or Lois, or Louie. You never row me if I'm a bit late when I've been with them. . . . It's just Maggie, because you don't like her.

MOTHER *(with emphasis)*: No, I *don't* like her—and I *can't* say I do.

ERNEST: But why not? Why not? She's as good as I am—and I'm sure you've nothing against her—have you, now?

MOTHER *(shortly)*: No, I don't know I've anything against her.

ERNEST: Well, then, what do you get so wild about?

MOTHER: Because I don't like her, and I never shall, so there, my boy!

ERNEST: Because you've made up your mind not to.

MOTHER: Very well, then.

ERNEST *(bitterly)*: And you did from the beginning, just because she happened to care for me.

MOTHER *(with coldness)*: And does nobody else care for you, then, but her?

ERNEST *(knitting his brows and shaking his hands in despair)*: Oh, but it's not a question of that.

MOTHER *(calmly, coldly)*: But it is a question of that.

ERNEST *(fiercely)*: It isn't! You know it isn't! I care just as much for you as ever—you know I do.

MOTHER: It looks like it, when night after night you leave me sitting up here till nearly eleven—and gone eleven sometimes——

ERNEST: Once, Mother, once—and that was when it was her birthday.

MOTHER *(turning to him with the anger of love)*: And how many times is it a quarter to eleven, and twenty to?

ERNEST: But you'd sit up just the same if I were in; you'd sit up reading—you know you would.

MOTHER: You don't come in to see.

ERNEST: When I am in, do you go to bed before then?

MOTHER: I do.

ERNEST: Did you on Wednesday night, or on Tuesday, or on Monday?

MOTHER: No; because you were working.

ERNEST: I was *in*.

MOTHER: I'm not going to go to bed and leave you sitting up, and I'm not going to go to bed to leave you to come in when you like . . . so there!

ERNEST *(beginning to unfasten his boots)* : Alright—I can't help it, then.

MOTHER : You mean you won't.

> *There is a pause.* ERNEST *hangs his head, forgetting to unlace his boot further.*

ERNEST *(pathetically)* : You don't worry our Nellie. Look, she's out now. You never row her.

MOTHER : I do. I'm always telling her.

ERNEST : Not like this.

MOTHER : I do! I called her all the names I could lay my tongue to last night.

ERNEST : But you're not nasty every time she goes out to see Eddie, and you don't for ever say nasty things about *him*. . . .

> *There is a moment of silence, while he waits for an answer.*

ERNEST : And I always know you'll be sitting here working yourself into a state if I happen to go up to Herod's Farm.

MOTHER : Do I?—and perhaps you would, if you sat here waiting all night——

ERNEST : But, Ma, you don't care if Nellie's out.

MOTHER *(after brooding awhile; with passion)* : No, my boy, because she doesn't mean the same to me. She has never understood —she has not been—like you. And now—you seem to care nothing—you care for *any*thing more than home : you tell me nothing but the little things : you used to tell me everything; you used to come to me with everything; but now—I don't *do* for you now. You have to find somebody else.

ERNEST : But I can't help it. I can't help it. I have to grow up—and things are different to us now.

MOTHER *(bitterly)* : Yes, things *are* different to us now. They never used to be. And you say I've never tried to care for her. I have— I've tried and tried to like her, but I can't, and it's no good.

ERNEST *(pathetically)* : Well, my dear, we shall have to let it be, then, and things will have to go their way. *(He speaks with difficulty.)* You know, Mater—I don't care for her—really—not half as I care for you. Only, just now—well, I can't help it, I can't help it. But I care just the same—for you—I do.

MOTHER *(turning with a little cry)* : But I thought you didn't!

> *He takes her in his arms, and she kisses him, and he hides his face in her shoulder. She holds him closely for a moment;*

then she kisses him and gently releases him. He kisses her. She gently draws away, saying, very tenderly:

MOTHER : There!—Nellie will be coming in.

ERNEST *(after a pause)*: And you do understand, don't you, Mater?

MOTHER *(with great gentleness, having decided not to torment him)*: Yes, I understand now. *(She bluffs him.)*

ERNEST *takes her hand and strokes it a moment. Then he bends down and continues to unfasten his boots. It is very silent.*

I'm sure that hussy ought to be in—just look at the time!

ERNEST : Ay, it's scandalous!

There are in each of their voices traces of the recent anguish, which makes their speech utterly insignificant. Nevertheless, in thus speaking, each reassures the other that the moment of abnormal emotion and proximity is passed, and the usual position of careless intimacy is reassumed.

MOTHER *(rising)*: I shall have to go and call her—a brazen baggage!

There is a rattle of the yard gate, and NELLIE *runs in, blinking very much.*

NELLIE *(out of breath; but very casually)*: Hello, our Ernest, you home?

MOTHER : Yes, miss, and been home long ago. I'll not have it, my lady, so you needn't think it. You're not going to be down there till this time of night! It's disgraceful. What will his mother say, do you think, when he walks in at past eleven?

NELLIE : She can say what she likes. Besides, she'll be in bed.

MOTHER : She'll hear him, for all that. I'd be ashamed of myself, that I would, standing out there slobbering till this time of night! I don't know how anyone can be such a fool!

NELLIE *(smiling)*: Perhaps not, my dear.

MOTHER *(slightly stung)*: No, and I should be sorry. I don't know what he wants running up at this time of a night.

NELLIE : Oh, Mother, don't go on again! We've heard it a dozen times.

MOTHER : And you'll hear it two dozen.

ERNEST, *having got off his shoes, begins to take off his collar and tie.*

NELLIE *sits down in the arm-chair.*

NELLIE *(dragging up the stool and beginning to unlace her boots)*:

I could hear my father carrying on again. Was he a nuisance?

MOTHER : Is he ever anything else when he's like that?

NELLIE : He *is* a nuisance. I wish he was far enough! Eddie could hear every word he said.

ERNEST : Shame! Shame!

NELLIE *(in great disgust)* : It is! *He* never hears anything like that. Oh, I was wild. I could have killed him!

MOTHER : You should have sent him home; then he'd not have heard it at all.

NELLIE : He'd only just come, so I'm sure I wasn't going to send him home then.

ERNEST : So you heard it all, to the mild-and-bitter end?

NELLIE : No, I didn't. And I felt such a fool!

ERNEST : You should choose your spot out of earshot, not just by the garden gate. What did you do?

NELLIE : I said, "Come on, Eddie, let's get away from this lot." I'm sure I shouldn't have wondered if he'd gone home and never come near again.

MOTHER *(satirically)* : What for?

NELLIE : Why—when he heard that row.

MOTHER : I'm sure it was very bad for him, poor boy.

NELLIE *(fiercely)* : How should you like it?

MOTHER : I shouldn't have a fellow there at that time at all.

ERNEST : You thought a father-in-law that kicked up a shindy was enough to scare him off, did you? Well, if you choose your girl, you can't choose your father-in-law—you'll have to tell him that.

NELLIE *has taken off her shoes. She stands in front of the mirror and uncoils her hair, and plaits it in a thick plait which hangs down her back.*

MOTHER : Come, Ernest; you'll never want to get up in the morning.

NELLIE *(suddenly)* : Oh! There now! I never gave him that rose. *(She looks down at her bosom and lifts the head of a rather crushed rose.)* What a nuisance!

ERNEST : The sad history of a rose between two hearts :

> "Rose, red rose, that burns with a low flame,
> What has broken you?
> Hearts, two hearts caught up in a game
> Of shuttlecock—Amen!"

NELLIE *(blushing)*: Go on, you soft creature! *(Looks at the rose.)*
ERNEST: Weep over it.
NELLIE: Shan't!
ERNEST: And pickle it, like German girls do.
NELLIE: Don't be such a donkey.
ERNEST: Interesting item: final fate of the rose.

> NELLIE *goes out; returns in a moment with the rose in an egg-cup in one hand, and a candle in the other.*
> *The* MOTHER *rises.*

ERNEST: I'll rake, Mother.

> NELLIE *lights her candle, takes her shawl off the table, kisses her mother good night, and bids her brother good night as he goes out to the cellar.*
> *The* MOTHER *goes about taking off the heavy green table-cloth, disclosing the mahogany, and laying a doubled table-cloth half across. She sets the table with a cup and saucer, plate, knife, sugar-basin, brown-and-white teapot and tea-caddy. Then she fetches a tin bottle and a soiled snapbag, and lays them together on the bare half of the table. She puts out the salt and goes and drags the pit-trousers from the cupboard and puts them near the fire.*
> *Meanwhile* ERNEST *has come from the cellar with a large lump of coal, which he pushes down in the fireplace so that it shall not lodge and go out.*

MOTHER: You'll want some small bits.—And bring a few pieces for him in the morning.
ERNEST *(returning to the cellar with the dust-pan)*: Alright! I'll turn the gas out now.

> *The* MOTHER *fetches another candle and continues her little tasks. The gas goes suddenly down and dies slowly out.*
> ERNEST *comes up with his candlestick on a shovelful of coal. He puts the candle on the table, and puts some coal on the fire, round the "raker". The rest he puts in the shovel on the hearth. Then he goes to wash his hands.*
> *The* MOTHER, *leaving her candle in the scullery, comes in with an old iron fire-screen which she hangs on the bars of the grate, and the ruddy light shows over and through the worn iron top.*
> ERNEST *is heard jerking the roller-towel. He enters, and goes*

to his mother, kissing her forehead, and then her cheek, stroking her cheek with his finger-tips.

ERNEST : Good night, my dear.

MOTHER : Good night.—Don't you want a candle?

ERNEST : No—blow it out. Good night.

MOTHER *(very softly)* : Good night.

There is in their tones a dangerous gentleness—so much gentleness that the safe reserve of their souls is broken.

ERNEST *goes upstairs. His bedroom door is heard to shut.*

The MOTHER *stands and looks in the fire. The room is lighted by the red glow only. Then in a moment or two she goes into the scullery, and after a minute—during which running of water is heard—she returns with her candle, looking little and bowed and pathetic, and crosses the room, softly closing the passage door behind her.*

END OF ACT III

Altitude: a fragment

(1924)

CHARACTERS

MARY
SPUD
CLARENCE
MILKMAN
IDA
MRS SPRAGUE
MABEL
INDIAN
TONY
ELIZABETH

SCENE I: *Kitchen of Mabel's house at Taos.*
SCENE II: *Another room in the house.*

The curtain rises, revealing the kitchen of MABEL'S *house at Taos.* MARY *stands in the sunny doorway, chanting to herself, saying "Om" resoundingly.*

MARY: This country is waiting. It lies spell-bound, waiting. The great South-West, America of America. It is waiting. . . . What for? What for?

    Enter SPUD, *taking in the situation at a glance.*

SPUD: Hello! Hasn't the cook come?

MARY: Good morning! No sign of her as yet. . . . Isn't morning wonderful, here at this altitude, in the great South-West? Does it kindle no heroic response in you, young Intellectual?

SPUD: I don't know. Maybe I'd better kindle a fire in the stove.

MARY: Quite right! Homage to the god of fire. Wait! An apron! Let me do it. The fire in this house is the woman's fire. The fire in the camp is the man's fire. You know the Indians say that?

SPUD: No, I didn't know it till you told me.

MARY: Oh, young Intellectual! It is a Woman Mediator you are pining for. The Woman Redeemer!

SPUD: Maybe! Does this look like an apron?

MARY (*girding on the apron, and busy at the stove*): To do, to know, and to be! Hamlet had hold of only one-third of the twisted string.

    Enter CLARENCE *in rose-coloured trousers and much jewellery.*

CLARENCE: Oh, good morning, Mary! Good morning, Spud.—Why, Mary, won't you let Emilia do that?

MARY: Do you see any Emilia in the neighbourhood?

CLARENCE: Why, no, I don't. Is it possible she's not coming? Oh, what a calamity!

MARY: A contretemps, not a calamity, young Idealist. The heroic nature is ready for every emergency. Woman is the great go-between. When the cook does not turn up, *I* am the cook. Mary and Martha should be one person.

SPUD: What about Magdalene?

MARY: The men will play *her* role.

CLARENCE: Oh, but do let me do this.

MARY: Do what?

CLARENCE: Make a fire and all that.

MARY: The wood-box is empty: bring in some wood.

> *He goes out.*

SPUD: Oh, I wish Mabel weren't so temperamental.

MARY: Thank God for Mabel's temperament, young Intellectual. Where would you be without it?

SPUD: Why, I might get my coffee.

MARY: You get more than coffee from Mabel.

SPUD: Maybe I do. But it's rough on an empty stomach.

> *Enter* CLARENCE; *lays wood on kitchen table.*

MARY: In the wood-box, young Dreamer!

CLARENCE: Oh, so sorry!

MARY: Brains and dreams won't start a stove. Hands, muscles, and common-sense must be ready for any emergency, in the new mystic we are bringing into the world.

CLARENCE: I'll take Mabel her breakfast in bed. That will be much the best.

> *The* MILKMAN *suddenly appears at the door.*

MILKMAN: How much? Got the empty bottles? Any cream?

SPUD: Oh, yes! Let's have cream!

CLARENCE: Mabel only lets us have it on Sundays.

MARY: A pint of cream, two quarts of milk. The cook will give you the bottles to-morrow.

> *Exit* MILKMAN, *slamming the screen door.* CLARENCE *follows him out and rings the gong loudly.*

SPUD: Why, what is he ringing for?

MARY: No doubt he thinks the bell will bring the breakfast, as the rooster thinks he brings the sun with his noise. It is all part of the male vanity. Woman brings the breakfast, meanwhile.

SPUD: And I suppose she has some hand in making the sun rise, too?

MARY: Certainly. It is the great creative spirit of Woman, the perfected Woman, that keeps the sun in stable equilibrium.

SPUD *(sniggering)*: Do you say she keeps the sun in her stable?

> *Enter* IDA.

IDA: Oh-h! I thought it was breakfast.

MARY: Lay the table, Ida.

IDA: For *everybody*?

> *Enter* MRS SPRAGUE *in white muslin. She hovers, then sits at table and looks benignly at the stray bits of wood left there by* CLARENCE, *who re-enters at this moment.*

CLARENCE: Oh—er, Good morning! Good morning, Mrs Sprague; how did you sleep? Good morning, Ida!

IDA: We're supposed to be laying the table.

MRS SPRAGUE *(picks up a tumbler and wanders around with it):* Oh yes! Oh yes!

> MABEL *pops in through the dining-room door.*

MABEL: Where's breakfast? Where's Emila? Who rang that bell?

CLARENCE: *I* rang the bell, Mabel. I thought we might as well all know that cook isn't coming.—*Won't* you go back to bed? *Please* do! You'll be *so* much more comfortable.

MABEL *(rushing at stove)*: Where's the coffee? Where's the coffee-pot? Is that water boiling?

MARY: Mabel, *I* am making the coffee.

MABEL: It's got to boil. It's got to boil several minutes. I want it *strong*, so it's got to boil.

MARY: Mabel, you may trust many things to me, the least of them being the coffee. Won't you all sit down and discuss the situation, while I solve it?

MABEL: The bacon! *(rushes into pantry and emerges with a side of bacon)* Who can cut bacon *thin*? It's got to be cut *thin*. I want it dry. Cut it, somebody, and *I'll* cook it.

CLARENCE *(with dignity)*: I'll cut it, Mabel. Where is a knife?

> MABEL *rushes across and produces a huge knife.* CLARENCE *proceeds to saw bacon, on the table-cloth.*

IDA: Not on the table-cloth, Clarence.

MABEL *(snatching knife)*: Not so *thick*! Somebody cut the bacon who can cut it *thin*. *(Silence.)* Spud, come and cut the bacon.

SPUD *(reluctantly)*: I'll try. My God, be careful with that knife; you look like a Chicago aesthetic. *(Crouches on floor to cut bacon.)*

> *Enter* INDIAN.

INDIAN *(in doorway)*: Hello!

MABEL: Hello, Joe! No cook this morning. You know how to cook?

INDIAN : No.

MARY : Will one of our young Intellectuals go to the well for water?

MABEL *(to Indian)* : Fetch a pail of water, Joe.

> JOE *goes out with pail.*

MARY : Don't you notice, the moment an Indian comes into the landscape, how all you white people seem so *meaningless*, so ephemeral?

IDA : Why, yes! I was just thinking how ephemeral you all looked when Joe picked up the pail.

MABEL *(snorts)* : It *is* extraordinary! It's because the Indians have *life*. They have *life*, where we have *nerves*. Haven't you noticed, Mary, at an Indian dance, when the Indians all sit banked up on one side, and the white people on the other, how *all* the life is on the Indian side, and the white people seem so dead? The Indians are like glowing coals, and the white people are like ashes.

IDA : Well, Mabel, and which side are you on?

MABEL *(snorts again)* : The Indian!

MARY : There is something which *combines* the red and the white, the Indian and the American, and is greater than either.

MABEL *(rushing at* SPUD*)* : That's enough bacon, Spud.

SPUD *(rising)* : I don't know that I feel so *ashy* at an Indian dance.

IDA : No, neither do I, Spud.

> SPUD *examines his finger, critically.*

CLARENCE : And *I certainly* don't get any glow from the Indians.

MABEL : Well, you all know what I mean. And you do *all feel* it. Anyway, you *look* it.

IDA : Perhaps we're the ashes of your stormy past, Mabel, and you see in the Indians the red glow of your future.—But, my dear, it's all red paint.

CLARENCE : Exactly : the paint they've daubed on their faces.

SPUD : The danger signal.

MRS SPRAGUE : Have you cut your finger?

SPUD : A little.

IDA : Suck it, Spud.

SPUD : I *am* sucking it.

> JOE *re-enters with the pail.*

INDIAN : Here's the water.

MABEL : Alright, Joe. You can go and chop some wood if you like.

JOE *grunts, doesn't like, but goes out.* MABEL *rushes at the stove.*

MABEL: *I'll* fry the bacon, Mary.

MARY: Mabel, *I am* officiating at this altar.

MABEL: But I want my bacon dry, *dry!* You others can have it as you want it, but I want mine dry.

MARY: You shall have it as dry as the Arizona desert, Mabel.

IDA: Oh, what about Professor Mack? Is he still desiccating in the Arizona desert, studying the habits and misbehaviours of the Cactus?

MABEL: He's coming here.

IDA: Why, how thrilling! Don't you feel awfully bucked, Mary?

MARY: Professor Mack and I have had a perfect correspondence all our lives. This is the first time we shall have slept under the same roof.

IDA: How extraordinary! I wonder what the *roof* will feel about it.

MABEL: Let's sit down now.

> *They all sit at table.*

Well . . . *(ominously)* here we all are.

SPUD: Minus a few of us.

MABEL: How are you, Alice? You've not said anything yet.

MRS SPRAGUE: Why, I'm fine, Mabel. How are you?

MABEL: Fine! *(snorts)* How is everybody? How are you, Spud? Ida?

SPUD: Fine!

IDA: Fine!

MABEL: Mary, how d'you feel this morning?

MARY: Why, fine!

CLARENCE: If you were going to ask me how I feel, Mabel, I feel fine, perfectly fine. It's *wonderful* to be here.

MABEL: Ye-es! You're *looking* marvellous. But you're not going down to the Plaza in those trousers?

CLARENCE: Why, yes. I wasn't going to take them off to go down town.

MABEL: What's the idea?

CLARENCE: As you said, we all *feel* so fine, I thought I'd try to look as fine as I felt.

MABEL: But why in trousers? Why look it in trousers?

CLARENCE: But why not? You wouldn't have me try to look it

without trousers. No, Mabel! If we *feel* wonderful, and we *are* perhaps rather wonderful, I think it's up to us to come out in our own feathers.

MABEL: Yes, but why feather your legs?

CLARENCE: But why not?

MABEL: It's an exhibitionist complex.

IDA: Mabel, I don't think you can quite say that. I *admire* rose-coloured trousers.

MABEL: Yes, alright, indoors. But not to go down to the Plaza. They're all wrong in the Plaza. Think how the people will *jeer*—and then talk. Another sign of vice from over here.

CLARENCE: But what does it matter whether they jeer and talk—I shall go perfectly unconscious of them, in my rose-coloured trousers.

MABEL: You won't! You can't! You'll be conscious all the time. You'll be conscious all the time that they're jeering at you, and then you'll get all tied up over it afterwards.

CLARENCE: I assure you, Mabel, I *should* have gone to the Plaza in my rose-coloured trousers *perfectly* unconscious of everybody, if you hadn't started this difficulty.

MABEL: I bet you wouldn't. You *couldn't*. Anyhow, what do you want to go to the Plaza for in rose-coloured trousers? *What* are you conscious of, when you wear them?

CLARENCE *(with hauteur)*: Of *feeling* wonderful, and, I hope, of looking it.

MABEL: Clarence! You know everybody will just say you look a fool. Not wonderful at all.

CLARENCE: I thought it didn't matter what the crowd in the Plaza says. Anyhow, you've squashed my efforts. I shall go and take off my trousers and never put them on again.

IDA: But you'll put on others, won't you?

CLARENCE: Yes, *grey* ones.

IDA: But Clarence! Wait. Why don't you walk up and down this room a few times before *us*, and see how you feel: and we'll say whether you're wonderful, or exhibitionist, or whatever it is.

CLARENCE: No. I shall go and take them right off.

MARY: Stick to your guns, young Aesthete.

IDA: Stick to your trousers, anyhow. No, I mean it quite fairly. Walk up and down a few times past the sink. Yes:—there!

CLARENCE *walks. Enter* JOE.

MABEL *(irritably)*: Hello, Joe! How're you feeling, hm?

INDIAN: Fine!

MABEL: Can you stay help wash dishes? Put some water in the kettle.

> JOE *crosses in front of* CLARENCE, *who is walking up and down.*

CLARENCE: Excuse me, Joe, will you keep still a minute.

MABEL: I *told* him to fill the kettle.

CLARENCE: Mabel, I am acting at the request of the majority.

MABEL: You're a pure exhibitionist. I don't care about majorities, anyhow. Leave off exhibiting yourself.

IDA: Oh, but you're *fine*, Clarence! I'm *all* for rose-coloured trousers.

CLARENCE: I shall go and take them right off.

IDA: No! No! They're wonderful.

MARY: Let us appeal to true, unspoiled taste, and hear what the vital American has got to say. Joe, what do you think of his trousers?

INDIAN: Fine!

> *Enter* TONY.

MABEL: Here's Tony! Let's ask Tony. He sees both sides. Tony, Clarence is going to the Plaza in those trousers. What you think of it?

TONY *(seating himself at table)*: Make a guy of himself, sure.

MARY: You wouldn't go down to the Plaza in them, Tony?

TONY: Me? No. I wouldn't.

MARY: And you, Joe; would you go to the Plaza in those trousers?

INDIAN: No Mam! They're fine for a dance, for an Indian.

MABEL: That's it! You give them to Joe, Clarence.

CLARENCE: I shall not, Mabel. But I shall go and take them *right* off, and never put them on again.

IDA: Don't, Clarence! Oh, don't!

MARY: The Indian has spoken.

IDA: Then let the Jew speak. I'm a Jew, and my people are good at speaking. Clarence, I implore you, don't haul down your flag. Keep your trousers. *I'll* walk down to the Plaza with you.

MABEL: *Ida!* Prepare for the consequences.

IDA: What consequences, Mabel?

MABEL: All the *talk*. What'll Andrew say?

IDA: Why I'll have him paint a portrait of Clarence *in* the trousers.

SPUD: Keep them, Clarence.

MRS SPRAGUE: They're a lovely colour; they make a bright note.

MARY: I wash my hands of them.

MABEL: But it's so *babyish!*

CLARENCE: I shall take them *right* off!

Flounces out. A silence.

MRS SPRAGUE: You know, voices have told me that Clarence is a great Initiator.

MABEL: Initiator of *what*, Alice?

IDA: The fashion in rose-coloured trousers. I agree with him entirely.

MRS SPRAGUE: No. If we take care of him, and protect him, and *love* him, he may be a Great Teacher.

MABEL: Well, I protect him, preventing him making a guy of himself.

MARY: I think the Indians are *always* right. I doubt if any young man is capable of having a revelation. I doubt *really* if any *man* is capable of having a revelation. Next time I *really* believe it will be a *Woman*. The next Redeemer will probably, almost certainly, be a Woman.

MABEL: Meaning yourself, Mary? Why shouldn't *I* have the revelation?

MARY: You're not perfect, Mabel. I'm glad you're not, for I have hardly any place in my life for a woman who is both rich and perfect.

MABEL: Tony!

TONY: What?

MABEL: Like a fried egg?

TONY: Yes, I think so.

MABEL: Well, get up and fry it then. There's no cook to-day.

MARY: How are you this morning, Tony? It's so good to sit next you.

TONY: I'm fine.

MABEL: The Indians *do* feel fine. They always feel fine. That's because they live right. They've got something that white people haven't got. We've got to get it. That's what we're here for. That's what I married Tony for: to try and get that wonderful something that they've got and that white people haven't.

TONY *(Getting up at last and looking around vaguely)*: Where the eggs?

MABEL: Can't you find any? Well, maybe there aren't any. Have some marmalade.

TONY: Well, I guess I eat a can of sardines.

MABEL: Tony, you don't want a can of sardines for breakfast!

TONY: Guess I do!

MABEL: Oh, dee-ar!

      TONY *unwinds sardines.*

MARY: Mabel, when you say the Indians have that wonderful thing that white people haven't got, I think *I* have it.—Joe, more wood on the fire.—The Indians have the rhythm of the earth. The earth in America has a *special* rhythm, the marvellous American rhythm. And here in Taos that rhythm is at its height.

IDA: You mean altitude?

MARY: I mean the *perfect* rhythm. The white people still haven't got the rhythm of America, the perfect rhythm, of American earth. The Indians have had it so long, maybe they're in danger of losing it. The new revelation will come when the white people, when some white *Woman* gets the perfect rhythm of the American earth. And I think if I stay here all summer *(looks meaningly at Mabel)*, I shall get it.

MABEL: Well, *stay* all the summer, and let's see you get it. We want something to happen. Here we all are, a group of more or less remarkable people, in a remarkable place, at a remarkable altitude. If something doesn't happen of itself, let's *make* it happen. Let's make a Thing!

      Enter ELIZABETH, *eating an apple and shedding large tears.*
What's the matter, Elizabeth?

ELIZABETH: Why I'm so mad at Contentos.

MABEL: What's he done, then?

ELIZABETH: Why he's broken his bridle *again,* and got away.

MABEL: Where is he?

TONY: I tell you to take a rope——

MABEL: Go get a rope and catch him.

      Enter CLARENCE *in grey flannels.*

IDA: Oh, dear, the glory has departed.

CLARENCE: Yes, it intended to depart.

IDA: Too bad.

MABEL: Spud, you finished? Go get the poppies before the sun spoils them. Hurry, now.

SPUD: Well, let me drink my coffee first.

> *Drinks hurriedly and departs.*

IDA: Spud's queer this morning.

CLARENCE: Spud always seems queer, to *me*.

MABEL: Spud *is* queer.—I wonder what it is; whether we can't fix it.

MRS SPRAGUE: He has such a swell disposition. I wonder what it can be?

CLARENCE: I don't know. Of course it mayn't *mean* anything, but I heard his door banging *all* night last night. It really seemed mysterious.

MRS SPRAGUE: It was my door. There's no catch on it. It makes me nervous in the night.

IDA: Oh! Why doesn't Mabel have a catch *put* on the door? Of course it makes you nervous, banging in the wind.

MABEL: I forget about it, every day.

CLARENCE: *I'll* put a catch on the door.

> *Exit.*

IDA: Will he do it, do you think?

MABEL: Who, Clarence? Maybe. But he's more likely to try a safety pin.

IDA: Mabel, you can say the Indians feel fine *all the time*, and that we ought to feel the same; but what I want to know is, what do you mean by feeling fine? Feeling up to the mark, and so on?

MABEL: Oh no, none of those dreary things. I mean feeling good. You have that good feeling, don't you know, when you expand— and you make everybody around you feel wonderful. I know I do it myself. You can't help it—they've *got* to feel good, just because of the thing that's in you. You radiate life, and the people around you feel good. Haven't you seen me do it? Don't you feel it come from me?

IDA: Ye-es, maybe I do. But what does this feeling good mean? Is it just good spirits?

MABEL: No! Not any of that. Tony, you explain how the Indians feel when they feel good.

TONY (*chewing a sardine*): Well, the Indians, they feel the sun.

They feel the sun inside them, and they feel good. Like what the sun inside them, and they love everybody.

IDA: Sunshine, Tony, or moonshine inside them?

MARY *(heavily)*: Let *me* explain what it is. The sun is overhead, and the earth is underfoot. We live between the two——

> *At that moment, the telephone rings;* SPUD *enters with poppies,* ELIZABETH *behind him.* MABEL *jumps to the telephone;* SPUD *poses with poppies;* ELIZABETH *gets a cup and pours herself coffee. All speak at once.*

MABEL: Hello!

ELIZABETH: Guess I'll have a cup of coffee.

SPUD: Aren't the poppies beautiful!

MABEL *(at telephone)*: You, Ida! *(*IDA *goes to the telephone.)* Elizabeth, you drinking coffee? Leave off! It's not good for you. Go get some vases for the poppies.

ELIZABETH: Why, I can drink just a cup!

> *Exit* ELIZABETH *and* SPUD.

IDA *(from phone)*: Telegram from Andrew.

MABEL: What saying? *(*IDA *hangs up receiver and holds her head in both hands.)*

CURTAIN

SCENE II

Another room in the house.

ELIZABETH: Spud, why don't you come and ride with me now?

SPUD: Why, I don't know, Elizabeth. I guess I'm busy.

ELIZABETH: Oh, busy! What at?

SPUD: I don't know.—Write a *pome*.

ELIZABETH: A pome! Why don't you do that after dinner?

SPUD: I might not feel like it.

ELIZABETH: Well, why do it at all?

SPUD: Oh, I don't know. Why do anything?

ELIZABETH: Because it's fun! Let's go riding up the canyon. Yes, do. It'll be lots of fun. Won't you?

SPUD: No, I don't think so—really!

ELIZABETH: Oh, why do you always act *mean*?

SPUD: I don't, do I? I don't want to.

ELIZABETH: But you do. Why do you if you don't want to? What do you say you want to write a *pome* for, instead of going a ride up the canyon with me. I call that acting mean.

SPUD: But how——?

ELIZABETH: Why, because it is.

SPUD: Because you want me to go riding up the canyon when I don't want to. Isn't that acting mean, when you want me to do a thing I don't want to.

ELIZABETH: Well, you ought to want to. You don't want to want to, that's where it's so mean of you. If you wanted to want to, you'd want to.

SPUD: Why?

ELIZABETH: Because it would be *fun*. Lots of fun.

SPUD: But I tell you I don't like fun. I don't care for it.

ELIZABETH: Oh go on! Oh my, don't you just act *mean*!

SPUD: And I *hate* lots-of-fun.

ELIZABETH: Why, it's impossible, and so you don't hate it. You just want to act mean to me.

SPUD: I don't see that *at all*.

ELIZABETH: Of course you do——

Enter IDA *with a tragic face.*

IDA: The poppies are all coming to pieces while you two children stay flirting here. Sic transit gloria mundi.

ELIZABETH: Who's sick then?

SPUD: And we've not been flirting.

ELIZABETH: If people are so *mean*——

SPUD: Do you mean me? Am I mean?

ELIZABETH: Yes, I do mean you. You are mean.

SPUD: Why am I?

ELIZABETH: Ah, goodness, starting that all over again.

IDA: Why *are* you mean, anyway, Spud?

SPUD: Because I won't go riding up the canyon with Elizabeth when I don't want to.

ELIZABETH: But he *ought* to want to.

IDA: Why not sacrifice yourself, Spud?

SPUD: I won't.

IDA: Why won't you?

SPUD: Because I *don't want to.*

IDA: But there must be a reason why you don't want to.

SPUD: Why? Does everything have a reason?

IDA: Yes. How not?

SPUD: Well, I don't know the reason why I don't want to, if there is any reason beyond just not wanting to.

ELIZABETH: The reason is *meanness.*

IDA *(sighing)*: I should have thought it would be awfully nice to ride up the canyon on a lovely summer morning with a fair and bonny maid—Love's young dream and all that sort of thing.

ELIZABETH: Ugh! Ida! For goodness' sake!

SPUD: That's exactly it. I don't want to fall in love with Elizabeth and possibly have her falling in love with me.

ELIZABETH: *Im*possibly, not possibly, Spud don't wanter! Till *I* want is to have *fun.*

SPUD: And every time you say it, I loathe *fun* more. I hate fun. I loathe it.

ELIZABETH: Well then, you must be just crazy. Everyone wants fun when they're young. It's only natural.

SPUD: Well then, I don't. Maybe I'm not young and natural.

ELIZABETH: You don't act young, so you can't be natural. A don't-wanter isn't natural.

IDA: But Spud, why shouldn't you fall in love with Elizabeth? She's a very nice girl.

ELIZABETH *(snorts)*: Why sure!

IDA: Wouldn't it be awfully good for you to fall in love with her? Wouldn't it mean much more life for you?

SPUD: No!!! It wouldn't! I tell you I'm not going to fall in love with a *girl*, and go dangling around. I object to it all.

IDA: But suppose you couldn't help yourself?

ELIZABETH: Yea-a! What then?

SPUD: But I can help myself—and I intend to help myself. I'm not going to fall in love with some fool girl, and get *married.* Married! Ugh! The very thought of it makes me sick with myself.

ELIZABETH: Ida's been married twice; and she's married now, and her husband's coming here to stay. Nice sort of manners you've got, Spud Johnson.

SPUD: I'm awfully sorry about Ida. I mean I don't want to hurt her feelings. But the very word marriage does something to me. Marriage! Marriage! Marriage!

ELIZABETH: Marriage!

IDA: Marriage! Perhaps you're right, Spud. But *we* were always brought up to think it the most desirable thing on earth.

ELIZABETH: Oh I don't think that. Only I *do* want some fun while I'm young, Spud.

SPUD: Well, I don't. I always avoid fun, if I can.

IDA: And you don't want *love*, Spud?

SPUD: Lo-o-ve! God, no! I'd rather take castor oil.

ELIZABETH: Love! L-o-o-ve! Much you know about it.

IDA: Well, I hope you don't know much more, child.

ELIZABETH: I don't know anything at all, but it might be fun! Lots of fun.

IDA: Yes, it might. What a pity it so rarely is.

SPUD: There you are, Ida. You only want me to touch pitch because you've touched it.

IDA: Maybe it's because I'm a woman. But what *do* you want, Spud?

SPUD: I'll tell you. I don't know myself.

ELIZABETH: He's only a don't-wanter, he is. All he wants is to act mean, that's all he wants. He's worse than Contentos.

IDA: Well, we all have our own difficulties.

ELIZABETH: I should say we do!

MABEL *(suddenly through door)*: Oh de-ar! What are you all *doing*? Where are those *vases*?

ELIZABETH *drops vase.*

ELIZABETH: There goes one of them.

CURTAIN

Noah's Flood: a fragment

CHARACTERS

NOAH
SHEM (the Utterer) I am, it is.
KANAH (the Echoer) it was, it shall be.
HAM (Heat)
SHELAH (Flux)
JAPHET (encompassing, spreading, Father of All :
also Destroyer)
COSBY (female-male. Kulturträger)

1ST MAN: What ails the sun, that his mornings are so sickly?

2ND MAN: You heard what the Old One said: the sun is dark with the anger of the skies.

1ST MAN: The Old One is sly. Himself is angry, so he says the anger breathes from the hollows of the sky. We are not fools altogether. What think you? Are the sons of men more stupid than the sons of God?

3RD MAN: I don't think! The Old One and his demi-god sons, what are they? They are taller than the sons of men, but they are slower. They are stronger, but it seems to me they are duller. Ask women what they think of the sons of Noah, the demi-gods! Ah, the sons of God! They follow at the heels of the daughters of men, and the daughters of men laugh beneath the black beards, as they laugh when the bull snorts, and they are on the safe side of the wall. Big is the bull by the river, but a boy leads him by the nose. So, if you ask me, do we lead these big ones, these demi-gods, old Noah and his sons, Shem and Ham and Japhet.

1ST MAN: If we had the secret of the red flutterer.

3RD MAN: Ha! I have the name of that Bird. Ham told a woman that the name is Fire.

1ST MAN: Fire! It is a poor name. What is its father, and who its mother?

3RD MAN: Nay, that Ham did not tell. It is a secret of these demi-gods. But I tell you. It comes out of an egg. And the Old One knows where the eggs of that bird called Fire are laid. So he gathers them up, for his house.

2ND MAN: He shall tell us.

3RD MAN: No, he will never tell us. But his sons may. Because if we knew the secret of the red bird they call Fire, and could find the eggs and have the young ones flutter in our houses, then we should be greater than Noah and his sons. The sons of men already are wittier than the sons of God. If we had the scarlet chicken they call Fire, between our hands, we could do away with the sons of God, and have the world for our own.

1ST MAN: So it should be. The sons of men are numberless, but these sons of God are few and slow. The sons of men know the secret of all things, save that of the red flutterer. The sons of men are the makers of everything. The sons of God command and chide, but what can they make, with their slow hands? Why are they lords, save that they guard the red bird which should now be ours. What name do they give it, again?

3RD MAN: Fire.

1ST MAN: Fire! Fire! And that is all their secret and their power: merely Fire! Already we know their secret.

3RD MAN: Ham told it to a woman, and even as she lay with him she laughed beneath his beard, and mocked him.

1ST MAN: Yet this red bird hatches the pale dough into bread, into good dark bread. Let us swear to catch the red bird, and take it to our houses. And when it has laid its eggs, we will kill the demi-gods, and have the earth to ourselves. For the sons of men must be free.

2ND MAN: Yes, indeed! Free! Free! Is it not a greater word than Fire? We will kill the demi-gods and be free. But first we must catch the red bird, take him alive, in a snare.

1ST MAN: Ah, if we could! For Ham has told us that the feathers shine like feathers of the sun, with warmth, even hotter than the sun at noon.

2ND MAN: Then it were very good if we had him, seeing the sun in heaven has lost his best feathers, and limps dustily across the heavens like a moulting hen. Ah men, have you learnt what it is to shiver?

3RD MAN: Have we not! Even in the day-time shivers seize us, since the sun has moulted his rays. And shivering in the day-time is like dying before one's hour. The death-shiver is on us. We must capture the red bird, so that he flutters his wings in our houses and brightens our flesh, as the moulting sun used to do, till he fell poor and mean.

2ND MAN: You know what Shem says? He says there are three birds: the little red bird in the houses of the demi-gods——

3RD MAN: The one Ham calls Fire. We must lay hold of that one.

2ND MAN: Then the bigger bird of the sun, that beats his yellow wings and makes us warm, and makes the ferns unroll, and the fern-seed fall brown, for bread.

3RD MAN: Ay, the bird of the sun! But he is moulting, and has lost his ray-feathers and limps through grey dust across the sky. He is

not to be depended on. Let us once get hold of the red chick Ham
calls Fire, and we will forget the sick sun of heaven. We need our
sun in our grasp. A bird in the hand is worth two in the bush.

2ND MAN: Yet you know what Shem says. Far, far away beyond
the yellow sun that flies across the sky every day, taking the red
berries to his nest, there lives the Great White Bird, that no man
has ever seen.

3RD MAN: Nor no demi-god either.

2ND MAN: In the middle of the tree of darkness is a nest, and in
the nest sits the Great White Bird. And when he rises on his nest
and beats his wings, a glow of strength goes through the world.
And the stars are the small white birds that have their nests
among the outer leaves. And our yellow sun is a young one that
does but fly across from the eastern bough to the western, near
us, each day, and in his flight stirs with his feathers the blue dust
of space, so we see him in the blue of heaven, flashing his sun-
pinions. But beyond the blue fume of the sky, all the time, beyond our seeing, the Great White Bird roosts at the centre of
the tree.

3RD MAN: Hast thou seen thy Great White Bird, fool?

2ND MAN: I? No!

3RD MAN: When dost thou expect to see him?

2ND MAN: I? Never!

3RD MAN: Then why dost thou talk of him?

2ND MAN: Because Shem told me.

3RD MAN: Shem! He is fooling thee. Did he tell thee the secret of
the little red bird?

2ND MAN: That, no!

3RD MAN: That, no! Rather will he tell thee of a Great White
Duck that no man ever did see or ever will see. Art thou not
a fool?

2ND MAN: Nay, for listen! Shem says that even the yellow sun
cannot fly across from the eastern bough to the western, save on
the wind of the wings of the Great White Bird. On the dead air he
cannot make heading. Likewise, Shem says, the air men breathe
is dead air, dead in the breast, save it is stirred fresh from the
wings of the Great White Bird.

3RD MAN: The air in my breast is not dead.

2ND MAN: And so it is, the sun struggles in grey dust across the heavy sky, because the wings of the Great White Bird send us no stir, there is no freshness for us. And so we shiver, and feel our death upon us beforehand, because the Great White Bird has sunk down, and will no more wave his wings gladly towards us.

1ST MAN: And pray, why should *he* be moping?

2ND MAN: Because the sons of men never breathe his name in answer. Even as the ferns breathe fern-seed, which is the fume of their answer to the sun, and the little green flowers that are invisible make a perfume like the sky speaking with a voice, answering deep into heaven, so the hearts of men beat the warmth and wildness of an answer to the Great White Bird, who sips it in and is rejoiced, lifting his wings. But now the hearts of men are answerless, like slack drums gone toneless. They say: We ourselves are the Great White Birds of the Universe. It is we who keep the wheel going!—So they cry in impertinence, and the Great White Bird lifts his wings no more, to send the wind of newness and morning into us. So we are stale, and inclining towards deadness. We capture the yellow metal and the white, and we think we have captured the answerer. For the yellow gold and the white silver are pure voices of answer calling still from under the oldest dawn, to the Great White Bird, as the cock crows at sunrise. So we capture the first bright answerers, and say: Lo! we are lords of the answer.—But the answer is not to us, though we hold the gold in our fist. And the wings of the Bird are slack.

1ST MAN: What is all this talk? Is the humming-bird less blue, less brilliant?

2ND MAN: It is Shem's word, not mine. But he says, the Great White Bird will waft his wings even to the beast, for the beast is an answerer. But he will withhold his draught of freshness from the new beast called man, for man is impertinent and answerless. And the small white birds, the stars, are happy still in the outer boughs, hopping among the furthest leaves of the tree, and twittering their bright answer. But men are answerless, and dust settles on them; they shiver, and are woe-begone in spite of their laughter.

1ST MAN: Nay, thou art a mighty talker! But thy Great White Bird is only a decoy-duck to drag thee into obedience to these demi-gods, who cannot stoop to sweep the fern-seed for themselves, but must bid the children of men.—And thou art a fool duck decoyed into their net. Did Japhet ever talk of a Great White Bird? And Japhet is shrewd. Japhet says: Ah, you sons of men, your life is a predicament. You live between warm and cold; take care. If you fall into great heat, you are lost, if you slip down the crevices of cold, you are gone for ever. If the waters forsake you, you are vanished, and if the waters come down on you, you are swept away. You cannot ride on the heat nor live beneath the waters. The place you walk on is narrow as a plank across a torrent. You must live on the banks of the stream, for if the stream dries up, you die, but if the stream flows over its banks, likewise you die. Yet of the stream you ask not whence it cometh nor whither it goeth. It travels for ever past you, it is always going, so you say. The stream is there! I tell you, watch lest it be not there. Watch lest the banks be gone beneath the flood. For the waters run past you like wolves which are on the scent. And waters come down on you like flocks of grasshoppers from the sky, alighting from the invisible. But what are the wolves running for, and what hatched the flying waters in mid-heaven? You know not. You ask not. Yet your life is a travelling thread of water for ever passing. Ask then, and it shall be answered you. Know the whither and the whence, and not a wolf shall slip silently by in the night, without your consent. Ask and it shall be answered unto you. Ask! Ask! and all things shall be answered unto you, as the cock answers the sun. Oh, wonderful race of Askers, there shall be no answer ye shall not wing out of the depths. And who answers, serves.—So says Japhet, and says well. And if we had the red flutterer, it should answer to us, and all things after should answer to us for their existence. And we should be the invincible, the Askers, those that set the questions.

3RD MAN: It is so. If we had the red bird in our hand, we could force the sun to give himself up in answer; yea, even the Great White Bird would answer in obedience. So we could unleash the waters from the ice, and shake the drops from the sky, in answer to our demand. The demi-gods are dumb askers, they get half-answers from us all. What we want is the red bird.

1ST MAN: It is true. That is all we need.

2ND MAN: Then let us take it. Let us steal it from their house, and be free.

3RD MAN: It is the great word: let us be free. Let us yield our answer no more, neither to gods nor demi-gods, sun nor inner sun.

1ST MAN: Men, masters of fire, and free on the face of the earth. Free from the need to answer, masters of the question. Lo, when we are lords of the question, how humbly the rest shall answer. Even the stars shall bow humbly, and yield us their reply, and the sun shall no more have a will of his own.

2ND MAN: Can we do it?

1ST MAN: Can we not! We are the sons of men, heirs and successors of the sons of God. Japhet said to me: The sons of men cannot capture the gift of fire: for it is a gift. Till it is given to them, by the sons of God, they cannot have it.—I said to him: Give us the gift.—He said: Nay! for ye know not how to ask. When ye know how to ask, it shall be given you.

3RD MAN: So! What they will not give, we will take.

2ND MAN: Yes, we will take it, in spite of them. We are heirs of the gods and the sons of God. We are heirs of all. Let us take the flutterer and be free. We have the right to everything; so let us take.

1ST MAN: Japhet said: it is a gift!

    Enter NOAH.

[Unfinished]